GUIDE TO

AMERICAN

BIOGRAPHY

Part I—1607-1815

MARION DARGAN

Foreword by DUMAS MALONE

GREENWOOD PRESS, PUBLISHERS
WESTPORT, CONNECTICUT

Library of Congress Cataloging in Publication Data

Dargan, Marion.
    Guide to American biography.

    Reprint of the ed. published by the University of
New Mexico Press, Albuquerque.
        CONTENTS: pt. 1. 1607-1815.--pt. 2. 1815-1933.
        1. United States--Biography--Bibliography.
I. Title.
Z5305.U5D323   016.92'0073   73-13455
ISBN 0-8371-7134-2

Originally published in 1949 by the Unviersity of New Mexico Press,
Albuquerque

Reprinted with the permission of the University of New Mexico Press

Reprinted in 1973 by Greenwood Press,
a division of Williamhouse-Regency Inc.

Library of Congress Catalogue Card Number 73-13455

ISBN 0-8371-7134-2

Printed in the United States of America

PREFACE

Many friends and acquaintances have helped to make this book possible. William E. Dodd, beloved teacher at the University of Chicago, did much to stimulate my interest in the personalities of American history. The example of Carl Russell Fish, of the University of Wisconsin, gave me the idea of teaching a course in American biography. Dr. Louise P. Kellogg, research associate of the State Historical Society of Wisconsin, kindly allowed me to read Professor Fish's manuscript on "Representative Americans," while his widow gave me permission to adapt to my bibliography the excellent organization which her husband had worked out for his course.

I began work on this GUIDE to meet the needs of my own students in a year course on American biography. However, the University of New Mexico Committee on Publications encouraged me to publish it, and made helpful suggestions as to its preparation. The University Committee on Research granted funds to further the project, while the Personnel Office provided clerical help. Dr. Josiah Russell, Head of the Department of History, and Dean T. C. Donnelly lightened my teaching load the second semester of the year 1948-49 to enable me to complete the present volume.

My colleagues at the University of New Mexico and other friends have aided me in one way or another. Those who helped chiefly by discussing with me the people and references to be included are: Ralph Douglass, L. L. Haas, Julia Keleher, Victor Kleven, Howard L. Mathany, T. M. Pearce, Frank Reeve, Conrad Richter, Dane Smith, Grace Thompson Edmister, C. V. Wicker, and Dorothy Woodward. Dr. Dudley Wynn, of the University of Colorado, and Miss Frances Gillmor, of the University of Arizona, made helpful suggestions. Dean Hector Lee and Dr. Charles Scott, both of Chico State College, and Prof. Jerome C. Hixson of De Pauw University, contributed ideas used in the introduction, while Miss Katherine Simons read and helpfully criticized several drafts of that document. Dean France Scholes, Miss Wilma Shelton, and Dr. George Arms helped me considerably with the bibliographical forms used. Dr. Arms went over the entire manuscript and was very helpful in many ways.

Without the constant encouragement and generous aid of librarians, this book would never have appeared. Their interest in the project has spurred me on, and so has my desire to repay the debt I owe them. They have taught me much about reference books, helped me with my forms, and joined in the constant search for books and references. I am indebted especially to the following members of the staff of the University of New Mexico Library: Helen Hefling, Ruth Russell, Genevieve Porterfield, Nancy Trammell, and Virginia Williams. During my stay at the Huntington Library, Miss Mary Isabel Frye helped me to find books and references, while Dr. Lyle Wright advised me on problems in bibliography. I wish also to acknowledge the courtesy and helpfulness of members of the staffs of the public libraries of Albuquerque, San Diego, and Los Angeles.

Dr. Guy Stanton Ford, Managing Editor of the American Historical Review, gave me permission to summarize comments made on books in that journal. Numerous correspondents have encouraged me to persevere with my task.

Many of my students have worked with me to make the references accurate. Mrs. Jane Harbour, Mrs. Shirley Ramsey, Mrs. June Stovall, and Mr. Milton Rohane typed the manuscript. My son, Lt. j. g. Marion Dargan, and my wife, Lena Dargan, read the proof with me. The latter also helped in countless other ways, managing household responsibilities so as to leave me leisure to do research.

Albuquerque, New Mexico,   MARION DARGAN
June 12, 1949.

FOREWORD

To students or readers who want to explore and understand the past, the value of biography now requires no arguing. This is not to say that the dicta of Carlyle and Emerson that the history of the world is but the biography of great men, and that properly there is no history except biography, are or should be accepted. There is no single approach to the past which should be emphasized exclusively. Many sorts of history are indispensable: political, economic, social, intellectual. History consists of everything that has happened, and when we view the past from some particular angle we do so merely for purposes of convenience. The various varieties of history simply represent different ways of looking at the same thing; and in practice the emphasis varies with the taste of individuals and the circumstances of a particular period.

At all times there is a larger political framework in which human life is set; there are institutions of government, and ways of making a living; there are ideas which provide a climate of opinion. Also, at all times there are persons, and it is they who make the scene itself significant. Surely there is no better way to vivify and illuminate history than to personalize it by means of biography. The past comes alive when we become acquainted with the actors on the scene, not merely as members of groups but as individuals. We cannot recreate them all, of course. There are too many of them, and relatively few of them have left a record. Most of the time we have to confine ourselves to leaders.

There are obvious disadvantages to this situation, for we should try to see the past through the eyes of common as well as uncommon men and women. No wise teacher wants his pupils to spend all their time looking at the mountain peaks; they must also be made aware of the plains and valleys. But—to change the figure of speech—one of the rare privileges of the student and reader is that he can associate in the realm of the spirit with the greatest men of the past, if he so wishes. He can walk and talk with Franklin or Emerson or Lincoln in a way that he could hardly have expected to do had he been contemporary with any one of them. If he should prefer less elevated company he can easily find that also. In the recorded history of the United States alone there are heroes and villains of every hue; there are subjects for any taste. Here one can find overwhelming proof of the adage that truth is stranger than fiction.

For these and other reasons, a guide to biographical literature is a sort of menu—an invitation to a feast which will last as long as life. If the individual often seems lost in the mass, in our age, this makes biography all the more appealing. It is personalized history and a perpetual reminder of the importance of persons.

DUMAS MALONE

New York, May 15, 1949

CONTENTS

vii

INTRODUCTION[1]

THE PURPOSE OF THE GUIDE

This is twofold: first, to furnish a working bibliography for individuals and groups who wish to pursue the study of American civilization by reading about the men and women who made America, or who are representative of its various generations, sections, and fields of interest.

Second, to assist reference librarians in one of the many fields of knowledge in which they are called upon to serve the reading public. I trust that this little book will save them many steps and add to their efficiency.

THE ADVANTAGES OF THE BIOGRAPHICAL APPROACH

At the age of eighty-three, Justice Oliver Wendell Holmes wrote that he remembered his grandmother well, and that "she remembered moving out of Boston when the British troops came at the beginning of the Revolution."[2] In view of the brevity of our history, it is easy to arrange a systematic course of reading which will include representative Americans from each period of our history. The individuals selected for study might be arranged in seven generations, then divided into regional groups. They should also represent different social classes and occupations.

This idea of approaching American history by doing systematic reading on individuals who represent different ages and sections is no novelty. Probably most readers have become tired of browsing and have tried to introduce some system into their reading. Certainly the idea has been used in college and university courses from New England to the Pacific Coast. Carl

---

1. The first part of this introduction was used in a paper on "The Biographical Approach to American History," which was read at a joint session of the American Historical Association and the National Council for Social Studies, Cleveland, Ohio, Dec. 29, 1947. A slightly different version appeared in *The Journal of Higher Education,* March, 1949.
2. Biddle, Francis. *Mr. Justice Holmes* (1942), p. 21.

Russell Fish was an outstanding pioneer in this field. He had a rare gift for understanding personalities, and worked out an excellent organization for such a course, dividing the people he discussed into six generations and sub-dividing them into state or sectional groups. His "Representative Americans" was very popular at the University of Wisconsin,[3] and also at both Harvard and Stanford where he sometimes taught in the summer. His public lectures on "Founders of the Republic" were also in great demand throughout Wisconsin. There is no doubt that American biography was taught with remarkable success by Professor Fish.

Since 1936, I have taught a year course in American biography in the University of New Mexico and have found such pleasure and enjoyment in this work that I wish to call attention to the advantages of the biographical approach. Teachers of both history and English would do well to consider them carefully.

A course in American biography makes a strong appeal to the interests of the students. Many high schools give excellent courses in American history in the senior year. Consequently university students are likely to regard another course in United States history as a repetition of what they have already had. But a course in biography will appeal to them as something new and different. Nor will the industrious student be disappointed. Being able to concentrate on personalities and to use the results of recent research, he should be able to arrive at a deeper understanding of old friends, as well as a wider acquaintance of the personnel of American history.

Biography makes history more dramatic.[4] Students find it more exciting to read a life of Grant or Lee than to study a history of the Civil War. The interest and suspense of a well-written biography enables the reader to rely largely on involuntary

---

3. Shortly after Fish's death, Dr. Louise P. Kellogg wrote that Prof. Fish's "Representative Americans" was "the most popular course in Wisconsin's curriculum." *Wisconsin Mag. of Hist.*, vol. 16 (1932) , p. 99.

4. In writing this section, I found Allan Nevin's *The Gateway to History* (1938) very helpful. Read Chapter XII, "Biography and History."

attention. Consequently, students are sometimes inclined to conclude that biography is the royal road to learning in the field of history.

The approach used in the biography course is not only different; it is as broad as life itself. It includes the artist, doctor, writer as well as the soldier, merchant, and politician. Many students will be able to do some of their work on people in their special fields of interest. Some of their reading can be correlated with courses in English, government, and science. If students are required to give special reports, they may be given first choice in their major fields. Students who are debating the question of their life work find it helpful to read biographies of people who followed the professions they are considering. In this way several of my own students were able to get previews of the professions they are practising today.

Biography possesses much of the appeal that fiction has: the emphasis on the individual, on incident, dialogue, and characterization. Although there are many inferior biographies, the English language is especially rich in great biographies, characterized by patient scholarship, fair interpretation, and literary charm. Books like *Benjamin Franklin* by Carl Van Doren and *Grover Cleveland* by Allan Nevins make biography a fascinating field in which to work.

Public libraries report that biography is one of the most popular non-fiction subjects with the general reading public. This means that biography is one of the most potent forces affecting the lives of people who read. It also suggests the probability that a comprehensive biography course will be influential in directing the reading of students after graduation. Publishers find it easy to sell biographies of people who are already known to the reading public. Students who complete a year course in American biography are reasonably sure to retain memories that will stimulate them to further reading when they have more leisure. Naturally some discussions satisfy the desire for information. We teachers need to cultivate the knack of saying just enough about a book to sharpen the desire to read it. The effect will vary with the individual, but the effort is worthwhile. The habit of reading biography is one of the richest prizes a university graduate can take with him when he leaves the campus. For biography is the key which enables one to enter into exciting action, to enjoy the companionship of great minds, to be inspired by noble lives.

If one wishes to take the most practical method of developing the historical judgment and critical ability of his students, he may do well to start with biography rather than history. Many historical works are packed with important facts which have been condensed by experts. An immature student finds it difficult to condense them further. Biographies contain many nonessential facts. They practically force one to learn the facts of most significance.

Students are frequently slow to take a critical attitude toward works of history. One might read an entire volume of *The History of the United States* by Edward Channing without presuming to criticize the work of such a famous historian. But a biography is so personal that the reader can hardly escape the question of the author's fairness toward his leading characters. If he defends his hero on every occasion and hurls angry epithets at those who oppose him, even the most inexperienced reader will see that the book is biased. Some one has said that gossips apply instinctively the criticism which has to be carefully taught to graduate students. Readers of biography find a bit of gossip now and then and have to be on guard against accepting everything they read.

I believe in using a variety of material: autobiographies, books of collective biography, and various types of biography— the popular biography, including both the laudatory and the debunking, and scholarly biographies such as Freeman's *Lee* and Randall's *Lincoln*. Students are more likely to continue to read biographies if they are allowed to find their own level. Furthermore, the necessity of distinguishing between various types of biography will give them opportunities to develop their critical faculties.

One critic recommended a popular life of Thomas Paine as "a good book to read in the subway." One might suggest an even more valuable use which books of this class may serve. University clinics tell us that we should learn to read better and faster, that we should increase our speed from 150 words a minute to from 400 to 600 words a minute. Biographies furnish good material for practice, especially those of the popular type. If the student is required to read two biographies of the same person, he can learn to skim facts already familiar and concentrate on the new material in the second book.

One more point. In a democratic society the men and women who occupy key positions are selected by the people. Choosing the best individuals for places of trust is one of our most important responsibilities. If handled properly, the biography course may render future citizens better equipped to evaluate current leaders and to see them in their true perspective. Thus wider use of the biography course may tend to give us better leaders and better government.

To recapitulate: the course in American biography promises many advantages. The novelty of the approach makes a strong appeal to the interests of students who appreciate the opportunity of meeting new people and of becoming more intimately acquainted with already familiar ones. Many of the books used are dramatic and exciting; some rank high as literature. The course gives the student opportunities to read about people who are of special interest to him, and to improve his reading speed and his ability to pick out what is significant. There is hope that he will become more critical of the books he reads, as well as more expert in judging leaders of his own generation.

CHOOSING THE PEOPLE TO STUDY

This is one of the major problems of the biography course. Each teacher will naturally make his own decisions. However, in my desire to be of assistance, I have taken the responsibility for suggesting certain names. Naturally, there will be considerable difference of opinion as to the number of people to be considered, the individuals most worthy of attention, and the time to be allotted to various sections, periods, and individuals. I trust that the publication of this bibliography will save much time for other teachers, and that they may find all the more pleasure in supplementing my list where they feel it needs it.

Washington and Lincoln are generally accepted as the two greatest Americans. But, if one asks either a social gathering or a history seminar as to the five greatest, the result is likely to be lively disagreement. If the number is raised to forty, the disagreement will be still livelier. Such is the conclusion of Dr. Dumas Malone in an article in which he lists forty men who are probably generally accepted as "American Immortals."[5] Many teachers of history will disagree with Dr. Malone here and there, but no one would deny that he should be a very competent judge in such matters. As editor of the *Dictionary of American Biography,* he had to pass on the relative importance of over 13,500 people included in that monumental work.

THE STANDARDS BY WHICH INDIVIDUALS WERE SELECTED

There is no general agreement as to the yardstick by which the people to be studied should be selected. Dr. Malone admits that he and his staff of experts had some difficulty in finding "an acceptable criterion of greatness." Naturally they gave weight to "achievement," "historical importance," and "personality." These concepts have been helpful in choosing the people included in this GUIDE, but they are not infallible. What did Mary Todd Lincoln achieve? How shall one compare the achieve-

---

5. Malone, Dumas. "Who are the American Immortals." *Harpers,* 174 (1937) : 544-48. The forty names listed by Dr. Malone would be very helpful in planning a one-semester course in American biography. See also "A Decade of Biographical Contributions to Recent American History," by Arthur S. Link in the *Mississippi Valley Historical Review,* March, 1948. This paper was read in somewhat briefer form at a joint session of the American Historical Association and the National Council for Social Studies, at Cleveland, Dec. 29, 1947.

ments of Benedict Arnold and Sidney Lanier? How shall one judge individuals who are "great" when measured by one standard, but not when measured by another? Shall Chief Joseph of the Nez Percé—an expert fighter and "the noblest Indian of them all"—be omitted because he is historically less important than the revengeful old man who gave his name to the Black Hawk War? Shall one emphasize tangible achievements to such an extent that influential educators will be omitted because they devoted themselves to building character rather than to writing books?[6]

Other concepts used in selecting the names listed in the GUIDE are the availability of interesting material and the desire to find representatives of various sections for each generation and various fields of interest. I have also sought to aid writers who wish to revive a few interesting individuals who have largely been forgotten.

Probably five out of six of these concepts will be generally accepted as valid, even though there will be disagreement as to their application. The one whose validity is sure to be questioned is the idea of giving recognition to obscure individuals. Some will object that this may lead to leaving out more worthwhile people. Every teacher should certainly guard against such a result. On the other hand, both teachers and students find a peculiar pleasure in talking about some of the "forgotten men." I still remember the intense interest which Professor William E. Dodd aroused when he told his students at the University of Chicago about Deveraux Jarratt, a poor teacher and clergyman in the Virginia back-country, who "almost became a gentleman"

6. There is a story that a South Carolinian was stranded in Kentucky some years ago. Forced to request a loan from a stranger he was directed to a man who was originally from his own state. The latter tested him by asking: "Whom do you regard as the great living South Carolinian?" The needy one replied instantly, "James H. Carlisle, President of Wofford College." Upon which his questioner replied, "O. K., I'll lend you whatever you want; but if you had said 'Ben Tilman,' I wouldn't have given you a cent!" Whether this is a true story or not, the people of South Carolina were sharply divided as to the greatness of these two sons—the one a beloved teacher, the other a political leader whose loyal followers made him governor of the state and its ⌐epresentative in the United States Senate for twenty-three years.

by the time of his death in 1801. Later I experienced a similar thrill when I read a fascinating article by Verner W. Crane on Christian Priber, the German who sought to establish a Utopia among the Cherokees in the first half of the eighteenth century. Some will think it a waste of time to discuss such individuals. But the popularity of *Lost Men of American History* by Stewart Holbrook (1946) suggests that the reading public is much interested in "the forgotten man."

THE GENERATIONS OF AMERICAN HISTORY FROM 1607 TO 1815

Professor Fish divided the early period into four generations, given below. It is helpful if we associate a few names with each.

Generations		*Massachusetts*	*Virginia*
First,	1607-1660	John Winthrop	John Rolfe
Second,	1660-1715	Samuel Sewall	Nathaniel Bacon
Third,	1715-1760	Jonathan Edwards	William Byrd II
Fourth,	1760-1815	John Adams	Thomas Jefferson[7]

One has to be a little arbitrary in fitting long-lived individuals like Benjamin Franklin (1706-1790) into this scheme, but it is a good working arrangement. By associating contemporaries, the student can avoid having to memorize dates for each individual. Furthermore, he finds much to think about as he reviews successive generations. The first generation is made up of Indians and transplanted Englishmen. When do the native-born whites come to outnumber those who were foreign-born? In which generation was the genuine American no longer a rarity? What were his characteristics? Are the people cited really representative of their generation and the colony or state in which each lived? Was there a steady progress in education with each succeeding generation?

---

7. The second part of the GUIDE, which will be published later, will cover three generations as follows: Fifth, 1815-1850; Sixth, 1850-1901; and Seventh, 1901 to the present. In writing this introduction, I have drawn most of my illustrations from Part I. Occasionally, however, I have found it desirable to refer to Part II.

A Practical Textbook for the Biography Course

Some may think that if Lytton Strachey or Gamaliel Bradford had given us a volume of sketches on just the right people, it would be an ideal text for the course in American biography. I agree, however, with the college president who said: "The trouble with textbooks is that they take the sport out of learning. Their authors have had all the excitement of the chase . . . and leave the student only the dead quarry." In quoting this in the preface of his text on American history, Professor Hicks adds: "The wise teacher will assure his students that there is plenty of game still uncaught, and that the text merely points the way to the chase."[8] With so many good biographies and books of collective biography—so many new and often conflicting points of view—it would be a shame to tie students down to an ordinary text, if one were available, or even to a set of lectures by one individual. Thomas Carlyle defined a university as "a collection of books." Every college or university library will contain many books that can be used in such a course. What one needs is an outline, listing the people to be studied and the best books and articles on them.

Methods of Conducting the Biography Course

Perhaps it may be of interest for the compiler of this book to describe the way he handles his own course.

I ask my students to follow the order of the Guide fairly closely, but get some variety by varying the regional representatives considered from year to year. We cover the first four generations in one semester, the last three, the next. This can be done in a course meeting two hours a week, but three hours a week is better.

I plan to cover three or four people each day. We frequently have a brief identification of someone considered previously. A member of the class then gives an oral report on someone for whom the library has a good full-length biography. Com-

---

8. Hicks, John D. *The American Nation* (1945), p. vi.

ments by the teacher are followed by group discussion of two persons about whom the library has a variety of material. This discussion is guided by the teacher with the aid of cards, indicating the references read by each student. The remaining time may be used for a brief lecture, especially when there is need to cover a third or fourth person quickly, or when the best material on the subject is not available in the university library.

A Working Bibliography

The Guide does not pretend to be complete, but it should be a useful tool. It aims to help students and readers find the best books and articles on representative Americans. It is not intended to be exhaustive. I have tried to omit older books and articles that have been replaced by better ones, but to include others which are still useful. Students wishing to supplement this bibliography in any way should use some of the aides listed on page 134.

The Guide is intended to be selective; it is also intended to serve all sorts of people. Serious students might prefer a brief bibliography which included only full-length biographies of the most scholarly type. Certainly the comments and reviews cited will make it easy for discriminating readers to pick out such books. At the same time readers who lack the time or inclination to read two to six volumes on one person will be directed to the best popular biographies and articles. Experience shows that the reading of popular biographical material leads sometimes to the most important consequences. Certainly the reader who knows something of George Washington or Thomas Jefferson can anticipate hours of pleasure in checking his impressions against the findings of the most thorough research men in the field.

The Classifications Used in the Bibliographies

Perhaps a few words of comment on the kinds of material cited in the bibliographies may help students and reference workers to use the book efficiently.

ORIGINAL SOURCES. Autobiographies, diaries and letters are given under this heading. No attempt is made to cite all of the works of the writers included in the GUIDE. Brief extracts from their writings are cited, especially when these throw light on the author. Space is lacking to list the various editions of a person's works. The *Dictionary of American Biography* should be consulted for this information.

BIOGRAPHY. Most biographies are listed in only one place in the GUIDE. The full title and the date of publication are given. The reference on the next line cites a review of the book. The comment usually reflects the point of view of this review. Since the biographies of a person are arranged alphabetically by the author's names, the most scholarly book may appear alongside of a popular biography of the debunking school. However, careful reading of the comments and reviews will help the student to select books which will appeal especially to him.

COLLECTIVE BIOGRAPHY. Strictly speaking, this term includes books that discuss two or more individuals. For convenience, I use it to include articles in periodicals, too, as many of these reappear in books of collective biography. The two references are given together so that the student will know that they are the same. Histories of American literature may also be put under this heading. Books or articles emphasizing literary criticism are either put under "special aspects," or omitted altogether. Some books of collective biography contain chapters on a number of people, while others ramble from one individual to another. Books of the first type are easier to use, but the passing references in the other books are often quite stimulating and suggestive.[9]

---

9. An example of the first type listed early in the GUIDE is *The Virginia Plutarch* by Philip Alexander Bruce, 2 vols. (1929). The first volume of this book contains chapters on four Virginians of the First Generation. Another excellent example of the same type is *Builders of the Bay Colony* by Samuel E. Morison (1930), which covers seven representatives of the First Generation. One of the first examples of the second type that we come to in the GUIDE is *Saints and Strangers* by George Findley Willison (1945).

HISTORY. Books of history are concerned with the general rather than the particular; with the times rather than the individual. They give excellent background material. Frequently they give the reader a good idea of the career of the individual in whom he is interested, especially if he is an outstanding leader. The rapid reader gets an excellent idea of his man in action, and this may help to correct the bias which a biographer is likely to have for his subject. Reading about the actions of a man, the thoughtful reader will find it helpful to jot down his characteristics—along with the most striking occasions on which he exhibited these traits. For instance, in an advanced course it seems a waste of time to go over the story of John Adams' life again, or to recount the various offices he held at one time or another. It is certainly more interesting and instructive to recall the occasions on which he displayed industry, moral courage, good judgment of men and women, and so forth. It requires patience to work out a person's characteristics from a narrative history, but the results are likely to be remembered.

Naturally, the works of some historians are much more useful in a biography course than those of others. It is only occasionally that it seems worth while to refer to writers like Charles Beard, Herbert L. Osgood, and Charles M. Andrews, who emphasize economic interpretation, or the institutional approach. Francis Parkman, Claude Bowers, and William E. Dodd are more helpful, as they all reflect a strong interest in personalities. Especially valuable are the histories which frequently depart from a historical narrative to sketch the careers or analyze the personalities of leaders.

Books of history frequently refer briefly to two or more of the people listed in the same chapter of the GUIDE. In some cases it seems possible to avoid repeating the references. Thus, readers finding a reference to *The Founding of New England* by James Truslow Adams (1921) at the beginning of the chapter on Plymouth (First Generation), may infer that Adams discusses most of the people cited. In similar fashion, finding a reference to *The Old South* by William E. Dodd under Governor Berkeley, they might be left to infer that the chapter would necessarily deal with Bacon, too, since the two men were so closely associated. While this is quite true, I have given references to Dodd's book under both of these names. The chapter on "The First American Civil War" disposes of Bacon, but references to Berkeley run through the book.

SPECIAL ASPECTS. The books and articles cited under this category always deal with some particular topic connected with a person—never with his life as a whole. Haworth writes of Washington as a farmer, Knollenberg as a military commander, Wecter of the history of Washington's reputation and why the American people made a hero of him. All these books come under special aspects.

BIOGRAPHIES OF CONTEMPORARIES. Cross references are given only in rare cases, as a systematic use of them might practically double the size of the book. A student reading extensively on James Madison will scarcely need to be directed to the books on Jefferson. Cross-references are given, however, where the relationship is somewhat obscure, or where the reference to a contemporary is especially pointed, or provocative.[10]

THE CHECK-LIST OF BOOKS FREQUENTLY CITED. Many of the books listed under categories other than "biography" are cited over and over again. Full bibliographical information regarding them is given in the check-list (pp. 121-133). This list will help the teacher in ordering books for the course and deciding which ones to put on reserve. It will also help students to locate books and references. In case there are two or more

---

10. Recent illustrations are the references to Mary Ball Washington and Lord Fairfax in the first two volumes of *George Washington* by Douglas Freeman (1948). When students find that scholars disagree on fact or interpretation we may expect consideration of the evidence, lively discussion, and perhaps further inquiry. Sometimes there may be more heat than light, but use of conflicting authorities arouses the spirit of inquiry and adds considerable interest to class discussions, and should lead to a search for facts.

Another illustration of the kind of thing cited under "Biographies of Contemporaries" is Mark Twain's rather candid comment on Bret Harte.

editions of a book, the date given in the check-list will indicate the edition used in working out the pages.[11] Students sometimes have trouble locating Parrington's *Main Currents in American Thought,* vol. I, because the Reserve Book Room may have it listed as *The Colonial Mind.* Schnittkind and Schnittkind are also troublesome, since they write under the pseudonyms of Thomas and Thomas. Tyler's *History of American Literature during the Colonial Period* is referred to by a short title. When a book has two or three co-authors or editors, first names and initials are dropped after the first reference. All of these matters can be cleared up through the check-list. This will also help the individual reader to choose books likely to appeal to him. If the comment interests you, read the review. Selecting your books with care will give added interest to the course.

---

11. When a book dealing with more than one person is cited in the body of the work with the date of publication, this indicates that it is not included in "The Check-List of Books Frequently Cited."

FIRST GENERATION, 1607-1660

CHAPTER I. VIRGINIA

POWHATAN—   ?-1618   —Emperor of Virginia
ORIGINAL SOURCES: Stedman, E. C., and E. M. Hutchinson, eds.
Library of American Literature, 1:27-29.
COLLECTIVE BIOGRAPHY: Bruce, P. A. *The Virginia Plutarch,*
1:1-11.
Wertenbaker, T. J., in *DAB,* 15:160.

POCAHONTAS—?-1617—Indian Princess and Ances-
tress of the "F.F.V.'s"
ORIGINAL SOURCES: Hart, Albert B., ed. *American History Told
by Contemporaries,* 1:214-19.
Stedman and Hutchinson. *Library of American Literature,*
1:10-21.
Trent, W. P., and B. W. Wells, eds. *Colonial Prose and Poetry,*
1:12-22.
BIOGRAPHY: Fletcher, J. G. *John Smith—also Pocahontas,* 105-
06, 124-28, 246-65, 269-70, 281-84.
COLLECTIVE BIOGRAPHY: Bruce, P. A. *Virginia Plutarch,* 1:28-
42.
Gives an interesting explanation of the rescue of Smith.
Peattie, D. C. "America's First Great Lady." *Read. Dig.,* 50
(1947) :91-94.
Wertenbaker, T. J., in *DAB,* 16:18.
SPECIAL ASPECTS: Cooke, J. E. "Did Pocahontas Really Rescue
Captain John Smith?" *Mag. of Amer. Hist.,* 13 (1885) :398-
403.
Deane, Charles. "Pocahontas and Captain Smith." *Mag. of
Amer. Hist.,* 13 (1885) :492-94.
Keiser, Albert. *The Indian in American Literature,* 1933, Chap-
ter I, "The Pocahontas Legend."

JOHN SMITH—1579-1631—Soldier of Fortune and Advertiser

ORIGINAL SOURCES: Arber, Edward, and A. G. Bradley, eds. *Travels and Works of Captain John Smith,* 2 vols., 1910.

The best edition. The introduction is an able argument for Smith's reliability.

Tyler, L. G., ed. *Narratives of Early Virginia, 1606-1625.* (Original Narratives of Early American History, 1907.)

AHR, 13:909. Includes the most important sources for the London company period. 294 pages are from Smith's works.

Stedman and Hutchinson. *Library of American Literature,* 1:3-10.

BIOGRAPHY: Chatterton, E. K. *Captain John Smith.* 1927.

N. E. Quar., 1:254. A lively narrative which defends its hero from the charge of being one of the seventeenth century's most picturesque liars.

Fletcher, John Gould. *John Smith—also Pocahontas.* 1928.

Outlook, 150:1332, Dec. 12, 1928. Somewhat iconoclastic, but retains some legends, including that of the rescue by Pocahontas.

COLLECTIVE BIOGRAPHY: Adams, James T., in *DAB,* 17:294-96.

Basso, Hamilton. *Main Stream,* 8-10.

Bruce, P. A. *Virginia Plutarch,* 1:12-27.

Doyle, J. A., in *DNB,* 18:478-81.

Morison, S. E. *Builders of the Bay Colony,* 7-14.

Tyler, M. C. *History of American Literature,* 1:18-38.

HISTORY: Andrews, C. M. *The Colonial Period of American History,* 1934.

For a brief appraisal by a recent historian of the value of Smith's services, *see,* 1:142, note.

Brown, Alexander. *Genesis of the United States,* 2 (1891): 1005-10.

Hostile.

Fiske, John. *Old Virginia and Her Neighbors,* 1 (1899):94-178.

Tyler, L. G. *England in America,* 43-64; 150-52 (American Nation series, V, 1904).

SPECIAL ASPECTS: Bassett, J. S., in *Cambridge History of American Literature,* 1:14-19.

Jalbert, H. H. "Captain John Smith, Jack of all Trades and Master of Most." *Mentor,* 14 (1926) :39-40.

Hazard, Lucy. *The Frontier in American Literature,* 49-55.

Henry, W. W. "A Defense of Captain John Smith." *Mag. of Amer. Hist.,* 25 (1891) :300-13.

Howe, Henry. *Prologue to New England,* (1943) :234-71.
Describes Smith's services in exploring and advertising New England.

Kunitz, S. J., and Howard Haycraft. *American Authors,* 698-99.

Morse, J. M. "John Smith and His Critics: a Chapter in Colonial Historiography." *Jour. of South. Hist.,* 1 (1935) :123-37.

Wecter, Dixon. *The Hero in American History,* 17-25.

JOHN ROLFE—1585-1622—Agricultural Experimentor

ORIGINAL SOURCES: Tyler, L. G. *Narratives of Early Virginia,* 235-44.
Letter stating his reasons for marrying Pocahontas.
Also in Stedman and Hutchinson, *Library of American Literature,* 1:17-21.

COLLECTIVE BIOGRAPHY: Seccombe, Thomas, in *DNB,* 17:157.

Wertenbaker, T. J., in *DAB,* 16:117.

HISTORY: Osgood, H. L. *The American Colonies in the Seventeenth Century,* 1:69-76.

SIR THOMAS DALE—?-1619—Governor: Was He Hard Boiled or Kindly?

COLLECTIVE BIOGRAPHY: Bruce, P. A. *Virginia Plutarch,* 1:43-56.
Sympathetic.

Laughton, Sir John Knox, in *DNB,* 5:385.

Wertenbaker, T. J., in *DAB,* 5:34.

HISTORY: Chitwood, O. P. *History of Colonial America,* 77-78.
Hostile.

———. *Justice in Colonial America,* (1905) :13-16.
Hostile.

Johnston, Mary. *Pioneers of the Old South,* 73-92. (Chronicles of America, V, 1918.)

CHAPTER II. PLYMOUTH

HISTORY: Adams, James Truslow. *The Founding of New England.* 1921.

AHR, 27:129. The best short history. Maintains that the majority of the immigrants to New England were indifferent to Puritanism. Chapter V introduces all of the important people of Plymouth.

WILLIAM BREWSTER—   1567-1644   —Founder

COLLECTIVE BIOGRAPHY: Henderson, T. F., in *DNB,* 2:1212.

Plooij, Daniel. *The Pilgrim Fathers from a Dutch Point of View.*

Usher, R. G., in *DAB,* 3:29.

Willison, G. F. *Saints and Strangers.*

HISTORY: Usher, R. G. *The Pilgrims and Their History.*

WILLIAM BRADFORD—1589-1657—Governor and Historian

ORIGINAL SOURCES: Bradford, William. *Bradford's History of Plymouth Plantation, 1606-1648.* Ed. by William T. Davis. (Original Narratives of Early American History, 1908).

AHR, 14:385. One of the most interesting sources for American colonization. The introduction gives the chief facts of Bradford's life.

COLLECTIVE BIOGRAPHY: Bassett, J. S., in *Cambridge History of American Literature,* 1:19-23.

Henderson, T. F., in *DNB,* 2:1069.

Kunitz and Haycraft. *American Authors,* 93-94.

Morison, S. E., in *DAB,* 2:559.

Plooij, Daniel. *The Pilgrim Fathers from a Dutch Point of View.*

Tyler, M. C. *History of American Literature,* 1:116-26.

Walker, Williston. *Ten New England Leaders,* 3-48.

Willison, G. F. *Saints and Strangers.*

HISTORY: Usher, R. G. *The Pilgrims and Their History.*

SPECIAL ASPECTS: Bradford, E. F. "Conscious Art in Bradford's *History of Plymouth Plantation,*" *N. E. Quar.,* 1 (1928):133-57.

SQUANTO—   ?-1622   —A Friendly Indian

COLLECTIVE BIOGRAPHY: Morison, S. E., in *DAB*, 17:487.

Willison, G. F. *Saints and Strangers.*

HISTORY: Adams, C. F. *Three Episodes of Massachusetts History*, 1:23-44.

MASSASOIT—   ?-1661   —A Noble Savage

COLLECTIVE BIOGRAPHY: Adams, James T., in *DAB*, 12:380.

Willison, G. F. *Saints and Strangers.*

HISTORY: Hutchinson, Thomas. *The History of the Colony and Province of Massachusetts Bay.* 1936. Vol. 1.

MILES STANDISH—1584-1656—"Captain Shrimp"

COLLECTIVE BIOGRAPHY: Carlyle, E. I., in *DNB*, 18:882.

Usher, R. G., in *DAB*, 17:500.

Willison, G. F. *Saints and Strangers.*

HISTORY: Usher, R. G. *The Pilgrims and Their History*, 110-26, index.

THOMAS MORTON OF MERRY MOUNT—1622-
1647—Adventurer and Trader

ORIGINAL SOURCES: Bradford, William, in Stedman and Hutchinson. *Library of American Literature*, 1:107-11, 147-51.

Mussey, J. B., ed. *Yankee Life by Those Who Lived It*, 459-66, 487-88.

Trent and Wells. *Colonial Prose and Poetry*, 1:70-79.

Warfel, H. R., R. H. Gabriel, and S. T. Williams, eds. *The American Mind*, 15-18.

COLLECTIVE BIOGRAPHY: Adams, James T., in *DAB*, 13:267.

Goodwin, Gordon, in *DNB*, 13:1055-7.

Morison, S. E. *Builders of the Bay Colony*, 14-19.

Sheahan, H. B. *Book of Gallant Vagabonds* (1925), 137-74.

Willison, G. F. *Saints and Strangers.*

HISTORY: Adams, C. F. *Three Episodes of Massachusetts History*, 1:162-82, 194-208, 342-51.

Hutchinson, Thomas. *The History of the Colony and Province of Massachusetts Bay.* 1936. Vols. 1-2.

Usher, R. G. *The Pilgrims and Their History,* 137-41.

SPECIAL ASPECTS: Connors, D. F. "Thomas Morton of Merry Mount: His First Arrival in New England." *Amer. Lit.,* 11 (1939):160-66.

CHAPTER III. MASSACHUSETTS BAY

JOHN WINTHROP—1587-1649—Governor and Historian

ORIGINAL SOURCES: Forbes, A. B., ed. *Winthrop Papers,* 4 vols., 1929-1943.

AHR, 32:328; 35:627; 37:556; 49:745. These valuable documents give much information on the Winthrop family in England and America and on Puritan life in New England. Vol. 4 is especially valuable for the light it throws on the personality and influence of John Winthrop.

Hosmer, J. K., ed. *Winthrop's Journal, 1630-1649,* 2 vols. (Original Narratives of Early American History, 1908) .

The best edition of one of the most valuable contemporary accounts of the establishment of an American colony.

Stedman and Hutchinson. *Library of American Literature,* 1: 291-309.

Trent and Wells. *Colonial Prose and Poetry,* 1:90-119.

COLLECTIVE BIOGRAPHY: Adams, J. T., in *DAB,* 20:408.

Kunitz and Haycraft. *American Authors,* 828-29.

Morison, S. E. *Builders of the Bay Colony,* 51-104.

Parrington, V. L. *Main Currents in American Thought,* 1:38-50.

Seccombe, Thomas, in *DNB,* 21:697.

Tyler, M. C. *History of American Literature,* 1:128-36.

Willison, G. F. *Saints and Strangers.*

HISTORY: Adams, J. T. *The Founding of New England.*

Andrews, C. M. *Colonial Period of American History.* Vol. 1.

Hart, A. B., ed. *Commonwealth History of Massachusetts,* 1: 159-67.

Hutchinson, Thomas. *The History of the Colony and Province of Massachusetts Bay.* 1936. Vols. 1-2.

Osgood, H. L. *American Colonies in the Seventeenth Century,* Vol. 1.

Wertenbaker, T. J. *The Puritan Oligarchy.*

SPECIAL ASPECTS: Gray, Stanley. "The Political Thought of John Winthrop." *N. E. Quar.,* 3 (1930) :681-705.

Johnson, E. A. J. "Economic Ideas of John Winthrop." *N. E. Quar.,* 3 (1930) :235-50.

NATHANIEL WARD—1578-1652—Lawmaker and Wit

ORIGINAL SOURCES: Stedman and Hutchinson. *Library of American Literature,* 1:276-85.

COLLECTIVE BIOGRAPHY: Dewey, E. H., in *DAB,* 19:433.

Harris, C. A., in *DNB,* 20:785.

Morison, S. E. *Builders of the Bay Colony,* 217-43.

Parrington, V. L. *Main Currents in American Thought,* 1:76-81.

Tyler, M. C. *History of American Literature,* 1:227-41.

JOHN COTTON—   1584-1652   —First Bostonian

ORIGINAL SOURCES: Hart, A. B. *American History Told by Contemporaries,* 1:335-39.

Trent and Wells. *Colonial Prose and Poetry,* 1:156-81.

Warfel, Gabriel, and Williams. *American Mind,* 25-27.

COLLECTIVE BIOGRAPHY: Adams, J. T., in *DAB,* 4:460.

Frothingham, P. R. *All These,* (1927) :17-44.

Kunitz and Haycraft. *American Authors,* 182-84.

Parrington, V. L. *Main Currents in American Thought,* 1:27-37.

Plooij, Daniel. *The Pilgrim Fathers from a Dutch Point of View.*

Sweet, W. W. *Makers of Christianity,* 5-12.

Tyler, M. C. *History of American Literature,* 1:210-16.

Walker, Williston. *Ten New England Leaders,* 49-94.

Willison, G. F. *Saints and Strangers.*

History: Holliday, Carl. *Woman's Life in Colonial Days.* 1922.

Hutchinson, Thomas. *The History of the Colony and Province of Massachusetts Bay,* 2 (1936) :370-73, 381-91.

Wertenbaker, T. J. *The Puritan Oligarchy,* 21-24, index.

Special Aspects: Morison, Samuel Eliot. *The Puritan Pronaos: Studies in the Intellectual Life of New England in the Seventeenth Century.* 1936.

ANNE BRADSTREET— c.1612-1672 —Poetess

Original Sources: Ellis, John H., ed. *Works of Anne Bradstreet in Prose and Poetry.* 1867, 1932.

The introduction gives a good sketch of the author.

Collective Biography: Bell, Margaret. *Women of the Wilderness,* (1938) :177-92.

Humphreys, Jennett, in *DNB,* 2:1094.

Kunitz and Haycraft. *American Authors,* 94-95.

Morison, S. E. *Builders of the Bay Colony,* 320-36.

Richardson, L. N., in *DAB,* 2:577.

Tyler, M. C. *History of American Literature,* 1:277-92.

History: Wertenbaker, T. J. *The Puritan Oligarchy,* 101-4.

Special Aspects: Morison, Samuel Eliot. *The Puritan Pronaos: Studies in the Intellectual Life of New England in the Seventeenth Century.* (1936) :213-18, index.

JOHN ELIOT— 1604-1690 —Apostle to the Indians

Collective Biography: Adams, J. T., in *DAB,* 6:79.

Byington, Ezra H., in *Papers Amer. Soc. Church Hist.,* 8 (1897) : 109-45.

Kunitz and Haycraft. *American Authors,* 248-49.

Morison, S. E. *Builders of the Bay Colony,* 289-319.

Parrington, V. L. *Main Currents in American Thought,* 1:81-84.

Parrington, V. L., Jr. *American Dreams: a Study of American Utopias,* (1947) :3-10.

Sweet, W. W. *Makers of Christianity,* 197-205.

Tedder, H. R., in *DNB,* 6:607.

Walker, Williston. *Ten New England Leaders,* 136-74.
Willison, G. F. *Saints and Strangers.*

CHAPTER IV. CONNECTICUT AND RHODE ISLAND

History: Sweet, W. W. *Religion in Colonial America,* Chapter IV, "The Massachusetts Rebels and the Dispersion of the Puritans."

THOMAS HOOKER — 1586?-1647 — Puritan Liberal

Collective Biography: Adams, J. T., in *DAB,* 9:199.
Archibald, W. S. *Thomas Hooker* (Tercentenary Commission of Connecticut, No. 4, 1933).
Bates, E. S. *American Faith,* 151-54.
Blankenship, Russell. *American Literature,* 97-100.
Goodwin, Gordon, in *DNB,* 9:1189.
Kunitz and Haycraft. *American Authors,* 379-80.
Parrington, V. L., in *Cambridge History of American Literature,* 1:45-48.
———. *Main Currents in American Thought,* 1:53-62.
Tyler, M. C. *History of American Literature,* 1:193-203.
History: Andrews, Charles M. *Colonial Period of American History,* 2:67-99.
Hutchinson, Thomas. *The History of the Colony and Province of Massachusetts Bay.* 1936.
Wertenbaker, T. J. *The Puritan Oligarchy.*
Special Aspects: Miller, Perry. "Thomas Hooker and the Connecticut Democracy." *N. E. Quar.,* 4 (1931) :663-712.
Morison, Samuel Eliot. *The Puritan Pronaos: Studies in the Intellectual Life of New England in the Seventeenth Century.* 1936.

JOHN WINTHROP, JR.—1605-1676—Scientist and Industrial Pioneer

Collective Biography: Adams, J. T., in *DAB,* 20:411.

Doyle, J. A., in *DNB*, 21:702.

Kingsbury, F. J., in *Am. Antiq. Soc. Proc.*, N. S., 12 (1898) :295-306.

Morison, S. E. *Builders of the Bay Colony*, 269-88.

HISTORY: Hutchinson, Thomas. *The History of the Colony and Province of Massachusetts Bay.* 1936. Vol. I.

ROGER WILLIAMS— c. 1603-1682 —"Firebrand"

ORIGINAL SOURCES: Stedman and Hutchinson. *Library of American Literature*, 1:246-53.

BIOGRAPHY: Brockunier, S. H. *The Irrepressible Democrat: Roger Williams.* 1940.

AHR, 46:921. An understanding study which attributes Rhode Island democracy to the reaction against the theocracy and the influence of the frontier.

Easton, Emily. *Roger Williams, Prophet and Pioneer.* 1930.

N. E. Quar., 3:571. Gives a good portrait of Williams, and contributes to our knowledge of his early life. Fails to grapple with such controversial questions as the cause of his banishment from Massachusetts.

Ernst, James E. *Roger Williams, the New England Firebrand.* 1932.

AHR, 38:568. The first full-length biography. This was written from the liberal standpoint by one of Parrington's students. It emphasizes Williams' public career rather than his personality.

COLLECTIVE BIOGRAPHY: Bates, E. S., *American Faith*, 135-50.

Brockunier, S. H., in *DAB*, 20:286.

Dos Passos, John. *The Ground We Stand On*, 23-183.

Hamlin, Fred. *Land of Liberty*, 20-34.

High, Stanley, in *There Were Giants in the Land*, 56-66.

Kunitz and Haycraft. *American Authors*, 820-21.

Parrington, V. L., in *Cambridge History of American Literature*, 1:43-45.

———. *Main Currents in American Thought*, 1:62-75.

Especially recommended. Williams was one of Parrington's favorite characters.

Peattie, D. C. "Roger Williams—First Modern American." *Read. Dig.*, 49 (1946) :65.

Seeger, Allan. *They Worked for a Better World*, (1939) :12-33.

Sweet, W. W. *Makers of Christianity,* 47-61.

Thomas, Henry and D. L. *Living Biographies of American Statesmen,* 3-15.

Tyler, M. C. *History of American Literature,* 1:241-63.

Willison, G. F. *Saints and Strangers.*

HISTORY: Adams, J. T. *Founding of New England.*

Andrews, Charles M. *Colonial Period of American History,* 2:1-36.

Hutchinson, Thomas. *The History of the Colony and Province of Massachusetts Bay.* 1936. Vol. I.

Tyler, L. G. *England in America,* 212-18, 235-38.

Wertenbaker, T. J. *The Puritan Oligarchy,* 215-18, 228-29.

SPECIAL ASPECTS: Ernst, James E. *The Political Thought of Roger Williams.* 1929.

AHR, 35:172. This study deals with Williams' life as well as his unique theory of the individual and the state.

Stead, G. A. "Roger Williams and the Massachusetts Bay." *N. E. Quar.,* 7 (1934) :235-57.

ANNE HUTCHINSON— 1591-1643 —"America's First Clubwoman"

ORIGINAL SOURCES: Hart, A. B. *American History Told by Contemporaries,* 1:382-87.

BIOGRAPHY: Augur, Helen. *An American Jezebel: the Life of Anne Hutchinson.* 1930.

N. E. Quar., 3:358. The most sensational biography. Is vituperative toward Mrs. Hutchinson's enemies.

Curtis, Edith. *Anne Hutchinson: a Biography.* 1930.

AHR, 36:206. A sympathetic biography which pictures the Boston social leader "badgered by a circle of angry men." Leaves the reader in doubt whether she was a harmless non-conformist or a menace to the state.

Rugg, Winifred K. *Unafraid: a Life of Anne Hutchinson.* 1930.

N. E. Quar., 3:358. A careful study, fair to both Mrs. Hutchinson and her opponents.

COLLECTIVE BIOGRAPHY: Adams, James T., in *DAB,* 9:436.

Bates, E. S. *American Faith,* 135-46.

Goodwin, Gordon, in *DNB,* 10:337.

Read, H. E. *Fighters for Freedom*, 177-78.

History: Adams, C. F. *Three Episodes of Massachusetts History*, 1:363-532; 2:533-78.

Adams, J. T. *Founding of New England*.

Holliday, Carl. *Woman's Life in Colonial Days*, (1922) :39-43.

Hutchinson, Thomas. *History of the Colony and Province of Massachusetts Bay*, Vols. 1-2.

Extract in Isidore Abramowitz, ed. *Great Prisoners*, 307-40.

Wertenbaker, T. J. *The Puritan Oligarchy*, 89-90, 219-23.

Special Aspects: Morgan, E. S. "The Case Against Anne Hutchinson." *N. E. Quar.*, 10 (1947) :635-49.

SECOND GENERATION, 1660-1715

CHAPTER V. VIRGINIA

SIR WILLIAM BERKELEY—1606-1677—Tyrant

COLLECTIVE BIOGRAPHY: Bruce, P. A., in *DAB*, 2:217.
——. *Virginia Plutarch*, 1:71-85.
Bullen, A. H., in *DNB*, 2:368.
Hamlin, Fred. *Land of Liberty*, 34-45.
HISTORY: Dodd, W. E. *The Old South: Struggles for Democracy*, (1937) :235-54, index.

NATHANIEL BACON—1647-1676—"The Greatest Figure of the First Century of American History"

ORIGINAL SOURCES: Andrews, C. M., ed. *Narratives of the Insurrections, 1675-1690*, 9-142 (Original Narratives of Early American History, 1915) .
Hart, A. B. *American History Told by Contemporaries*, 1:242-46.
Stedman and Hutchinson. *Library of American Literature*, 1:445-58.
BIOGRAPHY: Wertenbaker, Thomas J. *Torchbearer of the Revolution: the Story of Bacon's Rebellion and Its Leader.* 1940.
AHR, 47:135. A dramatic narrative which pictures Bacon and his followers as heroes rather than rebels and traitors.
COLLECTIVE BIOGRAPHY: Bruce, P. A., in *DAB*, 1:482.
——. *Virginia Plutarch*, 1:86-101.
Henderson, T. F., in *DNB*, 1:837.
HISTORY: Dodd, William E. *The Old South: Struggles for Democracy*, (1937) :235-55
SPECIAL ASPECTS: Wecter, Dixon. *The Hero in America*, 25-30.

RICHARD LEE II—1647-1714—"A Belated Elizabethan"

COLLECTIVE BIOGRAPHY: Hendrick, B. J. *The Lees of Virginia*, 27-46.

Schriftsgeisser, Karl. *Families,* 156-59.
Wright, L. B. *First Gentlemen of Virginia,* 212-34.
Also in *Huntington Lib. Quar.,* 2 (1938):1-35.

THOMAS HELLIER—c.1650-1678—Indentured Servant and Criminal

ORIGINAL SOURCES: Phillips, Ulrich B., ed. *Plantation and Frontier,* 1:357-65 (Documentary History of American Industrial Society, I, 1910).

WILLIAM FITZHUGH— 1651-1701 —Aristocrat

ORIGINAL SOURCES: Hart, A. B. *American History Told by Contemporaries,* 1:301-6.
COLLECTIVE BIOGRAPHY: Knott, H. W. H., in *DAB,* 6:438.
Wright, L. B. *First Gentlemen of Virginia,* 154-86.

WILLIAM RANDOLPH OF TURKEY ISLAND —1651-1711—Founder of the Family

COLLECTIVE BIOGRAPHY: Eckenrode, H. J. *The Randolphs,* 31-43.
Woodfin, Maude H., in *DAB,* 15:371.

WILLIAM BYRD I— 1652-1704 —The Emigrant

ORIGINAL SOURCES: Bassett, J. S., ed. *The Writings of Colonel William Byrd.* 1901.
This book is concerned mainly with the second William Byrd, but the introduction gives a brief sketch of his father.
COLLECTIVE BIOGRAPHY: Wertenbaker, T. J., in *DAB,* 3:382.
Wright, L. S. *First Gentlemen of Virginia,* 312-21.

FRANCIS NICHOLSON— 1655-1728 —Professional Governor

ORIGINAL SOURCES: Wright, L. B. "William Byrd's Opposition to Governor Francis Nicholson." *Jour. of South. Hist.,* 11 (1945) :68-79.
COLLECTIVE BIOGRAPHY: Bruce, P. A. *Virginia Plutarch,* 1:102-17.

Doyle, J. A., in *DNB*, 14:457.

Ford, W. C., in *Mag. of Amer. Hist.*, 29 (1893) :498-513.

Labaree, L. W., in *DAB*, 13:499.

HISTORY: Barnes, V. F. *The Dominion of New England.* 1923.

Hutchinson, Thomas. *The History of the Colony and Province of Massachusetts Bay.* 1936. Vols. 1-3.

Osgood, H. L. *American Colonies in the Seventeenth Century*, Vol. 3.

———. *American Colonies in the Eighteenth Century*, Vols. 1-4. Use index in vol. 4.

SPECIAL ASPECTS: McCulloch, Samuel Clyde. "The Fight to Depose Governor Francis Nicholson—James Blair's Affidavit on June 7, 1704." *Jour. of South. Hist.*, 12 (1946) :403-22.

JAMES BLAIR—1655-1743—"The Leading Virginia Clergyman of His Day"

COLLECTIVE BIOGRAPHY: Grossart, A. B., in *DNB*, 2:623.

Sweet, W. W. *Makers of Christianity*, 12-20.

Swem, Earl G., in *DAB*, 2:335.

HISTORY: Sweet, W. W. *Story of Religions in America*, 57-60.

SPECIAL ASPECTS: Lonn, Ella. *The Colonial Agents of the Southern Colonies*, 114-18.

ROBERT ("KING") CARTER—1663-1732—"The Richest and One of the Most Influential Men in Virginia"

ORIGINAL SOURCES: Wright, L. B., ed. *Letters of Robert Carter, 1720-1727: the Commercial Interests of a Virginia Gentleman.* 1940.

AHR, 28:428. Although Carter was one of the most powerful men in Virginia, he gives expression to many of the complaints of the tobacco planter.

COLLECTIVE BIOGRAPHY: Paullin, Charles O., in *DAB*, 3:541.

Wright, L. B. *First Gentlemen of Virginia*, 248-85. Also in *Huntington Lib. Quar.*, 1 (1937):3-61.

ROBERT BEVERLEY II— 1673-1722 —"Historian and Iconoclast"

ORIGINAL SOURCES: Beverley, Robert. *The History and Present State of Virginia.* Ed. by Louis B. Wright. 1947.

AHR, 53:832. A reprint of an excellent history of Virginia published in 1705. The introduction adds much to our knowledge of the author.

Stedman and Hutchinson. *Library of American Literature,* 2: 265-72.

COLLECTIVE BIOGRAPHY: Harrison, Fairfax, in *DAB,* 2:233.

Wright, L. B. *First Gentlemen of Virginia,* 286-311.

SPECIAL ASPECTS: Wright, L. B., "Beverly's History . . . of Virginia (1705), a Neglected Classic." *Wm. and Mary Quar.,* Third Series, 1 (1944) :49-64.

CHAPTER VI. NEW ENGLAND

KING PHILIP— ?-1676 —Indian Statesman

ORIGINAL SOURCES: Lincoln, C. H., ed. *Narratives of the Indian Wars, 1675-1699* (Original Narratives of Early American History, 1913) .

COLLECTIVE BIOGRAPHY: Britt, Albert. *Great Indian Chiefs,* 29-66.

Stearns, H. P., in *DAB,* 14:534.

HISTORY: Hutchinson, Thomas. *The History of the Colony and Province of Massachusetts Bay,* 1 (1936) :235-63.

MARY WHITE ROWLANDSON— 1635-1678 Indian Captive

ORIGINAL SOURCES: Lincoln, C. H. *Narratives of the Indian Wars,* 107-66.

Mussey, J. B. *Yankee Life by Those Who Lived It,* 387-407.

Proc. of the Amer. Antiquarian Soc., N. S., 12 (1898) :401-9.

Stedman and Hutchinson. *Library of American Literature,* 2:52-62.

Warfel, Gabriel, and Williams. *American Mind,* 66-72.

COLLECTIVE BIOGRAPHY: Britt, Albert. *Great Indian Chiefs,* 60-66.

SPECIAL ASPECTS: Keiser, Albert. *The Indian in American Literature.* 1933. Chapter II, "Puritan Wrath and Indian Captives."

HANNAH DUSTIN— 1657-? —Frontier Woman

ORIGINAL SOURCES: Lincoln, C. H. *Narratives of the Indian Wars,* 263-66.

COLLECTIVE BIOGRAPHY: Adams, J. T., in *DAB,* 5:554.

HISTORY: Parkman, Francis. *Count Frontenac and New France,* (1932) :405-7.

SIR EDMUND ANDROS—1637-1714—Illegal Despot or Loyal Official?

COLLECTIVE BIOGRAPHY: Barnes, V. F., in *DAB,* 1:300.
Sympathetic.
Low, S. J., in *DNB,* 1:411.

HISTORY: Adams, J. T. *Founding of New England,* 411-30.

Andrews, C. M. *Colonial Period of American History,* Vol. 3.

Barnes, Viola F. *The Dominion of New England: a Study in British Colonial Policy.* 1923.

AHR, 30:373. A sympathetic treatment of an important experiment in colonial administration.

Channing, Edward. *History of the United States,* 2:52-60, 173-85, 196-202.
Hostile.

SPECIAL ASPECTS: Wright, L. B. "William Byrd's Defense of Sir Edmund Andros." *Wm. and Mary Quar.,* Third Series, 2 (1945) :47-62.

INCREASE MATHER—1639-1723—"The Greatest American of His Generation"

ORIGINAL SOURCES: Burr, G. L., ed. *Narratives of Witchcraft Cases, 1648-1706* (Original Narratives of Early American History, 1914) .

Stedman and Hutchinson. *Library of American Literature*, 2:75-106.

Warfel, Gabriel, and Williams. *American Mind*, 45-49.

BIOGRAPHY: Murdock, Kenneth Ballard. *Increase Mather, the Foremost American Puritan*. 1925.

AHR, 31:531. Standard biography. The author is reluctant to criticize Mather and gives too much space to the political activities of a man whose main concern was religion. He denies that Increase and Cotton Mather were largely to blame for the witchcraft troubles. *See esp.*, pp. 287-316.

COLLECTIVE BIOGRAPHY: Bates, E. S. "The Puritan Mathers." *Amer. Merc.*, 46 (1939) :400-02.

Kunitz and Haycraft. *American Authors*, 515-17.

Malone, Dumas. *Saints in Action*, 39, 50, 53.

Murdock, K. B., in *DAB*, 12:390.

Parrington, V. L. *Main Currents in American Thought*, 1:99-106.

Tyler, M. C. *History of American Literature*, 2:67-73.

Walker, Williston. *Ten New England Leaders*, 175-216.

HISTORY: Barnes, V. F. *The Dominion of New England*. 1923.

Chitwood, O. P. *History of Colonial America*, 286f.

Hutchinson, Thomas. *The History of the Colony and Province of Massachusetts Bay*, 1 (1936) :310-13, 329-35, 343-51.

Morison, S. E. *Harvard College in the Seventeenth Century*, 2:473-537, index.

Sweet, W. W. *Story of Religions in America*, 88-93.

SPECIAL ASPECTS: Morison, Samuel Eliot. *The Puritan Pronaos: Studies in the Intellectual Life of New England in the Seventeenth Century*. 1936.

Wertenbaker, T. J. *The Puritan Oligarchy*. 1947.

Placed much of the blame for the witchcraft troubles on the Mathers. This, however, is denied by Murdock, *op. cit.*, and by S. E. Morison. *The Puritan Pronaos . . .* (1936), pp. 248-57.

JOSEPH DUDLEY—1647-1720—Native Son, but Unpopular Governor

BIOGRAPHY: Kimball, Everett. *The Public Life of Joseph Dud-*

ley: a Study of the Colonial Policy of the Stuarts in New England, 1660-1715. 1911.

AHR, 17:158. A careful piece of research which makes out the best case possible for a loyal but unpopular official.

COLLECTIVE BIOGRAPHY: Adams, J. T., in *DAB,* 5:481.

HISTORY: Adams, J. T. *Revolutionary New England,* 60-76.

Barnes, V. F. *The Dominion of New England.* 1923.

SIR WILLIAM PHIPS— 1650-1694 —"Typical Sea Captain"?

ORIGINAL SOURCES: Burr, George L. *Narratives of the Witchcraft Cases, 1648-1706* (Original Narratives of Early American History, 1914) .

Mather, Cotton. "Life of Sir William Phips," in K. B. Murdock, ed., *Selections from Cotton Mather,* 149-283 (American Authors series, 1926) .

———. *Life of Sir William Phipps.* Ed. by Mark Van Doren. 1929.

Written to justify his father's part in the appointment of Phips as governor of Massachusetts, Cotton Mather's life interprets an essentially modern man as a pious old seaman. Unreliable.

BIOGRAPHY: Lounsberry, Alice. *Sir William Phips: Treasure Fisherman and Governor of the Massachusetts Bay Colony.* 1941.

N. E. Quar., 14:583. A fictionized biography which gives a fairly accurate picture of the rise of a poor shepherd to fortune and power. However, the author is not convincing in her interpretation of the governorship.

COLLECTIVE BIOGRAPHY: Barnes, V. F., in *DAB,* 14:551.

Doyle, J. A., in *DNB,* 15:1122-23.

HISTORY: Chitwood, O. P. *History of Colonial America,* 284-91.

Karraker, C. K. *The Hispaniola Treasure.* 1934.

Books, July 22, 1934, p. 7. A detailed account of how Phips located a Spanish ship wrecked forty years before and salvaged $1,500,000 from it.

SPECIAL ASPECTS: George, R. H. "Treasure Trove of William Phips." *N. E. Quar.,* 6 (1933) :294-318.

Karraker, C. K. "The Treasure Expedition." *N. E. Quar.,* 5 (1932) :731-52.

SAMUEL SEWALL— 1652-1730 —"A Puritan Pepys"

ORIGINAL SOURCES: Burr, G. L. *Narratives of the Witchcraft Cases*, 386-87.

"Diary of Samuel Sewall, 1674-1729," in *Mass. Hist. Soc. Coll.*, Fifth Series, Vols. 5-7 (1878-1882).

A vivid and intimate account of the daily activities of a Puritan gentleman for over fifty years. Far from being a disagreeable fanatic, the author reveals himself as an honest and amiable man who liked fine clothes and good food and drink. One of the most interesting parts of the diary describes his unsuccessful courtship of Madame Winthrop when he was sixty-eight years old. He married another widow two years later.

————. *Samuel Sewall's Diary.* Ed. by Mark Van Doren. (An American Bookshelf, 1927.)

Bookman, 66:465. An abridged edition of the above.

Extracts in J. B. Mussey. *Yankee Life by Those Who Lived It*, 77-78, 108-17, 343-46, 409-10.

Van Doren, Mark. *Autobiography of America*, 32-41.

Warfel, Gabriel, and Williams. *American Mind*, 60-64.

COLLECTIVE BIOGRAPHY: Adams, J. T., in *DAB*, 16:610.

Kunitz and Haycraft. *American Authors*, 683-84.

Lawrence, H. W. "Samuel Sewall, Revealer of Puritan New England." *So. Atl. Quar.*, 33 (1934) :20-37.

Parrington, V. L. *Main Currents in American Thought*, 1:88-97.

Tyler, M. C. *History of American Literature*, 2:99-103.

SPECIAL ASPECTS: Morison, Samuel Eliot. *The Puritan Pronaos: Studies in the Intellectual Life of New England in the Seventeenth Century.* 1936.

COTTON MATHER—1663-1728—"The American"

ORIGINAL SOURCES: Burr, G. L. *Narratives of the Witchcraft Cases*, (1914) :89-144, 203-88.

Mussey, J. B. *Yankee Life by Those Who Lived It*, 333-43, 407-09.

Stedman and Hutchinson. *Library of American Literature*, 2:114-66, 346-52.

Van Doren, Mark. *Autobiography of America*, 25-31.

Warfel, Gabriel, and Williams. *American Mind*, 49-59.

BIOGRAPHY: Boas, R. P. and L. S. *Cotton Mather, Keeper of the Puritan Conscience.* 1928.

Nation, 128:137, Jan. 30, 1929. A skillful psychologist undertakes to explain "the seeming contradictions of Cotton Mather's neurotic character."

Wendell, Barrett. *Cotton Mather: the Puritan Priest.* 1891, 1926.

The standard biography.

COLLECTIVE BIOGRAPHY: Basso, Hamilton. *Main Stream,* 14-22.

Canby, H. S. *Classic Americans,* 22-28.

Hamlin, Fred. *Land of Liberty,* 20-34.

Kunitz and Haycraft. *American Authors,* 514-15.

Malone, Dumas. *Saints in Action,* 40, 50, 53.

Murdock, K. B., in *DAB,* 12:386.

Parrington, V. L. *Main Currents in American Thought,* 1:106-17.

Prejudiced.

Read, H. E., *Fighters for Freedom,* 179-82.

Tyler, M. C. *History of American Literature,* 2:73-90.

HISTORY: Morison, S. E. *Harvard College in the Seventeenth Century,* 2:548-54, index.

Murdock, K. C., in A. B. Hart. *Commonwealth History of Massachusetts,* 2:323-54.

Wertenbaker, T. J. *The Puritan Oligarchy.*

SPECIAL ASPECTS: Nordell, P. G. "Cotton Mather in Love." *Harper's,* 153 (1926) :566-72.

Tuttle, J. H. "The Libraries of the Mathers." *Am. Antiq. Soc., Proc.,* N. S., 20 (1910) :269-356.

Waters, R. E. "Biographical Technique in Cotton Mather's *Magnalia.*" *Wm. and Mary Quar.,* Third Series, 1 (1945) : 154-63.

SPECIAL ASPECTS: Morison, Samuel Eliot. *The Puritan Pronaos: Studies in the Intellectual Life of New England in the Seventeenth Century.* 1936.

SARAH KEMBLE KNIGHT— 1666-1727 —Teacher and Business Woman

ORIGINAL SOURCES: Winship, G. P., ed. *The Journal of Madame Knight.* 1920.

The best edition of a sprightly account of a journey made in 1704 from Boston to New York and return. The introductory note gives a brief sketch of the author.

Deane, W. R., ed. "Journey of Madame Knight from Boston to New York in 1704." *Littell's Living Age,* Third Series, 57 (1858) :963-80.

Extracts in Hart, A. B. *American History Told by Contemporaries,* 2:224-29; Mussey, J. B. *Yankee Life by Those Who Lived It,* 450-500; Stedman and Hutchinson. *Library of American Literature,* 2:248-64; Trent and Wells. *Colonial Prose and Poetry,* 327-46.

COLLECTIVE BIOGRAPHY: Gunn, Sidney, in *DAB,* 10:468.

Kunitz and Haycraft. *American Authors,* 443-44.

Parrington, V. L. *Main Currents in American Thought,* 1:137-38.

HISTORY: Hewes, Amy, in Hart, A. B. *Commonwealth History of Massachusetts,* 2:379-83.

CHAPTER VII. THE MIDDLE COLONIES

JACOB LEISLER—   1640-1691   —Rebel

ORIGINAL SOURCES: Andrews, C. M. *Narratives of the Insurrections,* (1915) :320-54.

Hart, A. B. *American History Told by Contemporaries,* 1:544-47.

COLLECTIVE BIOGRAPHY: Pargellis, Stanley, in *DAB,* 11:156.

Ulmann, Albert. *New Yorkers,* 38-56.

HISTORY: Andrews, C. M. *Colonial Period of American History,* 3:125-37.

Channing, Edward. *History of the United States,* 2:205-09, 295-96.

Faust, A. B. *The German Element in the United States,* 1 (1909) :13-26.

RICHARD COOTE, EARL OF BELLOMONT—
1636-1701—Able Administrator

COLLECTIVE BIOGRAPHY: Spencer, C. W., in *DAB*, 4:418.

Stephens, H. M., in *DNB*, 4:1088.

HISTORY: Adams, J. T. *Revolutionary New England*, 48-59.

Hutchinson, Thomas. *The History of the Colony and Province of Massachusetts Bay*, 2 (1936) :84-90.

Myers, Gustavus. *History of the Great American Fortunes*, 1 (1911) :28-32.

SPECIAL ASPECTS: Parsons, C. W. "Bellomont and Rasle in 1699." *Mag. of Amer. Hist.*, 13 (1885) :346-52.

WILLIAM KIDD—1645?-1701—Gentleman or Pirate?

ORIGINAL SOURCES: Jameson, J. F., ed. *Privateering and Piracy in the Colonial Period: Illustrative Documents*, (1923) :190-256.

AHR, 29:564. Includes a rather full record of the career of Kidd, but leaves the reader uncertain of his guilt.

BIOGRAPHY: Bonner, Willard Hallam. *Pirate Laureate: the Life and Legends of Captain Kidd*. 1947.

Booklist, 43:358. A scholarly attempt to distinguish between fact and fiction.

COLLECTIVE BIOGRAPHY: "Captain Kidd A Martyr, Not A Pirate:" *Current Opinion*, 78 (1925) :79-80.

"Captain Kidd, Pirate or Gallant Gentleman?" *Literary Digest*, 84:34-40, Feb. 28, 1925.

Cooper, H. H. "William Kidd, Gentleman." *Amer. Merc.*, 3 (1924) :337-46.

Gilder, J. B. "Was Captain Kidd a Pirate?" *Outlook*, 130:551-53, Apr. 5, 1922.

Gosse, Philip, in Eve Partridge, ed. *Pirates, Highwaymen and Adventurers*, (1927) :83-85.

James, Marquis. *They Had Their Hour*, 31-52.

Sympathetic.

Laughton, Sir John Knox, in *DNB*, 11:93.

Monaghan, Frank, in *DAB*, 10:367.

"Scapegoat, Will-o'-the-Wisp?" *Time,* 29:75-76, May 24, 1937.

Sternbeck, Alfred. *Filibusters and Buccaneers,* (1942) :231-45. Sympathetic.

"Why Captain Kidd Was No Pirate." *Literary Digest,* 93:62-67, May 7, 1927.

HISTORY: Osgood, H. L. *American Colonies in the 18th Century,* Vol. 1.
See index in vol. 4.

SPECIAL ASPECTS: "Pirate Gold: Tale of Chests, Four Maps, Captain Kidd and the South Seas." *Literary Digest,* 123:25-26, May 22, 1937.

EDWARD HYDE, LORD CORNBURY—1661-1723— Black Sheep

COLLECTIVE BIOGRAPHY: Tanner, E. P., in *DAB,* 4:441.

HISTORY: Chitwood, Oliver. *History of Colonial America,* 301, 308-10.

Osgood, H. L. *American Colonies in the Eighteenth Century,* 1:219-25; 2:39, 57-94.

CALEB HEATHCOTE—1665-1720—Typical Northern Aristocrat

BIOGRAPHY: Fox, Dixon Ryan. *Caleb Heathcote, Gentleman Colonist: the Story of a Career in the Province of New York, 1692-1721.* 1926.
AHR, 34:159. A vivid narrative of a successful business man and office holder who did much to promote the Anglican Church in America.

COLLECTIVE BIOGRAPHY: Fox, D. R., in *DAB,* 8:491.

WILLIAM PENN— 1644-1718 —Practical Utopian

ORIGINAL SOURCES: Comfort, William W., and others, eds. *Remember William Penn, 1644-1944.* 1944.
AHR, 50:808. Features quotations from Penn's writings which emphasize his contributions to the spiritual growth of man and the development of political institutions.

Myers, A. C., ed. *Narratives of Early Pennsylvania, West New Jersey, and Delaware, 1630-1707* (Original Narratives of Early American History, 1912) .

Stedman and Hutchinson. *Library of American Literature*, 2:227-29.

BIOGRAPHY: Brailsford, Mabel R.   *The Making of William Penn*. 1930.

AHR, 37:131. Excellent analysis of the factors which produced "one of the most baffling characters in all history." Deals with Penn's early life—prior to his coming to America.

Comfort, William Wister. *William Penn, 1644-1718: a Tercenary Estimate*. 1944.

AHR, 50:134. Excellent appraisal by a Quaker scholar. Sympathetic, objective, and brief.

Dobree, Bonamy. *William Penn, Quaker and Pioneer*. 1932.

AHR, 38:600. A picturesque life written in pleasing style by a brilliant English biographer. Describes Penn as a courtier rather than as a colonizer. Mildly critical while most biographies are somewhat eulogistic.

Hull, William I. *William Penn: a Topical Biography*. 1937.

AHR, 44:400. A unique study which departs from the chronological order followed by most biographies. Regards Penn as one of the greatest men of all time.

Pound, Arthur. *The Penns of Pennsylvania and England*. 1932.

MVHR, 19:579. Vivid sketches of the founder of Pennsylvania, his father and the later members of the family. Especially good on the European background.

Vulliamy, C. E. *William Penn*. 1934.

AHR, 40:172. A well-balanced, readable biography which gives an accurate impression of Penn's relations with the men and forces of the seventeenth century.

COLLECTIVE BIOGRAPHY: Bates, E. S. *American Faith*, 184-97.

Best, Agnes. *Rebel Saints*, 136-94.

Kelsey, R. W., in *DAB*, 14:433.

Read, H. E. *Fighters for Freedom*, 193-97.

Rigg, J. M., in *DNB*, 15:756.

Sweet, W. W. *Makers of Christianity*, 62-72.

Thomas and Thomas. *Living Biographies of American Statesmen*, 19-31.

HISTORY: Andrews, C. M. *Colonial Period of American History*, Vol. 3.

Channing, Edward. *History of the United States*, 2:102-27.

Jones, R. M. *The Quakers in the American Colonies*, (1923): 423-36.

Osgood, H. L. *American Colonies in the Seventeenth Century,* Vol. 2.

Russell, Elbert. *The History of Quakerism,* (1942) :117-20; index.

SPECIAL ASPECTS: Beatty, E. C. O. *William Penn as Social Philosopher.* 1939.

AHR, 45:723. A readable study which gives considerable biographical material. The author explains Penn's inconsistencies by pointing out that he was a practical man rather than a systematic philosopher.

Dorfman, Joseph. *Economic Mind in American Civilization,* 1:78-92, index.

THIRD GENERATION, 1715-1760

CHAPTER VIII. GEORGIA AND THE CAROLINAS

JAMES EDWARD OGLETHORPE— 1696-1785
—Founder of Georgia

ORIGINAL SOURCES: Warfel, Gabriel, and Williams. *American Mind*, 78-81.

BIOGRAPHY: Ettinger, Amos A. *James Edward Oglethorpe, Imperial Idealist*. 1936.

AHR, 42:145. An erudite study rather than a popular biography. Gives a balanced treatment of Oglethorpe's work as a soldier and administrator, but is inclined to overrate him as an author and liberal political philosopher.

COLLECTIVE BIOGRAPHY: Ettinger, A. A., in *DAB*, 14:1.

McConnell, F. J. *Evangelicals, Revolutionists and Idealists*, 13-40.

Venables, E., in *DNB*, 14:937.

HISTORY: Corry, J. P. *Indian Affairs in Georgia, 1732-1756*. 1936.

Coulter, E. M. *Short History of Georgia*.

Crane, Verner W. *The Southern Frontier, 1670-1732* (1928): 303-25.

———. "The Philanthropists and the Genesis of Georgia." *AHR*, 27 (1921):63-69.

Osgood, H. L. *American Colonies in the Eighteenth Century*, 3:48-51, 66-68, 396-97, 502-10.

SPECIAL ASPECTS: Boys, R. C. "General Oglethorpe and the Muses." *Ga. Hist. Quar.*, 31 (1947):19-29.

GEORGE WHITEFIELD—1714-1770—"The Greatest Preacher of the 18th Century"

COLLECTIVE BIOGRAPHY: Egbert, D. D., and D. M. Lee. *Princeton Portraits*, 295-98.

Gordon, Alexander, in *DNB*, 21:85-92.

McCartney, C. E. *Six Kings of the American Pulpit,* (1942):
9-52.

McConnell, F. J. *Evangelicals, Revolutionists and Idealists,*
69-100.

Starr, Harris E., in *DAB,* 20:124.

Sweet, W. W. *Makers of Christianity,* 108-16.

HISTORY: Osgood, H. L. *American Colonies in the Eighteenth
Century,* 2:501-502; 3:112-15, 409, 417-27, 438-39, 525.

Sweet, W. W. *Story of Religion in America,* 157, 190-92, 205-6,
211-12, 215, 234, 246-50.

Wright, Richardson. *Hawkers and Walkers in Early America.*
1927.

SPECIAL ASPECTS: Haviland, Thomas. "Of Franklin, Whitefield,
and the Orphans." *Ga. Hist. Quar.,* 29 (1945) :211-16.

CHRISTIAN GOTTLIEB PRIBER— ff. 1734-1744
—Philosopher or French Spy Among the Cherokees?

ORIGINAL SOURCES: Adair, James. *History of the American Indians,* (1930) :240-43.

Mereness, N. D., ed. *Travels in the American Colonies* (1916):
246-50.

COLLECTIVE BIOGRAPHY: Crane, Verner W., in *DAB,* 15:210.

———. "A Lost Utopia of the First American Frontier." *Sewanee
Rev.,* 27 (1919) :48-61.

HISTORY: Corry, J. P. *Indian Affairs in Georgia, 1732-1756,*
(1936) :109-10.

Phillips, U. B. *Life and Labour in the Old South,* 65-66.

ELIZABETH LUCAS PINCKNEY (ELIZA LUCAS) —
c. 1722-1793—Typical Southern Lady?

ORIGINAL SOURCES: Stedman and Hutchinson. *Library of American Literature,* 2:445-47.

BIOGRAPHY: Ravenel, Harriott Horry. *Eliza Lucas* (Women of
Colonial and Revolutionary Times, 1896) .

AHR, 2:376. This brief life by a direct descendant contains letters extend-
ing from 1739 to 1786. They reveal "a most interesting personality, a

colonial girl of excellent sense, industry, studiousness, and capacity for business . . ."

COLLECTIVE BIOGRAPHY: Beard, Annie E. *America Through Women's Eyes,* 33-41.

(R. E. P., first Baron Ernle) . "Two American Women." *Quar. Rev.,* 186 (1897) :53-63.

Also in *Living Age,* 215 (1897):90-91, 96-102.

HISTORY: Holliday, Carl. *Woman's Life in Colonial Days.* 1932.

McCrady, Edward. *South Carolina under the Royal Government, 1719-1776.* (1899) .

Spruill, J. C. *Women's Life and Work in the Southern Colonies.* 1938.

GABRIEL JOHNSTON—1699-1752—Scholar in Politics

COLLECTIVE BIOGRAPHY: Ashe, Samuel A. *Biographical History of North Carolina,* 4 (1906) :187-93.

Heck, E. L. W., in *DAB,* 10:140.

HISTORY: Ashe, S. A. *History of North Carolina,* Vol. 1, 1908.

Chitwood, O. P. *History of Colonial America,* 328-31, 561.

Gipson, L. H. *British Empire Before the American Revolution,* 2 (1936) :157-64.

Osgood, H. L. *American Colonies in the Eighteenth Century,* 4:149-74.

CHAPTER IX. VIRGINIA AND MARYLAND

ALEXANDER SPOTSWOOD—   1676-1740
—"Virginia's Best Administrator"

ORIGINAL SOURCES: Warfel, Gabriel, and Williams. *American Mind,* 75-78.

BIOGRAPHY: Dodson, Leonidas. *Alexander Spotswood, Governor of Colonial Virginia, 1710-1722.* 1932.

AHR, 38:798. This study throws much light on the personality of a dominant official and the economic forces he encountered. Did he remain loyal to the crown? Did he become a Virginian himself?

COLLECTIVE BIOGRAPHY: Bruce, P. A. *Virginia Plutarch*, 1:118-34.

Dodson, Leonidas, in *DAB*, 17:467.

Doyle, J. A., in *DNB*, 18:817.

HISTORY: Ingle, Edward. "Governor Spotswood's Horseshoe Campaign, 1716, as Related to the Romance of Cathay." *Mag. of Amer. Hist.*, 17 (1887) :295-306.

WILLIAM BYRD II—1674-1744—Cultured Aristocrat

ORIGINAL SOURCES: Bassett, John S. *The Writings of Colonel William Byrd.* 1901.

Forum, 34:85. Contains an excellent biographical sketch by the editor, as well as several interesting journals of travel written by Byrd for his own amusement. These include "The History of the Dividing Line," "A Journey to the Land of Eden," and "Progress to the Mines."

Boyd, W. K., ed. *William Byrd's Histories of the Dividing Line Betwixt Virginia and North Carolina.* 1929.

AHR, 35:416. This reprint includes the *Secret History*, "the malicious diary which the witty author formulated from his field notes immediately after the survey of 1728 . . ."

Van Doren, Mark, ed. *A Journey to the Land of Eden, and Other Papers.* 1928.

Sat. Rev. of Lit., 5:163, Sept. 29, 1928. These notes on Byrd's travels give us an interesting picture of nature and human nature in the raw, as seen by a keen observer who possessed a strong sense of humor.

Wright, Louis B., and Marion Tinling, eds. *Secret Diary of William Byrd of Westover, 1707-1712.* 1941.

Jour. of South. Hist., 8:110. An unusually frank revelation of the diarist and of eighteenth century manners. Excellent introductory sketch of Byrd's career.

Woodfin, Maude H., ed. *Another Secret Diary of William Byrd of Westover, 1739-1741.* 1942.

AHR, 49:108. Contains many references to plantation life and to prominent Virginians—Blair, Gooch, Dinwiddie, and others.

Wright, L. B. "A Shorthand Diary of William Byrd of Westover." *Huntington Lib. Quar.*, 2 (1939) :489-96.

For brief selections from Byrd's writings, *see*, G. L. Paine, ed. *Southern Prose Writers*, 3-4; Stedman and Hutchinson, *Library of American Literature*, 2:302-09; Trent and Wells, *Colonial Prose and Poetry*, 3:35-43;

Mark Van Doren, ed. *Autobiography of America,* 52-64; Warfel, Gabriel, and Williams. *American Mind,* 72-75.

BIOGRAPHY: Beatty, Richmond Croom. *William Byrd of Westover.* 1932.

AHR, 38:377. A study which shows more understanding of Byrd as a politician than as a writer and amateur scientist. Should be supplemented by reading the secret diaries.

COLLECTIVE BIOGRAPHY: Bruce, P. A. *Virginia Plutarch,* 1:135-54.

Tyler, M. C. *History of American Literature,* 2:270-78.

Wertenbaker, T. J., in *DAB,* 3:383.

Wright, L. B. *First Gentlemen of Virginia,* 312-47.
Best and most recent account.

Wright, L. B., and Marion Tinling. "William Byrd of Westover: an American Pepys." *So. Atl. Quar.,* 39 (1940) :259-74.

SPECIAL ASPECTS: Lonn, Ella. *The Colonial Agents of the Southern Colonies,* 118-23.

Masterson, James R. "William Byrd in Lubberland." *Amer. Lit.,* 9 (1937) :153-70.

Tyler, Dorothy. "Modern Education and William Byrd of Westover." *So. Atl. Quar.,* 43 (1944) :174-80.

Woodfin, Maude H. "William Byrd and the Royal Society." *Va. Mag. Hist. and Biog.,* 40 (1932) :23-34, 111-23.

SAMUEL DAVIES—1723-1761—Leader in the Great Awakening

ORIGINAL SOURCES: Davies, Samuel. "A Parson's Call to Arms." Stedman and Hutchinson. *Library of American Literature,* 2:447-49.

COLLECTIVE BIOGRAPHY: Egbert and Lee. *Princeton Portraits,* 42-45.

Hughes, J. G., Jr., in *Branch Hist. Papers of Randolph-Macon College,* 4 (1914) :65-79.

Pomfret, J. E., in *DAB,* 5:102.

Sweet, W. W. *Makers of Christianity,* 94-98.

HISTORY: Gewehr, Wesley M. *The Great Awakening in Virginia, 1740-1790,* (1930) :68-105.

Sweet, W. W. *Story of Religions in America,* 215-17.

SIR JOHN RANDOLPH—c. 1693-1736—Lawyer and Scholar

COLLECTIVE BIOGRAPHY: Eckenrode, H. J. *The Randolphs,* 44-51.

Woodfin, Maude H., in *DAB,* 15:361.

SPECIAL ASPECTS: Lonn, Ella. *The Colonial Agents in the Southern Colonies,* 123-25, 154.

ROBERT DINWIDDIE—1693-1770—"Discoverer of Washington"

BIOGRAPHY: Koontz, Louis K. *Robert Dinwiddie: His Career in American Colonial Government and Westward Expansion.* 1941.

AHR, 47:347. A defense which overlooks Dinwiddie's faults and magnifies his virtues. Based on inadequate research.

COLLECTIVE BIOGRAPHY: Wertenbaker, T. J., in *DAB,* 5:316.

Koontz, L. K. "Robert Dinwiddie: a Chapter in the American Colonial Frontier." *Pacific Hist. Rev.,* 5 (1936) :359-67.

HISTORY: Bailey, Kenneth P. *The Ohio Company of Virginia and the Westward Movement, 1748-1792,* (1939) :57-58, index.

THOMAS, LORD FAIRFAX—1693-1781—Friend of Washington

COLLECTIVE BIOGRAPHY: Harrison, Fairfax, in *DAB,* 6:255.

Wheatley, Richard. "The Fairfaxes of Yorkshire and Virginia." *Mag. of Amer. Hist.,* 13 (1885) :217-36.

See esp., 224-29.

BIOGRAPHIES OF CONTEMPORARIES: Freeman, Douglas S. *George Washington,* 1:186-88, 329ff., 501ff., index.

Hughes, Rupert. *George Washington,* Vol. 1.

Stephenson, Nathaniel, and W. H. Dunn. *George Washington,* 1:20-21, 33-34, 37, 51, 285.

RICHARD BLAND— 1710-1776 —"Retrospective Politician"

COLLECTIVE BIOGRAPHY: Swem, E. G., in *DAB*, 2:354.

Tyler, M. C. *Literary History of the American Revolution*, 1:229-31.

ALEXANDER HAMILTON— 1712-1756 —Physician, Traveler, and Social Historian

ORIGINAL SOURCES: Bridenbaugh, Carl, ed. *Gentleman's Progress: The Itinerarium of Dr. Alexander Hamilton, 1744.* 1948. *Wm. and Mary Quar.*, Third Series, 6:123. The authentic but lively journal of a journey in the northern colonies made by a young Scottish physician. The author was a witty writer, a good mixer, a curious and sharp observer. His journal throws much light on eighteenth century types.

COLLECTIVE BIOGRAPHY: Richardson, Hester D., in *DAB*, 8:170.

CHAPTER X. THE MIDDLE COLONIES

JOHN PETER ZENGER— 1697-1746 —Newspaper Editor and Publisher

COLLECTIVE BIOGRAPHY: Engle, W., in W. C. Howey, ed. *Fighting Editors*, (1948) :9-18.

Hart, C. S. *General Washington's Sons of Israel and Other Forgotten Heroes of History*, (1937) :87-105.

Morris, Richard B., in *DAB*, 20:648.

Ulmann, Albert. *New Yorkers*, 38-56.

Wolseley, R. E. "Apostle of a Free Press." *Jour. of Educ.*, 129 (1946) :236-38.

HISTORY: Bleyer, W. G. *Main Currents in the History of American Journalism*, (1927) :63-66.

Jones, R. W. *Journalism in the United States*, (1947) :89-101.

Lee, J. M. *History of American Journalism*, (1923) :39-43.

Mott, F. L. *American Journalism*, (1941) :31-42.

Osgood, H. L. *American Colonies in the Eighteenth Century*, 2:452-61.

Payne, G. H. *History of Journalism in the United States,* (1920): 48-58, index.

SPECIAL ASPECTS: Peattie, D. C. "Freedom on Trial: the Zenger Case." *Read. Dig.,* 51 (1947) :41-44.

ANDREW HAMILTON—   ?-1741   —Philadelphia
Lawyer

COLLECTIVE BIOGRAPHY: Spencer, Charles W., in *DAB,* 8:181.

HISTORY: Osgood, H. L. *American Colonies in the Eighteenth Century,* 2:460-62, 552; 4:48, 52-54.

WILLIAM (1673-1745) AND GILBERT TENNENT
—1703-1764—Frontier Educators

COLLECTIVE BIOGRAPHY: Egbert and Lee. *Princeton Portraits,* 32-34.

Starr, Harris E., in *DAB,* 18:366-69, 370-71.

HISTORY: Gewehr, W. M. *The Great Awakening in Virginia,* (1930) :5, 10, 57-58, 91, 222.

Sweet, W. W. *Story of Religion in America,* 179-80, 203-04, 206.

JOHN BARTRAM—   1699-1777   —"First Native
American Botanist"

ORIGINAL SOURCES: Harper, Francis, ed. "John Bartram: Diary of a Journey Through the Carolinas, Georgia, and Florida." *Trans. Am. Philos. Soc.,* N. S., Vol. 33, pt. 1 (1944) :1-20.

BIOGRAPHY: Earnest, Ernest. *John and William Bartram, Botanists and Explorers, 1699-1823.* 1940.

AHR, 47:202. An authoritative study of a father and son who "occupy a distinguished place in the development of American culture."

COLLECTIVE BIOGRAPHY: Faris, John T. *Romance of Forgotten Men,* (1928) :24-34.

Peattie, Donald C., in *DAB,* 2:26.

Tracy, Henry C. *American Naturists,* (1930) :29-35.

True, Rodney H. *Bartonia: Proc. of the Philadelphia Botanical Club,* Dec. 31, 1931.

Youmans, William J. *Pioneers of Science in America,* (1896) : 24-39.

SPECIAL ASPECTS: Barnhart, John H. "Significance of John Bartram's Work to Botanical and Horticultural Knowledge." *Bartonia: Proc. of the Philadelphia Botanical Club*, Dec. 31, 1931, pp. 24-34.

———. "Note on John Bartram's First Interest in Botany." *Ibid.*, 35-37.

Goodwin, Mary F. "Three Eighteenth Century Gardens." *Va. Quar. Rev.*, 10 (1934) :218-33.

Kraus, Michael. "Scientific Relations Between Europe and America in the Eighteenth Century." *Scientific Mo.*, 105 (1942) :259-72.

Pyle, Howard. "Bartram and His Garden." *Harper's*, 60 (1880) : 321-30.

CONRAD WEISER—1696-1760—Farmer and Indian Agent

ORIGINAL SOURCES: Weiser, Conrad. "Journal of a Tour to the Ohio," (1748) in Ruben Gold Thwaites, ed. *Early Western Travels*, 1:18-44.

BIOGRAPHY: Graeff, Arthur D. *Conrad Weiser, Pennsylvania Peacemaker*. 1943.

AHR, 51:770. A careful study which presents Weiser as the agent who carried out Pennsylvania's "good neighbor" policy toward the Six Nations. It reproduces the atmosphere of the Pennsylvania Dutch pioneers who "farmed their way to peace."

Wallace, Paul A. W. *Conrad Weiser, 1696-1760: Friend of Colonists and Mohawk*. 1945.

AHR, 51:506. An excellent study of Indian affairs which includes considerable source material. Unfortunately, the book fails to present this "foremost German of the colonial period" as the colorful figure he really was.

COLLECTIVE BIOGRAPHY: Bridenbaugh, Carl, in *DAB*, 19:614.

SIR WILLIAM JOHNSON— 1715-1774 —Superintendent of Indian Affairs

BIOGRAPHY: Pound, Arthur, and Richard E. Day. *Johnson of the Mohawks: a Biography of Sir William Johnson, Irish Immigrant, Mohawk War Chief, American Soldier, Empire Builder*. 1930.

AHR, 36:408. Fascinating story of an Irish pioneer in the Mohawk Valley who kept the Six Nations friendly to the English. While he was very unconventional in his private life, Sir William was probably the most important man in America at the time of his death in 1774.

Seymour, Flora W. *Lords of the Valley, Sir William Johnson and His Mohawk Brothers.* 1930.

AHR, 36:408. A brief popular biography which fails to emphasize the significance of Sir William's services.

COLLECTIVE BIOGRAPHY: Chichester, H. Manners, in *DNB,* 10:938.

Dailey, W. N. P., in *Chronicles of Oklahoma,* 22 (1944) :164-75.

Seymour, Flora W. *Indian Agents of the Old Frontier,* (1941) : 6-8.

Stevens, Wayne E., in *DAB,* 10:124.

HISTORY: Clarke, T. Wood. *The Bloody Mohawk.* 1940.

AHR, 46:481. A sort of who's who of New York in the colonial period. It describes the services of Sir William Johnson and gives a sympathetic interpretation of the Iroquois and the Loyalists. Perpetuates some questionable traditions.

BIOGRAPHIES OF CONTEMPORARIES: P. A. W. Wallace, in his *Conrad Weiser,* describes Johnson as "a politician who worked best in the half light."

ISRAEL PEMBERTON—1715-1779—Merchant and Quaker Leader

BIOGRAPHY: Thayer, Theodore. *Israel Pemberton, King of the Quakers.* 1943.

AHR, 50:136. Careful and impartial study of a merchant and philanthropist who strove to preserve Quaker principles in Pennsylvania and maintain peace with the Indians.

COLLECTIVE BIOGRAPHY: Bacon, Elizabeth M., in *DAB,* 14:412.

JOHN WOOLMAN—1720-1772—"An American Saint"

ORIGINAL SOURCES: Gummere, Amelia Mott, ed. *The Journal and Essays of John Woolman.* 1922.

AHR, 28:586. The biographical introduction makes a worthwhile contribution to our knowledge of Woolman.

Extracts in Stedman and Hutchinson. *Library of American Literature,* 3:78-85; Trent and Wells. *Colonial Prose and Poetry,* 3:296-314; Warfel, Gabriel, and Williams. *American Mind,* 96-100.

BIOGRAPHY: Whitney, Janet. *John Woolman: American Quaker.* 1942.

AHR, 48:655. A vivid presentation of the New Jersey tailor as a man of affairs and a humanitarian "troubled by the evils of the world."

COLLECTIVE BIOGRAPHY: Blankenship, Russell. *American Literature,* 134-36.

Canby, H. S. *Classic Americans,* 28-34.

Dalglish, D. N. *People Called Quakers,* (1938) :57-83.

Pomfret, John E., in *DAB,* 20:516.

Riley, Woodbridge, in *Cambridge History of American Literature,* 1:86-89.

Smith, C. F., in *DNB,* 21:904.

Tyler, M. C. *Literary History of the American Revolution,* 2:339-46.

HISTORY: Jones, R. M. *The Quakers in the American Colonies,* (1923) :391-416.

SPECIAL ASPECTS: Dorfman, Joseph. *Economic Mind in American Civilization,* 1:195-204.

BENJAMIN FRANKLIN—1706-1790—"The Most Versatile American of the Eighteenth Century"

ORIGINAL SOURCES: Bigelow, John, ed. *The Life of Franklin Written by Himself,* 3 vols., 1874.

The best edition of the *Autobiography.* Includes selections from Franklin's correspondence which continues the story after 1757.

Goodman, Nathan G., ed. *Benjamin Franklin's Own Story: His Autobiography Continued from 1759 to His Death in 1790 With a Biographical Sketch Drawn from His Writings.* 1937.

AHR, 44:209. Includes the Autobiography and a narrative which covers the years he spent in England as colonial agent and in France as commissioner.

———, ed. *A Benjamin Franklin Reader.* 1945.

AHR, 51:761. Selections from Franklin's works which reveal many aspects of his life and thought. They include the *Autobiography* and a brief biographical sketch by the editor.

Mott, F. L., and C. E. Jorgenson, eds. *Benjamin Franklin: Representative Selections* (American Writers series, 1936) .

Amer. Lit., 9:90. The extracts given are designed to illustrate the growth of Franklin's mind. The introduction presents the thesis that "Franklin may best be understood by relating all of his thought to an essential unity in the light of scientific deism, tempered by his debt to Puritanism, classicism and neo-classicism."

Van Doren, Carl, ed. *Benjamin Franklin: Autobiographical Writings.* 1945.

Nation, 162:82, Jan. 19, 1946. An excellent companion volume to Van Doren's biography of Franklin. Recommended for consecutive reading or browsing at odd moments.
Condensed in *Read. Dig.*, 48:143-68.

———, ed. *Letters and Papers of Benjamin Franklin and Richard Jackson, 1753-1785.* 1947.

Weekly Book Rev., July 13, 1947, p. 3. Jackson was a well informed lawyer and a member of Parliament who served as a colonial agent and a member of the Board of Trade. The letters which passed between these two friends are largely concerned with politics.

Selections from Franklin's writings may be found in Stedman and Hutchinson. *Library of American Literature,* 3:3-49; Trent and Wells. *Colonial Prose and Poetry,* 190-236; Warfel, Gabriel, and Williams. *American Mind,* 104-30; Charles Warner, ed. *Library of the World's Best Literature,* 10:5925-63.

BIOGRAPHY: Becker, Carl L. *Benjamin Franklin: a Biographical Sketch.* 1946.

Wm. and Mary Quar., Third Series, 4:231. This little volume is a reprint of Becker's brilliant article in the *DAB*. The best brief biography. The review gives a few corrections.

*Bruce, W. C. *Benjamin Franklin Self Revealed: a Biographical and Critical Study Based Mainly on His Own Writings,* 2 vols., 1917.

AHR, 24:487. Through skillful use of the topical method, the author gives us a brilliant and comprehensive estimate of Franklin. Did the eighteenth century produce a wiser and abler man?

Fay, Bernard. *Franklin, the Apostle of Modern Times.* 1929.

AHR, 35:663. A readable study by a French scholar, who presents some new material on the later loves of Franklin and on the part Masonry played in his life.

Russell, Phillips. *Benjamin Franklin, the First Civilized American.* 1926.

---

* Awarded the Pulitzer Prize.

New Repub., 48:303, Nov. 3, 1926. A lively presentation of the gayer side of Franklin, but not a full length portrait.

*Van Doren, Carl. *Benjamin Franklin*. 1938.

AHR, 46:160. The best biography. An authentic portrait based on wide research and written with rare literary charm.

Selections in H. V. Prochnow, ed. *Great Stories from Great Lives*, 284-92.

Van Doren, Carl. *Selected by Himself*, 309-434 (Viking Portable Library, 1945).

COLLECTIVE BIOGRAPHY: Bates, E. S. *American Faith*, 218-33.

Becker, Carl L., in *DAB*, 6:585.

Bridenbaugh and Bridenbaugh. *Rebels and Gentlemen*, 304-58.

Brown, C. R. *They Were Giants*, 1-34.

Brown, L. F., and G. B. Carson. *Men and Centuries of European Civilization*, 442-53.

Canby, H. S. *Classic Americans*, 34-35.

Over-emphasizes the influence of Quakerism.

Dos Passos, John. *Ground We Stand On*, 187-205.

Egbert and Lee. *Princeton Portraits*, 314-16.

Guedalla, Phillip. *Fathers of the Revolution*, 215-34.

Describes Franklin as "the first high priest of the religion of efficiency." Also in *Forum*, 75 (1926):37-49.

Kunitz and Haycraft. *American Authors*, 285-87.

O'Higgins, Harvey. *American Mind in Action*, 155-79.

Parrington, V. L. *Main Currents in American Thought*, 1:164-78.

Peattie, Donald C., in *Read. Dig.*, 45 (1944) :57-61.

Sherman, Stuart P. *Americans*, 28-62.

Penetrating estimate.

———, in *Cambridge History of American Literature*, 1:90-110.

Thomas and Thomas. *Fifty Great Americans*, 1-11.

———. *Living Biographies of American Statesmen*, 35-50.

Tyler, M. C. *Literary History of the American Revolution*, 2:359-81.

Van Doren, Carl, in *There Were Giants in the Land*, 68-74.

Van Loon, H. W. *Van Loon's Lives*, (1943) :767-98.

---

* Awarded the Pulitzer Prize.

Walton, John. *Makers of the U. S. A.,* 5-18.

Wilstach, Paul. *Patriots off their Pedestals,* 47-77.

HISTORY: Burlingame, Roger. *March of the Iron Men.* 1938.

Davidson, Philip. *Propaganda and the American Revolution.* 1941.

Klingberg, Frank J. *The Morning of America.* 1941.

Miller, John C. *Origins of the American Revolution.* 1943.

SPECIAL ASPECTS: Biancolli, Louis, ed. *The Book of Great Conversations,* 100-05.

A dramatic version of Franklin's skirmish with the British Secretary of State for America.

Blair, Walter. *Horse Sense in American Humor,* 1-23.

Boynton, P. H. *America in Contemporary Fiction,* 1-20.

Burlingame, Roger. *Inventors Behind the Inventor,* 16-33.

Crane, Verner W. *Benjamin Franklin, Englishman and American* (The Colver Lectures in Brown University, XIX, 1936).

AHR, 42:786. A "brilliant reappraisal of Franklin's social philosophy and political theory . . ." The author believes that Franklin "was secretly a dominion home-ruler at a time when his public utterances were more conciliatory to Parliament."

Crowther, James G. *Famous American Men of Science,* 17-155.

Dix, J. P. "Benjamin Franklin, Father of American Ingenuity." *Social Stu.,* 39 (1948) :16-24.

Dorfman, Joseph. *Economic Mind in American Civilization,* xi, 1:178-95, index.

Fay, Bernard. *The Two Franklins: Fathers of American Democracy.* 1933.

AHR, 39:741. Deals with Franklin's relations with his grandson, Benjamin F. Bache.

Ford, Paul Leicester. *The Many-sided Franklin.* 1899.

AHR, 5:579. Gives a vivid portrayal of Franklin as a scientist, politician, diplomatist, etc. Written with rare humor. Also in *Century,* 57 (1899).

Grampp, W. D. "Political Economy of Poor Richard." *Jour. Pol. Econ.,* 55 (1947) :132-41.

Holliday, Carl. *Woman's Life in Colonial Days.* 1922.

Jaffe, Bernard. *Men of Science in America,* (1944) :23-51.

James, Marquis. *They Had Their Hour,* Chapter III, "Franklin the Electrician."

Jernegan, M. W. "Benjamin Franklin's Electrical Kite and Lightning Rod." *N. E. Quar.,* 1 (1928) :180-96.

Ross, Earle D. "Franklin and Agriculture." *Jour. Pol. Econ.,* 37 (1929) :52-72.

Russell, Phillips. "Franklin in Paris." *McNaught's Mo.,* September, 1926.

Condensed in *Read. Dig.,* Mar., 1927, 60-88.

Spiller, Robert E., and others, eds. *Literary History of the United States,* 1:101-12.

Van Doren, Carl, ed. *Meet Dr. Franklin.* 1943.

AHR, 50:140. A series of papers on various aspects of "the many-sided Franklin" which correct popular misconceptions and contribute substantially to our knowledge.

Wecter, Dixon. *The Hero in America,* 50-80.

Williams, David. "More Light on Franklin's Religious Ideas." *AHR,* 43 (1938) :803-13.

Wright, L. B. "Franklin's Legacy to the Gilded Age." *Va. Quar. Rev.,* 22 (1946) :268-79.

Willson, Beckles. *America's Ambassadors to France,* 1-16.

CHAPTER XI. NEW ENGLAND

WILLIAM SHIRLEY—1694-1771—Able and Popular Governor of Massachusetts

BIOGRAPHY: Wood, George Arthur. *William Shirley, Governor of Massachusetts, 1741-1756: a History.* 1920.

AHR, 26:545. A definitive study of an English official who worked for the welfare of his colony.

COLLECTIVE BIOGRAPHY: Adams, James T., in *DAB,* 17:120.

Doyle, J. A., in *DNB,* 18:142.

Unsatisfactory.

Winsor, Justin, in *Mag. of Amer. Hist.,* 20 (1888) :368-71.

HISTORY: Adams, J. T. *Revolutionary New England.*

Osgood, H. L. *American Colonies in the Eighteenth Century,*
Vols. 3-4.

SIR WILLIAM PEPPERRELL—   1696-1759
—Merchant and Soldier

ORIGINAL SOURCES: Lincoln, Charles H., ed. "The Journal of
Sir William Pepperrell in the Expedition Against Louis-
bourg." *Am. Antiq. Soc. Proc., N. S.,* 20 (1909) :133-83.

COLLECTIVE BIOGRAPHY: Adams, James T., in *DAB,* 14:456.

Harris, Alexander, in *DNB,* 15:798.

Pound, Arthur. *Native Stock,* 3-41.

Stevens, J. A., in *Mag. of Amer. Hist.,* 2 (1878) :673-84.

HISTORY: Hutchinson, Thomas. *The History of the Colony and
Province of Massachusetts Bay,* Vols. 2-3, 1936.

PETER FANEUIL—   1700-1743   —Merchant

Adams, James T., in *DAB,* 6:262.

Weeden, W. B. *Economic and Social History of New England,*
2:465-70, 608-36.

JONATHAN EDWARDS— 1703-1758 —Speculative
Philosopher and Hell-Fire Preacher

ORIGINAL SOURCES: Faust, Clarence H., and Thomas H. Johnson, eds. *Jonathan Edwards: Representative Selections* (American Writers series, 1935) .

Mussey, J. B. *Yankee Life by Those Who Lived It,* 346-57.

Van Doren, Carl, ed. *Benjamin Franklin and Jonathan Edwards: Selections from Their Writings* (Modern Student's
Lib., 1920) .

Williams, Stanley, ed. "Six Letters of Jonathan Edwards to
Joseph Bellamy." *N. E. Quar.,* 1 (1928) :226-42.

Selections from Edwards' writings may be found in Trent and Wells.
Colonial Prose and Poetry, 3:143-89; Stedman and Hutchinson. *Library
of American Literature,* 2:373-411; Warfel, Gabriel, and Williams.
American Mind, 81-96; Charles Warner. *Library of the World's Best
Literature,* 9:5175-5188.

BIOGRAPHY: McGiffert, Arthur C., Jr. *Jonathan Edwards.* 1932.

N. E. Quar., 5:395. Brief but excellent portrait of the man.

*Winslow, Ola Elizabeth. *Jonathan Edwards, 1703-1758.* 1940. *AHR*, 46:417. The most complete and scholarly account. Emphasizes his life rather than his ideas.

COLLECTIVE BIOGRAPHY: Bates, E. S. *American Faith*, 207-14.

Blankenship, Russell. *American Literature*, 120-25.

Canby, H. S. *Classic Americans*, 9-22.

Christie, Francis A., in *DAB*, 6:30.

Egbert and Lee. *Princeton Portraits*, 40-42.

Gordon, Alexander, in *DNB*, 6:541.

Kunitz and Haycraft. *American Authors*, 243-44.

More, P. E., in *Cambridge History of American Literature*, 1:57-71.

Parrington, V. L. *Main Currents in American Thought*, 1:152-63.
Prejudiced.

Schneider, H. W., in *Encyclopedia of the Social Sciences*, 5:436.

Sweet, W. W. *Makers of Christianity*, 75-87.

Tyler, M. C. *History of American Literature*, 2:177-92.

Walker, Williston. *Ten New England Leaders*, 217-66.

HISTORY: Adams, J. T. *Revolutionary New England*, 170-74.

Holliday, Carl. *Woman's Life in Colonial Days.* 1932.

Seldes, G. V. *The Stammering Century*, (1928) :13-35.

Sweet, W. W. *Religion in Colonial America*, 282-84.

————. *The Story of Religions in America*, 185-89, 192-94.

SPECIAL ASPECTS: Carpenter, F. I. "The Radicalism of Jonathan Edwards." *N. E. Quar.*, 4 (1931) :629-44.

Faust, C. H. "Jonathan Edwards as a Scientist." *Amer. Lit.*, 1 (1930) :393-404.

Holliday, Carl. *Woman's Life in Colonial Days.* 1932.

Keller, C. R. *The Second Great Awakening in Connecticut*, (1942) :29-31, 229.

Miller, Perry. "Jonathan Edwards' Sociology of the Great Awakening." *N. E. Quar.*, 21 (1948) :50-77.

---

* Awarded the Pulitzer Prize.

Pitkanen, Allan. "Jonathan Edwards—Scourger of the Wicked."
Social Stu., 37 (1946) :269-71.

Spiller, Robert E., and others, eds. *Literary History of the United States,* 1:71-81.

Weeden, W. B. *Economic and Social History of New England,* 2:700-06.

Gives an interesting comparison of Edwards and Franklin.

THOMAS HANCOCK— 1703-1764 —Smuggler and War Profiteer

COLLECTIVE BIOGRAPHY: Edelman, Edward, in *DAB,* 8:220.

———, in *Jour. Econ. & Bus. Hist.,* 1 (1928) :77-104.

HISTORY: Baxter, W. T. *The House of Hancock: Business in Boston, 1724-1775* (Harvard Studies in Business History, 1945).

AHR, 51:326. The section dealing with Thomas Hancock constitutes over three fourths of the book and is "a real contribution to American business history." Read Chapter I, "Introduction to Thomas"; also pp. 223-24.

ROBERT FEKE—c. 1705-c. 1750—"The Best Portrait Painter in the Colonies Before Copley"

BIOGRAPHY: Foote, Henry W. *Robert Feke, Colonial Portrait Painter.* 1930.

AHR, 36:650. An attempt to reconstruct the life of a quiet unobtrusive man who, save for the superior portraits he painted, left few traces of himself.

COLLECTIVE BIOGRAPHY: Coburn, F. W., in *DAB,* 6:312.

HISTORY: Flexner, J. T. *American Painting,* 130-47.

SPECIAL ASPECTS: ———. "Aristocratic Visions: The Art of Robert Feke." *Mag. of Art,* 40 (1947) :2-7.

EPHRAIM WILLIAMS—1714-1755—Frontier Fighter Who Founded a College

COLLECTIVE BIOGRAPHY: Genzmer, George H., in *DAB,* 20:259.

Pound, Arthur. *Native Stock,* 77-105.

LORD JEFFERY AMHERST— 1717-1797 —British Commander

BIOGRAPHY: Long, J. C. *Lord Jeffery Amherst, a Soldier of the King.* 1933.

AHR, 39:318. A graphic narrative based on family papers. Was the commander a great soldier, or "only a capable one with fortune on his side"?

COLLECTIVE BIOGRAPHY: Mayo, Lawrence Shaw, in *DAB,* 1:256.

ROBERT ROGERS—1731-1795—Military Hero and Playwright

COLLECTIVE BIOGRAPHY: Pound, Arthur. *Native Stock,* 109-48.

Souslby, B. H., in *DNB,* 17:138.

Tyler, M. C. *Literary History of the American Revolution,* 1:150-51.

FOURTH GENERATION, 1760-1815

Dodd, William E. "The Declaration of Independence." *Va. Quar. Rev.*, 2 (1926) :334-49.

Contains many brief but intriguing references to individuals.

Nevins, Allan. *The American States During and After the Revolution, 1775-1789.* 1924.

MVHR, 11:581. An illuminating synthesis which describes "what was going on in the individual commonwealths . . ." Refers in passing to a large number of the leaders of this generation. Not usually cited in individual bibliographies.

CHAPTER XII. PENNSYLVANIA, NEW JERSEY, AND DELAWARE

HISTORY: Wertenbaker, Thomas J. *The Golden Age of Colonial Culture,* Chapter IV, "Culture with a 'Thee and a Thou': Philadelphia."

Bridenbaugh and Bridenbaugh. *Rebels and Gentlemen: Philadelphia in the Age of Franklin.* 1942.

AHR, 48:574. A fascinating portrait of America's largest city. Furnishes excellent background and passing glimpses of citizens who distinguished themselves in various fields.

CHARLES READ—c. 1713-1774—Farmer, Official, and Merchant

BIOGRAPHY: Woodward, Carl. *Ploughs and Politicks: Charles Read of New Jersey and His Notes on Agriculture, 1715-1774.* 1941.

AHR, 47:879. "Book I" is a careful biography of a forgotten colonial who was an authority on agriculture and who was well acquainted with the important people of New Jersey and Pennsylvania in his day.

COLLECTIVE BIOGRAPHY: Woodward, C. F., in *DAB*, 15:419.

ANTHONY BENEZET— 1713-1784 —Teacher and Philanthropist

ORIGINAL SOURCES: Benezet, Anthony. "An Early Protest

Against the Slave Trade," in Stedman and Hutchinson. *Library of American Literature,* 2:490-92.

BIOGRAPHY: Brookes, George S. *Friend Anthony Benezet.* 1937. *AHR,* 43:648. The first full-length biography. Follows the topical method of presentation.

COLLECTIVE BIOGRAPHY: Egbert and Lee. *Princeton Portraits,* 313-14.

Gummere, Amelia M., in *DAB,* 2:177.

CHRISTOPHER LUDWICK—1720-1801—Baker and Spy

COLLECTIVE BIOGRAPHY: Faris, John T. *The Romance of Forgotten Men,* (1928) :89-102.

Fitzpatrick, J. C. *The Spirit of the Revolution,* (1924) :139-57.

Holbrook, S. H. "A Forgotten Worthy of '76." *Amer. Merc.,* 61 (1945) :416-20.

Jackson, Joseph, in *DAB,* 11:497.

BENJAMIN WEST— 1728-1820 —Artist and Social Lion

COLLECTIVE BIOGRAPHY: Einstein, Lewis. *Divided Loyalties,* 283-325.

Fielding, Mantle, in *DAB,* 20:6.

Flexner, James T. *America's Old Masters,* 19-100.

Lee, Cuthbert. *Early American Portrait Painters,* 83-98.

McSpadden, J. W. *Famous Painters of America,* 1-42.

Monkhouse, Cosmo, in *DNB,* 20:1235.

HISTORY: Flexner, J. T. *American Painting,* 176-93.

Neuhaus, Eugen. *History and Ideals of American Art,* 23-24.

JOHN DICKINSON—1732-1808—"Spokesman of the Colonial Whigs"

ORIGINAL SOURCES: Warfel, Gabriel, and Williams. *American Mind,* 139-45.

Stedman and Hutchinson. *Library of American Literature,* 3:175-80.

BIOGRAPHY: Stillé, Charles J. *Life and Times of John Dickinson, 1732-1808.* 1891.

Mag. of Amer. Hist., 25:427. The standard biography. By nature a conservative, this country gentleman and lawyer pursued a rather hesitant course and refused to sign the Declaration of Independence. The author defends him from the charges of insincerity and political apostasy made against him in contemporary newspapers and pamphlets.

COLLECTIVE BIOGRAPHY: Adams, J. T., in *DAB,* 5:299.

Harrison, Robert, in *DNB,* 5:940.

Parrington, V. L. *Main Currents in American Thought,* 1:219-32.

Sharpless, Isaac. *Provincial Leaders of Provincial Pennsylvania,* (1919):224-43.

HISTORY: Davidson, Philip. *Propaganda and the American Revolution.* 1941.

Miller, J. C. *Origin of the American Revolution.* 1943.

Tyler, M. C. *Literary History of the American Revolution,* 1:234-41; 2:21-34.

JOHN MORGAN—1735-1789—Medical Director of Continental Army

COLLECTIVE BIOGRAPHY: Flexner, J. T. *Doctors on Horseback,* 3-53.

Peeling, J. H., in *DAB,* 13:172.

FRANCIS HOPKINSON—1737-1791—Philadelphia's First Dilettante

ORIGINAL SOURCES: Stedman and Hutchinson. *Library of American Literature,* 3:236-51.

BIOGRAPHY: Hastings, George Everett. *Life and Works of Francis Hopkinson.* 1926.

AHR, 32:894. Standard biography written with admirable detachment.

COLLECTIVE BIOGRAPHY: Bridenbaugh and Bridenbaugh. *Rebels and Gentlemen,* 104-06, 152-54, 228-29, index.

Ewen, David. *Composers of Yesterday,* 223-25.

Hastings, G. E., in *DAB,* 9:220.

Kunitz and Haycraft. *American Authors,* 385-86.

Parrington, V. L. *Main Currents in American Thought,* 1: 252-55.

Tyler, M. C. *Literary History of the American Revolution,* 1:162-71; 2:130-57.

SPECIAL ASPECTS: Sonneck, Oscar G. T. *Francis Hopkinson: the First American Poet-Composer.* 1905.

THOMAS PAINE— 1737-1809 —"America's First
Liberal"

ORIGINAL SOURCES: Clark, Harry Hayden, ed. *Thomas Paine: Representative Selections* (American Writers series, 1944) .

AHR, 50:143. Contains a valuable introduction which gives the best analysis available of Paine's ideas and their sources.

Foner, Philip S., ed. *The Complete Writings of Thomas Paine,* 2 vols., 1945.

AHR, 51:724. Contains an excellent biographical essay.

Peach, Arthur W., ed. *Selections From the Writings of Thomas Paine.* 1928.

Selections from Paine's writings may be found in Isidore Abramowitz. *Great Prisoners,* 377-91; Stedman and Hutchinson. *Library of American Literature,* 3:219-35; Warfel, Gabriel, and Williams. *American Mind,* 148-61.

BIOGRAPHY: Best, Mary Agnes. *Thomas Paine, Prophet and Martyr of Democracy.* 1927.

AHR, 34:135. A popular biography, strongly prejudiced in Paine's favor.

Conway, Moncure D. *Life of Thomas Paine,* 2 vols., 1892.

Pol. Sci. Quar., 8:349. The standard biography, based on wide research but prejudiced in Paine's favor.

Smith, Frank. *Thomas Paine, Liberator.* 1938.

AHR, 44:857. Recognized at the time of its publication as "by far the best account of Paine since Conway's study." Regards Paine as "a great figure" and gives a vivid description of the exciting times in which he lived.

Woodward, Wm. E. *Thomas Paine, America's Godfather.* 1945.

AHR, 51:328. A brief popular life written to refute charges that Paine was a "filthy little atheist," that he drank to excess, and that he seduced Mrs. Bonneville.

COLLECTIVE BIOGRAPHY: Bert, Struthers, in *There Were Giants in the Land,* 104-13.

Bradford, Gamaliel. *Damaged Souls,* 51-84.

Brinton, Crane, in *DAB,* 14:159.

Calverton, V. F. "Thomas Paine, God-intoxicated Revolutionary." *Scribner's,* 95 (1934) :15-22.

Connell, J. M. "Thomas Paine—the Man He Was." *Hibbert Jour.,* 35 (1937) :213-26.

Dodd, William E., in *Amer. Merc.,* 21 (1930) :477-83.

Fausset, Hugh I'Anson. *Poets and Pundits,* (1947) :235-44.

Fichter, J. H. *Roots of Change,* (1939) :65-86.

Kunitz and Haycraft. *American Authors,* 589-91.

McConnell, F. J. *Evangelicals, Revolutionists and Idealists,* 101-31.

Parrington, V. L. *Main Currents in American Thought,* 1:327-41.

Read, H. E. *Fighters for Freedom,* 198-203.

Seager, Allan. *They Worked for a Better World,* 34-55.

Stephen, Leslie, in *DNB,* 15:69.

Thomas and Thomas. *Fifty Great Americans,* 41-49.

Tyler, M. C. *Literary History of the American Revolution,* 1:452-74; 2:35-50.

Ulmann, Albert. *New Yorkers,* 57-76.

Woodward, W. E., in *Amer. Merc.,* 61 (1945) :72-79.

SPECIAL ASPECTS: Clark, H. H. "Toward a Reinterpretation of Thomas Paine." *Amer. Lit.,* 5 (1933) :133-45.

Dorfman, Joseph. *Economic Mind in American Civilization,* 1:447-59.

Lewis, Joseph. *Thomas Paine, Author of the Declaration of Independence.* 1947.
AHR, 52:799. Unconvincing. Paine never claimed to have had any part in writing the Declaration of Independence.

Miller, Perry. "Thomas Paine, Rationalist." *Nation,* 162:228-30, Feb. 23, 1946.

Penniman, Howard. "Thomas Paine—Democrat." *Amer. Pol. Sci. Rev.,* 37 (1943) :244-62.

Seitz, D. C. "Thomas Paine, Bridge Builder." *Va. Quar. Rev.,* 3 (1927) :571-84.

Smith, Frank. "New Light on Paine's First Year in America, 1775."*Amer. Lit.*, 1 (1930) :347-71.

Spiller, Robert E., and others, eds. *Literary History of the United States*, 1:137-41.

Sykes, Norman, in F. J. C. Hearnshaw, ed. *Social and Political Ideas of the Revolutionary Period*, (1931) :100-40.

Wecter, Dixon. "Hero in Reverse." *Va. Quar. Rev.*, 18 (1942) : 243-59.

WILLIAM BARTRAM— 1739-1823 —Traveler and Naturalist

ORIGINAL SOURCES: Van Doren, Mark, ed. *The Travels of William Bartram*. 1928.

Nation, 126:326, Mar. 21, 1928. One of the most delightful descriptions of travel and exploration in early American literature.

Stedman and Hutchinson. *Library of American Literature*, 4:3-15.

BIOGRAPHY: Earnest, Ernest. *John and William Bartram, Botanists and Explorers, 1699-1823*. 1940.

COLLECTIVE BIOGRAPHY: Bridenbaugh and Bridenbaugh. *Rebels and Gentlemen*, 310-17.

Cooper, Lane, in *DAB*, 2:28.

Stone, Witmer. "The Work of William, Son of John Bartram." *Bartonia: Proc. of the Philadelphia Botanical Club*, Dec. 31, 1931, pp. 20-23.

SPECIAL ASPECTS: Fagin, N. B. *William Bartram, Interpreter of the American Landscape*. 1933.

MVHR, 20:413. A dissertation which emphasizes Bartram's literary influence rather than his life or scientific attainments. The author however suggests that the Quaker scientist was an unerring observer and "a brilliant interpreter of nature."

CHARLES WILLSON PEALE— 1741-1827 —"The Artist of the Revolution"

BIOGRAPHY: Sellers, Charles Coleman. *Charles Willson Peale*, 2 vols., 1947.

AHR, 53:552. A sympathetic but candid biography of Peale and his family.

The book is not concerned with aesthetic criticism, but with the career of the portrait painter, patriot, and Jack-of-all-trades, and those of his artistic sons.

COLLECTIVE BIOGRAPHY: Flexner, J. T. *America's Old Masters,* 171-244.

Lee, Cuthbert. *Early American Portrait Painters,* 103-22.

Sellers, Horace W., in *DAB,* 14:344.

ANTHONY WAYNE—1745-1796—Reckless Warrior—
but Cautious

BIOGRAPHY: Boyd, Thomas A. *Mad Anthony Wayne.* 1929.

Outlook, 153:270, Oct. 16, 1929. Splendid portrait based on careful study.

Wildes, Harry E. *Anthony Wayne, Trouble Shooter of the American Revolution.* 1941.

AHR, 47:619. Well balanced study which emphasizes the Ohio campaign and Wayne's attempts to make a living at business and farming. Is rather rhetorical, but shows extensive use of manuscript material.

COLLECTIVE BIOGRAPHY: Downes, Randolph C., in *DAB,* 19:563.

HISTORY: Jacobs, J. R. *The Beginning of the U. S. Army,* (1947) :124-88.

BENJAMIN RUSH—1745-1813—"Stormy Medico of
the Revolution"

ORIGINAL SOURCES: Corner, George W., ed. *The Autobiography of Benjamin Rush.* 1948.

N. Y. Times, Nov. 7, 1948, p. 4. A vivid picture of a man who was one of the leading physicians of Philadelphia, physician-general of the army, and member of the Continental Congress.

Runes, Dagobert D., ed. *The Selected Writings of Benjamin Rush.* 1941.

Wm. and Mary Quar., Third Series, 5:283. A collection of Rush's essays on science, medicine, education, government, and reform.

BIOGRAPHY: Goodman, Nathan G. *Benjamin Rush, Physician and Citizen, 1746-1813.* 1934.

AHR, 41:196. An excellent account of the activities of a versatile man. However, the book gives little on his personality.

COLLECTIVE BIOGRAPHY: Flexner, J. T. *Doctors on Horseback,* 57-120.

Ford, Paul Leicester. "Dr. Rush and General Washington." *Atlantic,* 75 (1895) :633-40.

Shryrock, Richard H., in *DAB,* 16:227.

Wallis, J. K., in Willard Thorp, ed. *Lives of Eighteen from Princeton,* (1947) :51-67.

HUGH HENRY BRACKENRIDGE—   1748-1816
—"An Outstanding Pioneer of Culture in Western Pennsylvania"

BIOGRAPHY: Newlin, Claude Milton. *The Life and Writings of Hugh Henry Brackenridge.* 1932.

AHR, 38:769. An interesting study of a lawyer and writer involved in the Whiskey Rebellion who was the leading citizen of Pittsburgh for a generation. Read Chapter XIV, which describes the curious part Brackenridge played in his efforts to moderate the course of the Whiskey Rebellion.

COLLECTIVE BIOGRAPHY: Newlin, C. M., in *DAB,* 2:544.

Parrington, V. L. *Main Currents in American Thought,* 1:390-95.

Tyler, M. C. *Literary History of the American Revolution,* 2:210-24, 297-302.

HISTORY: Baldwin, Leland D. *Pittsburgh: the Story of a City,* (1937) :117-28.

Describes his activities in the Whiskey Rebellion.

Ferguson, R. J. *Early Western Pennsylvania Politics.* 1938.

SPECIAL ASPECTS: Eakin, Myrl I. "Hugh Henry Brackenridge— Lawyer." *Western Pa. Hist. Mag.,* 20 (1937) :163-75.

Williams, Mildred. "Hugh Henry Brackenridge as a Judge of the Supreme Court of Pennsylvania, 1799-1816." *Western Pa. Hist. Mag.,* 10 (1927) :210-23.

STEPHEN GIRARD—   1750-1831   —Merchant and Financier

COLLECTIVE BIOGRAPHY: Beard, A. E. *Our Foreign Born Citizens,* (1946) :141-46.

Lingelbach, W. E., in *DAB,* 7:319.

Minnigerode, Meade. *Certain Rich Men,* 3-30.

PHILIP FRENEAU—   1752-1832   —"That Rascal Freneau"

ORIGINAL SOURCES: Clark, Harry Hayden, ed. *Poems of Freneau.* 1929.

Contains a biographical and critical introduction by the editor.

Marsh, Philip, ed. "Madison's Defense of Freneau." *Wm. and Mary Quar.,* Third series, 3 (1946) :269-80.

Warfel, Gabriel, and Williams. *American Mind,* 209-17.

BIOGRAPHY: Leary, Lewis. *That Rascal Freneau: a Study in Literary Failure.* 1941.

Amer. Lit., 14:82. The definitive biography. Leary gives a sympathetic picture "of the vicissitudes of a journalist during the early years of the American Republic."

Pattee, Fred Lewis. "The Life of Philip Freneau," in his *Poems of Philip Freneau, Poet of the American Revolution,* Vol. I, pp. xiii-cxii, 1902.

Atlantic, 94:855. An excellent account of Freneau's adventures as student, sailor, sea-captain, British prisoner, and literary man.

COLLECTIVE BIOGRAPHY: Mott, F. L. *American Journalism,* (1941) :124-27.

Parrington, V. L. *Main Currents in American Thought,* 1:368-81.

Pattee, F. L., in *DAB,* 7:27.

———. *Side-Lights on American Literature,* 250-92, 1922.

Tucker, S. M., in *Cambridge History of American Literature,* 1:180-83.

Tyler, M. C. *Literary History of the American Revolution,* 1:171-83, 413-25; 2:246-75.

SPECIAL ASPECTS: Keiser, Albert. *The Indian in American Literature,* 1933, Chapter III, "The Indian Comes Into His Own."

Lee, Hector. "Philip Freneau as a War Propagandist in 1775." *Utah Academy of Sciences, Arts, and Letters,* 23 (1945) :73-81.

Marsh, P. M. "Jefferson and Freneau." *Am. Scholar,* 16 (1947) : 201-10.

———. "The Griswold Story of Freneau and Jefferson." *AHR,*
51 (1945) :68-73.

Spiller, Robert E., and others, eds. *Literary History of the
United States,* 1:169-75.

SARAH WISTER— 1761-1804 —Diarist

ORIGINAL SOURCES: Myers, A. C., ed. *Sally Wister's Journal, a
True Narrative, Being a Quaker Maiden's Account of Her
Experiences With Officers of the Continental Army, 1777-
1778.* 1902.

The diary of a vivacious girl who met many soldiers during the Revolution.

COLLECTIVE BIOGRAPHY: Bridenbaugh and Bridenbaugh. *Rebels
and Gentlemen,* 97, 115.

Lingelbach, Anna L., in *DAB,* 20:434.

NANCY SHIPPEN—1763-1841—A Belle of the Revolutionary Period

ORIGINAL SOURCES: Armes, Ethel, ed. *Nancy Shippen, Her Jour-
nal Book: the International Romance of a Young Lady of
Fashion of Colonial Philadelphia With Letters to Her and
About Her.* 1935.

AHR, 43:409. Fascinating story of a beauty who had many suitors, but married the wrong one. Throws much light on the manners of the day.

CHAPTER XIII. NEW YORK

HISTORY:Wertenbaker, Thomas J. *The Golden Age of Colonial
Culture,* Chapter III, "Father Knickerbocker Becomes Aesthetic: New York."

ROBERT R. LIVINGSTON— 1718-1775 —Head of
the Clan

ORIGINAL SOURCES: Stedman and Hutchinson. *Library of American Literature,* 3:371-79.

COLLECTIVE BIOGRAPHY: Bonham, M. L., Jr., in Samuel F.
Bemis, ed. *American Secretaries of State,* 1:115-89.

Hayes, Robert C., in *DAB*, 11:319.

BARON VON STEUBEN— 1730-1794 —Drillmaster

COLLECTIVE BIOGRAPHY: Armstrong, O. K. "He Transformed a Rabble into an Army." *Read. Dig.*, 52 (1948) :137-40.

BIOGRAPHY: Palmer, John McAuley. *General Von Steuben.* 1937.

AHR, 43:894. A biography which discards the "hoary myths concerning the hero's ancestry and career in Germany" and carefully appraises his contribution toward the success of the American Revolution.

COLLECTIVE BIOGRAPHY: Palmer, John McAuley, in *DAB*, 17:601.

MICHEL-GUILLAUME JEAN DE CREVECOEUR SAINT JOHN DE CREVECOEUR) —1735-1813
—Farmer and Traveler

ORIGINAL SOURCES: Crèvecoeur, Michel Guillaume St. Jean de. *Letters from an American Farmer*, ed. by Warren B. Blake. (Everyman's Library, 1912.)

———. *Letters from an American Farmer*, ed. by W. P. Trent and Ludwig Lewisohn. 1904.

Atlantic, 94:847. These charming letters reflect the reaction of a French immigrant to life in America. Apparently he was tempted to abandon civilization and seek peace and happiness among the Indians.

———. *Sketches of Eighteenth Century America: More "Letters From an American Farmer,"* ed. by H. L. Bourdin, R. H. Gabriel, and S. T. Williams. 1925.

MVHR, 14:74. Hitherto unpublished letters concerned largely with colonial life and the treatment of Loyalists by American Patriots.

Selections from Crèvecoeur's writings can be found in: Stedman and Hutchinson. *Library of American Literature*, 3:138-46; Mark Van Doren. *Autobiography of America*, 65-73; Warfel, Gabriel, and Williams. *American Mind*, 172-84.

BIOGRAPHY: Mitchell, Julia P. *St. Jean de Crèvecoeur.* 1916.

COLLECTIVE BIOGRAPHY: Bourdin, Henry L., and Stanley T. Williams. "The American Farmer Returns." *No. Am. Rev.*, 222 (1925) :135-40.

Canby, H. S. *Classic Americans*, 45-49.

Kunitz and Haycraft. *American Authors,* 192-93.

Parrington, V. L. *Main Currents in American Thought,* 1:140-47.

Tyler, M. C. *Literary History of the American Revolution,* 2:347-58.

Williams, Stanley T., in *DAB,* 4:542.

GEORGE CLINTON— 1739-1812 —Champion of States Rights

BIOGRAPHY: Spaulding, Ernest W. *His Excellency George Clinton (1739-1812), Critic of the Constitution.* 1938.

AHR, 44:144. Interesting but detailed study of a man who was seven times governor of New York.

COLLECTIVE BIOGRAPHY: Monaghan, Frank, in *DAB,* 4:226.

HISTORY: Adams, Henry. *History of the United States During the Administrations of Jefferson and Madison,* 9 vols.

Nevins, Allan. *American States during and after the Revolution,* 246-47, index.

JOHN JAY— 1745-1829 —Defender of Liberty

ORIGINAL SOURCES: Stedman and Hutchinson. *Library of American Literature,* 3:325-34.

BIOGRAPHY: Monaghan, Frank. *John Jay.* 1935.

AHR, 41:551. An entertaining study which throws much new light on Jay's personality and many activities. Disparages contemporaries who opposed his policies.

Pellen, George. *John Jay* (American Statesmen series, 1890).

A good biography based largely on family papers.

COLLECTIVE BIOGRAPHY: Bemis, Samuel F., in *DAB,* 10:5.

Umbreit, K. B. *Lives of the Chief Justices,* 1-50.

HISTORY: Becker, Carl. *Every Man His Own Historian,* (1935): 284-98.

Bemis, Samuel F. *Jay's Treaty: a Study in Commerce and Diplomacy.* 1923.

AHR, 29:345. *See especially,* 203-06.

SPECIAL ASPECTS: Bemis, S. F., in *American Secretaries of State,* 1:193-285.

STEPHEN AND ELIZA JUMEL—   c. 1754-1832
—Wine Merchants

BIOGRAPHY: Duncan, William Cary. *The Amazing Madame Jumel.* 1935.

Books, Feb. 17, 1935, p. 18. The incredible story of a woman who rose from poverty to riches. The author maintains that the Hamilton-Burr duel was over her!

COLLECTIVE BIOGRAPHY: Albion, Robert G., in *DAB,* 10:246.

Minnigerode, Meade. *Lives and Times,* 1-49.

AARON BURR—   1756-1836   —Adventurer

ORIGINAL SOURCES: Van Doren, Mark. *Autobiography of America,* 210-27.

BIOGRAPHY: Schachner, Nathan. *Aaron Burr: a Biography.* 1937.

AHR, 43:901. The author presents new evidence in his effort to defend Burr from charges of deliberate murder, political opportunism, and treason. W. F. McCaleb welcomes the book as evidence that the old lies have been discredited, and that "the story of Burr's life is nearing completion." *Books,* Oct. 21, 1937, p. 6. Henry Commager describes the book as "mostly passionate and prejudiced." *See also,* discussion by Schachner and Commager, *ibid.,* Oct. 3, 1937, p. 22.

Wandell, Samuel H., and Meade Minnegerode. *Aaron Burr: a Biography Compiled from Rare, and in Many Cases, Unpublished Sources,* 2 vols., 1925.

AHR, 31:801. A dramatic and eloquent defense which suggests that Burr was "mentally insecure from the start."

COLLECTIVE BIOGRAPHY: Bradford, Gamaliel. *Damaged Souls,* 87-120.

Also in *Harper's,* 146 (1922):67-76.

Cox, I. J., in *DAB,* 3:314.

Egbert and Lee. *Princeton Portraits,* 257-59.

McCartney, C. E. *Men Who Missed It,* (1940) :9-13.

Prochnow, H. V. *Great Stories From Great Lives,* 171-73.

Seitz, D. C. *The "Also Rans,"* (1928) :1-37.

HISTORY: Adams, Henry. *History of the U. S.,* Vols. 2 and 3.

Klingberg, Frank J. *The Morning of America.* 1941.

THEODOSIA BURR—1783-1813—Devoted Daughter

COLLECTIVE BIOGRAPHY: Bradford, Gamaliel. *Wives,* 91-124.
Also in *Atlantic,* 135:661-70.
Dobson, E. R., in *DAB,* 3:322.
Minnegerode, Meade. *Lives and Times,* 97-150.
Peacock, V. T. *Famous American Belles of the Nineteenth Century,* (1901) :18-38.

ALEXANDER HAMILTON—   1757-1804
—Washington's Prime Minister

ORIGINAL SOURCES: Prescott, Fred C., ed. *Alexander Hamilton and Thomas Jefferson: Representative Selections* (American Writers series, 1934) .
Van Doren, Mark. *Autobiography of America,* 202-09.
Warfel, Gabriel, and Williams. *American Mind,* 310-18.

BIOGRAPHY: Ford, Henry James. *Alexander Hamilton.* 1920.

Nation, 112:186, Feb. 2, 1921. A discriminating study, though somewhat biased in favor of Hamilton. Is fair to Burr, but not to Jefferson. Regards Hamliton's political philosophy as true, but fails to explain why he held it.

Oliver, Frederick Scott. *Alexander Hamilton: an Essay on American Union.* 1906.

AHR, 12:398. An admiring Englishman pays tribute to Britain's chief friend in America in the 1790's, and aims many "striking phrases and characterizations" at Jefferson and John Adams.

Schachner, Nathan. *Alexander Hamilton.* 1946.

AHR, 53:350. This biography is "more thorough, accurate, and impartial than any of its predecessors." It leaves his public career undimmed, but not his private life.

Smertenko, Johan Jacob. *Alexander Hamilton.* 1932.

Books, Dec. 18, 1932, p. 12. The author thinks Hamilton's struggles were largely motivated by his desire to overcome the handicap of his birth. Too much emphasis on "interpretation."

COLLECTIVE BIOGRAPHY: Agar, Herbert. *The People's Choice,* 27-30, 45-48, 55-59, index.
Guedalla, Philip. *Fathers of the Revolution,* 251-62.
Johnson, G. W. *American Heroes and Hero Worship,* (1943) : 54-93.

Loth, David, in L. V. Prochnow, *Great Stories From Great Lives,*
163-70.

Nevins, Allan, in *DAB,* 8:171.

O'Higgins, Harvey. *American Mind in Action.*

Parrington, V. L. *Main Currents in American Thought,* 1:292-
307.

Thomas and Thomas. *Fifty Great Americans,* 76-87.

————. *Living Biographies of American Statesmen,* 71-87.

Ulmann, Albert. *New Yorkers,* 77-106.

Vandenberg, Arthur H., in *Life,* 23:64-69, July 7, 1947.

Wilstach, Paul. *Patriots off their Pedestals,* 97-117.

HISTORY: Bowers, Claude. *Jefferson and Hamilton.*
The point of view is hostile to Hamilton. Read especially Chapter II,
"Hamilton: A Portrait."

Klingberg, Frank J. *The Morning of America.* 1941.

SPECIAL ASPECTS: Beard, C. A. *Economic Origins of Jeffersonian
Democracy.* 1915.

Dorfman, Joseph. *The Economic Mind in American Civilization,* 1:404-17, index.

Hendrick, B. J. *Bulwark of the Republic.*

Kunitz and Haycraft. *American Authors,* 332-34.

Marsh, P. M. "Hamilton and Monroe." *MVHR,* 34 (1947):
459-68.

Munro, W. B. *The Makers of the Unwritten Constitution,*
(1930):27-50.

Schachner, Nathan. "Legacy of Alexander Hamilton." *Amer.
Merc.,* 63 (1946):720-25.

Schlesinger, Arthur M., Jr. *The Age of Jackson,* 9-16.

Whiteley, Emily Stone. *Washington and His Aides-de-Camp.*
1936.

ROBERT FULTON—   1765-1815   —Inventor

COLLECTIVE BIOGRAPHY: Burlingame, Roger. *Inventors Behind
the Inventor,* 34-63.

Flexner, J. T. *Steamboats Come True.* 1944.

Lee, Cuthbert. *Early American Painters,* 295-305.

Mitman, C. W., in *DAB*, 7:68.

Thomas and Thomas. *Fifty Great Americans*, 97-104.

Ulmann, Albert. *New Yorkers*, 107-34.

HISTORY: Burlingame, Roger. *March of the Iron Men*. 1938.

WALTER BUTLER—?-1781—Loyalist and Legend- ary Villain?

ORIGINAL SOURCES: "Walter Butler's Journal . . ." in *Canadian Hist. Rev.*, 1 (1920).

COLLECTIVE BIOGRAPHY: Ross, Frank Edward, in *DAB*, 3:367.

HISTORY: Swiggett, Harold. *War Out of Niagara, Walter Butler and the Tory Rangers*. 1933.

MVHR, 20:279. This young Loyalist is usually described as a fiend. Swiggett says that actually he frequently restrained the Indians from murdering prisoners, women, and children. He did fail to check his savage allies at Cherry Valley, where the Indians outnumbered his men and were furious over the recent destruction of their towns.

CHAPTER XIV. CONNECTICUT

ISRAEL PUTNAM—1718-1790—Farmer and Soldier

COLLECTIVE BIOGRAPHY: Adams, James T., in *DAB*, 15:281.

Seitz, Don. *Uncommon Americans*, 108-23.

ROGER SHERMAN— 1721-1793 —"Cordwainer Statesman"

COLLECTIVE BIOGRAPHY: Boyd, Julian P., in *DAB*, 17:88.

———. "Roger Sherman, Portrait of a Cordwainer Statesman." *N. E. Quar.*, 5 (1932) :221-36.

SAMUEL PETERS—1735-1826—"An Early Writer of American Whoppers"

ORIGINAL SOURCES: Peters, Samuel. *General History of Connecticut*. Ed. by S. J. McCormick. 1877.

An entertaining, but unreliable account by an embittered Tory. The so-called "Blue laws" of New Haven constitute the most notorious part of the book.

COLLECTIVE BIOGRAPHY: Calder, I. M., in *DAB*, 14:511.

Middlebrook, Samuel. "Samuel Peters: a Yankee Munchausen." *N. E. Quar.*, 20 (1947) :75-87.

BENEDICT ARNOLD—1741-1801—"Greedy Traitor"

BIOGRAPHY: Sellers, Charles Coleman. *Benedict Arnold, the Proud Warrior*. 1930.

Nation, 132:588, May 27, 1931. A lively narrative, which however presents nothing new. Makes the salient features of Arnold's character stand out, and thus presents ample explanation for his treason.

COLLECTIVE BIOGRAPHY: Adams, Randolph G., in *DAB*, 1:362.

Bradford, Gamaliel. *Damaged Souls*, 19-50.

Also in *Harper's*, 146 (1923) :243-52; and Gamaliel Bradford. *Portraits and Personalities*, 19-39.

Garnett, Richard, in *DNB*, 1:579.

Holbrook, S. H. *Lost Men of American History*, 42-44.

James, Marquis. *They Had Their Hour*, 104-18.

HISTORY: Klingberg, Frank J. *The Morning of America*. 1941.

Van Doren, Carl. *Secret History of the American Revolution: an Account of the Conspiracies of Benedict Arnold and Numerous Others*. 1941.

N. Y. Times, Oct. 12, 1941, p. 1. A fascinating book based on the British headquarter's papers in the Clements Library. Van Doren makes it clear "that Arnold was not driven to treason by carping criticism, by misunderstanding, by failure to achieve promotion; it is clear that he deliberately embraced treason for its financial rewards." He concludes: "No other American officer made as much money out of the war as Arnold did."

Selections in *Carl Van Doren: Selected by Himself*. (Viking Portable Library, 1945.)

MARGARET ARNOLD— 1760-1834 —"Designing Hussy"?

COLLECTIVE BIOGRAPHY: Bradford, Gamaliel. *Wives*, 55-88.

Also in *Harper's*, 151 (1925) :23-33.

HISTORY: Van Doren, Carl. *Secret History of the American Revolution: an Account of the Conspiracies of Benedict Arnold and Numerous Others*. 1941.

N. Y. Times, Oct. 12, 1941, p. 1. Was the beautiful and hysterical Peggy

involved in her husband's treason? Did she egg him on and help him
with his plans? Is there conclusive proof, or is this a mystery?

OLIVER ELLSWORTH—1745-1807—Legislator and Chief Justice

COLLECTIVE BIOGRAPHY: Brown, William Garrott. "The Early
Life of Oliver Ellsworth." *AHR,* 10 (1905) :534-64.
———. "A Continental Congressman: Oliver Ellsworth, 1777-
1784." *Ibid.:* 751-81.
Drew and Lee. *Princeton Portraits,* 246-49.
Umbreit, K. B. *Our Eleven Chief Justices,* 79-110.
Woodbine, George Edward, in *DAB,* 6:111.

JOHN LEDYARD— 1751-1789 —World Traveler

Stedman and Hutchinson. *Library of American Literature,*
3:416-22.
BIOGRAPHY: Augur, Helen. *Passage to Glory: John Ledyard's
America.* 1946.
Weekly Book Rev., Jan. 13, 1946, p. 3. A fine adventure story of "the
American Marco Polo" who foresaw America's destiny in the Pacific.
Tends to exaggerate his importance.
COLLECTIVE BIOGRAPHY: Ghent, W. J., in *DAB,* 11:93.
Seitz, Don. *Uncommon Americans,* 231-41.
Sheahan, Henry Beston. *Book of Gallant Vagabonds,* (1925) :
19-53.
HISTORY: Brebner, John Bartlet. *The Explorers of North Amer-
ica, 1492-1806,* (1933) :458-63.
Mirsky, Jeanette. *The Westward Crossings,* 223-37.

TIMOTHY DWIGHT— 1752-1817 —"A Yankee Christian Gentleman"

ORIGINAL SOURCES: Mussey, J. B. *Yankee Life by Those Who
Lived It.*
Warfel, Gabriel, and Williams. *American Mind,* 217-27.
BIOGRAPHY: Cunningham, Charles E. *Timothy Dwight: a Biog-
raphy.* 1942.
AHR, 48:577. A fresh and sympathetic study which maintains that the

real founder of Yale University was both a defender of the orthodoxy of his day and a forerunner of the new age.

COLLECTIVE BIOGRAPHY: Blankenship, Russell. *American Literature,* 185-86.

Brooks, Van Wyck. *The World of Washington Irving,* (1944) : 60-65.

Howe, M. A. *Classic Shades,* 16-40.

Howard, Leon. *The Connecticut Wits,* (1943) :79-111, 342-401.

Kunitz and Haycraft. *American Authors,* 239-40.

Parrington, V. L. *Main Currents in American Thought,* 1:357-63.

Starr, Harris E., in *DAB,* 5:573.

Sweet, W. W. *Makers of Christianity,* 237-44.

Tyler, M. C. *Three Men of Letters,* (1895) :71-127.

SPECIAL ASPECTS: Leary, Lewis. "The Author of the Triumph of Infidelity." *N. E. Quar.,* 20 (1947) :377-85.

JOEL BARLOW—1754-1812—"The Most Original of the Hartford Wits"

ORIGINAL SOURCES: Warfel, Gabriel, and Williams. *American Mind,* 232-41.

COLLECTIVE BIOGRAPHY: Adams, Martin Ray. *Studies in the Literary Background of English Radicalism,* (1947) :23-82.

Dorfman, Joseph. "Joel Barlow: Trafficker in Trade and Letters." *Pol. Sci. Quar.,* 59 (1944) :83-100.

Dos Passos, John. *The Ground We Stand On,* 256-380.

Howard, Leon. *The Connecticut Wits,* (1943) :133-65, 271-341.

Kunitz and Haycraft. *American Authors,* 54-55.

Marble, Annie Russell. *The Hartford Wits,* 22-28 (Publications of the Tercentenary Commission of the State of Connecticut, LIX, 1936).

Parrington, V. L. *The Connecticut Wits,* (1926), pp. IX-LVII.

———. *Main Currents in American Thought,* 1:382-89.

Tinker, Chauncey Brewster. *Essays in Retrospect,* (1948) : 37-42.

Willson, Beckles. *America's Ambassadors to France,* 102-17.

Zunder, Theodore A., and Stanley T. Williams, in *DAB*, 1:609.

SPECIAL ASPECTS: Adams, M. R. "Joel Barlow, Political Romanticist." *Amer. Lit.*, 9 (1937) :113-53.

Boynton, Percy H. "Joel Barlow Advises the Privileged Orders." *N. E. Quar.*, 12 (1939) :477-99.

Dorfman, Joseph. *The Economic Mind in American Civilization*, 1:459-71, index.

Howard, Leon. "Joel Barlow and Napoleon." *Huntington Lib. Quar.*, 2 (1938) :37-51.

Tyler, M. C. *Three Men of Letters*, (1895) :129-80.

Zunger, T. A. *The Early Days of Joel Barlow, a Connecticut Wit*. 1934.

N. E. Quar., 8:127. An accurate but detailed narrative of the life of Barlow to 1787.

BENJAMIN TALLMADGE— 1754-1835 —Soldier-Businessman-Humanitarian

BIOGRAPHY: Hall, Charles S. *Benjamin Tallmadge: Revolutionary Soldier and American Businessman*. 1943.

MVHR, 30:597. This biography throws new light on Washington's secret service, Federalist party activities in Congress, and commerce and manufacturing.

COLLECTIVE BIOGRAPHY: Irwin, Ray W., in *DAB*, 18:284.

ELI WHITNEY—1765-1825—"The Inventor of Mass Production"

BIOGRAPHY: Burlingame, Roger. *Whittling Boy*. 1941.

Sat. Rev. of Lit., 23:19, Mar. 1, 1941. Fictionized narrative of the amazing career of a man whose cotton gin and interchangeable parts affected America most significantly.

COLLECTIVE BIOGRAPHY: Blake, W. P., in *Papers of the New Haven Historical Society*, 5 (1894) :109-31.

Burlingame, Roger. *Inventors Behind the Inventor*, 115-43.

Gray, Thomas, Jr. "The South Still Gropes in Eli Whitney's Shadow." *Ga. Hist. Quar.*, 20 (1936) :345-55.

Mitman, C. W., in *DAB*, 20:157.

Roe, J. W. *Connecticut Inventors*, 20-22 (Publications of the

Tercentenary Commission of the State of Connecticut,
XXXIII, 1934).

HISTORY: Burlingame, Roger. *March of the Iron Men,* (1938):
170ff, 186ff, index.

CHAPTER XV.   RHODE ISLAND, NEW HAMPSHIRE, AND VERMONT

STEPHEN HOPKINS— 1707-1785 —Merchant and
Politician

COLLECTIVE BIOGRAPHY: Richman, I. B., in *DAB*, 9:219.

Tyler, M. C. *Literary History of the American Revolution,*
1:63-69.

HISTORY: Adams, J. T. *Revolutionary New England,* 160, 197,
268-69, 297, 406.

Nevins, Allan. *American States,* (1924), 225-26.

ETHAN ALLEN—1738-1789—Green Mountain Rebel

BIOGRAPHY: Holbrook, Stewart H. *Ethan Allen.* 1940.

AHR, 46:668. A vivid picture of a fierce frontier leader and land speculator.

Pell, John. *Ethan Allen.* 1939.

Books, Dec. 1, 1939, p. 1. A vivid biography of a picturesque but brutal
and unscrupulous man who fought red-coats and Yorkers alike. The
book is the product of industrious research, an entertaining style, and a
skillful use of local color.

COLLECTIVE BIOGRAPHY: Doane, Gilbert H., in *DAB*, 1:188.

Rife, Clarence W. "Ethan Allen, an Interpretation." *N. E.
Quar.,* 2 (1929) :561-84.

Seitz, Don. *Uncommon Americans,* 195-208.

Tyler, M. C. *Literary History of the American Revolution,*
2:228-37.

HISTORY: Thompson, Charles Miner. *Independent Vermont.*
1942.

N. E. Quar., 15:378. A scholarly history which comes to the loyal Vermont
conclusion that, "in his ability to dramatize himself, to make himself

the blazing embodiment of the cause of Vermont," Ethan Allen "was of inestimable service" to his state as well as to his land company.

SPECIAL ASPECTS: Anderson, G. P. "Who Wrote 'Ethan Allen's Bible'?" *N. E. Quar.,* 10 (1937) :585-96.

Doten, Dana. "Ethan Allen's 'Original Something.'" *N. E. Quar.,* 11 (1938) :361-66.

Koch, G. A. *Republican Religion: the American Revolution and the Cult of Reason.* 1933.

Amer. Pol. Sci. Rev., 27:1023. An excellent account of the efforts of Thomas Paine, Ethan Allen, and others to establish deism as a popular religious movement.

Pell, John. "Ethan Allen's Literary Career." *N. E. Quar.,* 2 (1925) :585-602.

Schantz, B. T. "Ethan Allen's Religious Ideas." *Jour. Rel.,* 18 (1938) :183-217.

NATHANIEL GREENE—1742-1786—Militant Quaker
with Stiff Knee

COLLECTIVE BIOGRAPHY: Adams, R. G., in *DAB,* 7:569.

HISTORY: Klingberg, Frank J. *The Morning of America.* 1941.

Van Tyne, Charles H. *The War of American Independence.** 1929.

Whitton, F. E. *American War of Independence.* 1931.

BENJAMIN THOMPSON, COUNT RUMFORD—
1753-1814—"Wandering Scientist"

Stedman and Hutchinson. *Library of American Literature,* 3:494-503.

COLLECTIVE BIOGRAPHY: Cummings, A. D. "Eighteenth Century's Fuel Efficiency Expert." *Discovery,* 8 (1947) :120-23, 151-52.

Davis, Tenney L., in *DAB,* 18:449.

Einstein, Lewis. *Divided Loyalties,* 114-50.

Jaffe, Bernard. *Men of Science in America,* (1944) :52-77.

SPECIAL ASPECTS: Brown, Sanborn, and Kenneth Scott. "Count

---

* Won the Pulitzer Prize.

Rumford: International Informer." *N. E. Quar.,* 21 (1948) : 34-49.

GILBERT STUART— 1755-1828 —Portrait Painter

BIOGRAPHY: Whitley, W. T. *Gilbert Stuart.* 1932.

MVHR, 19:418. Stuart hated writing letters, consequently he has been neglected by biographers. The author, however, has produced an interesting book, based on thorough research. It still leaves some gaps in our knowledge of the artist's career.

COLLECTIVE BIOGRAPHY: Einstein, Lewis. *Divided Loyalties,* 384-87.

Flexner, J. T. *America's Old Masters,* 247-312.

Irwin, Grace. *Trail-Blazers of American Art,* (1930) :1-19.

Lee, Cuthbert. *Early American Portrait Painters,* 15-46.

McSpadden, J. W. *Famous Painters of America,* 71-108.

Morgan, John Hill, in *DAB,* 18:164.

HISTORY: Neuhaus, Eugen. *History and Ideals of American Art,* 33-42.

CHAPTER XVI. MASSACHUSETTS

HISTORY: Adams, James Truslow. *New England in the Republic, 1776-1850.* 1926.

AHR, 32:614. A provocative book which reverses the tendency to magnify the virtues of New England. Adams attributes Shay's Rebellion to the greed and stupidity of the ruling oligarchy, and pictures the Otises "figuring out whether they should make one or two hundred per cent out of the soldiers' winter clothes," when these soldiers were dying of cold and starvation at Valley Forge. In dealing with the years after 1815, he emphasizes the narrow sectionalism of the region, and its backwardness in educational and industrial matters. Good for background rather than for any connected account of individuals.

Wertenbaker, Thomas J. *The Golden Age of Colonial Culture,* Chapter II, "The Puritan Begins to Play: Boston."

THOMAS HUTCHINSON—1711-1780—"One of the Finest Representatives of Colonial America"

ORIGINAL SOURCES: Hutchinson, Thomas. *The History of the Colony and Province of Massachusetts Bay.* 1936.

Trent and Wells. *Colonial Prose and Poetry*, 3:251-60.

Warfel, Gabriel, and Williams. *American Mind*, 100-04.

BIOGRAPHY: Hosmer, James Kendall. *Life of Thomas Hutchinson, Royal Governor of the Province of Massachusetts Bay*. 1896.

Atlantic, 78:122. Writing a generation before the appearance of the *DAB*, Hosmer could scarcely vie with Carl Becker in paying tribute to Massachusetts' chief Tory at the beginning of the Revolution. However, when the biographer of Samuel Adams can deal justly with his chief opponent, we have convincing evidence that American historians were becoming less partisan and more broad-minded.

COLLECTIVE BIOGRAPHY: Becker, Carl L., in *DAB*, 9:439.

Einstein, Lewis. *Divided Loyalties*, 153-88.

Laughton, Sir John Knox, in *DNB*, 10:343-46.

Parrington, V. L. *Main Currents in American Thought*, 1:194-206.

Tyler, M. C. *Literary History of the American Revolution*, 2:394-411.

HISTORY: Fiske, John. *Essays, Historical and Literary*, 1 (1907) : 1-51.

Davidson, Philip. *Propaganda and the American Revolution*. 1941.

Miller, J. C. *Origins of the American Revolution*. 1943.

Schlessinger, A. M. *The Colonial Merchants and the Revolution*. 1918.

SPECIAL ASPECTS: Dorfman, Joseph. *The Economic Mind in American Civilization*, Vol. 1.

Mayo, L. S. "Thomas Hutchinson and his History of Massachusetts Bay." *Amer. Antiq. Soc. Proc.*, N. S., 41 (1931) :321-39.

SAMUEL ADAMS—1722-1803—"Father of the American Revolution"

BIOGRAPHY: Harlow, Ralph Volney. *Samuel Adams, Promoter of the American Revolution: a Study in Psychology and Politics*. 1923.

AHR, 29:568. An original book in that the author attempts to interpret his subject through the new psychology. Maintains that Adams was probably a neurotic with an inferiority complex and a sense of frustration. The author gives few new facts, and lacks the necessary data on the childhood and youth for a sound psychoanalysis.

Miller, John C. *Samuel Adams, Pioneer in Propaganda.* 1936.

AHR, 42:788. A vigorous narrative which shows how this bold leader united the country yeomen of Massachusetts and the Boston mechanics against the aristocrats; and then intrigued to put the radicals in control of the Continental Congress. Useful also for Otis, Hancock, and John Adams.

COLLECTIVE BIOGRAPHY: Becker, Carl L., in *DAB*, 1:95.

Guedalla, Philip. *Fathers of the Revolution,* 235-49.

Holbrook, S. H. *Lost Men of American History,* 11-32.

Also in *Amer. Merc.,* 59 (1944) :741-48.

Parrington, V. L. *Main Currents in American Thought,* 1:233-47.

Tyler, M. C. *Literary History of the American Revolution,* 2:1-8; 13-16.

Umbreit, K. C. *Founding Fathers,* 175-99.

HISTORY: Davidson, Philip. *Propaganda and the American Revolution.* 1941.

Hutchinson, Thomas. *The History of the Colony and Province of Massachusetts Bay.* 1936. Vol. 3.

Klingberg, Frank J. *The Morning of America.* 1941.

Miller, John C. *The Origins of the American Revolution.* 1943.

Schlessinger, A. M. *The Colonial Merchants and the Revolution.* 1918.

PAUL REVERE—1735-1818—Patriot and Silversmith

ORIGINAL SOURCES: Mussey, J. B. *Yankee Life by Those Who Lived It,* 416-20.

BIOGRAPHY: Forbes, Esther. *Paul Revere and the World He Lived In.** 1942.

Yale Rev., 32:161. Readable account which rescues the silversmith from the legends which Longfellow popularized.

---

* Won the Pulitzer Prize.

COLLECTIVE BIOGRAPHY: Forbes, Esther, in *There Were Giants in the Land,* 153-60.

James, Marquis. *They Had Their Hour,* 69-82.

Kellock, Katherine, in *DAB,* 15:514.

SPECIAL ASPECTS: "Life Follows the Route of Paul Revere." *Life,* 20:122-25, Apr. 22, 1946.

JOHN HANCOCK—1736-1793—Genuine Patriot or Muddle-headed Businessman?

BIOGRAPHY: Allan, Herbert S. *John Hancock: Patriot in Purple.* 1948.

AHR, 54:371. The best biography of a long neglected man. Maintains that Hancock possessed organizing ability of the highest order and was at one time "the most powerful political figure" in America. *Read especially,* pp. 356-66.

COLLECTIVE BIOGRAPHY: Adams, James T. "Portrait of an Empty Barrel." *Harper's,* 161 (1940) :425-34.

——, in *DAB,* 7:218.

Peterson, C. S. *First Governors of the Forty-eight States,* (1947) : 12-14.

Umbreit, K. C. *Founding Fathers,* 162-74.

HISTORY: Baxter, W. T. *The House of Hancock.* 1945.

AHR, 51:326. The author is quite hostile towards John, and regards him as a business failure whose incompetence caused the closing of the business. He also calls him a pariah for joining the American cause.

Hutchinson, Thomas. *The History of the Colony and Province of Massachusetts Bay.* 1936. Vol. 3.

Miller, John C. *The Origins of the American Revolution.* 1943.

Schlessinger, A. M. *The Colonial Merchants and the Revolution.* 1918.

SPECIAL ASPECTS: Dickerson, O. M. "John Hancock: Notorious Smuggler or Near Victim of British Revenue Racketeers?" *MVHR,* 32 (1946) :517-40.

JOHN S. COPLEY— 1737-1815 —Portrait Painter

COLLECTIVE BIOGRAPHY: Coburn, Frederick W., in *DAB,* 4:423.

Einstein, Lewis. *Divided Loyalties,* 326-56.

Flexner, J. T. *America's Old Masters,* 102-67.

Lee, Cuthbert. *Early American Portrait Painters,* 51-78.

McSpadden, J. W. *Famous Painters of America,* 45-69.

Martin, Sir Theodore, in *DNB,* 14:1102.

HISTORY: Caffin, Charles H. *The Story of American Painting,* (1907) :10-11, 16-22, 44.

SPECIAL ASPECTS: Flexner, James T. *American Painting,* (1947): 194-243.

   JOHN ADAMS—   1735-1826   —Peace Maker

ORIGINAL SOURCES: Van Doren, Mark. *Autobiography of America,* 166-73, 188-91.

Warfel, Gabriel, and Williams. *American Mind,* 197-304.

BIOGRAPHY: Chinard, Gilbert. *Honest John Adams.* 1933.

AHR, 39:541. A balanced biography. Emphasizes Adams' conscientious devotion to his country without overlooking his personal defects.

COLLECTIVE BIOGRAPHY: Adams, J. T. *The Adams Family,* 7-115.

Bruce, D. K. E. *Revolution to Reconstruction,* 43-84.

Ford, Worthington Chauncey, in *DAB,* 1:72.

Milhollen, H. D., and Milton Kaplan. *Presidents on Parade,* 30-36.

Perling, J. J. *Presidents' Sons,* (1947) :1-29.

Thompson, C. L. "John Adams: Forgotten President." *Cur. Hist.,* 14 (1948) :14.

Umbreit, K. C. *Founding Fathers,* 104-61.

Wilstach, Paul. *Patriots Off Their Pedestals,* 118-44.

HISTORY: Bowers, Claude. *Jefferson and Hamilton.*

Mead, Edwin D., in A. B. Hart. *Commonwealth History of Massachusetts,* 3:212-50.

Miller, J. C. *Origins of the American Revolution.* 1943.

SPECIAL ASPECTS: Adams, Randolph G. *Political Ideas of the American Revolution,* (1922) :86-108.

Booth, Edward T. *Country Life in America,* 3-37.

Dorfman, Joseph. *The Economic Mind in American Civilization*, 1:417-33, index.

————. "The Regal Republic of John Adams." *Pol. Sci. Quar.*, 59 (1944) :227-47.

Hedges, J. B. "John Adams Speaks His Mind." *AHR*, 47(1942): 806-09.

Morse, Anson D. "The Politics of John Adams." *AHR*, 4(1899): 292-312.

Pollard, James E. *Presidents and the Press*, 36-51.

Robathan, D. M. "John Adams and the Classics." *N. E. Quar.*, 19 (1946) :91-98.

Smith, Don. *Peculiarities of the Presidents*, 41.

Spengler, Joseph J. "The Political Economy of Jefferson, Madison, and Adams," in David K. Jackson, ed. *American Studies in Honor of William Kenneth Boyd*, (1940) :3-59.

Tyler, M. C. *Literary History of the American Revolution*, 1:93-98.

Von Abele, Rudolph. "World of John Adams." *Amer. Merc.*, 67 (1948) :66-73.

Walsh, C. M. *Political Science of John Adams*. 1915.

BIOGRAPHIES OF CONTEMPORARIES: Oliver, Frederick Scott. *Alexander Hamilton: an Essay on American Union*. 1906.

Maintains that Adams made an "undignified peace" with France in order to checkmate Hamilton.

ABIGAIL ADAMS— 1744-1818 —"America's First Emancipated Woman"

ORIGINAL SOURCES: Mitchell, Steward, ed. *New Letters of Abigail Adams, 1788-1801*. 1947.

AHR, 53:553. These revealing letters to her sister contain many bitterly partisan comments on current politics. The introduction includes an excellent essay on the "Fall of John Adams."

BIOGRAPHY: Bobbe, Dorothie. *Abigail Adams, the Second First Lady*. 1929.

Outlook and Ind., 151:389, Mar. 6, 1929. A readable biography which bears testimony to Abigail's piety, her ability as a letter-writer, and her resentment of man's tyranny over woman.

Whitney, Janet. *Abigail Adams.* 1947.

AHR, 53:553. A vivid picture of a devoted and intelligent housewife. The author is quite sympathetic, and fails to indicate that Mrs. Adams was a strong partisan of her husband and that both were jealous of Washington.

COLLECTIVE BIOGRAPHY: Bradford, Gamaliel. *Portraits of American Women,* 1-33.

Also in *Atlantic,* 120 (1917):340-50.

Hamilton, J. G. de R. "Abigail Adams: A Joy Forever." *Scribner's,* 87 (1930) :64-74.

Stephenson, Martha T., in *DAB,* 1:35.

Whitton, Mary Ormsbee. *First First Ladies, 1789-1865,* 20-38.

HISTORY: Bowers, Claude. *Jefferson and Hamilton.*

SPECIAL ASPECTS: Forbes, A. B. "Abigail Adams, Commentator." *Proc. Mass. Hist. Soc.,* 66 (1942) :126-53.

STEPHEN BURROUGHS—   1765-1840   —Rogue

ORIGINAL SOURCES: MacVeagh, Lincoln, ed. *Memoirs of the Notorious Stephen Burroughs.* 1925.

New Repub., 41:202, Jan. 14, 1925. Impersonating a minister, passing counterfeit money, breaking jail, and rape were among the charges against this schoolmaster, who traveled from New Hampshire to Georgia and back to Canada.

Extracts in J. B. Mussey. *Yankee Life by Those Who Lived It,* 73-75, 96-103, 167-70, 295-306, 366-71.

FRANCIS CABOT LOWELL— 1775-1817 —Textile
Manufacturer

COLLECTIVE BIOGRAPHY: Faulkner, Harold V., in *DAB,* 11:456.

Greenslet, Ferris. *The Lowells and Their Seven Worlds,* (1946) :124, 126-30, 155-59, 186, index.

HISTORY: Coburn, F. W. *History of Lowell and Its People.* 1920. Vol. 2.

SPECIAL ASPECTS: Ware, C. F. *Early New England Cotton Manufacture,* (1931) :61-65, 71.

CHAPTER XVII. SOUTH CAROLINA

History: Wertenbaker, Thomas J. *The Golden Age of Colonial Culture*, Chapter VII, "Rice, Indigo, and Elegance: Charleston."

*McCrady, Edward. *The History of South Carolina under the Royal Government, 1719-1776.* 1899.

AHR, 5:358. After covering the period down to 1765, the author describes the social conditions of the province at or before that date, then traces the political history of the next decade.

———. *The History of South Carolina in the Revolution, 1775-1780.* 1900.

AHR, 7:165. A well-balanced account of the first part of the Revolution in the state.

Wallace, David Duncan. *The History of South Carolina.* 4 vols. 1934-35.

AHR, 43:885. The most scholarly history of the state. It reveals thorough knowledge and deep insight. Vol. 2 deals with the period with which we are concerned; the index is in Vol. 3.

JOHN STUART— c. 1700-1779 —Superintendent of Indian Affairs for the Southern Colonies

Collective Biography: Jackson, G. B., in *Tenn. Hist. Mag.,* Sept. 1917.

Siebert, Wilbur H., in *DAB,* 18:172.

History: Alden, John Richard. *John Stuart and the Southern Colonial Frontier.* 1944.

AHR, 50:545. A careful study of the southern frontier and the efforts of leaders to maintain peace between the colonies and the Indians. Alden presents Stuart as "the equal if not the superior in ability and character" of Sir William Johnson. *Read especially,* pp. 156-75.

Shaw, Helen L. *British Administration of the Southern Indians, 1756-1783.* 1931.

Special Aspects: Hamer, Philip M. "John Stuart's Indian Policy during the Early Months of the American Revolution." *MVHR,* 17 (1930) :351-66.

---

* All of these state histories contain frequent but scattered references to the leaders listed.

HENRY LAURENS—1724-1792—Merchant, Planter, Congressman

BIOGRAPHY: Wallace, D. D. *Life of Henry Laurens.* 1915.

AHR, 21:818. A scholarly and discriminating biography of a high-minded gentleman who withdrew from the slave trade for reasons of conscience. Since he was not a rebel by nature, the process by which he became a patriot is of special interest.

COLLECTIVE BIOGRAPHY: Albion, R. G., in *DAB,* 11:32.

SPECIAL ASPECTS: Schlessinger, A. M. *The Colonial Merchants and the American Revolution.* 1918.

CHRISTOPHER GADSDEN— 1724-1805 —Merchant and Radical Leader

ORIGINAL SOURCES: Gadsden, Christopher. "Letters of Christopher Gadsden, 1778." *AHR,* 3 (1897) :83-89.

COLLECTIVE BIOGRAPHY: Meriweather, R. L., in *DAB,* 7:82.

Renick, E. I., in *Pubs. Southern Hist. Assn.,* July, 1898.

SPECIAL ASPECTS: Davidson, Philip. *Propaganda and the American Revolution.* 1941.

Schlessinger, A. M. *The Colonial Merchants and the American Revolution.* 1918.

FRANCIS MARION—1732-1795—"The Swamp Fox"

COLLECTIVE BIOGRAPHY: Meriweather, R. L., in *DAB,* 12:283.

Smith, Helena H., in *There Were Giants in the Land,* 196-206.

THOMAS SUMTER— 1734-1832 —Guerrilla Leader and Senator

BIOGRAPHY: Gregorie, Anna King. *Thomas Sumter.* 1931.

AHR, 38:168. A scholarly but "thoroughly human biography" of "a typical American" who rose from humble origins. His life as a guerrilla leader shows that the Revolution in South Carolina was "a ruthless civil war."

COLLECTIVE BIOGRAPHY: ———, in *DAB,* 18:219.

JOHN RUTLEDGE—1739-1800—Gifted and Devoted Leader

ORIGINAL SOURCES: Drayton, John. *Memoirs of the American Revolution,* 1 (1821) :131-41, 166-79.

BIOGRAPHY: Barry, Richard. *Mr. Rutledge of South Carolina,* 1942.

AHR, 48:801. A readable biography which stresses the best known activities of Rutledge and advances rather wide claims regarding his significance.

COLLECTIVE BIOGRAPHY: Barnwell, R. W., Jr. "Rutledge, 'the Dictator.' " *Jour. of South. Hist.,* 7 (1941) :215-24.

Umbreit, K. C. *Our Eleven Chief Justices,* 51-78.

WILLIAM HENRY DRAYTON— 1742-1779
—Brilliant and Eccentric Leader

ORIGINAL SOURCES: Drayton, John. *Memoirs of the American Revolution.* 1821.

The author gathered his information regarding the beginning of the Revolution in South Carolina and neighboring states very largely from the papers of his father, William Henry Drayton. The introduction gives a brief sketch of the life of his father.

COLLECTIVE BIOGRAPHY: Dargan, Marion, in *DAB,* 5:448.

SPECIAL ASPECTS: Davidson, Philip. *Propaganda and the American Revolution.* 1941.

———. "Whig Propagandists of the American Revolution." *AHR,* 39 (1934) :442-53.

Schlessinger, A. M. *The Colonial Merchants and the American Revolution.* 1918.

DENMARK VESEY—c. 1767-1822—A Representative
of the Other Half of the Population

COLLECTIVE BIOGRAPHY: Gregorie, A. K., in *DAB,* 19:258.

Higginson, T. W., in *Atlantic,* 7 (1861) :728-44.

Holbrook, S. H. *Lost Men of American History,* 111-14.

CHAPTER XVIII. NORTH CAROLINA

HERMON HUSBANDS—1724-1795—Restless Quaker
Agitator

ORIGINAL SOURCES: Henderson, Archibald, ed. "Hermon Husbands' Continuation of the Impartial Relation." *N. C. Hist. Rev.*, 18 (1941) :48-81.

BIOGRAPHY: Lazenby, Mary Elinor. *Hermon Husbands, a Story of His Life.* 1940.

MVHR, 28:137. A sympathetic biography of a substantial property owner who became involved in rebellion in North Carolina and Pennsylvania.

COLLECTIVE BIOGRAPHY: Hamilton, J. G. de R., in *DAB*, 4:427.

HISTORY: Ashe, S. A. *Biographical History of North Carolina.* 1905. Vol. 2.

SPECIAL ASPECTS: Bassett, John S. "The Regulators of North Carolina." *Ann. Report Am. Hist. Assn.*, 1894, Vol. II (1895).

ANNA CATHARINA ERNST   —1726-1816
—A Moravian Settler

ORIGINAL SOURCES: Fries, Adelaide L. *The Road to Salem.* 1944.

AHR, 50:180. The autobiography of an unusual woman who grew up among the Moravians in Pennsylvania, then went as a bride to North Carolina. Here she came in contact with leaders of the church and of the colony, Indian raiders, Regulators, and patriots. An intensely human document.

WILLIE JONES—1741-1801—Aristocratic Leader of the Democracy

ORIGINAL SOURCES: Hoyt, W. D., Jr. "Letters From Willie Jones to His Son at the University of North Carolina, 1796-1801." *N. C. Hist. Rev.*, 19 (1942) : 376-80.

COLLECTIVE BIOGRAPHY: Hamilton, J. G. de R., in *DAB*, 10:210. Robinson, B. P. "Willie Jones of Halifax. " *N. C. Hist. Rev.*, 18 (1941) :1-26, 133-70.

HISTORY: Ashe, S. A. *History of North Carolina.* 1925. Vol. II. DeMond, Robert O. *The Loyalists in North Carolina during the Revolution.* 1940.

DAVID FANNING— 1755-1825 —Indian Trader and Loyalist

COLLECTIVE BIOGRAPHY: Adams, James Truslow, in *DAB*, 6:264.

History: Ashe, S. A. *Biographical History of North Carolina,* 5:90-97.

DeMond, Robert O. *The Loyalists in North Carolina during the Revolution.* 1940.

CHAPTER XIX. VIRGINIA

History: Wertenbaker, Thomas J. *The Golden Age of Colonial Culture,* Chapter VI, "The Mind of the Tobacco Aristocrat: Williamsburg."

GEORGE WASHINGTON—1732-1799—Heroic Myth
or Red Blooded Virginian?

Original Sources: Chinard, Gilbert, ed. *George Washington as the French Knew Him: a Collection of Texts.* 1940.

AHR, 47:198. Estimates by French officers, diplomats, and travelers. Highly eulogistic.

Fitzpatrick, John C., ed. *The Diaries of George Washington, 1748-1799,* 4 vols., 1925.

AHR, 31:540. A matter of fact record which tells how Washington spent his time, but not what he thought! During the Revolution, Washington was too busy to keep diaries. After the war his entries sometimes tell of fox hunts, card games or horse races, but are largely concerned with plantation routine. Such entries as "women grubbing in the swamp," "the women were spreading dung as yesterday" show that the slaves worked hard at Mount Vernon.

Stedman and Hutchinson. *Library of American Literature,* 3:146-74.

Biography: Fay, Bernard. *George Washington, Republican Aristocrat.* 1931.

AHR, 37:764. The author justifies his sub-title by a study of "feudalism in Virginia." He gives a fair treatment of the Jumonville episode and the Genet mission.

Fitzpatrick, John C. *George Washington Himself: a Commonsense Biography written from his Manuscripts.* 1933.

AHR, 40:142. As the archivist of the Library of Congress, Mr. Fitzpatrick edited the most recent edition of Washington's writings. He dwells mostly on the period down to the close of the Revolution. He seeks to scotch "the Sally Fairfax myth" and to defend the political and military reputation of his subject.

Hughes, Rupert. *George Washington: I. The Human Being and the Hero, 1732-1762.* 1926.

Ind., 117:623, Nov. 27, 1926.

———. *II. The Rebel and the Patriot, 1762-1777.* 1928.

Nation, 126:159, Feb. 8, 1928.

———. *III. The Saviour of the States, 1777-1781.* 1930.

AHR, 36:412. Aroused great indignation in some quarters, but is now recognized as a conscientious effort to humanize Washington. Seeks to strip him of legend and let him speak for himself. Contends that he was in love with Sally Fairfax, denies that he had ever been in a real battle before the Revolution, or that he knelt in the snow at Valley Forge. Gives a realistic picture of the hardships which the commander-in-chief faced from day to day during the war.

Sears, Louis Martin. *George Washington.* 1932.

AHR, 37:764. Portrays "the real Washington, great and noble, with enough human weaknesses to make his fellowmen feel that he is not an unattainable ideal, but an inspiring example."

Stephenson, Nathaniel Wright, and Waldo Hilary Dunn. *George Washington,* 2 vols., 1940.

AHR, 46:928. A dynamic interpretation of Washington as the leader who shaped the destinies of America. The authors defend their hero from the charges made by Rupert Hughes and Charles Francis Adams.

Thayer, Wm. Roscoe. *George Washington.* 1922.

AHR, 28:366. An orthodox work, which, however, emphasizes the human traits of Washington.

Woodward, W. E. *George Washington, the Image and the Man.* 1926.

AHR, 32:611. A debunker's biography which takes Washington off his pedestal. Charges that he was in love with Sally Fairfax, and denies that he was a good general, or a man of ideas. Declares that he was more interested in property rights than in human rights. Summarizes Washington's qualities and concludes that he was a great man, though not of first rate ability. Makes caustic references to Washington's contemporaries.

COLLECTIVE BIOGRAPHY: Agar, Herbert. *The People's Choice,* 3-31.

Bradford, Gamaliel. *Portraits and Personalities,* 1-18.

Bruce, David K. E. *Revolution to Reconstruction,* 3-40.

Bruce, Philip A. *Virginia Plutarch,* 1:155-72; 2:1-18.

Dodd, William E. "George Washington, Nationalist," in *Ann. Report, Am. Hist. Assn.*, (1932) :133-48.

Egbert and Lee. *Princeton Portraits*, 317-29.

Fish, C. R. "George Washington, the Man." *Ill. State Hist. Soc. Trans.*, (1932) :21-40.

Fitzpatrick, John C., in *DAB*, 19:509.

Guedalla, Philip. *Fathers of the Revolution*, 189-212.
Also in *Harper's*, 150 (1924):98-106.

Hamlin, Fred. *Land of Liberty*, 66-84.

Hughes, Rupert, in *There Were Giants in the Land*, 187-93.

Kingdon, Frank. *Architects of the Republic*, 7-85.

Little, Shelby, in M. A. Hyde, *Modern Biography*, (1943) :61-68.

Read, H. E. *Fighters for Freedom*, 204-09.

Thomas and Thomas. *Fifty Great Americans*, 12-22.

———. *Living Biographies of American Statesmen*, 53-68.

Umbreit, K. B. *Founding Fathers*, 235-332.

Van Loon, Hendrick. *Van Loon's Lives*, 68-127.

Wilstach, Paul. *Patriots Off Their Pedestals*, 24-46.

HISTORY: Jacobs, J. R. *The Beginnings of the U. S. Army*. 1947.

Klingberg, Frank J. *The Morning of America*. 1941.

SPECIAL ASPECTS: Adams, Charles Francis. *Studies Military and Diplomatic*. 1911.

AHR, 17:613. Presents the thesis that Washington was not a military genius, but "a positively bad general" who was saved by the incompetence of Howe. Chapter II, "The Battle of Long Island," originally appeared in *AHR*, 1 (1896):650-70.

Ambler, Charles H. *George Washington and the West*. 1936.

MVHR, 23:405. A well-written account of Washington's work as a surveyor, militia leader, land speculator, and promoter of internal improvements in the west. The book adds nothing new, and occasionally refers to Washington as though he were a kind of "superman."

Booth, E. T. *Country Life in America*, 38-75.

Corbin, John. "The Unknown Washington." *Scribner's*, 86 (1929) :255-64.

———. "Washington and Sally Fairfax." *Ibid.*, 402-13.

———. "Washington and the American Union." *Ibid.*, 487-97.

Dorfman, Joseph. *The Economic Mind in American Civilization.* Vol. 1.

Haworth, Paul Leland. *George Washington, Country Gentleman: Being an Account of His Home Life and Agricultural
Activities.* 1925.

Published in 1915 as *George Washington, Farmer. AHR*, 21:858. Shows
how Washington acquired his vast lands and contends that he was a
successful farmer. Readable but not altogether convincing.

Knollenberg, Bernhard. *Washington and the Revolution, a Reappraisal: Gates, Conway, and the Continental Congress.*
1940.

AHR, 47:350. This challenging study presents evidence to rehabilitate
Gates and to show that the Conway Cabal was the result of Washington's imagination. It shows that the commander-in-chief was not the
perfect character imagined by Sparks, but a human being who sometimes
sought to evade laws, blame others for his own mistakes, and imagine
opposition where there was a mere difference of opinion.

O'Neill, E. H. *A History of American Biography,* Chapter VI,
"Washington: False and Real."

Deals with a number of biographers of Washington from Mason Weems to
Rupert Hughes.

Peattie, D. C. "First Farmer of the Land." *Read. Dig.*, 48(1946):
5-8.

Sears, L. M. "George Washington and the French Revolution—
the First Phase," in Avery Craven, ed. *Essays in Honor of
William E. Dodd,* 15-29.

Smith, Don. *Peculiarities of the Presidents.* 1946.

Spaulding, Oliver L., Jr. "The Military Studies of George
Washington." *AHR*, 29 (1924) :675-80.

Stephenson, N. W. "The Romantics and George Washington."
AHR, 39 (1934) :274-83.

Communication from Rupert Hughes on Stephenson's Comments. *Ibid.*, 794-97.

Wecter, Dixon. *The Hero in America,* 99-147.

DEVEREUX JARRATT—1732-1801—Leader in the
Great Awakening

COLLECTIVE BIOGRAPHY: Chorley, E. Clowes. *Men and Movements in the American Episcopal Church,* (1946) :1-25.

Sweet, W. W. *Makers of Christianity,* 102-8.

HISTORY: Goodwin, E. L. *The Colonial Church in Virginia.* 1927.

SPECIAL ASPECTS: Smith, J. W. "Devereaux Jarratt and the Beginnings of Methodism in Virginia." *The John P. Branch Hist. Papers of Randolph-Macon Coll., No. 1,* (1901) :3-21.

PATRICK HENRY—1736-1799—Illiterate Backwoods
Orator Who Plotted to Make Himself Dictator?

ORIGINAL SOURCES: Stedman and Hutchinson. *Library of American Literature,* 3:214-18.

BIOGRAPHY: Axelrad, Jacob. *Patrick Henry: the Voice of Freedom.* 1947.

Jour. of South. Hist., 14:120. A readable popular narrative which pictures Henry as the fiery champion of the people against both Tidewater aristocracy and English officials, but does not explain his shift from radicalism to conservatism.

Henry, William Wirt. *Patrick Henry: Life, Correspondence and Speeches,* 3 vols., 1891.

Atlantic, 70:408. A good history of Virginia from 1765 to 1799.

Tyler, M. C. *Patrick Henry* (American Statesmen series, 1887) .

Atlantic, 61:276. A sympathetic, well-written biography which defends Henry from Jefferson's charges.

COLLECTIVE BIOGRAPHY: Bruce, P. A. *Virginia Plutarch,* 1:173-94.

Dodd, William E., in *DAB,* 8:554.

Kunitz and Haycraft. *American Authors,* 360-61.

Peterson, C. S. *First Governors of the Forty-eight States,* 24-28.

Umbreit, K. C. *Founding Fathers,* 200-34.
Quite favorable.

Wilstach, Paul. *Patriots Off Their Pedestals,* 78-96.

HISTORY: Klingberg, Frank J. *The Morning of America.* 1941.

Miller, J. C. *Origins of the American Revolution.* 1943.

SPECIAL ASPECTS: Dodd, William E. "Virginia Takes the Road to Revolution," in Carl Becker and Others, eds. *The Spirit of '76,* 101-35.

Jones, Edgar D. *Lords of Speech,* (1938) :1-16.

BIOGRAPHIES OF CONTEMPORARIES: Malone, Dumas. *Jefferson, the Virginian.* 1947.

Gives an excellent portrait.

THOMAS JEFFERSON— 1743-1826 —"A Major Prophet of Individual Freedom and Human Dignity"

ORIGINAL SOURCES: Davis, Richard B., ed. *Correspondence of Thomas Jefferson and Francis Walker Gilmer, 1814-1826.* 1946.

Amer. Lit., 18:260. Some of these letters deal with the literary and scientific interest of these two cultivated Virginians. Others grew out of Gilmer's mission to England and Scotland to obtain professors for the new university.

Ford, Paul L., ed. *Autobiography of Thomas Jefferson.* 1914.

Mayo, Bernard, ed. *Jefferson Himself: the Personal Narrative of a Many-Sided American.* 1942.

Jour. of South. Hist., 9:264. Well-selected material from Jefferson's writings—arranged topically.

Stedman and Hutchinson. *Library of American Literature,* 3:265-85.

Turner, Lynn W.; "Thomas Jefferson Through the Eyes of a New Hampshire Politician." *MVHR,* 30 (1943) :205-14.

Van Doren, Mark. *Autobiography of America,* 161-65, 192-201.

Warfel, Gabriel, and Williams. *American Mind,* 241-50.

BIOGRAPHY: Adams, James Truslow. *The Living Jefferson.* 1936.

MVHR, 23:264. A mixture of biography, the history of liberalism, and an attack upon the New Deal.

Bowers, C. G. *The Young Jefferson, 1743-1789.* 1945.

AHR, 50:810. A readable account of Jefferson's early and middle years. Written in brilliant style, but not abreast of recent research.

———. *Jefferson and Hamilton: the Struggle for Democracy in America.* 1925.

AHR, 31:543. An entertaining, dramatic narrative of our first party conflicts. Frankly partial to Jefferson.

———. *Jefferson in Power: the Death Struggles of the Federalists.* 1936.

AHR, 43:413. A dramatic account of Jefferson's administration written to correct Henry Adams and other Federalist historians. Contains excellent thumb-nail sketches of friends and enemies.

Chinard, Gilbert. *Thomas Jefferson, the Apostle of Americanism.* 1929.

AHR, 35:378. Excellent biography by a French scholar who refutes the charge that Jefferson borrowed his democracy from French radicals. Emphasis on intellectual aspects.

Hirst, F. W. *Life and Letters of Jefferson.* 1926.

AHR, 31:799. An Englishman vigorously defends his hero from the charges made by the biographers of Hamilton. Emphasizes Jefferson as a man of letters and a scientist.

Kimball, Marie (Goebel). *Jefferson: the Road to Glory, 1743-1776.* 1943.

AHR, 49:109. Readable scholarly account of the early years. Shows that Jefferson was not the son of "an ignorant backwoodsman," that he was a rather gay young aristocrat before he "went studious" under the influence of Lawyer Wythe; and that he was very much in love with Martha Wayles.

———. *Jefferson: War and Peace, 1776-1784.* 1947.

AHR, 53:556. A sympathetic, well-written account of Jefferson during the Revolution. The author describes the social revolution he promoted in Virginia; defends his record as governor; describes the way he worked on his *Notes on Virginia*.

Malone, Dumas. *Jefferson and His Time,* Volume 1, *Jefferson the Virginian.* 1948.

AHR, 54:150. Jefferson is difficult to understand because he was reticent about his private affairs. Dr. Malone, however, writes about him "as though he were in the next room." He has given us a rich and comprehensive biography, written with clarity and understanding.

Nock, Albert Jay. *Jefferson.* 1926.

AHR, 32:339. An "entertaining, challenging book" which upholds Beard's economic interpretation of the Constitution, and maintains that Jefferson rendered great service to agriculture, although he was neither "a good practical farmer" nor a popular leader.

Padover, S. D. *Jefferson.* 1942.

AHR, 48:356. Readable, accurate study. Fair to Jefferson and his enemies. Emphasis on personal life.

COLLECTIVE BIOGRAPHY: Agar, Herbert. *The People's Choice,* 32-71.

Beard, Charles A. "Thomas Jefferson: a Civilized Man." *MVHR*, 30 (1943):159-70.

Bowers, C. G., in *There Were Giants in the Land,* 130-36.

Bruce, D. K. E. *Revolution to Reconstruction,* 85-136.

Dodd, W. E. *Statesmen of the Old South,* 1-88.

Hamlin, Fred. *Land of Liberty,* 84-106.

Hofstedter, Richard. *American Political Tradition and the Men Who Made It,* 18-43.

Johnson, Gerald. *American Heroes and Hero Worship,* (1943) : 54-93.

Knoles, George H. "Thomas Jefferson, Crusader for Freedom." *Social Stu.,* 3 (1942) :297-304.

Malone, Dumas, in *DAB,* 10:17.

———. "Polly Jefferson and her Father." *Va. Quar. Rev.,* 7 (1931) :81-95.
A personal picture. Sympathetic.

Parrington, V. L. *Main Currents in American Thought,* 1:342-56.

Peattie, Donald C. "Thomas Jefferson, Architect of Democracy." *Read. Dig.,* 42 (1943) :1-5.

———. *Journey into America,* 3-12.

Russell, Phillips. "Thomas Jefferson, Social Architect," in Durling and Watt. *Biography,* 91-112.

Tyler, M. C. *Literary History of the American Revolution,* 1:494-98.

Umbreit, K. C. *Founding Fathers,* 1-103.
Unsympathetic.

Wilstach, Paul. *Patriots Off Their Pedestals,* 145-81.

HISTORY: Adams, Henry. *The History of the United States During the Administrations of Jefferson and Madison,* 9 vols., 1890-91.
Reprinted in 4 vols., 1930. Condensed edition edited by Herbert Agar, 2 vols., 1947.

Hunt, Gaillard, ed. *The First Forty Years of Washington Society.* 1906.
AHR, 12:669. Shows that the attitude of Margaret Bayard Smith towards Jefferson changed from prejudice to ardent admiration and friendship. Mrs. Smith gives an entertaining account of Jefferson's home life.

Klingberg, Frank J. *The Morning of America.* 1941.

SPECIAL ASPECTS: Basso, Hamilton. *Mainstream,* 23-43.

Beard, Charles A. *Economic Origins of Jeffersonian Democracy.* 1915.

MVHR, 3:99. A frank attempt to explain Jeffersonian democracy by means of economic determinism.

———. "Jefferson in America Now." *Yale Rev.,* 25 (1936): 241-57.

Becker, Carl. "What Is Still Living in the Political Philosophy of Thomas Jefferson." *AHR,* 48 (1943) :691-706.

Bemis, S. F., in S. F. Bemis, ed. *American Secretaries of State,* 2:3-93.

Booth, Edward T. *Country Life in America,* 75-103.

Boyd, J. P.· "New Light on Jefferson and his Great Task." *N. Y. Times,* Apr. 13, 1947, p. 17.

Bowers, C. G. "Jefferson, Master Politician." *Va. Quar. Rev.,* 2 (1926) :321-33.

Chinard, Gilbert. "Jefferson's Influence Abroad." *MVHR,* 30 (1943) :171-86.

David, R. B., ed. "Postscript on Thomas Jefferson and his University Professors." *Jour. of South. Hist.,* 12 (1946) :422-32.

Dix, J. P. "Thomas Jefferson, Father of American Democracy," in *Social Stu.,* 38 (1947) :357-66.

Dorfman, Joseph. *The Economic Mind in American Civilization,* 1:433-47, index.

Dumbauld, Edward. *Thomas Jefferson, American Tourist.* 1946.

Foote, Henry W. *Thomas Jefferson, Champion of Religious Freedom, Advocate of Christian Morals.* 1947.

Goodspeed, E. J. "Thomas Jefferson and the Bible." *Harvard Theol. Rev.,* 40 (1947) :71-76.

Gould, W. D. "The Religious Opinions of Thomas Jefferson." *MVHR,* 20 (1933) :191-209.

Gramp, W. D. "Re-examination of Jeffersonian Economics." *South. Econ. Jour.,* 12 (1946) :263-82.

Griswold, A. W. "Agrarian Democracy of Thomas Jefferson." *Amer. Pol. Sci. Rev.,* 40 (1946) :657-81.

Kimball, Marie (Goebel). "The Epicure of the White House." *Va. Quar. Rev.,* 9 (1933) :71-81.

Knoles, George H. "The Religious Ideas of Thomas Jefferson." *MVHR,* 30 (1943) :187-204.

Koch, Adrienne. *The Philosophy of Thomas Jefferson.* (Columbia Studies in American Culture, 1943).

AHR, 49:739. An excellent "analytical and critical study of the origins of Jefferson's ideas on the universe, man, and society."

Lehmann-Hartleben, Karl. *Thomas Jefferson: American Humanist.* 1947.

N. Y. Times, Nov. 16, 1947, p. 9. A penetrating analysis of Jefferson's views of the Greek and Roman classical writers.

Malone, Dumas. "Jefferson and the New Deal." *Scribner's,* 93 (1933) :356-59.

Marsh, Phillip. "Vindication of Mr. Jefferson." *So. Atl. Quar.,* 45 (1946) :61-67.

Martin, P. "Jefferson's True Love." *Sat. Eve. Post,* 218:22-23, Apr. 13, 1946.

Merriam, Charles E. *History of American Political Theories,* 19-26.

Morais, H. M. *Deism in Eighteenth Century America* (Columbia University Studies in History, Economics and Public Law, 1934).

No. Am. Rev., 238:476. An interesting study which shows that deism "had a far stronger influence on the culture of the ante-bellum South than is generally known."

Pollard, James E. *Presidents and the Press,* 52-95.

———. *Am. Phil. Soc. Proc.,* Vol. 87, No. 3, "Thomas Jefferson," 1943.

AHR, 49:356. Gives the papers read before the society in celebration of the bicentennial of Jefferson.

Ruck, William S. "Jefferson the Architect." *Va. Quar. Rev.,* 8 (1932) :139-43.

Sanders, G. V. "Thomas Jefferson's Inventions." *Pop. Sci.,* 148 (1946) :104-13.

Schachner, Nathan. "Jefferson: a Slippery Politician." *Amer. Merc.,* 46 (1939) : 49-55.

———. "Jefferson: the Man and the Myth." *Ibid.*, 65 (1947) : 46-52.

Smith, Don. *Peculiarities of the Presidents.*

Spengler, Joseph J. "The Political Economy of Jefferson, Madison, and Adams," in David K. Jackson, ed. *American Studies in Honor of William Kenneth Boyd*, (1940) :3-59.

Stephenson, Nathaniel Wright. *Typical Americans and Their Problems* (Scripps College Papers, No. 3, 1930) , 1-19.

Wecter, Dixon. *The Hero in America*, 148-80.

Willson, Beckles. *America's Ambassadors to France*, (1928) : 17-39.

Wilstach, Paul. "Jefferson's Little Mountain." *Nation. Geog. Mag.*, 55 (1929) :481-503.

———. "Jefferson out of Harness." *Amer. Merc.*, 4 (1925) :63-68.

Wiltse, Charles M. *The Jeffersonian Tradition in American Democracy.* 1935.

AHR, 53:149. A scholarly study which maintains that Jefferson derived his political philosophy from England and America rather than from France.

Woodfin, Maude H. "Contemporary Opinion in Virginia of Thomas Jefferson," in Avery Craven, ed., *Essays in Honor of William E. Dodd*, (1935) :30-85.

BIOGRAPHIES OF CONTEMPORARIES: Fitzpatrick, John C. *George Washington Himself.* 1933.

Censures Jefferson severely.

Oliver, F. S. *Alexander Hamilton.* 1906.

Attributes Jefferson's founding a new party to motives of personal spite.

PHILIP VICKERS FITHIAN— 1747-1776
—Schoolmaster

ORIGINAL SOURCES: Fithian, Philip Vickers. *Journal and Letters of Philip Vickers Fithian, 1773-1774; a Plantation Tutor of the Old Dominion.* Ed. by Hunter Dickinson Farish. 1943.

Jour. of South. Hist., 9:561. The diary and letters of a Princeton student who tutored in the home of Robert Carter on the eve of the Revolution. Especially interesting because of the tolerance of this puritanical theologian for customs and institutions that were strange to him.

———. *Philip Vickers Fithian: Journal, 1775-1776, Written on the Virginia-Pennsylvania Frontier and in the Army around New York.* Ed. by Robert G. Albion and Leonidas Dodson. 1934.

AHR, 40:381. The author, a Presbyterian circuit-rider and later an army chaplain, gives the result of his keen observation of daily life on the frontier and the reactions of that section to the outbreak of the revolution.

Trent and Wells. *Colonial Prose and Poetry,* 3:315-31.

SPECIAL ASPECTS: Holliday, Carl. *Woman's Life in Colonial Days.* 1922.

JAMES MADISON—1750-1836—"The Father of the Constitution"

ORIGINAL SOURCES: Adair, Douglass, ed. "Autobiography." *Wm. and Mary Quar.* Third Series, 2 (1945) :191-209.

Hunt, Gaillard, ed. *The First Forty Years of Washington Society.* 1906.

Stedman and Hutchinson. *Library of American Literature,* 3:429-44.

BIOGRAPHY: Brant, Irving. *James Madison, the Virginia Revolutionist.* 1941.

Books, Sept. 28, 1941, p. 4. A sympathetic study of the first thirty years. Shows that although a shy scholar rather than a man of action, Madison was a young man of independent views.

———. *James Madison, the Nationalist, 1780-1787.* 1948.

AHR, 54:153. This full-length study describes Madison as a man who worked for radical reforms in Virginia, but for a strong government for the nation. Gives harsh characterizations of some of Madison's contemporaries.

Gay, Sydney H. *James Madison* (American Statesmen series, 1884).

A lively but prejudiced narrative which describes Madison as an intellectual weakling who fell under the evil influence of Jefferson.

Hunt, Gaillard. *The Life of James Madison.* 1902.

AHR, 9:170. A judicious history of Madison's times, which relegates his personality and his relations to his contemporaries to the background. He is described as a solemn man who vacillated between the influence of Hamilton and Jefferson.

Smith, Abbot Emerson. *James Madison, Builder: a New Estimate of a Memorable Career.* 1937.

AHR, 44:141. The author says that Madison was "almost insignificant personally," that he was not "distinguished as a counsellor" at the Philadelphia Convention, and that he "cut a pathetic figure" as president. He gives, however, a good presentation of what Madison contributed to American political and constitutional development.

COLLECTIVE BIOGRAPHY: Adair, Douglass, in Willard Thorp, ed. *Lives of Eighteen from Princeton*, 137-57.

Agar, Herbert. *The People's Choice*, 72-79.

Bowers, C. G., in *There Were Giants in the Land*, 130-36.

Bruce, D. K. E. *Revolution to Reconstruction*, 137-68.

Bruce, P. A. *Virginia Plutarch*, 2:57-75.

Egbert and Lee. *Princeton Portraits*, 250-57.

Pratt, Julius W., in *DAB*, 12:184.

Smith, Don. *Peculiarities of the Presidents*. 1946.

Thomas and Thomas. *Living Biographies of American Statesmen*, 139-50.

Wilstach, Paul. *Patriots Off Their Pedestals*, 211-41.

HISTORY: Adams, Henry. *The History of the United States During the Administrations of Jefferson and Madison*, 9 vols., 1890-91.

Reprinted in 4 vols., 1930. Condensed edition edited by Herbert Agar, 2 vols., 1947.

Fiske, John. *Essays, Historical and Literary*, 1:183-218.

Klingberg, Frank J. *The Morning of America*. 1941.

SPECIAL ASPECTS: Burns, Edward McN. *James Madison: Philosopher of the Constitution*. 1938.

AHR, 44:998. Gives a brief biographical introduction, then a full discussion of the character and purpose of the Constitution as presented in the writings of its chief framer.

Dorfman, Joseph. *The Economic Mind in American Civilization*. Vol. 1.

Hill, Charles E., in S. F. Bemis, ed. *American Secretaries of State*, 3:2-148.

Pollard, James Edward. *Presidents and the Press*, 96-115.

Schaedler, Louis C. "James Madison, Literary Craftsman." *Wm. and Mary Quar.*, Third Series, 3 (1946):515-33.

Spengler, Joseph J. "The Political Economy of Jefferson, Madison, and Adams," in David K. Jackson, ed. *American Studies in Honor of William Kenneth Boyd,* (1940) :3-59.

DOLLY PAYNE MADISON—1768-1849—"Our Most Famous First Lady"

ORIGINAL SOURCES: Cutts, Lucia B., ed. *Memoirs and Letters of Dolly Madison.* 1886.

Entertaining letters of an intelligent woman who took a lively interest in what was going on around her.

BIOGRAPHY: Anthony, Katharine. *Dolly Madison, Her Life and Times.* 1949.

N. Y. Times, Jan. 23, 1949, p. 6. The best biography of a woman of great simplicity and kindness who achieved remarkable success as a social leader.

Dean, Elizabeth L. *Dolly Madison, the Nation's Hostess.* 1928.

N. Y. Times, May 6, 1928, p. 5. Throws an interesting light on Washington society during the early years.

COLLECTIVE BIOGRAPHY: Bradford. *Wives,* 127-60.

Also in *Va. Quar. Rev.,* 1:1-18; and Durling and Watt. *Biography,* 365-82.

Malone, Dumas, in *DAB,* 12:181.

Minnigerode, Meade. *Some American Ladies,* 89-132.

Whitton, Mary Ormsbee. *First First Ladies, 1789-1865,* 54-70.

HISTORY: Hunt, Gaillard, ed. *The First Forty Years of Washington Society.* 1906.

AHR, 12:669. Gives an interesting account of Mrs. Madison in Washington and at her Virginia home, but rejects the story of how she saved Washington's picture in 1814.

JOHN MARSHALL—   1755-1835   —Chief Justice

BIOGRAPHY: Beveridge, Albert J. *The Life of John Marshall,* *
4 vols., 1916-1919.

AHR, 22:666; 25:515. A scholarly and readable work which describes Marshall as a very human man who could laugh at his own sufferings at Valley Forge, and who had a genius for winning and holding friends. Beveridge gives an excellent description of Marshall's personality and of his influence on the development of the Constitution. Beveridge was a strong partisan, however, and devoted too much space to the times in which Marshall lived. *Read especially,* Vol. I, Chapters 1-5 (early life and marriage); II, Chapter 5, "The Man and the Lawyer"; IV, Chapter 2, "Marshall and Story"; Chapter 9, "The Supreme Conservative."

---

* Won the Pulitzer Prize.

Thayer, J. B. *John Marshall* (Riverside Biographical series, 1901).

COLLECTIVE BIOGRAPHY: Abbott, Lawrence. *Twelve Great Modernists,* (1927) :127-50.

Adams, James T., in *Am. Scholar,* 1 (1932) :261-64.

Bruce, P. A. *Virginia Plutarch,* 2:76-96.

Corwin, Edward S., in *DAB,* 12:315.

Kunitz and Haycraft. *American Authors,* 511-12.

Parrington, V. L. *Main Currents in American Thought,* 2:20-27.

Peattie, D. C., "John Marshall—Inspired Justice." *Read. Dig.,* 51 (1947) :46-52.

Seagle, William. *Men of Law,* (1947) :269-305.

Thomas and Thomas. *Living Biographies of American Statesmen,* 109-21.

———. *Fifty Great Americans,* 67-75.

Umbreit, Kenneth. *Lives of the Chief Justices,* 111-96.

Wilstach, Paul. *Patriots Off Their Pedestals,* 182-210.

HISTORY: Corwin, Edward S. *John Marshall and the Constitution: a Chronicle of the Supreme Court* (Chronicles of America, XVI, 1919).

MVHR, 7:394. Gives "a vivid picture of Marshall as a man" and "an entirely new impression of his statesmanship and his place in American political life." *Read especially,* Chapter 8, "Among Friends and Neighbors."

Klingberg, Frank J. *The Morning of America.* 1941.

SPECIAL ASPECTS: C. M. S. "The Home Life of Chief Justice Marshall." *Wm. and Mary Quar.,* 2nd ser., 12 (1932) :67-69.

Dodd, William E. "Chief Justice Marshall and Virginia, 1813-1821." *AHR,* 12 (1907) :776-87.

Foran, William A. "John Marshall as a Historian." *AHR,* 43 (1947) :51-64.

Morison, S. E. "The Education of John Marshall." *Atlantic,* 126 (1920) :45-54.

Munro, W. B. *Makers of the Unwritten Constitution,* 53-81.

MARQUIS DE LAFAYETTE— 1757-1834 —French Aristocrat Who Championed American Liberty?

BIOGRAPHY: Gottschalk, Louis. *Lafayette Comes to America.* 1935.

AHR, 42:310. Claims that Lafayette came to America—not because he espoused American ideas—but because he wished to win glory by fighting the hated English and thus prove to his "in-laws" that he was not inferior. Did he live up to the role thrust upon him?

———. *Lafayette Joins the American Army.* 1937.

MVHR, 25:90. A study of the development of the marquis which seeks to explain how a rich young aristocrat "became in his later years the outstanding liberal of his day."

———. *Lafayette and the Close of the American Revolution.* 1942.

AHR, 48:354. Throws light on the development of Lafayette's ideals of liberty and on the coördination of the Americans and the French in the Yorktown Campaign.

Whitlock, Brand. *La Fayette,* 2 vols., 1929.

Jour. Mod. Hist., 2:281. An uncritical biography which contains many errors.

COLLECTIVE BIOGRAPHY: Monaghan, Frank, in *DAB*, 10:535.

Guedalla, Philip. *Fathers of the Revolution,* 263-84.

Woodward, W. E., in *There Were Giants in the Land,* 123-29.

JAMES MONROE— 1758-1831 —"The Last of the Virginia Dynasty"

BIOGRAPHY: Cresson, W. P. *James Monroe.* 1946.

AHR, 52:518. An authentic portrait of Monroe with a fair estimate of his strong and weak points. Also excellent estimates of his political associates from Jefferson to Jackson.

COLLECTIVE BIOGRAPHY: Beard, Charles Austin. *Presidents in American History,* 30-33, 166-67.

Bruce, David K. *Revolution to Reconstruction,* 171-92.

Bruce, P. A. *Virginia Plutarch,* 2:97-114.

Perkins, Dexter, in *DAB*, 13:87.

Thomas and Thomas. *Living Biographies of American Statesmen,* 153-65.

HISTORY: Klingberg, Frank J. *The Morning of America.* 1941.

SPECIAL ASPECTS: Hill, C. E., in S. F. Bemis. *American Secretaries of State,* 3:3-151.

Marsh, Philip. "Hamilton and Monroe." *MVHR,* 34 (1947): 459-68.

Pollard, J. E. *Presidents and the Press,* 116-26.

Smith, Don. *Peculiarities of the Presidents,* 28, 31, 77, and 114.

JOHN RANDOLPH— 1773-1833 —"Southside Statesman"

ORIGINAL SOURCES: Van Doren, Mark. *Autobiography of America,* 228-50.

BIOGRAPHY: Adams, Henry. *John Randolph* (American Statesmen series, 1882).
Bitter and unforgiving.

Bruce, William Cabell. *John Randolph of Roanoke, 1773-1833; a Biography Based Largely on New Material,* 2 vols., 1922.

AHR, 29:347. The author does a better job in describing Randolph as a man than as a politician. He gives an adequate discussion of the break with Jefferson, but devotes too much space to a family scandal.

Johnson, Gerald W. *Randolph of Roanoke: a Political Fantastic.* 1929.

N. Y. Times, Apr. 21, 1929, p. 5. A well written and penetrating study of an enigmatic American. Less sympathetic than Bruce.

COLLECTIVE BIOGRAPHY: Bradford, Gamaliel. *Damaged Souls,* 123-56.
Also in *Harper's,* 146 (1923):507-15.

Bruce, P. A. *Virginia Plutarch,* 2:115-32.

Eckenrode, H. J. *The Randolphs,* 188-226.

Malone, Dumas, in *DAB,* 15:363.

HISTORY: Adams, Henry. *History of the United States.*
Hostile.

Bowers, C. G. *Jefferson in Power,* 99-113.

CHAPTER XX. MARYLAND

HISTORY: Wertenbaker, Thomas J. *The Golden Age of Colonial Culture,* Chapter V, "Intellectual Life Around the Punch Bowl: Annapolis."

LAMBERT WICKES— 1735-1777 —The First Naval Officer to Command an American Warship in European Seas

BIOGRAPHY: Clark, William Bell. *Lambert Wickes, Sea Raider and Diplomat: the Story of a Naval Captain of the Revolution.* 1932.

AHR, 38:128. A valuable contribution to naval history, although it fails to present a clear-cut picture of this gallant and patriotic naval officer.

COLLECTIVE BIOGRAPHY: Bolander, Louis H., in *DAB,* 20:180.

JOHN CARROLL—1735-1815—First Catholic Bishop in U. S.

COLLECTIVE BIOGRAPHY: Warfel, Gabriel, and Williams. *American Mind,* 250-52.

Purcell, Richard, in *DAB,* 3:526.

CHARLES CARROLL OF CARROLLTON—1737-1832—Leading Catholic

BIOGRAPHY: Smith, Ellen Hart. *Charles Carroll of Carrollton.* 1942.

AHR, 48:799. This biography of the signer of the Declaration of Independence who helped to inaugurate the first railroad emphasizes the personality rather than his political career. Described as "the richest man in America," Carroll was at times generous and tolerant; at other times, rather close.

COLLECTIVE BIOGRAPHY: Wroth, Lawrence C., in *DAB,* 3:522.

JONATHAN BOUCHER— 1738-1804 —Militant Loyalist

ORIGINAL SOURCES: Bouchier, Jonathan,* ed. *Reminiscences of an American Loyalist, 1738-1789: being the Autobiography of the Rev. Jonathan Boucher.* 1925.

MVHR, 12:593. The memoirs of an Englishman who taught school in Virginia, then served as an Anglican rector in Maryland. Here he was closely associated with Governor Eden, whom he served in various ways. While he married a Virginia girl, he preached loyalist sermons, keeping his loaded pistols handy to prevent any interruption. Later he returned to England, where he suffered many hardships.

Trent and Wells. *Colonial Prose and Poetry,* 3:288-95.

---

* A grandson of Jonathan Boucher, although he spelled his name differently.

COLLECTIVE BIOGRAPHY: Johnson, Allen, in *DAB*, 2:473.

Parrington, V. L. *Main Currents in American Thought,* 214-18.

Walker, Robert G. "Jonathan Boucher: Champion of the Minority." *Wm. and Mary Quar.,* Third Series, 2 (1945) : 3-14.

FRANCIS ASBURY— 1745-1816 —Bishop of the Wilderness

BIOGRAPHY: Tipple, Ezra Squier. *Francis Asbury, the Prophet of the Long Road.* 1916.

AHR, 22:679. While the author shows a lack of system and an abundance of denominational fervor, he does give a clear-cut picture of the real founder of the Methodist Church in America.

Asbury, Herbert. *A Methodist Saint.* 1927.

New Repub., 50:280, April 27, 1927. "A history of the rise of Methodism in America rather than a life of its first bishop."

COLLECTIVE BIOGRAPHY: Day, Richard E. *Beacon Lights of Grace,* (1947) :89-101.

Johnson, Allen, in *DAB,* 1:379.

JOHN PAUL JONES—1747-1792—"The Father of the American Navy"

ORIGINAL SOURCES: Stedman and Hutchinson. *Library of American Literature,* 3:380-87.

BIOGRAPHY: Johnson, Gerald W. *First Captain: the Story of John Paul Jones.* 1947.

AHR, 53:549. A readable popular biography which makes some assertions without presenting evidence.

Lorenz, Lincoln. *John Paul Jones: Fighter for Freedom and Glory.* 1943.

AHR, 49:115. A comprehensive study based on wide research. Shows that the pre-eminence of Jones in the American navy was due to his ability and character rather than to luck.

Russell, Phillips. *John Paul Jones: Man of Action.* 1927.

AHR, 33:922. A somewhat fictionized biography which gives a vivid and fairly accurate impression of the naval hero.

Thomson, Valentine. *Knight of the Seas: the Adventurous Life of John Paul Jones.* 1939.

AHR, 46:161. An interesting biography based on new material from foreign archives. While the author "seems oblivious to certain defects in the commodore's character," he presents him as a very human figure.

COLLECTIVE BIOGRAPHY: Alden, Carroll Storrs, and Ralph Earle. *Makers of Naval Tradition*, 7-36.

Paullin, Charles O., in *DAB*, 10:183.

Thomas and Thomas. *Fifty Great Americans,* 58-66.

Warner, J. H. "John Paul Jones: Fighting Sentimentalist." *So. Atl. Quar.*, 47 (1948) :35-44.

HISTORY: Alden, C. S., and A. Wescott. *The United States Navy.* 1934.

AHR, 49:320. Emphasizes naval operations rather than personalities.

SPECIAL ASPECTS: Mahan, A. T. "John Paul Jones in the Revolution." *Scribner's,* 24 (1898) :22-36, 204-19.

ALBERT GALLATIN—   1761-1849   —Financier

ORIGINAL SOURCES: Gallatin, James. *A Great Peace Maker: the Diary of James Gallatin, Secretary to Albert Gallatin, 1813-1827.* 1915.

MVHR, 2:433. This seventeen year old lad was quite proud of the tact and humor with which his father kept peace between John Quincy Adams and Clay. One might be inclined to discount his testimony somewhat, but it is well substantiated by Adams himself.

BIOGRAPHY: Adams, Henry. *The Life of Albert Gallatin.* 1879, 1943.

AHR, 49:543. The standard biography—written by a famous historian while editing the Gallatin papers.

COLLECTIVE BIOGRAPHY: Johnson, Carman C. "Albert Gallatin of Western Pennsylvania." *Western Pa. Hist. Mag.*, 8 (1925) : 98-103.

Muzzey, David S., in *DAB*, 7:103.

HISTORY: Baldwin, Leland D. *Whiskey Rebels,* (1939) :51-55, 176-82, index.

SPECIAL ASPECTS: Dorfman, Joseph. *The Economic Mind in American Civilization.* Vol. 1.

ELIZABETH PATTERSON BONAPARTE—1785-1879—Society Belle

COLLECTIVE BIOGRAPHY: Genzmer, George H., in *DAB*, 2:428.

McCartney, C. E., and Gordon Dorrance. *The Bonapartes in America.* 1939.

Books, June 8, 1939, p. 11. An entertaining book about some colorful personalities, all of whom lived in America at one time or another. Elizabeth Patterson married Napoleon's youngest brother, Jerome, a naval officer, in December, 1803. When Napoleon refused to recognize the marriage, Miss Patterson was given a pension and returned to America with her young son.

Peacock, Virginia T. *Famous American Belles of the Nineteenth Century,* (1901) :39-60.

CHAPTER XXI. THE TRANS-APPALACHIAN SETTLEMENTS

JOHN SEVIER—1745-1815—Heroic Defender of the Frontier or Land Speculator?

ORIGINAL SOURCES: "The Diary of John Sevier." *Tenn. Hist. Mag.,* Oct., 1919, Apr., 1920.

BIOGRAPHY: Driver, Carl Samuel. *John Sevier, Pioneer of the Old Southwest.* 1932.

MVHR, 20:115. An interesting study which raises the intriguing question: Should we think of "Nolchucky Jack" as a "heroic defender of frontier homes and firesides against the ravages of Tories and Indians," or as a land speculator whose chief motive throughout life concerned "the possibilities of gain through the acquisition of land in the Indian country . . ."?

COLLECTIVE BIOGRAPHY: Bruce, P. A. *Virginia Plutarch,* 1:306-28.

Whitaker, Arthur P., in *DAB,* 16:602.

HISTORY: Abernethy, T. P. *From Frontier to Plantation in Tennessee,* (1932).

Williams, S. C. *History of the Lost State of Franklin.* 1924.

DANIEL BOONE—1734-1820—Typical Frontiersman?

ORIGINAL SOURCES: Van Doren, Mark. *Autobiography of America,* 297-303.

BIOGRAPHY: Bakeless, John Edwin. *Master of the Wilderness: Daniel Boone.* 1939.

Books, Sept. 10, 1939, p. 3. Entertaining but fully documented. Some of the stories are frankly marked as legendary.

Thwaites, Rueben Gold. *Daniel Boone.* 1903.

Standard biography based on the Draper manuscripts in the Wisconsin Historical Society.

COLLECTIVE BIOGRAPHY: Ghent, W. J., in *DAB,* 2:441.

Thomas and Thomas. *Fifty Great Americans,* 32-40.

HISTORY: Bruce, H. Addington. *Daniel Boone and the Wilderness Road.* 1910.

Nation, 91:610, Dec. 22, 1910. A popular account of Boone's early life and of the settlement of Kentucky.

Henderson, Archibald. *The Conquest of the Old Southwest,* (1920) :130-59.

SPECIAL ASPECTS: Alvord, Clarence. "The Myth of Daniel Boone." *Ill. State Hist. Soc. Jour.,* 19 (1926) :16-30.

Very critical.

Kellogg, Louise Phelps. "The Fame of Daniel Boone." *Ky. St. Hist. Soc. Reg.,* 32 (1934) :187-98.

A defense.

Wecter, Dixon. *The Hero in America,* 181-89.

RICHARD HENDERSON—1735-1785—Promoter of the Transylvania Colony

COLLECTIVE BIOGRAPHY: Cotteril, Robert Spencer, in *DAB,* 8:530.

HISTORY: Henderson, Archibald. *The Conquest of the Old Southwest,* (1920) :216-36.

SPECIAL ASPECTS: ———. "Richard Henderson and the Occupation of Kentucky, 1775." *MVHR,* 1 (1914) :241-63.

———. "Richard Henderson: the Authorship of the Cumberland Compact and the Founding of Nashville." *Tenn. Hist. Mag.,* Sept., 1916.

———. "The Creative Forces in Westward Expansion: Henderson and Boone." *AHR,* 20 (1914) :86-107.

SAMUEL MASON— c. 1750-1803 —"Desperado and River Pirate"

COLLECTIVE BIOGRAPHY: Ghent, W. J., in *DAB*, 7:374.

HISTORY: Rothert, Otto A. *The Outlaws of Cave-in-Rock.* 1924.
MVHR, 11:151. An interesting book which seeks to give the authentic story of some of the most notorious outlaws in early American history.

GEORGE ROGERS CLARK— 1752-1818 —Settler, Warrior, and Archaeologist

BIOGRAPHY: Bodley, Temple. *George Rogers Clark, His Life and Public Services.* 1926.
AHR, 22:883. Eulogistic.
James, James Alton. *The Life of George Rogers Clark.* 1928.
AHR, 34:353. Still the only adequate interpretation of a baffling personality. James is the best authority on the life of Clark, but his claim that the western leader was in military control of the Old Northwest when this region was ceded to the United States is controversial. Bemis says there is no evidence that Clark's conquest had much influence in determining the boundary. S. F. Bemis, *The Diplomacy of the American Revolution*, p. 219n.

COLLECTIVE BIOGRAPHY: Bruce, P. A. *Virginia Plutarch*, 1:269-86.

Bodley, Temple. "National Significance of George Rogers Clark." *MVHR*, 11 (1924):165-89.

James, J. A., in *DAB*, 4:127.

———. "An Appraisal of the Contributions of George Rogers Clark to the History of the West." *MVHR*, 17 (1930):98-115.

SPECIAL ASPECTS: Kellogg, Louise P. "The Early Biographers of George Rogers Clark." *AHR*, 35 (1930):295-302.

JAMES WILKINSON— 1757-1825 —"The Most Finished Rascal in American Annals"

BIOGRAPHY: Jacobs, James Ripley. *Tarnished Warrior: Major General James Wilkinson.* 1938.
AHR, 45:909. A convincing picture of an engaging adventurer. The best biography—based on extensive research.
Shreve, Royal Oran. *The Finished Scoundrel.* 1933.
MVHR, 20:573. A rather hastily written biography. The author is a

popularizer rather than a research man, and was not up to date on the recent monographic material when he wrote his book.

HISTORY: Jacobs, James Ripley. *The Beginning of the United States Army, 1783-1812.* 1947.

EPHRAIM McDOWELL— 1771-1830 —Backwoods Surgeon

COLLECTIVE BIOGRAPHY: Ashburn, P. M., in *DAB*, 12:27.

Flexner, J. T. *Doctors on Horseback,* 121-62.

JEAN LAFITTE— fl. 1809-1821 —"Pirate Patriot"

BIOGRAPHY: Saxon, Lyle. *Lafitte the Pirate.* 1930.

Outlook, 156:549, Dec. 3, 1930. Entertaining rather than critical.

COLLECTIVE BIOGRAPHY: Bridgewater, William, in *DAB*, 10:540.

Lister, W. B. "Portrait of a Pirate." *Amer. Merc.,* 7 (1926) : 214-19.

Peattie, Donald C. "Jean Lafitte, Pirate Patriot." *Read. Dig.,* 45 (1944) :37-40.

HISTORY: Fortier, Alcee. *History of Louisiana.* 1904. Vol. 3.

Guyarre, Charles. *History of Louisiana.* 1866. Vol. 4.

SPECIAL ASPECTS: Dobie, J. F. "Mystery of Lafitte's Treasure." *Yale Rev.,* 18 (1928) :116-34.

Ramsdell, Charles, Jr. "Why Jean Lafitte Became a Pirate." *Southwestern Hist. Quar.,* 43 (1940) :465-71.

CHAPTER XXII. THE INDIAN COUNTRY

PONTIAC—c. 1720-1769—Hero of a Great Conspiracy?

BIOGRAPHY: Peckham, Howard Henry. *Pontiac and the Indian Uprising.* 1947.

AHR, 53:547. An excellent study based in part on manuscripts and monographs not available to Parkman. Pictures the illiterate Ottawa chief as only one of several leaders, and a rather shadowy figure at that.

Marquis, Thomas Guthrie. *The War Chief of the Ottawas: a Chronicle of the Pontiac War* (Chronicles of Canada, XV, 1915).

Collective Biography: Adams, Randolph G., in *DAB,* 15:62.
Britt, Albert. *Great Indian Chiefs,* 95-125.

History: Parkman, Francis. *The Conspiracy of Pontiac,* 2 vols., 1851.

A dramatic narrative by a brilliant historian who may have exaggerated Pontiac's role. Should be used with caution.

Pound, Arthur. *Detroit: Dynamic City.* 1945.

Also in Flanagan, John T., ed. *America Is West,* (1945):66-73.

Seymour, Flora Warren. *The Story of the Indian,* (1929) :22-44.

Wrong, George M. *Canada and the American Revolution,* (1935) :71-114.

ALEXANDER McGILLIVRAY—c. 1759-1793—"The Most Influential Border Character of His Generation"

Original Sources: Caughey, John Walton. *McGillivray of the Creeks* (The Civilization of the American Indian, 1938) .

AHR, 45:242. In addition to the correspondence of the Creek leader there is an excellent sketch of his life. Caughey contends that he was always loyal to his own people and should be regarded as a great American patriot.

Collective Biography: Foreman, Carolyn Thomas. "Alexander McGillivray, Emperor of the Creeks, 1740-1793." *Chron. Oklahoma,* 7 (1929) :106-20.

Whitaker, Arthur P., in *DAB,* 12:50.

———. "Alexander McGillivray, 1783-1789." *N. C. Hist. Rev.,* 5 (1928) :181-203.

———. "Alexander McGillivray, 1789-1793." *N. C. Hist. Rev.,* 5 (1928) :289-309.

TECUMSEH—1768-1813—The Greatest Statesman of His Race

Biography: Raymond, Ethel T. *Tecumseh: a Chronicle of the Last Great Leader of His People* (Chronicles of Canada, XVII, 1915) .

This full length biography combines sound scholarship and an interesting style.

COLLECTIVE BIOGRAPHY: Britt, Albert. *Great Indian Chiefs,* 126-55.

Crane, Katharine E., in *DAB,* 18:358.

Seitz, Don. *Uncommon Americans,* 183-94.

HISTORY: Adams, Henry. *History of the United States.*

Ogg, Frederic A. *The Old Northwest,* 131-50 (Chronicles of America, XIX, 1921).

Seymour, Flora Warren. *The Story of the Red Man,* (1929): 89-109.

WILLIAM CLARK— 1770-1838 —Army Officer and Explorer

BIOGRAPHY: Bakeless, John. *Lewis and Clark, Partners in Discovery.* 1947.

N. Y. Times, Dec. 28, 1947, p. 3. This combination biography gives a lively impression of the younger brother of George Rogers Clark and a dramatic account of the famous expedition to the Oregon country. Clark named a Montana river for the girl with whom he was wildly in love and later married. He had a long and happy career.

COLLECTIVE BIOGRAPHY: Kellogg, L. P., in *DAB,* 4:141.

Thwaites, R. G., in *Mo. Hist. Soc. Coll.,* 2:1-24.

SPECIAL ASPECTS: Lindley, Harlow. "William Clark, the Indian Agent." *MVHA Proc.,* 1908-09, pp. 63-75.

MERIWETHER LEWIS— 1774-1809 —Explorer and Governor of Louisiana

ORIGINAL SOURCES: Quaife, Milo M., ed. "The Journals of Captain Meriwether Lewis and Sergeant John Ordway, Kept on the Expedition of Western Exploration, 1803-1806." *Wis. Hist. Soc. Coll.,* Vol. 22 (1916).

AHR, 22:882. The journal of Captain Lewis is only forty-six pages and describes his journey from Pittsburgh to the rendezvous opposite the mouth of the Missouri. Sergeant Ordway's journal describes the journey to the Pacific Ocean and back to St. Louis.

Thwaites, R. G., ed. *Original Journals of the Lewis and Clark Expedition,* 7 vols., 1904-05.

BIOGRAPHY: Bakeless, John. *Lewis and Clark, Partners in Discovery.* 1947.

N. Y. Times, Dec. 28, 1947, p. 3. This excellent study gives an interesting account of the personality and career of Lewis. Apparently he was more of an aide to Jefferson than a secretary. He contrasts sharply with Clark. At the age of thirty-five, he described himself as a lonely and melancholy old bachelor. Did he commit suicide in that crude Tennessee cabin, or was he murdered?

COLLECTIVE BIOGRAPHY: Kellogg, L. K., in *DAB,* 11:219.

Bruce, P. A. *Virginia Plutarch,* 2:38-56.

HISTORY: Brebner, John Bartlet. *The Explorers of North America, 1492-1806,* (1933) :464-82.

SPECIAL ASPECTS: Guinness, Ralph B. "The Purpose of the Lewis and Clark Expedition." *MVHR,* 20 (1933) :90-100.

SACAGAWEA*— c. 1787-1812? —Interpreter of the
Lewis and Clark Expedition

ORIGINAL SOURCES: Luttig, John C. *Journal of a Fur-Trading Expedition on the Upper Missouri, 1812-1813.* Ed. by Stella M. Drum. 1920.

AHR, 26:839. Toussaint Charbonneau and his wife went with this expedition led by Manuel Lisa of St. Louis. Perhaps the most interesting entry in this hitherto unknown journal kept by Lisa's clerk is one which notes the death from "putrid fever" of "the Wife of Charbonneau, a Snake Squaw." The name is given as "Sakakawea."

Thwaites, R. G., ed. *Original Journals of the Lewis and Clark Expedition,* 7 vols., 1904-05.

Nation, 79:216, Sept. 15, 1904. Lewis gave the Indian squaw little recognition, referring to her only once. Clark, however, speaks of her with affection and gratitude. In one entry he says of her: "To her I ascribe equal fortitude and resolution with anyone on board."

COLLECTIVE BIOGRAPHY: Ghent, W. J., in *DAB,* 16:278.

Hebard, Grace, in *Jour. of Amer. Hist.,* Sept., 1907.

While Sacagawea has been widely honored, she has also been the subject of a long controversy. In spite of Luttig's record of her death in Dakota in 1812, Miss Hebard identifies her with an Indian woman who died in Wyoming in 1884.

Robinson, Doane, in *So. Dak. Hist. Coll.,* 12 (1924) :71-84.

The Secretary of the South Dakota Historical Society denies that the Wyom-

---

* THE GUIDE follows the *Dictionary of American Biography* in the spelling of proper names. Other variations may appear in the titles of books or articles.

ing woman of Miss Hebard's paper could possibly have been the interpreter of the Lewis and Clark Expedition.

HISTORY: Hebard, Grace Raymond. *Sacajawea: A Guide and Interpreter of the Lewis and Clark Expedition, with an Account of the Travels of Toussaint Charbonneau, and of Jean Baptiste, the Expedition Papoose.* 1933.

MVHR, 20:280. A full length restatement of the thesis Miss Hebard advanced in 1907.

Mirsky, Jeanette. *Westward Crossings,* 238-344 (*in passim*).

BIOGRAPHIES OF CONTEMPORARIES: Bakeless, John. *Lewis and Clark.* 1947.

Recognizes Sacagawea as "a valiant companion and interpreter," but denies that she "guided the Corps of Discovery." Accepts Miss Hebard's thesis.

ZEBULON MONTGOMERY PIKE   —1779-1813
—Explorer and Spy?

COLLECTIVE BIOGRAPHY: Crichton, Kyle, in *Scribner's,* 82 (1927):462-67.

A popular article which suggests that Pike acted as a spy for the Burr conspirators.

Hafen, LeRoy, in *DAB,* 14:599.

HISTORY: Hart, Stephen Harding, and Archer Butler Hulbert, eds. *Zebulon Pike's Arkansas Journal: in Search of the Southern Louisiana Purchase Boundary Line.* 1932.

MVHR, 20:117. Reproduces the part of Pike's book which describes his journey from Missouri until his capture by the Spaniards on the upper Rio Grande. Also gives a sketch of the life of Pike by Hart, and an excellent essay on the purpose of the expedition by Hulbert. The latter denies that Pike acted as a spy, and argues that he was making an ordinary routine investigation of the boundary.

Hulbert, Archer Butler, ed. *Southwest on the Turquoise Trail: the First Diaries on the Road to Santa Fe.* 1933.

MVHR, 20:583. This collection of documents relating to the early history of the Santa Fe Trail contains Pike's account of his trip from northern New Mexico to Chihuahua and back to Natchitoches.

CHECK-LIST OF BOOKS CITED FREQUENTLY

This list includes books cited at least three times in this volume. A few important books have been added, although they are not cited in the body of the work. Books found especially useful in the early period are marked with a dagger [†]. Books that were awarded a Pulitzer Prize are marked with an asterisk [*].

Abramowitz, Isidore, ed. *The Great Prisoners: the First Anthology of Literature Written in Prison.* Dutton, 1946. 879 pp. $4.95.

Sat. Rev. of Lit., 29:25, Apr. 13, 1946. An unusual collection in which the world's most prominent "jailbirds" are allowed to speak for themselves. Early Americans included are Anne Hutchinson, William Penn, and Thomas Paine.

Adams, James T. *The Adams Family.* Little, 1930. 364 pp. o. p. 1948.

AHR, 36:410. An interpretative sketch of the rise of a famous family. Much emphasis on the family characteristics.

*Adams, James Truslow. *The Founding of New England.* 1921. o. p. 1948.

AHR, 27:129. The best short history. Maintains that the majority of the immigrants to New England were indifferent to Puritanism. Chapter V introduces all of the important people of Plymouth.

*Agar, Herbert. *The People's Choice from Washington to Harding: A Study in Democracy.* Houghton, 1933. 337 pp. $3.50.

AHR, 39:577. Brilliant sketches by the American born editor of *The English Review*. Seeks to prove that democracy has failed. Rates John Quincy Adams with Washington; detests Grant and Harding.

*Andrews, Charles McLean. *The Colonial Period of America History.* Yale Univ. Press, 1934-38, 4 vols. $4.50 ea.

AHR, 40:347; 42:782; 43:647; 44:920. The best history of the colonial period. The author, however, stresses British policy rather than individual colonists or the factors that made them different from Englishmen.

Basso, Hamilton. *Mainstream.* Reynal, 1943. 246 pp. o. p. 1948.

N. Y. Times, Nov. 28, 1943, p. 4. Provocative and readable sketches of ten representative Americans from John Smith and Cotton Mather to the two Roosevelts.

Bates, Ernest S. *American Faith: Its Religious, Political, and Economic Foundations.* W. W. Norton & Co., 1940. 479 pp. o. p. 1948.

Sat. Rev. of Lit., 21:6, Mar. 30. A popular sketch of the religious history of America. Shows a decided interest in radicals such as Anne Hutchinson and Roger Williams, the Shakers and Rappites.

Bemis, Samuel F., ed. *American Secretaries of State and their Diplomacy.* Knopf, 1927-29. 10 vols. o. p. 1948.

Reviews in *AHR,* vols. 33-35. This valuable work contains a scholarly and readable sketch of each man who served as Secretary of State down to Charles Evans Hughes.

Beston, Henry, ed. *American Memory.* Rinehart, 1937. 498 pp. $1.00.

Books, Dec. 12, p. 3. Discriminating selections from the diaries, letters, and speeches of nearly 200 men and women of the American past.

Blair, Walter. *Horse Sense in American Humor from Benjamin Franklin to Ogden Nash.* University of Chicago Press, 1942. 341 pp. $2.75.

AHR, 48:413. A readable account of a group of entertaining and influential writers.

Blankenship, Russell. *American Literature as an Expression of the National Mind.* Holt, 1931. 731 pp. $4.25.

New Repub., 69:52, Nov. 25, 1931. A good, one volume history of American literature written by a former student of Parrington. Gives the accepted opinions of each author clearly and briefly.

Booth, Edward T. *Country Life in America: as Lived by Ten Presidents of the United States.* Knopf, 1937. 276 pp. $3.75.

Weekly Book Rev., Oct. 26, 1947, p. 2. An interesting discussion of the farm backgrounds of ten presidents from Washington to Coolidge.

Bowers, Claude G. *Jefferson and Hamilton: the Struggle for Democracy in America.* Houghton, 1925. 531 pp. $4.00.

AHR, 31:543. This entertaining, popular study of the conflict which made the United States a democratic republic includes many excellent pen pictures of contemporaries.

———. *Jefferson in Power: the Death Struggles of the Federalists.* Houghton, 1936. $4.00.

AHR, 43:413. A dramatic account of Jefferson's administration written to correct Henry Adams and other Federalist historians. Contains excellent thumb-nail sketches of friends and enemies.

Bradford, Gamaliel. *Damaged Souls.* Houghton, 1923. 285 pp. $2.50.

Outlook, 134:334, July 4, 1923. An outstanding exponent of the new biography seeks to portray the character and inner motives of seven rather discredited men. The attitude is sympathetic rather than ruthless.

———. *Wives.* Harper, 1925. 298 pp. o. p. 1948.

Bookman, 62:500. Six of these women were wives of men prominent in American history. Perhaps the sketches of Dolly Madison and Theodosia Burr are among the best Bradford has done.

Britt, Albert. *Great Indian Chiefs: a Study of Indian Leaders in the Two Hundred Year Struggle to Stop the White Advance.* McGraw-Hill, 1938. 280 pp. o. p. 1948.

Soc. Studies, 29:278. Sketches of eight Indian warriors who resisted the Anglo-American advance. The book is a historical narrative—there is little criticism of the Indians or of the United States' policy.

Brown, Charles R. *They Were Giants.* Macmillan, 1934. 279 pp. o. p. 1948.

N. Y. Times, Mar. 4, p. 16. Graphic character studies from Franklin to David Starr Jordan. Intended for "ardent hero-worshippers" rather than for addicts of the debunking school.

Bruce, David Kirkpatrick Este. *Revolution to Reconstruction.* Doubleday, 1939. 486 pp. o. p. 1948.

Christian Science Monitor, April 29, 1929, p. 10. These sketches of the presidents from Washington to Lincoln are fuller than those of Agar, but lack his brilliance.

Bruce, Philip Alexander. *The Virginia Plutarch.* 2 vols. Univ. of N. C. Press, 1929. 327 pp., 353 pp. $7.50.

AHR, 35:885. Popular sketches of thirty-two natives or residents of Virginia. The tone is usually sympathetic: there is no debunking.

Burlingame, Roger. *Inventors Behind the Inventor.* Harcourt, 1947. 211 pp. $3.00.

N. Y. Times, Nov. 9, 1947, p. 65. An interesting book which honors the unknown heroes who did the preliminary work on inventions.

Cambridge History of American Literature. Ed. by William P. Trent and others. Macmillan, 1945. 3 vols. in one. Imperial edition. $4.95.

AHR, 24:100, 702; 26:812. This co-operative work lacks unity. Is inferior to Tyler in places. Shows little sympathy for the Mathers, slights Samuel Sewall, has a good chapter on Franklin. The one volume edition has three indices.

*Channing, Edward. *History of the United States.* Macmillan, 1905-25. 6 vols. $5.25 ea.

AHR, 11:390; 14:364; 18:603; 23:190. The best history of the United States from colonial times to the end of the Civil War from a single pen. Characterized by a direct narrative style, an over-emphasis of the Atlantic coast and some prejudice against England and her representatives in America. Gives more on personalities than either Andrews or Osgood.

Chitwood, Oliver Perry. *A History of Colonial America.* Harper, 1931, 1948. $4.50.

N. C. Hist. Rev., 9:209. A scholarly and readable book. Chitwood pays more attention to personalities than do other textbooks of colonial history.

Dictionary of American Biography. Ed. by Allen Johnson and Dumas Malone. Scribner's, 1928-36. 20 vols. o. p. Reprint of 1946, 11 vols. $115.00.

Reviews in *AHR,* vols. 35-43. The articles possess a high degree of accuracy and cover the subject's career and personality. Excellent bibliographies. Cited as *DAB.*

Dictionary of National Biography. Ed. by Leslie Stephen and Sidney Lee. Oxford, 1885-1900. Reprint of 1938 (including first supplement) , 22 vols. $200.00.

This British work contains sketches of important leaders in the American colonies. Cited as *DNB.*

Dorfman, Joseph. *The Economic Mind in American Civilization, 1606-1865.* Viking Press, 1946. 2 vols. $10.00.

AHR, 52:140. A useful study which combines biographical material with summaries of economic writing.

Dos Passos, John. *The Ground We Stand On: Some Examples from the History of a Political Creed.* Harcourt, 1941. 420 pp. $3.50.

N. E. Quar., 15:152. An outstanding novelist defends American democracy in brilliant sketches of Roger Williams, Franklin, Samuel Adams, Jefferson, Joel Barlow, and Hugh Brackenridge.

Eckenrode, H. J. *The Randolphs: the Story of a Virginia Family.* Bobbs-Merrill, 1946. 310 pp. $3.50.

AHR, 52:517. A popular book which argues the thesis "that there was something in the Randolph blood and spirit that enabled its men to lead in an aristocratic society but doomed them to frustration in a democratic state, especially the vulgar democracy of the age of Jackson."

Egbert, Donald Drew, and Diane Martindell Lee. *Princeton Portraits.* Princeton Univ. Press, 1947. 360 pp. $15.00.

AHR, 53:634. Gives pictures and biographical sketches of professors, presidents, and alumni.

Einstein, Lewis. *Divided Loyalties: Americans in England Dur-*

ing the War of Independence. Houghton, 1933. 369 pp.
o. p. 1948.

AHR, 39:578. Brief but charming sketches. Not all of these men were torn by conflicting loyalties. They include British spies, Loyalists, and artists.

Ewen, David, ed. *Composers of Yesterday: a Biographical and Critical Guide to the Most Important Composers of the Past.* Wilson, 1937. 488 pp. $5.00.

Booklist, 33:211. Brief sketches of famous composers and lists of their principal compositions.

Flexner, James Thomas. *American Painting: First Flowers of Our Wilderness.* Houghton, 1947. 368 pp. $10.00.

AHR, 53:631. A readable and scholarly book on relationship between American life and the painters of the Colonial Period.

——. *America's Old Masters: First Artists of the New World.* Viking, 1939. 422 pp. o. p. 1948.

AHR, 46:422. This book contains well written biographical sketches of four early American artists, well chosen illustrations, and a good bibliography.

——. *Doctors on Horseback: Pioneers of American Medicine.* Viking, 1937. 370 pp. $2.75.

New Repub., 93:204, Dec. 22, 1937. Sketches of seven extraordinary men who performed kitchen operations, established medical schools, and carried on research. Well written.

Guedalla, Philip. *Fathers of the Revolution.* Putnam, 1926. 302 pp. o. p. 1948.

N. Y. Times, June 13, 1926, p. 1. Impressionistic sketches of men connected with the Revolution. Written by an Englishman with irony and wit.

Hamlin, Fred. *Land of Liberty: Being an Informal History of the Common People and Their Heroes.* Crowell, 1947. 354 pp. $3.50.

AHR, 53:550. A journalistic and lively account of popular heroes like Jefferson, Lincoln, Whitman, and F. D. R. Contains many brief sketches, some errors.

Hart, Albert Bushnell, ed. *American History Told by Contemporaries.* Macmillan, 1897-1929. 5 vols. $4.25 ea. $20.00 set.

Seeks to give extracts from diaries and contemporary narratives rather than public documents.

——. *Commonwealth History of Massachusetts, Colony, Prov-*

ince, and State. States History Company, 1928-30. 5 vols. o. p. 1948.

AHR, 34:375; 35:181, 890; 36:842. An excellent history which possesses a unity sometimes lacking in coöperative works. Usually the interpretations are up-to-date, the treatment impartial. In the first two volumes, there is an occasional tendency "to laud the activities of Massachusetts at the expense of other colonies."

Hendrick, Burton J. *Bulwark of the Republic: a Biography of the Constitution.* Little, 1937. 467 pp. $5.00.

Yale Rev., 27:161. Vivid sketches of leaders closely associated with the history of the constitution.

———. *The Lees of Virginia: Biography of a Family.* Little, 1935. 455 pp. o. p. 1948.

AHR, 42:140. A well written history, illustrating the influence of aristocracy in America. Certain eighteenth century representatives receive the fullest treatment.

Hofstadter, Richard. *The American Political Tradition and the Men Who Made It.* Knopf, 1948. 378 pp. $4.00.

AHR, 54:612. These fresh and original estimates emphasize the outstanding leaders themselves rather than their ideas.

Holbrook, Stewart H. *Lost Men of American History.* Macmillan, 1946. 370 pp. $4.00.

AHR, 52:746. Interesting sketches of over 125 people who somehow missed fame. The author tries to cover too many people and makes some sweeping generalizations.

Hutchinson, Thomas. *History of the Colony and Province of Massachusetts Bay.* Ed. by Lawrence S. Mayo. Harvard University Press, 1936. 3 vols. $15.00.

AHR, 42:557. This scholarly history is an important source for the Fourth Generation. While the narrative reflects the partisanship of the author, his portraits of some of the leaders are "skillfully drawn" and even sympathetic.

James, Marquis. *They Had Their Hour.* Bobbs, 1934. 324 pp. o. p. 1948.

N. Y. Times, Mar. 11, 1934, p. 4. Mr. James' version of these dramatic episodes from American history are intensely interesting but not always convincing.

Kingdon, Frank. *Architects of the Republic.* Beechhurst, 1947. 284 pp. $3.50.

N. Y. Times, Jan. 4, 1948, p. 9. An interesting and inspiring study of four leaders and their main ideas. Strives to put Washington back on his pedestal, over-emphasizes Jefferson's political interests. Some factual errors.

Klingberg, Frank J. *The Morning of America.* Appleton-Century, 1941. 479 pp. o. p. 1948.

AHR, 47:423. A readable survey which covers American history from 1763 to 1829, but with special emphasis on the first twenty-six years of this period. The author, a university professor of history, stresses personalities and "good" stories about people, as well as political and military history.

Lee, Cuthbert. *Early American Portrait Painters.* Yale Univ. Press, 1929. 350 pp. o. p. 1948.

Yale Rev., 20:422. Brief sketches, for the general reader, of painters who were born in the American colonies. Each sketch is followed by an annotated catalogue of examples of the artist's work in public collections.

Lonn, Ella. *The Colonial Agents of the Southern Colonies.* Univ. of N. C. Press, 1945. 438 pp. $5.00.

AHR, 51:133. This scholarly work is primarily the study of an institution. However, Chapter VIII, "The Personnel in the Agencies," and scattered references throw light on the character and activities of the men who held the office.

McConnell, Francis John. *Evangelicals, Revolutionists and Idealists: Six English Contributors to American Thought and Action.* Abingdon-Cokesbury, 1942. 184 pp. $1.50.

Christian Century, 59:1530, Dec. 9, 1942. These stimulating essays by a Methodist bishop show that a soldier and a deist joined with preachers and reformers to make the Eighteenth Century better.

McSpadden, Joseph Walker. *Famous Painters of America.* Dodd, 1916. 417 pp. o. p. 1948.

Dial, 61:477, Nov. 30, 1916. Popular sketches of West, Copley, Stuart and others considered as men rather than as artists.

Milhollen, Hirst D., and Milton Kaplan. *Presidents on Parade: a Pictorial History.* 1948.

AHR, 54:218. Two experts on the Library of Congress staff prepared this attractive album which gives about a dozen pictures of each president. Some of the captions seem to exaggerate the importance of mediocre men like Pierce and Harding.

Minnigerode, Meade. *Lives and Times: Four Informal American Biographies.* Putnam, 1925. 215 pp. o. p. 1948.

Ind., 114:386, Apr. 4, 1925. Vivid and entertaining sketches that emphasize the human interest of early Americans like Theodosia Burr and Stephen Jumel.

————. *Some American Ladies.* Putnam, 1926. 287 pp. o. p. 1948.

New Repub., 47:181, June 30, 1926. Contains sketches of the wives of three of the early presidents. These are vivid and entertaining, but lack somewhat in character analysis.

Mirsky, Jeannette. *The Westward Crossings: Balboa, Mackenzie, Lewis and Clark.* Knopf, 1946. 365 pp. $4.00.

AHR, 52:745. Entertaining account of explorers who sought to reach the Pacific by crossing North America.

Morison, Samuel Eliot. *Builders of the Bay Colony.* Houghton, 1930. 365 pp. $5.00.

AHR, 36:405. Well written essays on men and women "who represent the various aspects of life" in Massachusetts during the first generation.

Mussey, June Barrows, ed. *Yankee Life by Those Who Lived It.* Knopf, 1947. 543 pp. $6.00.

A revised edition of a book published by Stackpole in 1937 with the title, *We Were New England.* This gives fascinating selections from the diaries and autobiographies of about thirty-six New Englanders. The authors include such worthies as Jonathan Edwards and P. T. Barnum, as well as rascals like Thomas Morton, Stephen Burroughs, and Henry Tufts. The earlier edition was reviewed in *Books,* Dec. 12, 1937, p. 3.

Neuhaus, Eugen. *The History and Ideals of American Art.* Stanford University Press, 1931. 441 pp. o. p. 1948.

Yale Rev., 21:188. Readable, understanding "chapters on painters of landscapes, winter, and the sea, scenes of Indian and frontier life, American types, and other specialties . . ." The information is biographical—not technical.

Osgood, Herbert Levi. *The American Colonies in the Seventeenth Century.* Macmillan, 1904-07. 3 vols. o. p. 1948.

AHR, 11:397; 13:605. A thorough, detailed study which emphasizes the institutional approach. Maintains "that through the Stuart period ran a more or less definite policy which aimed to subordinate the colonies to the royal will."

————. *The American Colonies in the Eighteenth Century.* Columbia Univ. Press., 1924-25. 4 vols. $20.00.

AHR, 31:533. An accurate study of the period from 1689 to 1763. Gives judicious estimates of a half dozen governors cited in the GUIDE.

Parrington, Vernon Louis. *Main Currents in American Thought.* (Vol. I, *The Colonial Mind, 1620-1800;* Vol. II, *The Romantic Revolution in America, 1800-1860;* Vol. III,

Beginnings of Critical Realism in America, 1860-1920.) Harcourt, 1927-30. 413, 493, 429 pp. $6.00 ea. (Students' ed., 3 vols. in one, 1930, $4.50.)

N. Y. Times, May 1, 1927, p. 3; Nov. 9, 1930, p. 1. An excellent history of American literature from a liberal standpoint. Is partial to Roger Williams but unfair to conservatives such as Thomas Hutchinson and John Marshall. The last volume was completed to 1900 only.

Peattie, Donald Culross. *Green Laurels: The Lives and Achievements of the Great Naturalists.* Simon & Schuster, 1936. 368 pp. o. p. 1948.

Books, July 19, 1936, p. 1. A vivid account of the adventures and ideas of the great naturalists. Devotes three chapters to Americans from Bartram to Rafinesque.

Plooij, Daniel. *Pilgrim Fathers from a Dutch Point of View.* N. Y. University Press, 1932. 154 pp. o. p. 1948.

AHR, 38:374. The author summarizes documents which he recently found in Holland. These throw new light on the Pilgrims, but do not greatly change our estimate of them.

Pollard, James E. *The Presidents and the Press.* Macmillan, 1947. 866 pp. $5.00.

Weekly Book Rev., Apr. 27, 1947, p. 2. Gives an accurate and entertaining story of the relations between the presidents and the newspapers.

Pound, Arthur. *Native Stock: the Rise of the American Spirit Seen in Six Lives.* Macmillan, 1931. 267 pp. o. p. 1948.

N. E. Quar., 5:164. Entertaining sketches of forgotten New Englanders who fought the French about the middle of the eighteenth century. Also one business man who advocated canal-building.

Pratt, Fletcher. *Eleven Generals.* Sloane, 1949. 355 pp. $5.00.

Sat. Rev. of Lit., April 23, 1949, p. 14. The author passes up Washington and Grant and deals with less known individuals like Nathaniel Greene and Sheridan. His vivid essays "combine criticism and story-telling as few students of the military art can hope to do."

Prochnow, Herbert Victor, ed. *Great Stories from Great Lives: a Gallery of Portraits from Famous Biographies.* Harper, 1944. 404 pp. $3.50.

N. Y. Times, June 11, 1944, p. 17. Extracts from modern biographies describing decisive moments in the lives of people from George Washington to Lou Gehrig and Will Rogers.

Read, Harlan E. *Fighters for Freedom.* Dodd, 1946. 287 pp. $2.75.

Weekly Book Rev., Dec. 8, p. 26. Compact, readable sketches of men who have fought in the battle for human freedom. Includes eight Americans.

Schlesinger, Arthur M. *Paths to the Present.* Macmillan, 1949. 317 pp. $3.00.

AHR, 24:104. This original and stimulating volume contains two essays of special interest to students of American biography. The first, "What then is the American, this New Man?" (Reprinted from *AHR,* 48 (1943): 225-44) throws much light on the evolution of the American character during the colonial period. The second, "A Yardstick for Presidents" indicates how fifty-five historians have ranked our highest executives.

Schnittkind, Henry Thomas (Henry Thomas, pseud.), and Dana Arnold Schnittkind (Dana Lee Thomas, pseud.). *Fifty Great Americans: Their Inspiring Lives and Achievements.* Doubleday, 1948. 468 pp. $4.00.

Booklist, 44:351. Enjoyable sketches of fifty American celebrities ranging from Franklin and Washington to Knute Rockne and George Gershwin. Thirty-nine of the sketches have been previously published.

——. *Living Biographies of American Statesmen.* Garden City Pub. Co., 1942. 323 pp. $1.98.

Books, Nov. 1, 1942, p. 28. The authors have a gift for recording significant events and delineating personality in a minimum of words.

Schriftgiesser, Karl. *Families.* Howell, Soskin & Co., 1940. 444 pp. o. p. 1948.

Books, Oct. 27, 1940, p. 25. An interesting study of personal characteristics handed down in such families as the Adamses, Lees, Vanderbilts, and Roosevelts. These brief essays are based on secondary works, but are sprightly and fairly accurate.

Seitz, Don Carlos. *Uncommon Americans.* Bobbs, 1925. 328 pp. o. p. 1948.

Outlook, 141:640, Dec. 23, 1925. Sketches of twenty-two unusual individuals who refused to conform.

Sherman, Stuart P. *Americans.* Scribner's, 1922. 336 pp. o. p. 1948.

Bookman, 47:86. A brilliant collection of essays that range from Franklin to Theodore Roosevelt.

Smith, Don. *Peculiarities of the Presidents: Strange and Intimate Facts Not Found in History.* Wilkinson Press, 1946. 185 pp.

A collection of interesting stories which "bring out the human side of the presidents." Undocumented.

Spiller, Robert Ernest, and others, eds. *Literary History of the United States.* 1948. 3 vols. $25.00.

N. Y. Times, Dec. 5, 1948, p. 4. These fresh evaluations of American writers from Captain John Smith to Faulkner were written by over fifty authors but read like a "freely flowing narrative." Vol. 3 contains excellent bibliographies.

Sweet, William Warren. *Makers of Christianity.* Holt, 1937. 351 pp. o. p. 1948.

AHR, 44:722. Most of the forty-odd sketches are of Protestants. Church organization is emphasized rather than ideas or changes in religious thought.

————. *Religion in Colonial America.* Scribner's, 1942. 367 pp. $3.00.

AHR, 49:488.

————. *The Story of Religion in America.* Harper, 1930. 571 pp. $4.00.

Books, Dec. 7, 1930, p. 41. The history of religious sects from colonial times on.

There Were Giants in the Land: Twenty-eight Historic Americans as Seen by Twenty-eight Contemporary Americans. Farrar, 1942. 242 pp. $2.00.

Books, Sept. 13, 1942, p. 5. A book of essays sponsored by the Treasury Department about citizens who served their country at a time of crisis.

Thomas, Henry, pseud. *See* Schnittkind, H. T.

Thorp, Willard, ed. *The Lives of Eighteen from Princeton.* Princeton Univ. Press, 1946. 356 pp. $3.75.

Wm. and Mary Quar., Third Series, 4:239. Excellent interpretive essays which emphasize "the humanistic contribution of these first Princeton leaders." They merit careful reading.

Trent, William P., and Benjamin W. Wells. *Colonial Prose and Poetry.* Crowell, 1929. 3 vols. in one. o. p. 1948.

Nation, 74:75, Jan. 23, 1902. Gives selections which show individual genius and the development of the national mind.

Tyler, Lyon Gardiner. *England in America, 1580-1652* (The American Nation, IV, 1904). Harper. $2.25.

AHR, 10:869. The author shows a lively interest in colonial beginnings, but is somewhat biased against New England. He takes an optimistic view of political liberalism in Virginia, but slights the struggle for democracy in Massachusetts and over-emphasizes the hanging of Quakers and witches in that colony.

Tyler, Moses Coit. *History of American Literature During the Colonial Time.* Putnam, 1878. 2 vols. o. p. 1948.

Mag. of Amer. Hist., 3:209. A thorough and exhaustive study. The year 1676 marks the dividing line between the volumes.

————. *Literary History of the American Revolution, 1763-1783.* Putnam, 1897. 2 vols. Reprint, Barnes and Noble, 1941. 2 vols. o. p. 1948.

AHR, 2:738; 46:988. An excellent study which does justice to Patriots and Tories alike. The year 1776 marks the dividing line between volumes.

Ullmann, Albert. *New Yorkers: Stuyvesant to Roosevelt.* Chaucer Head, 1929. 267 pp. o. p. 1948.

Nation, 128:491, Apr. 17, 1929. Interesting sketches of famous men who lived in New York at one time or another. Includes Thomas Paine and Edgar Allen Poe.

Umbreit, Kenneth Bernard. *Founding Fathers: Men Who Shaped Our Tradition.* Harper, 1941. 344 pp. $3.50.

Books, Nov. 30, 1941, p. 16. Sketches of six leaders of the Revolution, three from Massachusetts, three from Virginia. The sketches are impressionistic, entertaining, and provocative. The author shows a bias in favor of Patrick Henry and against Jefferson.

————. *Our Eleven Chief Justices: a History of the Supreme Court in Terms of Their Personalities.* Harper, 1938. 539 pp. $3.75.

Books, Nov. 27, 1938, p. 8. The lawyer-author shows that the opinions of the Chief Justices have been affected by their personalities and their political views, but maintains that they have been free from economic influences. He gives many anecdotes of their college days and personal habits, but ignores the charges made by Gustavus Myers in his *History of the Supreme Court.*

Usher, Roland G. *The Pilgrims and Their History.* Macmillan, 1918. o. p. 1948.

AHR, 24:514. A readable volume which gives the entire history of the Plymouth Colony.

Van Doren, Mark, ed. *An Autobiography of America.* Boni, 1929. 737 pp. o. p. 1948.

N. E. Quar., 3:365. The period ending in 1815 is portrayed vividly in twenty-three contemporary accounts.

Walker, Williston. *Ten New England Leaders.* Burdett, 1901. 471 pp. o. p. 1948.

Nation, 73:92, Aug. 1, 1901. The author shows great discrimination and makes his characters stand out clearly.

Wecter, Dixon. *The Hero in America: a Chronicle of Hero Worship.* Scribner's, 1941. 517 pp. o. p. 1948.

AHR, 47:341. As Carlyle wrote a century ago on the heroes of autocratic Europe, so Wecter has written on the heroes of democratic America. By tracing the rise and decline in reputations of major and minor heroes, he throws light on the changing ideals of the American people.

Wertenbaker, Thomas J. *The Golden Age of Colonial Culture.* New York University Press, 1942. 171 pp. $3.00.

N. E. Quar., 15:732. Brief chapters summarizing the cultural claims of the six leading towns of 18th Century America. The author slights literature in favor of other arts; makes some interesting generalizations. Useful for background—not cited for individuals.

———. *The Puritan Oligarchy: the Founding of American Civilization.* Scribner's, 1947. 359 pp. $5.00.

AHR, 53:824. Deals mainly with the efforts of leaders to establish a Bible commonwealth in Massachusetts and why they failed.

Willison, George Findlay. *Saints and Strangers: Being the Lives of the Pilgrim Fathers and Their Families, with Their Friends and Foes.* Harcourt, 1945. 513 pp. $3.75.

Wm. and Mary Quar., Third Series, 3:297. An entertaining work which rediscovers the Pilgrims. The author goes to extremes in debunking, and is not abreast of recent scholarship.

Wilstach, Paul. *Patriots Off Their Pedestals.* Bobbs, 1927. 241 pp. o. p. 1948.

Outlook, 147:157, Oct. 5, 1927. Informal sketches which claim that Washington sometimes rolled with laughter on the lawn, that Marshall was frequently the life of the party, and that even solemn Madison had his gay moments.

Wright, Louis Booker. *First Gentlemen of Virginia: Intellectual Qualities of the Early Colonial Ruling Class.* Huntington Lib., 1940. 373 pp. o. p. 1948.

AHR, 46:663. Scholarly and readable study of the literary interests of half a dozen aristocrats from 18th century Virginia.

HOW TO SUPPLEMENT THE GUIDE

Teachers using the GUIDE will find it interesting to add new people to give variety to the course and new references to keep it up-to-date.

Most of the books of collective biography cited include other people who might be used in the course. For a quick survey of their contents, see the *Standard Catalogue for Public Libraries* (Wilson, 1940), *Biography by Americans, 1658-1936,* by Edward H. O'Neill (University of Pennsylvania Press, 1939, $4), or the L.C. cards. The book reviews and the *Book Review Digest* usually mention some of the people discussed, but do not give all the names. The *DAB* suggests new people who might be used in every chapter of the GUIDE.

A time-saving method of keeping informed regarding the new biographies is to read the appropriate reviews in the *American Historical Review* (Macmillan, $5 a year) and the *Weekly Book Review* (*N. Y. Herald Tribune,* $2 a year). The quickest way to keep up with the new articles is by using the *Biography Index* (Wilson, 1946-; price on application).

The card catalogue of any library will give many titles not listed in the GUIDE. Critical estimates of the best of these books can be found in the annotated bibliographies of the *DAB*. Reviews of them can be located through "Writings on American History" by Grace Griffin (*Annual Report of the American Historical Association,* 1918-1943) and the *Book Review Digest* (1906).

Many of the books listed in the GUIDE contain helpful bibliographies. One of the best and most recent is given in the third volume of the *Literary History of the United States* by Spiller and others (Macmillan, 1949). These bibliographies are very scholarly, but cover writers only.

ABBREVIATIONS USED IN THE GUIDE

Am. Antiq. Soc. Proc. American Antiquarian Society, Proceedings
AHR. American Historical Review
Amer. Lit. American Literature
Amer. Merc. American Mercury
Am. Phil. Soc. Proc. American Philosophical Society, Proceedings
Amer. Pol. Sci. Rev. American Political Science Review
Am. Scholar. American Scholar
Ann. Report Am. Hist. Assn. American Historical Association, Annual Report
Ann. Report Smithsonian Inst. Smithsonian Institution, Annual Report
Atlantic. Atlantic Monthly
Books. New York Herald Tribune, Books
Chron. Oklahoma. Chronicles of Oklahoma
DAB. Dictionary of American Biography
DNB. Dictionary of National Biography
Ga. Hist. Quar. Georgia Historical Quarterly
Harper's. Harper's Magazine
Harvard Theol. Rev. Harvard Theological Review
Huntington Lib. Quar. Huntington Library Quarterly
Ill. State Hist. Soc. Trans. Illinois State Historical Society, Transactions
Ill. State Hist. Soc. Jour. Illinois State Historical Society, Journal
Ind. New York Independent
Jour. Econ. & Bus. Hist. Journal of Economic and Business History
Jour. Mod. Hist. Journal of Modern History
Jour. of South. Hist. Journal of Southern History
Jour. Pol. Econ. Journal of Political Economy
Jour. Rel. Journal of Religion
Mag. of Amer. Hist. Magazine of American History
Mag. of Art. Magazine of Art
MVHA Proc. Mississippi Valley Historical Association, Proceedings
MVHR. Mississippi Valley Historical Review
Mo. Hist. Soc. Coll. Missouri Historical Society, Collections
Nation. Geog. Mag. National Geographic Magazine
N. E. Quar. New England Quarterly
New Repub. New Republic
N. Y. Times. New York Times
No. Am. Rev. North American Review
N. C. Hist. Rev. North Carolina Historical Review
Pol. Sci. Quar. Political Science Quarterly
Proc. Mass. Hist. Soc. Massachusetts Historical Society, Proceedings
Pubs. Southern Hist. Assn. Southern Historical Association, Publications
Quart. Rev. Quarterly Review
Sat. Eve. Post. Saturday Evening Post
Sat. Rev. of Lit. Saturday Review of Literature
Scientific Mo. Scientific Monthly
Scribner's. Scribner's Magazine
Social Stu. Social Studies
So. Atl. Quar. South Atlantic Quarterly
South. Econ. Jour. Southern Economic Journal
Southwestern Hist. Quar. Southwestern Historical Quarterly
Tenn. Hist. Mag. Tennessee Historical Magazine
Trans. Am. Philos. Soc. American Philosophical Society, Transactions
Va. Mag. Hist. Virginia Magazine of History and Biography
Va. Quar. Rev. Virginia Quarterly Review
Weekly Book Rev. New York Herald Tribune Weekly Book Review
Western Pa. Hist. Mag. Western Pennsylvania Historical Magazine
Wis. Hist. Soc. Coll. State Historical Society of Wisconsin Collections
Wm. and Mary Quar. William and Mary Quarterly
Yale Rev. Yale Review

SUBJECT INDEX*

---

* Not intended to be exhaustive.

INDEX

GUIDE TO

AMERICAN

BIOGRAPHY

Part II—1815-1933

MARION DARGAN

GREENWOOD PRESS, PUBLISHERS
WESTPORT, CONNECTICUT

The purpose of this book is to summarize the personal side of American history. It may be years before the student hears of William Phips or Philip Hone, or arrives at an accurate appraisal of Jefferson Davis. Many, important in their day, become forgotten men, or misunderstood men. I hope, then, to introduce some of the rising generation to many new people, and to help them become better acquainted with others.

I decided to close the Seventh Generation at the turning point of 1933, and to leave out people still living. This allows more space for outstanding personalities, and may permit teachers to spend more time on their sections of the country, or the type of history in which their classes are most interested.

Readers should be careful to read the Introduction, Part I, pp. 1-14, which will enable them to use the book more intelligently. The Subject Index (pp. 503-06) will prove very useful in following the special interests of the students. Epithets sometimes give the popular view.

I would never have persevered with such a comprehensive project without the encouragement, counsel, and assistance of colleagues, friends, librarians, and students, too numerous to mention. A number of my colleagues at the University of New Mexico and friends in other institutions helped by reading pages of the manuscript falling in their fields, suggesting omissions and additions. Professor George Arms was especially helpful in the field of literature, and Professors George Winston Smith and Davidson B. McKibben in history. Mr. Thomas W. Gerity, Miss Genevieve Porterfield, and Mr. Arthur DeVolder gave much assistance in locating references. Professor William T. Hutchinson, of the University of Chicago, and Professor Bell Wylie, of Emory University, suggested some of the epithets used. Professors William Dabney, W. P. Albrecht, and George Smith helped to finish up the Seventh Generation. I wish also to acknowledge my indebtedness to Mr. E. B. Mann and Mr.

Fred E. Harvey of the University of New Mexico Press, and to the editors who kindly permitted me to use the reviews in their periodicals. My wife typed the manuscript and read the proof with me.

MARION DARGAN

Albuquerque, New Mexico
Nov. 7, 1951

CONTENTS

FIFTH GENERATION, 1815-1850

CHAPTER XXIII. NEW ENGLAND

Adams, J. T. *New England in the Republic, 1776-1850.* 1926.

AHR, 32:614. "An interesting and provocative book" which describes "the continual struggle of the common man to realize the doctrines of the Revolution in the life of the community." "A secondary topic throughout is the gradual growth of sectionalism." Most of our New Englanders for this generation are referred to in passing. See index.

Whitley, E. M. "Between the Acts at Ghent," *Va. Quar. Rev.,* 5 (1929) :18-30.

NOAH WEBSTER— 1758-1843 —"Schoolmaster to America"

Biography: Shoemaker, E. C. *Noah Webster, Pioneer of Learning.* 1936.

N. E. Quar., 9:723. After 1783, Americans had to attain political unity and achieve cultural unity. In his biography Dr. Shoemaker tells how Noah Webster, "a vain, callow country schoolmaster twenty-five years of age" devoted his life to "the task of teaching unity through his universal adoption of the American language."

Warfel, H. R. *Noah Webster, Schoolmaster to America.* 1936.

Sat. Rev. of Lit., 14:11, May 9, 1936. The best biography of a versatile thinker and writer who was a pioneer in many fields. Born a conservative Calvinist, Webster at one time was a radical like Tom Paine, but later became a staunch Federalist. The author has "a tendency to emphasize Webster's Americanism as perhaps too unique and distinctive, to the neglect of the contemporary Americanism of men such as Freneau,* the Hartford Wits, Royall Tyler, and Brookden Brown."

Extract in Prochnow, H. V., ed. *Great Stories from Great Lives,* 293-96.

Collective Biography: Clifton, J. L. *Ten Famous American Educators,* 100-22.

Fox, D. R., and A. M. Schlesinger. *The Cavalcade of America,* (2nd ser., 1939) :211-27.

Holbrook, S. H. *Lost Men of American History,* 87-90.

---

* Freneau and Joel Barlow were older than Noah Webster and are listed in the Fourth Generation (1760-1815). See Part I, pp. 68, 78.

Malone, Kemp, in *DAB*, 19:594.

Russell, F. A. *American Pilgrimage*, 1-15.

JOHN QUINCY ADAMS—1767-1848—A Jeffersonian from New England

ORIGINAL SOURCES: Adams, C. F., ed. "Letters of John Quincy Adams, 1811-1814." *Proceedings of the American Antiquarian Society*. N. S., 23 (1913) :110-69.

Ford, W. C., ed. *Writings of John Quincy Adams. Vol. I, 1779-1769.* 1913.

AHR, 18:818. Every reader of Adams' *Diary* "knows the variety and wealth of his observations during a half-century of public service and a residence of a quarter-century at European courts." The *Writings* relate "chiefly to the public life of the second Adams," but include "many letters of rare biographical interest." Mr. Ford has carefully selected material which supplies the gaps in the *Diary*.

——. *Writings of John Quincy Adams. Vol. II, 1796-1801.* 1913.

AHR, 19:653. When Adams was enroute to Portugal, he learned he had been appointed minister to Prussia. He was instructed to renew our treaty with that kingdom and to watch France. He became convinced "that the French Directory meant to revolutionize America, as it had Holland and the lesser states of Europe, with the aid of a discontented domestic faction. Having signed the treaty, Adams spent some time in traveling in Germany and in translating from German. However, matters of personal interest are excluded "rather rigorously from this volume."

——. *Writings of John Quincy Adams. Vol. III, 1801-1810.* 1914.

AHR, 20:173. "The third installment of Adams' *Writings* covers . . . the most critical period in his long public career." He entertained "serious doubts as to his usefulness in public life," and spent much time preparing himself for a professorship at Harvard.

——. *Writings of John Quincy Adams. Vol. IV, 1811-1815.* 1914.

AHR, 20:861. "Items of biographical interest abound in this volume." His motives in declining an appointment to the Supreme Court are set forth in letters to President Madison and to John Adams. Long residence abroad seemed to emancipate Adams "from the narrow provincialism of his section." He wrote that he was not "displeased to hear that Ohio, Kentucky, Indiana, and Louisiana were rapidly being peopled by Yankees."

——. *Writings of John Quincy Adams. Vol. V, 1814-1816.* 1916.

AHR, 21:356. The letters to Mrs. Adams "are full of entertaining comments on the daily life of the writer and his colleagues." They lead one to question the impression "that the five American commissioners were so often rent with discussion that their personal relations were embittered." Much space in this volume is given to Adams' new diplomatic mission to England. The problem of the Spanish South American colonies makes its appearance, and three of Adams' despatches foreshadow "his subsequent policy as Secretary of State."

———. *Writings of John Quincy Adams. Vol. VI, 1816-1819.* 1916.

AHR, 22:180. Adams served as Secretary of State during these years, and this volume shows that he was well-fitted for the post when he assumed office.

———. *Writings of John Quincy Adams. Vol. VII, 1820-1823.* 1917.

AHR, 23:871. This seventh volume touches on a variety of subjects in our relations with Great Britain and other nations. "The thoroughgoing quality of Adams' work as Secretary of State stands out in his instructions to Henry Middleton for the mission to Russia . . . No other contemporary American statesman could have written with so wide a vision of European affairs."

Koch, Adrienne, and William Peden, eds. *The Selected Writings of John Quincy Adams.* 1946.

AHR, 52:514. The letters and papers included reveal the intellectual qualities of father and son, and "the close spiritual and intellectual relationship" between them.

Nevins, Allan, ed. *The Diary of John Quincy Adams, 1794-1845. American Political, Social and Intellectual Life from Washington to Polk.* 1928, 1951.

AHR, 34:886; *Sat. Rev. of Lit.*, 34:17, Aug. 13, 1951. The introduction to this abridged edition includes a penetrating analysis of the author. The 1951 edition includes "brief biographical notes on the persons who figure most prominently in the narrative."

Tatum, E. H., Jr. "Ten Unpublished Letters of John Quincy Adams, 1796-1837," *Huntington Library Jour.*, 4 (1940) :369-88.

Van Doren, Mark. *An Autobiography of America,* 166-73.

BIOGRAPHY: Bemis, S. F.* *John Quincy Adams and the Foundations of American Foreign Policy.* 1950.

---

* Awarded the Pulitzer Prize.

AHR, 55:621. Using the Adams papers in the Massachusetts Historical Society, the author has written a convincing account of Adams' diplomatic career from 1795 to 1829. The book gives much on his private life, but little on the domestic questions of his administration.

Bobbe, Dorothie. *Mr. and Mrs. John Quincy Adams, an Adventure in Patriotism.* 1930.

Books, Sept. 14, 1930, p. 1. A fresh and lively narrative, although it contributes nothing new.

Clark, B. C. *John Quincy Adams: Old Man Eloquent.* 1932.

N. E. Quar., 6:209. A popular biography which sketches an interesting career "with sympathy, with vivacity, and with fidelity."

COLLECTIVE BIOGRAPHY: Adams, J. T. *The Adams Family,* 119-228.

Extract in Myers, C. L. *Readings in Biography,* 344-49.

Agar, Herbert. *The People's Choice,* 91-106.

Beard, C. A. *Presidents in American History,* 34-7, 168-69.

Brogan, D. W. *American Themes,* 11-24.

Bruce, D. K. E. *Revolution to Reconstruction,* 194-245.

Ford, W. C., in *DAB,* 1:84.

Schriftgeiser, Karl. *Families,* 21-30.

HISTORY: Agar, Herbert. *The Price of Union,* 205-10, 217-31.

Bowers, C. G. *Party Battles of the Jackson Period.*

SPECIAL ASPECTS: Cresson, W. P. *Diplomatic Portraits: Europe and the Monroe Doctrine One Hundred Years Ago.* (1923): 185-232.

Ford, W. C. "John Quincy Adams and the Monroe Doctrine," *AHR,* 7 (1902) :676-96; 8 (1902) :28-52.

Perkins, Dexter, in Bemis, S. F., ed. *American Secretaries of State,* 4:3-111.

Perling, J. J. *Presidents' Sons,* 1-49.

Pollard, J. E. *Presidents and the Press,* 126-43.

Spiller, R. E. *The American in England,* 119-34.

Wold, E. C. *Mr. President, How is Your Health?* 43-45.

BENJAMIN SILLIMAN—1779-1864—Pioneer American Chemist and Geologist

BIOGRAPHY: Fulton, J. F., and E. H. Thompson. *Benjamin Silliman, 1779-1864.* 1947.

N. Y. Times, Nov. 1, 1947, p. 7. The career of the first Professor of Chemistry and Natural History at Yale is studied in connection with "the development of science itself . . ."

COLLECTIVE BIOGRAPHY: Warren, Charles, in *DAB*, 17:160.

DANIEL WEBSTER— 1782-1852 —Politician or Statesman?

BIOGRAPHY: Adams, S. H. *The Godlike Daniel*. 1930.

N. Y. Times, Oct. 26, 1930, p. 3. In his dramatic sketch, "Mr. Adams shows a great deal of penetration and imagination" in general, "but in these crucial cases, the successive climaxes of Webster's astounding career, he fails."

*Fuess, C. M. *Daniel Webster*. 2 vols. 1930.

AHR, 37:565. In this review Professor Arthur C. Cole calls the book "a most important contribution to Webster literature." He describes it as a well-balanced study which gives local color, but no cumbersome detail, and avoids "the extremes of muckraking" and "hero worship." Reviewing the same book (*N. E. Quar.*, 4:358-63) Professor Frederick Merk remarks that Fuess failed to seize a wonderful opportunity to give "a scholarly reassessment of Webster's career," and merely put the conventional facts into an entertaining narrative which lacks scholarship.

Ogg, F. A. *Daniel Webster*. (American Crisis Biographies, 1914.)

AHR, 20:673. An accurate, judicious study—somewhat lacking in enthusiasm for a man who has been described as "perhaps the greatest forensic figure the world has ever seen."

COLLECTIVE BIOGRAPHY: Benet, S. V., in *There Were Giants in the Land*, 4-9.

Bradford, Gamaliel. *As God Made Them*, 3-42.

Also in *Harper's*, 155 (1927) :372-81.

Cole, A. C., in *DAB*, 19:585.

Fiske, John. *Essays, Historical and Literary*, 363-409.

Hubbard, Elbert. *Little Journeys to the Homes of American Statesmen*, 2:183-206.

Johnson, G. W. *America's Silver Age*, 71-81, 197-202.

Kunitz and Haycraft. *American Authors*, 709-91.

Lodge, H. C., in *Cambridge History of American Literature*, 2:92-103.

---

* The summaries of two different reviews given here are intended to remind students *once and for all* that historians sometimes differ radically in their estimates of the same book. Read it for yourself.

Parrington, V. L. *Main Currents in American Thought,* 2:304-16.

Seitz, D. C. *The "Also Rans,"* 110-25

Thomas and Thomas. *Fifty Great Americans,* 116-26.

HISTORY: Bowers, Claude. *Party Battles of the Jackson Period.*

SPECIAL ASPECTS: Current, R. N. "Webster's Propaganda and the Ashburton Treaty," *MVHR,* 34 (1947) :187-200.

Duniway, C. A. "Daniel Webster and the West," *Minn. Hist.,* 9 (1928) :3-15.

———, in *American Secretaries of State,* 5:3-64.

Foster, H. D. "Webster's Seventh of March Speech," *AHR,* 27 (1922) :245-70.

Spiller, et al. *Literary History of the United States,* 1:540-51.

LOWELL MASON— 1792-1872 —The Pioneer in
Public School Music

BIOGRAPHY: Rich, A. L. *Lowell Mason, the Father of Singing Among the Children.* 1946.

AHR, 52:388. A brief but thorough study of a hymn writer and musical educator who did much to democratize music.

COLLECTIVE BIOGRAPHY: Martens, F. H., in *DAB,* 12:371.

EDWARD THOMPSON TAYLOR— 1793-1871
—"Father Taylor"—"One of the Greatest American
Preachers of His Generation"

BIOGRAPHY: Haven, Gilbert, and Thomas Russell. *Life of Father Taylor.* 1904.

COLLECTIVE BIOGRAPHY: Bartol, C. A. "Edward Thompson Taylor, the Boston Bethel Preacher," *Century,* 33 (1887) :579-83.

MacDonald, Allan. "A Sailor Among Transcendentalists," *N. E. Quar.,* 8 (1935) :307-19.

Starr, H. E., in *DAB,* 18:321.

SPECIAL ASPECTS: Whitman, Walt. "Father Taylor and Oratory," *Century,* 33 (1887) :583-84.

HORACE MANN—   1796-1859   —Educator

ORIGINAL SOURCES: Wood, Playsted, ed. *One Hundred Years Ago,* (1948) :379-81.

BIOGRAPHY: Hinsdale, B. A. *Horace Mann and the Common School Revival in the United States.* 1898.

AHR, 4:743. Mr. Hinsdale concentrates upon Horace Mann as an educator. He pays little attention to him as a man.

Norton, A. O., ed. *Horace Mann.* (Education Classics, 1931).

COLLECTIVE BIOGRAPHY: Cassidy, F. P., in *Cath. Educ. Rev.,* 44 (1946) :453-60.

Clifton, J. L. *Ten Famous American Educators,* 7-27.

Fenner, M. S., and E. C. H. Fishburn. *Pioneer American Educators,* 17-24.

———, in *Nat'l Ed. Assoc. of the U. S. Future Teachers of America; sixth yearbook,* (1946) :8-15.

Graves, F. P. *Great Educators of Three Centuries,* 249-73.

Malone, Dumas. *Saints in Action,* 114-48.

Morgan, J. E., ed. *Horace Mann at Antioch: Studies in Personality and Higher Education.* 1939.

Booklist, 35:132, Dec. 15, 1938. A volume of miscellaneous material which includes "125 pages of biography and some history of Antioch College, as well as some of Mann's addresses."

Swift, F. H., in *DAB,* 12:240.

SPECIAL ASPECTS: Curti, M. E. *Social Ideas of American Educators,* 101-38.

Fenner, M. S., and E. C. H. Fishburn, "Horace Mann and Teacher Education," *Jour. Education,* 129 (1946) :210-12.

———. "Horace Mann: Prophet of Education," *NEA Jour.,* 35 (1946) :219-22.

Knight, E. W. "More Evidence of Horace Mann's Influence in the South," *Educ. Forum,* 12 (1948) :167-84.

Roberts, Josephine. "Horace Mann and the Peabody Sisters," *N. E. Quar.,* 18 (1945) :164-80.

Slosson, E. E. *American Spirit in Education,* (1921) :68-69, 124-37.

WILLIAM HICKLIN PRESCOTT—   1796-1859
—Brilliant Historian—Master of Literary Style

ORIGINAL SOURCES: Charvat, William, and Michael Kraus, eds. *William Hicklin Prescott: Representative Selections.* (American Writers, 1943).

Amer. Lit., 15:315. The introduction discusses "Prescott's spiritual environment, his scholarship, his conception of history, his style and manner of writing, his political ideas, his place in literary criticism, and his general reputation." There are 12 pages of bibliography and 463 pages of selections from Prescott's works.

Mood, Fulmer, and Granville Hicks, eds. "Letters to Dr. Channing on Slavery and the Annexation of Texas, 1837." *N. E. Quar.*, 5 (1932) :587-601.

Wolcott, Roger. *The Correspondence of William Hicklin Prescott, 1833-1847.* 1925.

AHR, 31:545. Many of these letters relate to collecting materials for *Phillip II*, and show "the extreme care of Prescott to find and use old manuscripts and other original sources." "They also reveal to what an extent Prescott's work was aided by his friends," especially Pascual de Gayangos, "an eminent Spanish scholar and historian."

COLLECTIVE BIOGRAPHY: Angus-Butterworth, L. M., in *So. Atl. Quar.*, 44 (1945):217-26.

Merriman, R. B., in *DAB*, 15:196.

Putman, Ruth, in *Cambridge History of American Literature*, 2:123-31.

Thorpe, F. N., in *Library of the World's Best Literature*, 20: 11707-804.

SPECIAL ASPECTS: Bassett, J. S. *The Middle Group of American Historians*, 211-23, 312-13.

Brooks, V. W. *The Flowering of New England*, 135-46, 327-31, 499-502.

Charvat, William. "Prescott's Political and Social Attitudes." *Amer. Lit.*, 13 (1941) :320-30.

Gooch, G. P. *History and Historians in the 19th Century*, 412-16.

Jameson, J. F. *History of Historical Writing in America*, 113-18.

Means, P. A. "A Re-examination of Prescott's Account of Early Peru," *N. E. Quar.,* 4 (1931) :645-62.

Nevins, Allan, in Macy, John, ed. *American Writers on American History,* 226-33.

MARY LYON— 1797-1849 —Pioneer in Higher Education for Women

COLLECTIVE BIOGRAPHY: Adams, E. L., and W. D. Foster. *Heroines of Modern Progress,* 30-57.

Bradford, Gamaliel. *Portraits of American Women,* 65-97.

Also in *Atlantic,* 122 (1918) :785-96.

Fox, D. R., and A. M. Schlesinger. *The Cavalcade of America,* (2nd ser., 1939) :193-210.

Goodsell, Willystine. *Pioneers of Women's Education in the United States,* 227-303.

Howe, M. A. D. *Classic Shades,* 41-77.

Wooley, M. E., in *DAB,* 11:531.

HISTORY: Woody, Thomas. *History of Women's Education in the United States,* 1 (1929) :348ff., 357ff., 361f., 372f.

SPECIAL ASPECTS: Slosson, E. E. *American Spirit in Education,* (1921) :241-45.

BRONSON ALCOTT— 1799-1888 —"The Most Transcendental Member of the 'Transcendental Club' "

ORIGINAL SOURCES: Miller, Perry, ed. *The Transcendentalists,* 150-56, 303-14.

Shepard, Odell, ed. *The Journals of Bronson Alcott.* 1938.

Amer. Lit., 10:500. Professor Shepard has done a splendid job in selecting representative material which defines Alcott well. The book is designed for the general reader, as well as the special student. The introduction "is perhaps the finest brief statement of Alcott's significance to be found anywhere." It "rightly emphasizes that the secret of Alcott's strength lies in his reciprocal relations with the great men who were his friends."

BIOGRAPHY: Morrow, H. W. *Father of Little Women.* 1927.

N. Y. Times, Oct. 23, 1927, p. 4. The biography of a pioneer educator who proved too progressive for Boston in the 1820's.

Shepard, Odell. *Pedlar's Progress: the Life of Bronson Alcott.* 1937.

Amer. Lit., 9:380. The biography of a Yankee pedlar who had "an almost messianic urge to teach . . ." The book is based on Alcott's journals, and is "a history of Alcott's mind from the subject's point of view, a kind of . . . apologia pro vita sua. As such it ranks among the great American literary biographies."

COLLECTIVE BIOGRAPHY: Bates, E. C., in *DAB*, 1:139.

Booth, E. T. *God Made the Country*, 186-201.

Brooks, V. W. *The Flowering of New England*, 228-51

Carpenter, F. L. "Bronson Alcott: Genteel Transcendentalist," *N. E. Quar.*, 13 (1940) :34-38.

Goddard, H. C., in *Cambridge History of American Literature*, 1:336-39.

SPECIAL ASPECTS: Hoeltze, H. H. *Sheltering Tree: a Story of the Friendship of Ralph Waldo Emerson and Amos Bronson Alcott.* 1943.

Sat. Rev. of Lit., 26 (1943):56. "A charming book" which "continues Alcott's well-merited rehabilitation."

Mead, David. "Some Ohio Conversations of Amos Bronson Alcott," *N. E. Quar.*, 22 (1949) :358-72.

McCuskey, Dorothy. *Bronson Alcott, Teacher.* 1940.

AHR, 46:721. "A competent, detailed story" of Alcott's "career as a teacher and educator." Miss McCuskey presents him "as an experimenter in the classroom, as the sponsor of new methods of pedagogy, and as the solicitous guide of little children."

GEORGE BANCROFT—   1800-1891   —"Renegade Scholar"

ORIGINAL SOURCES: Miller, Perry, ed. *The Transcendentalists*, 422-29.

BIOGRAPHY: Howe, M. A. D. *Life and Letters of George Bancroft.* 2 vols. 1908.

AHR, 14:150. Bancroft is allowed to speak for himself in these volumes, which represent "a selection from the great mass of Bancroft papers" skillfully pieced together. The letters evidence "the remarkable range and character of his acquaintance. They give few details regarding his methods and work as a historian." The book seems to show that Bancroft was "more highly regarded outside of historical circles than within them . . ."

*Nye, R. B. *George Bancroft, Brahmin Rebel.* 1944.

AHR, 50:559. A brisk narrative, "much more occupied with Bancroft the politician than with Bancroft the historian." Mr. Howe emphasized the genial personality of the man; Mr. Nye measures him "against the background of his time, concluding that he "was in many ways in advance of his period . . ." He declares that Bancroft "was consistent with his political principles, since in leaving his Boston Brahminism "he was but following his belief in the common man as the instrument of the Almighty."

COLLECTIVE BIOGRAPHY: Brooks, V. W. *The Flowering of New England,* 126-34.

Faris, J. T. *Men Who Conquered,* 123-34.

Howe, M. A. D., in *DAB,* 1:564.

Long, O. W. *Literary Pioneers,* 108-58.

Schlesinger, A. M., Jr. *The Age of Jackson,* 159-65.

Scott, Austin, in *Library of World's Best Literature,* 3:1433-39.

Sloane, W. M. "George Bancroft—in Society, in Politics, in Letters," *Century,* 33 (1887) :473-87

Vincent, L. H. *American Literary Masters,* 101-19.

HISTORY: Gooch, G. P. *History and Historians in the 19th Century,* (1928) :403-7.

SPECIAL ASPECTS: Bassett, J. S. *The Middle Group of American Historians,* 138-210.

Dawes, N. H., and F. T. Nichols. "Revaluing George Bancroft," *N. E. Quar.,* 6 (1933) :278-93.

Jameson, J. F. *The History of Historical Writing,* 100-10.

Kraus, Michael. "George Bancroft, 1834-1934," *N. E. Quar.,* 7 (1934) :662-86.

———. *A History of American History,* 215-39.

Also in *MVHR,* 19 (1932) :77-86.

Stewart, Watt, in Hutchinson, W. T., ed. *Essays in Historiography,* 1-25.

Willson, Beckles. *America's Ambassadors to England, 1785-1929,* 248-70.

---

* Awarded the Pulitzer Prize.

ORESTES AUGUSTUS BROWNSON— 1803-1876
—Seeker for Intellectual and Spiritual Certainty

ORIGINAL SOURCES: Miller, Perry, ed. *The Transcendentalists,* 45-47, 84-88, 92-94, 102-03, 106-23, 180-86, 189-91, 205-09, 240-46, 434-46.

BIOGRAPHY: Maynard, Theodore. *Orestes Brownson: Yankee, Radical, Catholic.* 1943.

AHR, 49:796. Written to correct earlier lives of Brownson and the idea that he went into the Catholic church to seek peace. Mr. Maynard throws off on Brownson's early Protestant associates and their doctrines. He describes Brownson as a burly, tempestuous figure who had "the largest and most luminous mind produced by Catholicism in America."

Schlesinger, A. M., Jr. *Orestes A. Brownson: A Pilgrim's Progress.* 1939.

Amer. Lit., 12:377. This erudite biography "is mainly a study of the various creeds and logical schemes through which Brownson hastened in his attempt to understand and reform a refractory world. If the author had made discriminatory use of details, he "might have given us a better insight into Brownson as a human being . . . But his writing is devoid of those 'little things and apparently trivial happenings' which, as Gamaliel Bradford tells us, are essential to expose the 'bare soul.'"

COLLECTIVE BIOGRAPHY: Bates, E. S., in *DAB,* 3:178.

Gabriel, R. H. *The Course of American Democratic Thought,* 54-59.

Parsons, Wilfred. "Orestes Brownson: an American Marxist before Marx," *Sewanee Rev.,* 47 (1939) :317-23.

SPECIAL ASPECTS: Caponigri, A. R. "Brownson and Emerson: Nature and History," *N. E. Quar.,* 18 (1945) :368-90.

Corrigan, Sister M. F. *Some Social Principles of Orestes A. Brownson.* 1939.

Amer. Lit., 12:376. Sister Corrigan "pictures Brownson as being keenly appreciative of the fundamental principles of the Catholic Church; and . . . maintains that Brownson's exposition of their applicability to social problems of his day offers a sound solution for social problems today."

Ryan, T. R. "Brownson's Love of Truth," *Catholic World,* 116: 537-44.

RALPH WALDO EMERSON— 1803-1882 —Sage of Concord and the Universe

ORIGINAL SOURCES: *Carpenter, F. I. *Ralph Waldo Emerson: Representative Selections.* (American Writers, 1934).

Amer. Lit., 6:480. "A highly satisfactory selection of Emerson's prose and verse." "Modernity . . . is the keynote of the introduction, which suggests most of the leading aspects of Emerson's thought 'in terms of the present day.' " "A number of factual errors occur in the editor's work."

Miller, Perry, ed. *The Transcendentalists,* 168-71, 173-80, 192, 196-98, 247-51, 375-81, 494-502.

Perry, Bliss, ed. *Heart of Emerson's Journal.* 1926.

Nation, 123:368, Oct. 13, 1926. Selections from the 10-volume edition described at the time of publication as "the best single book to which to go for a picture of the living Emerson." The *Journals* are significant because "they show Emerson in the act of becoming a writer."

Rahv, Philip, ed. *Discovery of Europe,* 139-60.

Rusk, R. L., ed. *The Letters of Ralph Waldo Emerson.* 6 vols. 1939.

AHR, 45:914. A notable work which throws much light on the development of Emerson's philosophical ideas and the important position he occupies in the intellectual history of America. The letters—especially those to Margaret Fuller—reveal a more human and intimate Emerson than we have hitherto known.

BIOGRAPHY: Brooks, V. W. *The Life of Emerson.* 1932.

Amer. Lit., 5:70. An interesting experiment in the art of the new biography. Mr. Brooks avoids many pitfalls, but his drive for dramatic effect leads to some exaggeration.

Extract in Prochnow, H. V., ed. *Great Stories from Great Lives,* 198-203.

Firkins, O. W. *Ralph Waldo Emerson.* 1915.

Nation, 101:436, Oct. 7, 1915. Mr. Firkins was the first biographer of Emerson to use the *Journal* published between 1909 and 1914. His book is "written in the pointed, epigrammatic style of Emerson himself . . ." The first half of the book is biographical, the rest is devoted to "a criticism of Emerson's literary art and an exposition of his philosophy."

Rusk, R. L. *The Life of Ralph Waldo Emerson.* 1949.

AHR, 55:381. The definitive biography which emphasizes Emerson's per-

---

* For more extensive bibliographies, see Carpenter, pp. xlix-lvi; *Cambridge History of American Literature,* 1 (1917) :551-56; Spiller, et al. *Literary History of the United States,* (1948) :492-501.

sonality and the people he met on his travels. Emerson "becomes more understandable and 'human,' more interested in social enterprises of many sorts, and more practicable." Professor Rusk presents his original findings in readable style and "with innumerable pieces of fresh evidence . . ."

Woodberry, G. E. *Life of Ralph Waldo Emerson.* (English Men of Letters, 1907)

Nation, 84:179, Feb. 21, 1907. "The critical chapters rather overbalance the narrative, but by no means the least satisfactory portion of Professor Woodberry's book is that which deals with the boyhood of Emerson and his life in Concord." The book also gives a good analysis of Emerson's character and of "the influence that surrounded the child and youth."

COLLECTIVE BIOGRAPHY: Abbott, L. F. *Twelve Great Modernists,* 195-221.

Booth, E. T. *God Made the Country,* 186-201.

Brooks, V. W. *Emerson and Others,* 3-105.

———. *The Flowering of New England,* 196-209, 286-97.

Dewey, John. *Characters and Events,* 1:69-77.

Gabriel, R. H. *American Democratic Thought,* 39-47.

Kunitz and Haycraft. *American Authors,* 252-55.

Lowell, J. R., in Peterson, Houston, ed. *Great Teachers,* 331-40.

McNulty, J. B. "Emerson's Friends and the Essay on Friendship," *N. E. Quar.,* 19 (1946) :390-4.

Mencken, H. L. *Mencken Chrestomathy,* 477-78.

More, P. L., in *Cambridge History of American Literature,* 1 (1917) :349-62.

Mowatt, R. B. *Americans in England,* 123-36.

Parrington, V. L. *Main Currents in American Thought,* 2:386-99.

Payne, W. M. *Leading American Essayists,* 135-240.

Russell, F. A. *American Pilgrimage,* 253-65.

Sherman, Stuart. *Americans,* 63-121.

Stephen, Leslie. *Studies of a Biographer,* 4:121-55.

Spiller, R. E., in *Literary History of the United States,* 2:350-87.

Thomas and Thomas. *Fifty Great Americans,* 145-55.

Van Doren, Mark, in *DAB,* 6:132.

Vincent, L. H. *American Literary Masters,* 147-86.

SPECIAL ASPECTS: Bailey, E. J. *Religious Thought in the Greater American Poets,* 47-69.

Bradley, S. L. "Emerson, and the Pioneer," *Amer. Lit.,* 19 (1947) :231-44.

Brownell, W. C. *American Prose Masters,* 133-204.

Canby, H. S. *Classic Americans,* 143-83.

Down, L. H. "Emerson and Dr. Channing: Two Men from Boston," *N. E. Quar.,* 20 (1947) :516-34.

Foerster, Norman. *American Criticism,* 52-110.

————. *Nature in American Literature,* 37-68.

Glicksberg, C. I. "Bryant on Emerson the Lecturer," *N. E. Quar.,* 12 (1939) :530-4.

Hummel, Hermann. "Emerson and Nietzsche," *N. E. Quar.,* 19 (1946) :63-84.

Lowell, J. R. "Emerson the Lecturer," in *My Study Windows,* (1871) :375-84.

Marchand, Ernest. "Emerson and the Frontier," *Amer. Lit.,* 3 (1931) :149-74.

Matthiessen, F. O. *American Renaissance,* 3-75.

Perry, Bliss. *Emerson Today.* (The Louis Clark Vanuxem Foundation Lectures, 1931).

Amer. Lit., 3:495. Professor Perry has given readers "the best of his opinions" and "information concerning Emerson." This is perhaps "the best short discussion of Emerson in print."

Quinn, P. F. "Emerson and Mysticism," *Amer. Lit.,* 21 (1950) : 397-414.

Roberts, J. R. "Emerson's Debt to the Seventeenth Century," *Amer. Lit.,* 21 (1949) :298-310.

Scudder, Townsend. *The Lonely Wayfaring Man: Emerson and Some Englishmen.* 1936.

Amer. Lit., 8:487. An entertaining account of Emerson's visits to England and his friendship with Carlyle and others.

Spiller, R. E. *The American in England,* 229-34.

Winters, Yvor. *In Defense of Reason,* 262-82, 477-79, 577-603.

NATHANIEL HAWTHORNE—1804-1864—Realist
of Souls

ORIGINAL SOURCES: Arvin, Newton, ed. *The Heart of Hawthorne's Journals.* 1929.

Amer. Lit., 2:517. The passages given are representative. The introduction points out elements which give the journals their importance: ideas recorded there which were developed into tales or novels, the descriptions of nature and the characterizations of people. The volume will be welcomed by readers; scholars will regret that Mr. Arvin failed to give us a reliable text.

Hawthorne, Julian. *Nathaniel Hawthorne and his Wife.* 1884.
This book by Hawthorne's son is the authorized life and letters.

Stewart, Randall, ed. *The American Notebooks by Nathaniel Hawthorne.* 1932.

Amer. Lit., 5:75. Previous to the publication of this book students knew Hawthorne's *American Notebooks* in an edition edited by his wife, Sophia. She omitted words and passages of which she disapproved. Now Mr. Stewart has given us an authentic version, thus permitting us a more accurate impression of Hawthorne, who seems much more human.

*Warren, Austin, ed. *Nathaniel Hawthorne: Representative Selections.* (American Writers, 1934) .

Professor Warren's "chief concern has been to trace the development of Hawthorne's religious, ethical, political, social, and literary ideas—to study his mind. And I have sought to interpret his writings in the light of his personality and aims." A bibliography and 368 pages of selections and notes follow.

BIOGRAPHY: Arvin, Newton. *Hawthorne.* 1929.

Nation, 129:554, Nov. 13, 1929. "Mr. Arvin has had the wisdom and the courage to write a study of Hawthorne that relies for its interest on straightforward portraiture and especially on candid and careful literary criticism."

Cantwell, Robert. *Nathaniel Hawthorne; American Years.* 1948.

Weekly Bk. Rev., Nov. 7, 1948, p. 1. This book "deals with Hawthorne's life only up to the publication of 'The Scarlet Letter,' and is presumably to be completed by a second volume at some later date. It contains some new material, chiefly relating to Hawthorne's mother's family, to Sophia Peabody's sojourn in Cuba during her young womanhood, and to the voyages made by Hawthorne's father as a mariner."

---

* See also Warren, pp. lxxv-lxxxix; *Cambridge History of American Literature,* 2 (1918) :415-24; Spiller, et al. *Literary History of the United States,* 3 (1948) : 544-53.

Gorman, H. S. *Hawthorne: a Study in Solitude.* (Murray Hill Biographies, 1927).

Nation, 125:482, Nov. 2, 1927. Mr. Gorman's brief study reveals inadequate knowledge of Puritan backgrounds. He is too hasty in dismissing movement around Hawthorne, but "has penetrated to the heart of his problem and has stripped from Hawthorne the tangle of maudlin eulogy which has so long covered his reputation."

James, Henry. *Nathaniel Hawthorne.* (English Men of Letters, 1879).

This monograph is the first extended study ever made of an American writer. It still remains one of the best, and it is one of the most satisfactory of the earlier books of James.

Also in Wilson, Edmund, ed. *Shock of Recognition,* 425-565.

Mather-Jackson, E. A. *Nathaniel Hawthorne: a Modest Man.* 1940.

Amer. Lit., 13:73. "Hawthorne is seen more clearly in his personal relationships in Mr. Mather's book* than in any previous biography. . . . The author has drawn freely upon recent biographies of Hawthorne's contemporaries, Hawthorne's letters . . . and the notebooks" to make the book "particularly rich in personal detail."

Stewart, Randall. *Nathaniel Hawthorne: a Biography.* 1948.

Weekly Bk. Rev., Nov. 7, 1948, p. 1. Professor Stewart's biography "is an important contribution to scholarship because it adds materially . . . to our factual information about Hawthorne. It has very real interest for the general reader because it also proposes some radical changes in the interpretation of Hawthorne's personality.

Van Doren, Mark. *Nathaniel Hawthorne.* (American Men of Letters, 1949).

Sat. Rev. of Lit., 32:11, Apr. 30, 1949. "Here, at last . . . is a Hawthorne in whom one can believe . . . a Hawthorne who is not only credible but whom one understands appreciably better than one did before Mr. Van Doren wrote his book. . . . [It] is essentially a criticism of Hawthorne's work to which a good deal of biography has been made to contribute."

Woodberry, G. E. *Nathaniel Hawthorne.* (American Men of Letters, 1902).

Dial, 34:147, Mar. 1, 1902. Professor Woodberry's volume on Hawthorne . . . has been described as the most discriminating biography ever written in this country. It is certainly a very solid and admirable piece of work, mingling narrative and criticism in exactly the right proportion."

---

* The author used the pseudonym of Edward Mather.

COLLECTIVE BIOGRAPHY: Brooks, V. W. *The Flowering of New England,* 210-27, 268-85, 374-87, 460-77.

Erskine, John, in *Cambridge History of American Literature,* 2:16-31.

———. *Leading American Novelists,* 179-273.

Parrington, V. L. *Main Currents in American Thought,* 2:442-50.

Sherman, S. P. *Americans,* 122-52.

Williams, S. T., in *Literary History of the United States,* 1:416-40.

SPECIAL ASPECTS: Beers, H. A. *Four Americans,* 33-57.

Blair, Walter. "Color, Light and Shadow in Hawthorne's Fiction," *N. E. Quar.,* 15 (1942) :74-94.

Bromfield, Louis, in Macy, J. A., ed. *American Writers on American Literature,* 97-104.

Brooks, V. W. *Chilmark Miscellany,* 207-19.

Brown, E. K. "Hawthorne, Melville, and Ethan Brand," *Amer. Lit.,* 3 (1931) :72-75.

Brownell, W. C. *American Prose Masters,* 63-130.

Canby, H. S. *Classic Americans,* 226-62.

Cowie, Alexander. *Rise of the American Novel,* 327-62.

Cowley, Malcolm. "Hawthorne in Solitude," *New Repub.,* 119: 19-23, Aug. 2, 1948.

———. "Hawthorne in the Looking-glass," *Sewanee Rev.,* 56 (1948) :545-63.

Davidson, E. H. *Hawthorne's Last Phase.* 1949.

N. E. Quar., 24:101. This book seeks "to account for Hawthorne's premature senility and the corresponding or consequent failure of his creative power" and to make a "literary analysis of his methods of composition, including the relations of his note-books to his 'Romances.'"

Faust, Bertha. *Hawthorne's Contemporaneous Reputation.* 1939.

Amer. Lit., 12:373. "A competent and useful survey," which maintains that Hawthorne was fortunately not affected "as a writer by the criticisms of his contemporaries . . ."

Hall, L. S. *Hawthorne, Critic of Society.* (Yale Studies in English, 1944) .

AHR, 51:170. "The thesis of this book is that Hawthorne was transformed in the years between his Brook Farm days (1842) and the years of his Liverpool Consulship (1853-1856) from a sharp critic of American mores into a champion of the opportunistic democracy of his time. In the earlier phase he was dissatisfied with his society; in his later years he found America's mode of existence 'the best the world had to offer.' "

Hawthorne, Manning. "Nathaniel Hawthorne at Bowdoin," *N. E. Quar.,* 13 (1940) :246-79.

Hayford, Harrison. "Hawthorne, Melville and the Sea," *N. E. Quar.,* 19 (1946) :435-52.

Hazard, L. L. *The Frontier in American Literature,* 27-40.

Hicks, Granville. *Great Tradition,* 1-31.

Howe, Irving. "Hawthorne and American Fiction," *Am. Merc.,* 68 (1949) :367-74.

Leavis, Q. D. "Hawthorne as Poet," Part I, *Sewanee Rev.,* 59 (1951) :179-205.

Mathiessen, F. O. *American Renaissance,* 192-241, 316-68.

Mills, Barris. "Hawthorne and Puritanism," *N. E. Quar.,* 21 (1948) :78-102.

More, P. E. *Shelburne Essays,* 1st ser., (1904) :22-50; 2nd ser., (1905) :173-87.

Poe, E. A. *Hawthorne Tales.* 1847.

Also in Wilson, Edmund, ed. *Shock of Recognition,* 154-69.

Schubert, Leland. *Hawthorne the Artist.* 1944.

Amer. Lit., 16:352. Mr. Schubert shows that Hawthorne was an artist in "his use of structure, line, mass, movement, contrast, variety, rhythm, color, sound, and so on." His book contains much that is "extremely illuminating."

Schneider, H. W. *History of American Philosophy,* 133-44.

———. *The Puritan Mind,* 256-64.

Snell, G. D. *Shapers of American Fiction,* 117-29.

Stephens, Leslie, in *Hours in a Library,* 1 (1875) :204-37.

Ticknor, Caroline. *Glimpses of Authors,* 31-42.

Turner, Arlin. *Hawthorne as Editor: Selections from his Writings in the American Magazine of useful and entertaining knowledge.* (La. State Univ. Studies, 1941) .

Amer. Lit., 13:271. Mr. Turner defines Hawthorne's rather "hurried, inadequate, and unoriginal" role as a magazine editor at the age of thirty-two. These pages fail to reveal the writer's ability to analyze human nature.

Van Doren, Carl. *American Novel,* 58-83.

Voight, G. P. "Hawthorne and the Roman Catholic Church," *N. E. Quar.,* 19 (1946) :394-97.

Wallace, Archer. *Religious Faith of Great Authors,* 30-55.

Warren, Austin. "Hawthorne's Reading," *N. E. Quar.,* 8 (1935) : 480-97.

Winters, Yvor. *In Defense of Reason,* 157-75.

WILLIAM LLOYD GARRISON— 1805-1879 —Outstanding Leader or "Dead Weight Upon the Abolition Cause"?

ORIGINAL SOURCES: Abramowitz, Isidore. *Great Prisoners,* 572-77.

BIOGRAPHY: Korngold, Ralph. *Two Friends of Man: the Story of William Lloyd Garrison and Wendell Phillips and their Relationship with Abraham Lincoln.* 1950.

AHR, 55:928. A vivid and provocative book which accepts the two abolitionists rather uncritically. However, "Mr. Korngold is unconvincing in portraying Garrison as the unchallenged leader of the abolitionist forces mobilized in the 1830's . . ." It is interesting to note that he disapproves of the failure of the reformer to champion the cause of white labor in New England.

Swift, Lindsay. *William Lloyd Garrison.* (American Crisis, 1911).

Nation, 93:35, July 13, 1911. The best short biography. The point of view is that slavery "disappeared when it did chiefly because William Lloyd Garrison and his followers stirred the conscience of the nation to the depths, and made the continuance of the institution seem a crime."

COLLECTIVE BIOGRAPHY: Eddy, Sherwood, and Kirby Page. *Makers of Freedom,* 11-31.

Fuess, C. M., in *DAB,* 7:168.

Higginson, T. W. *Contemporaries,* (1899) :244-56.

Madison, C. A. *Critics and Crusaders,* 3-38.

Malone, Dumas. *Saints in Action,* 66-70.

Read, H. E. *Fighters for Freedom,* 256-61.

Seldes, G. V. *The Stammering Century*, (1928) :239-47.

Tyler, A. F. *Freedom's Ferment*, 410-15.

Villard, O. G. *Some Newspapers and Newspaper-Men*, 302-15.

HISTORY: *Barnes, G. H. *The Anti-Slavery Impulse, 1830-1844.* 1933.

AHR, 39:747. "Professor Barnes contends that Garrison as a leader was but 'a name, an embodied motto, a figurehead of fanaticism.' His 'promiscuous villification of all individuals, institutions and beliefs with which he did not agree so alienated churches and ministers that actually he became a dead weight upon the abolition cause.' "

Nye, R. B. *Fettered Freedom: Civil Liberties and the Slavery Controversy, 1830-1860.* 1949.

AHR, 55:162. A stimulating and suggestive study dealing with "the reactions of the American people, during one central period and on one specific issue to the civil liberties tradition." Professor Nye "concludes that the abolition crusade succeeded because it 'managed to merge antislavery with civil liberties.' " Unlike Professor Barnes, he scarcely concerns himself "with comparative estimates of antislavery workers . . ."

BIOGRAPHIES OF CONTEMPORARIES: Thomas, B. P. *Theodore Weld, Crusader for Freedom.* 1950.

MVHR, 37:722. Mr. Thomas portrays Garrison as a leader who caused dissension in the ranks of the abolitionists by his autocratic movements, his violent attacks on the clergy, his tangential activity in minor reform movements, and his radical no-government. In the judgment of the author, "it was really Garrison's enemies (particularly southern newspapers) who gave him fame." Abolitionists differed as to "the relative importance of Garrison and Weld as leaders." Historians still do.

HENRY WADSWORTH LONGFELLOW— 1807-1882 —"The Best Loved American Poet of His Generation"

ORIGINAL SOURCES:† Shepard, Odell. *Henry Wadsworth Longfellow: Representative Selections.* (American Writers, 1934) .

In his preface, Professor Shepard says that his selections from Longfellow's poems were made with a three-fold purpose: "first of all, to present Longfellow as he was, without excessive regard to the rise and fall of his fame or to the more superficial changes in literary fashion that have affected

---

*See page 167.

† See also Shepard, pp. lvii-lxii; *Cambridge History of American Literature*, 2 (1917) :425-36; Spiller, et al. *Literary History of the United States*, 3 (1948): 622-26.

his reputation; secondly, to show his 'representative value' as an American product of the nineteenth century; and, lastly, to indicate his influence in the shaping of the American mind." The volume contains an excellent introduction.

BIOGRAPHY: Gorman, H. S. *A Victorian American: Henry Wadsworth Longfellow.* 1926.

N. Y. World, Oct. 24, 1926, p. 9. Mr. Gorman's biography is the story—not of a great poet—but of a happy successful man who was in tune with his generation."

Hawthorne, Hildegarde. *The Poet of Craigie House: the Story of Henry Wadsworth Longfellow.* 1936.

Amer. Lit., 8:234. Miss Hawthorne weaves "imaginative conversations and picturesque incidents from authentic facts taken from his [Longfellow's] journals and letters," and seeks to give "a lively and popular story, without sacrificing any of the important details essential to a full-length study." She dwells "at some length upon the romantic periods of love, the short courtship and almost equally short years of marriage to Mary Potter, and the protracted wooing of Frances Appleton. The essential details of the biography are accurate, but there are "many minor errors . . .'"

Longfellow, Samuel. *Life of Henry Wadsworth Longfellow, with Extracts from His Journals and Correspondence.* 2 vols. 1886.

Atlantic, 57:702. A faithful portrait by the poet's younger brother, a Unitarian clergyman.

Thompson, Lawrance. *Young Longfellow (1807-1843).* 1938.

Amer. Lit., 11:469. An interesting study which "removes some of the bearded dignity with which Samuel Longfellow endowed the poet, and substitutes a confused and romantic young man with a gift of song." The result is that the poet "becomes more likeable and understandable because he seems more human."

COLLECTIVE BIOGRAPHY: Bradford, Gamaliel. *Biography and the Human Heart,* 37-62.

Bronson, W. C., in *DAB,* 11:382.

Brooks, V. W. *The Flowering of New England,* 147-71, 303-8, 443-50, 508-12.

Howells, W. D. *Literary Friends and Acquaintances,* 178-211.

Kunitz and Haycraft. *American Authors,* 476-79.

Long, O. W. *Literary Pioneers,* 159-98.

Shepard, Odell, in *Literary History of the United States,* 1:587-606.

Stedman, E. C. *Poets of America,* 180-224.

Trent, W. P., in *Cambridge History of American Literature,* 2: 32-41.

Wendell, Barrett. *A Literary History of America,* 378-92.

SPECIAL ASPECTS: Bailey, E. J. *Religious Thought in the Greater American Poets,* 108-36.

Colton, Arthur. "Longfellow: an Essay in Reputation," *Bookman,* 76 (1933) :128-33.

Hatfield, J. T. *New Light on Longfellow: with Special Reference to His Relations to Germany.* 1933.

Amer. Lit., 5:374. The trend toward fairer evaluation of Longfellow has been greatly aided by Professor Hatfield, who presents "a wealth of unknown details concerning the poet's relation to Germany." It is significant that in his student days Longfellow was strongly attracted to Germany and German poetry, and that it was he who was the first to suggest the trek toward educational methods which was later emphasized at Harvard under President Eliot.

Johnson, C. L. "Longfellow's Beginnings in Foreign Languages," *N. E. Quar.,* 20 (1947) :317-28.

OLIVER WENDELL HOLMES—1809-1894—"Autocrat of the Breakfast Table"

ORIGINAL SOURCES: Hayakawa, S. I., and H. M. Jones. *Oliver Wendell Holmes: Representative Selections.* (American Writers, 1939) .

Amer. Lit., 11:331. This useful volume gives a sound estimate of Holmes from the point of view of the present day. There is "an adequate discussion of Holmes' relation to science," "the selections are well chosen, and they include materials from Holmes' less technical prose upon medical subjects."

BIOGRAPHY: Howe, M. A. D. *Holmes of the Breakfast Table.* 1939.

N. Y. Times, Apr. 23, 1939, p. 3. Mr. Howe "draws a simple but arresting portrait of this 'epicure in words,' this incorrigible talker and lecturer; this humane physician." This brief biography makes Holmes live again— the boy who listened to Margaret Fuller, the old professor who examined William James on anatomy.

Morse, J. T. *Life and Letters of Oliver Wendell Holmes.* 2 vols. 1896.

Dial, 20:299, May 16, 1896. "Taken together, the memoir and the letters form a complete and most engaging portraiture . . ."

Tilton, E. M. *Amiable Autocrat: a Biography of Dr. Oliver Wendell Holmes.* 1947.

AHR, 53:645. An accurate portrait. Miss Tilton's book is thoroughly documented and restrained in its conclusions. It "has made any other biography unnecessary for many years to come."

COLLECTIVE BIOGRAPHY: Allen, Devere, ed. *Adventurous Americans,* 18-37.

Ballantine, W. G. "Oliver Wendell Holmes as a Poet and as a Man," *No. Am. Rev.,* 140 (1909) :178-93.

Brooks, V. W. *The Flowering of New England,* 343-58, 487-98.

Clark, H. H. "Oliver Wendell Holmes, a Reinterpretation," *N. E. Quar.,* 12 (1939) :19-34.

Fox, D. R., and A. M. Schlesinger. *Cavalcade of America,* (2nd ser., 1939) :324-39.

Fuller, H. D., in Macy, John, ed. *American Writers on American Literature,* 153-63.

Grattan, C. H. "Oliver Wendell Holmes," *Am. Merc.,* 4 (1925) :37-41. •

Howe, M. A. D., in *DAB,* 9:169.

———. "Dr. Holmes, the Friend and Neighbor," *Yale Rev.,* 7 (1918) :562-78.

Howells, W. D. *Literary Friends and Acquaintances,* 146-77.

Matthews, Brander, in *Cambridge History of American Literature,* 2:224-40.

Parrington, V. L. *Main Currents in American Thought,* 2:451-59.

Shepard, Odell, in *Literary History of the United States,* 1:587-606.

Stedman, E. C. *Poets of America,* 273-303.

Stephen, Leslie. *Studies of a Biographer,* 2:149-82.

Wendell, Barrett. *Literary History of America,* 407-25.

SPECIAL ASPECTS: Bailey, E. J. *Religious Thought in the Greater American Poets,* 137-57.

Brooks, V. W. "Dr. Holmes: Forerunner of the Moderns," *Sat. Rev. of Lit.*, 14 (1936) :3-4, 13-15.

Canby, H. S. "Breakfast with Dr. Holmes," *Sat. Rev. of Lit.*, 5 (1929) :617.

Flanagan, J. T. "Dr. Holmes Advises Young Ignatius Donnelly," *Amer. Lit.*, 13 (1941) :59-61.

Lockensgard, Hjalmar. "Holmes Quizzes the Professors," *Amer. Lit.*, 13 (1941) :157-62.

Townsend, F. S. "The Religion of Oliver Wendell Holmes," *Methodist Rev.*, 91 (1909) :605-11.

BIOGRAPHIES OF CONTEMPORARIES: Bowen, C. D. *Yankee from Olympus*, 14-94.

MARGARET FULLER— 1810-1850 —Journalist and Social Reformer

ORIGINAL SOURCES: Miller, Perry, ed. *The Transcendentalists*, 331-39, 366-72, 402, 404-07, 457-64.

Orr, E. W., ed. "Two Margaret Fuller Manuscripts," *N. E. Quar.*, 11 (1938) :794-802.

Rahv, Philip, ed. *Discovery of Europe*, 161-72.

Rostenberg, Leona, ed. "Diary of Timothy Fuller in Congress, January 12-March 15, 1818," *N. E. Quar.*, 12 (1939) :521-29.

——. "Margaret Fuller's Roman Diary," *Jour. Modern Hist.*, 17 (1940) :209-20.

——. "Mazzini to Margaret Fuller, 1847-49," *AHR*, 47 (1941) : 73-80.

Wade, Mason, ed. *The Writings of Margaret Fuller.* 1941.

Amer. Lit., 14:87. A reprint intended "to rescue Margaret Fuller the writer from the obscurity and neglect to which fate and the attentions of her friends and relatives have brought her."

BIOGRAPHY: Anthony, Katharine. *Margaret Fuller: a Psychological Biography.* 1921.

Current Opinion, 70:222. An interesting biography written by an ardent feminist who used the methods of psychoanalysis.

Bell, Margaret. *Margaret Fuller: a Biography.* 1930.

Amer. Lit., 3:227. A popular biography which fails to shed new light. However, "Miss Bell writes with the lively style of a good novelist . . ."

Stern, M. B. *The Life of Margaret Fuller.* 1942.

Amer. Lit., 14:87. Miss Stern seeks "to make Margaret Fuller live again as a dynamic, evolving creature, to show her in her surroundings, and reveal her in countless scenes and attitudes, with her pupils, her friends, her lovers. The book is the fictional portrait of a very astonishing lady, built up on a basis of fact, witness the huge bibliography appended. It is a beautiful piece of imaginative reconstruction, and will probably remain the most graphic of the many lives that have been written or may yet be written about the Cambridge bluestocking."

Extract in Prochnow, H. V., ed. *Great Stories from Great Lives,* 276-81.

Wade, Mason. *Margaret Fuller, Whetstone of Genius.* 1940.

AHR, 46:721. A readable biography which rescues Margaret Fuller from legend, but is inclined to view her "as a social barometer of the intellectual and social currents of her time."

COLLECTIVE BIOGRAPHY: Anthony, Katharine, in *DAB,* 7:63.

Bradford, Gamaliel. *Portraits of American Women,* 131-63.

Also in *No. Am. Rev.,* 210 (1919) :109-21.

Brooks, V. W. *The Flowering of New England,* 236-42, 377-79, 428-31.

Goddard, H. C., in *Cambridge History of American Literature,* 1:342-43.

Madison, C. A. *Critics and Crusaders,* 94-113.

O'Higgins, O. W. *The American Mind in Action,* 300-27.

Parrington, V. L. *Main Currents in American Thought,* 2:426-34.

SPECIAL ASPECTS: Hess, M. W. "Margaret Fuller and Browning's Childe Roland," *Personalist,* 28 (1947) :376-83.

Randel, W. P. "Hawthorne, Channing, and Margaret Fuller," *Amer. Lit.,* 10 (1939) :472-76.

Stern, M. B. "Margaret Fuller and The Dial," *So. Atl. Quar.,* 40 (1941) :11-21.

BIOGRAPHIES OF CONTEMPORARIES: Brooks, V. W. *The Life of Emerson.* 1932.

THEODORE PARKER— 1810-1860 —"Yankee
Crusader"

ORIGINAL SOURCES: Miller, Perry, ed. *The Transcendentalists,*
226-31, 259-83, 315-24, 414-21, 449-57, 484-93.

BIOGRAPHY: Commager, H. S. *Theodore Parker.* 1936. 1947.

AHR, 42:365. A valuable and provocative study which seeks to view men
and events through Parker's eyes. Professor Commager does full justice to
Parker's "native vigor," his "encyclopedic learning," and "hard-hitting
eloquence."

COLLECTIVE BIOGRAPHY: Christie, F. A., in *DAB,* 14:238.

Commager, H. S. "The Dilemma of Theodore Parker," *N. E.
Quar.,* 6 (1933) :257-77.

Malone, Dumas. *Saints in Action,* 41, 54, 126.

SPECIAL ASPECTS: Commager, H. S. "Tempest in a Boston Tea
Cup," *N. E. Quar.,* 6 (1933) :651-75.

Newbrough, G. F. "Reason and Understanding in the Works of
Theodore Parker," *So. Atl. Quar.,* 47 (1949) :64-75.

Smith, H. S. "Was Theodore Parker a Transcendentalist?" *N. E.
Quar.,* 23 (1950) :351-64.

ELIHU BURRITT— 1810-1879 —An Early Peace
Advocate

BIOGRAPHY: Curti, M. E. *The Learned Blacksmith: the Letters
and Journals of Elihu Burritt.* 1937.

Amer. Lit., 9:485. A brief biography of the Connecticut Yankee blacksmith
who crusaded for peace, improved education, the abolition of slavery, and
other reforms.

COLLECTIVE BIOGRAPHY: Curti, M. E., in *DAB,* 3:328.

SPECIAL ASPECTS: Curti, M. E. "Henry Wadsworth Longfellow
and Elihu Burritt," *Amer. Lit.,* 7 (1935) :315-28.

WENDELL PHILLIPS— 1811-1884 —"The Silver-
tongued Abolitionist"

BIOGRAPHY: Korngold, Ralph. *Two Friends of Man: the Story of
William Lloyd Garrison and Wendell Phillips and their Relationship with Abraham Lincoln.* 1950.

Jour. South. Hist., 16:228. Mr. Korngold gives a warm defense of two New
England radicals, which shows "no real understanding of southern slavery

but accepts the propaganda of Garrison and Phillips as truly portraying conditions in the Old South." The author also does not take into account the significant studies of the New York abolitionists and of the western anti-slavery movement by Barnes and Damond, who de-emphasize the importance of Garrison and Phillips and elevate the contributions of Weld, the Tappan brothers, the Grimké sisters, and Birney."

COLLECTIVE BIOGRAPHY: Blan, J. L. "Scholar in a Republic," in *American Philosophic Addresses,* (1946) :261-84.

Fuess, C. M., in *DAB,* 14:546.

Hofstadter, Richard. *American Political Tradition,* 135-61.

Hubbard, Elbert. *Little Journeys to the Homes of Eminent Orators,* 505-54.

Madison, C. A. *Critics and Crusaders,* 60-79.

Morris, Charles. *Heroes of Progress in America,* 199-204.

Wildman, Edwin. *Famous Leaders of Character in America,* (1922) :71-80.

Woodberry, G. E. *Heart of Man and Other Papers,* (1922) :299-323.

Smalley, G. W., in *Library of World's Best Literature,* 20:11409-412.

SAMUEL COLT—　　1814-1862　　—Inventor and Manufacturer

BIOGRAPHY: Rohan, Jack. *Yankee Arms Maker: the Incredible Career of Samuel Colt.* 1935.

Books, Oct. 6, 1935, p. 10. "Mr. Rohan's biography of Samuel Colt is an excellent example of painstaking effort to piece together the incidents and events of a remarkable industrial career. Leaders of industry seldom receive such careful research and impartial consideration as Mr. Rohan has displayed in this book. It was a difficult book to write, for it took years to come in contact with the necessary letters and documents, and it is an absorbing book to read."

COLLECTIVE BIOGRAPHY: Mitman, C. W., in *DAB,* 4:318.

SPECIAL ASPECTS: Webb, W. P. *The Great Plains,* (1931) :170-73, 176-79.

HENRY DAVID THOREAU—　1817-1862　—"The Village Rebel"

ORIGINAL SOURCES: *Crawford, B. V., ed. *Henry David Thoreau:*

---

* See also Crawford, pp. lix-lxix; *Cambridge History of American Literature,* 2 (1917) :411-15; Spiller, et al. *Literary History of the United States,* 3 (1948) :742-46.

Representative Selections. (American Writers, 1934).

Amer. Lit., 7:228. This volume contains an excellent introduction. The selections from Thoreau's writings reveal his growth "both as an observer of his times and as a literary artist." "The text of the selections is that of the first editions and periodical appearances of Thoreau's writings . . ."

Miller, Perry, ed. *The Transcendentalists,* 324-30, 396-402.

Shepard, Odell, ed. *The Heart of Thoreau's Journals.* 1927.

Teale, E. W., ed. *Walden, or Life in the Woods.* 1946.

Toney, Bradford, ed. *The Journals of Henry David Thoreau.* 14 vols. 1951.

N. Y. Times, May 20, 1951, p. 1. Thoreau, who irritated his contemporaries, continues to be popular because "he is so stimulating a thinker and so extraordinarily fine a writer. That he is both is as clear from the *Journals* as it is from *Walden* itself. Famous passages include his description of a snow-storm, his encounters with wild beasts, his 'outburst concerning the gold rush and the whole philosophy of men who "live by luck without contributing any value to society," ' and his protest against building a railroad that may manage to run over many of the persons it is supposed to benefit."

Whicher, G. F., ed. *Walden and Selected Essays.* 1947.

BIOGRAPHY: Atkinsion, J. B. *Henry Thoreau: the Cosmic Yankee.* 1927.

N. Y. Times, Nov. 20, 1927, p. 1. A good portrait of Thoreau, but not a detailed biography.

Bazalgette, Leon. *Henry Thoreau, Bachelor of Nature.* 1924.

N. Y. Times, Dec. 7, 1924, p. 2. A lively, picturesque narrative which attempts to popularize a dead man who was never popular in his lifetime.

Canby, H. S. *Thoreau.* 1939.

Amer. Lit., 12:112. This book, "excellent in large part, suffers from certain handicaps and shortcomings." Mr. Canby's interest in Thoreau came too late "for him to talk" with old timers who knew Thoreau and Sanborn, his first biographer. "The second part of the book, the story of Thoreau between the time of John's death and his sojourn at Walden, seems too much concerned with Thoreau's love of women . . . The third part is "the best . . ." here Mr. Canby brings Thoreau to authorship and is able "to exchange the shaky biographical ground of Sanborn and secondary sources for the firm ground of Thoreau's own journal."

Extract in Prochnow, H. V., ed. *Great Stories from Great Lives,* 102-07.

Krutch, J. W. *Henry David Thoreau*. (American Men of Letters, 1948).

N. Y. Times, Oct. 3, 1948, p. 4. A critical biography by "a temperate thinker with a singularly penetrating mind and a lucid literary style."

Whicher, G. F. *Walden Revisited: a Centennial Tribute to Henry David Thoreau*. 1945.

AHR, 51:170. A brief but "delightfully written biography and reappraisal of Thoreau."

COLLECTIVE BIOGRAPHY: Adams, R. W., and H. S. Canby, in *DAB*, 18:491.

Booth, E. T. *God Made the Country*, 186-201.

Brooks, V. W. *The Flowering of New England*, 286-302, 359-73, 422-42.

Canby, H. S., in *There Were Giants in the Land*, 161-68.

Hazard, L. L. *The Frontier in American Literature*, 164-71.

Madison, C. A. *Critics and Crusaders*, 174-93.

Payne, W. M. *Leading American Essayists*, 241-316.

Phelps, W. L. *Howells, James, Bryant and Other Essays*, 66-95.

Russell, F. A. *American Pilgrimage*, 199-215.

Scudder, Townsend, in *Literary History of the United States*, 1:388-415.

Shepard, Odell. "Paradox of Thoreau," *Scribner's*, 48 (1920) : 335-42.

Stern, M. B. "Approaches to Biography," *So. Atl. Quar.*, 45 (1946) :362-71.

Stevenson, R. L. *Familiar Studies of Men & Books*, 113-49.

SPECIAL ASPECTS: Allen, Frank, ed. *Men of Concord and Some Others as Portrayed in the Journal of Henry David Thoreau*. 1936.

Amer. Lit., 9:267. A compilation of the "most gossipy passages from Thoreau's writings about his neighbors of Concord." The book emphasizes "the neighborliness of Thoreau, who was America's most parochial writer after all, interpreting universal experience in terms of Concord."

Brawner, J. P. "Thoreau as a Wit and Humorist," *So. Atl. Quar.*, 44 (1945) :170-76.

Brooks, V. W. "Thoreau at Walden," in Balch, Marston. *Modern Short Biographies*, 255-73.

Canby, H. S. *Classic Americans,* 184-225. (Thoreau's social thinking).

———. "Thoreau: a New Estimate," *Sat. Rev. of Lit.,* 32:15-16, Dec. 3, 1949.

Cook, R. L. *Passage to Walden.* 1949.

Sat. Rev. of Lit., 32:52, Apr. 16, 1949. Mr. Cook passes up the biographical approach and discusses the special aspects which interest him: Thoreau's travels in Concord, other writers on nature, Thoreau's attitude toward man, his study of the Indians, his mysticism in his approach to nature, his physical skill, his attitude toward craftsmanship, and his writings.

Dabbs, J. M. "Thoreau: the Adventurer as Economist," *Yale Rev.,* 36 (1947) :667-72.

De Armond, Fred. "Thoreau and Schopenhauer: an Imaginary Conversation," *N. E. Quar.,* 5 (1932) :55-64.

Foerster, Norman. *Nature in American Literature,* 69-142.

Ford, N. A. "Henry David Thoreau, Abolitionist," *N. E. Quar.,* 19 (1946) :359-71.

Hoeltje, H. H. "Thoreau and the Concord Academy," *N. E. Quar.,* 21 (1948) :103-09.

———. "Thoreau as a Lecturer," *N. E. Quar.,* 19 (1946) :485-94.

Hurd, H. E. "Henry David Thoreau—a Pioneer in the Field of Education," *Education,* 49 (1929) :372-76.

Keiser, Albert. *The Indian in American Literature,* 209-32.

Kwiat, J. J. "Thoreau's Philosophical Apprenticeship," *N. E. Quar.,* 18 (1945) :51-69.

MacMechan, Archibald, in *Cambridge History of American Literature,* 2:1-15.

Manning, C. A. "Thoreau and Tolstoy," *N. E. Quar.,* 16 (1943) : 234-43.

More, P. E. "Thoreau's Journal," in *Shelburne Essays* (5th ser., 1928) :106-31.

Van Doren, Mark. *Henry David Thoreau, a Critical Study.* 1916.

Nation, 103:614, Dec. 28, 1916. "For solid, demolishing criticism of Thoreau, one will look in vain for anything more effective than the present volume; Lowell's spirited attack is, by comparison, weak and superficial."

Whitford, Kathryn. "Thoreau and the Woodlots of Concord,"
N. E. Quar., 23 (1950) :291-306.

BIOGRAPHIES OF CONTEMPORARIES: Barrus, Clara. *The Life and Letters of John Burroughs,* 2:327-37.

CHAPTER XXIV. NEW YORK AND PENNSYLVANIA

JOHN JACOB ASTOR— 1763-1848 —"America's
First Millionaire"

BIOGRAPHY: Porter, K. W. *John Jacob Astor, Business Man.* 2
vols. (Harvard Studies in Business History, 1931).

AHR, 37:769. A detailed study based largely on primary sources. While
"the personal side of Astor's life is by no means neglected," it has been
subordinated to his business career.

Smith, A. D. H. *John Jacob Astor, Landlord of New York.* 1929.

New Republic, 59:80, June 5, 1929. A popular narrative which pays more
attention to the development of the fur trade than to the character of
Astor.

COLLECTIVE BIOGRAPHY: Ghent, W. J., in *DAB,* 1:397.

Hubbard, Elbert. *Little Journeys to the Homes of Great Business Men,* 201-29.

Minnigerode, Meade. *Certain Rich Men,* 33-49.

Muggah, M. G., and P. H. Raihle. *Meet Your Neighbor,* 20-23.

Myers, Gustavus. *History of Great American Fortunes,* (1936) :
93-96, 127-30, 665-67.

O'Connor, Harvey. *The Astors.* 1941.

Books, Apr. 13, 1941, p. 5. An entertaining but unsympathetic family biography. Mr. O'Connor says that the founder of the American family
made his fortune from the China trade—rather than from furs—and that
intelligent men like Washington Irving frequented his house.

Schriftgeisser, Karl. *Families,* 246-55, 266-71.

Wildman, Edwin. *Builders of America,* 195-209.

HISTORY: Fuller, G. W. *History of the Pacific Northwest,* 95-
109.

Monaghan, James. *Overland Trail,* 64-92.

SPECIAL ASPECTS: Gras, N. S. B., and H. M. Larsons, eds. *Casebook in American Business History*, 76-98.

Porter, K. W. "Myths after Astor," *Bus. Hist. Soc. Bul.*, 10 (1936) :1-7.

AMOS EATON— 1776-1842 —Scientist

BIOGRAPHY: McAllister, E. M. *Amos Eaton, Scientist and Educator, 1776-1842.* 1941.

AHR, 47:621. A sympathetic biography of a farmer's son who did much to arouse interest in botany and geology.

COLLECTIVE BIOGRAPHY: Merrill, G. P., in *DAB*, 5:605.

PHILIP HONE— 1780-1851 —Merchant and Society Leader

ORIGINAL SOURCES: Nevins, Allan. *The Diary of Philip Hone, 1828-1851.* 2 vols. 1927.

Nation, 126 (1928):98. A valuable book by the one-time mayor of New York which reflects "the mental process of the Whig aristocracy," and gives an intimate picture of the social life of the day. The introduction gives a biographical sketch of the diarist, and many of the people of the Fifth Generation appear in the diary.

COLLECTIVE BIOGRAPHY: Nevins, Allan, in *DAB*, 9:192.

WASHINGTON IRVING— 1783-1859 —The First American Man of Letters to Receive European Recognition

ORIGINAL SOURCES: *Pochmann, H. A., ed. *Washington Irving: Representative Selections.* (American Writers, 1934).

Amer. Lit., 6:479. "The most informative volume in existence concerning Washington Irving." Mr. Pochmann makes a deft use of new facts, he adjusts "controversial points of view," he adopts "new approaches. . . ." Excellent bibliography.

Rahv, Philip, ed. *Discovery of Europe*, 94-101.

Williams, S. T., ed. *The Journal of Washington Irving.* 1931.

Amer. Lit., 4:336. While this record comes on the heels of Irving's Dresden residence, "there is no hint of the reputed unhappy love experience with

---

* See also Pochmann, pp. xciii-cx; *Cambridge History of American Literature*, 1 (1917) :245-59; Spiller, et al. *Literary History of the United States*, 3 (1948) :578-83.

Emily Foster." On the contrary, it contains one of the very rare passages in his writings describing his youthful betrothed, Matilda Hoffman, in a well-hidden but touching recollection. More significant are the passages revealing his sources and methods in writing his next book.

———. "Washington Irving's First Stay in Paris," *Amer. Lit.*, 2: 15-20.

BIOGRAPHY: Hellman, G. S. *Washington Irving, Esquire, Ambassador at Large from the New World to the Old.* 1925.

Yale Rev., 15:1411, Jan., 1926. Mr. Hellman gives a picture of Irving as "one of the earliest American protagonists of culture and perhaps the first real interpreter of America to Europe. Stress is placed upon Irving's public services, as when his tact and influence helped to avoid war between France and the United States, and again when he paved the way for the settlement of the Oregon boundary dispute. Nobody can leave this volume without new love for Washington Irving, gentle, high-minded, unfailingly courteous spirit, unsurpassed apostle of the sweetness of life."

Williams, S. T. *The Life of Washington Irving.* 2 vols. 1935.

AHR, 42:357. A definitive biography which shows "the important part played by Irving as the first prominent American to gain for his country the good will of Europe." The reviewer confesses himself "perplexed by Professor Williams' refusal to accept as an established fact Irving's proposal of marriage to Emily Foster."

COLLECTIVE BIOGRAPHY: Brooks, V. W. *The World of Washington Irving*, 127-37, 152-66, 249-54, 284-92, 358-60.

Mowatt, R. B. *Americans in England*, 103-22.

Parrington, V. L. *Main Currents in American Thought*, 2:203-11.

Payne, W. M. *Leading American Essayists*, 43-134.

Putman, G. H., in *Cambridge History of American Literature*, 1:245-59.

Russell, F. A. *American Pilgrimage*, 165-82.

Spiller, R. E. *The American in England*, 258-61, 275-92, 294-99.

Taylor, W. F. *History of American Letters*, 93-101.

Ulmann, Albert. *New Yorkers*, 146-67.

Williams, S. T., in *DAB*, 9:505.

———, in *Literary History of the United States*, 1:242-52.

SPECIAL ASPECTS: Bowers, C. G. *The Spanish Adventure of Washington Irving.* 1940.

Amer. Lit., 12:255. This book is "mildly agreeable reading," but it shows carelessness and "never exhibits penetrative evaluation of Irving either as a writer or as a diplomat in Spain."

Canby, H. S. *Classic Americans*, 67-97.

Carver, George. *Alms for Oblivion*, 181-99.

McDermott, J. F., ed. *The Western Journals of Washington Irving*. 1944.

MVHR, 32:111. A vivid portrayal of Irving's trip to the Oklahoma plains in 1832. This supplements his *Tour of the Prairies.*

Mott, F. L. *Golden Multitudes*, 70-76.

Snell, G. D. *Shapers of American Fiction, 1798-1947*, 105-17.

EMMA HART WILLARD— 1787-1870 —"America's Pioneer in the Education of Women"

BIOGRAPHY: Lutz, Alma. *Emma Willard, Daughter of Democracy*. 1929.

Outlook, 152:188, May 29, 1929. Emma Willard founded a seminary "where she demonstrated that intensive education would not ruin female health nor dancing, female morals." Miss Lutz has used "rich stores of material, including many letters to make an absorbing book. . . . She has told a good story well."

COLLECTIVE BIOGRAPHY: Goodsell, Willystine. *Pioneers of Women's Education in the United States*, 15-112.

Lutz, Alma, in *DAB*, 20:231.

HISTORY: Woody, Thomas. *History of Women's Education in the United States*. 1929. 1:305f., 310ff., 344ff., 400f., 434f., 458f.

SPECIAL ASPECTS: Taylor, J. M. *Before Vassar Opened*. 1914.

Rev. of Revs., 50:113. Dr. Taylor's work covers the early experiments of seminaries and colleges for women from the opening of Emma Willard's Troy Seminary for Women in 1821 down to the consideration of the curriculum of Vassar and other women's colleges at the present time."

JAMES FENIMORE COOPER— 1789-1851 —"A Pioneer Among American Novelists"

ORIGINAL SOURCES: Rahv, Philip, ed. *Discovery of Europe*, 119-27.

*Spiller, R. E., ed. *James Fenimore Cooper: Representative Selections*. (American Writers, 1936).

* See also Spiller, pp. xc-cii; *Cambridge History of American Literature*, 1 (1917):530-34; Spiller, et al. *Literary History of the United States*, 3 (1948):450-55.

Amer. Lit., 8:348. This anthology of Cooper's critical prose has an excellent introduction which "includes a discussion of the critical prose, the social criticism in the novels, and two sections on 'The Pleasure and Business of the Novel' and 'The Purpose and Art of the Novel.' "

BIOGRAPHY: Boynton, H. W. *James Fenimore Cooper.* 1931.

Amer. Lit., 3:332. A "more authentic portrait than may be found in any earlier biography." The early chapters covering the years down to 1819 are especially well done.

Grossman, James. *James Fenimore Cooper.* (American Men of Letters, 1949).

Amer. Lit., 22:195. The author gives the main facts in Cooper's colorful career "in as much detail as a short biography permits." He summarizes the plots of Cooper's novels "with considerable literary skill." "His discussion of the Anti-Rent novels . . . is excellent, for here he uses his legal knowledge of the struggle between the patroon landlords and their tenants."

Lounsbury, T. R. *James Fenimore Cooper.* (American Men of Letters, 1883).

Atlantic, 51:540. An excellent study, more critical than biographical. Mr. Lounsbury "by his diligence and critical acumen has really rescued Cooper from oblivion."

Phillips, M. E. *James Fenimore Cooper.* 1913.

Nation, 96:210, Feb. 27, 1913. "A personal sketch of the man himself, not a new estimate of his writings."

Spiller, R. E. *Fenimore Cooper: Critic of His Times.* 1931.

Amer. Lit., 4:404. A book in which "Mr. Spiller brings to us the rich fruits of his study of Cooper's life, writings, and ideas." It is "a readable biography," which gives some new material, but still leaves "a dozen perplexing questions about Cooper's life and writings unanswered."

COLLECTIVE BIOGRAPHY: Brooks, V. W. *World of Washington Irving,* 214-33, 315-36, 399-425.

Erskine, John. *Leading American Novelists,* 51-129.

Parrington, V. L., Jr. *American Dreams,* 22-26.

Parrington, V. L. *Main Currents in American Thought,* 2:222-57.

Snell, G. B. *Shapers of American Fiction,* 15-27.

Van Doren, Carl, in *Cambridge History of American Literature,* 1:293-306.

——, in *DAB,* 4:400.

Williams, S. T., in *Literary History of the United States*, 1:253-69.

SPECIAL ASPECTS: Brownell, W. C. *American Prose Masters*, 3-60.

Canby, H. S. *Classic Americans*, 97-142.

Clavel, Marcel. *Fenimore Cooper and his Critics: American, British and French Criticism of the Novelist's Early Work.* 1938.

Amer. Lit., 10:498. Professor Clavel is a thorough student of Cooper. In his book he publishes for the first time "Cooper's own notes on his novels. . . ." Brief as these are, their inclusion "makes the book indispensable to anyone who would again review his literary career."

Clemens, Samuel. "Fenimore Cooper's Literary Offenses," *No. Am. Rev.*, 161 (1895) :1-2.

———. "Fenimore Cooper's Further Literary Offenses," *N. E. Quar.*, 19 (1946) :291-301.

Grossman, James. "James Fenimore Cooper: an Uneasy American," *Yale Rev.*, 40 (1951) :696-709.

Hazard, L. L. *The Frontier in American Literature*, 97-117.

Keiser, Albert. *The Indian in American Literature*, 101-43.

Lawrence, D. H. *Studies in Classic American Literature*, 50-92.

Leisey, E. E. *American Historical Novel*, (1950) :9-12, 56-57.

Mott, F. L. *Golden Multitudes*, 70-76.

Ross, J. F. *The Social Criticism of Fenimore Cooper.* (Univ. of Cal. Studies in English, 1933).

Amer. Lit., 5:201. Among other things Mr. Ross gives a sound "exposition of the major accusation brought by Cooper against Jacksonian America; namely that it was perverting the admirable principle of civil and political equality into a social dogma . . ." Some of the evidence concerning Cooper the critic is ignored, or slighted, by Mr. Ross.

Russell, J. A. "Cooper: Interpreter of the Real and Historical Indian," *Jour. of Amer. Hist.*, 23 (1930) :41-71.

Spiller, R. E. "Fenimore Cooper: Critic of His Times," *Amer. Lit.*, 1 (1929) :131-48.

Spiller, R. E., ed. "Fenimore Cooper's Defense of Slave-owning America," *AHR*, 35 (1930) :575-82.

Spiller, R. E. *The American in England*, 318-45.

Stanford, Alford, in Macy, John, ed. *American Writers on American Literature,* 72-80.

Waples, Dorothy. *The Whig Myth of James Fenimore Cooper.* 1938.

Amer. Lit., 10:376. A spirited but scholarly "denunciation of the blackening of Cooper's character by the Whig press of the Jacksonian period . . ." Perhaps Miss Waples has "overemphasized Cooper's political connections with the Democratic party," and the support given him "by the Democratic press at the time of the libel suits." There are a few errors, but this interesting book contains a surprising "wealth of new or little-known material . . . concerning Cooper's life and the reception of his works . . ."

Winters, Yvor. *In Defense of Reason,* (1947) :176-99.

PETER COOPER—   1791-1863   —Philanthropist

BIOGRAPHY: Nevins, Allan. *Abram S. Hewitt, with Some Account of Peter Cooper.* 1935.

AHR, 41:557. Abram Hewitt's father-in-law, Peter Cooper, "possessed a distinction of character that made him . . . one of the most prominent private citizens of the Republic. He exemplified the finest community spirit of the generation that all but remembered the living Franklin, whom he resembled in his homely devotion to civic service."

Mack, E. C. *Peter Cooper, Citizen of New York.* 1949.

AHR, 55:999. Professor Mack does not "capitalize on his subject's well-known eccentricities," but gives him "the affectionate full-length treatment that this fine American deserves." The book shows careful research and is well written. The background traces the development of New York City from "the small town of Cooper's boyhood to the teeming metropolis of his old age."

COLLECTIVE BIOGRAPHY: Brown, C. R. *There Were Giants,* 80-102.

Hubbard, Elbert. *Little Journeys to the Homes of Great Business Men,* 233-60.

McCausland, Elizabeth. "Cooper Union," *Mag. Art,* 40 (1947) : 242-44, 282-84, 322-24.

Parker, W. B., in *DAB,* 4:409.

Ulmann, Albert. *New Yorkers,* 197-212.

SAMUEL FINLEY BREESE MORSE—   1791-1872
—Inventor and Artist

BIOGRAPHY: *Mabee, Carleton. *The American Leonardo: a Life of Samuel F. B. Morse.* 1943.

---

* Awarded the Pulitzer prize.

AHR, 49:127. A scholarly, humane biography which enriches "our understanding of Morse, especially of his character, mind and career as an artist." The book is well-documented and well written, but it exaggerates the versatility of Morse.

COLLECTIVE BIOGRAPHY: Fox, D. R., and A. M. Schlesinger, eds. *Cavalcade of America*, 1st ser., (1937) :154-70.

Genzmer, G. H., in *DAB*, 13:247.

Iles, George. *Leading American Inventors*, (1912) :119-75.

Ulmann, Albert. *New Yorkers*, 170-96.

SPECIAL ASPECTS: Burlingame, Roger. *Inventors Behind the Inventor*, 64-89.

Morse, E. L. "Samuel F. B. Morse, the Painter," *Scribner's*, 51 (1912) :346-59.

Spiller, R. E. *The American in England*, 94-98.

LUCRETIA COFFIN MOTT— 1793-1880 —Quaker Reformer and Preacher

BIOGRAPHY: Hare, L. C. M. *The Greatest American Woman, Lucretia Mott*. 1937.

Nation, 145:299. Lucretia Mott "was a rare and saint-like person with an unusual mind." She was "an excellent Quaker preacher" who advocated abolition, temperance and the emancipation of women. Mr. Hare gives the main facts of her life, but fails to justify the title of his book.

COLLECTIVE BIOGRAPHY: Jenkins, A. E., in Foster, W. D., ed. *Heroines of Modern Religion*, 88-113.

Morris, Charles. *Heroes of Progress in America*, 219-25.

Williams, M. W., in *DAB*, 13:288.

CORNELIUS VANDERBILT— 1794-1877 —"The Greatest Self-made Native American Businessman of the Early Nineteenth Century"

BIOGRAPHY: Lane, W. J. *Commodore Vanderbilt: an Epic of the Steam Age*. 1942.

AHR, 48:139. The author carefully avoids being sensational and emphasizes Vanderbilt's business career, An authentic biography.

COLLECTIVE BIOGRAPHY: Andrews, Wayne. *The Vanderbilt Legend; the Story of the Vanderbilt Family, 1794-1940*. 1941.

N. Y. Times, Jan. 26, 1941, p. 1. An honest book in which "the facts speak for themselves. They speak eloquently. And so we see the cold-hearted, domineering profane figure of the Dutch ferry boy from Staten Island as he really must have been . . . The first 180 pages are devoted to the Commodore, and they touch upon every facet of his life, from his almost brutal boyhood to his hymn-singing old age."

Harlow, A. F., in *DAB*, 14:169.

Josephson, Matthew. *The Robber Barons*, 12-20, 66-74, index.

Minnigerode, Meade. *Certain Rich Men*, 103-33.

Myers, Gustavus. *History of the Great American Fortunes*, (1936) :273-76, 318-34.

Russell, Bertrand. *Freedom Versus Organization*, 301-10.

Scroggs, W. O. *Filibusters and Financiers*. 1916.

SPECIAL ASPECTS: Gras, N. S. B., and H. M. Larsons, eds. *Casebook in American Business History*, 359-72.

WILLIAM CULLEN BRYANT— 1794-1878 —Poet and Editor

ORIGINAL SOURCES: *McDowell, Termaine, ed. *William Cullen Bryant: Representative Selections*. (American Writers, 1935) .

Amer. Lit., 7:357. The introduction gives an excellent estimate of Bryant in the light of recent research.

BIOGRAPHY: Bigelow, John. *William Cullen Bryant*. (American Men of Letters, 1890) .

Harper's, 80:769. A brief biography by an intimate friend.

COLLECTIVE BIOGRAPHY: Brenner, Rica. *Twelve American Poets Before 1900*, 23-47.

Brooks, V. W. *The World of Washington Irving*, 234-61.

Leonard, W. E., in *Cambridge History of American Literature*, 1:260-78.

McDowell, Termaine, in *Literary History of the United States*, 1:294-305.

Parrington, V. L. *Main Currents in American Thought*, 2:238-46.

Pattee, F. L. *Side-Lights on American Literature*, 293-326.

---

* See also McDowell, pp. lxxiii-lxxxii; *Cambridge History of American Literature*, 1 (1917) :517-21; Spiller, et al. *Literary History of the United States*, 3 (1948) :422-27.

Phelps, W. L. "William Cullen Bryant, Father of American Poetry," *Ladies Home Journal*, 40 (1923) :14ff.

——. *Howells, James, Bryant, and Other Essays*, (1924) :1-30.

Stedman, E. C. *Poets of America*, 62-94.

SPECIAL ASPECTS: Bailey, E. J. *Religious Thought in the Greater American Poets*, 10-31.

Foerster, Norman. "Nature in Bryant's Poetry," *So. Atl. Quar.*, 17 (1918) :10-17.

——. *Nature in American Literature*, (1923) :7-19.

Glicksberg, C. L. "Bryant and the United States Review," *N. E. Quar.*, 7 (1934) :687-701.

——. "William Cullen Bryant and Fanny Wright," *Amer. Lit.*, 6 (1935) :427-32.

——. "William Cullen Bryant and the Nineteenth-Century Science," *N. E. Quar.*, 23 (1950) :91-96.

Laurence, Arthur. "Bryant and the Berkshire Hills," *Century*, 28 (1895) :368-75.

McDowell, Tremaine. "Cullen Bryant Prepares for College," *So. Atl. Quar.*, 30 (1931) :125-33.

——. "Cullen Bryant at Williams College," *N. E. Quar.*, 1 (1928) :443-66.

——. "Bryant and The North American Review," *Amer. Lit.*, 1 (1929) :14-26.

——. "William Cullen Bryant and Yale," *N. E. Quar.*, 3 (1930) : 706-16.

Nevins, Allan. *The Evening Post: a Century of Journalism*. 1922.

AHR, 28:553. The best account of Bryant's long career as an editor. It reveals his political liberalism, and shows that he gave the *Post* "balance, dignity and power for half a century," and that he and his associate, John Bigelow, gave the paper "a literary and scholarly flavor, as evidenced, for example, by its famous controversy on the editorial misdemeanors of President Jared Sparks . . ." Incidentally he "accumulated half a million dollars as a fair and fearless editor." He was a pioneer in championing worthy causes such as Central Park, the modern apartment house, and the international copyright.

Strong, A. H., in *American Poets and Their Theology* (1916) : 3-48.

FRANCES WRIGHT— 1795-1852 —Crusader for Social Justice

BIOGRAPHY: Perkins, A. J. G., and Theresa Wolfson. *Frances Wright, Free Enquirer: the Study of a Temperament.* 1939.

AHR, 46:224; *Amer. Lit.,* 12:129. An excellent biography which throws much light on the personality of one of the most interesting and fascinating women of the Fifth Generation. However, the authors fail to relate Miss Wright's ideas adequately to the Enlightenment, to Benthamism, and to other patterns of thought.

Waterman, W. R. *Frances Wright.* (Columbia Univ. Studies in History, Economics, and Public Law, 1924).

AHR, 30:614. An excellent biography based on Miss Wright's papers and contemporary newspapers.

COLLECTIVE BIOGRAPHY: Anthony, Katharine, in *DAB,* 20:549.

JAMES GORDON BENNETT— 1795-1872 —Father of the Yellow Journal

BIOGRAPHY: Carlson, Oliver. *The Man Who Made News: James Gordon Bennett.* 1942.

AHR, 48:606. A readable narrative that contends that as editor of the New York *Herald* Bennett was the first American to view the newspaper "as a purveyor of up-to-the-minute news rather than as a literary journal or party organ." Mr. Carlson fails to understand Bennett or his times, and does not give an adequate explanation of his "devious political course. . . ." There are some errors in the book, which however is "the best book on an important American figure . . ."

Seitz, D. C. *James Gordon Bennett: Father and Son: Proprietors of the New York Herald.* 1928.

N. Y. Times, Nov. 25, 1928, p. 9. James Gordon Bennett and his son constituted "the longest newspaper dynasty we Americans have known." They were a bold pair who broke traditions and printed things formerly shielded from the public gaze. Mr. Seitz is a former newspaperman and his book is "somewhat journalistic."

COLLECTIVE BIOGRAPHY: Beard, A. E. S. *Our Foreign-Born Citizens,* 59-64.

Lee, J. M. *History of American Journalism,* 193-200.

Mott, F. L. *History of American Journalism,* 229-38.

Nevins, Allan, in *DAB,* 2:195.

Villard, O. G. *Some Newspapers and Newspaper Men,* (1923): 273-81.

HISTORY: Levermore, C. H. "The Rise of Metropolitan Journalism," *AHR,* 6 (1901) :446-65.

ALEXANDER DALLAS BACHE— 1806-1867
—Physicist and "Key Figure in the Intellectual
Development of America"

BIOGRAPHY: Odgers, M. M. *Alexander Dallas Bache: Scientist and Educator, 1806-1867.* (Penna. Lives, 1947) .

AHR, 53:851. A very readable biography of a teacher and educator. "A key figure in the development of America at a time when many of our education and scientific institutions were becoming established."

COLLECTIVE BIOGRAPHY: Baurer, L. A., in *DAB,* 1:461.

JOHN AUGUSTUS ROEBLING— 1806-1869 —He
Designed Brooklyn Bridge

BIOGRAPHY: Schuler, Hamilton. *The Roeblings—a Century of Engineers, Bridge-Builders and Industrialists.* 1931.

Steinman, D. B. *The Builders of the Bridge: the Story of John Roebling and His Son.* 1945.

AHR, 51:136. The senior Roebling was a native of Germany who brought a colony of immigrants to the United States in 1831. The others settled down to farming. Roebling became "a builder of bridges, of railroad suspension bridges." Using wire ropes—his own invention—he built bridges across the two rivers at Pittsburgh, and across the Niagara and the Ohio. But his "greatest triumph was the Brooklyn Bridge." He designed this bridge, introducing "many new plans" in its construction. However, he "suffered an accident while working on the bridge and died," so his son took over the job. Mr. Steinman, himself a "noted bridge-builder and engineer," has given us "a dramatic biography of two notable members of his profession . . ."

COLLECTIVE BIOGRAPHY: Tilden, C. J., in *DAB,* 16:86.

SPECIAL ASPECTS: Muller, E. "Epic Human Story of Brooklyn Bridge," *Read. Dig.,* 52 (1948) :75-80.

EDWIN FORREST—1806-1872—"Earliest American-
Born Actor of the First Rank"

BIOGRAPHY: Moses, M. J. *The Fabulous Forrest: the Record of an American Actor.* 1930.

N. Y. Times, July 20, 1930, p. 5. Mr. Moses seems more interested "in Forrest the man than Forrest the actor . . . For much of the volume one is presented with a mass of conflicting evidence on Forrest's personality," but in the concluding chapter the author gives "a vivid picture of the actor in a few bold, unbiased strokes of characterization."

COLLECTIVE BIOGRAPHY: Barrett, Lawrence, in Matthews, Brander, and Lawrence Hutton. *Actors and Actresses of Great Britain and the United States*, 4 (1886) :33-67.

Eaton, W. P., in *DAB*, 6:529.

Seitz, D. C. *Uncommon Americans*, 291-312.

BIOGRAPHIES OF CONTEMPORARIES: Jefferson, Joseph. *"Rip Van Winkle": The Autobiography of Joseph Jefferson*, (1950): 121-30.

EDGAR ALLAN POE— 1809-1849 —"The Most Widely Read of America's Classic Authors"

ORIGINAL SOURCES: *Alterton, Margaret, and Hardin Craig. *Edgar Allan Poe: Representative Selections*. (American Writers, 1935).

N. E. Quar., 8:624. This little volume contains "an able introduction discussing the relation of Poe's philosophic-literary principles to his practices in his art, a capable selection of texts from Poe's fiction, criticism, and poetry, and a vast paraphernalia of bibliography, notes, and criticism."

Laverty, C. D., ed. "Poe in 1847," *Amer. Lit.*, 20 (1948) :163-68.

Ostrom, J. W., ed. *Letters of Edgar Allan Poe*. 2 vols. 1948.

Herald-Tribune Wk. Bk. Rev., Dec. 19, 1948, p. 1. This edition, with its elaborate critical apparatus, "is an indispensable tool for any student of Poe's life."

BIOGRAPHY: Allen, Hervey. *Israfel: the Life and Times of Edgar Allan Poe*. 1926. Rev. ed. 1934.

Amer. Lit., 7:223. A readable biography which brings out "as never before Poe's indebtedness to his environment, in Philadelphia especially . . ."

Quinn, A. H. *Edgar Allan Poe: a Critical Biography*. 1941.

Amer. Lit., 14:168. The best biography. While no unfavorable evidence has been suppressed or modified, whenever possible Mr. Quinn interprets "the facts in the light most favorable to Poe." The book "contains a large amount of new material," and eliminates "the false and unauthentic."

Woodberry, G. E. *Life of Edgar Allan Poe*. (American Men of Letters, 1885).

---

* See also Alterton and Craig, pp. cxix-cxxxiii; *Cambridge History of American Literature*, 2 (1917) :452-68; Spiller, et al. *Literary History of the United States*, 3 (1948) : 689-96.

Atlantic, 55:705. "Mr. Woodberry has done for Poe the greatest service which one man can render another. He has told the truth about him." A revised edition in two volumes appeared in 1909. It is still one of the best biographies, and some critics prefer it to Quinn.

COLLECTIVE BIOGRAPHY: Allen, Hervey, in *DAB,* 15:19.

Brooks, V. W. *Chilmark Miscellany,* 187-207, 303-09.

————. *The World of Washington Irving,* 337-61, 443-56.

Bruce, P. H. *The Virginia Plutarch,* 2:188-206.

Campbell, Killis, in *Cambridge History of American Literature,* 2:55-69.

Cargill, Oscar. *Intellectual America,* 176-310.

Matthiessen, F. O., in *Literary History of the United States,* 1: 321-42.

————, in *Sewanee Rev.,* 54 (1946) :175-205.

Parrington, V. L. *Main Currents in American Thought,* 2:57-59.

Russell, F. A. *American Pilgrimage,* 216-33.

Schnittkind, H. T. *Living Biographies of Great Poets,* 233-45.

Stedman, E. C. *Poets of America,* 255-73.

Thomas and Thomas. *Fifty Great Americans,* 164-72.

Ulmann, Albert. *New Yorkers,* 213-31.

SPECIAL ASPECTS: Alderman, E. A. "Edgar Allan Poe and the Universty of Virginia," *Va. Quar. Rev.,* 1 (1925) :78-84.

Bailey, E. J. *Religious Thought in the Greater American Poets,* 32-46.

Brownell, W. C. *American Prose Masters,* 207-67. Perhaps the most acute criticism.

Bruce, P. A. "Background of Poe's University Life," *So. Atl. Quar.,* 10 (1911) :212-26.

Campbell, Killis. *The Mind of Poe and Other Studies.* 1933.

New Republic, 76:27, Aug. 16, 1933. Professor Campbell shows "that far from being aloof from his time, Poe had many alliances with it. An important chapter gives the results of scrutinizing Poe's works for their autobiographical elements."

Collins, Joseph. *The Doctor Looks at Biography,* 168-76.

Fagin, N. B. *Histrionic Mr. Poe.* 1949.

Nation, 169:186, Aug. 20, 1949. A convincing and entertaining book that holds that "the mystery of Poe's life and the attraction of his works are largely explained by Poe's theatrical associations."

Foerster, Norman. *American Criticism*, 1-51.

Haycraft, Howard. *Art of the Mystery Story: a Collection of Critical Essays*, (1946) :158-77.

Hoole, W. S. "Poe in Charleston, S. C.," *Amer. Lit.*, 6:78-80.

Kent, C. W. "Poe's Student Days at the University of Virginia," *Bookman*, 13 (1901) :430-40; 44 (1916) :517-25.

Krutch, J. W. *Edgar Allan Poe: a Study in Genius*. 1926.

Sat. Rev. of Lit., 2:834, June 5, 1926. This is "a provocative little book, one of the best of many recent attempts to determine what light psychoanalysis throws on literature." However, his zeal for his thesis has led Professor Krutch into some errors of fact.

Lawrence, D. H. *Studies in Classic American Literature*, 93-120.

Also in Wilson, Edmund, ed. *The Shock of Recognition*, 966-84.

Marchand, Ernest. "Poe as Social Critic," *Amer. Lit.*, 6 (1934) : 28-43.

Markham, Edwin, in Macy, J. A., ed. *American Writers on American Literature*, 135-52.

Mencken, H. L. *Mencken Chrestomathy*, 479-81.

Snell, G. D. *Shapers of American Fiction, 1798-1947*, 45-60.

Whitman, S. H. *Edgar Poe and His Critics*. 1949.

Jour. South. Hist., 16:90. A reprint of a protest originally published eleven years after Poe's death. The pamphlet was "the first authoritative and convincing reply of any length to Griswold and those who took their cue from him."

Wilson, J. S. "The Devil Was in It," *Am Merc.*, 24 (1931) :215-20.

———. "Young Man Poe," *Va. Quar. Rev.*, 2:238-53.

Winters, Yvor. *In Defense of Reason*, 234-61.

JOHN HUMPHREY NOYES— 1811-1886   —The Founder of Oneida Community

BIOGRAPHY: Parker, R. A. *Yankee Saint: John Humphrey Noyes and the Oneida Community*. 1935.

Weekly Book Rev., Oct. 27, 1935, p. 18. A well-balanced study of an extraordinary man who rebelled against conventional morality.

COLLECTIVE BIOGRAPHY: Bidwell, P. W., in *DAB*, 13:589.

Holbrook, S. H. *Lost Men of American History*, 255-58.

ABRAM STEVENS HEWITT— 1822-1903 —Iron Master, Mayor and Congressman

BIOGRAPHY: Nevins, Allan. *Abram S. Hewitt, with Some Account of Peter Cooper*. 1935.

AHR, 41:557. A history of "the Cooper-Hewitt family and its work in industry, politics, and philanthropy . . ." Peter Cooper set his son-in-law, Abram Hewitt, in the way to become a progressive iron-master. After visiting England and Europe to study the new steel processes developed there, Hewitt established the first open-hearth furnaces in America. During the Railroad strike of 1877, he defended labor. His intimacy with Samuel Tilden led to his election to Congress, where he served for twelve years. He was mayor of New York for one term, and kept in touch with municipal affairs, promoting tenement house reform and parks in congested areas. He also served as a trustee of Columbia University and of the Carnegie Institution. After his death ex-mayor Seth Low said "New York seems lonely without Mr. Hewitt."

COLLECTIVE BIOGRAPHY: Parker, W. B., in *DAB*, 8:604.

Shepard, E. M. "Abram S. Hewitt, a Great Citizen," *Rev. of Reviews*, 27 (1903) :164-67.

Tyler, A. F. *Freedom's Ferment*, 184-95.

CHAPTER XXV. CHESAPEAKE BAY REGION

WILLIAM THORNTON—1759-1828—Architect and Inventor

COLLECTIVE BIOGRAPHY: Caemmerer, H. P. "Architects of the United States Capitol," *So. Atl. Quar.*, 44 (1945) :202-16.

Kimball, Fiske, in *DAB*, 18:504.

SPECIAL ASPECTS: Hunt, Gaillard. "William Thornton and Negro Colonization," *Proc. Am. Antiquarian Soc.*, Apr., 1920.

ANNE NEWPORT ROYALL —1769-1854 —Early Newspaper Woman

BIOGRAPHY: Jackson, G. S. *Uncommon Scold: the Story of Anne Royall*. 1937.

AHR, 44:453. An interesting account of a picturesque character. The old lady's comments and descriptions are not wholly accurate, "but they furnish many interesting details, especially of the philanthropic and reform movements which she so thoroughly detested." The account of her trial as a common scold is quite a legal curiosity.

Porter, S. H. *Life and Times of Anne Royall.* 1909.

COLLECTIVE BIOGRAPHY: Blakenhorn, Heber. "The Grandma of The Muckrakers," *Am. Merc.,* Sept., 1927.

Bridenbaugh, J. H., in *DAB,* 16:204.

Wright, R. L. *Forgotten Ladies,* 156-86.

ROGER BROOKE TANEY— 1777-1864 —Eminent Jurist or Politician in the Chief Justice's Black Robe?

BIOGRAPHY: Palmer, B. W. *Marshall and Taney, Statesmen of the Law.* 1939.

AHR, 45:717. A popular book. "It is vigorously and pungently written and seems, in the main, to be an accurate portrayal."

Smith, C. W., Jr. *Roger B. Taney: Jacksonian Jurist.* 1936.

N. Y. Times, Feb. 16, 1936, p. 18. "This book is not a biography of the author of the Dred Scott decision but is a solid and heavily documented study of his political theory and his work in constitutional interpretation. As such it is valuable."

Steiner, B. C. *Life of Roger Brooke Taney, Chief Justice of the U. S. Supreme Court.* 1922.

AHR, 28:556. A biography which strips "the eulogistic varnish from the most authentic of the earlier portraits of its hero," and adds "a number of unflattering details." The book is "far too long. The pages bristle with details, which reveal little or nothing of Taney's character, his point of view, or the real measure of his public services."

Swisher, C. B. *Roger B. Taney.* 1935.

AHR, 43:415. A definitive biography in line with the recent tendency to recognize Taney as one of our greatest chief justices. Mr. Swisher gives us "a living historical portrait" of the man, and a higher estimate of the Justice than that given by Burgess Rhodes and William Graham Sumner.

COLLECTIVE BIOGRAPHY: Swisher, C. B., in *DAB,* 18:289.

Umbreit, K. B. *Our Eleven Chief Justices,* 196-246.

WINFIELD SCOTT— 1786-1866 —Troubleshooter

BIOGRAPHY: Elliott, C. W. *Winfield Scott: the Soldier and the Man.* 1937.

AHR, 43:655. "A definitive biography" based on wide research. The author, however, fails to explain why a man who frequently quarreled with his colleagues was so successful in settling border disputes! "Scott's faults are not spared," yet they are subordinated to those qualities which made him "a great soldier and a useful citizen . . ." The book "is not entirely free from error."

Smith, A. D. H. *Old Fuss and Feathers: the Life and Exploits of Lt. Gen. Winfield Scott*. 1937.

AHR, 43:655. A popular biography which in spite of a surprising number of errors gives "a fair idea of Scott's personality and services to his country . . ."

COLLECTIVE BIOGRAPHY: Bruce, P. A. *The Virginia Plutarch*, 1: 171-88.

Gance, W. A., in *DAB*, 16:505.

Lewis, Lloyd. "Old Fuss and Feathers," *Am. Merc.*, 24 (1931): 480-89.

Seitz, D. C. *The "Also Rans,"* 125-44.

Stone, Irving. *They Also Ran*, 119-89.

JOHN TYLER—   1790-1862   —"His Accidency the President"

BIOGRAPHY: Chitwood, O. P. *John Tyler, Champion of the Old South*. 1939.

AHR, 46:171. Professor Chitwood gives an adequate account of Tyler as a Virginia politician; but is not wholly abreast of recent research in dealing with the bank controversy and foreign affairs.

COLLECTIVE BIOGRAPHY: Abernethy, T. P., in *DAB*, 19:88.

Agar, Herbert. *The People's Choice*, 138-43.

Levin, P. R. *Seven by Chance*, 8-54.

Young and Middleton. *Heirs Apparent*, 121-29.

HISTORY: Agar, Herbert. *The Price of Union*, 296-301.

Bowers, C. G. *Party Battles of the Jackson Period*.

SPECIAL ASPECTS: Lambert, O. D. *Presidential Politics in the United States, 1841-1844*. 1936.

AHR, 43:164. "In this book Mr. Lambert takes for his key to an understanding of Tyler's unhappy administration the conflicting personal ambitions and maneuverings of the leading political figures for the presidency in 1844. . . . The reviewer takes issue "with Mr. Lambert's interpretation of the causes of this situation." She argues that Tyler acted on principles, and that the author "confuses Clay and his followers with the Whig party."

Perling, J. J. *Presidents' Sons*, 86-107.

Pollard, J. E. *Presidents and the Press*, 211-25.

DUFF GREEN— 1791-1875 —"Independent Editor"

COLLECTIVE BIOGRAPHY: Green, F. M. "Duff Green, Militant Journalist of the Old School," *AHR*, 52 (1947) :247-64.

Green, F. M., in *DAB*, 7:540.

SPECIAL ASPECTS: Green, F. M. "Duff Green: Industrial Promoter," *Jour. South. Hist.*, 2 (1936) :3-28.

FRANCIS PRESTON BLAIR—1791-1876—Journalist and Politician

BIOGRAPHY: Smith, W. E. *The Francis Preston Blair Family in Politics.* 1933.

AHR, 39:350. Blair was a Kentuckian whom Jackson called to Washington in 1831 to edit the *Globe*. For fifteen years this was "probably the most influential Democratic journal in the country." Blair "exercised great potential political power" as a friend of both Jackson and Van Buren. After the election of President Polk, however, he drifted away from the Democratic party and along with his sons, Montgomery and Junior, joined the Republican party. After the death of Lincoln the Blairs "drifted back into the Democratic fold." Using the family papers, Professor Smith has given us an excellent "political history of the Blair family."

COLLECTIVE BIOGRAPHY: Clay, T. M. "Two Years with Old Hickory," *Atlantic*, 60 (1887) :187-99.

Smith, W. E., in *DAB*, 2:332.

HISTORY: Bowers, C. G. *Party Battles of the Jackson Period*, 160-67.

DRED SCOTT—   C. 1795-1858   —Slave

COLLECTIVE BIOGRAPHY: Barclay, T. S., in *DAB*, 16:488.

Holbrook, S. H. *Lost Men of American History*, 160-63.

SPECIAL ASPECTS: Hodder, F. H. "Some Phases of the Dred Scott Case," *MVHR*, 16 (1929) :3-22.

Stenberg, R. R. "Some Political Aspects of the Dred Scott Case," *MVHR*, 19 (1933) :571-77.

Warren, Charles. *Supreme Court in American History*, 2:279-319.

BIOGRAPHIES OF CONTEMPORARIES: Swisher, C. B. *Roger B. Taney*, (1935) :485ff.

JOHN PENDELTON KENNEDY— 1795-1870
—Novelist of Virginia Life

ORIGINAL SOURCES: Wynne, James, in *Harper's*, 25 (1862) :335-40.

BIOGRAPHY: Gwarhmey, E. M. *John Pendelton Kennedy*. 1931.

Amer. Lit., 4:76. "An array of documents affording some new information on the life of John Pendelton Kennedy" but not a well-organized biography.

COLLECTIVE BIOGRAPHY: Parrington, V. L. *Main Currents in American Thought*, 2:46-56.

Wade, J. D., in *Literary History of the United States*, 1:307-10.

Williams, M. W., in *DAB*, 10:333.

SPECIAL ASPECTS: Campbell, Killis. "The Kennedy Papers," *Sewanee Rev.*, 25 (1917) :1-19, 193-208, 348-60.

Moore, J. R. "Kennedy's Horse-Shoe Robinson: Fact or Fiction?" *Amer. Lit.*, 4:160-66.

MARGARET O'NEALE EATON— 1796-1879
—Adventuress

ORIGINAL SOURCE: Eaton, Margaret O'Neale Timberlake. *The Autobiography of Peggy Eaton*. 1932.

BIOGRAPHY: Pollack, Queena. *Peggy Eaton: Democracy's Mistress*. 1931.

MVHR, 18:256. The picturesque career of the tavern-keeper's daughter whose husband became Secretary of War is traced with charm but with much detail.

COLLECTIVE BIOGRAPHY: Abernethy, T. P., in *DAB*, 14-41.

Croffut, W. A. *American Procession*, 82-95.

Minnigerode, Meade. *Some American Ladies*, 241-87.

Peacock, V. T. *Famout American Belles of the 19th Century*, 69-79.

HISTORY: Bowers, C. G. *Party Battles of the Jackson Period*, 116ff.

BIOGRAPHIES OF CONTEMPORARIES: *Burke, P. W. *Emily Donelson of Tennessee,* 1:179-90.

HARRIET TUBMAN— 1800?-1913 —"Moses of Her People"

BIOGRAPHY: Conrad, Earl. *Harriet Tubman.* 1943.

AHR, 49:541. The "first full-length biography of a woman born in slavery in Maryland." The author tells how she "conducted from two to three hundred slaves" through the underground railway, and how she served as a scout, a spy and a nurse. The author charges that white publishers refused to publish this story of "an American heroine of yesterday."

FREDERICK DOUGLASS— 1817?-1895 —Negro Abolitionist

BIOGRAPHY: Foner, P. S.*The Life and Writings of Frederick Douglass.* Vol. I, *Early Years, 1817-1849;* Vol. II, *Pre Civil War Decade, 1850-1860.* 1950.

Jour. of Negro Hist., 35:320. "The first portion, roughly one-fifth, of each of these volumes is a standard 'life and times' treatment: in the remaining four-fifths of each volume Douglass speaks in his own words."

Graham, Shirley. *There Was Once a Slave: the Heroic Story of Frederick Douglass.* 1947.

AHR, 53:356. A fictionized biography which dramatizes Douglass while adhering closely to fact.

Quarles, Benjamin. *Frederick Douglass.* 1948.

AHR, 54:156. A well-written biography of a colorful figure who rose "by his own efforts and forceful personality not only to be the leading person of his race but to be recognized as an outstanding American . . ." The book is based on extensive research, is impartial, and gives a sound estimate of Douglass' influence.

Washington, B. T. *Frederick Douglass.* 1907.

AHR, 13:624. An unusually well-written study which presents Douglass as an object lesson for his race.

COLLECTIVE BIOGRAPHY: Brawley, B. G. *Negro Builders and Heroes,* 61-66.

DuBois, W. E. B., in *DAB,* 5:406.

Herndon, Angelo, in *There Were Giants in the Land,* 137-43.

Moxcey, M. E., in Lotz, P. H., ed. *Rising Above Color,* 58-65.

---

* See page 206.

Roger, J. A. *World's Great Men of Color,* 537-49.
HISTORY: Franklin, J. H. *From Slavery to Freedom: a History of American Negroes,* (1947) : see index.
SPECIAL ASPECTS: Dreer, Herman. *American Literature by Negro Authors,* (1950) :116-21, 187-88.

CHAPTER XXVI. CAROLINA AND GEORGIA

THOMAS COOPER—1759-1839—Versatile Scholar or Wild-eyed Radical?

BIOGRAPHY: Malone, Dumas. *The Public Life of Thomas Cooper, 1783-1839.* 1926.

AHR, 32:618. A "remarkably vivid" picture of "a most fascinating personality as contemporaries saw him."

COLLECTIVE BIOGRAPHY: Jaffe, Bernard. *Men of Science in America,* 78-103.

Malone, Dumas, in *DAB,* 4:414.

SPECIAL ASPECTS: Malone, Dumas. "The First Years of Thomas Cooper in America, 1794-1801," *So. Atl. Quar.,* 22 (1923) :139-56.

WILLIAM GASTON— 1778-1844 —North Carolina Legislator & Jurist

BIOGRAPHY: Schauinger, J. H. *William Gaston, Carolinian.* 1949.

MVHR, 37:123. "A fairly complete and well-balanced account of Gaston's career." Mr. Schauinger used a variety of sources in gathering his material; unfortunately his book contains a number of errors.

COLLECTIVE BIOGRAPHY: Connor, R. D. W., in *DAB,* 7:180.

Hannon, W. B. "Judge William Gaston, Statesman and Jurist," *Jour. Am. Irish Historical Society,* 10 (1911) :253-58.

HISTORY: Ashe, S. A. *Biographical History of North Carolina,* 2:99-108.

JOEL ROBERTS POINSETT—1779-1851—Father of the Smithsonian Institution

BIOGRAPHY: Rippy, J. F. *Joel R. Poinsett, Versatile American.* 1935.

AHR, 42:152. Using the Poinsett papers in the Historical Society of Pennsylvania, Rippy has written an interesting brief biography of a neglected figure. Poinsett used too direct methods to be an effective diplomat in South America or Mexico. His wide travel made him a nationalist in South Carolina during the Nullification crisis, but he represented a minority. His "most effective service was as Secretary of War under Van Buren."

COLLECTIVE BIOGRAPHY: Rippy, J. F., in *DAB*, 15:30.

SPECIAL ASPECTS: "Flower that Symbolizes Christmas," *Pan. Am. Union Bul.*, 81 (1947) :689-90.

JOHN CALDWELL CALHOUN—1782-1852—"The Most Influential Defender of the Old South"

ORIGINAL SOURCES: Boucher, C. S., and R. P. Brooks, eds. "Correspondence Addressed to John C. Calhoun, 1837-1849," in *Ann. Report of the Amer. Hist. Assoc.*, 1 (1929) :127-533.

Jameson, J. F., ed. "Correspondence of John C. Calhoun," in *Ann. Report of the Amer. Hist. Assoc.*, 1899; vol. 2, 1900.

Waring, A. N. "Letters of John C. Calhoun to Patrick Noble, 1812-1837," *Jour. South. Hist.*, 16 (1950) :64-73.

BIOGRAPHY: *Coit, M. L. *John C. Calhoun: American Portrait.* 1950.

AHR, 55:910. This "warm, sympathetic account of Calhoun's career," is "an excellent synthesis" of his life and times. It is based on wide research and shows keen understanding. Miss Coit's interpretation varies in detail from Hofstadter and Current; she agrees in some respects with Schlesinger. She is inclined to exaggerate the Carolinian's achievements somewhat. Her book is the best one-volume biography.

Holst, Hermann. *John C. Calhoun.* 1882.

Hunt, Gaillard. *John C. Calhoun.* (American Crisis, 1908.)

AHR, 14:368. Pictures Calhoun as neither god nor monster, but as a man who was forced to adapt himself to a changing environment.

Meigs, W. M. *The Life of John Caldwell Calhoun.* 2 vols. 1917.

AHR, 23:872. A careful study based on wide research. Says Calhoun derived his nationalism from Jefferson and the frontier. Concludes that the Carolinian's fight to form a Southern bloc headed by Virginia was defeated by Editor Thomas Ritchie.

Styron, Arthur. *The Cast-Iron Man: John C. Calhoun and American Democracy.* 1935.

---

* Awarded the Pulitzer Prize.

AHR, 42:362. The author throws little light on Calhoun's personality and give an inadequate explanation of why an ardent nationalist became a champion of sectionalism.

Wiltse, C. M. *John C. Calhoun, Nationalist, 1782-1828.* 1944.

———. *John C. Calhoun, Nullifier, 1829-1839.* 1949.

AHR, 50:550, 55:161. An able and sympathetic study, based on wide research. It refutes the idea that Calhoun was a political trickster, or traitor, and presents him as an attractive personality and an understandable leader of the South. Mr. Wiltse maintains that the South Carolinian originally favored broad use of Federal powers and championed state's rights only when he saw that Northern protectionists had perverted the nationalist doctrine to sectional ends. These two volumes are the best biography of Calhoun we have and the best study of the age of Jackson. A third volume will follow.

COLLECTIVE BIOGRAPHY: Agar, Herbert. *The People's Choice,* 125-28.

Bradford, Gamaliel. *As God Made Them,* 87-127.

Dodd, W. E. *Statesmen of the Old South,* 91-167.

Hendrick, B. J. *Bulwark of the Republic,* 213-33, 280-82.

Hofstadter, Richard. *American Political Tradition,* 67-91.

Johnson, G. W. *America's Silver Age,* 38-47.

Macartney, C. L. N. *Men Who Missed It,* 22-30.

Phillips, U. B., in *DAB,* 3:411.

Seitz, D. C. *The "Also Rans,"* 53-76.

Smith, M. B. *The First Forty Years of Washington Society.* 1906.

Thompson, C. L. "John C. Calhoun, Apostle of the South," *Current Hist.,* 14 (1948) :146-52.

Young and Middleton. *Heirs Apparent,* 79-93.

HISTORY: Bowers, C. G. *Party Battles of the Jackson Period.*

SPECIAL ASPECTS: Carpenter, J. T. *The South as a Conscious Minority.*

Current, R. N. "John C. Calhoun, Philosopher of Reaction," *Antioch Rev.,* 3 (1943) :223-34.

Fitzsimons, M. A., "Calhoun's Bid for the Presidency, 1841-1844," *MVHR,* 38 (1951) :39-60.

Gabriel, R. H. *American Democratic Thought,* 103-110.

Hay, T. R. "John C. Calhoun and the Presidential Campaign of 1824," *No. Car. Hist. Rev.,* 12 (1935) :20-44.

Jacobson, J. M. *Development of American Political Thought,* 414-25.

Merriam, C. E. *American Political Theories,* 267-304.

———. "The Political Philosophy of John C. Calhoun," in Garner, J. W., ed. *Studies in Southern History and Politics,* (1914) :319-38.

Pinckney, C. C. "John C. Calhoun from a Southern Standpoint," *Lippincott's Mo. Mag.,* 62 (1898) :81-90.

Rayback, J. G. "Presidential Ambitions of John C. Calhoun, 1844-1848," *Jour. South. Hist.,* 14:331-56.

Schultz, H. S., "A Century of Calhoun Biographies," *So. Atl. Quar.,* 50 (1951) :248-54.

Sioussat, St. G. L., in Bemis, S. F., ed. *American Secretaries of State,* 5:127-233.

Stephenson, N. W. *Lectures on Typical Americans* (Scripps College Papers, Nov. 3, 1930) :21-38.

———. "Calhoun, 1812, and After," *AHR,* 31 (1926) :701-07.

Wiltse, C. M. "Critical Southerner: John C. Calhoun on the Revolution of 1848," *Jour. South. Hist.,* 15 (1949) :299-310.

———. "John C. Calhoun and the A. B. Plot," *Jour. South. Hist.,* 13 (1947) :46-61.

Wilson, F. G. *The American Political Mind,* 219-30.

JOHN ENGLAND— 1786-1842 —Catholic Bishop of Charleston

BIOGRAPHY: Grant, D. F. *John England: American Christopher.* 1949.

Jour. South. Hist., 16:86. "A brief but impressive biography of the first [Roman Catholic] bishop of Charleston." "Mrs. Grant presents ample evidence of his militant but tempered defense of Catholic doctrine and practise," but fails to give an ordered account of "the great bishop's constructive work to make his church and its priesthood an integral part of the South and of the United States."

Guilday, Peter. *Life and Times of John England, 1786-1842.* 2 vols. 1927.

AHR, 33:674. A well-written, objective biography of a strong personality who labored against many obstacles to build up the Catholic church in the Carolinas and Georgia.

COLLECTIVE BIOGRAPHY: Purcell, R. J., in *DAB,* 6:161.

BIOGRAPHIES OF CONTEMPORARIES: Schauinger, J. H. *William Gaston, Carolinian.* 1949.

JAMES HENRY HAMMOND— 1786-1857 —Planter and Political Leader

BIOGRAPHY: Merritt, Elizabeth. *James Henry Hammond, 1807-1864.* (Johns Hopkins Studies, 1923) .

AHR, 29:611. "An excellent study of a brilliant but eccentric planter who served as Governor of South Carolina and United States Senator, then moved to Texas in 1855.

COLLECTIVE BIOGRAPHY: Hamilton, J. G. de R., in *DAB,* 8:207.

AUGUSTUS BALDWIN LONGSTREET— 1790-1870 —Educator and Humorist

BIOGRAPHY: Wade, J. D. *Augustus Baldwin Longstreet: a Study of the Development of Culture in the South.* 1924.

AHR, 30:181. An entertaining biography of a talented Georgian who was by turns a lawyer, journalist, Methodist minister and college president, but who is best known as the author of *Georgia Scenes.*

COLLECTIVE BIOGRAPHY: Aswell, J. R., ed. *Native American Humor,* 54-59, index.

Hudson, A. P. *Humor of the Old Deep South,* 315-31.

Meine, F. J. *Tall Tales of the Southwest,* 17-21.

Parrington, V. L. *Main Currents in American Thought,* 2:166-72.

Wade, J. D., in *DAB,* 11:390.

SPECIAL ASPECTS: Wade, J. D., in Odum, H. W., ed. *Southern Pioneers in Social Interpretation,* 117-40.

HUGH SWINTON LEGARÉ— 1797-1843 —"The Most Cultivated Mind in the South Before the Civil War"

BIOGRAPHY: Rhea, Linda. *Hugh Swinton Legaré, a Charleston Intellectual.* 1934.

AHR, 40:350. Dr. Rhea gives a better treatment of Legaré as a literary man than as an officeholder and politician.

COLLECTIVE BIOGRAPHY: Hamilton, J. G. de R., in *DAB,* 11:144.

Parrington, V. L. *Main Currents in American Thought,* 2:114-24.

Ramage, B. J. "Legaré's Youth," *Sewanee Rev.,* 10 (1902) :43-55.

——. "Legaré, the Statesman," *ibid,* 10 (1902) :167-80.

WILLIAM GREGG—   1800-1867   —"The Father of Southern Cotton Manufacture"

BIOGRAPHY: Mitchell, Broadus. *William Gregg, Factory Master of the Old South.* 1928.

AHR, 34:399. A brief biography which gives the main facts in the life of a Virginian who established a factory in South Carolina and sought to raise the standard of living for the poor whites. The author fails to reveal "where Gregg found his best markets."

COLLECTIVE BIOGRAPHY: Mitchell, Broadus, in *DAB,* 7:599.

FRANCIS LIEBER—   1800-1872   —German Refugee Who Taught Political Science in Carolina and New York

BIOGRAPHY: Freidal, Frank. *Francis Lieber, Nineteenth-Century Liberal.* (Southern Biography, 1948) .

AHR, 55:160. "An exceptionally adequate biography" of a European refugee who became "the first outstanding American scholar" in the field of political science.

COLLECTIVE BIOGRAPHY: Dorfman, Joseph, and R. G. Tugwell, "Francis Lieber, German Scholar in America," *Columbia Univ. Quar.,* 30 (1938) :159-90, 267-93.

Parrington, V. L. *Main Currents in American Thought,* 2:93-98.

Sears, L. M. "The Human Side of Francis Lieber," *So. Atl. Quar.,* 27 (1928) :42-61.

Vincent, J. M., in *DAB,* 11:236.

SPECIAL ASPECTS: Curti, Merle. "Francis Lieber and Nationalism," *Huntington Library Quar.,* 4 (1941) :263-92.

Freidal, Frank. "Francis Lieber, Charles Sumner, and Slavery," *Jour. South. Hist.,* 9 (1943) : 75-93.

WILLIAM LOWNDES YANCEY— 1814-1863
—Ardent Secessionist

ORIGINAL SOURCES: Dumond, D. L. *Southern Editorials on Secession.* 1931.

COLLECTIVE BIOGRAPHY: Brown, W. G. *The Lower South in American History,* (1903) :115-54.

Dumond, D. L., in *DAB*, 20:592.

SPECIAL ASPECTS: Seitz, D. C. *Famous American Duels,* 310-16.

CRAWFORD WILLIAMSON LONG— 1815-1878
—Discoverer of Anasthesia?

COLLECTIVE BIOGRAPHY: Flexner, J. T. *Doctors on Horseback,* 293-310, 333-52.

Fulton, J. F., in *DAB*, 11:374.

Leonardo, R. A. *Lives of Master Surgeons,* 261-62.

Robinson, Victor. *Victory Over Pain,* 83-92.

SPECIAL ASPECTS: Boland, F. K. *The First Anesthetic: the Story of Crawford Long.* 1950.

Ga. Hist. Quar., 35:169. "A valuable contribution to the history of Medicine."

CHAPTER XXVII. THE OLD NORTHWEST

WILLIAM HENRY HARRISON— 1773-1841 —"Old Tippecanoe"

BIOGRAPHY: Cleaves, Freeman. *Old Tippecanoe: William Henry Harrison and His Time.* 1939.

Books, Jan. 21, 1940, p. 5. A first-class biography based on considerable research which suggests that Harrison was a better Indian fighter than he was a statesman.

Goebel, D. B. *William Henry Harrison, a Political Biography.* (Indiana Historical Collections, 1926) .

AHR, 32:895. A scholarly and readable biography which emphasizes Harrison's political and military activities.

Green, J. A. *William Henry Harrison: His Life and Times.* 1941.

AHR, 48:132. A eulogistic biography. The author is justified in estimating Harrison as a generous and kindly man, but critical historians cannot accept his assumption that our ninth president was a great public figure.

COLLECTIVE BIOGRAPHY: Booth, E. T. *Country Life in America,* 148-68.

Goebel, D. B., in *DAB,* 8:348.

Levin, P. R. *Seven by Chance,* 8-17.

SPECIAL ASPECTS: Perling, J. J. *Presidents' Sons,* 73-85.

Pollard, J. E. *Presidents and the Press,* 201-11.

JOHN CHAPMAN—1774-1847—"Johnny Appleseed"

COLLECTIVE BIOGRAPHY: Coulter, F. C. "American Pioneer," *House and Gard.,* 89 (1946) :104-05.

Haley, W. D., in *Harper's,* 43 (1871) :830-36.

Lindsay, Vachel. "In Praise of Johnny Appleseed," *Century,* 102 (1921) :545-52.

Also ———, in *Collected Poems,* 82-90.

Peattie, D. C., in *DAB,* 4:17.

SPECIAL ASPECTS: Price, Robert. "A Boyhood for 'Jonny Appleseed,'" *N. E. Quar.,* 17 (1944) :381-93.

———. "The New England Origins of 'Jonny Appleseed,'" *N. E. Quar.,* 12 (1939) :454-69.

Wecter, Dixon. *The Hero in American History,* 193-98.

DANIEL DRAKE—   1785-1852   —"The Father of Western Medicine"

ORIGINAL SOURCES: Horine, E. P., M.D., ed. *Pioneer Life in Kentucky, 1785-1800.* 1948.

AHR, 54:225. A collection of letters of Dr. Drake describing the frontier conditions of his youth. This frontier doctor was a predecessor of Mark Twain "whom in background and literary qualities of vividness and humor he somewhat resembles . . ." The letters "were not designed as a literary performance. They were merely the offhand familiar talk of a father to his children."

Rosen, George, and Beate Caspari-Rosen, eds. *400 Years of a Doctor's Life,* 6-11, 33-34, 63-66.

COLLECTIVE BIOGRAPHY: Flexner, J. T. *Doctors on Horseback,* 165-234.

Mathews, A. P., in *DAB*, 5:426.

HISTORY: *Buley, R. C. *The Old Northwest*, 2:543-45.

WILLIAM BEAUMONT—1785-1853—Army Doctor

ORIGINAL SOURCES: Beaumont, William. *William Beaumont's Formative Years; Two Early Notebooks, 1811-1821.* 1946.

Rosen, George, and Beate Caspari-Rosen, eds. *400 Years of a Doctor's Life,* 365-66.

COLLECTIVE BIOGRAPHY: Flexner, J. T. *Doctors on Horseback,* 237-92.

Vaughan, V. C., in *DAB*, 2:104.

PETER CARTWRIGHT— 1785-1872 —Backwoods Preacher

ORIGINAL SOURCES: Stone, Irving, and Richard Kennedy, eds. *We Speak for Ourselves,* 403-08.

Strickland, W. P., ed. *Autobiography of Peter Cartwright, the Backwoods Preacher.* 1857.

Extract in Flanagan, J. T., ed. *America is West,* 165-69.

BIOGRAPHY: Grant, H. H. *Peter Cartwright, Pioneer.* 1931.

Christian Century, 48:380, Mar. 18, 1931. Mrs. Grant describes Peter Cartwright as a "vigorous, vital, and picturesque figure" who "rode herd on the saints and sinners of the frontier." He fought slavery and intemperance and sought to make the world "safe for Methodism."

COLLECTIVE BIOGRAPHY: Bates, E. S., in *DAB*, 3:546.

Chamberlin, M. H., in *Trans. of the Ill. State Hist. Soc.,* (1902) : 47-56.

Flexner, J. T. *Doctors on Horseback,* 165-234.

Miller, B. W. *Ten Famous Evangelists,* 52-58.

Tyler, A. F. *Freedom's Ferment,* 35-40.

JAMES HALL—1793-1868—"Literary Pioneer of the Illinois Country"

BIOGRAPHY: Flanagan, J. T. *James Hall, Literary Pioneer of the Ohio Valley.* 1941.

---

* Awarded the Pulitzer Prize.

AHR, 48:373. A biography of a frontier judge who fought outlaws, but is best remembered for his writings about pioneer life.

COLLECTIVE BIOGRAPHY: Scott, F. W., in *DAB*, 8:134.

HISTORY: Buley, R. C. *The Old Northwest,* 2:539-90.

Rusk, R. L. *The Literature of the Middle Western Frontier,* 1: 171-77, 2:74-84.

CATHARINE ESTHER BEECHER—   1800-1878
—Educator and Reformer

COLLECTIVE BIOGRAPHY: Beecher, C. E. *Educational Reminiscences and Suggestions.* 1874.

Also in Barnard, Henry, in *Amer. Jour. of Educ.,* 28:65-94.

Chase, W. J., in *DAB,* 2:125.

Goodsell, Willystine. *Pioneers of Women's Education in the United States,* 113-226.

Mussey, J. B., ed. *Yankee Life by Those Who Lived It,* 379-80.

Stowe, L. B. *Saints, Sinners and Beechers,* 73-137.

Thorp, M. F. *Female Persuasion,* (1949) :11-55.

HISTORY: Woody, Thomas. *History of Women's Education in the United States,* vol. I, see index.

ROBERT DALE OWEN—   1801-1877   —"Social Reformer"

BIOGRAPHY: Leopold, R. W. *Robert Dale Owen: a Biography.* (Harvard Historical Studies, 1940)

AHR, 47:150. A scholarly biography of a versatile reformer who worked with his father, Robert Owen, in the experimental community at New Harmony, Indiana, and who later "conducted a free-thought, feminist, anticlerical journal in association with Frances Wright . . ." He also served as a member of the legislature of Indiana, and later as a member of Congress. Dale was a gifted man, but Dr. Leopold thinks his versatility was a hindrance to his success.

Pancoast, Elinor, and A. E. Lincoln. *The Incorrigible Idealist: Robert Dale Owen in America.* 1940.

Amer. Lit., 12:394. Robert Dale Owen was a leader in the radical movement of the 1820's—labor, education, women's rights, birth control. But later, when the Abolitionists came in, "Owen gravitated to the other side, advocated Texan annexation, denounced the Wilmot Proviso as unconstitutional, and helped forbid in 1850, the immigration of free Negroes into Indiana."

COLLECTIVE BIOGRAPHY: Fichter, J. H. *Roots of Change*; 87-111.

Mitchell, Broadus, in *DAB*, 14:118.

Mumford, Lewis. *The Story of Utopias*. 1922.

Bookman, 56:769, Feb., 1923. Analysis and criticism of various utopian schemes from Plato to H. G. Wells.

HISTORY: Bestor, A. E., Jr. *Backwoods Utopias: the Sectarian and Owenite Phases of Communitarian Socialism in America: 1663-1829*. 1950.

AHR, 55:923. Professor Bestor has made a thorough study of "the Owenite movement and offers a very credible explanation for its popularity in America, its weakness, and its early collapse." He concentrates largely on Robert Owen, his two sons and the educators and scientists attracted by the experiment at New Harmony, Indiana.

Young, Marguerite. *Angel in the Forest: a Fairy Tale of Two Utopias*. 1945.

AHR, 51:162. This story of New Harmony, Indiana, deals with the communistic and socialistic experiments of Father Rapp and Robert Owen. The book was written "after much research" but the facts are "embroidered with fancy, humor, and a touch of irony which, to some extent, detract from the history."

THEODORE DWIGHT WELD— 1803-1895
—"Forgotten Abolitionist"

ORIGINAL SOURCES: Barnes, G. H., and D. L. Dumond, eds. *Letters of Theodore Dwight Weld, Angelina Grimké, Weld, and Sarah Grimké, 1822-1844*. 2 vols. 1934.

AHR, 41:162. These letters—some of them love letters—were found about 1930 "in an old trunk in a Massachusetts farmhouse." They throw much light on Weld's character and have given us a new interpretation of the anti-slavery movement.

BIOGRAPHY: Thomas, B. P. *Theodore Weld, Crusader for Freedom*. 1950.

AHR, 56:912. Accepting Barnes' "highly eulogistic statement of Weld's stature," and giving less attention to Garrison's New England "coteria," Mr. Thomas "centers his tale on Weld" and his followers. One unfortunate result of Mr. Thomas' effort to depict Weld as a man of central significance is that many others active in anti-slavery in the 1830's are made to appear run-of-the-mill by contrast.

COLLECTIVE BIOGRAPHY: Barnes, G. H., in *DAB*, 19:625.

HISTORY: Barnes, G. H. *The Anti-Slavery Impulse, 1830-1844.* 1933.

AHR, 39:747. A new interpretation of the anti-slavery movement based upon new material. Professor Barnes shows that Weld—rather than Garrison—was "the driving force behind the movement . . ." Weld was forgotten because he constantly shunned publicity.

*Nye, R. B. *Fettered Freedom: Civil Liberties and the Slavery Controversy, 1830-1860.* 1949.

CHAPTER XXVIII. THE OLD SOUTHWEST

ANDREW JACKSON— 1767-1845 —Certainly a Democrat With a Big "D" But Was He a Democrat With a Little "d"?

ORIGINAL SOURCES: Bassett, J. S. *Correspondence of Andrew Jackson.* 6 vols. 1926-1933.

AHR, 31:807, 32:898, 34:359, 35:380, 37:171, 39:749. These reviews and the corresponding chapters of Professor Bassett's *Life* are the best guides for the use of these papers. The General Index is given in vol. 7, and each of the other volumes has a very useful preface.

BIOGRAPHY: Bassett, J. S. *The Life of Andrew Jackson.* 2 vols. 1911. 2 vols. in one. 1916.

AHR, 17:624. A biography based "almost exclusively upon manuscript sources." It gives a "wealth of personal detail" but not a history of the times. The chapter on personal characteristics "shows much skill in analysis." It is debatable, however, whether Jackson "threw the task of judging upon the common man." Did he not "by sheer force of will and the happy chance of opportunity . . . so commend his ideas to the masses that the masses came to think them their own?"

James, Marquis. *Andrew Jackson: The Border Captain.* 1933.

———. *Andrew Jackson: Portrait of a President.* 1937. Also in 2 vols. in one. 1938.

AHR, 43:654. Mr. James "writes from the viewpoint of the 'new' biography, representing its emphasis upon the conception of a biography as a portrait and its insistence upon the 'human' side of such writing." He is very successful in dealing with the personal side of Jackson's life. He is quite thorough in treating the presidential campaigns, the Eaton affair, and

---

* See page 161.

the struggle with Biddle. He is inclined to neglect minor problems, but gives "a highly dramatized account" of Jackson's death.

Johnson, G. W. *Andrew Jackson: an Epic in Homespun.* 1927.

Books, Oct. 30, 1927, p. 3. Mr. Johnson adds no new information, but he tells his story "with a vigor and spirit that are sure to hold the attention of the average reader . . ."

Extract in Hyde, M. A. *Modern Biography,* 138-89.

COLLECTIVE BIOGRAPHY: Abernethy, T. P., in *DAB,* 9:526.

Agar, Herbert. *The People's Choice,* 111-29.

Ashley, M. P. *Mr. President,* 169-231.

Booth, E. T. *Country Life in America,* 104-28.

Brogan, D. W. *American Themes,* 219-26.

Bruce, D. K. E. *Revolution to Reconstruction,* 245-72.

Hamlin, Fred. *Land of Liberty,* 144-64.

Hofstadter, Richard. *American Political Tradition,* 44-66.

James, Marquis, in *There Were Giants in the Land,* 40-47.

Peattie, D. C. "Old Hickory—Great American," *Read. Dig.,* 52 (1948) :123-28.

Schlesinger, A. M. "Legacy of Andrew Jackson," *Am. Merc.,* 64 (1947) :168-73.

Somit, Albert. "New Papers: Some Sidelights upon Jacksonian Administration," *MVHR,* 35 (1948) :91-98.

Thomas and Thomas. *Living Biographies of American Statesmen,* 169-83.

Thompson, C. L. "Andrew Jackson: the People's Choice," *Current Hist.,* 14 (1948) :224-29.

HISTORY: Agar, Herbert. *The Price of Union,* 211-76.

Bowers, C. G. *Party Battles of the Jackson Period.*

Channing, Edward. *History,* 4:511-20; 5:365-402, 422-32, 442-55.

Ogg, F. A. *The Reign of Andrew Jackson: a Chronicle of the Frontier in Politics.* (Chronicles of America, 1919) .

AHR, 26:115. "In Mr. Ogg's volume the honest, virile, irascible, chivalric, iron-willed, patriotic 'General' Jackson and his battles with Indians, law-breakers, red-coats, nullifiers, aristocrats, John Adams, John Marshall, and the Whigs stand out in fresh and strong lines again."

*Schlesinger, A. M., Jr. *The Age of Jackson.* 1945.

AHR, 51:510. A stimulating re-interpretation which advances the thesis that Jacksonian democracy owed its chief support to eastern workingmen rather than to "the intermittent radicalism of the West and South . . ." Mr. Schlesinger writes with a lively and pungent style, and his book is well organized.

SPECIAL ASPECTS: Abernethy, T. P. "Jackson and the Rise of Southwestern Democracy," *AHR*, 33 (1927) :64-77.

Barker, E. C. "President Jackson and the Texan Revolution," *AHR*, 12 (1907) :788-809.

Catterall, R. C. H. *The Second Bank of the United States.* 1903.

AHR, 8:787. Having used the papers of Nicolas Biddle, Mr. Catterall presents new opinions and new evidence on "the origin of Jackson's antagonism to the United States Bank" and on "Clay's relationship to the struggle for a recharter."

Dodd, W. E. "Jackson and his Enemies," *Century,* 111 (1926) : 734-45.

———. "The Making of Andrew Jackson," *ibid,* 531-38.

Hoyt, W. D., ed. "Zachary Taylor on Jackson and the Military Establishment, 1835," *AHR,* 51 (1946) :480-84.

Klingberg, F. J. "Personal Traits of President Andrew Jackson," *Historical Outlook,* 14 (1923) :10-14.

Perling, J. J. *Presidents' Sons,* 359-74.

Pollard, J. E. *Presidents and the Press,* 147-81.

Russell, Bertrand. *Freedom Versus Organization,* 255-67.

Seitz, D. C. *Famous American Duels,* 123-68.

Sternberg, R. R. "Jackson's 'Rhea Letter' Hoax," *Jour. South. Hist.,* 2 (1936) :480-96.

Walker, A. S. "Andrew Jackson: Frontier Democrat," *East Tenn. Hist. Soc. Pubs.,* 18 (1946) :59-86.

Wecter, Dixon. *The Hero in America,* 199-221.

BIOGRAPHIES OF CONTEMPORARIES: Burke, P. W. *Emily Donelson of Tennessee.* 2 vols. 1941.

AHR, 49:365. Mrs. Burke did considerable research in privately owned manuscripts, as well as in those in the Library of Congress and other institutions. Consequently she has added much to what we know of the

---

* Condensed, with some new material added, in *New Rep.,* 114 (Mar. 25-June 3, 1946) .

personal relationships of Jackson and social life in Washington. Emily Donelson belonged to one of Tennessee's first families. She was Rachel Jackson's niece, and married Andrew Jackson Donelson, her cousin, and the ward of the future President. At the age of twenty-one, Mrs. Donelson became Jackson's "Lady of the White House." The book is "a gossipy, anecdotal, and somewhat romanticized history" of this influential family.

RACHEL JACKSON—1767-1828—"Beloved Rachel"

COLLECTIVE BIOGRAPHY: Minnegerode, Meade. *Some American Ladies,* 183-240.

Whitton, M. O. *First First Ladies, 1789-1865,* 116-35.

BIOGRAPHIES OF CONTEMPORARIES: *Burke, P. W. *Emily Donelson of Tennessee,* 1:15-28ff.

SEQUOYAH— 1770-1843 —"The Ablest Intelligence Produced Among the American Indians"

BIOGRAPHY: Foreman, Grant. *Sequoyah.* (Civilization of the American Indian, 1938).

AHR, 45:247. A skillful presentation of practically all that is known of the inventor of the Cherokee alphabet.

COLLECTIVE BIOGRAPHY: Ghent, W. J., in *DAB,* 16:586.

Sweetser, K. D. *Book of Indian Braves,* 55-75.

EPHRAIM McDOWELL— 1771-1830 —Pioneer in Abdominal Surgery

BIOGRAPHY: Schachner, August. *Ephraim McDowell, "Father of Ovariotomy" and Founder of Abdominal Surgery.* 1921.

AHR, 27:616. A readable biography in "our sparse literature of medical heroes."

COLLECTIVE BIOGRAPHY: Ashburn, P. M., in *DAB,* 12:27.

THOMAS SPALDING— 1774-1851 —"Progressive Planter"

BIOGRAPHY: Coulter, E. M. *Thomas Spalding of Sapelo.* (Southern Biography, 1940).

AHR, 46:935. A well written narrative based on scattered sources. Thomas Spalding is largely forgotten today, but his career helps the student to understand the economic development of the South.

---

* See page 206.

COLLECTIVE BIOGRAPHY: Green, F. M., in *DAB*, 17:426.

LORENZO DOW—   1777-1834   —"Crazy Dow"

ORIGINAL SOURCES: Dowling, John, ed. *The Dealings of God, Man, and the Devil; as Exemplified in the Life, Experience, and Travels of Lorenzo Dow. To Which is Added, The Vicissitudes of Life, by Peggy Dow.* 1856.

BIOGRAPHY: Sellers, C. C. *Lorenzo Dow, The Bearer of the Word.* 1928.

N. E. Quar., 2:339. A vivid life of a picturesque itinerant preacher who used the natural gifts of a Connecticut Yankee to peddle Christianity from Ireland and Canada to Mississippi Territory.

COLLECTIVE BIOGRAPHY: Wade, J. D., in *DAB*, 5:410.

FELIX GRUNDY— 1777-1840 —"The Most Skillful Criminal Lawyer of the Southwest"

BIOGRAPHY: Parks, J. H. *Felix Grundy, Champion of Democracy.* (Southern Biography, 1940).

AHR, 46:680. A scholarly biography of a politician forgotten today apparently because he lacked settled convictions.

COLLECTIVE BIOGRAPHY: Abernethy, T. P., in *DAB*, 8:32.

EDMUND PENDLETON GAINES—   1777-1849 —Fiery General Who Promoted National Security and Humane Indian Policy

BIOGRAPHY: Silver, J. W. *Edmund Pendleton Gaines, Frontier General.* (Southern Biography, 1949).

AHR, 55:623. A well-written narrative of the long career of an "eccentric but able military leader" whose non-conformity got him into endless troubles. Gaines' third wife was Myra Clark Whitney, who finally won her case against the city of New Orleans forty years after the General's death.

COLLECTIVE BIOGRAPHY: Hamilton, J. G. de R., in *DAB*, 7:92.

BIOGRAPHIES OF CONTEMPORARIES: Harmon, N. B. *The Famous Case of Myra Clark Gaines.* 1946.

AHR, 52:396. "Mr. Harmon tells the story of the distinguished but loose-living Daniel Clark of old New Orleans" and the courageous and persistent fight of his daughter to win judgment against the city of New Orleans.

HENRY CLAY— 1777-1852 —War Hawk and
Conciliator

BIOGRAPHY: Mayo, Bernard. *Henry Clay, Spokesman of the New West.* 1937.

AHR, 43:652. This—the first of three projected volumes carries the story down to the declaration of war in 1812. Professor Mayo sketches the whole environment in detail—social, economic and political.

Van Deusen, G. G. *The Life of Henry Clay.* 1937.

AHR, 43:652. The best brief biography of Clay. Knowledge of background is either assumed, or given in the fewest possible words.

COLLECTIVE BIOGRAPHY: Bradford, Gamaliel. *As God Made Them,* 43-85.

Coulter, E. M., in *DAB,* 4:173.

Fuller, H. B. *The Speakers of the House,* (1909) :32-59, 158-61.

Johnson, G. W. *America's Silver Age,* 1-37, 48-55.

Macartney, C. E. *Men Who Missed It,* 14-21.

Orth, S. P. *Five American Politicians,* 171-294.

Seitz, D. C. *The "Also Rans,"* 77-95.

Stone, Irving. *They Also Ran,* 35-58.

Wildman, Edwin. *Builders of America,* 21-40.

HISTORY: Bowers, C. G. *The Party Battles of the Jackson Period,* 171-226.

Poage, G. R. *Henry Clay and the Whig Party.* 1937.

Yale Rev., 25:831. A well-organized study based on "a large mass of newspaper and manuscript materials . . ."

SPECIAL ASPECTS: Burton, T. E., in Bemis, S. F., ed. *American Secretaries of State,* 4:115-58.

Seitz, D. C. *Famous American Duels,* 227-50.

ZACHARY TAYLOR— 1784-1850 —"Old Rough and Ready"—"The Forlorn Soldier Who Ventured Into Politics"

BIOGRAPHY: Dyer, Brainerd. *Zachary Taylor.* (Southern Biography, 1946) .

AHR, 52:521. An objective study which presents Taylor as a man of courage and decision, if not a master of strategy or a great statesman. Professor Dyer has given us an excellent biography, well-organized and "practically free from errors, factual and typographical."

Hamilton, Holman. *Zachary Taylor: Soldier of the Republic.* 1941.

Jour. South. Hist., 7:406. A "superior biography" which presents Zachary Taylor "as an able, stouthearted, self-sacrificing frontier soldier" who spent almost forty years on the frontier. The most important contribution of the book is concerned with Taylor's "peacetime activities in the United States army . . . He reflected typical officer attitudes in being able to see the Indian point of view, in hating whisky sellers and in despising speculators and fur-trading companies."

McKinley, S. B., and Silas Bent. *Old Rough and Ready: the Life and Times of Zachary Taylor.* 1946.

AHR, 52:523. A popular biography which fails "to contribute anything that is really new." The authors failed to make adequate use of the Marcy Papers and made some inaccurate and irrelevant statements.

COLLECTIVE BIOGRAPHY: Stephenson, W. H., in *DAB,* 18:349.

SPECIAL ASPECTS: Castaneda, C. E. "Relations of General Scott with Santa Anna," *Hispanic AHR,* 29 (1949) :455-73.

Pollard, J. E. *Presidents and the Press,* 256-67.

ALEXANDER PORTER—   1785-1844   —"Typical
Leader of the Old South"

BIOGRAPHY: Stephenson, W. H. *Alexander Porter, Whig Planter of Old Louisiana.* (University Studies, 1934) .

AHR, 41:391. "A scholarly, satisfying biography" of "a witty and genial" Irish immigrant who became a successful planter and lawyer. Popular in spite of the aristocratic ideas he made no attempt to conceal, he served his adopted country as legislator, judge and United States senator.

COLLECTIVE BIOGRAPHY: Stephenson, W. H., in *DAB,* 15:81.

JOHN JAMES AUDUBON— 1785-1851 —The Bird
Man

ORIGINAL SOURCES: Peattie, D. C., ed. *Audubon's America: Narratives and Experiences.* 1940.

Sat. Rev. of Lit., 22:7, Oct. 12, 1940. Selections from Audubon's occasional writings and from his journals. They include his description of his journey down the Mississippi, the various kinds of birds and wild animals he saw, his character sketches of various frontier types, his meeting with the extraordinary Rafinesque.

BIOGRAPHY: Arthur, S. C. *Audubon: an Intimate Life of the American Woodsman.* 1937.

N. Y. Times, July 4, 1937, p. 4. "The author has made an intimate study of the birds of Louisiana. The book is rich in quotations, and presents some less admirable features of Audubon's character.

Herrick, F. H. *Audubon the Naturalist: a History of his Life and Time.* 2 vols. 1917.

AHR, 23:669. The first adequate biography. Gives new facts concerning Audubon's early life. Shows that while a life-long student of birds, he was thirty-five years of age when he conceived the idea of publishing his *Birds of America.*

Muschamps, E. A. *Audacious Audubon: the Story of a Great Pioneer, Artist, Naturalist and Man.* 1929.

Amer. Lit., 2:203. A brief life in which the facts are decorated with fancy.

Rourke, C. M. *Audubon.* 1936.

New Repub., 89:23, Nov. 4, 1936. A romantic, but well-written book which gives a lively idea of the man and the world in which he lived.

Extract in Hamilton, E. B., ed. *How They Started,* 265-86.

COLLECTIVE BIOGRAPHY: Bolton, S. K. *Famous Men of Science,* 20-29.

Brooks, V. W. *The World of Washington Irving,* 138-51, 247-48.

Geiser, S. W. *Naturalists of the Frontier,* 79-94.

Hylander, C. J. *American Scientists,* 35-43.

Jordon, D. S. *Leading American Men of Science,* 71-88.

Peattie, D. C. *Green Laurels,* 216-43.

Peattie, D. C., and E. R. Dobson, in *DAB,* 1:423.

Spiller, R. E. *The American in England,* 68-71.

Weeks, Mangum. "On John James Audubon," *So. Atl. Quar.,* 41 (1942) :76-87.

HISTORY: Buley, R. C. *The Old Northwest,* 2:586-89.

SPECIAL ASPECTS: Audubon, M. R. "Audubon's Story of his Youth," *Scribner's,* 13:267-87.

Beard, A. E. *Our Foreign-Born Citizens,* 39-48.

Peattie, D. C. *Singing in the Wilderness: a Salute to John James Audubon.* 1935.

Sat. Rev. of Lit., 12:19, Oct. 12, 1935. A somewhat sentimental attempt to dramatize scenes in Audubon's life.

Shelly, D. A. "John James Audubon, Artist," *Mag. Art,* 39 (1946) :170-75.

Sutton, G. M. "Audubon—Pioneer American Bird Artist," *Audubon Mag.,* 53 (1951) :31-7.

GIDEON LINCECUM— 1793-1874 —Frontier Physician, Indian Trader, Botanist

ORIGINAL SOURCES: "Autobiography of Gideon Lincecum," *Miss. Hist. Soc. Pubs.,* 8 (1904) :443-519.

Extract in Phillips, U. B. *Plantation and Frontier,* 2:185-96.

COLLECTIVE BIOGRAPHY: Geiser, S. W., in *DAB,* 11:241.

———. *Naturalists of the Frontier,* (1948) :199-214.

Also in *Southwest Rev.,* 15 (1929) :93-111.

SPECIAL ASPECTS: Hudson, A. P. *Humor of the Old Deep South,* 62-67, 126-50.

BENJAMIN LEONARD COVINGTON WAILES— 1797-1862—"Scientist and Planter"

BIOGRAPHY: Sydnor, C. S. *A Gentleman of the Old Natchez Region, Benjamin·L. C. Wailes.* 1938.

AHR, 44:654. The biography of a "dynamic ante-bellum Mississippian," as well as "a history of the evolving civilization in the Natchez region from its frontier days in 1800 to the beginning of the Civil War." This "versatile pioneer" served as a legislator and as assistant to the Choctaw Indian agent. Wailes "promoted a local athenaeum and lyceum," helped to establish the Mississippi Historical Society and made a geological survey of the state. Professor Sydnor's interesting book is based on the diary which Wailes kept regularly from 1852 to 1862, as well as other family papers.

COLLECTIVE BIOGRAPHY: Sydnor, C. S., in *DAB,* 19:315.

JOHN A. MURRELL— 1804-1844 —"The Great Western Land Pirate"

BIOGRAPHY: Phares, Ross. *Reverend Devil, a Biography of John A. Murrell.* 1941.

Jour. South. Hist., 7:404. A popular biography, based on much research. "The account of the capture and trial of the conspirators in the proposed slave insurrection at Lewingston, Mississippi, is a strange chapter in southern history. It is a colorful study in ante-bellum fear psychology and extra-judicial criminal procedure." The book is marred by a number of typographical errors.

COLLECTIVE BIOGRAPHY: Holmes, O. W., in *DAB*, 13:369.

Hudson, A. P. *Humor of the Old Deep South*, 336-48.

Phillips, U. B. *Plantation and Frontier*, 2:76-78.

SPECIAL ASPECTS: Marshall, Park. "John A. Murrell and Daniel Crenshaw," *Tenn. Hist. Mag.*, 6 (1920) :3-9.

JOHN JACOBUS FLOURNOY— 1808-1879
—"Champion of the Common Man?"

BIOGRAPHY: Coulter, E. M. *John Jacobus Flournoy, Champion of the Common Man in the Antebellum South*. 1942.

Wm. and Mary Quar., 2nd ser., 23:226. Flournoy was a fantastic character— "clearly a case for the pathologist or the psychiatrist." Professor Coulter calls him a champion of the common man, but the reviewer questions this. Did he command the respect of that class, or have any appreciable influence with it? Did "the reforms" he advocated reflect the demands of the poor whites, "the yeomen farmers and other moderate men of simple means?" "Perhaps his real claim to be remembered is his championship of a state institution for the deaf and dumb. Flournoy also reflected the prejudices of some of the common people, perhaps, when he attacked the prevalent system of college education with its emphasis on the classics, the 'fashionable learned languages.' "

HISTORY: Coulter, E. M. *College Life in the Old South* (1928) : 293-94.

CHAPTER XXIX. TEXAS

DAVID CROCKETT— 1786-1836 —Backwoods
Hunter and Congressman

ORIGINAL SOURCES: Garland, Hamlin, ed. *An Autobiography of David Crockett*. (Modern Student's Library, 1923) .

Loomis, C. G. "Davy Crockett Visits Boston," *N. E. Quar.*, 20 (1947) :396-400.

Stone, Irving, and Richard Kennedy, eds. *We Speak for Ourselves*, 147-51.

Thomason, J. W., Jr. *The Adventures of Davy Crockett, Told Mostly by Himself*. 1934.

Amer. Lit., 6:368. This book "purports to consist of the reprinted texts of the *Narrative* and the *Exploits.*" However, "practically all the passages critical of Andrew Jackson and his policies have been omitted."

BIOGRAPHY: Rourke, Constance. *Davy Crockett.* 1934.

Amer. Lit., 6:368. An exciting biography which integrates "the fact and fiction that have gathered together around the name of Crockett."

Extract in Hamilton, E. B., ed. *How They Started,* 3-44.

Extract in Van Doren, Carl, ed. *Modern American Prose,* 894-904.

COLLECTIVE BIOGRAPHY: Bechdolt, F. R. *Giants of the Old West,* 73-98.

Brooks, V. W. *The World of Washington Irving,* 379-83.

Foster, A. P., in *Tenn. Hist. Mag.,* 9 (1925) :166-77.

Ghent, W. J., in *DAB,* 4:555.

Parrington, V. L. *Main Currents in American Thought,* 2:172-79.

Seitz, Don. *Uncommon Americans,* 313-28.

HISTORY: Beard, C. A. *Rise of American Civilization,* 1:540-41.

Myers, J. M. *Alamo,* 135-52.

SPECIAL ASPECTS: Blair, Walter. *Horse Sense in American Humor,* 24-50.

Hazard, L. L. *The Frontier in American Literature,* 62-69.

Rourke, Constance. "Davy Crockett, Forgotten Facts and Legend," *Southwest Rev.,* 19 (1934) :149-61.

———. *American Humor,* 55-59.

Wade, J. D. "The Authorship of David Crockett's 'Autobiography,' " *Ga. Hist. Quar.,* 6 (1922) :265-68.

Wecter, Dixon. *The Hero in America,* 189-93.

STEPHEN FULLER AUSTIN—   1793-1836
—"Founder of Texas"

ORIGINAL SOURCES: Barker, E. C., ed. "The Austin Papers," *AHA Ann. Report, for the year 1919,* vol. II, (1924), 2 vols.; and *AHA Ann. Report for the year 1922,* (1928), 1 vol.

AHR, 30:839. Many of these documents concern legal and administrative affairs, but the volumes throw much light on the characters of Stephen Austin and of his father and mother.

BIOGRAPHY: Barker, E. C. *The Life of Stephen F. Austin, the Founder of Texas, 1793-1836.* 1925.

AHR, 32:348. The standard biography. It is factual rather than interpretative and reveals "the admirable character and winning personality of the man."

COLLECTIVE BIOGRAPHY: Barker, E. C., in *DAB,* 1:437.

———, in *MVHR,* 5 (1918) :20-35.

Also in *Southwestern Hist. Quar.,* 22 (1918) :1-17.

And in Barker, E. C., ed. *Readings in Texas History,* (1929) : 147-58.

SAM HOUSTON—   1793-1863   —"The Raven"

ORIGINAL SOURCES: Williams, A. W., and E. C. Barker, eds. *The Writings of Sam Houston, 1813-1863. Vol. I, 1813-1836.* 1938.

AHR, 45:414. These papers cover Houston's youthful activities in the militia and the regular army, and as Indian agent, his career in Congress and as governor of Tennessee. Giving no new clues to his "unfortunate marital tangle," they cover his later work as Indian agent on the frontier and in Washington. His relations with the Texans are covered from his visit in 1833 to his difficulties in organizing their army and government.

———. *Vol. II, July 16, 1814-March 31, 1842.* 1939.

Jour. South. Hist., 6:268. This volume covers the remainder of Houston's first administration as president of Texas, the period of Lamar's administration, and the first four months of Houston's second presidential term.

———. *Vol. III, December 20, 1822-January 31, 1844.* 1940.

Jour. South. Hist., 7:111. "With the exception of nine documents belonging to the period covered by Volumes I and II, the material presented in this volume falls within the period from April 1, 1842, to January 31, 1844." All of the documents fall "within the period of Houston's second administration as president of the Republic of Texas . . ."

———. *Vol. IV, September 29, 1821-February 23, 1847.* 1941.

Jour. South. Hist., 7:408. Almost half of this volume belongs to the period covered by the first three volumes and consists of documents "from the hitherto inaccessible collections in the possession of his (Houston's) grandchildren." The rest of the volume covers "the next three years beyond the date reached in Volume III." These papers indicate that Houston "consistently desired to see Texas become a part of the United States, and that he worked both directly and indirectly to bring this about on the most favorable terms possible for Texas."

————. *Vol. V, August 28, 1824-March 14, 1854; Vol. VI, January 30, 1828-February 25, 1858.* 1941.

Jour. South. Hist., 8:270. "With the exception of sixteen documents belonging to the period covered by the first four volumes, the material presented in these volumes falls within the period from March 1, 1847, to February 25, 1858, during all of which time Houston was a member of the United States Senate."

————. *Vol. VII, November, 1824-March, 1860; Vol. VIII, April, 1825-July, 1863,* with index. 1941.

Jour. South. Hist., 9:572. "With the exception of twenty-nine documents belonging to the years covered by the earlier volumes of this series, the material presented in these two volumes falls within the period from March 1, 1848, to Houston's death, on July 26, 1863. Thus they cover the last twelve months of his service as a United States senator from Texas, his uncompleted term as governor of the state during the secession controversy, and his two years in retirement after having been forced out of the governor's chair in March, 1861."

Wooten, D. G., Houston, Samuel, and Santa Anna. "The San Jacinto Campaign," in Barker, E. C., ed. *Readings in Texas History,* 298-316.

BIOGRAPHY: Creel, George. *Sam Houston, Colossus in Buckskin.* 1928.

IND, 121:117, Aug. 4, 1928. An interesting narrative of adventure. Eulogistic rather than critical.

James, Marquis. *The Raven, a Biography of Sam Houston, 1793-1863.* 1929.

MVHR, 17:464. "A vivid picture of Houston's boyhood in Virginia and Tennessee, of his rise in politics, of his relations to Eliza Allen and Tiona Rogers, and of his career to 1856 . . ." The account of Houston's life in the Indian country is also well done. "In the consideration of such topics as the relations of Houston and Jackson, Houston's attitude to annexation, and his career as Senator, there are evidences of historical and critical immaturity."

COLLECTIVE BIOGRAPHY: Bruce, Philip. *The Virginia Plutarch,* 2:133-50.

Caldwell, R. G., in *DAB,* 9:263.

Thomas and Thomas. *Fifty Great Americans,* 127-35.

HISTORY: Foreman, Grant. *Pioneer Days in the Old South-West,* (1926) :179-206.

SPECIAL ASPECTS: Moore, J. T. "Houston, the Greatest Comeback in American History," *Sat. Eve. Post*, 200-26-27, May 19, 1928.

Wilson, P. W. "Sam Houston's Secret," *No. Am. Rev.*, 229 (1930) :449-59.

CHAPTER XXX. THE FAR WEST

JOHN McLOUGHLIN— 1784-1857 —Father of Oregon

ORIGINAL SOURCES: Barker, B. B., ed. *Letters of Dr. John Mc-Loughlin written at Fort Vancouver, 1829-32.* 1948.

AHR, 55:179. This correspondence is virtually all with McLoughlin's subordinates in the Columbia District. The letters "illustrate the amazing thoroughness" with which McLoughlin ran this vast area.

Judson, K. B. "Dr. John McLoughlin's Last Letter to the Hudson Bay Company, as Chief Factor, in Charge of Fort Vancouver, 1845," *AHR*, 21 (1915) :104-9.

Rich, E. E., ed. *The Letters of John McLoughlin from Fort Vancouver to the Governor and Committee. First series, 1825-1838.* (Hudson Bay Co., 1941).

Canadian Hist. Rev., 24:203. With a few exceptions these letters represent yearly summaries of the progress of the district under McLoughlin's control, plus discussions of the problems which have arisen and the policies suggested by McLoughlin or the Governor and Committee at home. The introduction by Dr. W. K. Lamb gives an excellent outline of the development of the Columbia District during this phase of McLoughlin's career. This narrative affords a clear perspective of the main trends and illuminates the essential material contained in the letters themselves.

Rich, E. E., and W. K. Lamb, eds. *The Letters of John Mc-Loughlin from Vancouver to the Governor and Committee. Second series, 1839-1844.* (Hudson Bay Co., 1943).

Canadian Hist. Rev., 26:195. This volume "opens with McLoughlin's return in the autumn of 1839 after a year's furlough in England . . . The major theme is the open breach between McLoughlin and Sir George Simpson and the growing acerbity of their quarrel. It arose fundamentally from the clash of two vigorous and antagonistic temperaments."

Rich, E. E., ed. *The Letters of John McLoughlin from Fort Van-*

couver to the Governor and Committee. Third Series, 1844-1846. (Hudson Bay Co., 1944).

Canadian Hist. Rev., 27:210. This volume "sees to its end McLoughlin's services with the company, and covers the settlement of the Oregon boundary dispute and the retreat of the Company to Vancouver and the north."

BIOGRAPHY: Dye, E. E. *McLoughlin and Old Oregon.* 1936.

N. Y. Times, Oct. 18, 1936, p. 23. Mrs. Dye says that warfare would have broken out in Oregon "had it not been for the strength of character and sense of justice of one man—Dr. John McLoughlin . . ." The reprint of a book which first appeared 36 years ago.

Holman, F. V. *Dr. John McLoughlin, the Father of Oregon.* 1907.

AHR, 13:620. A fine tribute to the Canadian of Scotch-Irish ancestry who served as the chief factor of the Hudson Bay Company and preserved the peace between the British and the Americans during the joint occupation of Oregon.

Montgomery, R. G. *The White-Headed Eagle, John McLoughlin, Builder of an Empire.* 1934.

AHR, 40:763. This biography, based on careful research, "presents the personal life of Dr. John McLoughlin, . . . progress of his career with the fur companies of Canada, and the residence at Fort Vancouver from 1824 to 1846. He is pictured as the beneficent ruler of a vast empire, the kindly father and husband, the benefactor and friend of the Indian, missionary, and settler." Little effort has been made "to present McLoughlin in his character as a business manager of the Columbia River department of the Hudson Bay Company" or to give a complete picture of the many company activities directed by him.

COLLECTIVE BIOGRAPHY: Schafer, Joseph, in *DAB,* 12:134.

HISTORY: Fuller, G. W. *History of the Pacific Northwest,* 110-19.

SPECIAL ASPECTS: Merk, Frederick. "The Oregon Pioneers and the Boundary," *AHR,* 29 (1924) :681-99. Read especially 683, 686-90, 692-94.

JEDEDIAH STRONG SMITH— 1798-1831 —"The Original California Pathfinder"

ORIGINAL SOURCES: Dale, H. C., ed. *The Ashley-Smith Explorations and the Discovery of a Central Route to the Pacific, 1822-1829.* 1941.

AHR, 48:202. The first edition of this book (1918) was recognized as an "important contribution." The revised edition traces Smith's route with greater precision, . . . and describes more fully the relations between Smith and the Hudson Bay Company; the most important new source here is Sullivan's *Travels of Jedediah Smith* (1934)."

Sullivan, M. S. *The Travels of Jedediah Smith. A Documentary Outline including the Journal of the Great American Pathfinder*. 1934.

PHR, 4:181. "The ransacking of family papers and of official archives is gradually yielding original material which brings into sharper focus the blurred and hazy figure of one of the most extraordinary of American western explorers, Jedediah Smith." One hundred and fifty pages of this book "are devoted to the original material;" Mr. Sullivan uses only fifteen pages to supply "information about his hero."

COLLECTIVE BIOGRAPHY: Campbell, W. S. *Mountain Men*, 21-34, 62-71.

Gray, A. A. *Men Who Built the West*, 43-62.

Schafer, Joseph, in *DAB*, 17:290.

HISTORY: Cleland, R. G. *California: the American Period*, 46-60; index.

JOHN MARSH— 1799-1856 —California Pioneer

BIOGRAPHY: Lyman, G. D. *John Marsh, Pioneer*. 1930.

MVHR, 17:621. An interesting and realistic biography of a Harvard graduate who drifted from Fort Snelling (Minn.) to California.

COLLECTIVE BIOGRAPHY: Hunt, R. D. *California's Stately Hall of Fame*, 147-51.

Ray, P. O., in *DAB*, 12:301.

JOSEPH LANE— 1801-1881 —"Frontier Politician"

BIOGRAPHY: Kelly, Sister M. M. J. *The Career of Joseph Lane, Frontier Politician*. 1942.

AHR, 48:813. An "interesting and informative" biography of "a relatively obscure man who through native ability and considerable shrewdness attained some prominence as an officer in the Mexican War, as an Indian fighter," and as governor of Oregon and United States senator. As an Indian agent Lane had an unusual understanding of the Indian point of view. He "was one of the ablest and most vivid personalities of his time in western history."

COLLECTIVE BIOGRAPHY: Schafer, Joseph, in *DAB*, 10:579.

MARCUS WHITMAN—   1802-1846   —Pioneer
Missionary

BIOGRAPHY: Drury, C. M. *Marcus Whitman, M.D., Pioneer and Martyr.* 1937.

AHR, 44:154. A joint biography of Marcus and Narcissa Whitman. The author accepts the Perkins theory that the missionary and his wife were not fitted to do missionary work among the Oregon Indians.

Hulbert, A. B., and Dorothy Hulbert, eds. *Marcus Whitman, Crusader, Part I, 1802-1839.* (Overland to the Pacific, 1936) .

AHR, 42:560. This volume has three parts: a biography of Whitman from 1802 to 1839, letters to Samuel Parker and his "Report of a Tour West of the Rocky Mountains in 1835-1837," and a diary and letters relating to the missionary labours of the Whitmans, 1835-1839. "Each one of the three parts is a distinctive contribution." The biography of Whitman "is characterized by a sympathetic understanding and appreciation of the missionary point of view. The third section contains most of the new material."

———. *Marcus Whitman, Crusader. Part II, 1839 to 1843.* (Overland to the Pacific, 1938) .

AHR, 44:741. This volume is in two parts. The biographical section brings the story of Whitman's life down to his return to Oregon in 1843. It gives "a thorough and convincing picture of Marcus Whitman as man and as missionary." The second part consists of Oregon Mission Correspondence.

———. *Marcus Whitman, Crusader. Part III, 1843 to 1847.* (Overland to the Pacific, 1941) .

AHR, 47:887. This concluding volume covers the years 1843 to 1847. A continuation of the biography which ends with an excellent description of the massacre. The documents included leave one in doubt whether Whitman was primarily interested in ministering to the Indian or in promoting American immigration.

COLLECTIVE BIOGRAPHY: Schafer, Joseph, in *DAB,* 20:141.

HISTORY: Fuller, G. W. *History of the Pacific Northwest,* 128-34, 143-69.

SPECIAL ASPECTS: Bourne, E. G. "The Legend of Marcus Whitman," *AHR,* 6 (1901) :276-300.

Also in ———. *Essays in Historical Criticism,* (1901) :3-109.

Hulbert, A. B. "Undeveloped Factors in the Life of Marcus Whitman," in Willard and Goodykoontz, eds. *The Trans-Mississippi West,* 87-102.

THOMAS OLIVER LARKIN—   1802-1858
—"California's First Millionaire?"

BIOGRAPHY: Underhill, R. L. *From Cowhides to Golden Fleece: the Story of Thomas O. Larkin.* 1940, 1946.

Sat. Rev. of Lit., 22:27, May 25, 1940. "A great deal of California history is bound up with the career of Thomas O. Larkin"—a shrewd Yankee trader whose story "waited long for the adequate telling; but at last, received a biography, based on the study of 3,400 unpublished letters which no student of Western history can neglect, and which many general readers should find of interest."

COLLECTIVE BIOGRAPHY: Kelsey, R. W., in *DAB*, 10:617.

Parker, R. J. *Greater America*, 415-29.

HISTORY: Cleland, R. G. *History of California: the American Period*, 170-75.

De Voto, Bernard. *The Year of Decision*, 222-27.

Kelsey, R. W. *The U. S. Consulate in California.* (Publications of the Academy of Pacific Coast History, 1910) :165-267.

Kelsey, R. W. *The United States Consulate in California.* 1910.

Bemis and Griffin. *Guide to the Diplomatic History of the U. S.*, 266.

Kelsey "uses Larkin's papers to expose Polk's intrigue to instigate rebellion in California and to acquire it à la Texas."

Ogden, Adele, and Engel Sluiter, eds. *Greater California*, (1945) :415-29.

JOHN AUGUSTUS SUTTER— 1803-1880 —"Swiss
Adventurer—First Enthusiast for California"

BIOGRAPHY: Cendrars, Blaise. *Sutter's Gold.* 1926.

Sat. Rev. of Lit., 3:253, Oct. 30, 1926. "A superb book . . . one of the most fascinating biographical studies since Lytton Strachey published his *Eminent Victorians.*"

Dana, Julian. *Sutter of California: a Biography.* 1936.

PHR, 6:296. "A vivid, sympathetic, and yet journalistic account of John A. Sutter's life."

Gudde, E. G. *Sutter's own Story: the Life of John Augustus Sutter and the History of New Helvetia in the Sacramento Valley.* 1936.

PHR, 6:296. Sutter dictated his reminiscences to H. H. Bancroft in 1876.

Mr. Gudde has "rewritten the entire story in his own words. . . . Large gaps in the 'Reminiscences' have been filled in by material taken primarily from the 'New Helvetia Diary . . .' "

Wilbur, M. E. *John Sutter, Rascal and Adventurer.* 1949.

PHR, 18:400. A novelized biography which shows "a tendency to play up the sensational feature of Sutter's life," and "a marked prejudice against Mexico's regime in California as well as against the squatters who appropriated Sutter's domain."

Zollinger, J. P. *Sutter: the Man and His Empire.* 1939.

PHR, 9:85. After thorough research, Mr. Zollinger has produced "a masterpiece of literary skill" dealing with "a picturesque figure that appeared often in a conspicuous position amid the stirring events of a decade of western history." "It is doubtful whether we shall have a more readable biography of Johann Augustus Sutter, or one based upon additional manuscript material."

COLLECTIVE BIOGRAPHY: Bechdolt, F. R. *Giants of the Old West,* 179-204.

Faris, J. T. *Romance of Forgotten Men,* 225-48.

Ghent, W. J., in *DAB,* 18:224.

Gray, A. A. *Men Who Built the West,* 75-87.

Hunt, R. D. *California's Stately Hall of Fame,* 159-63.

Marshall, J. W., in Commager, H. S., and Allan Nevins, eds. *Heritage of America,* 551-54.

Zweig, Stefen. *Tide of Fortune,* (1940) :179-94.

SPECIAL ASPECTS: Zollinger, J. P. "John Augustus Sutter's European Background," *Cal. Hist. Soc. Quar.,* 14 (1935) :28-46.

JAMES OHIO PATTIE—1804-1850—Fur Trader and Explorer

ORIGINAL SOURCES: Flint, Timothy, ed. *Personal Narrative of James O. Pattie of Kentucky.* (Lakeside Classics, 1930) .

"Story of the adventures of an American trader and trapper in New Mexico and adjacent regions, 1824-30 . . ." The original edition appeared in 1831.

COLLECTIVE BIOGRAPHY: Ghent, W. J., in *DAB,* 14:310.

HISTORY: Cleland, R. G. *California: American Period,* 61-74.

JAMES BRIDGER— 1804-1881 —"Discoverer of South Pass"

BIOGRAPHY: Alter, J. C. *James Bridger, Trapper, Frontiersman, Scout and Guide: a Historical Narrative.* 1925.

Campbell, W. S. *Jim Bridger, Mountain Man: a Biography*. 1946.

Weekly Bk. Rev., Oct. 6, 1946, p. 6. A somewhat fictionalized biography, based mainly on other biographies.

COLLECTIVE BIOGRAPHY: Dale, H. C., in *DAB*, 3:33.

JOSEPH SMITH— 1805-1844 —Mormon Leader

BIOGRAPHY: Brodie, F. M. *No Man Knows My History: the Life of Joseph Smith, the Mormon Prophet*. 1945.

AHR, 51:725. Miss Brodie is a former resident of Utah, but she writes with great objectivity and has new material. She maintains "that the chief influence in drawing converts into the church was not Smith but the Book of Mormon." It, she says, "is one of the earliest examples of frontier fiction, the first long Yankee narrative that owes nothing to English literary fashions."

COLLECTIVE BIOGRAPHY: De Voto, Bernard, in *DAB*, 17:310.

SPECIAL ASPECTS: Cannon, M. H. "Further note on the Bankruptcy of Joseph Smith in Illinois," *Pacific History*, 15 (1946) :114-15.

Tyler, A. F. *Freedom's Ferment*, 86-107.

JOSIAH GREGG— 1806-1850 —Santa Fe Trader

ORIGINAL SOURCES: Fulton, M. G., ed. *Diary and Letters of Josiah Gregg*. 2 vols. (American Exploration and Travel, 1941, 1944).

AHR, 51:330. Documents that "fill a hitherto unexplained gap" in the life of "the famous author and Santa Fe trader." They cover "especially the decade 1840-1850."

COLLECTIVE BIOGRAPHY: Connelly, W. E. "Dr. Josiah Gregg, Historian of the Old Santa Fe Trail," *MVHA, Proc.,* 10 (1920) :334-48.

Ghent, W. J., in *DAB,* 7:597.

SPECIAL ASPECTS: Lee, J. T. "The Authorship of Gregg's *Commerce of the Prairies,*" *MVHR*, 16 (1930) :451-66.

JOHN CHARLES FRÉMONT—1813-1890—Explorer

BIOGRAPHY: Goodwin, Cardinal. *John Charles Frémont, 1813-1890: an Explanation of His Career*. 1930.

AHR, 36:417. A special study of critical parts of Frémont's life: the Bear Flag revolt, the Civil War and later railroad transactions. Little fresh information is given, but the interpretation is consistently hostile to Frémont.

Nevins, Allan. *Frémont: the West's Greatest Adventurer, being a Biography from certain hitherto unpublished Sources of General John C. Frémont together with his wife Jessie Benton Frémont.* 2 vols. 1928.

AHR, 33:894. A conservative biography rather than an attempt at psychoanalysis. Sympathetic, it presents Frémont as a distinguished explorer, though at times naive and reckless.

———. *Frémont, Pathfinder of the West.* 1939.

AHR, 45:478. In reviewing this book, Cardinal Goodwin points out that differences of opinion in regard to Frémont "have arisen largely from evaluation of his later career and interpretation of his character." Professor Goodwin concludes that the book "adds nothing to our knowledge of Frémont, but it is the best camouflage of the man that has appeared."

COLLECTIVE BIOGRAPHY: Campbell, W. S. *Mountain Men,* 235-49.

Croffut, W. A. *American Procession, 1855-1914,* 268-73.

Fox, D. R., and A. M. Schlesinger. *The Cavalcade of America* (2nd ser., 1939) :275-90.

Nevins, Allan, in *DAB,* 7:19.

Seitz, D. C. *The "Also Rans,"* 144-66.

Stone, Irving. *They Also Ran,* 139-58.

Zabriskie, G. A. "Pathfinder," *N. Y. Hist. Society Quar.,* 31 (1947) :4-17.

HISTORY: Cleland, R. G. *California: American Period,* 131-39, 194-210, index.

De Voto, Bernard. *The Year of Decision,* see index.

Monaghan, James. *Overland Trail,* 217-37.

BIOGRAPHIES OF CONTEMPORARIES: Zollinger, J. P. *Sutter.* (1939) . Abusive.

JESSIE BENTON FRÉMONT—   1824-1902
—Ghost-writer

ORIGINAL SOURCES: Frémont, J. B. *Souvenirs of My Time.* 1887.
Extract in Flanagan, J. T., ed. *America is West,* 451-58.

BIOGRAPHY: Phillips, C. C. *Jessie Benton Frémont, a Woman who made History.* 1935.

AHR, 42:565. A popular biography which fails to emphasize Jessie's domineering character.

Stone, Irving. *Immortal Wife: the Biographical Novel of Jessie Benton Frémont*. 1944.

N. Y. Times, Oct. 1, 1944, p. 4. A good blend of biography and fiction, though it cannot be cited as an authority on facts.

COLLECTIVE BIOGRAPHY: Dobson, E. R., in *DAB*, 7:18.

Duffus, R. L. "Frémont and Jessie," *Am. Merc.*, 6 (1925) :289-97.

Peacock, V. T. *Famous Belles of the 19th Century*, 123-47.

SARAH ELEANOR ROYCE— 1819-1891 —A Forty-niner

ORIGINAL SOURCES: Gabriel, H. E., ed. *A Frontier Lady: Recollections of the Gold Rush and Early California*. 1932.

Amer. Lit., 5:390. A "dramatic narrative" of the author's "experiences on the overland journey to California in '49" and "her reminiscences of the primitive and unlovely life in the early mining camps . . ." This straightforward narrative by the mother of Professor Josiah Royce of Harvard was not intended for publication. It is based partly on her diary and partly on recollections.

JOHN BIDWELL— 1819-1900 —"Father of Chico"

ORIGINAL SOURCES: Bidwell, John. *In California before the Gold Rush*. 1948.

PHR, 18:26. A reprint of articles on early California from the *Century*, November, 1890.

BIOGRAPHY: Hunt, R. D. *John Bidwell: Prince of California Pioneers*. 1942.

AHR, 48:879. "A well-written and well-organized biography of one of California's great pioneers." The author knew Bidwell personally and has a tendency to build him "into a greater figure than he actually was . . ."

COLLECTIVE BIOGRAPHY: Ghent, W. J., in *DAB*, 2:247.

WILLIAM CHAPMAN RALSTON— 1826-1875 —Robber-Baron and Philanthropist

BIOGRAPHY: Dana, Julian. *The Man who Built San Francisco: a Study of Ralston's Journey with Banners*. 1936.

AHR, 43:224. A popular book full of anecdotes about early San Francisco, rather than a biography.

Tilton, C. G. *William Chapman Ralston, Courageous Builder.* 1935.

COLLECTIVE BIOGRAPHY: Barclay, T. S., in *DAB*, 15:333.

Lyman, G. D. *Ralston's Ring: California Plunders of Comstock Lode.* 1937.

PHR, 7:82. Drawing his material mostly from contemporary newspapers and manuscripts, "Dr. Lyman has given us an excellent picture in fascinating style of Ralston and his ring of close associates."

SIXTH GENERATION, 1850-1901

CHAPTER XXXI, NEW ENGLAND

GERRIT SMITH—1797-1874—Backer of John Brown
and Jefferson Davis

ORIGINAL SOURCES: Fabian, R. C., ed. "Some Uncollected Letters of John Greenleaf Whittier to Gerrit Smith," *Amer. Lit.*, 22 (1950) :158-63.

BIOGRAPHY: Harlow, R. V. *Gerrit Smith, Philanthropist and Reformer.* 1939.

AHR, 45:417. An excellent biography of a Christian gentleman who used his wealth to promote reform.

COLLECTIVE BIOGRAPHY: Harlow, R. V., in *DAB*, 17:270.

SPECIAL ASPECTS: Harlow, R. V. "Gerrit Smith and the John Brown Raid," *AHR*, 38 (1932) :32-60.

DAVID GLASGOW FARRAGUT—1801-1870—"One
of the Most Aggressive Sea Fighters in History"

BIOGRAPHY: Lewis, C. L. *David Glasgow Farragut.* 2 vols. 1941-43.

AHR, 47:638; 49:319. The best biography. It represents Farragut as an upright Christian patriot, possessed of "judgment, courage, ambition, aggression, and audacity," but somewhat out of touch with his seamen.

COLLECTIVE BIOGRAPHY: Alden, C. S., and Ralph Earle. *Makers of Naval Tradition*, 146-75.

Choate, J. H. *American Addresses*, 27-47.

Croffut, W. A. *American Procession*, 256-68.

Frothingham, J. P. *Sea-Fighters from Drake to Farragut*, (1902) :335-96.

Hill, J. D. *Sea Dogs of the Sixties*, (1935) :3-62.

Lewis, C. L. *Famous American Naval Officers*, 215-51.

Paullin, C. O., in *DAB*, 6:286.

DOROTHEA LYNDE DIX— 1802-1887 —Reformer

BIOGRAPHY: Marshall, H. E. *Dorothea Dix, Forgotten Samaritan.* 1937.

AHR, 44:157. A scholarly and well-written biography which gives an "understanding explanation of Dorothea Dix's reasons for her remarkable humanitarian activities."

COLLECTIVE BIOGRAPHY: Abbott, Elizabeth, ed. *Some American Pioneers in Social Welfare,* (1937) :107-27.

Baker, C. H., in *DAB,* 5:323.

Beach, S. C. *Daughters of the Puritans,* 123-62.

Haggard, H. W. *Doctor in History,* (1934) :355-70.

Holbrook, S. H. *Lost Men of American History,* 136-42.

Morris, Charles. *Heroes of Progress in America,* 239-44.

Robinson, Victor. *White Caps,* (1946) :147-84.

SPECIAL ASPECTS: Deutch, Albert. *Mentally Ill in America,* (1946) :158-85.

Tyler, A. F. *Freedom's Ferment,* 304-07.

MARK HOPKINS—   1802-1887   —Educator

COLLECTIVE BIOGRAPHY: Fenn, W. W., in *DAB,* 9:215.

Spring, L. W., in Peterson, Houston, ed. *Great Teachers,* 77-99.

Thwing, C. F. *Guides, Philosophers and Friends,* 125-42.

SPECIAL ASPECTS: Howe, M. A. D. *Classic Shades,* 79-120.

ROBERT BENNET FORBES—   1804-1889   —"A Grand Old Man of Many Seas"

BIOGRAPHY: Connolly, J. B. *Canton Captain.* 1942.

Books, Jan. 18, 1942, p. 4. A vivid narrative of a member of a wealthy ship-owning family who followed the sea for most of his life.

COLLECTIVE BIOGRAPHY: Albion, R. G., in *DAB,* 6:508.

Henderson, D. M. *Yankee Ships in China Seas,* (1946) :147-68.

ELIZABETH PALMER PEABODY—   1804-1894 —"The Founder of the American Kindergarten"

ORIGINAL SOURCES: Miller, Perry, ed. *The Transcendentalists,* 140-50, 372-74, 464-69.

COLLECTIVE BIOGRAPHY: Adams, R. W., in *DAB,* 14:335.

Brooks, V. W. *The Flowering of New England,* 228-51.

Fenner, M. S., and E. C. Fishburn. *Pioneer American Educators,* 73-80.

Tharp, L. H. *The Peabody Sisters of Salem.* 1950.

AHR, 55:926. A readable reappraisal of three remarkable women: Elizabeth, a teacher who became the founder of the American kindergarten, Mary, who married Horace Mann, and Sophia, who married Hawthorne. A fascinating book based on careful research in letters and diaries, and introducing many fascinating personalities. Generally accurate and interesting.

JEAN LOUIS RODOLPH AGASSIZ— 1807-1873
—Swiss Naturalist

ORIGINAL SOURCES: James, William. *Memories and Studies,* (1911) :1-16.

BIOGRAPHY: Teller, J. D. *Louis Agassiz, Scientist and Teacher.* (Ohio Univ. Graduate Sc. Studies, 1947) .

COLLECTIVE BIOGRAPHY: Bolton, S. K. *Famous Men of Science,* (1946) :85-119.

Brooks, V. W. *The Flowering of New England,* 443-59.

Fenton, C. L., and M. A. Fenton. *Story of the Great Geologists,* (1945) :111-23.

Holder, C. F., and D. S. Jordan, eds. *Leading American Men of Science,* 147-69.

Husband, Joseph. *Americans by Adoption,* 37-55.

Hylander, C. J. *American Scientists,* 65-76.

Jaffe, Bernard. *Men of Science in America,* 233-57.

Jordon, D. S., and J. K. Jordon, in *DAB*, 1:114.

Roman, A. S., in *Sci. Am.,* 181 (1949) :48-51.

Shaler, N. S., in Peterson, Houston, ed. *Great Teachers,* 205-19.

Snyder, Mrs. E. E. *Biology in the Making,* (1940) :80-104.

Teller, J. D. "Louis Agassiz and Men of Letters," *Sci. Mo.,* 65 (1947) :428.

———. "Louis Agassiz, Teacher of Science," *Sch. Sci., and Math.,* 47 (1947) :729.

Thomas and Thomas. *Living Biographies of Great Scientists,* (1941) :167-84.

SPECIAL ASPECTS: Eliot, C. W. *Late Harvest,* (1924) :57-64.

Saidla, L. E., and W. E. Gibbs, eds. *Science and the Scientific Mind,* (1930) :249-64.

CHARLES FRANCIS ADAMS— 1807-1886 —Our Greatest Ambassador in the Sixties

ORIGINAL SOURCES: Ford, W. C., ed. *A Cycle of Adams Letters, 1861-1865.* 2 vols. 1920.

AHR, 26:546. "The chief interest in these letters, and it is great, is the same for the historian as for the general reader, that of personality. The three writers are all reasonably human, they are all strongly Adamses, and they are sharply distinguished from each other."

COLLECTIVE BIOGRAPHY: Ford, W. C., in *DAB,* 1:40.

Holbrook, S. H. *Lost Men of American History,* 178-97.

HISTORY: Adams, E. D. *Great Britain and the American Civil War.* 2 vols. 1925.

AHR, 31:154. A penetrating and impartial study. "The two volumes have the great merit of being thoroughly readable all through."

SPECIAL ASPECTS: Mowat, R. B. *Americans in England,* 186-201.

Perling, J. J. *Presidents' Sons,* 181-82.

PHINEAS TAYLOR BARNUM— 1810-1891 —"The Most Typical American"

ORIGINAL SOURCES: Abbott, Lyman. *Silhouettes of My Contemporaries,* 1-15.

Barnum, P. T. *Life of P. T. Barnum, Written by Himself.* 1855.
There were many editions of this book. They are generally accurate.

Mussey, J. B., ed. *Yankee Life by Those Who Lived It,* 218-22, 268-70, 321-23.

Stone, Irving, and Richard Kennedy, eds. *We Speak for Ourselves,* 69-76.

BIOGRAPHY: Finger, C. J. *Life of Barnum.* 1924.

Root, H. W. *The Unknown Barnum.* 1927.

Bookman, 67:324, May, 1928. "Mr. Root's biography is a sober, academic affair, quite free from those fictional arts with which biographers now dress up their material; and well documented with Barnum's own remarks. In these quiet and somewhat gray pages the Great Showman contrives constantly to shine by his own irresistible light."

Werner, M. R. *Barnum, 1810-1891.* 1923.

New Repub., 34:274, May 2, 1923. An entertaining biography based largely on the autobiography of this typical American.

COLLECTIVE BIOGRAPHY: Basso, Hamilton. *Main Stream,* 113-30.

Bluminfield, R. D. *R. D. B.'s Procession,* 55-59.

Bradford, Gamaliel. *Damaged Souls,* 189-221.

Also in *Atlantic,* 130 (1922) :82-92.

Britt, Albert. *Great Biographers,* (1936) :161-82.

Croffut, W. A. *American Procession,* 284-93.

Dibble, R. F. *Strenuous Americans,* 287-335.

———, in Balch, Marston, ed. *Modern Short Biographies,* 274-310.

Fox, D. R., and A. M. Schlesinger, eds. *Cavalcade of America,* 246-65.

Guedalla, Philip. *Supers and Supermen,* 281-86.

O'Higgins, H. J., and E. H. Reede. *American Mind in Action,* 132-54.

Paxson, F. L., in *DAB,* 1:636.

Rourke, C. M. *Trumpets of Jubilee,* 367-426.

Wildman, Edwin. *Famous Leaders of Industry,* 1st ser., (1920) : 17-34.

SPECIAL ASPECTS: Aldrich, Richard. *Musical Discourse,* (1928) : 218-41.

Dulles, F. R. *America Learns to Play,* (1910) :112-35.

Johnson, A. T., and Allen Tate, eds. *America Through the Essay,* (1938) :436-70.

CHARLES SUMNER— 1811-1874 —Chairman of
Foreign Relations Committee

ORIGINAL SOURCES: Chambrun, Marquis de. "Personal Recollections of Charles Sumner," *Scribner's,* 13 (1893) :153-64.

Johnson, A. B. "Recollections of Charles Sumner," *Scribner's,* 8 (1887) :475-90; 9 (1887) :101-14; 10 (1887) :224-29, 297-304.

Pierce, E. L. *Memoir and Letters of Charles Sumner.* 4 vols. 1877-93.

A "monumental work which Pierce erected to the memory of his hero" and intimate friend.

BIOGRAPHY: Grimke, A. M. *The Scholar in Politics: a Life of Charles Sumner.* 1892.

A shorter biography by a negro lawyer.

Haynes, G. H. *Charles Sumner.* (American Crisis, 1910) .

AHR, 16:154. "While Professor Haynes has assembled his material carefully and has written a clear, readable narrative, he is nevertheless very much under the spell of Sumner's compelling personality." He was "often doctrinaire and intemperate in speech . . . What escapes the biographer is the ignorance of Sumner respecting the actual institution of slavery. . . . What offended Sumner's conscience was slavery in the abstract. . . . The defects of Sumner's statesmanship were most conspicuous after the Civil War, when unluckily his influence was greatest."

Storey, Moorfield. *Charles Sumner.* (American Statesmen), 1900) .

AHR, 6:157. "A thoughtful and a sympathetic narrative of the statesman's career." The author was Sumner's secretary. Later he was a lawyer and diplomat.

COLLECTIVE BIOGRAPHY: Bradford, Gamaliel. *Union Portraits,* 231-61.

Haynes, G. H., in *DAB,* 18:208.

Higginson, T. W. *Contemporaries,* (1899) :280-93.

Hoar, G. F., in *Forum,* 16 (1894) :549-59.

Thomas and Thomas. *Living Biographies of American Statesmen,* 221-31.

Wildman, Edwin. *Famous Leaders of Character in America,* 43-52.

HISTORY: Beale, H. K. *The Critical Year,* (1930) : see index.

Rhodes, J. F. *History of the United States,* 7 vols. 1893-1906. See index.

Rhodes is severe toward Sumner, but the more recent historians are more severe.

Milton, G. F. *Age of Hate,* (1930) : see index.

SPECIAL ASPECTS: Dunning, W. A. *Reconstruction, Political and Economic,* (1907) : see index.

White, L. A. "Charles Sumner and the Crisis of 1860-61," in Craven, Avery, ed. *Essays in Honor of William E. Dodd,* (1935) :131-93.

BIOGRAPHIES OF CONTEMPORARIES: Nevins, Allan. *Hamilton Fish.* See index.

*HARRIET BEECHER STOWE—1811-1896—"The Most Widely Read American Novelist for Almost a Generation"

ORIGINAL SOURCES: Mussey, J. B., ed. *Yankee Life by Those Who Lived It,* 25-29.

Rammelkamp, C. H., ed. "Harriet Beecher Stowe's Reply," *MVHR,* 19 (1932) :261.

BIOGRAPHY: Gilbertson, Catherine. *Harriet Beecher Stowe.* 1937.

AHR, 43:949. A well-balanced, readable biography which includes fair estimates of the entire Beecher family.

Wilson, Forrest. *Crusader in Crinoline: the Life of Harriet Beecher Stowe.* 1941.

AHR, 63:636. A vigorous, sympathetic portrait of the author of the bestseller among American novels in the 1850's. Mr. Wilson presents "the Beecher-Stowe clan as a robust, migrating professional family of mid-nineteenth century vintage," and gives a "critical evaluation of all the writings of Mrs. Stowe."

COLLECTIVE BIOGRAPHY: Adams, E. C., and W. D. Foster. *Heroines of Modern Progress,* 88-119.

Anthony, Katharine, in *DAB,* 18:115.

Beech, S. C. *Daughters of the Puritans,* 209-47.

Bradford, Gamaliel. *Portraits of American Women,* 99-130.

Also in *Atlantic,* 122 (1918) :84-94.

Brooks, V. W. *The Flowering of New England,* 404-21.

Eaton, G. D., in *Am. Merc.,* 10 (1927) :449-59.

Malone, Dumas. *Saints in Action,* 75, 89-90, 92-94.

Myers, A. J. W., in Lotz, P. H., ed. *Women Leaders,* 109-17.

Rourke, C. M. *Trumpets of Jubilee,* 89-148.

Russell, F. A. *American Pilgrimage,* 82-98.

Stowe, L. B. *Saints, Sinners and Beechers,* 154-235.

Van Doren, Carl, in *Cambridge History of American Literature,* 3:69-73.

Whicher, G. F., in *Literary History of the United States,* 1:581-86.

---

* For a more complete bibliography see Spiller, et al. *Literary History of the United States,* 3 (1948) :736-38.

SPECIAL ASPECTS: Bushnell, G. H. *From Papyrus to Print,*
(1947) :185-89.

Boynton, P. H. *America in Contemporary Fiction,* 35-52.

Cowie, Alexander. *Rise of the American Novel,* 447-63.

Erskine, John. *Leading American Novelists,* 275-323.

Mott, F. L. *Golden Multitudes,* 114-22.

Phelps, W. L., in *Howells, James, Bryant, and other Essays,*
(1924) :181-206.

Trent, W. P., and John Erskine. *Great American Writers,* 197-
211.

HENRY WARD BEECHER—1813-1887—Clergyman

ORIGINAL SOURCES: Abbott, Lyman. *Silhouettes of My Contemporaries,* 213-39.

BIOGRAPHY: Olson, B. G. *Henry Ward Beecher.* (Hall of Fame,
1946).
A brief biographical sketch.

COLLECTIVE BIOGRAPHY: Bishop, J. B. *Notes and Anecdotes of
Many Years,* 35-43.

Brastow, L. O. *Representative Modern Preachers,* 98-142.

C. offut, W. A. *American Procession,* 56-81, 267-73.

Hamlin, Fred. *Land of Liberty,* 251-72.

Hibben, Patrick, in Murphy, M. E., et al., eds. *Treasury of
Brooklyn,* (1949) :126-38.

Higgins, P. L. *Preachers of Power,* (1950) :9-36.

Jones, E. D. *Lincoln and the Preachers,* (1948) :86-97.

Macartney, C. E. N. *Six Kings of the American Pulpit,* 86-124.

Rourke, C. M. *Trumpets of Jubilee,* 149-237.

Starr, H. E., in *DAB,* 2:129.

Stowe, L. B. *Saints, Sinners and Beechers,* 236-335.

*JOHN LOTHROP MOTLEY—   1814-1877
—"Representative of the Brahmin Spirit"

ORIGINAL SOURCES: Higby, C. P., and B. T. Schantz, eds. *John
Lothrop Motley: Representative Selections.* (American Writers, 1939).

---

* For a more complete bibliography see Higby and Schantz, pp. cxxxviii-
clxi; *Cambridge History of American Literature,* 2 (1917) :501-03; Spiller, et al.
Literary History of the United States, 3 (1948) :664-66.

N. E. Quar., 15:171. "This book represents Motley more fully than any other single volume. It contains (besides other matter) 364 pages expertly cut from the three great histories . . . an excellent 27-page annotated bibliography, a chronological table, and a collaborative critical introduction of 121 pages." Mr. Schantz discusses Motley's literary theory and his political and social attitudes; Mr. Higby, his histories and his career as a diplomat.

Howells, W. D. *Literary Friends and Acquaintances,* 93-97.

Lodge, H. C. "Some Early Memories," *Scribner's,* 53 (1913): 724-28.

Mildmay, H. S. J., ed. *John Lothrop Motley and His Family.* 1910.

AHR, 16:396. After Lowell, "Motley was the best of American writers . . . The correspondence with Bismarck is decidedly interesting. Most of the volume, however, is made up of letters from other members of Motley's family, chiefly his wife and his eldest daughter . . ."

BIOGRAPHY: Holmes, O. W. *John Lothrop Motley, a Memoir.* 1879.

A brief biography by an intimate friend.

Also in ———. *Writings,* 11 (1878) :329-526.

COLLECTIVE BIOGRAPHY: Blok, P. J. "A Tribute from Holland," *Nation,* 98:427-28, Apr. 16, 1914.

Brooks, V. W. *The Flowering of New England,* 334-42.

Cheyney, E. P., in *DAB,* 13:282.

Long, O. W. *Literary Pioneers,* 199-224.

Parrington, V. L. *Main Currents in American Thought,* 3:927-30.

Putman, Ruth, in *Cambridge History of American Literature,* 2:131-47.

Vincent, L. H. *American Literary Masters,* 359-76.

SPECIAL ASPECTS: Bassett, J. S. *The Middle Group of American Historians,* 223-32.

Gooch, G. P. *History and Historians of the 19th Century,* (1913) :416-19.

Jameson, J. F. *History and Historical Writing in America,* (1891) :117-21.

Lynch, Sister M. C. *The Diplomatic Mission of John Lothrop Motley to Austria, 1861-1867.* 1944.

AHR, 51:354. Suggests that Motley cared more for meeting the best people and for his writing than for observing developments in Vienna or Europe.

Nevins, Allan, in Macy, John, ed. *American Writers on American Literature*, 226-42.

Whipple, E. P. "Motley, the Historian," *Recollections of Eminent Men*, (1886) :155-203.

Also in *Harper's*, 58 (1879) :897-910.

Willson, Beckles. *America's Ambassadors to England*, 336-57.

AMELIA JENKS BLOOMER— 1818-1894 —Editor and Reformer

COLLECTIVE BIOGRAPHY: Kasten, M. A., in *DAB*, 2:385.

Thorp, Margaret. *Female Persuasion*, (1949) :107-42.

SPECIAL ASPECTS: Gonciar, Beth. "Amelia Jenks Bloomer, Advocate of Women's Trousers," *Hobbies*, 53 (1948) :118-19.

LYDIA ESTES PINKHAM— 1819-1883 —A Great Vegetable Compounder

BIOGRAPHY: Burton, Jean. *Lydia Pinkham is Her Name*. 1949.

Weekly Bk. Rev., Aug. 21, 1949, p. 6. Miss Burton has produced a "sound and wholly delightful biography" of an able business woman. Mrs. Pinkham was "a wise and kindly woman" who knew psychology and advertising and wrote thousands of letters to women all over the country.

Washburn, R. C. *The Life and Times of Lydia E. Pinkham*. 1931.

COLLECTIVE BIOGRAPHY: Genzmer, G. H., in *DAB*, 14:624.

Woodward, Helen. "Story of Lydia Pinkham," *Am. Merc.*, 70 (1950) :725-33.

*JAMES RUSSELL LOWELL—1819-1891—Poet and Diplomat

ORIGINAL SOURCES: Clark, H. H., and Norman Foerster, eds. *James Russell Lowell: Representative Selections*. (American Writers, 1947).

Amer. Lit., 20:351. These selections illustrate "Lowell's development as an unusually versatile man of letters, using a multitude of forms." Besides

---

* For a more complete bibliography see Clark, pp. cxliii-clxvi; *Cambridge History of American Literature*, 2 (1917) :544-54; Spiller, et al. *Literary History of the United States*, 3 (1948) :628-34.

an extensive bibliography, there is an introduction discussing Lowell's mental growth and Lowell as a critic.

Doyle, H. G. "Interesting Letter of James Russell Lowell," *Hispania,* 31 (1948) :398-400.

Greenslet, Ferris. *Under the Bridge,* 36, 51, 52, 60, 74, 76-77, 85-88, 111, 112, 198.

Howe, M. A. D., ed. *New Letters of James Russell Lowell.* 1932.

MVHR, 20:133. These letters to the poet's family and friends give glimpses of Lowell's contacts with British and French writers and of his annoyance at criticism of America and Americans.

Norton, C. E., ed. *The Letters of James Russell Lowell.* 1894, 1904.

BIOGRAPHY: Beatty, R. C. *James Russell Lowell.* 1942.

Nation, 155:521, Nov. 14, 1942. A study combining biography and literary criticism. Professor Beatty does full justice to Lowell's "abilities and his charm both as a man and as a writer, and to his significance in American life."

Greenslet, Ferris. *James Russell Lowell; His Life and His Work.* (American Men of Letters, 1905) .

Dial, 40:119, Feb. 16, 1906. "Mr. Greenslet's study of Lowell is admirably made. The result is a complete record of this many sided life and a really judicial discussion of the poet's place in literature." An excellent brief biography.

Scudder, H. E. *James Russell Lowell.* 2 vols. 1901.

Atlantic, 89:254. An excellent biography in which literary criticism is "subordinate to telling the story of a life."

COLLECTIVE BIOGRAPHY: Bradley, Sculley. "Lowell, Emerson and the Pioneer," *Amer. Lit.,* 19 (1947) :231-44.

Brooks, V. W. *The Flowering of New England,* 303-22, 499-525.

———. *New England: Indian Summer,* 24-27, 307-11.

Greenslet, Ferris. *The Lowells and their Seven Worlds.* 1946.

Amer. Lit., 19:186. "When Ferris Greenslet was writing his very sound brief biography of James Russell Lowell some forty years ago he became interested in various other members of the family . . . He strove to make this book . . . not so much the success story of a family as a chronicle play of New England history for three centuries, seen through the family's eyes and dramatized in its actions."

Hale, E. E. *James Russell Lowell and his Friends.* 1899.

Higginson, T. W. *Old Cambridge,* (1899) :145-96.

Howe, M. A. D., in *DAB,* 11:458.

Howells, W. D. *Literary Friends and Acquaintances*, (1900) : 212-50.

James, Henry, in *Library of the World's Best Literature*, 16: 9229-78.

Thorndike, A. H., in *Cambridge History of American Literature*, 2:245-57.

Vincent, L. H. *American Literary Masters*, 453-82.

SPECIAL ASPECTS: Bailey, E. J. *Religious Thought in the Greater American Poets*, 158-82.

Bernard, E. G. "New Light on Lowell as Editor," *N. E. Quar.*, 10 (1937) :337-41.

Blair, Walter. *Horse Sense in American Humor*, 82-101.

Brownell, W. C. *American Prose Masters*, 271-335.

De Mille, G. E. *Literary Criticism in America*, (1931) :49-85.

Foerster, Norman. *American Criticism*, 111-56.

———. *Nature in American Literature*, 143-75.

Galsworthy, John. *Addresses in America*, (1919) :1-10.

Hicks, Granville. *Great Tradition*, 1-31.

Lovett, R. M., in Macy, John, ed. *American Writers on American Literature*, 177-89.

Nadal, E. S. *A Virginian Village*, (1917) :148-83.

Orcutt, W. D. *From My Library Walls*, (1945) :179-83.

Perry, Bliss. *Praise of Folly*, (1923) :130-50.

Phelps, W. L., in *Howells, James, Bryant, and Other Essays*, 96-122.

Prichard, J. P., "Glance at Lowell's Classical Reading," *Amer. Lit.*, 21 (1950) :442-55.

Reilly, J. J. *James Russell Lowell as a Critic*. 1915.

Root, Elihu. *Men and Policies*, 58-62.

Smith, Bernard. *Forces in American Criticism*, (1939) :229-65.

Strong, A. H. *American Poets and their Theology*, 265-317.

Thompson, Francis. *Literary Criticism*, (1948) :307-13.

Trent, W. P., and John Erskine. *Great American Writers*, 134-69.

Voss, Arthur. "Backgrounds of Lowell's Satire in the Biglow Papers," *N. E. Quar.*, 23 (1950) :47-64.

Willson, Beckles. *America's Ambassadors to England*, 374-97.

Woodberry, G. E. *Makers of Literature*, (1900) :324-49.

———. *Studies of a Literateur*, (1921) :215-31.

SUSAN BROWNELL ANTHONY —1820-1906
—Feminist

COLLECTIVE BIOGRAPHY: Eddy, Sherwood, and Kirby Page. *Makers of Freedom*, 177-99.

Ferner, M. S., and E. C. Fishburn. *Pioneer American Educators*, 81-88.

Howe, M. A. D. *Causes and their Champions*, 195-233.

Malone, Dumas. *Saints in Action*, 84-113.

Morris, Charles. *Heroes of Progress in America*, 232-38.

Seitz, D. C. *Uncommon Americans*, 147-55.

Thomas and Thomas. *Fifty Great Americans*, 194-202.

———. *Living Biographies of Famous Women*, (1942) :163-75.

Starr, H. E., in *DAB*, 1:318.

Weitz, A. C. "Praise for a Valiant Soul," *NEA Jour.*, 39 (1950) : 103.

MARY BAKER EDDY—1821-1910—Religious Leader

BIOGRAPHY: Dakin, E. F. *Mrs. Eddy: the Biography of a Virginal Mind*. 1930.

Nation, 129:265. Returning from the World War with his old beliefs shattered, Mr. Dakin investigated Christian Science and its founder in the hope of finding something new. "His book is a story rather than either an attack or a panegyric, and is well documented so as to be difficult to dispute. Mr. Dakin writes of Mrs. Eddy with sympathy and some admiration. He admires her courage, will power, and shrewdness in raising herself in middle age from a useless life of neurotic invalidism to the dictatorship of a remarkably influential religion; he says she 'believed her doctrine with a belief that burned like fire.' . . . Mr. Dakin has done a service in writing of Mrs. Eddy from a factual rather than a controversial standpoint."

COLLECTIVE BIOGRAPHY: Johnson, Allen, in *DAB*, 6:7.

Hubbard, Elbert. *Little Journeys to the Homes of Great Teachers*, 2:327-75.

Milmine, Georgine. "Mary Baker Eddy: the Story of Her Life and the History of Christian Science," *McClure's,* 28 (1907) : 227-42, 339-54, 506-24, 608-27.

Seitz, D. C. *Uncommon Americans,* 276-90.

Thomas and Thomas. *Living Biographies of Religious Leaders,* (1942) :269-81.

Zweig, Stefan. *Mental Healers,* (1932) :101-248.

SPECIAL ASPECTS: Manwell, R. D., and S. B. Fahs. *Church Across the Street,* (1947) :229-43.

Orcutt, W. D. *Celebrities Off Parade,* 45-85.

Strachan, Pearl. "Landmarks of Mary Baker Eddy," *Christian Sci. Mon.,* 9-11, June 1, 1946.

GEORGE FRANCIS TRAIN— 1829-1904 —Business Man and Lecturer

ORIGINAL SOURCES: Train, G. F. *My Life in Many States and in Foreign Lands.* 1902.

BIOGRAPHY: Thornton, Willis. *The Nine Lives of Citizen Train.* 1948.

N. Y. Times, Nov. 14, 1948, p. 36. The biography of an eccentric who built clipper ships, introduced tramways into England, promoted the Union Pacific, ran for president, travelled around the world, lectured as "Champion Crank."

COLLECTIVE BIOGRAPHY: Carleton, W. "Meetings with George Francis Train," *Harper's W.,* 48:213, Feb. 6, 1904.

Outlook, 76:252-53, Jan., 1930.

Seitz, D. C. *Uncommon Americans,* 167-82.

FRANCIS PARKMAN—1823-1893—Historian of the Wilderness

ORIGINAL SOURCES: Tebbell, J. W., ed. *The Battle for North America.* 1948.

MVHR, 37:112. "A condensation into one volume of Francis Parkman's thirteen-volume work, *France and England in North America.*" The book "does not give an entirely accurate picture of Parkman, but the time has been changed." Mr. Tebbell has succeeded in making "at least some of the text available and palatable to the general reader."

*Schramm, W. L., ed. *Francis Parkman: Representative Selections*. (American Writers, 1938) .

AHR, 47:153. This book is valuable chiefly for the introduction, which includes essays on Parkman's life, his political and social philosophy, and his literary achievements.

Wade, Mason, ed. *The Journals of Francis Parkman*. 2 vols. 1947.

AHR, 54:438. These documents include records of Parkman's travels in New England, the West, Canada, and Europe. The *Oregon Trail* journal of 1846 (pp. 383-510) is especially interesting. The *Journals* include notes for the histories, and throw much light on Parkman's intellectual development.

BIOGRAPHY: Wade, Mason. *Francis Parkman: Heroic Historian*. 1942.

AHR, 48:748. A sympathetic study by a Catholic scholar. An excellent book, although the discovery of Parkman's diaries led the author to overemphasize the years of preparation.

COLLECTIVE BIOGRAPHY: Adams, J. T., in *DAB*, 14:247.

Bassett, J. S., in *Cambridge History of American Literature*, 3: 189-91.

———, in *Sewanee Rev.*, 10 (1902) :285-301.

Brooks, V. W. *New England: Indian Summer*, 169-83.

Kunitz and Haycraft. *American Authors*, 596-98.

Perry, Bliss. "Some Personal Qualities of Francis Parkman," *Yale Rev.*, 13 (1924) : 443-46.

Russell, F. A. *American Pilgrimage*, 134-49.

Vincent, L. H. *American Literary Masters*, 379-98.

HISTORY: Monaghan, James. *Overland Trail*, (1947) :295-317.

SPECIAL ASPECTS: Bourne, E. G. *Essays in Historical Criticism*, (1901) :277-87.

Also in *Atlantic*, 73 (1894) :664-74.

Fitch, G. H. *Great Spiritual Writers of America*, (1916) :103-10.

Nevins, Allan, in Macy, John, ed. *American Writers on American Literature*, 226-42.

Compares Parkman with Prescott and Motley.

---

* For fuller bibliographies, see Schram, pp. cxxi-cxiv; *Cambridge History of American Literature*, 4 (1921) :737; Spiller, et al. *Literary History of the United States*, 3 (1948) :680-82.

Saveth, E. N. *American Historians and European Immigrants,* 98-111.

Schafer, Joseph, in MVHR, 10 (1924) :351-64.

Also in *Wis. Mag. of Hist.,* 7 (1924) :265-80.

Schramm, W. L. "Parkman's Novel," *Amer. Lit.,* 9:218-27.

Smith, J. P., in Hutchinson, W. T., ed. *Essays in American Historiography,* 43-59.

Trent, W. P., and John Erskine. *Great American Writers,* 181-86.

Winsor, Justin, in *Atlantic,* 73 (1894) :660-64.

Wrong, G. M., in *Canadian Hist. Rev.,* 4 (1923) :289-303. Critical.

*EMILY DICKINSON— 1830-1886 —"The Leading American Poet of Her Generation"

ORIGINAL SOURCES: Bianchi, M. D., ed. *Emily Dickinson, Face to Face: Unpublished Letters with Notes and Reminiscences by her Niece.* 1932.

Sat. Rev. of Lit., 9:363, Jan. 7, 1933. This volume gives us "a new Emily Dickinson, a far more comprehensible and less enigmatic creature than the mythical sphinx of Amherst, a richer spirit and a more intimate human being."

Todd, M. L., ed. *Letters of Emily Dickinson.* 1931.

Amer. Lit., 4:318. "The definitive edition of the letters of a major American poet."

——. *Letters of Emily Dickinson.* 1951.

Sat. Rev. of Lit., May 19, 1951, p. 18. A new printing of the first collection which first appeared in 1894.

Ward, T. V. W., ed. *Emily Dickinson's Letters to Doctor and Mrs. Josiah Gilbert Holland.* 1951.

N. Y. Times, Apr. 22, 1951, p. 6. The ninety-three letters Emily Dickinson wrote to Dr. and Mrs. J. G. Holland, "two-thirds of them published here for the first time, are among the finest written by the American poet, and in their way inimitable."

Whicher, G. F. "Some Uncollected Poems of Emily Dickinson," *Amer. Lit.,* 20 (1948) :436-40.

---

* For fuller bibliography see Spiller, et al. *Literary History of the United States,* 3 (1948) :467-70.

Biography: Bianchi, M. D. *The Life and Letters of Emily Dickinson*. 1924.

N. Y. Times, Apr. 13, 1924, p. 7. Mrs. Bianchi takes a proprietory attitude toward her aunt, and is reticent regarding her lover.

Extract in Hyde, M. A., ed. *Modern Biography*, 80-86.

Pollitt, Josephine. *Emily Dickinson: the Human Background of her Poetry*. 1930.

Nation, 130:329, Mar. 19, 1930. Miss Pollitt seeks to prove that Emily's lover was Major Hunt, the husband of her girlhood friend, Helen Fiske. More important is "her study of the intellectual influence that touched the young poet."

Taggard, Genevieve. *The Life and Mind of Emily Dickinson*. 1930.

N. Y. Times, June 22, 1930, p. 3. Miss Taggard tries to prove that Emily's lover was George Gould, first an Amherst student and later a preacher of some renown. Her second task is to study Miss Dickinson's poetry "as a reflection on the mental and emotional states of which it was the product. The book is distinguished both for its penetration and its sympathy."

Whicher, G. F. *This Was a Poet: a Critical Biography of Emily Dickinson*. 1938.

Amer. Lit., 10:510. Professor Whicher's book "is more than a critical account of a poet and her times. It is a notable reappraisal and an authoritative re-creation."

Collective Biography: Bradford, Gamaliel. *Portraits of American Women*, 229-57.

Also in *Atlantic*, 124 (1919) :216-26.

Brooks, V. W. *Chilmark Miscellany*, 219-31.

——. *New England: Indian Summer*, 316-29.

Brown, R. W. *Lonely Americans*, (1929) :235-57.

Foerster, Norman, in *Cambridge History of American Literature*, 3:31-34.

Hartley, Marsden. *Adventurers in the Arts*, (1921) :198-206.

Josephson, Matthew. *Portrait of the Artist as American*, 139-98.

Kunitz and Haycraft. *American Authors*, 215-17.

Moore, Virginia. *Distinguished Women Writers*, (1934) :145-60.

Whicher, G. F., in *DAB*, 5:297.

Williams, S. T., in *Literary History of the United States,* 2:907-16.

Wood, Clement. *Poets of America,* 82-96.

SPECIAL ASPECTS: Bingham, M. T. *Ancestors' Brocades: the Literary Debut of Emily Dickinson.* 1945.

AHR, 51:171. A "footnote to literary history." Deals with the family feud and litigation; throws "little new light on Emily herself."

———. "Emily Dickinson's Earliest Friend," *Amer. Lit.,* 6 (1934) :191-92.

———. "Emily Dickinson's Handwriting—a Master Key," *N. E. Quar.,* 22 (1949) :229-34.

De Voto, Bernard, in *Harper's,* 190 (1945) :602-05.

Hicks, Granville. *Great Tradition,* 100-30.

Johnson, T. H. "Speaking of Books," *N. Y. Times Bk. Rev.,* Aug. 20, 1950, p. 2.

Loggins, Vernon. *I Hear America,* 14-22.

Lowell, Amy. *Poetry and Poets,* (1930) :88-108.

Trueblood, C. K., in Drake, W. A., ed. *American Criticism,* (1926) :291-307.

Whicher, G. F. "Emily's Suitors," *Forum,* 106 (1946) :162-66.

———. "Deliverance of Emily Dickinson, One of America's Greatest Poets," *Weekly Bk. Rev.,* Aug. 13, 1950, p. 2.

———. "In Emily Dickinson's Garden," *Atlantic,* 177 (1946) :64-70.

Winters, Yvor. *In Defense of Reason,* 283-99.

JAMES GILLESPIE BLAINE—   1830-1893
—Statesman or Politician?

ORIGINAL SOURCES: Blaine, J. G. *Twenty Years of Congress, from Lincoln to Garfield.* 2 vols. 1884-86.

DAB, 2:329. This book "stands high in character among works of its kind."

Dodge, M. A. (Gail Hamilton, pseud.) *Biography of James G. Blaine.* 1895.

AHR, 2:181. A volume of letters. Contains confidential correspondence between Garfield and his future Secretary of State. . . . This gives the key of Garfield's administration: "the Republican party was to be consolidated within, and the country aroused by a vigorous foreign attitude."

Volwiler, A. T., ed. *The Correspondence between Benjamin Harrison and James G. Blaine, 1882-1893.* (Memoirs of the American Philosophical Society, 1940).

AHR, 47:158. An "interesting collection" of some 350 items of correspondence between the two dominating Republicans of the 1880's.

BIOGRAPHY: *Muzzey, D. S. *James G. Blaine: a Political Idol of Other Days.* (American Political Leaders, 1934).

AHR, 41:554. The best biography. It does not clear up all the mysteries in Blaine's life, but gives a just estimate of his claim to statesmanship.

Russell, C. E. *Blaine of Maine.* 1931.

Books, Nov. 8, 1931, p. 10. A good account of Blaine's career, but the author is inaccurate and unfair in dealing with his times.

COLLECTIVE BIOGRAPHY: Bradford, Gamaliel. *American Portraits,* 115-41.

Also in *Atlantic,* 126 (1920) :509-19.

Fish, C. R., in *DAB,* 2:322.

Fuller, H. B. *The Speakers of the House,* (1909) :169-72, 175-82, 184-96.

Macartney, C. E. N. *Men Who Missed It,* 87-95.

Seitz, D. C. *The "Also Rans,"* 282-97.

Stone, Irving. *They Also Ran,* 231-50.

White, W. A. *Masks in a Pageant,* 63-107.

HISTORY: Rhodes, J. F. *History of the United States.* 8 vols. See vols. 3-8.

SPECIAL ASPECTS: Lockey, J. B., in *American Secretaries of State,* 7:263-97; 8:109-84.

Tyler, A. F. *The Foreign Policy of James G. Blaine.* 1927.

AHR, 33:676. A well-balanced account of Blaine's influence on foreign affairs.

BIOGRAPHIES OF CONTEMPORARIES: Dyke, J. C., ed. *Autobiography of Andrew Carnegie.* 1920.

†LOUISA MAY ALCOTT—   1832-1888   —"The
Author of *Little Women"*

ORIGINAL SOURCES: Cheney, E. D., ed. *Louisa May Alcott: her Life, Letters, and Journals.* 1889, 1928.

---

* Awarded the Pulitzer Prize.
† For fuller bibliography see Spiller, et al. *Literary History of the United States,* 3 (1948) :383-84.

Nation, 49:416. An intimate friend describes Miss Alcott's struggles with poverty and ill health and her experiences as an army nurse.

Pickett, Mrs. L. C. *Across My Path,* 105-10.

BIOGRAPHY: Anthony, K. C. *Louisa May Alcott.* 1938.

Amer. Lit., 11:854. This attempt of a popular biographer "to psychoanalyze Louisa Alcott and her parents" is unfortunate. While "Miss Anthony's scholarly background is usually sound," her Freudian interpretation fails to fit the known facts, to recommend itself to the reader as probable and to "explain phenomena otherwise inexplicable."

Meigs, Cornelia. *Invincible Louisa: the Story of the Author of Little Women.* 1933.

Amer. Lit., 6:97. Miss Meigs "sees in Miss Alcott a modern woman, eager for independence and a career, but without the modernist's clamor for 'self-expression'!" Her literary significance "consists in her inauguration of a fiction for the young drawn from life, not the fancy."

Stern, M. B. *Louisa May Alcott.* 1950.

N. Y. Herald Tribune Bk. Rev., Apr. 16, 1950, p. 4. "From the many un-critical and over-enthusiastic accounts of her (Louisa May Alcott) Miss Stern's book stands out by reason of its unfailing objectivity and good sense. For general readers it offers a compact and almost breathless nar-rative of a remarkable career, a success story on the Oliver Optic model. For literary scholars and social historians, who may be interested in Bronson Alcott as well as his daughter, it supplies a meticulous biblio-graphy . . . an elaborate set of notes on sources documenting every topic discussed, and a highly useful index."

COLLECTIVE BIOGRAPHY: Beach, S. C. *Daughters of the Puritans,* 251-86.

Bradford, Gamaliel. *Portraits and Personalities,* 133-53.

Brooks, V. W. *New England: Indian Summer,* 45-65.

Russell, F. A. *American Pilgrimage,* 150-64.

Talbot, Marion. "Glimpses of the Real Louisa May Alcott," *N. E. Quar.,* 11 (1938) :731-38.

Ticknor, Caroline, in *DAB,* 1:141.

Stern, M. B. "Louisa M. Alcott: an Appraisal," *N. E. Quar.,* 22 475-98.

SPECIAL ASPECTS: Gerould, Mrs. K. F. *Modes and Morals,* (1920) :182-98.

Leech, Margaret. *Reveille in Washington,* 222-24.

Stern, M. B. "Louisa Alcott, Trouper: Experiments in Theatri-cals, 1848-80," *N. E. Quar.,* 16 (1943) :175-97.

JAMES ABBOTT McNEILL WHISTLER— 1834-
1903—"America's Master Painter"

ORIGINAL SOURCES: Wolcott, J. G. *Fra Angelo Bomberto in the Underworld of Art; New Correspondence Concerning James A. McNeill Whistler and his Family*, by F. W. Coburn. 1946.

BIOGRAPHY: Laver, James. *Whistler*. 1930.

Sat. Rev. of Lit., 7:675, May 21, 1930. "A sympathetic and understanding study of a man both eccentric and charming" who had "an art of making enemies."

Pennell, Elizabeth, and Joseph Pennell. *The Life of Whistler*. 2 vols. 1908.

Bookman, 28:479. The authorized biography. Gives the first comprehensive account of Whistler's life and an analysis of his methods as an artist.

COLLECTIVE BIOGRAPHY: Baumer, W. H. *Not All Warriors*, 222-60.

Blumenfeld, R. D. *R. D. B.'s Procession*, 169-74.

Bradford, Gamaliel. *American Portraits*, 85-112.

Also in *Atlantic*, 127 (1921) :513-24.

Brown, R. W. *Lonely Americans*, 51-85.

Caffin, C. H. *American Masters of Painting*, 37-51.

Cortissoz, Royal, in *DAB*, 20:73.

Cox, Kenyon. *Old Masters and New*, 227-54.

Hubbard, Elbert. *Little Journeys to the Homes of Eminent Artists*, 151-81.

Irwin, Grace. *Trail-Blazers of American Art*, 76-94.

Josephson, Matthew. *Portrait of the Artist as American*, 44-69.

Key, J. T. "Recollections of Whistler," *Century*, 75 (1908) :928-32.

McCarthy, Justin. *Portraits of the Sixties*, (1903) :236-52.

McSpadden, J. W. *Famous Painters of America*, (1940) :221-71.

Seitz, D. C. *Uncommon Americans*, 209-20.

Starr, Sidney. "Personal Recollections of Whistler," *Atlantic*, 101 (1908) :528-37.

Thomas and Thomas. *Fifty Great Americans*, 209-18.

———. *Living Biographies of Great Painters*, 254-70.

SPECIAL ASPECTS: Cahill, Holger, in Cahill, Holger, and A. H. Barr, eds. *Art in America in Modern Times,* (1934) :7-13.

Cargill, Oscar. *Intellectual America,* 399-536.

Cheney, S. W. *Story of Modern Art,* (1941) :147-74.

Chesterton, G. K. *Heretics,* (1905) :234-46.

Cortissoz, Royal. *Art and Common Sense,* 179-216.

Hartmann, Sadakichi. *The Whistler Book; a Monograph of the Art of James McNeill Whistler, together with a careful study of his more important works.* 1924.

James, Henry. *Views and Reviews,* (1908) :207-14.

Lewisohn, S. A. *Painters and Personality,* (1948) :93-100.

Mather, F. J. *Estimates in Art,* 2nd ser., (1931) :89-101.

Mowat, R. B. *Americans in England,* 227-42.

Paris, W. F. *Personalities in American Art,* (1930) :9-20.

Parry, Sir E. A. *What the Judge Thought,* (1923) :111-30.

Pennell, Elizabeth, and Joseph Pennell. *Art of Whistler.* 1928.

Roof, K. M., in Cockayne, C. A., ed. *Modern Essays of Various Types,* (1927) :245-49.

Rothenstein, J. K. M. *Pot of Paint,* (1929) :87-121.

Symons, Arthur. *Studies in Seven Arts,* (1925) :78-97, 252-55, 269-73.

———. *Studies on Modern Painters,* (1925) :30-51.

Ticknor, Caroline. *Glimpses of Authors,* 286-92.

Van Dyke, J. C. *American Painting and Its Tradition,* 147-83.

CHARLES WILLIAM ELIOT— 1834-1926 —"The Most Influential Educator of His Generation"

ORIGINAL SOURCES: Peabody, F. G. *Reminiscences of Present-day Saints,* 295-306.

BIOGRAPHY: James, Henry. *Charles W. Eliot, President of Harvard University, 1869-1909.* 2 vols. 1930.

AHR, 36:618. A great biography which testifies to the number and quality of the bricks which Eliot "built into the walls of Harvard University," and gives a fine estimate of the man and his influence on higher education in America.

COLLECTIVE BIOGRAPHY: Brown, R. W. *Lonely Americans,* 15-47.

Davidson, Carter. "The Eras in Higher Education," *J. Higher Educ.,* 19 (1948) :289-94.

Howe, M. A. D. *Classic Shades,* 163-99.

Malone, Dumas. *Saints in Action,* 151, 155-59.

Perry, R. B., in *DAB,* 6:71.

Thwing, C. F. *Guides, Philosophers and Friends,* 3-35.

Wildman, Edwin. *Famous Leaders of Character in America,* 111-20.

SPECIAL ASPECTS: Babbitt, Irving, in Schilpp, P. A., ed. *Higher Education Faces the Future,* 187-204.

Carpenter, H. C. "Emerson, Eliot, and the Elective System," *N. E. Quar.,* 24 (1951) :13-34.

Chapman, J. J. *Memories and Milestones,* (1915) :165-90.

Eliot, S. A., in Strong, S. D., ed. *What I Owe my Father,* 49-60.

Frothingham, P. R. *All These,* (1928) :291-314.

Grandgent, C. H. *New Word: Essays,* (1929) :170-81.

PHILLIPS BROOKS— 1835-1893 —The Bishop

ORIGINAL SOURCES: Abbott, Lyman. *Silhouettes of my Contemporaries,* 240-57.

Peabody, F. G. *Reminiscences of Present-day Saints,* 157-78.

COLLECTIVE BIOGRAPHY: Brastow, L. O. *Representative Modern Preachers,* 195-251.

Britt, Albert. *Great Biographers,* (1936) :148-52.

Brown, C. R., in *There Were Giants,* 148-78.

Choate, J. H. *American Addresses,* 135-39.

Deland, Margaret, in *Atlantic,* 166 (1940) :29-37.

Dinsmore, C. A., in *DAB,* 3-83.

Higgins, P. L. *Preachers of Power,* (1950) : 39-56.

Howe, M. A. D. *Causes and their Champions,* 44-79.

Macartney, C. E. N. *Six Kings of the American Pulpit,* 128-54.

Malone, Dumas. *Saints in Action,* 42-43, 50, 54-55.

Rowe, H. K. *Modern Pathfinders of Christianity,* (1928) :219-29.

Thwing, C. F. *Friends of Men,* 3-29.

Vernon, A. W., in *Cambridge History of American Literature,* 3:218-25.

Wildman, Edwin. *Famous Leaders of Character in America,* 123-32.

SPECIAL ASPECTS: Scarlett, William. *Phillips Brooks: Selected Sermons.* 1949.

N. E. Quar., 23:279. "An excellent collection of the outstanding sermons of a great nineteenth century preacher."

WINSLOW HOMER—   1836-1910   —"America's Greatest Marine Painter"

BIOGRAPHY: Downes, W. H. *The Life and Works of Winslow Homer.* 1911.

Nation, 94:19, Jan. 4, 1912. An appreciative biography by the art critic of the *Boston Transcript* who was also an admiring friend.

Goodrich, Lloyd. *Winslow Homer; Publisher for the Whitney Museum of American Art.* 1944.

Library Jour., 69:760, Sept. 15, 1944. Lloyd Goodrich's biography "is a human, friendly study of a delightful American, New Englander to the core, as well as an analysis of the work of the distinguished artist."

COLLECTIVE BIOGRAPHY: Caffin, C. H. *American Masters of Painting,* 71-80.

Cortissoz, Royal. *American Artists,* (1923) :119-25.

Brinton, Christian. "Life and Work of Winslow Homer," *Scribner's,* 49 (1911) :9-23.

Downes, W. H., in *DAB,* 9:186.

Irwin, Grace. *Trail Blazers of American Art,* 39-58.

McSpadden, J. W. *Famous Painters of America,* 167-90.

Thomas and Thomas. *Living Biographies of Great Painters,* (1940) :299-312.

SPECIAL ASPECTS: Baldinger, W. S. "Art of Eakins, Homer, and Ryder; a Social Revaluation," *Art Quar.,* 9 (1946) :213-33.

Beam, P. C. "Winslow Homer's Father," *N. E. Quar.,* 20 (1947) : 51-74.

Cahill, Holger, and A. H. Barr, eds. *Art in Modern Times,* (1934) :7-13.

Cox, Kenyon. "Art of Winslow Homer," *Scribner's,* 56 (1914) : 377-88.

Hartley, Marsden. *Adventures in the Arts,* (1921) :42-49.

Mumford, Lewis. *Brown Decades,* (1931) :183-246.

Sanborn, Ashton. "Winslow Homer's Adirondack Guide," *Boston Museum Bul.,* 46 (1948) :48-51.

Van Dyke, J. C. *American Painting and its Tradition,* 89-114.

WILLIAM DEAN HOWELLS—1837-1920—Realistic Novelist

ORIGINAL SOURCES: Howells, Mildred, ed. *Life and Letters of William Dean Howells.* 1928.

Books, Nov. 25, 1928, p. 1. Especially valuable for Howell's correspondence with Henry James and Mark Twain.

*Kirk, Clara, and Rudolf Kirk, eds. *William Dean Howells: Representative Selections.* (American Writers, 1950) .

N. E. Quar., 23:544. "This book is sympathetic, accurate, and just. It exhibits careful scholarly editing and a great amount of exhaustive research. At the same time it makes interesting reading." To the introduction Professor and Mrs. Kirk "have added a valuable bibliography compiled by Professor George W. Arms and William M. Gibson." Some critics will dissent from certain statements in this excellent book.

COLLECTIVE BIOGRAPHY: Brooks, V. W. *New England: Indian Summer,* 23-44, 373-94.

Firkins, O. W., in *DAB,* 4:306.

Haight, G. H., in *Literary History of the United States,* 2:285-97.

Josephson, Matthew. *Portrait of the Artist as American,* (1930) : 139-98.

Kazin, Alfred. "Howells: a Late Portrait," *Antioch Rev.,* 1 (1941) :216-33.

Parrington, V. L. *Main Currents in American Thought,* 3:241-53.

---

* See also Kirk and Kirk, pp. clxviii-cxcix; *Cambridge History of American Literature,* 4 (1921) :656-57; Spiller, et al. *Literary History of the United States,* 3 (1948) :571-76.

Van Doren, C. C., in *Cambridge History of American Literature,* 3:77-85.

SPECIAL ASPECTS: Arms, G. W. "Howell's New York Novel:
Comedy and Belief," *N. E. Quar.,* 21 (1948) :313-25.

———. "The Literary Background of Howell's Social Criticism,"
Amer. Lit., 14 (1942) :267-71.

Brooks, V. W. *Chilmark Miscellany,* 231-45.

Clemens, S. L. *What is Man?* (1917) :228-39.

Cowie, Alexander. *Rise of the American Novel,* 653-701.

De Mille, G. E. *Literary Criticism in America,* (1931) :182-205.

Firkins, O. W. *William Dean Howells: a Study.* 1924.
A critical study rather than a biography.

Garland, Hamlin, in Macy, John, ed. *American Writers on
American Literature,* 285-97.

Gibson, W. M. "Mark Twain and Howells: Anti-Imperialists,"
N. E. Quar., 20 (1947) :435-70.

Hartwick, Harry. *Foreground of American Novel,* 315-40.

Hicks, Granville. *Great Tradition,* 68-99.

James, Henry, in Wilson, Edmund, ed. *Shock of Recognition,*
570-79.

Mencken, H. L. *Mencken Chrestomathy,* 489-92.

Morby, E. S. "William Dean Howells and Spain," *Hispan. Rev.,*
14 (1946) :187-212.

Morris, L. R. "Conscience in the Parlor: William Dean Howells," *Am. Scholar,* 18 (1949) :407-16.

Phelps, W. L., in *Howells, James, Bryant, and Other Essays,* 156-
80.

Smith, Bernard. *Forces in American Criticism,* (1939) :134-84.

Snell, G. D. *Shapers of American Fiction,* 198-211.

Taylor, W. F. *Economic Novel in America,* (1942) :214-81.

Ticknor, Caroline. *Glimpses of Authors,* 169-78.

Van Doren, C. C. *American Novel, 1789-1939,* 115-36.

HENRY ADAMS— 1838-1918 —"The Charming Pessimist"

ORIGINAL SOURCES: Adams, Henry. *The Education of Henry
Adams: an Autobiography.* 1918.

AHR, 24:422-34. Carl Becker explains why Adams regarded his life as a failure.

Extract in Wagenknecht, E. C., ed. *When I Was a Child,* 21-33.

Ford, W. C., ed. *Letters of Henry Adams, 1858-1891.* 1930.

AHR, 36:616. These letters are essential "for the study of one of the most interesting minds America has produced." They throw great light on the development of the author's mind years before he wrote the *Education.* They also discuss the personalities of Washington and London in the 1860's.

———. *Letters of Henry Adams, 1892-1918.* 1938.

AHR, 44:940. These later letters are interesting but add nothing of importance to our knowledge of their author, but there are "many extremely interesting passages about people and books."

Greenslet, Ferris. *Under the Bridge,* 28, 51, 84, 144-52, 185.

La Farge, Mabel. "Henry Adams: a Niece's Memories," *Yale Rev.,* 9 (1920) :271-85.

Laughlin, J. L. "Some Recollection of Henry Adams," *Scribner's,* 69 (1921) :576-85.

Rahv, Philip, ed. *Discovery of Europe,* 332-58.

Silver, A. W. "Henry Adams 'Diary of a Visit to Manchester,' " *AHR,* 51 (1945) :74-89.

Stone, Irving, and Richard Kennedy, eds. *We Speak for Ourselves,* 249-56.

BIOGRAPHY: Adams, J. T. *Henry Adams.* 1933.

AHR, 39:792. A delightful essay which attributes Adams' disappointment and disillusion to his feeling that his own achievements fell so far short of those of John and John Quincy.

Cater, H. D. *Henry Adams and his Friends.* 1947.

AHR, 52:738. "Dr. Cater has made the greatest contribution . . . to our knowledge of Henry Adams, the man." He adds over 600 letters to the other collections listed here. Furthermore the biographical introduction constitutes "the most faithful account of Henry Adams yet produced."

COLLECTIVE BIOGRAPHY: Adams, J. T. *The Adams Family,* (1930) :306-51.

Bassett, J. S., in *Cambridge History of American Literature,* 3: 198-200.

Becker, Carl. *Every Man his own Historian,* (1935) :143-68.

Bradford, Gamaliel. *American Portraits,* 29-57.

Also in *Atlantic,* 125 (1920) :623-34.

Brooks, V. W. *Chilmark Miscellany,* 287-96.

———. *New England: Indian Summer,* 90-94, 354-72, 474-90.

Bullard, F. L. "Abraham Lincoln and Henry Adams: a Contrast in Education," *Abraham Lincoln Quar.,* 1 (1941) :227-72.

Cournos, John. *Modern Plutarch,* 275-87.

Gabriel, R. H. *American Democratic Thought,* 259-68.

Johnson, Allen, in *DAB,* 1:61.

Kunitz and Haycraft. *American Authors,* 7-10.

MacDonald, William, in Macy, John, ed. *American Writers on American Literature,* 317-26.

Parrington, V. L. *Main Currents in American Thought,* 3:214-27.

Sherman, S. P. *Americans,* 288-315.

Spiller, R. E. "Henry Adams: Man of Letters," *Sat. Rev. of Lit.,* 30 (1947) :11-12.

———, in *Literary History of the United States,* 2:1080-1103.

Thwing, C. F. *Guides, Philosophers and Friends,* 223-38.

SPECIAL ASPECTS: Adams, J. T. *Tempo of Modern Life,* (1931) : 214-39.

Basso, Henry. "Henry Adams: a Mind in the Making," *New Yorker,* 23 (1947) :103-06, Mar. 29, 1947.

Beard, C. A. "Historians at Work: Brooks and Henry Adams," *Atlantic,* 171 (1943) :87-98.

Brooks, V. W. *Sketches in Criticism,* 198-210.

Commager, Henry, in Hutchinson, W. T., ed. *Essays in American Historiography,* 191-206.

Crothers, S. M. "Education in Pursuit of Henry Adams," *Yale Rev.,* 8 (1919) :580-95.

Delaney, S. P. "Man of Mystery," *No. Am. Rev.,* 216 (1922) :695-704.

Dickason, D. H. "Henry Adams and Clarence King," *N. E. Quar.,* 17 (1944) :229-54.

Ford, W. C. "Henry Adams, Historian," *Nation,* 106:674-75, June 8, 1918.

Glicksberg, C. I. "Henry Adams the Journalist," *N. E. Quar.*, 21 (1948) :232-36.

Hess, M. W. "Atomic Age and Henry Adams," *Cath. World,* 172 (1951) :256-63.

———. "Lin Yutang on Henry Adams," *America*, 84:16-18, Oct. 7, 1950.

Hind, C. L. *Authors and I*, 13-18.

Hume, R. A. *Runaway Star: an Appreciation of Henry Adams.* 1951.

N. Y. *Times,* Apr. 22, 1951, p. 22. Mr. Hume interprets Henry Adams as "a man of singular courage" who when disillusioned started to educate himself anew, studying geology, biology and physics, trying to discover 'an historical formula that should satisfy the condition of the stellar universe.' "

———. "The Style and Literary Background of Henry Adams with Attention to *The Education of Henry Adams,*" *Amer. Lit.*, 16 (1944) :296-315.

Irish, M. D. "Henry Adams: the Modern American Scholar," *Am. Scholar*, 1 (1932) :223-29.

Kraus, Michael. *A History of American History,* 321-35.

Kronenberger, Louis, in Cowley, Malcolm, and Bernard Smith, eds. *Books that Changed our Minds,* (1939) :45-57.

Miller, R. F. "Henry Adams and the Influence of Women," *Amer. Lit.*, 18 (1947) :291-98.

More, P. E. *Shelburne Essays,* 11th ser., (1921) :115-40.

Nichols, R. F. "The Dynamic Interpretation of History," *N. E. Quar.*, 8 (1935) :163-78.

Samuels, Ernest. *The Young Henry Adams.* 1948.

Booklist, 45:157, Jan. 1, 1949. "Not a biography but a study of Adams's intellectual development during the formative period of his career up to the time when, frustrated in his ambition toward statesmanship, he turned definitely to literature in which he later won renown with his histories . . ."

Saveth, E. N. *American Historians and European Immigrants, 1875-1925,* 65-89.

Sheldon, W. D. "Why Education Failed to Educate Henry Adams," *Sewanee Rev.*, 28 (1921) :54-65.

Whipple, T. K. *Spokesman*, 23-44.

Winters, Yvor. *In Defense of Reason*, 374-430.

Wright, Nathalia. "Henry Adams' Theory of History: a Puritan Defense," *N. E. Quar.*, 18 (1945) :204-10.

ALFRED THAYER MAHAN— 1840-1914 —"The Prophet of 'Manifest Destiny' "

ORIGINAL SOURCES: Westcott, Allan, ed. *Mahan on Naval Warfare; Selections from the Writings of Rear Admiral Alfred T. Mahan.* 1942.

New Repub., 106:156, Feb. 2, 1942. "From 1890 until his death in 1914, Admiral Mahan produced a flow of books and articles defining the principles of sea power and urging the United States to embrace those principles in cooperation with Great Britain, with special emphasis on our position in Asia and the Pacific."

BIOGRAPHY: Puleston, Captain W. B. *Mahan: the Life and Work of Captain Alfred Thayer Mahan, U. S. N.* 1939.

AHR, 45:422. Captain Puleston has skillfully woven together "the story of Mahan's life and an exposition of his ideas . . ." He does not attempt "to relate Mahan's ideas to the 'climate of opinion' in which they took shape," or to appraise "their influence upon the course of events."

Taylor, C. C. *The Life of Admiral Mahan.* 1920.

COLLECTIVE BIOGRAPHY: Alden, C. S., and Ralph Earle. *Makers of Naval Tradition*, 228-46.

Gabriel, R. H. *The Course of American Democratic Thought*, 344-51.

Lewis, C. L. *Famous American Naval Officers*, 255-74.

Sprout, M. T., in Earle, E. M., ed. *Makers of Modern Strategy*, (1943) :415-45.

West, R. S. *Admirals of American Empire; the Combined Story of George Dewey, Alfred Thayer Mahan, Winfield Scott Schley, and William Thomas Sampson.* 1948.

Westcott, Allen, in *DAB*, 12:206.

SPECIAL ASPECTS: Ellicott, J. M. "Sidelights on Mahan," *U. S. Naval Inst. Proc.*, 74 (1948) :1247-49.

Pratt, J. W., in Hutchinson, W. T., ed. *Essays in American Historiography*, 207-26.

JOHN FISKE—1842-1901—Popularizer of Evolution

ORIGINAL SOURCES: Abbott, Lyman. *Silhouettes of my Contemporaries*, 81-99.

*Fisk, Ethel. *The Letters of John Fiske*. 1940.

PHR, 10:388. "These letters form the best account we have of Fiske's life. He was "an immensely talented popularizer of history and evolution." The exigencies of a large family and his high standard of living led him "to exhaust his powers in constant and highly profitable lecture tours," and he died at the age of fifty-nine. Otherwise he might have had his great wish and succeeded Henry Adams at Harvard. "As a human being John Fiske was one of God's best."

Perry, T. S. "John Fiske: an Appreciation," *Atlantic*, 89 (1902) : 627-37.

BIOGRAPHY: Clark, J. S. *The Life and Letters of John Fiske*. 2 vols. 1917.

AHR, 23:878. Mr. Clark makes "Fiske's personality stand out clearly, using long extracts from his letters to his wife. He makes it clear that he considers "the attempt to reconcile religion and science the most valuable of Fiske's efforts." He makes no effort to "estimate the value of Fiske's historical work."

COLLECTIVE BIOGRAPHY: Adams, J. T., in *DAB*, 6:420.

Brooks, V. W. *New England: Indian Summer*, 89-114, 250-75.

Commager, H. S. *The American Mind*, 82-90.

Parrington, V. L. *Main Currents in American Thought*, 3:203-11.

SPECIAL ASPECTS: Hofstadter, R. I. *Social Darwinism in American Thought, 1860-1915*, 68-85.

Kraus, Michael. *History of American History*, 336-79.

Sanders, J. W., in Hutchinson, W. T., ed. *Essays in American Historiography*, 144-70.

Saveth, E. N. *American Historians and European Immigrants, 1875-1925*, 32-42.

Schneider, H. W. *History of American Philosophy*, 321-43.

Wiener, P. P. *Evolution and the Founders of Pragmatism*, (1949) : 129-51.

Werkmeister, W. H. *History of Philosophical Ideas in America*, 80-102.

---

* Fiske's daughter who married a Fisk without an "e."

*WILLIAM JAMES— 1842-1910 —Philosopher and Psychologist

ORIGINAL SOURCES: †Perry, R. B. *Thought and Character of William James; as Revealed in Unpublished Correspondence and Notes, Together with his Published Writings.* 2 vols. 1935.

Amer. Lit., 8:241. Professor Perry's long awaited study includes "not only the best available account of the early years of Henry James but also some thirty new letters written by the novelist."

———. "Common Enemy; Early Letters of Oliver Wendell Holmes, Jr., and William James," *Atlantic Harvest,* (1947): 647-60.

Raymond, M. E. "Memories of William James," *N. E. Quar.,* 10 (1937) :419-29.

COLLECTIVE BIOGRAPHY: Brooks, V. W. *New England: Indian Summer,* 250-75.

Clifton, J. L. *Ten Famous American Educators,* 212-33.

Cohen, M. R., in *Cambridge History of American Literature,* 3: 248-55.

Commager, H. S. *American Mind,* 91-107.

Grattan, C. H. *The Three Jameses: a Family of Minds.* 1932.

No. Amer. Rev., 234:574. "A book into which a great deal of painstaking and conscientious work has gone, an eminently sound interpretation of three extraordinarily fascinating characters. The background covers the whole history of America and is done with whatever attention seems necessary, but the emphasis is upon the men themselves, the elder James, a Swedenborgian closely connected with the transcendentalist movement in New England, and the two sons, the philosopher who wrote like a novelist, and the other who did just the reverse. . . . Mr. Grattan made a real contribution in this volume."

McElroy, H. C. *Modern Great Philosophers,* (1950) :71-84.

Perry, R. B., in *DAB,* 9:590.

Thomas and Thomas. *Fifty Great Americans,* 268-74.

———. *Living Biographies of Great Philosophers,* (1941) :295-305.

SPECIAL ASPECTS: Bixler, J. S. *Religion in the Philosophy of William James.* 1926.

---

* For a more complete bibliography see Spiller, et al. *Literary History of the United States,* 3 (1948) :590-93.
† Awarded the Pulitzer Prize.

Sat. Rev. of Lit., 3:422, Dec. 11, 1926. Professor Bixler's thesis is that William James "made his temperament the basis of his philosophy." However, his ultimate aim is "to prove the central position of religion in the thought of James . . . By means of copious quotations from letters and lectures he shows that James's pluralism and pragmatism were inspired by the kind of world that would satisfy his heart's desire."

Brooks, V. W. *Sketches in Criticism*, 37-45.

Curti, M. E. *Social Ideas of American Educators*, 429-58.

Dewey, John. *Characters and Events*, 1 (1929) :107-22.

Durant, W. J. *Story of Philosophy*, 530-77

Flournoy, Theodore. *The Philosophy of William James.* 1917.

Nation, 104:462. This little book was "expanded from an address given by the eminent Swiss psychologist immediately after Professor James' death. It is clearly and simply written and furnishes an admirable introduction to the study of William James—quite the best that we have seen."

Gabriel, R. H. *The Course of American Democratic Thought*, 280-89, index.

Hofstadter, R. L. *Social Darwinism in American Thought, 1860-1915*, 103-20.

Kallen, H. M., et al. *In Commemoration of William James: 1842-1942.* 1942.

Amer. Lit., 15:203. "A collection of essays and addresses by sixteen different authors on the subject of William James. Like all such collections, it is miscellaneous and uneven in quality, but the spirit of William James gives it unity, and some of the contributors give it distinction."

Macy, J. A. *Critical Game*, 175-89.

Mayhall, Jane. "William James and the Modern World," *Antioch Rev.*, 8 (1948) :291-305.

Miller, D. S., in Peterson, Houston, ed. *Great Teachers*, 223-28.

More, P. E. *Shelburne Essays*, 7th ser., (1910) :195-212.

Morris, Lloyd. *William James: the Essence of a Modern Mind.* (Twentieth Century Library, 1950) .

Amer. Lit., 23:271. "William James, unlike most professional philosophers, expressed his thoughts in a language that any intelligent reader can readily understand and therefore has never stood in great need of an interpreter. Lloyd Morris's little book . . . is rather a summary than an interpretation, and it is a great merit of the author that his style is as charming as that of James himself. Those who do not have time to read all of James's works, or who wish to refresh their memories, will find this book comprehensive and yet brief and readable."

Nathanson, Jerome. *Forerunners of Freedom,* (1941) :79-115.

Otto, M. C., and others. *William James, the Man and the Thinker, Addresses in Celebration of the Centenary of his Birth.* 1943.

Christian Century, 60:134, Feb. 3, 1943. "Many of the writers in these volumes sense the fact that the philosophy of William James yet has much to contribute to the liberation and vitalization of religious thought."

Perry, R. B. *In the Spirit of William James.* 1938.

Amer. Lit., 10:370. A brief study focusing attention on a few crucial problems: "how far was James's thought typically 'American'? Why was Josiah Royce, born on the Western frontier, much less 'American' in his philosophy than James, born in the East, and educated largely in Europe? . . . What should be the liberal attitude to illiberalism, i.e., to fascism?" The rest of the book tries to define "pragmatism," "experience," and "the limits of faith . . ." The book certainly "demonstrates the importance of James's thought to the modern world. . . ."

Royce, Josiah. *William James, and Other Essays of the Philosophy of Life,* (1911) :3-45.

Santayana, George. *Character and Opinions in the United States,* (1920) :64-96.

———, in Wilson, Edmund, ed. *Shock of Recognition,* 867-83.

Schneider, H. W. *History of American Philosophy,* 513-56.

Wickham, Harvey. *The Unrealists.* (1929) :29-67.

Winkler, J. K., and Walter Bromberg. *Mind Explorers,* (1939) : 146-83.

Werkmeister, W. H. *History of Philosophical Ideas in America,* 204-37.

Wiener, P. P. *Evolution and the Founders of Pragmatism,* (1949) :18-30, 97-128.

HENRY JAMES—1843-1916—An Un-American Snob or One of the Most Fascinating and Challenging American Novelists?

ORIGINAL SOURCES: Howe, M. D., ed. "Letters of Henry James to Mr. Justice Holmes," *Yale Rev.,* 38 (1949) :410-33.

La Farge, John, ed. "Henry James's Letters to the La Farges," *N. E. Quar.,* 22 (1949) :173-92.

Lubbock, Percy, ed. *The Letters of Henry James.* 2 vols. 1920.

Bookman, 51:364. "These letters bid fair to become a classic in English literature."

Matthiessen, F. O., and K. B. Murdock, eds. *Notebooks of Henry James*. 1947.

N. Y. Times, Dec. 7, 1947, p. 5. The novelist made these notes over a period of 33 years. They are his ideas for novels and short stories, and are accompanied with "a helpful introduction" and "a running commentary." A lady seated next to James at dinner gossips about a scandal, the artist begins to worry his idea, for to him literature is a game of skill.

Excerpt in *Atlantic*, 180 (1947) :145-46.

*Richardson, L. N., ed. *Henry James: Representative Selections*. (American Writers, 1941).

Amer. Lit., 14:91. This volume contains three critical essays, three literary portraits, and seven short stories. The introduction "touches on the most important points in James's life, themes, literary ideals, technique, and philosophy." Unfortunately the editor's style lacks precision, and this is "likely to go with looseness in thinking."

BIOGRAPHY: Brooks, V. W. *The Pilgrimage of Henry James*. 1925.

Bookman, 61:477, June, 1925. A brilliant study which "attempts to explain why Henry James made a failure of life." Mr. Brooks describes his continual struggle to find in England or America a setting suited to his nature and the demands of his profession.

Dupee, F. W. *Henry James*. (American Men of Letters, 1951).

N. Y. Times, Apr. 8, 1951, p. 5. "A thoroughly balanced and integrated assessment of Henry James' literary achievement, blended with a study of the novelist's highly original and curious personality."

COLLECTIVE BIOGRAPHY: Beach, J. W., in *Cambridge History of American Literature*, 3:96-108

Blackmur, R. P., in *Literary History of the United States*, 2: 1039-64.

Bradford, Gamaliel. *American Portraits*, 171-96.

Brooks, V. W. *New England: Indian Summer*, 224-49, 276-95, 395-408.

Brown, E. K. "James and Conrad," *Yale Rev.*, 35 (1946) :265-85.

---

* For a more complete bibliography see Richardson, pp. xci-cxi; *Cambridge History of American Literature*, 4 (1921) :671-75; Spiller, et al. *Literary History of the United States*, 3 (1948) :584-90.

Fadiman, Clifton. "The Revival of Interest in Henry James," *Herald-Tribune Wk. Bk. Rev.*, Jan. 14, 1945, p. 1-2.

Ford, F. M. *Portraits from Life*, (1937) :1-20.

Matthiessen, F. O., ed. *The James Family; including Selections from the Writings of Henry James, senior, William, Henry, and Alice James.* 1948.

N. E. Quar., 22-108. Professor Matthiessen makes "his 'group biography' a James family anthology by the judicious selection of characteristic writings by all of his principal figures." The reviewer predicts "that it will be a long time before another American family produces so rich and varied a volume of good reading. . . ."

Stein, Gertrude. *Four in America*, 119-59.

Van Doren, Carl, in *DAB*, 9:579.

Wilson, Edmund. *Triple Thinkers*, (1948) :88-132.

SPECIAL ASPECTS: Auden, W. H. "Henry James and the Artist in America," *Harper's*, 197 (1948) :36-40.

Beach, J. W. *The Method of Henry James.* 1918.

Booklist, 14:228, June, 1918. "A sincere study of the 'ideal and method' as developed especially in his various novels." The author considers that "the tone of *The Ambassadors* is the nearest we ever came to the very tone of Henry James. It is the tone of large and sociable speculation upon human nature, a tone at once grave and easy, light and yet deep, earnest and yet free from anxiety. It is the tone most of all, of the leisurely thinker, well assured that maturity can be the product only of time."

Boit, Louise. "Henry James as Landlord," *Atlantic*, 178 (1946) : 118-21.

Brownell, W. C. *American Prose Masters*, 339-400.

Cowie, Alexander. *Rise of the American Novel*, 702-42.

Eliot, T. S., in Wilson, Edmund, ed. *Shock of Recognition*, 854-65.

Firebaugh, J. J. "The Pragmatism of Henry James," *Va. Quar. Rev.*, 27 (1951) :419-35.

Hamilton, E. C. "Biographical and Critical Studies of Henry James, 1941-1948," *Amer. Lit.*, 20 (1949) :424-35.

Herrick, Robert, in Macy, John, ed. *American Writers on American Literature*, 298-316.

Hicks, Granville. *Great Tradition*, 100-30.

Hoskins, Katherine. "Henry James and the Future of the Novel," *Sewanee Rev.*, 54 (1946) :87-101.

Josephson, Matthew. *Portrait of the Artist as American*, 70-198, 265-88.

Leavis, F. R. *Great Tradition; George Eliot, Henry James, Joseph Conrad.* 1948.

Le Clair, R. C. "Henry James and Minnie Temple," *Amer. Lit.*, 21 (1949) :35-48.

Matthiessen, F. O. *Henry James: the Major Phase.* 1944.

Booklist, 41:136. A critical study of three novels by James. The author used Mr. James' unpublished notebooks "for illustrating the artistic intentions and personal psychology of James."

Nowell-Smith, S. H., ed. *Legend of the Master.* 1948.

Sat. Rev. of Lit., 31:16, May 29, 1948. This "collection of anecdotes, brief sketches, gossip, poignant sayings by James himself is fascinating reading."

Popkin, Henry. "The Two Theatres of Henry James," *N. E. Quar.*, 24 (1951) :69-83.

Roberts, Morris. "Henry James' Final Period," *Yale Rev.*, 31 (1947) :60-67.

Smith, J. A., ed. *Henry James and Robert Louis Stevenson, a Record of Friendship and Criticism.* 1948.

Amer. Lit., 23:245. "The record of a friendship of two writers of widely different temper and art, deeply respectful of each other's skills and deeply attached to one another."

Warren, Austin. *Rage for Order*, (1948) :142-61.

Winters, Yvor. *In Defense of Reason*, 300-43.

*EDWARD BELLAMY—1850-1898—Social Reformer and Author

BIOGRAPHY: Morgan, A. E. *Edward Bellamy.* 1944.

AHR, 50:575. A first biography somewhat inclined to exaggerate Bellamy's significance as a thinker.

COLLECTIVE BIOGRAPHY: Bakeless, John, in *DAB*, 2:163.

Brooks, V. W. *New England: Indian Summer*, 373-94.

Madison, C. A. *Critics and Crusaders*, 134-54.

Ticknor, Caroline. *Glimpses of Authors*, 112-21.

---

* For a more complete bibliography see Spiller, et al. *Literary History of the United States*, 3 (1948) :401-03.

Tarbell, I. M. "New Dealers of the Seventies," *Forum,* 92 (1934) :133-49.

SPECIAL ASPECTS: Forbes, A. B. "The Literary Quest for Utopia, 1880-1900," *Social Forces,* 6 (1927) :179-89.

Howells, W. D., in *Atlantic,* 82 (1898) :253-56.

Madison, C. A., in *N. E. Quar.,* 15 (1942) :444-66.

Mott, F. L. *Golden Multitudes,* 165-71.

Mumford, Lewis. *The Story of Utopias,* (1922) :159-69.

Parrington, V. L., Jr. *American Dreams,* 57-97.

Sadler, Elizabeth. "One Book's Influence: Edward Bellamy's 'Looking Backward,' " *N. E. Quar.,* 17 (1944) :530-55.

Schneider, H. W. *History of American Philosophy,* 193-207.

Shurter, R. L. "The Literary Work of Edward Bellamy," *Amer. Lit.,* 5 (1933) :229-34.

Taylor, W. F. *Economic Novel in America,* 184-213.

ALICE FREEMAN PALMER—1855-1902—The Girl Who Put Wellesley College on the Map

ORIGINAL SOURCES: Abbott, Lyman. *Silhouettes of my Contemporaries,* 59-80. •

An Academic Courtship: Letters of Alice Freeman and George Herbert Palmer, 1886-1887. With an Introduction by Caroline Hazard. 1940.

BIOGRAPHY: Palmer, G. H. *The Life of Alice Freeman Palmer.* 1908.

Bookman, 27:519. Husbands do not always make good biographers, but this is an exception.

COLLECTIVE BIOGRAPHY: Converse, Florence, in *DAB,* 14:173.

Fenner, M. S., and E. C. Fishburn. *Pioneer American Educators,* 105-12.

Leslie, E. A., in Lotz, P. H., ed. *Women Leaders,* 86-95.

Malone, Dumas. *Saints in Action,* 106-07.

Parkman, M. R. *Heroines of Service,* (1917) :31-58.

JOHN SINGER SARGENT— 1856-1925 —Artist and Painter

COLLECTIVE BIOGRAPHY: Caffin, C. H. *American Masters of Painting,* 55-67.

Cox, Kenyon. *Old Masters and New,* 255-65.

Irwin, Grace. *Trail-Blazers of American Art,* 167-92.

Law, F. A. *Modern Great Americans,* 234-47.

McSpadden, J. W. *Famous Painters of America,* 273-99.

SPECIAL ASPECTS: Cortissoz, Royal. *Art and Common Sense,* 217-46.

Cox, Kenyon. *Artist and Public,* (1914) :134-48.

Fry, R. E. *Transformations,* (1927) :125-35.

Mather, F. J. *Estimates in Art,* 2nd ser., (1931) :235-67.

Mellquist, Jerome. *Emergence of an American Art,* (1942) :44-59.

Mowat, R. B. *Americans in England,* 227-42.

Symons, Arthur. *Studies in Seven Arts,* (1925) :274-78.

Van Dyke, J. C. *American Painting and Its Tradition,* 243-70.

GEORGE WASHINGTON GOETHALS—1858-1928
—Military Engineer

COLLECTIVE BIOGRAPHY: Beard, A. E. S. *Our Foreign-Born Citizens,* 147-56.

Forbes, B. C. *Men Who are Making America,* 163-72.

Law, F. H. *Modern Great Americans,* 106-20.

Parkman, M. R. *Heroes of Today,* 161-97.

Rhodes, C. D., in *DAB,* 7:355.

Wildman, Edwin. *Famous Leaders of Industry,* 2nd ser., (1921) : 111-20.

SPECIAL ASPECTS: Bishop, J. B. *Notes and Anecdotes of Many Years,* 187-228.

WALTER CAMP— 1859-1925 —Father of Modern Football

BIOGRAPHY: Powell, H. W. H. *Walter Camp, the Father of American Football.* 1926.

Bookman, 64:635, Jan., 1927. A very readable book, which, however, leaves a few gaps in the life of one of the finest of American sportsmen.

COLLECTIVE BIOGRAPHY: Krout, J. A. *Annals of American Sport,* (Pageant of America, 1929) :238-42.

Literary Digest, 84 (1925) :72-75, Mar., 1928.

Osborn, N. G., in *DAB,* 3:444.

Outlook, 139 (1925) :440-41.

Outlook, 156 (1930) :661-63.

CHAPTER XXXII. NEW YORK

SARAH JOSEPHA HALE— 1788-1879 —Author and Editor

BIOGRAPHY: Entrikin, Isabelle. *Sarah Josepha Hale and Godey's Lady's Book.* 1946.

Finley, R. E. *The Lady of Godey's, Sarah Josepha Hale.* 1931.

Booklist, 28:196, Jan., 1932. "This noted feminist was for fifty years . . . the editor of *Godey's Lady's Book,* the forerunner of woman's magazines of today. She retired at the age of ninety. Through this magazine she advocated higher education for women. She established the first free sea-man's library at Boston and worked for child welfare, public playgrounds, and property rights for women. She was also a successful writer of children's books."

COLLECTIVE BIOGRAPHY: Lownsbery, Eloise. *Saints and Rebels,* (1937) :223-40.

Stern, B. M., in *DAB,* 8:111.

Wright, Richardson. *Forgotten Ladies,* 187-217.

SPECIAL ASPECTS: Schlesinger, A. M. *Learning How to Behave,* (1946) :15-26.

Walworth, Dorothy. "Sarah Hale and her Lady's Book," *Read. Digest,* 48 (1946) :42-46.

Wood, J. P. *Magazines in the United States,* (1949) :54-56.

THURLOW WEED— 1797-1882 —President-maker and "Governor of Governors"

ORIGINAL SOURCES: Weed, Harriet, ed. *The Autobiography of Thurlow Weed.* 1883.

Atlantic, 52:414. "Mr. Weed's autobiography shows . . . how significant and interesting to an old man are the incidents of early life and the circumstances out of which his education has come." But the author reveals less of himself than of his times.

BIOGRAPHY: Barnes, T. W. *Memoir of Thurlow Weed.* 1884.

Nation, 38:325. Weed was very "reticent in regard to the inside history of New York politics, and particularly in regard to the birth, life and tragic dissolution of the firm of Seward, Weed, and Greeley. It seems to be the object of this memoir (by a grandson) to fill up this and other similar gaps in the autobiography; and the work is done quite as satisfactorily as it could have been done by any second hand."

Van Deusen, G. G. *Thurlow Weed: Wizard of the Lobby.* 1947.

AHR, 53:122. A "painstaking, thorough, dependable research work," based almost entirely on original sources. Dr. Van Deusen presents the facts of Weed's career, but does not portray his relationships "as graphically as might be desired." The book needs an analysis of "the basic impulses that patterned Thurlow Weed." The author also fails to evaluate him as an editor who failed "to grow journalistically with the American press."

COLLECTIVE BIOGRAPHY: Croffut, W. A. *American Procession,* 205-25.

Boatfield, H. C., in *DAB,* 19:598.

Van Deusen, G. G. "Thurlow Weed: a Character Study," *AHR,* 49 (1944) :427-40.

SPECIAL ASPECTS: Hendrick, B. J. *Lincoln's War Cabinet,* 1-123.

Lamb, M. J. "Thurlow Weed's Home in New York City," *Mag. of Amer. Hist.,* 19 (1888) :1-20.

Van Deusen, G. G., ed. "Thurlow Weed's Analysis of William H. Seward's Defeat in the Republican Convention of 1860," *MVHR,* 34 (1947) :101-04.

WILLIAM HENRY SEWARD—   1801-1872   —"A Lovable Man and a Great Secretary of State"

ORIGINAL SOURCES: Seward, F. W., ed. "Autobiography of W. H. Seward from 1861 to 1864 with a Memoir of his Life and Selections from his Letters from 1831 to 1845. 1877." *Pol. Sci. Quar.,* 6 (1891) :711-24.

———. *Seward at Washington.* 2 vols. 1891.

BIOGRAPHY: Bancroft, Frederick. *The Life of William H. Seward.* 2 vols. 1900.

AHR, 6:152. A well-balanced biography covering Seward's leadership of the Whig party and his service as Secretary of State. Both sympathetic and critical.

COLLECTIVE BIOGRAPHY: Bradford, Gamaliel. *Union Portraits,* 197-229.

Croffut, W. A. *American Procession,* 226-35.

Hendrick, B. J. *Lincoln's War Cabinet,* 124-216.

Macartney, C. E. N. *Lincoln and his Cabinet,* 83-179.

——.*Men Who Missed It,* 37-43.

Perkins, Dexter, in *DAB,* 16:615.

Seitz, D. C. *The "Also Rans,"* 192-207.

HISTORY: Schlesinger, A. M., Jr. *The Age of Jackson,* 283-88.

SPECIAL ASPECTS: Dennett, Tyler. "Seward's Far-Eastern Policy," *AHR,* 28 (1932) :45-62.

Henderson, D. M. *Yankee Ships in China Seas,* (1947) :237-46.

Koht, Halvdan. "The Origin of Seward's Plan to Purchase the Danish West Indies," *AHR,* 50 (1945) :762-67.

Parry, Sir E. A. *What the Judge Thought,* (1923) :266-83.

Russell, W. H., in Nevins, Allan, ed. *America Through British Eyes,* 263-70.

Temple, H. W., in Bemis, S. F., ed. *American Secretaries of State,* 7:3-115.

Van Deusen, G. G., ed. "Thurlow Weed's Analysis of William H. Seward's Defeat in the Republican Convention of 1860," *MVHR,* 34 (1947) :101-04.

HAMILTON FISH— 1808-1893 —"Statesman Among Scoundrels"

BIOGRAPHY: Nevins, Allan. *Hamilton Fish: the Inner History of the Grant Administration.* 1936.

AHR, 42:802. A well-written life of a wealthy socialite who was the ablest member of Grant's cabinet. Shrewd thumb-nail sketches of contemporaries.

COLLECTIVE BIOGRAPHY: Current, R. N., in Salter, J. T., ed. *Public Men in and out of Public Office,* (1946) :210-24.

Fuller, J. V., in *DAB,* 6:397.

SPECIAL ASPECTS: Fuller, J. V., in Bemis, S. F., ed. *American Secretaries of State,* 7:125-216.

Wilson, Edmund. *American Jitters,* (1932) :10-27.

HORACE GREELEY— 1811-1872 —"The Most Important of American Editors"

ORIGINAL SOURCES: Greeley, Horace. *Recollections of a Busy Life.* 1868. New editions 1873, 1930.

DAB, 7:534. Gives a simple and concise statement of the main facts in his career and a frank revelation of the forces which influenced his tastes and thoughts.

BIOGRAPHY: Hale, W. H. *Horace Greeley, Voice of the People.* 1950.

Sat. Rev. of Lit., 33:42, Oct. 7, 1950. "This compact, swift-paced life, based on a thorough study of manuscript as well as printed sources, has special merit. Mr. Hale has digested his voluminous materials admirably, has formed a clear understanding of Greeley's outwardly simple but inwardly complex personality, and has given us a well-written narrative which never for a page loses interest. Mr. Hale's biography is a delightfully readable book, and is the best of the existing lives of Greeley. . . ."

Seitz, D. C. *Horace Greeley, Founder of the New York Tribune.* 1927.

Bookman, 64:740. A good popular biography.

Stoddard, H. L. *Horace Greeley: Printer, Editor, Crusader.* 1946.

AHR, 52:520. A newspaperman's "life of a great American editor." "From the stories he tells emerges a vivid Greeley—brilliant, industrious, changeable, perverse, resolute, independent, profane, lonely, and unhappy."

COLLECTIVE BIOGRAPHY: Bradford, Gamaliel. *As God Made Them,* 129-66.

Also in *Am. Merc.*, 1 (1924) :385-93.

Croffut, W. A. *American Procession,* 28-45, 56-81, 124-38, 236-55.

Macartney, C. E. N. *Men Who Missed It,* 69-76.

Nevins, Allan, in *DAB,* 7:528.

Rourke, C. M. *Trumpets of Jubilee,* 239-365.

Seitz, D. C. *The "Also Rans,"* 242-54.

Stone, Irving. *They Also Ran,* 1-34.

Wildman, Edwin. *Famous Leaders of Character in America,* 55-68.

HISTORY: Bowers, Claude. *Tragic Era,* see index.

Mott, F. L. *American Journalism,* 218-20, 267-78, 340-43, 371-74.

SPECIAL ASPECTS: Bishop, J. B. *Notes and Anecdotes of Many Years,* 8-34.

Deusen, G. G., in Earle, E. M., ed. *Nationalism and Interna-tionalism: Essays Inscribed to Carlton J. H. Hayes,* (1950) : 431-54.

Fahrney, R. L. *Horace Greeley and the Tribune in the Civil War.* 1936.

AHR, 43:420. An excellent analysis of Greeley's leadership during the war.

Isely, J. A. *Horace Greeley and the Republican Party, 1853-1861: a Study of the New York Tribune.* (Princeton Studies in History, 1947) .

AHR, 53:358. A valuable and much-needed study of Greeley's work in fos-tering the strength and shaping the policies of the Republican party. Greeley's role is difficult to evaluate since "party chiefs and even anti-slavery spokesmen distrusted him." Mr. Isely ranks him with Rhett and Ruffin as "one of those who brought sectional bitterness to a Civil War fruition which they perhaps did not intend."

Snyder, L. L., and R. B. Morris, eds. *Treasury of Great Report-ing,* 107-9, 116-19.

Van Zandt, R. "Horace Greeley, Agrarian Exponent of Ameri-can Idealism," *Rural Sociol.,* 13 (1948) :411-19.

Willison, G. F. *Here They Dug Gold,* (1946) :49-70.

JAMES MARION SIMS—   1813-1883   —"Giant of American Surgery"

ORIGINAL SOURCES: Rosen, George, and Beate Casperi-Rosen, eds. *400 Years of a Doctor's Life,* 34-36, 76-79, 171-78, 307-08, 338-39.

Sims, J. M. *The Story of My Life.* 1884.

BIOGRAPHY: Harris, Seale. *Woman's Surgeon; the Life Story of J. Marion Sims.* 1950.

MVHR, 37:730. "J. Marion Sims was a remarkable person. His scientific achievements as 'father of gynecology' are both substantial and fascinat-ing. His personality as portrayed by his able biographer, is no less fas-cinating. Sims' early career in South Carolina' and Alabama sheds con-siderable light on the state of medical practice in 1830's and 1840's and gives the social historian excellent documentation on the precariousness of life and health in the South . . . The author, himself a distinguished surgeon, has the literary skill to make the most of an already lively and important subject. The work is careful, detailed, and interesting."

COLLECTIVE BIOGRAPHY: Faris, J. T. *Men Who Conquered,* 34-45.

Kelly, H. A., in *DAB*, 17:186.

SPECIAL ASPECTS: Bierring, W. L., in Fishbein, Morris. *History of the American Medical Association, 1847-1947,* (1947):627-29.

SAMUEL JONES TILDEN— 1814-1886 —A Leader Fortunately Deserted by Followers in '77*

BIOGRAPHY: Flick, A. C. *Samuel Jones Tilden: a Study in Political Sagacity.* 1939.

AHR, 46:175. The Tilden papers, which were carefully sifted by the executors, were supplemented by many other sources. The success of a man who was personally insignificant—and no orator—is explained by the view that he "conquered through his ideas."

COLLECTIVE BIOGRAPHY: Flick, A. C., in *DAB,* 18:537.

Hirsch, M. D. "Samuel J. Tilden, the Story of a Lost Opportunity," *AHR,* 60 (1951):788-803.

ELIZABETH CADY STANTON—1815-1902—Leader in Woman's Rights Movement

ORIGINAL SOURCES: Stone, Irving, and Richard Kennedy, eds. *We Speak for Ourselves,* 319-25.

COLLECTIVE BIOGRAPHY: Adams, E. C., and W. B. Foster. *Heroines of Modern Progress,* 58-88.

Croffut, W. A. *American Procession,* 180-97.

Williams, M. W., in *DAB,* 17:521.

SPECIAL ASPECTS: Barth, Ramona. "Feminist Crusade," *Nation,* 167:71-73, July 17, 1948.

JOHN BIGELOW—1817-1911—Editor and Diplomat

BIOGRAPHY: †Clapp, Margaret. *Forgotten First Citizen: John Bigelow.* 1947.

AHR, 53:355. An admirable study of a man who was consul in Paris during the Civil War, helped to edit the *New York Evening Post* and to establish the New York Public Library.

COLLECTIVE BIOGRAPHY: MacDonald, William, in *DAB,* 2:258.

---

* See p. 318.
† Awarded the Pulitzer Prize.

HERMAN MELVILLE— 1819-1891 —Discoverer of the South Seas

ORIGINAL SOURCES: Melville, Herman. "Journal of Melville's Voyage in a Clipper Ship," *N. E. Quar.,* 2 (1929) :120-25.

Metcalf, E. M., ed. *Journal of a Visit to London and the Continent, by Herman Melville, 1849-1850.* 1948.

Herald Tribune, Nov. 28, 1948, p. 26. This journal of a business trip gives "sharp impressions of men and cities; it is (also) a veritable seedpot of ideas, scenes and characters which would germinate in his later works." The editor, the writer's granddaughter, in her notes provides "a quantity of new information about Melville drawn from manuscript collections not before explored by scholars."

Morison, S. E., ed. "Melville's 'Agatha' Letter to Hawthorne," *N. E. Quar.,* 2 (1929) :296-307.

*Thorp, Willard. *Herman Melville: Representative Selections.* (American Writers, 1938).

Amer. Lit., 11:92. "An excellent book." The introduction is "the sanest and soundest discussion of Melville's life and work which has been published" to date. . . . "This preliminary essay is practically free of factual errors." The bibliograhy, selections from Melville's prose and poetry and a chronological table complete the book.

BIOGRAPHY: Arvin, Newton. *Herman Melville.* (American Men of Letters, 1950).

Sat. Rev. of Lit., 33:21, Apr. 29, 1950. "Much new information about Melville's life remains unpublished. . . . Newton Arvin has masterfully handled his material to give us the best general book on Melville ever published."

Freeman, John. *Herman Melville.* (English Men of Letters, 1926).

Ind., 117:108, July 24, 1926. "For those who want a short story of Melville's life vividly and ably told, . . . this book is admirable."

Mumford, Lewis. *Herman Melville.* 1929.

Amer. Lit., 1:215. A combination of biography and critical analysis, with the emphasis on the latter. The chapters on *Moby Dick* and *Pierre* are especially good, but the former "has been overemphasized at the expense of Melville's other genuinely fine books, particularly *Pierre.* . . ."

Sedgwick, W. E. *Herman Melville: the Tragedy of Mind.* 1944.

---

* For more complete bibliographies see Thorp, pp. cxxxiii-clxi; Weaver, R. M. *Herman Melville, Mariner and Mystic,* (1921) :385-88; Spiller, et al. *Literary History of the United States,* 3 (1948) :647-54.

N. Y. Times, Jan. 21, 1945, p. 3. Mr. Sedgwick traces the development of Melville's mind with great sympathy and insight.

Stone, Geoffrey. *Melville.* (Great Writers of the World, 1949) .

Nation, 169:574, Dec. 10, 1949. "Mr. Stone's book on Melville is refreshing in at least one respect: it is written by a devout and instructed Catholic, and hence by a man who stands in a position of some intellectual detachment from Melville's work. Mr. Stone is not at the mercy of that work on its philosophical side as some of Melville's other expounders have been: he has been under no compulsion to elevate *Moby Dick* . . . to the status of a scripture, and this has set him free to look at it as one would look at a play of Shakespeare's or a novel of Dostoevski's."

Weaver, R. M. *Herman Melville: Mariner and Mystic.* 1921.

Nation, 114:20, Jan. 4, 1922. An early biography of Melville—valuable for the "judicious use of excerpts from his autobiographical works. . . ."

COLLECTIVE BIOGRAPHY: Bolitho, Hector, and John Mulgan. *Emigrants; Early Travelers to the Antipodes,* (1939) :155-67.

Booth, E. T. *God Made the Country,* 220-45.

Brooks, V. W. *Emerson and Others,* (1927) :169-205.

———. *The Times of Melville and Whitman,* 142-75.

Cournos, John. *Modern Plutarch,* 78-95, 127-34.

Gabriel, R. H. *American Democratic Thought,* 67-77.

Josephson, Matthew. *Portrait of the Artist as American,* 3-43.

Matthiessen, F. O. *American Renaissance,* 371-95.

Montgomery, E. R. *Story Behind Great Books,* (1946) :169-71.

Mumford, Lewis. "The Significance of Herman Melville," *New Repub.,* 56:212-14, Oct. 10, 1928.

Opitz, E. A. "Herman Melville: an American Seer," *Contemp. Rev.,* 170 (1946) :348-53.

Paullin, C. O., in *DAB,* 12:522.

Russell, F. A. *American Pilgrimage,* 119-33.

Spiller, R. E. "Melville: Our First Tragic Poet," *Sat. Rev. of Lit.,* 33:24-25, Nov. 25, 1950.

SPECIAL ASPECTS: Abele, R. V. "Melville and the Problem of Evil," *Am. Merc.,* 65 (1947) :592-98.

Anderson, C. R. *Melville in the South Seas.* 1939.

Amer. Lit., 11:85. Mr. Anderson gives us a full account of Melville's journeyings from 1841 to 1844 ("the most important years of his life") and a careful enquiry "into the proportions of autobiography, of borrowing, and of pure invention in the novels and tales which are based to a greater or less degree upon the author's adventures in the South Seas. . . ." On the whole, . . . Mr. Anderson's book is well written and interesting, thoroughly documented and informative."

Boynton, P. H. *More Contemporary Americans,* 29-50.

Braswell, William. "Melville as a Critic of Emerson," *Amer. Lit.,* 9 (1937) :317-34.

———. *Melville's Religious Thought: An Essay in Interpretation.* 1943.

Amer. Lit., 16:240. "A thoughtful provocative book" which does much to clarify dark passages in Melville's writing." It "opens with a survey of Melville's religious background and of the influences upon his thinking effected through family, friends, and books."

Canby, H. S. *Classic Americans,* 226-62.

Cowie, Alexander. *Rise of the American Novel,* 363-411.

Foster, E. S. "Melville and Geology," *Amer. Lit.,* 17 (1946) :50-65.

Gabriel, R. H. *The Course of American Democratic Thought,* 67-77.

Hart, J. D. "Melville and Dana," *Amer. Lit.,* 9 (1937) :49-55.

Hicks, Granville. *Great Tradition,* 1-31.

Huntress, Keith. "Melville's Use of a Source for White-Jacket," *Amer. Lit.,* 17 (1946) :66-74.

Maugham, W. S. *Great Novelists and their Novels,* (1948) :211-32.

Pattee, F. L. *Feminine Fifties,* 28-49.

Schneider, H. W. *History of American Philosophy,* 293-301.

Snell, G. D. *Shapers of American Fiction,* 60-78.

Stovall, Floyd. *American Idealism,* (1943) :55-78.

Walters, R. E. "Melville's Sociality," *Amer. Lit.,* 17 (1946) :33-49.

Weaver, R. M., in Macy, John, ed. *American Writers on American Literature,* 190-206.

Williams, M. L. "Two Hawaiian-Americans Visit Herman Melville," *N. E. Quar.,* 23 (1950) :97-99.

Winters, Yvor. *In Defense of Reason,* 200-33.

WALT WHITMAN—1819-1892—"Poet of Democracy"

ORIGINAL SOURCES: Frenz, H., ed. "Walt Whitman's Letters to Karl Knortz," *Amer. Lit.*, 20 (1948) :155-63.

Silver, R. G. "Whitman in 1850: Three Uncollected Articles," *Amer. Lit.*, 19 (1948) :301-17.

*Stovall, Floyd. *Walt Whitman: Representative Selections.* (American Writers, 1934).

Trowbridge, J. T. "Reminiscences of Walt Whitman," *Atlantic*, 89 (1902) :163-75.

BIOGRAPHY: Arvin, Newton. *Whitman.* 1938.

Books, Nov. 6, 1938, p. 8. Emphasizes Whitman's opinions on politics, economics and philosophy.

Bailey, J. C. *Walt Whitman.* (English Men of Letters, 1926).

Outlook, 143:548, Aug. 18, 1926. An excellent brief biography.

Barrus, Clara. *Whitman and Burroughs, Comrades.* 1931.

Amer. Lit., 4:398. A record of the comradeship of Whitman and Burroughs, as well as "a rich store of information about the life and personality of the poet."

Burroughs, John. *Whitman: a Study.* 1896.

Nation, 64:55, Jan. 21, 1897. A sympathetic study of Whitman's character and poetry.

Canby, H. S. *Walt Whitman, an American: a Study in Biography.* 1943.

AHR, 49:761. An excellent narrative of the poet's life, with expert literary criticism and "an authentic historical interpretation of Whitman's America as well."

Fausset, H. L'Anson. *Walt Whitman, Poet of Democracy.* 1942.

Sat. Rev. of Lit., 25:6, July 18, 1942. Using psychoanalysis, Mr. Fausset describes Whitman as "a split personality who never achieved integration in either his life or his art."

†Holloway, Emory. *Whitman: an Interpretation in Narrative.* 1926.

N. Y. Times, Oct. 10, 1926, p. 5. Professor Holloway's objective is "to draw the growth of Whitman's mind, to picture the 'man in himself,' to give a

---

* For fuller references see Stovall, pp. liii-lx; Allen, G. W. *Walt Whitman Handbook*, (1946) : read especially chapter one; *Cambridge History of American Literature*, 2 (1918) :551-81; Spiller, et al. *Literary History of the United States*, 3 (1948) :759-68.
† Awarded the Pulitzer Prize.

clear understanding of why Whitman was Whitman and so to orientate him in the scheme of the American life of his time and in himself."

Morris, H. S. *Walt Whitman: a Brief Biography with Reminiscences.* 1930.

N. Y. Times, June 29, 1930, p. 16. Short life by a personal friend who visited the poet during his last decade.

Perry, Bliss. *Walt Whitman: his Life and Work.* (American Men of Letters, 1906).

Outlook, 85:278, Feb. 2, 1907. "An adequate and candid account of Whitman's antecedents and conditions and of the outward happenings of his life."

Platt, I. H. *Walt Whitman.* 1904.

A very brief biography.

Roger, Cameron. *The Magnificent Idler, the Story of Walt Whitman.* 1926.

Bookman, 63:477, June, 1926. "Whitman . . . has never been better presented than in the mellow, easily read, friendly chapters of *The Magnificent Idler . . .*, in which Cameron Rogers pictures a genial egotist, a warm friend, a puzzled and groping soul."

Winwar, Frances. *American Giant: Walt Whitman and his Times.* 1941.

Books, Nov. 16, 1941, p. 2. A readable biography by a novelist. Some errors of hasty judgment.

Collective Biography: Bradford, Gamaliel. *Biography and the Human Heart,* 65-93.

Also in *Bookman,* 42 (1915) :533-48.

Brooks, V. W. *The Times of Melville and Whitman,* 122-41, 176-91, 217-33.

Canby, H. S., in *Literary History of the United States,* 1:427-98.

Gohdes, C. L. F. "Whitman and Emerson," *Sewanee Rev.,* 37. (1929) :79-93.

Holloway, Emory, in *Cambridge History of American Literature,* 2:551-81.

Josephson, Matthew. *Portrait of the Artist as American,* (1930) : 139-98.

Matthiessen, F. O. *American Renaissance,* 517-625.

O'Higgins, H. J., and E. H. Reede. *American Mind in Action,* 202-34.

Parrington, V. L. *Main Currents in American Thought,* 3:69-86.

Sherman, S. P. *Americans,* 153-85.

Also in Durling and Watt. *Biography,* 290-307.

Stedman, E. C. *Poets of America,* 349-95.

Van Doren, Mark, in *DAB,* 20:143.

——, in *There Were Giants in the Land,* 84-89.

Vincent, L. H. *American Literary Masters,* 485-506.

Wood, Clement. *Poets of America,* 35-55.

SPECIAL ASPECTS: Allen, G. W. *Walt Whitman Handbook.* 1946.

AHR, 51:765. "A well-integrated review of everything significant that has
been written about Whitman, set in logical order and supplemented by
the results of the author's own investigation. . . . Mr. Allen inclines, in
general, to be sympathetic with his subject but he is in no sense uncritical." Read especially chapters on "Growth of Walt Whitman Biography"
and "Whitman's Fundamental Ideas."

Brooks, V. W. *America's Coming of Age,* (1915) :109-29.

——. *Sketches in Criticism,* (1932) :178-89.

Bullet, G. W., in Brown, A. B., ed. *Great Democrat,* (1934) :651-
62.

Canby, H. S. *Classic Americans,* 308-51.

Campbell, Killis. "The Evolution of Whitman as Artist," *Amer.
Lit.,* 6 (1934) :254-63.

Cooke, A. L. "Whitman's Musical Background," *N. E. Quar.,* 19
(1946) :224-35.

Cowie, Alexander. *Rise of the American Novel,* 306-09.

Cowley, Malcolm. "Walt Whitman: the Miracle," *New Repub.,*
114 (1946) :385-88.

——. "Walt Whitman: the Secret," *ibid,* 481-84.

Foerster, Norman. *American Criticism,* 157-222.

——. *Nature in American Literature,* 176-220.

Furness, C. J. "Walt Whitman's Politics," *Am. Merc.,* 16 (1929) :
459-66.

Glicksberg, C. I. "Walt Whitman in 1862," *Amer. Lit.,* 6
(1934) :264-82.

Glicksberg, C. I., ed. *Walt Whitman and the Civil War.* 1933.

New Repub., 74:259, Apr. 12, 1933. "The editor of this volume has brought together a group of Whitman inedits which illuminates his biography for the period of the Civil War and a few years thereafter—newspaper articles, memoranda, letters, manuscripts, versions of poems, newspaper clippings and the like."

Hintz, H. W. *Quaker Influence in American Literature,* (1940): 59-75.

Macy, J. A. *Critical Game,* 203-11.

———. *The Spirit of American Literature,* (1908): 210-47.

More, P. E., in *Shelburne Essays,* 4th ser., (1906): 180-211.

Mumford, Lewis, in Piercy, J. K., ed. *Modern Writers at Work,* (1930): 175-83.

———. *The Golden Day,* (1926): 121-38.

Myers, H. A. "Whitman's Conception of the Spiritual Democracy," *Amer. Lit.,* 6 (1934): 239-53.

Oppenheim, James, in Macy, John, ed. *American Writers on American Literature,* 258-73.

Santayana, George. *Interpretations of Poetry and Religion,* (1900): 166-216.

Schyberg, Frederick. *Walt Whitman.* 1951.

N. Y. Times, Apr. 1, 1951, p. 4. This study by a Danish scholar is important for Mr. Schyberg's "searching examination and evaluation of the changes made by Whitman in successive editions of *Leaves of Grass* and his assessment of Whitman both as a symptom and as an influence in world literature."

Shepard, Esther. *Walt Whitman's Pose.* 1938.

Booklist, 34:314, May 1, 1938. "An attack on Whitman's ethics and personal honesty, which asserts that he drew the inspiration for his pose as an original American poet, and many of his ideas, from a novel by George Sand, and never admitted his indebtedness."

Spiegelman, Julia. "Walt Whitman and Music," *So. Atl. Quar.,* 41 (1942): 167-76.

Stovall, Floyd. "Main Drifts in Whitman's Poetry," *Amer. Lit.,* 4 (1932): 3-21.

Strong, A. H. *American Poets and their Theology,* 419-70.

Trent, W. P., and John Erskine. *Great American Writers,* 212-31.

Willard, C. B. *Whitman's American Fame: the Growth of his Reputation in America After 1892.* 1950.

N. E. Quar., 23:420. An interesting and useful book—"something between a history and an annotated bibliography. . . ." It discusses "Whitman's struggles for recognition in his own lifetime," and the efforts of Whitman's admirers to keep alive the discussion of his work after 1892 until its own merits and a changing taste had made it more widely acceptable.

BIOGRAPHIES OF CONTEMPORARIES: Barrus, Clara. *The Life and Letters of John Burroughs,* 2:100-04.

JULIA WARD HOWE— 1819-1910 —Author, Social Reformer, Poet

ORIGINAL SOURCES: Pickett, Mrs. L. C. *Across My Path,* 1-6.

BIOGRAPHY: Richards, L. E., and M. H. Elliott. *Julia Ward Howe.* 2 vols. 1915.

———. *Two Noble Lives.* 1911.

COLLECTIVE BIOGRAPHY: Adams, E. C., and W. B. Foster. *Heroines of Modern Progress,* 178-214.

Brooks, V. W. *New England: Indian Summer,* 115-39.

Malone, Dumas. *Saints in Action,* 84-113.

Orcutt, W. D. *Celebrities on Parade,* 133-91.

Parkman, M. R. *Heroines of Service,* 119-47.

Woollcut, Alexander, in *There Were Giants in the Land,* 24-29.

SPECIAL ASPECTS: Chapman, J. J. *Memories and Milestones,* (1915):235-45.

Humphrey, Grace. *Women in American History,* 154-63.

O'Higgins, H. J., and E. H. Reede. *American Mind in Action,* 251-76.

Van Doren, Carl, and C. L. Carmer. *American Scriptures,* 293-97.

HENRY JARVIS RAYMOND— 1820-1869 —Founder of *The New York Times*

BIOGRAPHY: Brown, Francis. *Raymond of the Times.* 1951.

N. Y. Times, Aug. 12, 1951, p. 1. A "scholarly and fascinating biography" of "the man who a century ago served journalism and national unity."

COLLECTIVE BIOGRAPHY: Davis, Elmer, in *DAB,* 15:408.

GEORGE TEMPLETON STRONG— 1820-1876 —Forgotten Lawyer

ORIGINAL SOURCES: Nevins, Allan, and M. H. Thomas, eds. *The Diary of George Templeton Strong.* 4 vols. To appear in 1952.

George Templeton Strong was a prominent New York attorney who was treasurer of the United States Sanitary Commission during the Civil War. He was a trustee of Columbia, a vestryman of Trinity, the President of the Philharmonic Society, and one of the founders of the Union League Club. This important diary is an interesting picture of New York and national life, 1835-1876. Furnishing an inside record of New York society and legal life, it also gives much musical and dramatic criticism, as well as views of Lincoln, Stanton, and other great men.

DANIEL EDGAR SICKLES—1820-1914—"The Hero of Gettysburg"

BIOGRAPHY: Pinchon, Edgcumb. *Dan Sickles, Hero of Gettysburg and "Yankee King of Spain."* 1945.

AHR, 51:552. A popular biography of a hero of the Dumas variety. It is undocumented but the general reader will find it fascinating.

COLLECTIVE BIOGRAPHY: Lanza, C. H., in *DAB,* 17:150.

JAY COOKE—   1821-1905   —Tycoon

BIOGRAPHY: Larson, Henrietta. *Jay Cooke: Private Banker.* (Harvard Studies in Business History, 1936) .

AHR, 43:662. "A scholarly reappraisal of the career of Jay Cooke" which emphasizes "his pioneering activities in the development of modern American investment banking."

COLLECTIVE BIOGRAPHY: Minnigerode, Meade. *Certain Rich Men,* 53-82.

Oberholtzer, E. P., in *DAB,* 4:383.

SPECIAL ASPECTS: Gras, N. S. B., and H. M. Larson, eds. *Casebook in American Business History,* 296-324.

CHESTER ALAN ARTHUR— 1830-1886 —Socialite and Spoilsman Who Made a Good President

ORIGINAL SOURCES: Wise, J. S. *Recollections of Thirteen Presidents,* 155-67.

BIOGRAPHY: Howe, G. F. *Chester A. Arthur: a Quarter-Century of Machine Politics.* (American Political Leaders, 1934) .

AHR, 41:172. Lacking the letters for a personal biography, "Mr. Howe has shown critical thoroughness and a sound critical temper" in using miscellaneous material, and he has made a distinct contribution in dealing with "Arthur's career in the New York state machine, and his record in the presidency."

COLLECTIVE BIOGRAPHY: Agar, Herbert. *The People's Choice,* 229-66.

Hathaway, E. V. *Book of American Presidents,* 209-25.

Levin, P. R. *Seven by Chance,* 147-76.

Paxson, F. L., in *DAB,* 1:373.

Root, Elihu. *Miscellaneous Addresses,* 109-13.

Young, K. H., and Louis Middleton. *Heirs Apparent,* 193-203.

SPECIAL ASPECTS: Perling, J. J. *Presidents' Sons,* 220-26.

Pollard, J. E. *Presidents and the Press,* 488-97.

JAY GOULD— 1836-1892 —Wizard of Wall Street

BIOGRAPHY: Warshow, R. I. *Jay Gould: the Story of a Fortune.* 1928.

Nation, 127:69, July 18, 1928. "A breezy yet convincing biography of the 'five-foot consumptive Napoleon of finance' whose utterly unscrupulous genius for turning everything he touched into gold makes King Midas and Aladdin look like third-raters."

COLLECTIVE BIOGRAPHY: Croffut, W. A. *American Procession,* 236-55, 274-83.

Hungerford, Edward. *Men of Erie: a Story of Human Effort,* (1946) :158-70.

Minnigerode, Meade. *Certain Rich Men,* 135-87.

Nevins, Allan, in *DAB,* 7:454.

SPECIAL ASPECTS: Grayson, T. J. *Leaders and Periods in American Finance,* 329-49.

Myers, Gustavus. *History of Great American Fortunes,* (1936) : 395-446, 478-503.

GROVER CLEVELAND— 1837-1908 —"The Outstanding President Between Lincoln and Theodore Roosevelt"

ORIGINAL SOURCES: Gilder, R. W. *Grover Cleveland, a Record of Friendship.* 1910.

Also in *Century,* 78 (1909) :483-503, 687-706, 846-60; 79 (1909) : 24-31.

Nevins, Allan, ed. *Letters of Grover Cleveland, 1850-1908.* 1935.

AHR, 40:765. Letters which reveal many human qualities such as a passion for fishing and an inclination to shun publicity.

Extract in Prochnow, H. V., ed. *Great Stories from Great Lives,* 362-73.

Wise, J. S. *Recollections of Thirteen Presidents,* 171-91.

BIOGRAPHY: McElroy, Robert. *An Authorized Biography.* 2 vols. 1923.

New Repub., 37 (1923):127. Well written narrative of a career which suggests that Puritan love of independence leads to negation. Usually impartial, but not in discussing the Pullman strike.

*Nevins, Allan. *Grover Cleveland: a Study in Courage.* 1932.

AHR, 39:351. A vivid portrait that shows that Cleveland's honesty and courage helped to put him in the presidential office, but did not give him the statesmanship to meet the new issues of the eighties and nineties.

COLLECTIVE BIOGRAPHY: Agar, Herbert. *The People's Choice,* 229-66.

Bradford, Gamaliel. *American Portraits,* 143-70.

Egbert, D. D., and D. M. Lee. *Princeton Portraits,* 225-29.

Faris, J. T. *Men Who Conquered,* 150-62.

Grayson, T. J. *Leaders and Periods of American Finance,* 376-92.

Hathaway, E. V. *Book of American Presidents,* 226-39.

Hofstadter, Richard. *American Political Tradition,* 162-82.

Nevins, Allan. "Cleveland: an Ill-appreciated Personality," *Am. Scholar,* 3 (1934) :133-43.

Paxson, F. L., in *DAB,* 4:205.

Root, Elihu. *Men and Policies,* 88-92.

———. *Miscellaneous Addresses,* 105-08.

Thomas and Thomas. *Living Biographies of American Statesmen,* 263-77.

White, W. A. *Masks in a Pageant,* 108-51.

Wildman, Edwin. *Famous Leaders of Character in America,* 153-64.

HISTORY: Agar, Herbert. *The Price of Union,* 542-54.

SPECIAL ASPECTS: Blake, N. M. "Background of Cleveland's Venezuelan Policy," *AHR,* 47 (1942) :259-77.

Knoles, G. H., ed. "Grover Cleveland on Imperialism," *MVHR,* 37 (1950) :303-04.

---

* Awarded the Pulitzer Prize.

Milton, G. F. *Use of Presidential Power, 1789-1943*, 154-72.

Perling, J. J. *Presidents' Sons*, 227-36.

Pollard, J. E. *Presidents and the Press*, 499-533.

Wickser, D. J. "Grover Cleveland: his Character, Background and Legal Career," *Am. Bar Assn. Jour.*, 33 (1947) :327-30.

WHITELAW REID— 1837-1912 —Editor and Diplomat

BIOGRAPHY: Cortissoz, Royal. *The Life of Whitelaw Reid*. 2 vols. 1921.

AHR, 27:135. An interesting and authoritative biography which sometimes assumes the role of defender.

COLLECTIVE BIOGRAPHY: Nevins, Allan, in *DAB*, 15:482.

SPECIAL ASPECTS: Willson, Beckles. *America's Ambassadors to England, 1785-1929*, 419-40.

———. *America's Ambassadors to France, 1777-1927*, (1928) :335-58.

Mott, F. L. *American Journalism*, 422-25.

JOHN PIERPONT MORGAN—1837-1913—"Symbol of an Era"

BIOGRAPHY: Allen, F. L. *The Great Pierpont Morgan*. 1949.

AHR, 55:167. This brief sketch is "the only scholarly, well balanced interpretation" of Morgan's career. A character study rather than a detailed narrative.

Excerpts in *Harper's*, 197 (1948) Dec.:25-37; 198 (1949) Jan.:61-71; Feb.:53-62.

Satterlee, H. L. *J. Pierpont Morgan: an Intimate Portrait*. 1939.

AHR, 45:929. This volume by Morgan's son-in-law throws light on the financier's early years, his services to art and religion, but little on his business affairs or the harder side of his personality. Unfortunately Morgan burned many of his papers.

Winkler, J. K. *Morgan the Magnificent: the Life of J. Pierpont Morgan*. 1930.

Sat. Rev. of Lit., 7:122, Sept. 13, 1930. A readable, popular biography which singles out the high spots.

COLLECTIVE BIOGRAPHY: Atwood, A. W., in *DAB*, 13:175.

Flynn, J. T. *Men of Wealth*, (1941) :452-513.

Anonymous. *Mirrors of Wall Street,* 43-57.

SPECIAL ASPECTS: Cannon, C. L. *American Book Collectors and Collecting,* 277-91.

Gras, N. S. B., and H. M. Larson, eds. *Casebook in American Business History,* 545-65.

Redmond, R. L. "Fabulous Mr. Morgan," *Art N.,* 48 (1949) :33-35.

Root, Elihu. *Miscellaneous Addresses,* 227-32.

Thompson, C. L. "Problems of Industrial Expansion; J. Pierpont Morgan: Consolidator," *Cur. Hist.,* 17 (1949) :90-95.

Wasson, R. G. *The Hall Carbine Affair: a Study in Contemporary Folklore.* 1941.

AHR, 51:382. An inquiry into the truth of Myers' story that Morgan got his start in 1861 by buying obsolete arms from one branch of the Federal Government and selling them to another.

Harris, Frank. *Latest Contemporary Portraits,* (1927) :221-30.

*JOHN BURROUGHS— 1837-1921 —Naturalist and Essayist

ORIGINAL SOURCES: Barrus, Clara, ed. *The Heart of Burrough's Journals.* 1928.

Amer. Lit., 1:228. Especially interesting are "the numerous remarks about Whitman and Emerson."

Perry, Bliss. *The Praise of Folly,* (1923) :63-72.

BIOGRAPHY: Barrus, Clara. *The Life and Letters of John Burroughs.* 2 vols. 1925.

Ind., 115:652, Dec. 5, 1925. An excellent biography by a friend and physician who was given many pages of autobiographical material.

————. *Our Friend, John Burroughs.* 1914.

Booklist, 10:345, May, 1914. "Nearly half of the book is compiled from a series of letters, autobiographical in character, written at the request of Miss Barrus, with bits of interviews to fill in the gaps. The other chapters describe the naturalist and his haunts with an appreciative human touch that is full of charm. It is this intimate treatment which makes the book more enjoyable than De Loach's *Rambles with John Burroughs.*"

COLLECTIVE BIOGRAPHY: Eastman, Fred. *Men of Power,* 4 (1940) :136-71.

———————————

* For a more complete bibliography see Spiller, et al. *Literary History of the United States,* 3 (1948) :427-28.

Foerster, Norman, in *DAB*, 3:330.

Law, F. H. *Modern Great Americans*, 37-49.

Sherman, S. P. *Mainstream*, 48-60.

Tracy, A. C. *American Naturalists*, (1930) :86-99.

Wildman, Edwin. *Famous Leaders of Character in America*, 167-76.

SPECIAL ASPECTS: Foerster, Norman. *Nature in American Literature*, 264-305.

Osborn, H. F. *Impressions of Great Naturalists*, (1928) :227-50.

WASHINGTON ROEBLING—1837-1926—Engineer

BIOGRAPHY: Steinman, D. B. *The Builders of the Bridge: the Story of John Roebling and his Son*. 1945.

AHR, 51:136. John Roebling died in 1869 just as the field work was beginning on Brooklyn Bridge, and Col. Washington Roebling, a graduate of Rensselaer Polytechnic and a veteran of the Civil War took over. In 1873 he was paralyzed by the dreaded caisson disease. For ten years he directed the work from his window in Brooklyn, while his wife made daily trips to the bridge to inspect the work and carry instructions to the men. When the bridge was opened in May, 1883, Col. Roebling sat at his window with his field glasses to see President Arthur and Grover Cleveland lead the parade across the bridge.

COLLECTIVE BIOGRAPHY: Tilden, C. J., in *DAB*, 16:89.

WILLIAM GRAHAM SUMNER—   1840-1910
—Economist and Sociologist

BIOGRAPHY: Starr, H. E. *William Graham Sumner*. 1925.

Ind., 115:191, Aug. 15, 1925. "Mr. Starr has written a faithful, uninspired book. It is not a great biography, but it is accurate and just; the hero worship or the romance with which one is tempted to enshroud so vigorous, unique a teacher is lacking. Perhaps too much so; perhaps this gnarled, rugged personality is judged by too sane, too unemotional an intellect."

COLLECTIVE BIOGRAPHY: Keller, A. G. "Discoverer of the Forgotten Man," *Am. Merc.*, 27 (1932) :257-70.

Smith, Mortimer. "W. G. Sumner; the Forgotten Man," *Am. Merc.*, 71 (1950) :357-66.

Starr, H. E., in *DAB*, 18:217.

SPECIAL ASPECTS: Barnes, H. E., ed. *Introduction to the History of Sociology*, 155-72.

Beach, W. G. *Growth of Social Thought,* (1939) :167-75.

Bogardus, E. S. *Development of Social Thought,* (1940) :324-51.

Chamberlain, Jack, in Cowley, Malcolm, and Bernard Smith, eds. *Books that Changed Our Minds,* (1939) :75-87. •

Dowie, M. R. *Sumner Today: Selected Essays with Comments by American Leaders.* 1940.

——. *The Forgotten Man and Other Essays.* 1919.

Ellwood, C. A. *Story of Social Philosophy,* (1938) :500-25.

Gabriel, R. H. *The Course of American Democratic Thought,* (1940) :237-50.

Hofstadter, R. I. *Social Darwinism in American Thought, 1860-1915,* 37-51.

Keller, A. G. *Reminiscences of William G. Sumner.* 1933.

Yale Rev., 23:389. This book is not a formal biography, but frank and amusing recollections by a former student and colleague.

Page, C. H. *Class and American Sociology from Ward to Ross,* (1940) :73-110.

Schneider, H. W. *History of American Philosophy,* 396-415.

JOHN WILLIAM BURGESS— 1844-1931 —Political Scientist

ORIGINAL SOURCES: Burgess, J. W. *Reminiscences of an American Scholar: the Beginnings of Columbia University.* 1934.

AHR, 40:154. "A revealing portrait of a powerful and fascinating personality who did much to promote American scholarship between 1870 and 1900. The book is not a contemporary record, but it is exceptionally well written."

COLLECTIVE BIOGRAPHY: Merriam, C. E., in *DAB,* 21 (supplement one) :132.

Saveth, E. N. *American Historians and European Immigrants, 1875-1925,* 42-51.

Shepard, W. R., in Odum, H. W., ed. *American Masters of Social Science,* (1927) :23-57.

SPECIAL ASPECTS: Kraus, Michael. *History of American History* 336-79.

BIOGRAPHIES OF CONTEMPORARIES: Butler, N. M. *Across the Busy Years,* Vol. I.

CHARLES FOLLEM McKIM— 1847-1909 —"One of the Greatest of Modern American Architects"

ORIGINAL SOURCES: Goldsmith, G. "I Remember McKim, Mead, and White," *Am. Inst. Arch. Jour.*, 13 (1950) :168-72.

BIOGRAPHY: Moore, Charles. *The Life and Times of Charles Follem McKim.* 1929.

AHR, 35:892. McKim was something of a puzzle to his parents and acquaintances. His biographer suggests that the secret force that made him a leader among artists was a profound appreciation of beauty as found in Greek and Roman architecture.

COLLECTIVE BIOGRAPHY: Cortissoz, Royal. *American Artists*, (1923) :303-12.

Moore, Charles, in *DAB*, 12:99.

SPECIAL ASPECTS: Choate, J. H. *American Addresses*, (1911) : 325-38.

Cortissoz, Royal. *Art and Common Sense*, 379-432.

Root, Elihu. *Miscellaneous Addresses*, 197-204.

JOSEPH PULITZER— 1847-1911 —Hearst's Chief Rival and Fellow Warmonger

BIOGRAPHY: Barrett, J. W. *Joseph Pulitzer and his "World."* 1941.

AHR, 47:895. This book is "essentially the work of a hero-worshiping reporter rather than a carefully documented study."

COLLECTIVE BIOGRAPHY: Alexander, Jack, in Drewry, J. E., ed. *Post Biographies of Famous Journalists*, (1942) :391-410.

Beard, A. E. S. *Our Foreign-Born Citizens*, 283-89.

Black, Alexander. *American Husbands*, 149-82.

Croffut, W. A. *American Procession*, 139-53.

Mott, F. L. *American Journalism*, 430-41.

Thomas and Thomas. *Fifty Great Americans*, 275-82.

Stone, Jack, in Howey, W. C., ed. *Fighting Editors*, (1948) :125-34.

Villard, O. G., in *DAB*, 15:260.

———. *Disappearing Daily*, (1944) :251-63.

———. *Some Newspapers and Newspaper Men*, 42-62.

ALEXANDER GRAHAM BELL—   1847-1922
—Inventor of the Telephone

BIOGRAPHY: Mackenzie, Katherine. *Alexander Graham Bell.* 1928.

Sat. Rev. of Lit., 5:607, Jan. 19, 1928. "This is a work well worth doing and it has been done well. One of America's greatest scientists is presented not only as a discoverer, but as a man; intensely alive, filled with enthusiasm about the world of ideas."

COLLECTIVE BIOGRAPHY: Beard, A. E. S. *Our Foreign-Born Citizens,* 49-58.

Colton, F. B. "Miracle Men of the Telephone," *Nat. Geo. Mag.,* 91 (1947) :273-316.

Dunlap, O. E. *Radio's 100 Men of Science,* (1944) :84-86.

Farrar, L. D. "Man Behind the Telephone," *Pub. Utilities,* 39: 332-41, Mar. 13, 1947.

Forbes, B. C. *Men Who are Making America,* 28-35.

Hathaway, E. V. *Partners in Progress,* 91-130.

Howe, G. W. O. "Alexander Graham Bell and the Invention of the Telephone," *Nature,* 159 (1947) :455-57.

Hylander, C. J. *American Inventors,* 126-39.

Langdon, W. C., in *DAB,* 2:148.

Law, F. H. *Civilization Builders,* 222-31.

———. *Modern Great Inventors,* 8-21.

Low, A. M. *They Made Your World,* (1949) :142-46.

Mann, F. J. "Alexander Graham Bell—Scientist," *Elec. Engineer,* 66 (1947) :215-29.

Ratcliff, J. D. *Modern Miracle Men,* 279-95.

Thomas and Thomas. *Fifty Great Americans,* 283-93.

———. *Life Stories of Great Inventors,* 151-66.

Wildman, Edwin. *Famous Leaders of Industry,* 1st ser., (1920) : 37-47.

SPECIAL ASPECTS: Watson, T. A. "How Bell Invented the Telephone," *Elec. Engineer,* 66 (1947) :232-36.

AUGUSTUS SAINT-GAUDENS—   1848-1907
—"America's Greatest Sculptor"

ORIGINAL SOURCES: Saint-Gaudens, Homer, ed. *Reminiscences of Augustus Saint-Gaudens.* 2 vols. 1913.

Yale Rev., 3:591. "Mr. Homer Saint-Gaudens, son of the sculptor, is a writer by profession; and, thoroughly informed in regard to his father's life and work, sympathetic and justly enthusiastic, he has succeeded in piecing together the scraps of reminiscences into an admirably coherent work. The united efforts of these two men have produced one of the most attractive books of the past year. It is really a history of American art presented through the life of an individual of heroic gifts and of delightful picturesqueness."

BIOGRAPHY: Cortissoz, Royal. *Augustus Saint-Gaudens.* 1907.

Dial, 43:423, Dec., 1916. "Mr. Cortissoz was fortunate in knowing the great artist personally, and some of his most delightful passages are those that embody intimate reminiscence. The bulk of the monograph, however, is criticism, needless to say of the most discriminating kind."

Also in *Outlook,* 84 (1906) : 199-208.

Hind, C. L. *Augustus Saint-Gaudens.* 1908.

Dial, 45:349, Nov. 16, 1908. Besides photographic-reproductions showing the development of the art of Saint-Gaudens, the author, an English sculptor, gives an appreciative essay. The book gives a "fair idea of the strength and the limitations of Saint-Gaudens."

COLLECTIVE BIOGRAPHY: Beard, A. E. S. *Our Foreign-Born Citizens,* 322-29.

Caffin, C. H. *American Masters of Sculpture,* (1903) : 1-17.

Cortissoz, Royal, in *DAB,* 16:296.

Cox, Kenyon. *Old Masters and New,* 266-85.

Husband, Joseph. *Americans by Adoption,* 121-39.

Irwin, Grace. *Trail Blazers of American Art,* 118-43.

McSpadden, J. W. *Famous Sculptors of America,* (1924) : 29-70.

Saint-Gaudens, Homer, ed. "Saint-Gaudens the Master," *Century,* 78 (1909) : 611-26.

SPECIAL ASPECTS: Cortissoz, Royal. *Painter's Craft,* Scribner, 1930, 401-12.

Cox, Kenyon. *Artist and Public,* (1914) : 169-228.

Taft, Lorado. *History of American Sculpture,* (1903) : see index.

———. *Modern Tendencies in Sculpture,* (1921) : 97-117.

JACOB AUGUST RIIS— 1849-1914 —"New York's Most Useful Citizen"

ORIGINAL SOURCES: Riis, J. A. *Making of an American.* 1901.

Bookman, 14:497. Mr. Riis writes an "absorbing autobiography, in which he shows concretely how one man became an American citizen, and a good citizen." One of the best autobiographies in American literature.

Also in *Outlook,* 67 (1901) :497.

BIOGRAPHY: Ware, Louise. *Jacob A. Riis: Police Reporter, Reformer, Useful Citizen.* 1938.

N. Y. Times, Apr. 17, 1938, p. 5. "A book that not only presents an engaging portrait of the man but recreates the background against which he moves so effectively. . . . There are also charming descriptions of the Riis family life."

COLLECTIVE BIOGRAPHY: Beard, C. A. *Rise of American Civilization,* 2:538-608.

Bleyer, W. G. *Main Currents,* 298-304.

Filler, Louis. *Crusaders of American Liberalism,* 45-48.

Husband, Joseph. *Americans by Adoption,* (1920) :139-53.

BIOGRAPHIES OF CONTEMPORARIES: Pringle, H. F. *Theodore Roosevelt,* see index.

Roosevelt, Theodore. *An Autobiography,* 168ff., 199-200, see index.

ALBERT GOODWILL SPALDING—   1850-1915
—"Sportsman and Merchant"

BIOGRAPHY: Bartlett, Arthur. *Baseball and Mr. Spalding.* 1951.

N. Y. Times, Feb. 25, 1951, p. 14. Albert Spalding was the first president of the Chicago White Stockings, and the founder of a sports-equipment empire. He was so closely connected with technical innovations "and with the game's spirited organizational maneuverings that the book is more than just a personal success story."

COLLECTIVE BIOGRAPHY: Kieran, John, in *DAB,* 17:420.

SAMUEL GOMPERS— 1850-1924 —"The Grand Old
Man of Labor"

ORIGINAL SOURCES: Frey, J. P. "Samuel Gompers as I Remember Him," *Am. Federationist,* 56 (1949) :6-9; 57 (1950) :6-9 Feb.; 9-11 Mar.

Gompers, Samuel. *Seventy Years of Life and Labor; an Autobiography.* 2 vols. 1925. 2 vols. in 1, 1943.

Outlook, 139:587. Although poorly arranged, these volumes furnish much information on Gompers and the A. F. of L. They reveal him as a sturdy figure who guided labor along conservative lines.

Stone, Irving, and Richard Kennedy, eds. *We Speak for Ourselves,* 337-43.

BIOGRAPHY: Harvey, R. H. *Samuel Gompers: Champion of the Toiling Masses.* 1935.

N. Y. Times Bk. Rev., June 16, 1935, p. 3. A revealing portrait.

COLLECTIVE BIOGRAPHY: Collins, Wilkie. "Great American," *Am. Federationist*, 57 (1950) :7-9.

Commons, J. R., in *DAB*, 7:369.

Friedman, L. M. *Pilgrims in a New Land*, (1948) :337-52.

Howe, M. A. D. *Causes and their Champions*, 157-94.

Madison, C. A. *American Labor Leaders*, (1950) :73-107.

Riesel, Victor. "Samuel Gompers—Little Giant of Labor," *Read. Dig.*, 57 (1950) :121-25.

Thompson, E. R. *Uncensored Celebrities*, (1919) :238-44.

SPECIAL ASPECTS: Fitch, J. A. "Samuel Gompers and the Labor Movement," *Survey*, 86 (1950) :289-92.

Thompson, C. L. "Labors' Problems: Real Wages," *Cur. Hist.*, 18 (1950) :154-62.

DAVID BELASCO— 1854-1931 —Dramatist and Producer

ORIGINAL SOURCES: Middleton, George. *These Things are Mine; the Autobiography of a Journeyman Playwright*, (1947) :273-90.

BIOGRAPHY: Winter, William. *Life of David Belasco.* 1918.

Booklist, 15:263, Apr., 1919. "Sympathetic chronicle of a courageous and picturesque career."

COLLECTIVE BIOGRAPHY: Busch, Nivens. *21 Americans*, 131-54.

Dickson, Samuel. *San Francisco is Your Home*, 159-63.

Eaton, W. P., in *DAB*, 21 (supplement one) :66.

Lewisohn, Ludwig. *Drama and the Stage*, (1922) :47-52.

SPECIAL ASPECTS: Brown, J. M. *Upstage*, (1930) :183-90.

Cole, Toby, and H. K. Chinoy, eds. *Actors on Acting*, (1949) : 498-505.

Nathan, G. J., in Moses, M. J., and J. M. Brown, eds. *American Theatre as Seen by its Critics*, (1934) :228-35.

HERBERT LEVI OSGOOD— 1855-1918 —Historian

BIOGRAPHY: Fox, D. R. *Herbert Levi Osgood: an American Scholar.* 1924.

AHR, 29:812. Professor Fox has shown "much insight and literary skill" in writing this brief but inspiring study of a quiet scholar who produced seven notable volumes on the institutional history of the American colonies.

COLLECTIVE BIOGRAPHY: Fox, D. R., in *DAB,* 14:78.

SPECIAL ASPECTS: Beatty, E. C. O., in Hutchinson, W. T., ed. *Essays in American Historiography,* 271-93.

Kraus, Michael. *History of American History,* 400-52.

Saveth, E. N. *American Historians and European Immigration, 1875-1925,* 191-99.

LILLIAN RUSSELL—1861-1922—"Glamour Girl of the Nineties"

BIOGRAPHY: Morell, Parker. *Lillian Russell: the Era of Plush.* 1940.

Sat. Rev. of Lit., 22:11, June 22, 1940. Popular biography of the Iowa-born girl who won fame and fortune on the American stage.

COLLECTIVE BIOGRAPHY: Blodget, L. P., in *DAB,* 16:246.

*WILLIAM SIDNEY PORTER—   1862-1910 —"O'Henry"

ORIGINAL SOURCES: Abramowitz, Isidore, ed. *Great Prisoners,* 669-77.

BIOGRAPHY: Davis, R. H., and A. B. Maurice. *Caliph of Bagdad; being Arabian Nights Flashes of the Life, Letters, and Works of O'Henry.* 1931.

New Repub., 67:348, Aug. 12, 1931. "An unusual book . . . yet while O'Henry is remembered at all, it will deserve to stand as the definitive account of the man and of his method."

Jennings, A. J. *Through the Shadows with O'Henry.* 1921.

Freeman, 4:430, Jan. 11, 1922. The author—a famous train robber pardoned by Roosevelt—knew Porter in the Ohio penitentiary and in Honduras. The two "became fast friends. His book is the history of this friendship."

Long, E. H. *O'Henry: the Man and His Work.* 1949.

Amer. Lit., 22:85. Mr. Long's concise biography "is pleasant to read and it takes a long step toward the 'definitive' biography of some future day."

Smith, C. A. *O'Henry, a Biography.* 1916.

---

* For further bibliography see Spiller, et al. *Literary History of the United States,* 3 (1948) :696-98.

Dial, 61:573, Dec. 28, 1916. "A work of rare charm and moving interest, a happy mean between the biographical and the critical study."

COLLECTIVE BIOGRAPHY: Black, Alexander. *American Husbands,* (1925) :149-82.

Cooper, F. T. *Some American Story Tellers,* (1911) : 225-44.

Hind, C. L. *Authors and I,* 136-41.

Russell, F. A. *American Pilgrimage,* 65-81.

Tinker, E. L., in *Reader's Digest Reader,* 44-45.

Van Doren, Carl, in *DAB,* 15:105.

Williams, B. C. *Our Short Story Writers,* (1922) :200-22.

SPECIAL ASPECTS: Courtney, L. W. "O'Henry's Case Reconsidered," *Amer. Lit.,* 14 (1943) :361-71.

Forman, H. J. "Mystery of O'Henry," *Read. Dig.,* 51 (1947) : 92-96.

Leacock, S. B. *Essays and Literary Studies,* (1916) :231-66.

Loggins, Vernon. *I Hear America,* 331-48.

Long, E. H. "O'Henry: the Man and his Work." *Antioch Rev.,* 9 (1949) :559.

Mais, S. P. B. *From Shakespeare to O'Henry,* (1923) :300-17.

Pattee, F. L. *Sidelights on American Literature,* (1922) :3-55.

Rollins, H. E. "O'Henry's Texas," *Texas Rev.,* 4 (1919) :295-307.

Smith, C. A. *Southern Literary Studies,* (1927) :158-67.

EDWARD WILLIAM BOK— 1863-1930 —Editor

ORIGINAL SOURCES: Bok, E. W. *Americanization of Edward Bok: the Autobiography of a Dutch Boy Fifty Years After.* 1920.

Bookman, 52:362. "Mr. Bok has done more than merely carry the reader with him along the pleasant paths which he has trod. He has thought deeply upon the problem of the immigrant and the result is a valuable contribution."

Frank, Glenn. *American Looks at his World,* 23-33.

COLLECTIVE BIOGRAPHY: Beard, A. E. S. *Our Foreign-Born Citizens,* 78-95.

Collins, Joseph. *The Doctor Looks at Biography,* 190-98.

Filler, Louis. *Crusaders of American Liberalism,* 148-51.

Dillard, Irving, in *DAB,* 21 (sup. 1) :91.

Orcutt, W. D. *Celebrities Off Parade,* 224-54.

Wood, J. P. *Magazines in the United States,* (1949) :105-20.

JAMES JOHN CORBETT—1866-1933—"Gentleman Jim"

ORIGINAL SOURCES: Stone, Irving, and Richard Kennedy, eds. *We Speak for Ourselves,* 101-07.

COLLECTIVE BIOGRAPHY: Collins, Joseph. *The Doctor Looks at Biography,* 295-99.

DeFord, M. A. *They were San Franciscans,* (1941) :274-94.

Fleischer, N. S. *Heavyweight Championship,* (1949) :105-15.

Inglis, W. O. *Champions off Guard,* 109-45.

Rice, Harold. *Within the Ropes: Champions in Action,* (1946) : 39-88.

LINCOLN STEFFENS—1866-1936—The Chief of the Muckrakers

ORIGINAL SOURCES: *The Autobiography of Lincoln Steffens.* 2 vols. 1931.

Nation, 132:415, Apr. 15, 1931. The story of a great reporter who won the confidence of crooked political bosses, and knew intimately Roosevelt, Wilson, and Harding.

Extract in Balch, Marston. *Modern Short Biographies and Autobiographies,* 49-60.

Hamilton, E. B. *How They Started,* 141-64.

Hyde, M. A. *Modern Biography,* 70-78.

Rahv, Philip, ed. *Discovery of Europe,* 514-26.

Stone, Irving, and Richard Kennedy, eds. *We Speak for Ourselves,* 364-70.

Wagenknecht, E. C. *When I was a Child,* 353-57.

COLLECTIVE BIOGRAPHY: Filler, Louis. *Crusaders for American Liberalism,* 90-101, 350-55.

Hunt, R. D. *California's Stately Hall of Fame,* 505-10.

Lydenberg, John. "Henry Adams and Lincoln Steffens," *So. Atl. Quar.,* 48 (1949) :42-64.

Madison, C. A. *Critics and Crusaders,* 395-418.

———. "Muckraker's Progress," *Va. Quar. Rev.,* 22 (1946) :405-20.

SPECIAL ASPECTS: Chamberlain, John. *Farewell to Reform: the Rise, Life and Decay of the Progressive Mind in America,* (1933) :see index.

Regier, C. C. *The Era of the Muckrakers,* (1932) :see index.

GEORGE HORACE LORIMER— 1868-1937 —"The Henry Ford of American Literature"

BIOGRAPHY: Tebbel, John. *George Horace Lorimer and the Saturday Evening Post.* 1948.

AHR, 54:218. "A judicious, accurate and fairly complete portrait of America's greatest popular magazine editor. The book is poorly organized, but one can skip the long lists of authors and their works to get the portrait of a remarkable man!"

STEPHEN CRANE— 1871-1900 —Poet and Novelist

BIOGRAPHY: Beer, Thomas. *Stephen Crane.* 1923.

New Repub., 37:153, Jan. 2, 1924. "While containing high praise for the author of *The Red Badge,* the volume is not written in unduly glowing terms nor with the air of the idol-worshipper."

Berryman, John. *Stephen Crane.* (American Men of Letters, 1950) .

Booklist, 47:187, Jan. 15, 1951. "In spite of an occasionally baffling style and a loose invocation of Freud, this biography of the rediscovered American poet and novelist gives a perceptive interpretation. The biographer seeks in the events of Crane's life—the aura of sanctity in his childhood, a haphazard education, experience as a journalist, his marriage to a prostitute—an explanation for Crane's genius. His literary evaluation of both poetry and prose is informed and lucid, and his picture of the man clean cut, but his explanation of the Oedipus complex root of Crane's art seems too glib and not completely satisfying."

Raymond, T. L. *Stephen Crane.* 1923. A short biography.

COLLECTIVE BIOGRAPHY: Ford, F. M. *Portraits from Life,* (1937) :21-37.

Garland, Hamlin, in *Yale Rev.,* 3 (1914) :494-506.

Josephson, Matthew. *Portrait of an Artist as American,* 232-63.

Westcott, Allan, in *DAB,* 4:506.

SPECIAL ASPECTS: Conrad, Joseph. *Notes on Life and Letters,* (1921) :49-52.

Elconin, V. A. "Stephen Crane at Ashbury Park," *Amer. Lit.,* 20 (1948) :275-89.

Gregory, Horace, and M. A. Zaturenska. *History of American Poetry,* 133-37.

Kazin, Alfred. *On Native Grounds,* 51-72.

Hartwick, Harry. *Foreground of American Fiction,* 21-44.

Hatcher, H. H. *Creating the Modern American Novel,* (1935): 12-20.

Hicks, Granville. *Great Tradition,* 131-63.

Loggins, Vernon. *I Hear America,* 9-31.

Van Doren, C. C. *American Novel, 1789-1939,* 225-44.

Wells, H. G., in Wilson, Edmund. *Shock of Recognition,* 661-71.

CHAPTER XXXIII. PENNSYLVANIA

THADDEUS STEVENS— 1792-1868 —"The Greatest Dictator Congress Ever Had"

BIOGRAPHY: Current, R. N. *Old Thad Stevens: a Story of Ambition.* 1942.

AHR, 48:821. A vivid, balanced biography which gives excellent sketches of contemporaries.

McCall, S. W. *Thaddeus Stevens.* (American Statesman, 1899).

AHR, 5:155. Mr. McCall has produced as "judicious and useful a volume as any in the series."

Miller, A. B. *Thaddeus Stevens.* 1939.

AHR, 45:478. A readable biography which leaves the reader to wonder whether "Old Thad" was motivated chiefly by love of the slave, or hatred of his master.

Singmaster, Elsie. *I Speak for Thaddeus Stevens.* 1947.

Weekly Bk. Rev., May 25, 1947, p. 18. A fictionalized biography.

Woodburn, J. A. *Life of Thaddeus Stevens.* 1913.

AHR, 19:177. "Mr. Woodburn's method has been to let Stevens tell his own story, . . . while Stevens's attitude toward slavery and reconstruction naturally claims the major portion of the space, his interest in education, and his democracy . . . receive due attention. The special interest of Mr. Woodburn, however, is in Stevens's financial views."

Woodley, T. F. *Thaddeus Stevens.* 1934.

Sat. Rev. of Lit., 12:20, Aug. 24, 1935. Being a Pennsylvanian attorney Mr. Woodley presents a fuller record of Stevens's activities before 1861. "Perhaps the chief contribution of this thorough but unskillfully written book is the evidence it offers for Stevens's sincerity which made him so power-ful a force in Reconstruction. It was this which, conjoined with unwisdom and prejudice, made his career so lamentable a calamity to the Southern whites, to the Republican party of the North, and in the end to the Negro race itself."

COLLECTIVE BIOGRAPHY: Nevins, Allan, in *DAB*, 17:620.

HISTORY: Bowers, C. G. *The Tragic Era,* 65-84, index.

Fish, Carl. *American Civil War,* 310-12.

SPECIAL ASPECTS: Thompson, C. L. "Thaddeus Stevens: Radical Republican," *Cur. Hist.,* 14 (1948) :277-82.

Woodburn, J. A. "The Attitude of Thaddeus Stevens toward the Conduct of the Civil War," *AHR,* 12 (1907) :567-83.

SIMON CAMERON— 1799-1889 —Secretary of War

BIOGRAPHY: Crippen, L. F. *Simon Cameron: Ante-Bellum Years.* (Men of America, 1942) .

AHR, 48:815. An able defense of Cameron's early career which seeks to rehabilitate his reputation.

McNair, J. B. *Simon Cameron's Adventure in Iron, 1837-1846.* 1949.

New biographical material.

COLLECTIVE BIOGRAPHY: Hendrick, B. J. *Lincoln's War Cabinet,* 1-123, 217-64.

Meneely, H. A., in *DAB,* 3:437.

Macartney, C. E. N. *Lincoln and his Cabinet,* 23-46.

JOHN GREENLEAF WHITTIER— 1807-1892 —Quaker Abolitionist and Poet

ORIGINAL SOURCES: Abbott, Lyman. *Silhouettes of My Contemporaries,* 126-35.

Field, Annie. *Authors and Friends.* 1897.

Nation, 64:168, Mar. 4, 1897. "It is a happy fortune which enables us to see so many writers of the famous Boston coterie through the eyes of an intelligent, cultivated, and sympathetic woman, whose opportunities for knowing them were of the best."

———. "Whittier: Notes of His Life and of His Friendships," *Harper's,* 86 (1893) :338-59.

BIOGRAPHY: Bennett, Whitman. *Whittier: Bard of Freedom.* 1941.

New Repub., 106:93, Jan. 19, 1942. "Undiscriminating in its admiration, and written in the too consciously 'folksy' style of the former press agent for Lasky, this biography has nevertheless the value of giving a fresh and fairly detailed account of the poet's important work for the antislavery movement."

Carpenter, G. R. *John Greenleaf Whittier*. 1903.

Nation, 77:450. An excellent summary of all the existing sources, including Whittier's correspondence with John Quincy Adams, Henry Clay and William Lloyd Garrison.

Higginson, T. W. *John Greenleaf Whittier*. (English Men of Letters, 1902).

Nation, 76:440, May 28, 1903. A well-rounded biography.

Mordell, Albert. *Quaker Militant: John Greenleaf Whittier*. 1933.

New Repub., 75:320, Aug. 2, 1933. "An interesting book" but Mr. Mordell fails to fuse his "psychological analysis, political history, literary criticism —into a coherent whole, to interpret the man, the politician, and the poet in the light of some genuinely unifying principle of understanding."

Pollard, J. A. *John Greenleaf Whittier, Friend of Man*. 1949.

N. E. Quar., 23:547. Dr. Pollard examines "Whittier's labors as politician and abolitionist, champion of the Indian, friend of the working man. . . . His views on government and his democratic ideals are for the first time stated in broad philosophical terms. We recognize Whittier's larger role in an age of general social re-evaluation," but we do not find adequate critical analysis of Whittier's poetry.

COLLECTIVE BIOGRAPHY: Brooks, V. W. *The Flowering of New England*. 388-403.

———. *New England: Indian Summer*, 45-65.

Mordell, Albert, in *DAB*, 20:173.

Perry, Bliss. "Whittier for Today," *Atlantic*, 100 (1907) :851-59.

Thomas and Thomas. *Living Biographies of Great Poets*, (1941) :265-76.

Vincent, L. H. *American Literary Masters*, 255-83.

SPECIAL ASPECTS: Bailey, E. J. *Religious Thought in the Greater American Poets*, 70-107.

Christman, L. H., in *John Ruskin, Preacher*, 56-74.

Fitch, G. H. *Great Spiritual Writers of America*, (1916) :87-94.

Foerster, Norman. *Nature in American Literature*, 20-36.

Griffin, M. L. "Whittier and Hayne: a Record of Friendship," *Amer. Lit.*, 19 (1947) :41-58.

Hintz, H. W. *Quaker Influence in American Literature,* (1940) : 76-86.

Howe, W. D., in Macy, John, ed. *American Writers on American Literature,* 125-34.

More, P. E. *Shelburne Essays,* 3rd ser., (1905) :28-53.

Ticknor, Caroline. *Glimpses of Authors,* 74-92.

Turner, Arlin. "Whittier Calls on George W. Cable," *N. E. Quar.,* 22 (1949) :92-96.

Trent, W. P., and John Erskine. *Great American Writers,* 134-69.

Schaedler, L. C. "Whittier's Attitude toward Colonial Puritanism," *N. E. Quar.,* 21 (1948) :350-67.

Smallwood, O. T. "Historical Significance of Whittier's Anti-Slavery Poems as Reflected by their Political and Social Background," *Negro Hist. Jour.,* 35 (1950) :150-73.

Stevens, J. S. *Whittier's Use of the Bible.* (Univ. of Maine Studies, 1930) .

Amer. Lit., 3:109. "Mr. Stevens has attempted a task that long needed to be done, but one which he has by no means completed."

Strong, A. H. *American Poets and their Theology,* 105-58, 322-27.

Wallace, Archer. *Religious Faith of Great Men,* 114-38.

DAVID DIXON PORTER—1813-1891—"Picturesque Sea-dog"

BIOGRAPHY: West, R. S., Jr. *The Second Admiral: a Life of David Dixon Porter, 1813-1891.* 1937.

AHR, 43:905. Admiral Porter was quite a controversial figure but Professor West shows that he "was an officer with a body of real achievement to his credit." He has written a "fascinating biography of a remarkable American."

COLLECTIVE BIOGRAPHY: Alden, C. S., and Ralph Earle. *Makers of Naval Tradition,* (1942) :176-202.

Lewis, C. L. *Famous American Naval Officers,* 99-127.

Paullin, C. O., in *DAB,* 15:85.

EDWIN McMASTERS STANTON—   1814-1869
—Administrator Who Organized the North for Victory

COLLECTIVE BIOGRAPHY: Bradford, Gamaliel. *Union Portraits,* 165-96.

Also in *Atlantic,* 116 (1915) :180-91.

Hendrick, B. J. *Lincoln's War Cabinet,* 217-64.

Macartney, C. E. N. *Lincoln and his Cabinet,* 297-358.

Meneely, A. H., in *DAB,* 17:517.

STEPHEN COLLINS FOSTER— 1826-1864 —"The Most Popular Song Writer in American History"

ORIGINAL SOURCES: Morneweck, E. F. *Chronicles of Stephen Foster's Family.* 2 vols. 1944.

Atlantic, 176:150. Letters and family recollections compiled by the composer's niece.

BIOGRAPHY: Howard, J. T. *Stephen Foster, America's Troubadour.* 1934.

MVHR, 21:415. "Foster is best remembered for his songs of the southern Negro," although "his contact with the South was slight." He "derived his chief inspiration to compose plantation melodies from the Negro minstrel show which in his time was a popular form of entertainment." Foster "realized what many an historian has failed to know: that Negro slavery had its softer side, its mutual and genuine affections."

Milligan, H. V. *Stephen Collins Foster: a Biography of America's Folk-Song Composer.* 1920.

N. Y. Evening Post, Oct. 23, 1920, p. 14. "By a careful sifting of material the author has sought to present an authentic account of Foster's career, taking special pains to dispel some of the legends that have grown up around his later years and death."

Walters, Raymond. *Stephen Foster: Youth's Golden Gleam; a Sketch of his Life and Background in Cincinnati, 1846-1850.* 1936.

N. Y. Times, Dec. 6, 1936, p. 16. "With the discovery of some new material, as well as the careful gathering together of facts already known, Dr. Walters has made an interesting and valuable picture of 'America's Troubadour' in these developing years, and of the Cincinnati that he knew."

COLLECTIVE BIOGRAPHY: Ewen, David, ed. *Composers of Yesterday,* 149-51.

Goldberg, Isaac. *Tin Pan Alley,* 43-45.

Long, Haniel. *Pittsburgh Memoranda,* (1935) :19-26.

Also in Beckwith and Coope, eds. *Contemporary American Biography,* 86-92.

Nevins, R. P. "Stephen C. Foster and Negro Minstrels," *Atlantic,* 20 (1887) :608-16.

Overmeyer, Grace. *Famous American Composers,* 35-54.

Palmer, C. W., in *DAB,* 6:557.

Spaeth, Sigmund. "Stephen Foster of 'Tin Pan Alley,' " *Etude,* 56 (1938) :711-12.

Also in Beckwith and Coope, eds. *Contemporary American Biography,* 69-77.

Thomas and Thomas. *Forty Famous Composers,* (1948) :171-77.

———. *Living Biographies of Famous Americans,* 129-36.

SPECIAL ASPECTS: Hodges, Fletcher. *Stephen Foster, Democrat.* 1946.

Howard, J. T. *Our American Music,* (1946) :184-98.

Pattee, F. L. *Feminine Fifties,* 307-21.

GEORGE BRINTON McCLELLAN— 1826-1885
—"The North's Greatest Commander" or Vacillating General Who Nearly Lost the War?

ORIGINAL SOURCES: Chesnut, M. B. *Diary from Dixie,* see index.

Myers, W. S. *The Mexican War Diary of George B. McClellan.* 1917.

AHR, 23:220. This little book reveals much regarding McClellan's personality and gives life-like pictures of the campaigns.

BIOGRAPHY: Eckenrode, J. H., and Bryan Conrad. *George B. McClellan, the Man Who Saved the Union.* 1942.

Jour. of South. Hist., 8:278. Two southern historians claim that politics kept McClellan from capturing Richmond and from occupying his rightful place in history.

Houser, M. L. *Lincoln and McClellan; Prepared for the Lincoln Group of Chicago.* 1946.

Myers, W. S. *General George Brinton McClellan: a Study in Personality.* 1934.

AHR, 40:764. Using extracts from McClellan's correspondence, the author presents his personality vividly and with the greatest sympathy. Military history is restricted to "a few illustrations." An "interesting" and "useful" book, but partial to McClellan.

COLLECTIVE BIOGRAPHY: Bradford, Gamaliel. *Union Portraits*, 1-32.

Also in *Atlantic*, 114 (1914) :508-19.

Croffut, W. A. *American Procession*, 226-35.

Hendrick, B. J. *Lincoln's War Cabinet*, 265-319.

Hungerford, Edward. *Men of Erie*, (1946) :180-99.

Macartney, C. E. N. *Men Who Missed It*, 62-68.

Maurice, Sir Frederick. *Statesmen and Soldiers of the Civil War*, 59-89.

Milton, G. F. *Conflict*, 100-20, 233-47.

Seitz, D. C. *The "Also Rans,"* 208-27.

Spaulding, O. L., in *DAB*, 11:581.

Stone, Irving. *They Also Ran*, 119-89.

HISTORY: Catton, Bruce. *Mr. Lincoln's Army.* 1951.

N. Y. Times, Feb. 25, 1951, p. 23. "Mr. Catton tells the story in journalistic order, beginning with Pope's fiasco at Second Bull Run, then going back to pick up the narrative of McClellan's rise. . . . He does enormous research and then presents "it in almost a motion picture . . . with brief, vivid close-ups of generals. Yet all is kept within a structure of sound analysis of the causes and meaning of events."

Fish, Carl. *American Civil War*, 259-60.

SPECIAL ASPECTS: Dowdey, Clifford. *Experiment in Rebellion*, 181-98.

Muldoon, S. J. *Psychic Experiences of Famous People*, (1947) : 91-98.

BIOGRAPHIES OF CONTEMPORARIES: Randall, J. G. *Lincoln the President.* 1945.

Regards McClellan as the North's greatest commander.

JOSEPH JEFFERSON—   1829-1905   —Actor

ORIGINAL SOURCES: Jefferson, Joseph. *Rip Van Winkle; Autobiography.* New Revised Edition, 1950.

Kirkus, 18:250, Apr. 15, 1950. "Still makes excellent reading, not only of the theatre of Jefferson's day but of an active, full, interesting life."

BIOGRAPHY: Winter, William. *Life and Art of Joseph Jefferson.* 1894.

COLLECTIVE BIOGRAPHY: Bradford, Gamaliel. *American Portraits,* 197-223.

——. *Portraits and Personalities,* 93-115.

Eaton, W. P., in *DAB*, 10:15.

SPECIAL ASPECTS: Cole, Toby, and H. K. Chenoy. *Actors on Acting,* (1949) :473-79.

Davis, L. L., in Moses, M. J., and J. M. Brown, eds. *American Theatres Seen by its Critics,* (1934) :75-78.

Frohman, Daniel. *Encore,* (1937) :106-25.

Ormsbee, Helen. *Backstage with Actors,* (1938) :145-67.

Winter, William. *Other Days,* (1908) :64-97.

ANDREW CARNEGIE— 1835-1919 —Steelmaker
Who Promoted Peace

ORIGINAL SOURCES: Van Dyke, J. C., ed. *Autobiography of Andrew Carnegie.* 1920.

AHR, 26:368. A notable autobiography, but does it reveal the steps by which a penniless immigrant became the most powerful figure in the steel industry?

Extract in Keyes, R. K., ed. *Lives of Today and Yesterday,* 14-22.

And in *Famous Fortunes,* 125-42.

BIOGRAPHY: Hendrick, B. J. *The Life of Andrew Carnegie.* 2 vols. 1932.

AHR, 38:777. This "official life" is an excellent biography—"scholarly, well proportioned, the result of years of research, and reasonably unbiased." It is apparently definitive "on the personal side of Carnegie's life."

Winkler, J. K. *Incredible Carnegie; the life of Andrew Carnegie, 1835-1919.* 1931.

New Repub., 69:248, Jan. 13, 1932. A readable, popular biography which gives interesting information on the Homestead strike, but throws little light on the development of the Scottish ironmaster.

COLLECTIVE BIOGRAPHY: Arnold, J. B. *Giants in Dressing Gowns,* (1942) :153-58.

Extract in Prochnow, H. V., ed. *Great Stories from Great Lives,* 145-46.

Basso, Hamilton. *Mainstream,* 84-112

Beard, A. E. S. *Our Foreign-Born Citizens,* 83-93.

Blumenfield, R. D. *R. D. B.'s Procession,* 232-36.

Dos Passos, John. *U. S. A.,* 1:264-65.

Forbes, B. C. *Men Who are Making America,* 36-43.

Grayson, T. J. *Leaders and Periods of American Finance,* 406-27.

Hathaway, E. V. *Partners in Progress,* 260-74.

Hubbard, Elbert. *Great Business Men,* 262-99.

Hendrick, B. J., in *DAB,* 3:499.

Husband, Joseph. *Americans by Adoption,* 91-103.

Johnson, Alvin. "Andrew Carnegie, Educator," *Jour. of Adult Ed.,* 8 (1936) :5-9.

Law, F. H. *Modern Great Americans,* 50-62.

Morris, Charles. *Heroes of Progress in America,* 325-34.

O'Higgins, H. J., and E. H. Reede. *American Mind in Action,* 111-62.

Root, Elihu. *Men and Policies,* 49-57.

Scott, J. B. "Andrew Carngie, November, 1835—August 11, 1919," *Pan Amer. Union Bul.,* 70 (1936) :8-18.

Sherman, S. P. *Americans,* 246-55.

Thomas and Thomas. *Fifty Great Americans,* (1948) :230-41.

Wildman, Edwin. *Famous Leaders of Industry,* 2nd ser., (1921) : 27-38.

Williams, J. H. H. *Men of Stress: Woodrow Wilson, Andrew Carnegie, Lord Leverhulme.* 1948.

SPECIAL ASPECTS: Gabriel, R. H. *The Course of American Democratic Thought,* 150-53, index.

Hazard, L. L. *The Frontier in American Literature,* 212-21.

Russell, Bertrand. *Freedom versus Organization,* 325-33.

GEORGE WESTINGHOUSE—1846-1914—"Inventor and Manufacturer"

BIOGRAPHY: Leupp, F. E. *George Westinghouse, his Life and Achievements.* 1918.

AHR, 24:283. Written for non-technical readers, Mr. Leupp's book is "a fascinating history of the more notable accomplishments of the great industrialist." Hampered by the absence of personal letters, the author used interviews to get "a fairly vivid picture of the man."

COLLECTIVE BIOGRAPHY: Caldwell, O. H., in *DAB,* 20:16.

Faris, J. T. *Men Who Conquered,* 69-74.

Hylander, C. J. *American Inventors,* 117-25.

Law, F. H. *Civilization Builders,* 37-39.

Wildman, Edwin. *Famous Leaders of Industry,* 1st ser., (1920) : 285-94.

SPECIAL ASPECTS: Grayson, T. J. *Leaders and Periods of American Finance,* 350-75.

Lydgate, W. A. "George Westinghouse: Master Inventor," *Read. Dig.,* 48 (1946) :91-4.

HENRY CLAY FRICK—1849-1919—Capitalist—Labor Baiter—Art Patron

BIOGRAPHY: Harvey, G. B. M. *Henry Clay Frick, the Man.* 1928.

New Repub., 54:223, Apr. 4, 1928. Readable success story of a Pennsylvania Dutch farm boy who became the Bismarck of the Homestead strike.

COLLECTIVE BIOGRAPHY: Forbes, B. C. *Men Who are Making America,* 131-43.

McDonald, P. B., in *DAB,* 7-29.

SPECIAL ASPECTS: Nixon, L. L. "Unique Philanthropy," *NEA Jour.,* 35 (1946) :31.

JOHN BACH McMASTER— 1852-1932 —The First United States Social Historian

BIOGRAPHY: Goldman, E. F. *John Bach McMaster, American Historian.* 1943.

AHR, 49:72. Mr. Goldman has given us "an engaging picture" of a very industrious professor too busy "launching a new type of history" to understand undergraduates.* He notes his indebtedness to Macauley, and praises him as a pioneer who found "a new approach to American history . . ." He fails to emphasize McMaster's "extensive use of newspapers" and his realization of the importance of the West. Mr. Goldman discusses McMaster's bias against the South, but fails to note that he gives too little attention to women in his many pages.

COLLECTIVE BIOGRAPHY: Lingelbach, W. E., in *DAB,* 12:140.

SPECIAL ASPECTS: Hutchinson, W. T., in his *Essays in American Historiography,* 122-43.

———. "John Bach McMaster, Historian of the American People," *MVHR,* 16 (1929) :23-49.

---

* Hutchinson lists a dozen prominent historians among McMaster's students. P. 125.

Kraus, Michael. *History of American History,* 380-95.

JOHN PHILIP SOUSA— 1854-1832 —Composer and Band Master

COLLECTIVE BIOGRAPHY: Goldberg, Isaac, in *Am. Merc.,* 27 (1932) :193-200.

Howard, J. T., in *DAB,* 17:407.

Hughes, Rupert. *Contemporary American Composers,* (1900) : see index.

Overmeyer, Grace. *Famous American Composers,* 90-106.

Whelbourn, Hubert. *Celebrated Musicians,* (1930) : see index.

SPECIAL ASPECTS: Taylor, Deems. *Of Men and Music,* (1937) : 58-61.

Larkin, C. H. "Stars and Stripes Forever Around the World," *Etude,* 64 (1946) :548-49.

DANIEL GUGENHEIM— 1856-1930 —Capitalist and Philanthropist

COLLECTIVE BIOGRAPHY: Forbes, B. C. *Men Who are Making America,* 173-80.

Lerner, Max, in *DAB,* 8:36.

O'Conner, Henry. *The Gugenheims,* (1937) :221-37.

Schriftgiesser, Karl. *Families,* 244-306.

CHAPTER XXXIV. CHESAPEAKE BAY

EDMUND RUFFIN— 1794-1865 —"Agriculturist and Publisher"

ORIGINAL SOURCES: Hamilton, J. G. de Roulhac, ed. *The Papers of Thomas Ruffin.* (Publications of the N. C. Hist. Commission, 1918) .

BIOGRAPHY: Craven, A. O. *Edmund Ruffin, Southerner: a Study in Secession.* 1932.

AHR, 38:775. An exceptionally well-written study of a man of many contradictions who worked for agricultural reform and secession.

COLLECTIVE BIOGRAPHY: Craven, A. O., in *DAB*, 16:214.

Dies, E. J. *Titans of the Soil*, (1949) :55-63.

MATTHEW FONTAINE MAURY—   1806-1873
—"The Pathfinder of the Seas"

ORIGINAL SOURCES: Dozer, D. M., ed. "Matthew Fontaine Maury's Letter of Instruction to William Lewis Herndon," *Hispan. Amer. Hist. Rev.*, 28 (1948) :212-28.

BIOGRAPHY: Lewis, C. L. *Matthew Fontaine Maury, the Pathfinder of the Seas.* 1927.

AHR, 33:925. An adequate biography of a loveable and inspiring naval officer who in spite of his lameness became an outstanding authority on oceanography.

COLLECTIVE BIOGRAPHY: Alden, C. S., and Ralph Earle. *Makers of Naval Tradition*, 111-29.

Heath, W., in *Cath. World*, 168 (1949) :349-53.

Jaffe, Bernard. *Men of Science in America*, 207-32.

Marmer, H. A., in *DAB*, 12:428.

Smith, C. A. *Southern Literary Studies*, 168-81.

ROBERT EDWARD LEE— 1807-1870 —A Military
Genius in Fact or Fiction?

ORIGINAL SOURCES: Blackford, C. M., III, ed. *Letters from Lee's Army, or Memoirs In and Out of the Army in Virginia During the War Between the States.* 1947.

AHR, 53:195. "This volume is the second Civil War book to come from the notable Blackford family of Lynchburg, Virginia."

Cabell, Branch. "Letters to General Lee," *Atlantic*, 177 (Mar. 1946) :81-84.

Chesnut, M. B. *Diary from Dixie*, see index.

Hoyt, W. M. D., ed. "Some Personal Letters of Robert E. Lee, 1850-1858," *Jour. South. Hist.*, 12 (1946) :557-70.

BIOGRAPHY: Bradford, Gamaliel. *Lee the American.* 1912.

Yale Rev., 2:359. A New England "psychographer" portrays a soul who was great in defeat as an example for the generation inclined to worship success.

Also in *Atlantic*, 106 (1910) :730-39; 108 (1911) :83-93, 220-27, 501-12.

Bruce, P. A. *Robert E. Lee.* 1907.

AHR, 13:389. A loyal Virginia historian pictures Lee as a hero free from faults, Jackson as the perfect lieutenant, Longstreet the chief scapegoat.

*Freeman, D. S. *R. E. Lee, a Biography.* 4 vols. 1934, 1935.

AHR, 40:534; 41:164. A biographer with remarkable powers of analysis and great literary skill has given us a biography worthy of Lee. His volumes present a vivid picture of the war as seen from Lee's headquarters. There is also frank criticism of the Confederate commander and his associates.

Read esp. Vol. 1, Chap. 25, "The Answer He Was Born to Make."

Vol. 3, Chap. 9, "Why Was Gettysburg Lost?"

Vol. 4, Chap. 10, "The Sword of Robert E. Lee." (Discussion of Lee's methods as military commander).

Chap. 22, "Lee's Theory of Education."

Chap. 27, "The Pattern of a Life."

Also in Prochnow, H. V., ed. *Great Stories from Great Lives,* 21-34.

Maurice, Sir Frederick. *Robert E. Lee, the Soldier.* 1925.

AHR, 30:840. An outstanding British military authority discusses Lee's campaigns in detail and rates him "above Wellington as a general."

White, H. A. *Robert E. Lee and the Southern Confederacy, 1807-1870.* (Heroes of the Nation, 1897).

Nation, 65:502. The best one-volume biography.

Collective Biography: Bradford, Gamaliel. *Portraits and Personalities,* 57-74.

Bruce, Philip. *The Virginia Plutarch,* 2:223-44.

Cournos, John. *Modern Plutarch,* 325-46, 359-64.

Eliot, Ellsworth, Jr. *West Point in the Confederacy,* 45-80.

Freeman, D. S., in *DAB,* 11:120.

———, in *There Were Giants in the Land,* 145-52.

Hendrick, B. J. *The Lees of Virginia,* 391-438.

Malone, Dumas. *Saints in Action,* 12-14, 21, 137.

Schriftgiesser, Karl. *Families,* 188-97

Thomas and Thomas. *Fifty Great Americans,* 156-63.

———. *Living Biographies of Famous Americans,* 139-49.

Walton, John. *Makers of the U. S. A.,* (1943) :65-74.

Westrate, E. V. *Those Fatal Generals,* (1936) :202-14.

Wildman, Edwin. *Famous Leaders of Character in America,* 17-26.

---

* Awarded the Pulitzer Prize.

History: *Dodd, W. E. *Lincoln or Lee,* (1928) :69-116.

Also in *Century,* 113 (1927) :661-73.

Fish, Carl. *American Civil War,* 262-64.

SPECIAL ASPECTS: Adams, C. F. *Lee at Appomattox,* (1902) :1-30, 376-429.

Colby, Elizabeth, and D. S. Freeman. "Robert E. Lee: Is His Military Genius Fact or Fiction?" *Current Hist.,* 29 (1928) : 36-47.

Collins, Joseph. *The Doctor Looks at Biography,* 183-87.

Flournoy, Mrs. M. H. *Essays: Historical and Critical,* 41-47, 51-56.

O'Connor, Robert. "Robert E. Lee: the Southern Saint," *Am. Merc.,* 68 (1949) :578-86.

Peattie, D. C. "Lee's Greatest Victory," *Read. Dig.,* 56 (1950) . 93-96.

Riley, F. L., ed. *General Robert E. Lee After Appomattox.* 1922.

AHR, 27:830. Reminiscences by students and professors who knew Lee when he sought as the head of an obscure college to contribute to the restoration of the South.

Rister, C. C. *Robert E. Lee in Texas.* 1946.

AHR, 52:396. The author thinks that the two and a half years Lee spent in Texas intensified his love for Virginia and thus affected his great decision in 1861.

Robert, J. C. "Lee the Farmer," *Jour. South. Hist.,* 30 (1937) : 422-40.

Wallace, Archer. *Religious Faith of Great Men,* 174-92.

Wecter, Dixon. *Hero in America,* 273-306.

RAPHAEL SEMMES— 1809-1877 —The Leading
Naval Officer of the CSA

BIOGRAPHY: Gosnell, Lt. Com. H. A. *Rebel Raider: Being an Account of Raphael Semmes's Cruise in the C.S.S. Sumter: Composed in Large Part of Extracts from Semmes's Memoirs of Service Afloat, Written in the year 1869.* 1948.

AHR, 54:165. "Mr. Gosnell has pruned away the unessential material and freed a story that has the swift excitement of an adventure classic." A brief but enjoyable volume.

Roberts, W. A. *Semmes of the Alabama.* 1938.

---

* See p. 352.

AHR, 44:100. An "interesting readable biography . . ."

COLLECTIVE BIOGRAPHY: Bradford, Gamaliel. *Confederate Portraits,* 217-46.

Cranwell, J. P. *Spoilers of the Sea,* 24-47, 79-110.

Robinson, W. J., Jr., in *DAB,* 16:579.

SPECIAL ASPECTS: Butler, P. R. "Cruise of the Sumter," *Blackwood's,* 263 (1948) :351-62.

Flournoy, Mrs. M. H. *Essays: Historical and Critical,* 69-75.

GEORGE HENRY THOMAS— 1816-1870 —A Southerner Who Fought for the North

COLLECTIVE BIOGRAPHY: Bradford, Gamaliel. *Union Portraits,* 97-129.

Also in *Atlantic,* 114 (1914) :218-30.

Spaulding, O. L., Jr., in *DAB,* 18:432.

HISTORY: Fish, Carl. *American Civil War,* 260.

CLARA HARLOWE BARTON— 1821-1912 —Angel of Mercy or Genius for Organization?

ORIGINAL SOURCES: Pickett, Mrs. L. C. *Across My Path,* 89-93.

BIOGRAPHY: Barton, W. E. *The Life of Clara Barton, Founder of the American Red Cross.* 2 vols. 1922.

AHR, 28:140. A full-length biography based on Miss Barton's journals and letters. The author analyzes the character of his kinswoman and does not spare her faults and mistakes. All criticism, however, leaves her a calm, persistent person who got things done.

Williams, B. C. *Clara Barton, Daughter of Destiny.* 1941.

Books, Nov. 23, 1941, p. 8. A fascinating biography, based on exclusive use of recently discovered letters and diaries.

Extract in Prochnow, H. V., ed. *Great Stories from Great Lives,* 178-85.

COLLECTIVE BIOGRAPHY: Fenner, M. S., and E. C. Fishburn. *Pioneer American Educators,* 97-104.

Howe, M. A. D. *Causes and Their Champions,* 3-43.

Humphrey, Grace. *Women in American History,* 189-206.

Law, F. H. *Civilization Builders,* 318-20.

Malone, Dumas. *Saints in Action,* 107-08.

Parkman, M. R. *Heroines of Service,* 61-85.

Peattie, D. C. *Journey into America,* (1943) :268-76.

Robinson, Victor. *White Caps,* (1946) :208-34.

Starr, H. E., in *DAB,* 2-18.

THOMAS JONATHAN JACKSON—   1824-1863
—Lee's Right-hand Man

ORIGINAL SOURCES: *Blackford, C. M., III, ed. *Letters from Lee's Army: Memoirs of Life In and Out of the Army in Virginia During the War Between the States.* 1947.

Chesnut, M. B. *A Diary from Dixie,* see index.

Douglas, Henry. *I Rode with Stonewall.* 1940.

Sat. Rev. of Lit., 23:6, Dec. 28, 1940. No conventional portrait, but a series of realistic glimpses from the pen of a young lawyer who fought under Jackson from Bull Run to Chancellorsville.

BIOGRAPHY: Cook, R. B. *Family and Early Life of Stonewall Jackson.* 3rd ed., revised. 1948.

Henderson, G. F. R. *Stonewall Jackson and the American Civil War.* 2 vols. 1898.

A fascinating biography by an English military critic. For a recent criticism, see Freeman, D. S. *The South to Posterity,* 159-67.

Tate, Allen. *Stonewall Jackson, the Good Soldier.* 1928.

Nation, 126:593, May 23, 1928. A military biography tersely written which describes Jackson's battles with admirable skill.

COLLECTIVE BIOGRAPHY: Bruce, Philip. *The Virginia Plutarch,* 2:245-68.

Freeman, D. S., in *DAB,* 9:556.

———. *Lee's Lieutenants,* l:xlii, 9-10, 122-30, 307-08, 311-24, 435-88; 2:7-10, 36-51, 81-132, 154-56, 193-202, 236-49, 499-500; 3: xl-xiii.

HISTORY: Fish, Carl. *American Civil War,* 257-58.

SPECIAL ASPECTS: Dabney, R. L., in Rosenberger, F. C., ed. *Virginia Reader,* (1948) : 419-30.

Deaderick, Barron. "Strategy in the Civil War," *Military Service,* (1946) :171-72.

Van Doren, Carl, and C. L. Carmer. *American Scriptures,* 133-40.

Wallace, Archer. *Religious Faith of Great Men,* 174-92.

---

* See p. 307.

DANIEL COIT GILMAN—1831-1908—"The Leader in Developing American Graduate Instruction"

BIOGRAPHY: Flexner, Abraham. *Daniel Coit Gilman: Creator of the American Type of University.* 1946.

AHR, 53:181. A lucid and comprehensive study of the "remarkable man who assembled that amazing group of brilliant men who attracted to Baltimore so large a proportion of the young men who were soon to achieve eminence in American and world scholarship."

Franklin, Fabian. *Daniel Coit Gilman.* 1910.

AHR, 53:181. "The only extended biography of this extraordinary man. . . . A competent and valuable study."

COLLECTIVE BIOGRAPHY: Faris, J. T. *Men Who Conquered,* 173-83.

Malone, Dumas. *Saints in Action,* 149-78.

Mitchell, S. C., in *DAB,* 7:299.

Thwing, C. F. *Guides, Philosophers and Friends,* 57-82.

JAMES EWELL STUART— 1833-1864 —Cavalry Leader "Second to None in Valour, in Zeal, and in Unflinching Devotion to His Country"

BIOGRAPHY: Blackford, Lt. Col. W. W. *War Years with Jeb Stuart.* 1945.

AHR, 51:518. Civil War reminiscences written in the 1890's by an officer in the Confederate Army. Blackford was devoted to Stuart, was a great admirer of Lee, "his dislike of Jefferson Davis and the Confederate government was unsurpassed . . . The entire story is woven around the military career of Jeb Stuart and might, therefore, be classed as a military biography. The battles, sieges, and raids are all described in vivid and realistic detail."

Thomason, J. W., Jr. *Jeb Stuart, 1833-1864.* 1930.

AHR, 36:653. An interesting military biography of one of the most picturesque figures of the Confederacy. Unfortunately there is no analysis of the function of cavalry as affected by the use of improved guns and trenches.

Also in *Scribner's,* 87:88 m-o, 1930.

COLLECTIVE BIOGRAPHY: Bradford, Gamaliel. *Confederate Portraits,* 35-62.

Also in *Atlantic,* 111 (1913) :98-109.

Bruce, Philip. *The Virginia Plutarch,* 2:268-86.

Freeman, D. S. in *DAB*, 18:170.

——. *Lee's Lieutenants*, l:xlviii, 275-302, 633-51; 2:xxiv-xxvi, 52-62, 68-73, 286-311, 397-412, 651-53; 3:xi, xxiv, xxxii, 1-5, 8-19, 51-73, 136-40, 162-71, 206-16, 248-63, 414-34.

Johnston, C. H. L. *Famous Cavalry Leaders*, (1908) :277-312.

SPECIAL ASPECTS: Deaderick, Barron. "Strategy in the Civil War," *Military Service*, (1946) :190-91.

Hergesheimer, Joseph. *Swords and Roses*, 267-93.

JOHN SINGLETON MOSBY—1833-1916—Guerrilla Leader

BIOGRAPHY: Jones, V. C. *Ranger Mosby*. 1944.

AHR, 50:354. A readable life of a rather unusual military leader who became a Republican after the Civil War.

COLLECTIVE BIOGRAPHY: Lanza, C. H., in *DAB*, 13:272.

JAMES GIBBONS—   1834-1921   —Archbishop of Baltimore

BIOGRAPHY: Will, A. S. *Life of Cardinal Gibbons, Archbishop of Baltimore*. 2 vols. 1922.

AHR, 29:154. An authoritative and intimate biography of an extraordinary man who was for a third of a century the ranking prelate of the Catholic church in America.

COLLECTIVE BIOGRAPHY: Agar, William, in *There Were Giants in the Land*, 30-37.

Finn, B. A. *Twenty-four American Cardinals*, (1948) :45-74.

Will, A. S., in *DAB*, 7:238.

KATE CHASE SPRAGUE—   1840-1899   —Society Leader

BIOGRAPHY: Phelps, M. M. *Kate Chase, Dominant Daughter: the Life Story of a Brilliant Woman and her Famous Father*. 1935.

AHR, 41:394. The tragic story of a beautiful woman who failed to make her father president, and married the wrong man. Unsympathetic, but just.

COLLECTIVE BIOGRAPHY: "Dashing Kate Chase and her Great Ambition," *Ladies Home Jour.*, 18 (1901) :11-12.

Hendrick, B. J. *Lincoln's War Cabinet*, 367-418.

Maury, J. W., and K. E. Crane, in *DAB*, 17:473.

Peacock, V. T. *Famous American Belles*, 206-29.

HISTORY: Bowers, C. G. *The Tragic Era*, 252-55, index.

Leech, Margaret. *Reveille in Washington*, 453-54, index.

RICHARD HENRY PRATT—1840-1924—"The Best Friend the Indians Ever Had"

BIOGRAPHY: Eastman, E. G. *Pratt, the Red Man's Moses*. (Civilization of the American Indian, 1935).

AHR, 41:781. Campaigning against hostile tribes in the 1860's, Captain Pratt gained a sympathetic understanding of them. Having been put in charge of a band of conquered braves in Oklahoma in 1878, he eventually founded the famous Carlisle Indian School. General Pratt was "a living dynamo" so his life-story is substantially the history of Indian education in this country. There are so many threads in the story the reader tends to lose contact with the loveable but obstinate personality who first turned Comanches and Cheyennes from fighting to seeking an education.

COLLECTIVE BIOGRAPHY: Bakeless, John, in *DAB*, 15:175.

LESTER FRANK WARD— 1841-1913 —Advocate of the Planned Society

BIOGRAPHY: Cape, E. P. *Lester F. Ward: a Personal Sketch*. 1922.

Amer. Jour. Soc., 28:479. The author of this volume was associated with Ward in the preparation of his *Glimpses of the Cosmos*. It throws little light on the years when he blazed "the earliest trail of American sociological thinking;" during which "he was in constant contact with many of the greatest thinkers of Europe and America."

COLLECTIVE BIOGRAPHY: Dealey, J. Q., in *DAB*, 19:430.

SPECIAL ASPECTS: Barnes, H. E., ed. *Introduction to the History of Sociology*, (1948) :173-90.

Beach, W. G. *Growth of Social Thought*, (1939) :141-52.

Bogardus, E. S. *Development of Social Thought*, (1940) :305-23.

Chugerman, Samuel. *Lester F. Ward, the American Aristotle: A Summary and Interpretation of his Sociology*. (Duke Univ. Press, 1939) .

New Repub., 101:119, Nov. 15, 1939. Mr. Chugerman's book is "both biographical and analytical." It devotes 77 pages to Ward's life and achievements and 481 pages to his scientific and sociological conceptions, ranging from biology through psychology and economics to ethics. Ward was an "amazing personality." In spite of severe wounds in the Civil War, he held a Government clerkship in Washington, acquired a working knowledge of a dozen languages and "covered natural science and sociology" with great thoroughness. During the last seven years of his life he taught sociology in Brown University.

Dealey, J. Q., in Odum, H. W., ed. *American Masters of Social Science,* (1927) :61-96.

Ellwood, C. A. *Story of Social Philosophy,* 526-52.

Gabriel, R. H. *The Course of American Democratic Thought,* 204-09.

Hofstadter, R. I. *Social Darwinism in American Thought, 1860-1915,* 52-67.

Page, C. H. *Class and American Sociology,* (1940) :33-43.

BELLE BOYD—   1843-1900   —Confederate Spy

BIOGRAPHY: Sigaud, L. A. *Belle Boyd: Confederate Spy.* 1945.

AHR, 50:854. An able and readable defense of a much maligned woman, written by an officer in the U. S. Intelligence Corps.

COLLECTIVE BIOGRAPHY: Kasten, M. A., in *DAB,* 2:524.

Hergesheimer, Joseph. *Swords and Roses,* 235-64.

Wright, Richardson. *Forgotten Ladies,* 253-86.

WILLIAM HENRY WELCH— 1850-1934 —Dean of
American Medicine

BIOGRAPHY: Flexner, Simon, and J. T. Flexner. *William Henry Welch and the Heroic Age of American Medicine.* 1941.

AHR, 47:899. The story of a remarkable man who did much to raise the standards of medical education. Based partly on the recollections of Simon Flexner, who was one of Dr. Welch's pupils and friends.

COLLECTIVE BIOGRAPHY: MacCallum, W. G., in *DAB,* 19:624.

CHAPTER XXXIV. CAROLINA, GEORGIA, AND
FLORIDA

ROBERT BARNWELL RHETT—   1800-1876
—"Father of Secession"

BIOGRAPHY: White, L. A. *Robert Barnwell Rhett, Father of Secession.* 1931.

AHR, 38:134. The author fails "to develop Rhett's actions out of his personality," or to convince the reader that he was a Southern nationalist rather than an ardent champion of states rights.

COLLECTIVE BIOGRAPHY: White, L. A., in *DAB,* 15:526.

SPECIAL ASPECTS: Carpenter, J. T. *The South as a Conscious Minority.* 1930.

BENJAMIN FRANKLIN PERRY— 1805-1886
—"South Carolina Unionist"

BIOGRAPHY: Kibler, L. A. *Benjamin F. Perry: South Carolina Unionist.* 1946.

AHR, 52:754. A careful and at times "vivid account of Perry's public and private life." Based on "a wealth of manuscript materials," the book follows the life of a country editor whom President Johnson appointed provisional governor of his native state.

COLLECTIVE BIOGRAPHY: Hamilton, J. G., in *DAB,* 14:483.

WILLIAM GILMORE SIMMS— 1806-1870 —"The Most Virile and Interesting Figure of the Old South"

BIOGRAPHY: Trent, W. P. *William Gilmore Simms.* (American Men of Letters, 1892).

Atlantic, 69:838. The standard biography—both sympathetic and critical.

COLLECTIVE BIOGRAPHY: Brooks, V. W. *The World of Washington Irving,* 291-314.

Parrington, V. L. *Main Currents in American Thought,* 2:125-36.

Van Doren, Carl, in *Cambridge History of American Literature,* 1:312-18.

———, in *DAB,* 17:171.

Wade, J. D., in *Literary History of the United States,* 1:311-13.

SPECIAL ASPECTS: Aswell, J. R., ed. *Native American Humor,* (1947) :303-17.

Cowie, Alexander. *Rise of the American Novel,* 228-46.

Erskine, John. *Leading American Novelists,* 131-78.

Hazard, L. L. *The Frontier in American Literature,* 70-74.

Higham, J. W. "The Changing Loyalties of William Gilmore Simms," *Jour. South. Hist.,* 9 (1943) :210-23.

Holman, C. H. "William Gilmore Simms's Picture of the Revolution as a Civil Conflict," *Jour. South. Hist.,* 15 (1949) :44-62.

——. "The Influence of Scott and Cooper on Simms," *Amer. Lit.*, 23 (1951) :203-18.

Hoole, W. S. "A Note on Simms's Visits to the Southwest," *Amer. Lit.*, 6 (1934) :334-36.

——. "William Gilmore Simms's Career as Editor," *Ga. Hist. Quar.*, 19 (1935) :47-54.

Jarrell, H. M. "Simms's Visits to the Southwest," *Amer. Lit.*, 5 (1933) :29-35.

Leisy, E. E. *American Historical Novel*, (1950) :12-13, 35-36, 104-06.

Van Doren, Carl. *American Novel, 1789-1939*, 43-57.

ROBERT TOOMBS—1810-1885—"Typical Southern Whig"

ORIGINAL SOURCES: Phillips, U. B., ed. *Correspondence of Robert Toombs, Alexander H. Stevens, and Howell Cobb.* (An. Report of AHA, vol. 2, 1911)

AHR, 19:916. The letters from Sept. 15, 1850, to Dec. 10, 1851, reflect the "'Constitutional Union' movement in Georgia, following the Compromise of 1850, which in Professor Phillips's opinion saved the union from immediate disruption. This view, ably argued in his *Life of Robert Toombs* . . . is illuminated very strikingly by these forty-three letters."

BIOGRAPHY: Phillips, U. B. *The Life of Robert Toombs.* 1913.

AHR, 19:663. A "painstaking and detailed" study by a master in the field of Georgia politics. Professor Phillips describes Toombs as one of an all-powerful triumvirate, yet allows him to remain a shadowy background figure. However, he fails to emphasize the personality of the Georgian, or to explain why he missed being made the president of the C. S. A.

COLLECTIVE BIOGRAPHY: Bradford, Gamaliel. *Confederate Portraits*, 183-216.

Hendrick, B. J. *Statesmen of the Lost Cause*, 57-84.

Patrick, R. W. *Jefferson Davis and his Cabinet*, 78-90.

Phillips, U. B., in *DAB*, 18:590.

ALEXANDER HAMILTON STEPHENS— 1812-1883—Rebel Vice-President

BIOGRAPHY: Pendleton, Louis. *Alexander H. Stephens.* (American Crisis, 1908) .

AHR, 14:155. "A decidedly interesting book" about a little, consumptive man who "was continually catching the attention, not of the South only, but the entire country. He could do this largely by virtue of an unusually appealing personality."

Von Abele, Rudolph. *Alexander H. Stephens: a Biography.* 1946.

AHR, 52:526. "Stephens' loquacity in speeches, books, and letters—especially letters . . . form the basis, under the discriminating skill of Rudolph Von Abele, of one of the best specimens of recent biographical literature. Stephens . . . was an interesting character, and Mr. Von Abele has made entertaining use of his many phrases . . . Mr. Von Abele is only twenty-four years old and with this extremely readable volume makes a promising start as biographer and historian."

COLLECTIVE BIOGRAPHY: Bradford, Gamaliel. *Confederate Portraits,* 151-81.

Hendrick, B. J. *Statesmen of the Lost Cause,* 57-84, 409-32.

Patrick, R. W. *Jefferson Davis and his Cabinet.* 1944.

Phillips, U. B., in *DAB,* 17:569.

SPECIAL ASPECTS: Carpenter, J. T. *The South as a Conscious Minority.* 1930.

Dowdey, Clifford. *Experiment in Rebellion,* (1946) :50-65.

HENRY WILLIAM RAVENEL— 1814-1887
—Botanist and Agricultural Writer

ORIGINAL SOURCES: Childs, A. R., ed. *The Private Journal of Henry William Ravenel, 1859-1887.* 1947.

AHR, 53:848. The keenly interesting diary of a cultivated gentleman, who was on intimate terms with scientists in America and Europe. Ravenel records his "experiments in botany, horticulture, and agriculture . . ." He also gives the reactions of a liberal Southerner who lived through secession, war, and reconstruction.

COLLECTIVE BIOGRAPHY: Childs, A. R., in *DAB,* 15:396.

WADE HAMPTON— 1818-1902 —Dashing Cavalry
Leader Who Kept Peace in 1877

ORIGINAL SOURCES: Chesnut, M. B. *Diary from Dixie,* see index.

BIOGRAPHY: Jerrell, H. M. *Wade Hampton and the Negro: the Road not Taken.* 1950.

MVHR, 37:736. Professor Jerrell cited the *Nation* and Governor Daniel Chamberlain "to justify the frustration of Radical Reconstruction," and "narrates . . . Hampton's part in restoring white supremacy" in South Carolina. He contends that the state "would have been saved from the extremes of Radicalism and its anti-Negro sequel had Hampton's liberal course been heeded." Gary and Tillman aided Hampton in his victory of 1877, but "prevented the fulfillment of pledges to the Negroes." Professor Jerrell rightly asserts that Hampton could not keep his pledge "because of white opposition." But the author does not prove that he wished to keep it. . . . According to Jerrell, Hampton persuaded enough Negroes to vote for him to secure his election in 1876 . . ." The reviewer declines to accept this view, saying he "cannot ignore the use of rifle clubs and tissue ballots as revealed by a mountain of congressional testimony."

Wells, E. L. *Hampton and his Cavalry in '64.* 1899.
Based largely on Hamilton's notes. *DAB,* 8:215.

Wellman, M. W. *Giant in Gray: a Biography of Wade Hampton of South Carolina.* 1949.
MVHR, 37:145. Mr. Wellman tells the story of the cavalry leader's "war years with the grace and clarity of a successful writer of fiction." Perhaps he "should have stopped there. His research on the Reconstruction period has been inadequate."

COLLECTIVE BIOGRAPHY: Easterby, J. H., in *DAB,* 8:212.

HISTORY: Phillips, U. B. *Life and Labor in the Old South.* 1929.
Wallace, D. D. *History of South Carolina,* see index.

JOSEPH EMERSON BROWN— 1821-1894 —Hillbilly Traitor to the C. S. A.?

BIOGRAPHY: Hill, L. B. *Joseph E. Brown and the Confederacy.* 1939.
AHR, 45:926. Although Brown has been called "the outstanding 'success' among all Georgia statesmen," Dr. Hill tries to make this war governor a traitor. Proven?

COLLECTIVE BIOGRAPHY: Brooks, R. P., in *DAB,* 3:141.
Hendrick, B. J. *Statesmen of the Lost Cause,* 324-62.
HISTORY: Coulter, E. M. *Confederate States,* 387-91, 540-46.

JAMES LONGSTREET— 1821-1904 —"Lee's War Horse" or "Traitor to the South"

ORIGINAL SOURCES: Longstreet, Lt. Gen. James. *From Manasas to Appomattox: Memoirs of the Civil War in America.* 1896.
Nation, 62:146. Longstreet's record established his reputation as a brave, cool-headed corps commander. His capacity to command an independent army was not fully tested. Lee "had fullest faith in Longstreet's ability and character."

BIOGRAPHY: Eckenrode, H. J., and Bryan Conrad. *James Longstreet, Lee's War Horse.* 1936.

AHR, 42:367. The authors concentrate largely on three phases of Longstreet's career: the use by Longstreet of his "physical bigness" to overcome personal opposition, "Lee's alleged subserviency to Longstreet and Longstreet's ardent desire for independent command and his failure after he attained it." The result is a sweeping but rather hasty indictment of Longstreet.

COLLECTIVE BIOGRAPHY: Bradford, Gamaliel. *Confederate Portraits,* 63-92.

Also in *Atlantic,* 110 (1912) :834-45.

Freeman, D. S., in *DAB,* 11:391.

———. *Lee's Lieutenants.* Vol. 3. *Gettysburg to Appomattox.* 1944.

AHR, 50:563. In telling the story of Gettysburg, Dr. Freeman concludes "the absence of Stuart, the indecision of Ewell and the sulking of Longstreet complicated adverse conditions of combat; but the traditional easy explanation of defeat at Gettysburg as the direct and exclusive result of the shortcomings of these three men cannot be sustained. Longstreet, he writes, is not the 'villain of the piece.' Instead, 'the mistakes of Lee and of Ewell and the long absence of Stuart were personal factors of failure as serious as Longstreet's'—a conclusion with which this reviewer is prepared to agree despite Longstreet's own revelation in his *Memoirs* of his reluctant hanging-back state of mind. While the author's judgment of Longstreet's part at Gettysburg is less harsh than that of some, it is made plain that Lee's 'war horse' was no more than a competent executive officer, not the great strategist that he fancied himself. 'Where Longstreet's planning was original it was not practical, and where it was practical it was not original,' Dr. Freeman remarks."

SPECIAL ASPECTS: Deaderick, Barron. "Strategy in the Civil War," *Military Service,* (1946) :175-76.

Longstreet, Helen. *Lee and Longstreet at High Tide: Gettysburg in the Light of the Official Records.* 1904.

AHR, 10:903. A vindication of "the untarnished memory of a great soldier." In 1867, when Longstreet wrote a New Orleans paper, advising acceptance of the liberal terms * offered the South, he was denounced as a "Traitor to the South." This cry was taken up by the uninformed, he was practically ostracized and lost the business by which he supported his family. Grant, who had been Longstreet's friend at West Point, made the Georgian Collector of the Port at New Orleans. This identified him with the Republican party of the South, and added to the popular prejudice against him. After the death of Lee, sensational charges first ap-

---

* Longstreet would have been one of those disfranchised by these terms.

peared that Longstreet had caused the loss of the battle of Gettysburg by disobedience of Lee's orders. For years Longstreet's conduct at that battle was a burning question among Southerners. Impartial historians acquitted Longstreet of anything that could be called disobedience." But it was developed that he believed the attack to be very unwise, and that, when first proposed, he had advised strongly against it." However, the old prejudice died out, and Longstreet became a welcome guest at Confederate reunions. Unfortunately, the charges were revived by General Gordon, when he published his *Reminiscences* in 1903.

Sanger, D. B. "Was Longstreet a Scapegoat?" *Infantry Jour.*, 43 (1936) :39-45.

BIOGRAPHIES OF CONTEMPORARIES: *Gordon, Lt. Gen. J. B. *Reminiscences of the Civil War.* 1903.

Nation, 78:374. "In connection with Gettysburg, the familiar accusation against Longstreet of dilatoriness on the last two days is reiterated. The weight of available evidence seems to sustain Gordon's categorical charge (p. 160) that Longstreet failed in the element of time to respond to Lee's command. But final decision should be reserved until after the publication of Longstreet's posthumous defense, understood to be in the press, under his widow's name. The great and merited devotion of every Confederate to Lee makes it easier for them to believe that a subordinate must have been at fault."

BENJAMIN HARVEY HILL— 1823-1882 —Georgia
Statesman

BIOGRAPHY: Pearce, H. J., Jr. *Benjamin H. Hill: Secession and Reconstruction.* 1928.

AHR, 35:423. A factual biography of "a champion of minority causes" who was usually ready to accept the will of the majority.

COLLECTIVE BIOGRAPHY: Pearce, H. J., Jr., in *DAB*, 9:25.

Harris, J. C. *Joel Chandler Harris, Editor and Essayist*, 14-34.

JABEZ LAMAR MONROE CURRY— 1825-1903
—Educator and Diplomat

BIOGRAPHY: Rice, J. P. *J. L. M. Curry: Southerner, Statesman, and Educator.* 1949.

AHR, 55:701. A brief biography of a Southerner of broad interests and

---

* Gordon is described as "the most important military figure in the history of Georgia. The head of the United Confederate Veterans (1890-1904), he was governor of Georgia and U. S. senator from Georgia. His *Reminiscences* was notable for "its entire lack of sectional rancor and its uniform generosity and fairness toward friend and foe alike." He died in Jan., 1904. *DAB*, 7:424.

strong personality. Educated at the University of Georgia and at Harvard, he was a lawyer, planter, Confederate soldier, minister, college president, and general agent of the Peabody Fund.

COLLECTIVE BIOGRAPHY: Malone, Dumas. *Saints in Action,* 114-48.

Mitchell, S. C., in *DAB,* 4:805.

SPECIAL ASPECTS: Curti, M. E. *Social Ideas of American Educators,* 261-87.

*HENRY TIMROD— 1828-1867 —Poet Laureate of the Confederacy

ORIGINAL SOURCES: Hubbell, J. B., ed. *The Last Years of Henry Timrod, 1864-1867.* 1941.

N. E. Quar., 15:173. A collection of unpublished records regarding literary relations between New England and the defeated South.

BIOGRAPHY: Thompson, H. T. *Henry Timrod: Laureate of the Confederacy.* 1929.

Amer. Lit., 1:224. "A brief biographical sketch introducing some personal reminiscences and family tradition . . . There is no critical estimate."

SPECIAL ASPECTS: Parks, E. W., in Timrod, Henry. *Essays of Henry Timrod,* 3-60.

HINTON ROWAN HELPER— 1829-1909 —"The Hated Helper"

COLLECTIVE BIOGRAPHY: Hamilton, J. G., in *DAB,* 8:517.

Holbrook, S. H. "Hinton Helper and his Crisis," *Am. Merc.,* 60 (1945) :108-13.

———. *Lost Men of American History,* 154-77.

Polk, William. "The Hated Helper," *So. Atl. Quar.,* 30 (1931) : 177-89.

Seitz, D. C. *Uncommon Americans,* 242-55.

HENRY MORRISON FLAGLER— 1830-1913 "Robber Baron Extraordinary of the Gilded Age"

ORIGINAL SOURCES: Lefevre, Edwin. "Flagler and Florida," *Everybody's Mag.,* Feb., 1910.

BIOGRAPHY: Martin, S. W. *Florida's Flagler.* 1949.

---

* For a more complete bibliography see Spiller, et al. *Literary History of the United States,* 3 (1948) :747-48.

AHR, 55:440. A friendly biography which skims over Flagler's part in the early history of the Standard Oil Company and devotes most of the book to his "increasing preoccupation with the Florida resort business after 1850 . . ."

COLLECTIVE BIOGRAPHY: Thompson, Holland, in *DAB*, 6:451.

ELIAS BOUDINOT— 1835-1890 —"Indian Editor"

BIOGRAPHY: Gabriel, R. H. *Elias Boudinot, Cherokee, and his America*. 1941.

PHR, 10:381. This story of an intelligent native Cherokee missionary, Elias Boudinot, "educated in the tradition of New England Puritanism" in Connecticut, and of his Yankee wife, Harriet Gold, is "an account of attempted racial adaptation which succeeded with these two individuals but left their peoples cold and hostile."

COLLECTIVE BIOGRAPHY: Thomas, D. Y., in *DAB*, 2:478.

LEONIDAS LAFAYETTE POLK—1837-1892—North Carolina's "Most Significant Citizen Between 1865 and 1900"

BIOGRAPHY: Noblin, Stuart. *Leonidas Lafayette Polk: Agrarian Crusader*. 1949.

AHR, 55:1002. A "scholarly account" of the contribution of the president of the Farmers' Alliance to the educational, agricultural, and political history of North Carolina. "A valuable portrait of a neglected agrarian leader."

COLLECTIVE BIOGRAPHY: Baumer, W. H. *Not All Warriors*, 102-49.

Hicks, J. D., in *DAB*, 15:40.

Poe, Clarence. "L. L. Polk: a Great Agrarian Leader in a Fifty-Year Perspective," *So. Atl. Quar.*, 41 (1942) :404-15.

SPECIAL ASPECTS: Hicks, J. D. "The Farmer's Alliance in North Carolina," *N. C. Hist. Rev.*, 2 (1925) :162-87.

Polk, L. L. "The Farmer's Discontent," *No. Amer. Rev.*, 153 (1891) :5-12.

*SIDNEY LANIER— 1842-1881 —"The Greatest of Southern Poets After Poe"

ORIGINAL SOURCES: Anderson, C. R., ed. *The Centennial Edition of the Works of Sidney Lanier*. Ten volumes. 1946.

---

* For fuller references see Spiller, et al. *Literary History of the United States*, 3 (1948) :605-08.

Weekly Bk. Rev., Aug. 25, 1946, p. 1. A biography by the editor is given in vol. I, pp. xxi-xc. The letters given in volumes 7 to 10 reflect Lanier's hunger for contact with other musicians and writers.

———. "Two Letters from Lanier to Holmes," *Amer. Lit.*, 18 (1947) :321-26.

Whicher, G. F. "Sidney Lanier's Letters," *Forum,* 106 (1946) : 354-58.

Biography: Lorenz, Lincoln. *The Life of Sidney Lanier.* 1935.

Amer. Lit., 8:232. A short popular biography.

Mims, Edwin. *Sidney Lanier.* 1905.

Nation, 82:60, Jan. 18, 1906. This book tells Lanier's life in a straightforward, if not brilliant, manner, and honestly attempts to characterize him as a man, a musician, a scholar, a poet, and a critic. Mr. Mims offers no explanation of the fact that while Lanier's utterances, views, and creations aroused widespread interest and elicited varied response, they have, nevertheless, failed to win at home or abroad general acceptance of his admirer's claims. Again, and chiefly, this book acknowledges, but totally fails to solve, the main problem before a writer on Lanier.

Starke, A. H. *Sidney Lanier: a Biographical and Critical Study.* 1933.

Amer. Lit., 5:275. "Although the author makes no claim to have written a complete and definitive biography of Lanier, he certainly offers the most detailed account of his life yet published, as well as the fullest and most minute study of his works. . . ."

Collective Biography: Bradford, Gamaliel. *American Portraits,* 59-83.

Also in *No. Amer.,* 211 (1920) :805-17.

Brooks, V. W. *Chilmark Miscellany,* 297-303.

———. *The Times of Melville and Whitman,* 351-77.

Clark, H. H., ed. *Major American Poets,* (1936) :611-49, 903-13.

Kunitz and Haycraft. *American Authors,* 449-51.

Miles, Dudley, in *Cambridge History of American Literature,* 2:331-46.

Mims, Edwin, in *DAB,* 10:601.

Starke, A. H. "William Dean Howells and Sidney Lanier," *Amer. Lit.*, 3 (1931) :79-82.

Williams, S. T., in *Literary History of the United States,* 2:899-916.

Wood, Clement. *Poets of America,* (1925) :68-81.

Special Aspects: Flournoy, Mrs. M. H. *Essays: Historical and Critical,* 89-96.

Foerster, Norman. *Nature in American Literature,* 221-37.

Graham, Philip. "Lanier and Science," *Amer. Lit.,* 4 (1932) : 288-92.

Mims, Edwin. *Great Writers as Interpreters of Religion,* (1943) :110-40.

Myers, J. A. *Fighters of Fate,* (1927) :174-81.

Spiller, R. E. "Sidney Lanier, Ancestor of Anti-realism," *Sat. Rev. of Lit.,* 31:6-7, Jan. 10, 1948.

Strong, A. H. *American Poets and their Theology,* 369-418.

Thorp, Willard. "Memorial to Lanier," *Va. Quar. Rev.,* 23 (1947) :123-38.

Williams, S. T., in Macy, John, ed. *American Writers on American Literature,* 327-41.

Wilson, Edmund. "Sidney Lanier and Stephen Foster," *New Yorker,* 22:134-42, Dec. 14, 1946.

BENJAMIN RYAN TILLMAN—   1847-1918
—"Pitchfork Ben"

Biography: Simkins, F. B. *Pitchfork Ben Tillman, South Carolinian.* 1944.

AHR, 50:570. A frank and authoritative account of a "dirt farmer" and intellectual (!) who wrested the control of South Carolina away from the tidewater aristocracy.

Collective Biography: Phillips, Russell. "The Plowboy from Edgefield," *Va. Quar. Rev.,* 8 (1932) :514-29.

Simkins, F. B., in *DAB,* 18:547.

History: Simkins, F. B. *The Tillman Movement in South Carolina.* 1926.

AHR, 32:176. An impartial account of the passing of the control of South Carolina from Wade Hampton and the aristocrats to Tillman and the small farmers.

History: Sullivan, Mark. *Our Times,* 3:231-34, 264f.

Special Aspects: Eubanks, J. E. *Ben Tillman's Baby: the Dispensary System of South Carolina, 1892-1915.* 1951.

Jour. South. Hist., 17:271. "A concise account of the history of South Carolina's Liquor Dispensary System from its inception under Governor Benjamin Tillman in 1892 until its demise in 1915. Mr. Eubanks opens with
a foreword and a first chapter which gives a sketch of the temperance
movement in the U. S."

Simkins, F. B. "Ben Tillman's View of the Negro," *Jour. South.
Hist.*, 3 (1937) :161-74.

*JOEL CHANDLER HARRIS— 1848-1908 —"Uncle Remus"

BIOGRAPHY: Brookes, S. B. *Joel Chandler Harris, Folklorist.*
1950.

Sat. Rev. of Lit., 33:42, Oct. 14, 1950. "This volume is primarily an attempt
at classifying, summarizing and examining the folklore element in the
writings of Joel Chandler Harris, with some background study of the
times and influences which shaped his writings. Mrs. Brookes, one happily notes, does convey the human and literary excellences of Harris's
tales, songs, and proverbs, although there is a tendency on her part to
smother her subject with encomium and panegyric."

Harris, J. C. *The Life and Letters of Joel Chandler Harris.* 1918.

Bookman, 48:426. This biography "has been written with as much good
judgment as affection by his daughter-in-law, Julia Collier Harris."

COLLECTIVE BIOGRAPHY: Genzmer, G. H., in *DAB*, 8:312.

Ticknor, Caroline. *Glimpses of Authors*, 152-68.

HISTORY: Buck, P. H. *The Road to Reunion.*

SPECIAL ASPECTS: Gaines, F. P. *The Southern Plantation*, 74-77.

Harris, J. C., ed. *Joel Chandler Harris: Editor and Essayist.* 1931.

Amer. Lit., 4:82. Mrs. Harris largely achieves her aim "to present the author
of the beloved Negro tales in a role that ought to endear him more than
ever to his fellow-southerners. . . ." She presents no adverse criticism.

——, in Odum, H. W., ed. *Southern Pioneers in Social Interpretation*, 141-64.

Hess, M. W. "Man Who Knew Uncle Remus," *Cath. World*, 166
(1947) :254-58.

Smith, C. A. *Southern Literary Studies*, 128-57.

Wade, J. D., in Johnson, A. T., and Allen Tate, eds. *America
Through the Essay*, (1938) :407-20.

---

* For a more complete bibliography see Spiller, et al. *Literary History of the
United States*, 3 (1948) :540-42.

HENRY WOODFIN GRADY—1850-1889—"A First-rate Newspaper Man" and "An Apostle of Good Will Between the North and the South"

BIOGRAPHY: Nixon, R. B. *Henry W. Grady, Spokesman of the New South.* 1943.

AHR, 49:511. A sympathetic biography based largely on manuscript material. The author emphasizes Grady's work as a newspaper man who chartered special trains to cover earthquakes, and managed at times to scoop the national press. He also describes the services of the young editor in promoting agriculture and manufacturing in the South, and in promoting baseball and better relations between the sections.

COLLECTIVE BIOGRAPHY: Crotty, Joseph, and William Engle, in Howey, W. C., ed. *Fighting Editors,* (1948) :51-58.

Wade, J. D., in *DAB,* 7:465.

SPECIAL ASPECTS: Rutherford, M. L. *The Saint in History and Literature,* 415-20.

THOMAS EDWARD WATSON—   1856-1922 —Populist Politician and Editor

BIOGRAPHY: Brewton, W. W. *The Life of Thomas E. Watson.* 1926.

Woodward, C. V. *Tom Watson, Agrarian Rebel.* 1938.

AHR, 44:661. A fair and authentic biography of a controversial figure in Georgia politics.

COLLECTIVE BIOGRAPHY: Wade, J. D. "Jefferson: New Style," *Am. Merc.,* 18 (1929) :293-301

Woodward, C. V., in *DAB,* 19:548.

SPECIAL ASPECTS: Johnson, G. W. *American Heroes and Hero-Worship,* 147-91.

McGill, Ralph. "Tom Watson: the People's Man," *New Repub.,* 119:16-20, Aug. 23, 1948.

Myers, Gustavus. *History of Bigotry in the United States,* 248-66.

"Passing of Tom Watson," *Outlook,* 132:228-29, Oct. 11, 1922.

"Tattler," "Thomas E. Watson: Knight Errant," *Nation,* 103: 440-41, Nov. 9, 1916.

JAMES BUCHANAN DUKE— 1856-1925 —Founder
of the Tobacco Trust

BIOGRAPHY: Jenkins, J. W. *James B. Duke, Master Builder.* 1927.

Boston Transcript, Feb. 21, 1928, p. 2. "No 'business novel' ever written is more dramatic than the life-story of this 'master-builder' of business."

Winkler, John. *Tobacco Tycoon; the Story of James Buchanan Duke.* 1942.

AHR, 48:832. A readable account of a man who cared little for money or social prestige but was driven by a lust for power.

COLLECTIVE BIOGRAPHY: Forbes, B. C. *Men Who Are Making America,* 68-75.

Mitchell, Broadus, in *DAB,* 5:497.

Wildman, Edwin. *Famous Leaders of Industry,* 1st ser., (1920) : 93-101.

HISTORY: Boyd, W. K. *The Story of Durham, City of the New South,* 77-96.

SPECIAL ASPECTS: Daniel, Jonathan. "Question," *Read. Dig.,* 52 (1948) :146.

CHAPTER XXXV. TENNESSEE, KENTUCKY, AND THE LOWER SOUTH

WILLIAM GANNAWAY BROWNLOW—1805-1877
—Editor and Storm Center of East Tennessee

ORIGINAL SOURCES: Brownlow, W. G. *Sketches of the Rise, Progress, and Decline of Secession, with a Narrative of Personal Adventures Among the Rebels.* 1862.

Larned, J. N. (Literature of American History, p. 221) "The book is intensely bitter in tone and interesting chiefly from the author's personality."

BIOGRAPHY: Coulter, E. M. *William G. Brownlow, Fighting Parson of the Southern Highlands.* 1937.

AHR, 43:419. A somewhat sympathetic study of a "dynamic and powerful personality" who used his power to punish those he hated.

COLLECTIVE BIOGRAPHY: Scott, F. W., in *DAB*, 3:177.

SPECIAL ASPECTS: Gabriel, R. H. *The Course of American Democratic Thought*, 53-54, 57, 58, 64.

Mott, F. L. *Golden Multitudes*, 165-71.

ANDREW JOHNSON—1818-1875—"The Only True and Outstanding Democrat Produced by the Old South"

ORIGINAL SOURCES: Wise, J. S. *Recollections of Thirteen Presidents*, 101-12.

BIOGRAPHY: Stryker, L. P. *Andrew Johnson: a Study in Courage.* 1929.

AHR, 35:139. In his effort to defend Johnson, Stryker adopts a partisan tone. He fails to show that Johnson had a policy of his own, that he was class conscious in his attitude toward his own section, and that his own character interfered with his success.

Winston, R. W. *Andrew Johnson, Plebian and Patriot.* 1928.

Nation, 126:645. A scholarly and restrained biography which rehabilitates the reputation "of a courageous and effective champion of popular rights and civil liberty."

COLLECTIVE BIOGRAPHY: Agar, Herbert. *The People's Choice*, 199-228.

Hathaway, E. V. *Book of American Presidents*, 170-85.

Levin, P. R. *Seven by Chance*, 83-145.

Sioussat, St. G. L., in *DAB*, 10:81.

Young, J. H., and Lamar Middleton. *Heirs Apparent*, 161-75.

HISTORY: Beale, H. K. *The Critical Year: a Study of Andrew Johnson and Reconstruction.* 1930.

AHR, 36:171. This scholarly study of the critical election of 1866 is sympathetic toward Johnson, though it does not rate him as high as does Claude Bowers or Robert Winston.

———. "On Rewriting Reconstruction History," *AHR*, 45 (1940) :807-27.

Bowers, Claude. *The Tragic Era*, see index.

Fish, Carl. *American Civil War*, 399.

Milton, G. F. *The Age of Hate: Andrew Johnson and the Radicals.* 1930.

AHR, 36:837. A scholarly and readable work which portrays Johnson "as an honest, intelligent, and thoroughly good President," whose constructive program was overwhelmed by a campaign of abuse and hate. Mr. Milton gives an excellent analysis of Johnson, including his weaknesses. There are some inaccuracies, and little attention is given to "the motives behind the hatreds of the day. . . ."

SPECIAL ASPECTS: Brown, Wenzell. "Fearless Andrew Johnson," *Am. Merc.,* 70 (1950) :608-17.

Dunning, W. A. "The Impeachment and Trial of President Johnson," in *Essays on the Civil War and Reconstruction,* (1931) :253-303.

Gipson, L. H. "The Statesmanship of President Johnson: a Study of the Presidential Reconstruction Policy," *MVHR,* 2 (1916) :363-83.

Perling, J. J. *Presidents' Sons,* 150-61.

Pollard, J. E. *Presidents and the Press,* 397-433.

Thompson, C. L. "Andrew Johnson and the Lost Cause," *Cur. Hist.,* 14 (1948) :336-41.

Strong, M. K. "Post-war Congressional Election," *ibid.,* 10 (1946) :435-41.

JEFFERSON DAVIS— 1808-1889 —Scapegoat for
Secession

ORIGINAL SOURCES: Blackford, W. W. *War Years with Jeb Stuart.* 1945.
Unfavorable to Davis.

Calendar of the Jefferson Davis Postwar Manuscripts in the Louisiana Historical Association Collection. 1943.

AHR, 50:188. "A paraphrased condensation of the documents preserved and in part assembled by Jefferson Davis and his wife in order to write a vindication of the Southern Confederacy."

Chesnut, M. B. *Diary from Dixie,* see index.

Fleming, W. L., ed. "Some Documents Relating to Jefferson Davis at West Point," *MVHR,* 7 (1920) :146-52.

Gilmore, J. R. "Our Visit to Richmond in 1864," *Atlantic Harvest,* 242-72.

Also in *Atlantic,* 14 (1864) :372-83.

———. "A Suppressed Chapter of History," *Atlantic,* 59 (1887) : 435-48.

Rowland, Dunbar, ed. *Jefferson Davis, Constitutionalist, his Letters, Papers, and Speeches.* Ten vols. 1923.

AHR, 29:352. These papers, "reasonably exhaustive, . . . tend to elevate the place in history of the President of the Confederacy . . ." They "utterly destroy the myth that Davis was a punctilious, exacting and quarrelsome martinet. . . . Nowhere does the reader find in these volumes evidence of personal dislikes, arbitrary decisions, and favoritism. . . . Davis showed every quality of character that one might envy in a high official or in a personal friend. And . . . Davis did show real military gifts." In the critical moments from 1863 to 1865, he "was the one who seemed to see the broad significance of events."

Russell, W. H., in Nevins, Allan, ed. *America Through British Eyes,* 270-73.

Wise, J. S. *Recollections of Thirteen Presidents,* 67-97.

Biography: Cutting, Elizabeth. *Jefferson Davis, Political Soldier.* 1930.

AHR, 36:611. A sympathetic study which presents Davis as "a great man and a statesman." Miss Cutting emphasizes diplomatic problems but overlooks the attitude of the great banking houses, which were not as dependent on cotton as they had been before 1860. The chronology of the book is confusing.

Dodd, W. E. *Jefferson Davis.* (American Crisis, 1907) .

AHR, 13:878. The best biography. A sympathetic yet judicial study which presents the Confederate president as a "man of high character and great ability who was responsible for no very considerable error of judgment. . . ."

Eckenrode, H. J. *Jefferson Davis, President of the South.* 1923.

AHR, 29:356. Mr. Eckenrode maintains that the Civil War was a conflict between Nordic and non-Nordic principles and that the South failed because of the inadequacy of Davis. The author is too dogmatic and presents "his interpretation unsupported by evidence. The book is practically undocumented."

McElroy, R. M. *Jefferson Davis; the Unreal and the Real.* 2 vols. 1937.

AHR, 44:160. Professor McElroy gives us a very liberal view of Davis. He pictures him as a gentle forgiving man, who opposed secession and sought to avoid a war.

Extract in Prochnow, H. V., ed. *Great Stories from Great Lives,* 155-57.

Tate, Allen. *Jefferson Davis, his Rise and Fall: a Biographical Narrative.* 1929.

MVHR, 16:570. A fresh interpretation which maintains that many of the misfortunes of the Confederacy were due to the indecision of Davis, his contempt for public opinion and the rigid quality of his mind.

Winston, R. W. *High Stakes and Hair Trigger: the Life of Jefferson Davis.* 1930.

AHR, 37:384. A popular biography which represents Davis as "a typical Southern aristocrat," partly responsible for both the Civil War and the failure of the Confederacy. The thesis is interesting and merits consideration, but the book is marred by some errors and inaccurate quotations.

COLLECTIVE BIOGRAPHY: Agar, Herbert. *The People's Choice,* 137-73.

Baumer, W. H. *Not All Warriors,* 52-101.

Bradford, Gamaliel. "Lee and Davis," *Atlantic,* 107 (1911) :62-72.

Dodd, W. E. *Statesmen of the Old South,* 171-235.

Hendrick, B. J. *Statesmen of the Lost Cause,* 12-56, 409-32.

Patrick, R. W. *Jefferson Davis and his Cabinet,* 27-45.

Stephenson, N. W., in *DAB,* 5:123.

Thomas and Thomas. *Living Biographies of American Statesmen,* 251-60.

HISTORY: *Channing, Edward. *History of the United States,* 6: 275-77, 624-28, index.

Coulter, E. M. *Confederate States,* 24-27, 104-11, 374-404, index.

Dowdey, Clifford. *Experiment in Rebellion,* 1-9, 141-55.

Fish, Carl. *American Civil War,* 174-75.

Hanna, A. J. *Flight into Oblivion.* 1938.

AHR, 45:179. This book deals with "the dispersion of the high civil officers of the Confederate States" in the spring of 1865. It includes three good adventure stories in the accounts of the escapes of Secretaries Benjamin and Breckinridge and Attorney-General Davis.

Milton, G. F. *Conflict.* 1941.

AHR, 48:136. Mr. Milton "thinks that the defeat of the South was due to faulty strategy, failure to utilize properly its more limited but sufficient resources, and to favoritisms, jealousies, and hatreds among Confederate leaders. He is particularly severe upon Jefferson Davis for his partiality to Bragg and Pemberton . . . and for his distrust of Johnson."

---

* The review of this volume suggests "Rowland's ten volume collection of Jefferson Davis's papers" was "here extensively exploited for the first time. . . ." *AHR,* 31:151.

SPECIAL ASPECTS: Carpenter, J. T. *The South as a Conscious Minority.* 1930.

Fleming, W. L. "The Early Life of Jefferson Davis," *MVHA, Proc.,* 9 (1915) :151-76.

Gabriel, R. H. *The Course of American Democratic Thought,* 116-19.

Maurice, Sir Frederick. "President Davis and General Joseph Johnston," *Atlantic,* 138 (1926) :52-61.

———. *Statesmen and Soldiers of the Civil War,* 3-58.

Nichols, R. F. "United States vs. Jefferson Davis," *AHR,* 31 (1926) :266-84.

Owsley, F. L. *State Rights in the·Confederacy.* 1925.

AHR, 31:591. State interference with the activities of the central government was either "the determining factor in the collapse of the Confederacy" or "a determining factor." Generally the tone of the book is "judicious and fair, though the author seems to feel that the actions of such men as Governors Brown of Georgia and Vance of North Carolina and the Stephens-Toombs faction in Congress was dictated solely by a desire to spite Davis, instead of by a mistaken idea of the best means of defending their states."

Patrick, R. W. *Jefferson and his Cabinet.* 1944.

AHR, 50:566. "Dr. Patrick is emphatic in his opinion that the collapse of the Confederacy was not due to weaknesses within its administration. He shows that Davis was an able and co-operative administrator who chose an efficient group of cabinet members upon whom he placed due responsibility, and that these members of his administration were not treated as mere clerks in their respective departments."

Stephenson, N. W. "A Theory of Jefferson Davis," *AHR,* 21 (1915) :73-90.

Von Abele, Rudolph. "Jefferson Davis, Nationalist," *Am. Merc.,* 64 (1947) :313-19.

Walmsley, J. E. "The Last Meeting of the Confederate Cabinet," *MVHR,* 6 (1919) :336-46.

Weyl, Nathaniel. *Treason,* 262-82.

BIOGRAPHIES OF CONTEMPORARIES: Coit, M. L. *John C. Calhoun.* 1950.

AHR, 55:911. Deals "too harshly" with Davis.

VARINA HOWELL DAVIS—1826-1906—"First Lady of the Confederacy"

ORIGINAL SOURCES: Chesnut, M. B. *Diary from Dixie,* see index.

Pickett, Mrs. L. C. *Across My Path,* 7-14.

BIOGRAPHY: Roland, Eron. *Varina Howell, Wife of Jefferson Davis.* Vol. I. 1928.

AHR, 33:926. "The interesting story of a very interesting woman," but the book "is based too much upon tradition" and "Mrs. Davis's *Memoirs* of her husband. . . ."

COLLECTIVE BIOGRAPHY: Bradford, Gamaliel. *Wives,* 161-98.

Also in *Harper's,* 151 (1925) :255-66.

Hergesheimer, Joseph. *Swords and Roses,* 67-97.

Stephenson, M. T., in *DAB,* 5:146.

JUDAH PHILIP BENJAMIN— 1811-1884 —"The Brains of the Confederacy"

BIOGRAPHY: Abrahams, R. D. *Mr. Benjamin's Sword.* 1948.

Butler, Pierce. *Judah P. Benjamin.* (American Crisis, 1907) .

AHR, 13:369. A readable and just life of a man who left no personal papers and whose greatest success was won in his new life in England.

Meade, R. D. *Judah P. Benjamin, Confederate Statesman.* 1943.

AHR, 49:506. An excellent biography based on years of research and a real understanding of a remarkable man. Born in the British West Indies and educated in Carolina, this intelligent Jew became a successful lawyer and sugar planter in Louisiana. Elected to the United States senate, in time he became a close friend and advisor of Jefferson Davis. Later he was a member of the Confederate President's Cabinet. When the Confederacy collapsed, Benjamin took refuge in England, shrewdly claiming British citizenship. At the age of 55, he was only beginning his most brilliant career as a commercial lawyer in England.

Rywell, Martin. *Judah Benjamin, Unsung Rebel Prince.* 1948.

COLLECTIVE BIOGRAPHY: Bradford, Gamaliel. *Confederate Portraits,* 121-50.

Also in *Atlantic,* 111 (1913) :795-806.

Goodhart, A. L. *Five Jewish Lawyers of the Common Law,* 4-15.

Hagan, H. H. *Eight Great American Lawyers,* (1933) :206-53.

Hamilton, J. A., in *DNB,* 2:222.

Hendrick, B. J. *Statesmen of the Lost Cause,* 153-87.

Kohler, M. J., in *Jewish Encyclopedia,* 3:28.

Lonn, Ella. *Foreigners in the Confederacy,* 62-65; index.

Patrick, R. W. *Jefferson Davis and his Cabinet,* 155-202.

Stephenson, N. W., and H. W. Knott, in *DAB,* 2:181.

HISTORY: Coulter, E. M. *Confederate States*, 120-21, 377-78, 381-82, index.

SPECIAL ASPECTS: Dowdey, Clifford. *Experiment in Rebellion*, 50-65, 322-33.

ALBERT GALLATIN BROWN— 1813-1880 —The Poor Man's Representative in Politics

BIOGRAPHY: Ranck, J. B. *Albert Gallatin Brown, Radical Southern Nationalist*. 1937.

AHR, 44:411. A scholarly and well-written biography of a unique figure. This native of South Carolina who drifted to frontier Mississippi was "one of the few non-aristocrats to reach high office in the ante-bellum South," and "one of the earliest and most intense advocates of Southern rights and secession in the Gulf states."

COLLECTIVE BIOGRAPHY: Riley, F. L., in *DAB*, 3:100.

JOSIAH GORGAS—1818-1883—Yankee Genius Who Served the C. S. A.

ORIGINAL SOURCES: Vandiver, F. E., ed. *The Civil War Diary of General Josiah Gorgas*. 1947.

So. Atl. Quar., 47:596. The book throws little light on Gorgas' activities as Chief of Ordnance for the Confederacy. It does give valuable comments on Davis and other Southern leaders, and on the conduct of the war.

COLLECTIVE BIOGRAPHY: Ramsdell, C. W., in *DAB*, 7:428.

SPECIAL ASPECTS: Vandiver, F. E. "Mexican War Experiences of Josiah Gorgas," *Jour. South. Hist.*, 13 (1947) :373-94.

NATHAN BEDFORD FORREST—   1821-1877 —Confederate Cavalry Leader

BIOGRAPHY: Henry, R. S. *"First With the Most" Forrest*. 1944.

AHR, 50:565. The "best biography" of an unschooled slave-trader who won fame as a cunning fighter.

COLLECTIVE BIOGRAPHY: Creel, George. *Sons of the Eagle*. (1927) :251-64.

Hergesheimer, Joseph. *Swords and Roses*, 205-31.

Seitz, D. C. *Uncommon Americans*, 124-37.

Spaulding, T. M., in *DAB*, 6:532.

SPECIAL ASPECTS: Deaderick, Barron. "Strategy in the Civil War," *Military Service*, (1946) :162-63.

SIMON BOLIVAR BUCKNER—   1823-1914
—Southern Gentleman

BIOGRAPHY: Stickles, A. M. *Simon Bolivar Buckner, Borderland Knight.* 1940.

AHR, 46:479. A scholarly biography of a colorful Southerner whose friendship with Grant helped to heal war wounds.

COLLECTIVE BIOGRAPHY: Coulter, E. M., in *DAB,* 3:234.

JOHN HUNT MORGAN— 1825-1864 —Confederate
Raider

BIOGRAPHY: Holland, C. F. *Morgan and his Raiders: a Biography of the Confederate General.* 1942.

AHR, 48:823. An entertaining narrative which emphasizes the personality of the great raider rather than military details. Morgan was a pioneer in dismounting cavalry for battle. The author thinks he would have been more significant but for the tendency of West Pointers to favor each other.

COLLECTIVE BIOGRAPHY: Lanza, C. H., in *DAB,* 13:174.

GEORGE WASHINGTON CABLE—   1844-1925
—"The Literary Discoverer of New Orleans"

BIOGRAPHY: Bikle, L. C. *George W. Cable, his Life and Letters.* 1928.

No. Amer., 226:adv., Dec., 1928. In this simply written narrative, Cable's daughter gives extracts from her father's letters and interesting incidents of his friendship with Mark Twain, Henry Ward Beecher, and Andrew Carnegie.

COLLECTIVE BIOGRAPHY: Pattee, F. L., in *DAB,* 3:392.

SPECIAL ASPECTS: Butcher, Philip. "George Washington Cable and Negro Education," *J. Negro Hist.,* 34 (1949) :119-34.

Cowie, Alexander. *Rise of the American Novel,* 556-67.

Hazard, L. L. *The Frontier in American Literature,* 76-78.

Hicks, Granville. *Great Tradition,* 32-67.

Orcutt, W. D. *From My Library Walls,* (1945) :225-28.

Pattee, F. L. *A History of American Literature since 1870,* (1922) :246-253.

Tinker, E. L. "Cable and the Creoles," *Amer. Lit.,* 5 (1934) :313-326.

Turner, Arlin. "Whittier Calls on George W. Cable," *N. E. Quar.,* 22 (1949) :92-96.

———. "Novelist and Reformer," *So. Atl. Quar.*, 48 (1949) :539-45.

BOOKER TALIAFERRO WASHINGTON—1859?-1915—Educator

ORIGINAL SOURCES: Abbott, Lyman. *Silhouettes of My Contemporaries*, 258-81.

Washington, B. T., in Rosenberger, F. C., ed. *Virginia Reader*, (1948) :490-94.

———. *Up From Slavery: an Autobiography*. 1901.

Nation, 72:281, Apr. 4, 1901. An impressive story of his struggle for education for himself and his people.

Stone, Irving, and Richard Kennedy, eds. *We Speak for Ourselves*, 257-63.

BIOGRAPHY: Mathews, B. J. *Booker T. Washington, Educator and Interracial Interpreter*. 1948.

AHR, 54:630. An excellent portrait which throws much light on the current conflict over civil rights.

COLLECTIVE BIOGRAPHY: Armstrong, O. K. "Booker T. Washington—Apostle of Good Will," *Read. Dig.*, 50 (1947) :25-30.

Brawley, B. G. *Negro Builders and Heroes*, (1937) :147-57.

Eddy, G. S., and Kirby Page. *Makers of Freedom*, 32-62.

Fenner, M. S., and E. C. Fishburn. *Pioneer American Educators*, 121-28.

Hagedorn, Hermann. *Americans*, 87-109.

Howe, M. A. D. *Causes and their Champions*, 234-66.

Hubbard, Elbert. *Little Journeys to the Homes of Great Teachers*, 183-216.

Morris, Charles. *Heroes of Progress in America*, 335-44.

Rogers, J. A. *World's Great Men of Color*, 2 (1947) :575-86.

Stokes, A. P., in *DAB*, 19:506.

Wildman, Edwin. *Famous Leaders of Character in America*, 225-35.

HISTORY: Franklin, J. H. *From Slavery to Freedom: a History of American Negroes*, (1947) :337-405.

Sullivan, Mark. *Our Times*, 3:129-47.

SPECIAL ASPECTS: Barton, R. C. *Witnesses for Freedom*, (1948) : 3-17.

Curti, M. E. *The Social Ideas of American Educators,* 288-309.

Dreer, Herman. *American Literature by Negro Authors,* (1950) : 121-26.

Farrison, W. E. "Booker T. Washington, a Study in Educational Leadership," *So. Atl. Quar.,* 41 (1942) :313-19.

Gill, D. M., and A. M. Pullen. *Adventures of Service,* (1938) : 58-67.

Gloster, H. M. *Negro Voices in American Fiction,* (1948) :17-22.

Work, M. N., in Odum, H. W., ed. *Southern Pioneers in Social Interpretation,* 165-82.

JOHN SHARP WILLIAMS— 1854-1932 —"An Old Fashioned Senator"

BIOGRAPHY: Osborn, G. C. *John Sharp Williams: Planter-Statesman of the Deep South.* 1943.

Jour. South. Hist., 9:582. "John Sharp Williams is an excellent subject for a biography, for he was a rare combination of real worth and colorful personality. His name frequently appeared in the newspapers and magazines of his day."

COLLECTIVE BIOGRAPHY: Sydnor, C. S., in *DAB,* 20:277.

CHAPTER XXXVI. OHIO AND INDIANA

WILLIAM TECUMSEH SHERMAN—   1820-1891 —Barbarian or Modern Realist?

ORIGINAL SOURCES: Chesnut, M. B. *Diary from Dixie,* 331-59, index.

"Diary of Major Connolly," *Transactions of the Illinois Hist. Soc.,* (1928) :215-438.

Howe, M. A. D., ed. *Hitchcock, Henry. Marching with Sherman; Passages from Letters and Campaign Diaries, Nov., 1864-May, 1865.* 1927.

Boston-Transcript, Nov. 19, 1927, p. 3. "This is a document of first-class importance for the Civil War period. A keen observer, an educated professional man and a discriminating judge of men and events, Major Hitchcock's estimates, reports and comments are exceedingly valuable.

Further, they are intimate and close-up from the position of their author and accurate because written on the field."

Upson, W. O. D., ed. *With Sherman to the Sea: the Civil War Letters, Diaries & Reminiscences of Theodore F. Upson.* 1943.

AHR, 49:158. This little book "contains a down to earth account of the Civil War experiences of an Indiana farm boy turned soldier." The realistic picture of war "is illumined with flashes of native humor and dignified by the young soldier's conviction of the rightness of his cause."

Sherman, W. T. *Memoirs of General William T. Sherman.* 2 vols. 1875.

Atlantic, 36:245. Sherman's style is clear and direct. He abounds in anecdotes and sometimes paints a picture in a few phrases. He makes free use of letters, orders, and reports.

Sherman, General W. T., and John. *The Sherman Letters.* 1894.

Larned, J. N. (Literature of American History, p. 252). "The letters by General Sherman are more numerous, . . . and are particularly frank and energetically express his antagonism to politicians and political methods."

Stone, Irving, and Richard Kennedy, eds. *We Speak for Ourselves,* 25-32.

BIOGRAPHY: Liddell-Hart, B. H. *Sherman: Soldier, Realist, American.* 1929.

AHR, 35:640. This "exhaustive and penetrating study of Sherman as a soldier and as a human being" is "the more valuable for proceeding from an English scholar. . . . In regard to the burning of Columbia, Captain Liddell-Hart says "Generals who plan to burn a city are unlikely to take up their quarters in the midst of it.""

Lewis, Lloyd. *Sherman, Fighting Prophet.* 1932.

MVHR, 20:126. "A very human biography. With a journalist's appreciation of reader interest, the author has borrowed heavily from personal narrative of the war to fill his book with human interest stories. . . . Skillfully woven into the narrative is an appreciation of the military importance of the Western Campaigns, and one sees in slow development the idea of living off the enemy country."

COLLECTIVE BIOGRAPHY: Bradford, Gamaliel. *Union Portraits,* 131-63.

Croffut, W. A. *American Procession,* 256-66.

Lewis, Lloyd, in Hamilton, E. B., ed. *How They Started,* 192-225.

Spaulding, O. L., in *DAB,* 17:93.

Westrate, E. V. *Those Fatal Generals,* (1936) :229-45.

HISTORY: Rhodes, J. F. "Sherman's March to the Sea," *AHR,* 6 (1901) :466-74.

SPECIAL ASPECTS: Birkenhead, F. E. C. *Turning Point in History,* (1930) :172-87.

Brown, J. M. "Sherman in the Saddle," *Sat. Rev. of Lit.,* 31:26-30, Feb. 28, 1948.

Miers, E. S. *The General Who Marched to Hell: William Tecumseh Sherman and His March to Fame and Infamy.* 1951.

N. Y. Times, June 3, 1951, p. 7. Sherman's campaign in Georgia and the Carolinas—"the first example, on any scale, of total war"—has sufficed to give its leader "rank as one of the world's great soldiers—perhaps the greatest soldier of the Civil War, saving Lee. . . . The march to the sea is a military epic, and it finds Mr. Miers at his best."

O'Connor, Richard. "Sherman: Imaginative Soldier," *Am. Merc.,* 67 (1948) :555-64.

Rhodes, J. F. "Who Burned Columbia?" *AHR,* 7 (1902) :485-93. 93.

RUTHERFORD BIRCHARD HAYES— 1822-1893
—President

ORIGINAL SOURCES: Abbott, Lyman. *Silhouettes of My Contemporaries,* 282-94.

Wise, J. S. *Recollections of Thirteen Presidents,* 133-42.

BIOGRAPHY: Eckenrode, H. J. *Rutherford B. Hayes, Statesman of Reunion.* 1930.

AHR, 36:456. The best life of Hayes. Develops the thesis that although elected by fraud, he effected a reunion of North and South that Tilden could not have brought about. The book is based on a careful study of the Hayes Papers. It is written in popular style and contains some generalizations and other statements impossible to prove.

COLLECTIVE BIOGRAPHY: Agar, Herbert. *The People's Choice,* 229-66.

Bassett, J. S. *Makers of a New Nation,* (1928) :105-28.

Brown, Wenzell. "Hayes the Forgotten President," *Am. Merc.,* 68 (1949) :169-77.

Creel, George. *Sons of the Eagle,* 311-22.

Croffut, W. A. *American Procession*, 205-25.

Goebel, D. B., and Julius Goebel. *Generals in the White House,* 202-65.

Hathaway, E. V. *American Presidents*, 198-208.

HISTORY: Woodward, C. V. *Reunion and Reaction: the Compromise of 1877 and the End of Reconstruction*. 1951.

Herald-Tribune Bk. Rev., May 13, 1951, p. 4. "Mr. Woodward has a story and a thesis. The story is an immensely complicated one of the real history of the bargain of 1877 that put Hayes in the White House and ended military reconstruction. The thesis is that this chapter of our history is to be understood chiefly in economic terms and that it was the concluding part of the Second American Revolution." See also Mr. Woodward's forthcoming new book on the New South.

SPECIAL ASPECTS: Perling, J. J. *Presidents' Sons*, 187-201.

Pollard, J. E. *Presidents and the Press*, 455-79.

Rhodes, J. F. *Historical Essays*, (1909) :243-64.

Wold, K. C. *Mr. President, How is Your Health?* 129-32.

LEWIS WALLACE—1827-1905—Writer and Man of Action

ORIGINAL SOURCES: Wallace, Lew. *An Autobiography*. 2 vols. 1906.

BIOGRAPHY: McKee, Irving. *"Ben Hur" Wallace: the Life of General Lew Wallace*. 1947.

PHR, 17:220. A stirring biography of "an active participant in Taylor's march into Mexico, the battle of Shiloh, the defense of Cincinnati and of Washington against Confederate raiders, the assassination of Lincoln and the trial of the "conspirators," the Lincoln County War and the depredations of Billy the Kid. Wallace was associated with many military men and literary figures. He was a forceful man who was always running into 'cliques.' "

COLLECTIVE BIOGRAPHY: Armstrong, W. P. "General Lew Wallace: Indiana Lawyer Who Won Fame as an Author," *Am. Bar Assn. Jour.*, 34 (1948) :283-86.

Holbrook, S. H. *Little Annie Oakley and other Rugged People,* 102-06.

Lingelbach, A. L., in *DAB*, 19:375.

Nickalson, Meredith. *The Hoosiers*, (1900) :180-99.

Tarkington, Booth, in *There Were Giants in the Land,* 75-82.

Ticknor, Caroline. *Glimpses of Authors,* 93-111.

SPECIAL ASPECTS: Mott, F. L. *Golden Multitudes,* 172-83.

Wallace, Archer. *Religious Faith of Great Men,* 30-55.

JAMES ABRAM GARFIELD—1831-1881—The Last President Born in a Log Cabin

ORIGINAL SOURCES: Hinsdale, M. L., ed. *Garfield-Hinsdale Letters, Correspondence between James Abram Garfield and Burke Aaron Hinsdale.* 1949.

AHR, 55:634. Letters which passed between Garfield and an Ohio teacher who was one of his former pupils.

Merritt, A. H., ed. "Two Unpublished Letters of James A. Garfield, Written While a Student at Williams College," *N. Y. Hist. Soc. Quar.,* 31 (1947) :129-38.

Wise, J. S. *Recollections of Thirteen Presidents,* 145-51.

BIOGRAPHY: Caldwell, R. G. *James A. Garfield, Party Chieftain.* (American Political Leaders, 1931).

AHR, 37:774. A scholarly and readable biography. Briefer than the earlier work by Smith. The author is generally favorable to his subject, yet he apparently assumes that Garfield's silence when attacked in public was due to a wish to conceal something compromising.

Smith, T. C. *The Life and Letters of James Abram Garfield.* 2 vols. 1925.

AHR, 31:550. A detailed study based on voluminous papers left by Garfield.

COLLECTIVE BIOGRAPHY: Agar, Herbert. *The People's Choice,* 229-66.

Goebel, D. B., and Julius Goebel. *Generals in the White House,* (1945) :202-65.

Hathaway, E. V. *Book of American Presidents,* 209-25.

Levin, P. R. *Seven by Chance,* 151-56, 163-68.

Paxson, F. L., in *DAB,* 7:145.

SPECIAL ASPECTS: Perling, J. J. *Presidents' Sons,* 202-19.

Pollard, J. E. *Presidents and the Press,* 480-88.

Wold, K. C. *Mr. President, How is Your Health?* 133-39.

BIOGRAPHIES OF CONTEMPORARIES: Eckenrode, H. J. *Rutherford B. Hayes.* 1930.

Denounces Garfield as "the trickiest politician of his age."

MARCUS ALONZO HANNA— 1837-1904 —President Maker

ORIGINAL SOURCES: Thompson, C. W. *Presidents I've Known and Two Near Presidents,* 15-37.

BIOGRAPHY: Beer, Thomas. *Hanna.* 1929.

N. Y. World, Nov. 29, 1929, p. 16. "Mark Hanna, who lives in the memory of the American people as a fat, pudgy man who wore an oversize suit covered with dollar signs, stands forth as a human being. . . ."

COLLECTIVE BIOGRAPHY: Cole, A. C., in *DAB,* 8:225.

Dibble, R. F. *Strenuous Americans,* 336-421.

Flynn, J. T. *Men of Wealth,* 383-421

O'Higgins, H. J., and E. H. Reede. *American Mind in Action,* 202-34.

White, W. A. *Masks in a Pageant,* 191-232.

SPECIAL ASPECTS: Beveridge, A. J. *Meaning of the Times,* 244-47.

JOHN DAVISON ROCKEFELLER— 1839-1937 —"The Most Hated Man in the Country" or "The Leading Hero of America's Heroic Age"

BIOGRAPHY: Flynn, J. T. *God's Gold: the Story of Rockefeller and His Time.* 1932.

Nation, 51:566, Dec. 7, 1932. The author wrote his book to defend Rockefeller. He maintains that of all the great American fortunes, Rockefeller's was "the most honestly acquired."

Latham, Earl, ed. *John D. Rockefeller, Robber Baron or Industrial Statesman?* 1949.

Nevins, Allan. *John D. Rockefeller: the Heroic Age of American Enterprise.* 2 vols. 1940.

AHR, 47:163. An authoritative biography based on family papers and many sources never used before. Professor Nevins concludes that his hero is significant as "a bold innovator in both industry and philanthropy" who "brought to the first a great unifying idea," and "to the second a stronger, more expert, and more enduring type of organization. Mr. Nevins's style is felicitous, and interest in his book holds up surprisingly well in view of the length." A review by Gustavus Myers (*Nation,* 151: 450, Nov. 9, 1940) is less favorable.

COLLECTIVE BIOGRAPHY: Flynn, J. T., in Hamilton, E. B., ed. *How They Started,* 45-72.

——. *Men of Wealth*, (1941) :422-51.

Forbes, B. C. *Men Who Are Making America*, 296-309.

Howe, M. A. D. *Causes and Their Champions*, 119-56.

Thomas and Thomas. *Fifty Great Americans*, 250-57.

——. *Living Biographies of Famous Americans*, 189-99.

Wildman, Edwin. *Famous Leaders of Industry*, 1st ser., (1920) : 213-26.

SPECIAL ASPECTS: Harris, J. C. *Joel Chandler Harris, Editor and Essayist*, 379-89.

Myer, Gustavus. *History of Great American Fortunes*, 700-04.

JAMES FORD RHODES— 1848-1927 —Objective Historian or Apologist for Big Business?

BIOGRAPHY: Howe, M. A. D. *James Ford Rhodes: an American Historian.* 1929.

AHR, 35:141. A delightful portrait of a man who retired from business at the age of 37 to write American history. Rhodes's letters are skillfully used to reveal his personality, but little is said about his methods as an historian.

COLLECTIVE BIOGRAPHY: Borome, Joseph. "James Ford Rhodes and Historical Scholarship," *N. E. Quar.*, 21 (1948) :379-83, 539.

Cushing, H. W. *Medical Career*, (1940) :233-44.

Kraus, Michael. *History of American History*, 336-79.

Miller, R. C., in Hutchinson, W. T., ed. *Essays in American Historiography*, 171-90.

Saveth, E. N. *American Historians and European Immigrants, 1875-1925*, 165-78.

*JAMES WHITCOMB RILEY— 1849-1916 —The Hoosier Poet

ORIGINAL SOURCES: Mitchell, M. B. *James Whitcomb Riley as I Knew Him; Real Incidents in the Early Life of America's Beloved Poet.* 1949.

Phelps, W. L., ed. *Life and Letters of James Whitcomb Riley.* 1930.

---

* See *Cambridge History of American Literature*, 4 (1921) :651-53. Spiller, et al. *Literary History of the United States*, 3 (1948) :703-05.

Amer. Lit., 3:350. The collection included hundreds of letters. Some of the most charming are to children.

BIOGRAPHY: Dickey, Marcus. *The Youth of James Whitcomb Riley*. 1919.

Wis. Lib. Bul., 15:269, Dec., 1919. "An intimate biography which carries the poet through youth and early manhood from his struggles to earn a living as a patent medicine vendor and a sign painter, to his final success as a poet."

————. *The Maturity of James Whitcomb Riley*. 1922.

Booklist, 19:188, Mar., 1923. "This completes the biography begun in *The Youth of James Whitcomb Riley* (*Booklist*, 16:278, May, 1920) telling of his ventures as a journalist, on the lecture platform, the publishing of his books and his friendships. An adequate record of the details of the poet's life."

COLLECTIVE BIOGRAPHY: Hofrihter, R. J. *Three Poets and Reality*, (1942) :3-8.

Howe, W. D., in *DAB*, 15:611.

Martin, J. B. *Indiana*, (1947) :101-12.

Wyatt, E. F. *Great Companions*, (1917) :182-90.

SPECIAL ASPECTS: Bowra, C. M. *Heritage of Symbolism*, (1943) : 56-97.

Beveridge, A. J. *Meaning of the Times*, (1908) :254-59.

Masters, E. L., in Shepard, Odell, and R. S. Hillyer, comps. *Essays of Today*, (1926-27) :342-62.

CHAPTER XXXVII. ILLINOIS

*ABRAHAM LINCOLN— 1809-1865 —"The Liberal Statesman"

ORIGINAL SOURCES: Angle, P. M., ed. *Abraham Lincoln: His Autobiographical Writings Now Brought Together for the First Time*. 1948.

N. Y. Times, Feb. 15, 1948, p. 16. "A narrative of Lincoln's life and thought (made up) by arranging excerpts from Lincoln's writings about himself

---

* For more complete bibliographies see Angle, P. M. *A Shelf of Lincoln Books: a Critical Selective Bibliography of Lincolniana*. 1946; Monaghan, Jay. *Lincoln Bibliography*, 1839-1939. 1945; Randall, J. G. *Lincoln the President*, 2 (1945) :343-400.

quoted in various biographies and articles, and by passages from his speeches and messages to Congress that seem most revealing. . . . The core of the present compilation is the third person autobiography which Lincoln wrote, soon after he was nominated for the presidency, at the request of John L. Scripps, a Chicago newspaper man."

———. *New Letters and Papers of Lincoln.* 1930.

AHR, 36:170. Angle includes some newspaper reports of Lincoln's speeches.

Basler, R. P., ed. *Abraham Lincoln: His Speeches and Writings.* 1946.

MVHR, 33:657. The best single-volume collection of Lincoln's writings. Texts of three-fourths of the selections were taken from original manuscripts or photostats.

Brown University, ed. *Lincoln Letters Hitherto Unpublished in the Library of Brown University and Other Providence Libraries.* 1927.

Cuthbert, Norma, ed. *Lincoln and the Baltimore Plot, 1861, from Pinkerton Records and Related Papers.* 1949.

AHR, 55:691. Pinkerton's report shows "that there were men in Baltimore who were talking about killing Lincoln . . ." but the evidence does not prove "that there was a deadly purpose behind their bombast. . . ."

Hertz, Emanuel. *Abraham Lincoln: a New Portrait.* 2 vols. 1931. The second volume consists of badly-edited letters and documents, many of which had been previously published by other editors.

Mearns, D. C. *The Lincoln Papers: the Story of the Collection with Selections to July 4, 1861.* 2 vols. 1948.

AHR, 54:624. Mearns presents more than five hundred documents from the Robert Todd Lincoln Collection. Introductory chapters present a history of the collection, describing those who had to do with it.

Pratt, H. E., ed. *Concerning Mr. Lincoln: in which Abraham Lincoln is Pictured as He Appeared to Letter Writers of His Time.* 1944.

AHR, 50:182. "Sixty-two letters and documents written by people who knew Lincoln. . . ." Most of these had never been published before.

Richardson, R. D., ed. *Abraham Lincoln's Autobiography.* 1948.

N. Y. Times, Feb. 15, 1948, p. 16. "Before Lincoln wrote the story of his life for John Scripps, he compiled a first person autobiographical narrative of some 600 words for Jesse W. Fell, an old friend. It is this account, together with some other Fell papers referring to Lincoln and with comment by Mr. Richardson, a Fell descendant, that makes up Abraham Lincoln's Autobiography."

Shaw, A. H., comp. and ed. *The Lincoln Encyclopedia: the Spoken and Written Words of A. Lincoln Arranged for Ready Reference.* 1950.

AHR, 55:992. Mr. Shaw gives about 5,000 brief quotations, most of them Lincoln's writings, and others from recorded accounts of Lincoln's addresses. He uncritically includes "several forgeries and spurious quotations."

Sparks, E. E. *The Lincoln-Douglas Debates of 1858.* 1908.

Stephenson, N. W., ed. *An Autobiography of Abraham Lincoln, Consisting of the Personal Portions of His Letters, Speeches, and Conversations.* 1926.

AHR, 32:624. Lincoln's Autobiography down to 1860 is supplemented with letters, state papers, and "a few well-authenticated conversations and stories." Through these documents Professor Stephenson "emphasizes his favorite theory that Lincoln first found himself in July, 1862, when he determined to use his authority over McClellan, that up to this time he had been a suppressed and hesitant character." Mr. Stephenson believes that Lincoln's delay at this time "was due to his conviction that a civilian executive should not interfere with a military commander until that commander had proved, both to him and the country, his inadequacy."

Stern, P. V. D., ed. *The Life and Writings of Abraham Lincoln.* 1940.

MVHR, 27:301. A fairly well selected anthology of Lincoln's writings.

Tracy, G. A., ed. *Uncollected Letters of Abraham Lincoln.* 1917. This compilation is marred by the inclusion of some forged material.

Extract in Angle, P. M., ed. *Lincoln Reader,* 308-09.

BIOGRAPHY: Angle, P. M., ed. *The Lincoln Reader.* 1947.

AHR, 53:124. "A republication of 179 selections from the writings of 65 authors, cemented into a unified biography by the running comment of the editor. . . . The better-known biographies are all represented. . . ."

Bancroft, George. *Abraham Lincoln, a Tribute.* 1908.

Books, 27:471. This is Bancroft's memorial address on the life and character of Lincoln, delivered February 12, 1866.

Barton, W. E. *President Lincoln.* 2 vols. 1933.

Sat. Rev. of Lit., 9:487, Mar. 18, 1933. Barton, a Congregational clergyman, wrote voluminously on Lincoln. His work, often diffuse and garrulous, has been superseded, but he did pioneer in thorough use of some Lincoln sources.

Extracts in Angle, P. M., ed. *Lincoln Reader,* 11-15, 23-25, 60-62, 198-200.

Beveridge, A. J. *Abraham Lincoln, 1809-1858.* 2 vols. 1928.

AHR, 34:616. Beveridge sought to write objective history without any interpretation or thesis. Using enormous industry and the sense of a trained lawyer in examining new sources he came as near doing this "as is humanly possible." There is an absence of sentimentality in his treatment.

Extracts in Angle, P. M., ed. *Lincoln Reader,* 9-11, 30-33, 78-82, 102-06.

Brogan, D. W. *Abraham Lincoln.* 1935.

Godfrey, R. B., Baron Charnwood. *Abraham Lincoln.* (Makers of the Nineteenth Century, 1916) .

AHR, 22:413. A graceful, highly useful short biography. Liberal in tone, its "contribution is not of new facts but of deep thought." There are some inaccuracies.

Oberholtzer, E. P. *Abraham Lincoln.* (American Crisis, 1904) .

AHR, 10:901. "Limited research and his 'standards of elegance' combined to prevent Professor Oberholtzer from really understanding Lincoln's life and background."

Randall, J. G. *Lincoln the President, Springfield to Gettysburg.* 2 vols. 1945.

AHR, 51:726. The finest of Lincoln biographies—a masterpiece of historical craftsmanship. Six chapters are devoted to Lincoln's life before the presidency. Exhaustive research, even-handed evaluation of evidence, and honest interpretation are its virtues.

Extracts in Angle, P. M., ed. *Lincoln Reader,* 248-54, 343-47.

Sandburg, Carl. *Abraham Lincoln: the Prairie Years.* 2 vols. 1926.

AHR, 31:809. These interesting volumes give evidence of wide, but often uncritical reading. There is poetic interpretation and lusty, dynamic zeal in the writing, but it does not meet all the historical requirements of a good biography.

Extracts in Angle, P. M., ed. *Lincoln Reader,* 5-7, 18-20, 33-35, 114-17, 222-25, 256-63.

———. *Abraham Lincoln: the War Years.* 4 vols. 1939.

AHR, 45:917. A vast panorama and kaleidoscopic portrait gallery of the Civil War generation, yet it is neither a complete history of the Civil War nor a definitive biography of Lincoln. Perhaps it is "a people's epic," but the writing is uneven and at times impeded by masses of quotation.

Extracts in Angle, P. M., ed. *Lincoln Reader,* 332-33, 336, 439-42, 447-49, 466-70, 497-504, 533-36.

————. *Storm Over the Land.* 1942

AHR, 48:658. A greatly condensed version of *The War Years*. Details have been thrown out, and the writing simplified.

Smith, T. V. *Lincoln: Living Legend.* 1940.

AHR, 46:990. Commemorative of Lincoln's Cooper Union Address of 1860. Smith's little essay "is the ripe product of a mind whose blending of philosophy and purposive politics is implicit in every paragraph."

Stephenson, N. W. *Lincoln: an Account of his Personal Life, Especially of its Springs of Action as Revealed and Deepened by the Ordeal of War.* 1922.

AHR, 28:596. Stephenson fails in his romantic attempt at character analysis, but he makes a valuable contribution in his narrative of Lincoln's struggle against the anti-slavery radicals of his party during the Civil War.

Tarbell, I. M. *The Life of Abraham Lincoln.* 2 vols. 1900.

AHR, 5:778. Incorporated newly discovered source materials. Realistic account. Removes "the air of miraculous growth" from Lincoln's early development. The appendix in volume two gives a number of previously unpublished documents.

Extract in Angle, P. M., ed. *Lincoln Reader*, 7-9.

Wagenknecht, E. C., ed. *Abraham Lincoln: His Life, Work, and Character: an Anthology of History and Biography, Fiction, Poetry, Drama, and Belles-Lettres.* 1947.

Sat. Rev. of Lit., 30:22, Nov. 15, 1947. Discriminating readers will find selections from Beveridge, Bradford, Randall, Sandburg, Tarbell, Wecter, and many other writers on Lincoln.

Wheare, K. C. *Abraham Lincoln and the United States.* (Teach Yourself History Library, 1949) .

AHR, 55:691. A brief biography giving the essential facts of Lincoln's life, "a shrewd estimate of the man, and an illuminating interpretation of the period in which Lincoln played his role."

Whitlock, Brand. *Abraham Lincoln.* c1909.

Books, 27:628. This biography has interest largely because it gives an interpretation of Lincoln by one of the most interesting figures of the "Progressive Era" in American history.

COLLECTIVE BIOGRAPHY: Agar, Herbert. *The People's Choice,* 174-94.

Booth, E. T. *Country Life in America*, 184-208.

Bradford, Gamaliel. *Portraits and Personalities*, 40-56.

Brogan, D. W. *American Themes*, 243-55.

Brown, R. W. *Lonely Americans*, 261-311

Also in Durling and Watt, eds. *Biography,* 113-33.

Bruce, D. K. E. *Revolution to Reconstruction,* 443-85.

Dodd, W. E. *Lincoln or Lee.* 1928.

Yale Rev., 18:372. "Professor Dodd's little essay . . . presents in a pungent and provocative way Lincoln as the personification of the ideals of Jeffersonian democracy in a mid-nineteenth-century generation. Lee is presented as personifying the aristocratic traditions and ideals which the eighteenth century bequeathed to the nineteenth. Dodd discusses the factors (and accidents) which brought about the triumph of Lincoln and the defeat of Lee in the spring of 1865. He raises the question as to what would have been the result in the pantheon of New World heroes had Lee won, as more than once he came so near doing. In his last sentence the author raises another question—'Is it Lincoln or Lee the country honors most today, honors by imitating?' "

Merriam, C. E. *Four American Party Leaders,* 1-21.

Nevins, Allan. *Emergence of Lincoln.* 2 vols. 1950.

N. Y. Times, Oct. 15, 1950, p. 1. "A tremendous amount of detailed research has been presented with the skill that makes the name of Allan Nevins synonymous with history at its best."

Parrington, V. L. *Main Currents in American Thought,* 2:152-60.

Randall, J. G., in *DAB,* 11:242.

Randall, R. P. "Mr. Lincoln: a Portrait by His Wife," *N. Y. Times Mag.,* Feb. 11, 1951, p. 9.

Schouler, James. *History of the U. S. Under the Constitution,* c1894-c1904, 6:624-33.

Stephenson, N. W., in *Cambridge History of American Literature,* 3:367-84.

HISTORY: Nicolay, J. G., and John Hay. *Abraham Lincoln: a History.* 10 vols. 1890.

Nation, 52:13, 34. When Lincoln took his young secretaries to Washington, they had hardly reached the White House before they were collecting material for a history of his administration. Being close friends and sharing Lincoln's confidence even before his election, it was natural that they should assume this task. They were given full co-operation by the President. After his death, Robert T. Lincoln, the president's son, encouraged them to continue, and lent them his father's papers. Before they began to write, six years were spent in arranging the papers and blocking out the chapters. When other duties allowed, the two secretaries collaborated for fifteen years, 1875-1890. The result was a co-operative work in the fullest sense. Each selected the chapters he would write and they were gone over carefully by his partner. The title indicates the nature of the product. Their subject was so important that his "biography" involved the retelling of much of the history of the country!

Special Aspects: Angle, P. M. *"Here I Have Lived," a History of Lincoln's Springfield, 1821-1865.* 1935.

MVHR, 23:273. An accurate study built upon the thesis that Springfield did much to mould Lincoln's personality and character. It "humanizes Lincoln's social life."

Armstrong, W. P. "Lincoln as Commander-in-Chief," *Sat. Rev. of Lit.*, 28:5-6, Feb. 10, 1945.

Ballard, Brigadier-General C. R. *The Military Genius of Abraham Lincoln.* 1926.

AHR, 32:934. "A good brief account of the military operations in Virginia with particular reference to Lincoln's leadership and control."

Baringer, W. E. *A House Dividing: Lincoln as President Elect.* 1945.

AHR, 51:517. The title is somewhat of an exaggeration since Baringer treats mostly the formation of Lincoln's cabinet. There is insufficient caution in the evaluation of evidence. Emphasis is upon description rather than upon analysis.

———. *Lincoln's Vandalia: a Pioneer Portrait.* 1949.

AHR, 55:382. "A careful re-examination of the forty-four weeks (scattered over more than four years) of Lincoln's first legislative experience. . . . Based on exhaustive research and carefully annotated, Dr. Baringer's little book is an authoritative account of a neglected period in Lincoln's biography."

———. *Lincoln's Rise to Power.* 1937.

AHR, 44:158. Lincoln's career from June, 1858, to November, 1860.

Basler, R. P., "Abraham Lincoln, Artist," *No. Am. Rev.*, 245 (1938):144-53.

———. *The Lincoln Legend: a Study in Changing Conceptions.* 1935.

MVHR, 22:589. Analysis of the writings about Lincoln, with an attempt to define phases in the development of the Lincoln legend.

Bullard, F. L. *Abraham Lincoln and the Widow Bixby.* 1946.

AHR, 53:125. "A scholarly piece of historical detective work."

Canby, H. S. "Whitman and Lincoln," *Sat. Rev. of Lit.*, 26:4, 20-21, Oct. 23, 1943.

Carman, H. J., and R. H. Luthin. *Lincoln and the Patronage.* 1943.

AHR, 49:314. Stresses Lincoln's skill as a practical politician in utilizing the patronage to hold "together diverse conflicting factions in common purposes."

Cole, A. C., "Lincoln's Election an Immediate Menace to Slavery in the States?" *AHR,* 36 (1931) :740-67. See Professor Hamilton's reply below.

———. "President Lincoln and the Illinois Radical Republicans," *MVHR,* 4 (1918) :417-36.

Croly, Herbert, "The Paradox of Lincoln," *New Repub.,* 21 (1920) :350-53.

Dodd, W. E., "Lincoln's Last Struggle," *Century,* 114 (1927) : 46-61.

———. "Rise of Abraham Lincoln," *ibid,* 113 (1927) :569-84.

Donald, David, "The Folklore Lincoln," *Ill. State Hist. Soc. Jour.,* 40 (1947) :377-96.

Dudley, H. M., "The Election of 1864," *MVHR,* 18 (1932) : 500-18.

Fish, Carl, "Lincoln and the Patronage," *AHR,* 8 (1902) :53-69.

Fite, E. D. *The Presidential Campaign of 1860.* 1911.

AHR, 17:628. The best account of Lincoln's election in 1860.

Hacker, L. M., "Lincoln and the Republicans," *Am. Merc.,* 62 (1946) :370-75.

Hamilton, J. G. de Roulhac, "Lincoln's Election an Immediate Menace to Slavery in the States?" *AHR,* 37 (1932) :700-11.

Harbinson, W. A., "Indiana Republicans and the Re-election of President Lincoln," *Ind. Mag. of Hist.,* 34 (1938) :42-64.

Harper, R. S. *Lincoln and the Press.* 1951.

AHR, 55:914. This book lists instances of mob violence against newspapers, arrests of editors, attempts to ban newspapers from the mail. "Nowhere is there any clear analysis of Lincoln's policy toward the press, especially of his position on censorship. Instead there are scattered accounts . . . of his dealings with individual editors. . . . There is nothing like an adequate sampling of press opinion upon the major events with which Lincoln was associated. . . . Mr. Harper is guilty of a number of factual errors that no student of the Civil War period ought to make."

Hesseltine, W. B. *Lincoln and the War Governors.* 1948.

AHR, 54:887. With great skill Professor Hesseltine shows how Lincoln was able to overcome both egotistical personalities and the State's rights fetish in the northern States.

Hofstadter, Richard. *The American Political Tradition,* 92-134.

Lewis, Lloyd. *Myths After Lincoln.* 1929.

MVHR, 16:413. Traces the development of the folk legends which after Lincoln's death led to the "apotheosis of Lincoln." Much of the folk hero portrait came from funeral orations and sermons.

Luthin, R. H., "Abraham Lincoln Becomes a Republican," *Pol. Sci. Quar.,* 59 (1944) :420-38.

———, "Abraham Lincoln and the Tariff," *AHR,* 49 (1944) : 609-29.

———. *The First Lincoln Campaign.* 1944.

AHR, 50:561. Much of this book considers the nomination of Lincoln; only fifty pages are concerned with the national inter-party contest. Good bibliography.

Maurice, Major General Sir Frederick Barton. *Statesmen and Soldiers of the Civil War; a Study of the Conduct of the War.* 1926.

McLaughlin, A. C., "Lincoln, the Constitution, and Democracy," *Abraham Lincoln Association Papers for 1936,* 25-39.

Milton, G. F. *Abraham Lincoln and the Fifth Column.* 1942.

AHR, 49:123. Lincoln's wartime problems in dealing with the Democratic opposition to his administration in the North. There is emphasis upon the Copperhead societies, Vallandigham, and Governor Horatio Seymour of New York. Written with brilliant facility, but there is evidence of hasty research.

Monaghan, Jay. *Diplomat in Carpet Slippers: Abraham Lincoln Deals with Foreign Affairs.* 1945.

AHR, 51:338. "None will challenge Mr. Monaghan's thesis that the diplomacy of the Civil War was very skillful and that Abraham Lincoln, from whom so little might reasonably have been expected in the direction of foreign affairs, rose to the challenge to a degree which seemed almost miraculous. The presumption seems to remain, however, that his greatest success was in the selection of those to whom he trusted the carrying out of the policies and from whom he accepted a great deal of very wise advice. *Diplomat in Carpet Slippers* is a challenging book. . . ."

Murr, J. E., "Lincoln in Indiana," *Ind. Mag. of Hist.,* 13 (1917) : 307-48.

Pargellis, Stanley, "Lincoln's Political Philosophy," *Abraham Lincoln Quar.,* 3 (1945) :275-90.

Paullin, C. O., "President Lincoln and the Navy," *AHR,* 14 (1909) :284-303.

Pollard, J. E. *Presidents and the Press,* 312-96.

Potter, D. M. *Lincoln and His Party in the Secession Crisis.* 1942.

AHR, 48:591. An ingenious work which attempts to prove that while Lincoln rejected compromise in the secession crisis he thought that he could maintain the union without war through a "policy of purposeful non-action."

Pratt, H. E. *The Personal Finances of Abraham Lincoln.* 1943.

AHR, 49:316. From Pratt's volume one gets the impression that "Lincoln was not a seeker after monetary wealth yet neither was he impecunious and totally indifferent to its acquisition."

Randall, J. G., "Civil and Military Relationships Under Lincoln," *Penn. Mag. of Hist. and Biog.,* 69 (1945) :199-206.

———. *Constitutional Problems Under Lincoln.* 1926.

AHR, 33:419. A scholarly, lucid work. "Lincoln's conception of the executive power was very broad, and his exercise of it very moderate."

———, "Lincoln and Fort Sumter," *Jour. of South. Hist.,* 3 (1937) :259-88.

*———. Lincoln and the South. (Fleming Lectures in Southern History, 1946) .

AHR, 52:194. Four lectures by an outstanding authority on Lincoln given at Louisiana State University. The first lists "the family ties and personal friendships which presumably gave Lincoln a sympathetic understanding of the Southern people and led him to frame a pattern for peace without vindictiveness." The other lectures discuss Lincoln's handling of the border states, his policy toward slavery, and his plans for reconstruction. These lectures are "a skillful blending of fact and interpretation."

———. *Lincoln, the Liberal Statesman.* 1947.

MVHR, 34:494. Eight of Professor Randall's superb essays on Lincoln and his era. Two of these appear here for the first time; the other six are reprinted from periodicals with revisions and full annotations.

———, "When War Came in 1861," *Abraham Lincoln Quar.,* 1 (1940) :3-42.

Riddle, D. W. *Lincoln Runs for Congress.* 1948.

AHR, 54:691. "Modestly Professor Riddle disclaims having found new Lin-

---

* In going through the *AHR,* I planned to work the Lincoln books up all together. However, when my colleague and friend, Professor George Smith, offered to write the comments on Lincoln, I was delighted to accept his very generous offer. Especially since I had found he really knew the Civil War period. But I said at once that I would like to comment on this book. My grandfather, Julius A. Dargan, signed the ordinance of secession that took South Carolina out of the union. But if he and Southerners generally had understood the situation as this great scholar sees it, there would have been no war.

coln sources as the basis for his carefully documented account, and it is true that this little volume does not materially alter the picture of the campaign as drawn by A. J. Beveridge or Harry E. Pratt. But *Lincoln Runs for Congress* is more exhaustive in research and more complete in detail than any previous study of this almost forgotten chapter of the Lincoln story. Professor Riddle's book is another example of the superior scholarly productions sponsored by the Abraham Lincoln Association.

Ross, E. D., "Lincoln and Agriculture," *Agri. Hist.*, 3 (1929) : 51-66.

Stamp, K. M., "Lincoln and the Strategy of Defense in the Crisis of 1861," *Jour. of South. Hist.*, 11 (1945) :297-323.

Thomas, B. P. *Lincoln's New Salem.* 1934.

MVHR, 22:103. A carefully documented account of the "origin, growth, decay, (and) . . . restoration of New Salem." There is little originality in the part of the book which deals with Lincoln's life in the Illinois frontier village."

———. *Portrait for Posterity: Lincoln and His Biographers.* 1947.

AHR, 53:847. A comparative study of Lincoln's biographers with analysis of the contribution that each important biographer has made to the development of the Lincoln portrait.

Tilley, J. S. *Lincoln Takes Command.* 1941.

AHR, 47:637. An attack on Lincoln by an Alabama lawyer who asserts that Lincoln deliberately provoked the Civil War. Contains errors of fact as well as unsound interpretations.

Townsend, W. H. *Lincoln and His Wife's Home Town.* 1929.

AHR, 35:677. "Mr Townsend's central theme is the importance of Lincoln's marriage into an 'aristocratic' Southern family as a factor in the development of his understanding of the South and of slavery."

Wecter, Dixon. *Hero in America,* 222-72.

Wesley, C. H., "Lincoln's Plans for Colonizing the Emancipated Negroes," *Jour. of Negro Hist.*, 4 (1919) :7-21.

Williams, K. P. *Lincoln Finds a General.* 2 vols. 1949.

AHR, 55:627. Williams is Professor of Mathematics at Indiana University and a former army officer. He demonstrates competence in military subjects of a technical nature, but his evaluation of Lincoln's relations to his generals, and the conduct of the war in the East to the autumn of 1863 are highly controversial.

Williams, T. H. *Lincoln and the Radicals.* 1941.

AHR, 47:890. Depicts President Lincoln's struggle against his "radical" critics within his own party, and especially his relations with the Committee on the Conduct of the War.

Wilson, C. R., "New Light on the Lincoln-Blair-Fremont 'Bargain' of 1864," *AHR*, 42 (1936) :71-78.

BIOGRAPHIES OF CONTEMPORARIES: Donald, David. *Lincoln's Herndon.* 1948.

AHR, 54:623. Mr. Donald has given us "an authoritative portrait" in "a book which is scholastic, yet intensely human and interesting." The treatment is "sympathetic, but impartially just."

Nicolay, Helen. *Lincoln's Secretary: a Biography of John G. Nicolay.* 1949.

AHR, 54:890. John George Nicolay was an immigrant German-American who became private secretary to Lincoln upon his nomination for the presidency. He shared this position with John Hay and later the two men collaborated on a ten-volume biography of Lincoln. Nicolay's daughter has told her father's story "with remarkable objectivity."

MARY TODD LINCOLN—	1818-1882	—Wife

ORIGINAL SOURCES: Keckley, E. H. *Behind the Scenes, or Thirty Years a Slave and Four Years in the White House.* 1868.

"The most illuminating document (on Mrs. Lincoln), on the whole, is the record of Mrs. Keckley, the colored seamstress at the White House. Mrs. Keckley was an intelligent observer, devoted to Mrs. Lincoln, and admitted to many intimate scenes and experiences."—Gamaliel Bradford.

BIOGRAPHY: Evans, W. A. *Mrs. Abraham Lincoln: a Study of Her Personality and Her Influence on Lincoln.* 1932.

AHR, 38:384. A medical man and psychologist seeks to vindicate the reputation of Mary Todd. Gives an adequate treatment of her influence on her husband.

Helm, Katherine, *Mary, Wife of Lincoln.* 1929.

New Repub., 59:348, Aug. 14, 1929. ". . . Miss Helm's work is purely a work of fiction, and rather undistinguished fiction at that. . . . Even though Miss Helm resorts to a stacking of the cards which would get any poker player shot in his chair, she does manage to make her heroine appear in the better light."

Sandburg, Carl, and P. M. Angle. *Mary Lincoln, Wife and Widow.* Part I, by Carl Sandburg; Part II, *Letters, Documents and Appendix,* by Paul M. Angle. 1932.

Books, Nov. 27, 1932, p. 1. "The author has given a sane and well reasoned story. His work is objective and fair. His conclusions always are well supported by evidence. In order to make sure of a fair hearing on disputed points the documents from which he has worked are edited and appended to the main study."

Extracts in Beckwith and Coope. *Contemporary American Biography,* 95-117.

COLLECTIVE BIOGRAPHY: Bradford, Gamaliel. *Wives,* 17-52.

Also in Balch, Marston, ed. *Modern Short Biographies,* 233-54.

Also in *Harper's,* 61 (1925) :489-98.

Leech, Margaret. *Reveille in Washington,* 285-310.

Randall, J. G., in *DAB,* 11:265.

Randall, R. P., "Mary Lincoln: Judgment Appealed," *Abraham Lincoln Quar.,* 5 (1949) :379-404.

An able and sympathetic re-appraisal of Lincoln's wife, with a deep insight into the Lincoln family relationships.

BIOGRAPHIES OF CONTEMPORARIES: Randall, J. G. *Lincoln the President.* 2 vols. 1945.

AHR, 51:726. "Events and personalities associated with Lincoln appear in a new light: no longer is the emotional Mary Todd the overbearing, bossy, and impossible-to-live-with wife that others have pictured her to be. . . ."

CYRUS HALL McCORMICK— 1809-1884
—Inventor and Manufacturer

BIOGRAPHY: Casson, H. N. *Cyrus Hall McCormick, His Life and Works.* 1909.

Book News Monthly, 28:480. "The whole story is vivaciously told in this volume of the life and work of McCormick. . . . The book is attractively gotten up, abundantly illustrated and very readable."

Hutchinson, W. T. *Cyrus Hall McCormick.* 2 vols. 1930, 1935.

AHR, 36:835; 41:780. Professor Hutchinson's biography "is the familiar story in American industrial history . . . of an early life of harsh experiences ripening into that of a daring, resourceful, aggressive man, neither asking nor giving quarter." In this "exhaustive biography," much space is given to litigation with rival inventors, the establishment and growth of the factory in Chicago, 1847-1884, McCormick's philanthropies, and his relations with the Presbyterian Church and the Democratic party.

COLLECTIVE BIOGRAPHY: Dies, E. J. *Titans of the Soil,* (1949) : 75-83.

Forbes, B. C. *Men Who Are Making America,* 240-49.

Hathaway, E. V. *Partners in Progress,* 184-227.

Hylander, C. J. *American Inventors,* 59-65.

Iles, George. *Leading American Inventors,* (1939) :276-314.

Kellar, H. A., in *DAB*, 11:604.

Law, F. H. *Civilization Builders,* 112-15.

McCormick, Cyrus. *The Century of the Reaper,* (1931) :1-88.

Morris, Charles. *Heroes of Progress in America,* 166-70.

Wildman, Edwin. *Famous Leaders of Industry,* 1st ser., (1920) : 167-78.

HISTORY: Tebbel, John. *An American Dynasty; the Story of the McCormicks, Medills, and Pattersons.* 1946.

A fascinating history of strong individuals in the newspaper world.

SPECIAL ASPECTS: McCormick, C. H., in *Famous Fortunes,* 143-58.

STEPHEN ARNOLD DOUGLAS—   1813-1861
—The Little Giant

BIOGRAPHY: Johnson, Allen. *Stephen A. Douglas: a Study in American Politics.* 1908.

AHR, 14:369. An analysis of Douglas's public life, which shows that he "consistently supported the principle of local self-government from the beginning of his political life," and which disproves "the commonly accepted belief that Douglas was guilty of truckling to the South." Professor Johnson gives a discriminating picture of his personality, which "brings out the finest trait of Douglas's character—his magnanimity."

Stevens, F. E., "Life of Stephen Arnold Douglas," *Ill. State Hist. Soc. Jour.* 1924.

AHR, 31:149. "A very inadequate picture of Douglas as the representative of western sectionalism. . . . Those who have been following the controversy over the origin of the repeal of the Missouri Compromise restriction 'will find Stevens does not point out' the importance in this connection of Douglas's plans for transcontinental railroad development."

COLLECTIVE BIOGRAPHY: Johnson, Allen, in *DAB,* 5:397.

Macartney, C. E. N. *Men Who Missed It,* 53-61.

Masters, E. L., in *Am. Merc.,* 22 (1931) :11-23.

Nevins, Allan, "Stephen A. Douglas: His Weaknesses and His Greatness," *Ill. State Hist. Soc. Jour.,* 42 (1949) :385-410.

Seitz, D. C. *The "Also Rans,"* 167-91.

Stone, Irving. *They Also Ran,* 213-50.

HISTORY: Milton, G. F. *The Eve of Conflict: Stephen A. Douglas and the Needless War.* 1934.

AHR, 40:531. An able and provocative work which maintains that Douglas made the greatest effort to use intelligence to save the nation from extremists. Not impartial.

SPECIAL ASPECTS: Carter, O. N., "Lincoln and Douglas as Lawyers," *Proceedings of the MVHA*, 4 (1911) : 213-40.

Dickerson, O. M., "Stephen A. Douglas and the Split in the Democratic Party," Proceedings of the *MVHA*, 7 (1914) :196-211.

Harmon, G. D., "Douglas and the Compromise of 1850," *Ill. State Hist. Soc. Jour.*, 21 (1929) :453-99.

Lynch, W. O., "The Character and Leadership of Stephen A. Douglas," *MVHR*, 10 (1923) :454-67.

Milton, G. F., "Douglas's Place in American History," *Ill. State Hist. Soc. Jour.*, 26 (1934) :323-48.

Orth, S. P. *Five American Politicians, a Study in the Evolution of American Politics,* (1906) :295-447.

BIOGRAPHIES OF CONTEMPORARIES: Beveridge, A. J. *Lincoln.* 1928.

Most biographers of Lincoln treat Douglas as a foil for their hero. Very sympathetic.

ULYSSES SIMPSON GRANT— 1822-1885
—"Stupid Butcher or Military Genius?"

ORIGINAL SOURCES: Chesnut, M. B. *Diary From Dixie,* see index.

Grant, U. S. *Personal Memoirs of U. S. Grant.* 2 vols. 1885-1886.

Nation, 42:172; 43:12. Grant's sentences have the directness and brevity of a man of action. They remind one of despatches from the field of battle.

BIOGRAPHY: Brooks, W. E. *Grant at Appomattox: a Study of the Man.* 1942.

AHR, 48:658. This book "recounts, pleasantly enough, the major events of Grant's life from Point Pleasant to Appomattox."

Extract in Prochnow, H. V., ed. *Great Stories From Great Lives,* 78-81.

Conger, Colonel A. L. *Rise of U. S. Grant.* 1931.

Books, June 14, 1931, p. 6. "Colonel Conger's study is a vigorous, though critical defense of Grant's early military career, and, based entirely on documentary evidence—chiefly the Records of the Rebellion—it carries conviction.

Coolidge, L. A. *Ulysses S. Grant.* 1917.

AHR, 22:885. In this biography "Grant . . . both man and boy . . . stands out more clearly than in any previous account. In fact, he emerges as an understandable human being and the main lines of characterization seem likely to be final."

Edmonds, F. S. *Ulysses S. Grant.* (American Crisis, 1915).

AHR, 21:183. A brief popular biography. "Mr. Edmonds writes in an easy style, and handles his subject with sympathy, but without excessive hero-worship."

Fuller, Colonel J. F. C. *The Generalship of Ulysses S. Grant.* 1929.

AHR, 35:891. In seeking to rehabilitate Grant's military reputation, Colonel Fuller pictures him as "eternally right"; blames his defeats on the short-comings of subordinates. Grant was usually thoughtful and considerate of others; his biographer's criticisms "are often trenchant and dogmatic." In spite of some faults, Colonel Fuller has written "a stimulating book."

Green, Horace. *General Grant's Last Stand: a Biography.* 1936.

AHR, 43:167. "This book is built around a thin bundle of pencil notes, written by Grant the invalid, when the cancer in his throat limited his speech. . . . These notes relate to whatever happened to be passing through Grant's mind and deal with biographical content scattered through his whole career." The book merits consideration but has limitations.

Also in *Harper's,* 170 (1935):533-40.

Hesseltine, W. B. *Ulysses S. Grant, Politician.* (American Political Leaders, 1935).

AHR, 41:553. After surveying Grant's life down to 1865 in two brief chapters, the author devotes the rest of his book to a careful study of the General's political career. His conclusion is that although Grant grew as a president, "his growth was that of a party politician."

*Lewis, Lloyd. *Captain Sam Grant.* 1950.

Sat. Rev. of Lit., 33:12, May 27, 1950. A careful study of Grant's early career, which describes his development as a kindly but fearless and determined young officer. It gives an amusing account of the Old West Point and a vivid narrative of the War with Mexico.

McCormick, R. R. *Ulysses S. Grant, the Great Soldier of America.* 1934.

AHR, 41:223. The purpose of this book is "to enhance the military reputation of General Grant." Colonel McCormick "has produced an interesting volume with very good battle accounts, the clearness of which is increased by the numerous excellent maps. He has pushed his thesis too

---

* Lewis died before he could finish his biography of Grant. See p. 362.

hard, however, in trying to prove his national, and even international, superlatives for Grant's generalship."

Woodward, W. E. *Meet General Grant.* 1928.

Books, Nov. 18, 1928, p. 7. A popular biography which has good thumbnail sketches of Lee, Sherman, and others. Also errors in fact and in interpretation.

COLLECTIVE BIOGRAPHY: Agar, Herbert. *The People's Choice,* 199-228.

Bach, C. A., and F. L. Paxson, in *DAB*, 7:492.

Burne, Lt. Col. A. H. *Lee, Grant, and Sherman.* 1939.

AHR, 45:177. This book deserves "careful reading by anyone interested in the military history of the Civil War. . . . The discussion of the military leadership is generally fair and constructive." The one limitation "is that it is written without any reference to economic, social, and political conditions in the Confederacy. Relation of the discussion to contemporary military events and conditions elsewhere would have aided in an understanding of the value and significance of the events and leadership under consideration." The book is marred by many errors.

Goebel, D. B., and Julius Goebel. *Generals in the White House,* 166-201.

HISTORY: Bowers, Claude. *The Tragic Era,* see index.

Fish, Carl. *American Civil War,* 264-67.

SPECIAL ASPECTS: Fischer, L. R., ed. "Grant's Letters to His Missouri Farm Tenants," *Agri. Hist.,* 21 (1947) :26-42.

Fuller, Major-General J. F. C. *Grant and Lee: a Study in Personality and Generalship.* 1933.

AHR, 40:384. Major-General Fuller "states that careful study of the Civil War led him to reverse the conventional school-book estimates of Grant and Lee. Grant emerges much more than the stupid butcher, while Lee, instead of being 'one of the greatest generals the world has ever seen seems one of the most incapable Generals-in-Chief in history.' The reader will probably remain unconvinced by Fuller's extreme conclusions. Both men are left with middling stature. Lee, it is claimed, was capable of brilliant tactical victories lacking decisive strategical results, while Grant loathed the tactical side of war with its slaughter, but the strategical side fascinated him. Enough is shown of the strong elements of Grant's character and ability to lift him out of the 'stupid butcher' category yet he remains considerably below Marlborough, Frederick, and other first-raters. Lee is criticized for his failure to remove incompetent subordinates, his poor supply service, and his failure to correct these faults by pressure on the Confederate government. It may be said in his defense that those weaknesses were inherent in the Confederacy itself, for the state-rights idea carried to its logical conclusion prevented effective con-centration of power, and by the time Lee was in a position to exert his influence upon the government, the harm had been done."

Grant, J. R., "A Boy in the White House," *Harper's*, 150 (1925) : 129-40; 333-41; 465-74.

Hutchins, R. M., ed. *Letters from Lloyd Lewis Showing Steps in the Research for His Biography of U. S. Grant*. 1950.

AHR, 56:137. These letters with their "infectious enthusiasm" shows that in November, 1947, the biographer confessed that Grant was "a mystery." A year later he added "there is no mystery. . . . Lewis then saw every-thing explained by the fact that in anything that interested Grant—be it mental arithmetic, pistol marksmanship, horses, or swimming—Grant could excell."

Maurice, Major General Sir Frederick Barton. *Statesmen and Soldiers of the Civil War*, 90-117

Perling, J. J. *Presidents' Sons*, 162-86.

Pollard, J. E. *Presidents and the Press*, 434-54.

Stein, Gertrude. *Four in America*, 3-81.

Wecter, Dixon. *Hero in America*, 307-40.

Woolley, E. C., "Grant's Southern Policy," in Garner, J. W., ed. *Studies in Southern History and Politics*, 179-200.

BIOGRAPHIES OF CONTEMPORARIES: Nevins, Allan. *Hamilton Fish: the Inner History of the Grant Administration*, 105-42, index.

PHILIP DANFORTH ARMOUR—   1832-1901
—Business Man and Philanthropist

BIOGRAPHY: Leech, Harper, and J. C. Carroll. *Armour and His Times*. 1938.

AHR, 45:181. The success story of a country boy who foresaw that the price of pork would go down with the Confederacy.

COLLECTIVE BIOGRAPHY: Ghent, W. J., in *DAB*, 1:347.

Grayson, T. J. *Leaders and Periods of American Finance*, 393-405.

Wildman, Edwin. *Famous Leaders of Industry*, 1st ser., (1920) : 3-14.

DWIGHT LYMAN MOODY— 1837-1899
—"The Greatest Evangelist of the Nineteenth Century"

ORIGINAL SOURCES: Abbott, Lyman. *Silhouettes of My Contemporaries,* 184-212.

Moody, P. D., in Strong, S. D., ed. *What I Owe to My Father,* 109-15.

BIOGRAPHY: Bradford, Gamaliel. *D. L. Moody, a Worker in Souls.* 1927.

Books, Nov. 13, 1927, p. 7. "Mr. Bradford's task . . . was to build up a personality from the fragmentary data which Dwight L. Moody left behind him, and he has done it carefully and with extraordinary analytical skill. . . ."

Moody, P. D. *My Father: an Intimate Portrait of Dwight Moody.* 1938.

N. E. Quar., 11:656. His youngest son gives us an intimate picture which emphasizes the human qualities of his father's greatness as a man and an American.

Moody, W. R. *The Life of Dwight L. Moody.* 1930.

COLLECTIVE BIOGRAPHY: Day, R. E. *Beacon Lights of Grace; Twelve Biographical Vignettes,* (1947):145-54.

Duffus, R. L., "The Hound of Heaven," *Am. Merc.,* 5 (1925): 424-32.

Rowe, H. K. *Modern Pathfinders of Christianity,* (1928):196-207.

Sweet, W. W. *Makers of Christianity,* (1939):235-78.

Weigle, L. A., in *DAB,* 13:103.

*JOHN HAY— 1838-1905
—Figurehead or Great Secretary of State?

ORIGINAL SOURCES: Dennett, Tyler, ed. *Lincoln and the Civil War in the Diaries and Letters of John Hay.* 1939.

AHR, 45:175. Hay's diary "is, like young Hay himself, sophisticated, full of literary sparkle, racy, opinionated, at times oversmart, and always colorful. In style it is urbane, debonair, saucy, playful, flippant to a degree, dotted with a scholar's foreign phrases, yet so redolent of Pike County. It is, of course, unique as a record of Lincoln, catching his casual talk,

---

* For a more complete bibliography see Spiller, et al. *Literary History of the United States.* 2 (1948):553-54.

giving close-up vignettes of his offhand moments, registering some of his pithiest anecdotes at the source, revealing his messages, decisions, and letters in the making, and opening otherwise closed doors upon the harrassed President's mental and emotional life. Since Lincoln had no Boswell (Herndon did not begin his biographical labors till after Lincoln's death) the Hay record finds its chief value in the preservation of fleeting pictures that would otherwise have been lost, pictures of Lincoln refusing to make 'points of etiquette & personal dignity,' reading Shakespeare to Hay, talking Shakespeare with Hackett, saving lives in court-martial reviews, receiving delegations, restraining his own impatience toward Meade after Gettysburg, listening to a regimental band, amusing himself with a Richmond editor's attack upon Jefferson Davis, and so on. For the men who passed before his eye the impish secretary had telling and often devastating thumbnail characterizations; if it was a pretty woman, the fact and degree of pulchritude were not likely to be omitted. Hay's prejudices colored his jottings as they later swayed the ten-volume biography. For Republican enthusiasm there is no apology. 'Haight is a good egg (wrote Hay, p. 41) he votes straight every time.' Despite his scorn for the radicals, Hay shared their prejudices against McClellan, and his comments on that general are to be used with caution."

BIOGRAPHY: *Dennett, Tyler. *John Hay: From Poetry to Politics.* 1933.

AHR, 39:544. A definitive biography which presénts a charming portrait and gives Hay his true place in history.

Thayer, W. R. *Life and Letters of John Hay.* 2 vols. 1915.

AHR, 21:831. The official archives of the Department of State not being open to him, Mr. Thayer warned readers he would produce a "personal biography" rather than a "public history." He did produce an interesting and charming book. However, under the circumstances, how can the reviewer call it "this definitive biography"? Did he say the final word on Hay's place in history?

COLLECTIVE BIOGRAPHY: Dennis, A. L. P., in *DAB,* 8:430.

Hinds, C. L. *Authors and I,* 124-29.

Kohlsaat, H. H. *From McKinley to Harding,* (1923) :72-75, 97, 105-06.

Parrington, V. L. *Main Currents in American Thought,* 3:173-79.

Thomas, B. P. *Portrait for Posterity,* 94-131.

Thwing, C. F. *Guides, Philosophers and Friends,* 267-87.

SPECIAL ASPECTS: Bishop, J. B., "A Friendship with John Hay," *Century,* 71 (1906) :773-80.

---

* Awarded the Pulitzer Prize.

——. *Notes and Anecdotes of Many Years,* 44-67.

Chapman, A. S., "The Boyhood of John Hay," *Century,* 78 (1909) :444-54.

Dennis, A. L. P., in Bemis, S. F., ed. *American Secretaries of State,* 9:115-89.

Hicks, Granville. *Great Tradition,* 68-99.

Root, Elihu. *Miscellaneous Addresses,* 91-103.

Willson, Beckles. *America's Ambassadors to England,* 398-418.

FRANCES ELIZABETH WILLARD—   1839-1898
—Prohibitionist

ORIGINAL SOURCES: Stone, Irving, and Richard Kennedy, eds. *We Speak for Ourselves,* 332-36.

Willard, F. E. *Glimpses of Fifty Years: the Autobiography of an American Woman.* 1889.

BIOGRAPHY: Earhart, Mary. *Frances Willard: From Prayers to Politics.* 1944.

AHR, 50:573. A scholarly but readable biography which rejects legend and presents Miss Willard as a very human personality, as well as a skillful politician.

COLLECTIVE BIOGRAPHY: Adams, E. C., and W. B. Foster. *Heroines of Modern Progress,* 215-44.

Anthony, Katharine, in *DAB,* 20:233.

Bartlett, E. R., in Lotz, P. H., ed. *Women Leaders,* 127-37.

Bradford, Gamaliel. *Portraits of American Women,* 195-225.

Clifton, J. L. *Ten Famous American Educators,* 167-87.

Dibble, R. F. *Strenuous Americans,* 183-256.

Fenner, M. S., and E. C. Fishburn. *Pioneer American Educators,* 89-96.

Howe, M. A. D. *Causes and Their Champions,* 80-118.

Malone, Dumas. *Saints in Action,* 84-113.

Parkman, M. R. *Heroines of Service,* (1917) :89-115.

Thomas and Thomas. *Living Biographies of Famous Women,* (1942) :279-91.

SPECIAL ASPECTS: Beveridge, A. J. *Meaning of the Times,* (1908) :248-53.

Muggah, M. G., and P. H. Raihle. *Meet Your Neighbor,* 72-75.

JOHN PETER ALTGELD— 1847-1902
—"Dangerous Friend of Anarchists" or "One of the Greatest and Most Beneficent Governors Illinois Ever Had?"

BIOGRAPHY: Barnard, Harry. *"Eagle Forgotten": the Life of John Peter Altgeld.* 1948.

AHR, 44:662. A popular biography which presents Altgeld's story in vivid fashion. The author tries to be impartial, "but occasionally leans backwards."

Browne, W. R. *Sympathetic Altgeld of Illinois: a Record of His Life and Work.* 1924.

N. Y. Times, June 20, 1924, p 3. Mr. Browne, although too warm an admirer to be scientifically critical, has written a convincing biography."

COLLECTIVE BIOGRAPHY: Madison, C. A. *Critics and Crusaders,* 366-94.

——, "John Peter Altgeld, Pioneer Progressive," *Antioch Rev.,* 5 (1945) :121-34.

Paxton, F. L., in *DAB,* 1:231.

Wish, Harvey, "Altgeld and the Progressive Tradition," *AHR,* 46 (1941) :813-31.

HISTORY: Bogart, E. L., and C. M. Thompson. *The Industrial State.* 1920.

AHR, 26:548. The reviewer recalls being roundly reproached for speaking well of Altgeld; says Chapter 8, "New Forces Astir" (by Agnes Dennis) is one of the best chapters in the book.

BIOGRAPHIES OF CONTEMPORARIES: Whitelock, Brand. *Forty Years of It.* 1914.

Nation, 98:367, Apr. 2, 1914. "No more interesting American autobiography has appeared in a good while."

WILLIAM RAINEY HARPER— 1856-1906
—First President of the University of Chicago

COLLECTIVE BIOGRAPHY: Malone, Dumas. *Saints in Action,* 107, 170-75.

Shorey, Paul, in *DAB,* 8:287.

Thwing, C. F. *Guides, Philosophers and Friends,* 163-78.

HISTORY: Goodpseed, T. W. *History of the University of Chicago.* 1916.

SPECIAL ASPECTS: Brown, Francis, in *Am. Jour. of Semitic Languages,* Apr., 1906.

*WILLIAM VAUGHN MOODY— 1869-1910
—"A Forerunner of the New Poets"

ORIGINAL SOURCES: Mackaye, Percy, ed. Moody, W. V. *Letters to Harriet.* 1936.

Booklist, 32:167, Feb., 1936. "Letters by the poet and dramatist, during the years 1901 to 1909, to Harriet Converse Tilden, who later became his wife. She was a woman of understanding and wide sympathies, whose Chicago home was a haven to many writers." The introduction includes a tribute to her and a sketch of Moody's life.

Mason, D. G., ed. *Some Letters of William Vaughn Moody.* 1913.

BIOGRAPHY: Henry, D. D. *William Vaughn Moody: a Study.* 1935.

Amer. Lit., 6:463. Mr. Henry has given us a useful book in collecting the available material on the life of William Vaughn Moody and "interpreting his poetry in the light of this experience."

COLLECTIVE BIOGRAPHY: Eaton, W. P., in *DAB,* 13:108.

SPECIAL ASPECTS: Gregory, Horace, and M. A. Zaturenska. *History of American Poetry, 1900-1940,* 25-43.

Loggins, Vernon. *I Hear America,* 33-70.

CHAPTER XXXVIII. KANSAS AND MISSOURI

JOHN BROWN— 1800-1859
—"Hero, Monomaniac or Criminal?"

ORIGINAL SOURCES: Abramowitz, Isidore, ed. *Great Prisoners,* 578-91.

BIOGRAPHY: Karsner, David. *John Brown, Terrible Saint.* 1934.

New Repub., 81:416. In the main a condensation of the biography by O. G. Villard which appeared in 1910.

Villard, O. G. *John Brown, 1800-1859: a Biography Fifty Years After.* Revised edition, 1943.

AHR, 49:356. The addenda summarizes new facts about Brown discovered since 1910. There are also many additions to the bibliography.

COLLECTIVE BIOGRAPHY: Bradford, Gamaliel. *Damaged Souls,* 157-88.

Cournos, John. *Modern Plutarch,* 207-34, 254-63.

---

* See *Cambridge History of American Literature,* 4 (1921) :650-51; Spiller, et al. *Literary History of the United States,* 3 (1948) :660-62.

Johnson, Allen, in *DAB*, 3:131.

Madison, C. A. *Critics and Crusaders*, 35-59.

Malone, Dumas. *Saints in Action*, 57-83.

SPECIAL ASPECTS: Malin, J. C. *John Brown and the Legend of Fifty-six*. (Memoirs of the American Philosophical Society, 1942).

AHR, 48:819. A critical study which concludes that the Browns migrated to Kansas for economic reasons—rather than to fight slavery. The book is well documented.

Snyder, L. L., and R. B. Morris, eds. *Treasury of Great Reporting*, 121-25.

Weyl, Nathaniel. *Treason*, 238-61.

CARL SCHURZ—   1829-1906
—"The Incarnation of Our National Conscience"

ORIGINAL SOURCES: Bancroft, Frederick, ed. *Speeches, Correspondence, and Political Papers of Carl Schurz*. 6 vols. 1913.

AHR, 19:376. The chief interest of these volumes is "their complete revelation of the man. Schurz's single-minded devotion to principle and his political honesty, as well as his personal limitations, are more clearly shown in these letters than in his published *Reminiscences*."

Harper's Weekly. Important for caricature of Schurz by Nast especially in 1872 and for editorials by Schurz.

Schafer, Joseph, ed. *Intimate Letters of Carl Schurz, 1841-1869*.

(Publications of the State Hist. Soc. of Wis., Collections, Vol. 30, 1928).

AHR, 35:178. These letters cover Schurz's German student days and his early manhood in America. Those to his wife are "the most interesting and instructive," and furnish "the deepest insight into the character of Schurz and the secret of his success. . . ."

Schurz, Carl. *The Reminiscences of Carl Schurz*. 3 vols. 1907-08.

AHR, 13:880. "A worthy record of a great career," which offers the greatest of contrast. Volume I describes the exciting adventures of a Prussian university student during the Revolution of '48. Volume II traces Carl's rise in American politics, his eloquent support of Lincoln, and his service record as a general in the Civil War. Volume III describes his opposition to Grant and to the Imperialism of 1898. Schurz's work as editor, lecturer, and cabinet member runs through volumes II and III. Frederick Bancroft and W. A. Dunning give a sketch of Schurz's political career, 1869-1906 in Volume III, pp. 311-455.

BIOGRAPHY: Easum, C. V. *The Americanization of Carl Schurz.* 1929.

MVHR, 17:483. This study of the first ten years (1852-1862) Schurz spent in America "explains how this German political refugee became a devoted American citizen." The book is based on research and "is written in a very entertaining fashion. . . ."

Fuess, C. M. *Carl Schurz, Reformer (1829-1906).* 1932.

Books, Apr. 17, 1932, p. 17. "A nicely balanced, sympathetic and just appraisal of the great independent. . . . Chapters on Schurz's connection with the Liberal Republican movement, with the new Indian policy, and with Civil Service reform are important contributions, embodying new material in our history."

Schafer, Joseph. *Carl Schurz, Militant Liberal.* (Wisconsin Biographies, 1930).

MVHR, 17:484. By selecting the more important activities of Schurz, and now and then quoting him, the biographer has succeeded admirably in revealing a very real personality.

COLLECTIVE BIOGRAPHY: Beard, A. E. S. *Our Foreign-Born Citizens,* 330-35.

Faust, A. B. *The German Element in the United States,* 2 vols. (1927) :index.

Husband, Joseph. *Americans by Adoption,* 56-73.

Ludwig, Emil, in Kranz, H. B., and Emil Ludwig, eds. *Twenty Exiles of History,* (1943) :301-18.

Morgan, B. Q., in Zucker, A. E., ed. *Forty-eighters,* (1950) :221-50.

Rhodes, J. F., in *Library of World's Best Literature,* 22:12974-94.

Villard, O. G., in *DAB,* 16:466.

Willkie, W. L., in *There Were Giants in the Land,* 207-16.

HISTORY: Bowers, Claude. *The Tragic Era,* see index.

Ross, E. D. *The Liberal Republican Movement.* (Cornell Studies, 1919).

AHR, 25:522. A thorough and impartial study.

SPECIAL ASPECTS: Choate, J. H. *American Addresses,* 297-301.

Donner, Barbara. "Carl Schurz the Diplomat," *Wis Mag. Hist. and Biog.,* 20 (1937) :291-309.

Fichter, J. H. *Roots of Change,* (1939) :242-64.

Fuess, C. M., "Carl Schurz, Henry Cabot Lodge, and the Campaign of 1884: a Study in Temperament and Political Philosophy," *N. E. Quar.*, 5 (1932) :453-82.

Mahaffey, J. H., ed. "Carl Schurz's Letters from the South," *Georgia Hist. Quar.*, 35 (1951) :222-57.

Van Doren, Carl, and C. L. Carmer. *American Scriptures*, 239-43.

BIOGRAPHIES OF CONTEMPORARIES: Paine, A. B. *Thomas Nast: His Period and His Pictures.* 1904.

When his ferocious attacks had sent Boss Tweed to jail, Thomas Nast, the German-American cartoonist, turned to a defense of Grant. Ironically enough, this led to a systematic ridicule of Schurz and other senators opposing the administration.

*SAMUEL LANGHORNE CLEMENS— 1835-1910
—Mark Twain

ORIGINAL SOURCES: Clemens, Clara. *My Father, Mark Twain.* 1931.

Clemens, S. L. *Mark Twain's Autobiography.* 1924.

Booklist, 21:108. Mark Twain's "voice rings from the grave with all its old warmth, wit, and candor." The book "follows no plan or sequence and the sudden changes from things of the moment to childhood recollections are at times disconcerting."

De Voto, Bernard, ed. *Mark Twain in Eruption: Hitherto Unpublished Pages About Men and Manners.* 1940.

Amer. Lit., 13:173. The student of Mark Twain who knows his *Autobiography* and Paine's *Biography* "will find little that is either genuinely novel or truly 'eruptive'" in this book. "For example, the animadversions on Theodore Roosevelt reproduced by Mr. De Voto bring many amusing details, but add nothing essentially new to what every informed reader of Mark Twain already knows about his dislikes for Roosevelt I. The book is really a supplement to the *Autobiography* and, like it, "its chief interest lies in the inimitable witticisms and caustic comments which Mark Twain made upon man and events."

Lorch, F. W., "Mark Twain's Philadelphia Letters in the Muscatine Journal," *Amer. Lit.,* 17 (1946) :348-52.

Paine, A. B., ed. *Mark Twain's Letters.* 1917.

Literary Digest, 55:42, Dec. 29, 1917. "A contribution to Mark Twain literature" and "a notable example of the way in which letters should be

---

* See *Cambridge History of American Literature,* 4 (1921) :635-39; Spiller, et al. *Literary History of the United States,* 3 (1948) :442-50.

compiled so as to reflect the true character of the person who wrote them."

Pattee, F. L., ed. *Mark Twain: Representative Selections.* (American Writers, 1935).

Amer. Lit., 7:350. "An attractive little book of selections containing an extensive introduction and a serviceable bibliography." Unfortunately copyrights made it necessary to exclude the *Autobiography* and the *Letters,* and Professor Pattee chose to use much space refuting Mr. Brooks's Freudian interpretation of Mark Twain.

Quick, Dorothy, in Wagenknecht, E. C., ed. *When I Was a Child,* 47-59, 193-99.

Rahv, Philip, ed. *Discovery of Europe,* 237-68.

Stone, Irving, and Richard Kennedy, eds. *We Speak for Ourselves,* 294-302.

Thomson, M. N., in Lorch, F. W., ed. "Doesticks and Innocents Abroad," *Amer. Lit.,* 20 (1949) :446-49.

Webster, S. C., ed. *Mark Twain, Business Man.* 1946.

Amer. Lit., 18:169. The correspondence with Charles L. Webster, Twain's editor, merely elaborates the fact that the humorist was "impulsive and temperamental, a hard man to work with, and that he was always trying to do a dozen things at once. . . . The real additions and corrections to the record come from the family correspondence, and from the reminiscences of the editor's mother, Annie Moffett Webster." Members of the Clemens and Webster families "emerge in clearer outline than before, and some of Paine's most romantic details of the humorist's youth suffer a deflation which extends to the conclusions drawn from them by the psychoanalytical critics."

Wecter, Dixon, ed. *Love Letters of Mark Twain.* 1949.

Herald-Tribune Bk. Rev., Nov. 7, 1949, p. 1. For gentle, serious-minded Olivia Langdon to marry a stormy, blasphemous man from the rowdy West seemed to invite disaster, but it didn't work out that way. The result was a happy marriage, and he changed her far more than she changed him.

Also in *Atlantic,* 180:33-39, Nov. 1947; 66-72, Dec., 1947; 181: 83-88, Jan., 1948.

———. *Mark Twain to Mrs. Fairbanks.* 1949.

Amer. Lit., 22:202. Mrs. Fairbanks for thirty years was Mark Twain's friend and literary advisor. She was a conventional woman who helped to refine him and purify his language.

BIOGRAPHY: Brashear, M. M. *Mark Twain, Son of Missouri.* 1934.

Amer. Lit., 6:460. Miss Brashear has done much "to dispel the notion that Mark Twain's Missouri of the 1840's and 1850's was as culturally barren and suppressive as some critics have alleged." She shows "that in spite of his assertions to the contrary, Mark Twain was not ignorant of books." In her most provocative and valuable chapter she "advances the theory that Mark Twain's literary provenience is to be sought chiefly among the writers of the eighteenth century." The book has some faults, but these do not detract from its importance

Brooks, V. W. *The Ordeal of Mark Twain.* 1920, 1933.

Rev. of Revs., 62:334. "Primarily a psychological study (but) full of biographical detail. . . ." Mr. Brooks tries to offer "a logical explanation of Mark Twain's well-known tendency to pessimism. To satisfy his own mind Mr. Brooks seems to have adopted a thesis which he feels bound to support by ingenious and plausible argument. As a clever and brilliant application of critical methods to a literary career, the book has few equals in American literature."

De Voto, Bernard. *Mark Twain's America.* 1932.

Amer. Lit., 4:399. The author's thesis is that Mark Twain was a frontier humorist. His literary intelligence was shaped by the life of the frontier and found expression in the themes and forms developed by the humor of the frontier. In spite of some faults, Mr. De Voto's book "is undoubtedly the most important of all books dealing with America's greatest humorist."

Ferguson, De Lancey. *Mark Twain: Man and Legend.* 1943.

Amer. Lit., 16:143. "This book," says its author, "aims to trace in detail Mark Twain's career as a writing man, passing over lightly, or ignoring, his multifarious non-literary doings. I have tried to examine the forces which made him a writer, to tell how he wrote his books and why he wrote them as he did! . . . This interesting and intelligent scheme for a literary man's biography has produced a book . . . which deserves a place among the better studies of Mark Twain."

Masters, E. L. *Mark Twain: a Portrait.* 1938.

Amer. Lit., 10:373. Mr. Masters maintains that Mark Twain's "political and economic adherences did much to tangle his rightful career." He asserts that this was "to expose the deep-seated economic, social, and political evils of the United States and with the weapon of satire to attack them. But instead of a satirist Mark Twain became a humorist, a mere buffoon, who, if he saw the evils corrupting American life, lacked the courage effectually to combat them. . . . His chief sin was his failure to espouse the proletarian cause. . . . Mr. Masters' book, then, has at least three serious faults: inaccurate reporting, unwarranted assumptions, and a confused philosophy. As a portrait of Mark Twain it does not deserve serious scholarly attention."

Paine, A. B. *Mark Twain, a Biography: the Personal and Literary Life of Samuel Langhorne Clemens.* 3 vols. 1912.

Booklist, 9:113. "The authorized life, based on close daily companionship with the great humorist for four years, a thorough study of his life here and abroad, and a large body of material contributed by his friends."

———. *Short Life of Mark Twain.* 1920.

Booklist, 17:113, Dec., 1920. "A condensation of the author's official biography in three volumes."

Wagenknecht, E. C. *Mark Twain: the Man and His Work.* 1935.

Sat. Rev. of Lit., 12:3, Oct. 12, 1935. "Professor Wagenknecht's critical biography . . . is a sane and accurate discussion of a man hard to analyse, and very difficult to estimate without exaggeration either of his tragic pessimism or his boisterous humor. This writer's sensible handling of the wife-suppression theory is excellent, and indeed his volume is the most useful, if not the most brilliant or penetrating, short book on Mark Twain."

COLLECTIVE BIOGRAPHY: Brooks, V. W. *Chilmark Miscellany,* 309-15.

———. *The Times of Melville and Whitman,* 448-64, 283-300.

Cournos, John. *Modern Plutarch,* 1-18, 33-39.

Croffut, W. A. *American Procession,* 169-79.

Dixon, Wecter, in *Literary History of the United States,* 2:917-39.

Doren, C. V., in *DAB,* 4:192.

Hagedorn, Hermann. *Americans,* 1-17.

Josephson, Matthew. *Portrait of the Artist as American,* 139-98.

Law, F. H. *Modern Great Americans,* 77-91.

O'Higgins, H. J., and E. H. Reede. *American Mind in Action,* 26-49.

Russell, F. A. *American Pilgrimage,* 16-32.

Thomas and Thomas. *Fifty Great Americans,* 219-29.

———. *Living Biographies of Famous Novelists,* (1943) :277-91.

HISTORY: Monaghan, James. *Overland Trail,* (1947) :374-91.

SPECIAL ASPECTS: Andrews, K. R. *Nook Farm: Mark Twain's Hartford Circle.* 1950.

Herald-Tribune Bk. Rev., Dec. 31, 1950, p. 5. The first detailed study of "the background, associations and accomplishments of Mark Twain's greatest and happiest period—the twenty years, 1871 to 1891, which he spent in Hartford."

Bellamy, G. C. *Mark Twain as a Literary Artist.* 1950.

Sat. Rev. of Lit., 33:30, Sept. 23, 1950. "Miss Bellamy writes delightfully and with vigorous freshness. Some of her phrases have a Twainian spice. Her summaries are convincing. The order and clarity of her argument show the influence of her profession as a teacher and literary critic without any shadow of pedantic dullness."

Benson, Ivan. *Mark Twain's Western Years.* 1938.

PHR, 7:282. A readable account of Samuel Clemens's career in the Far West. Mr. Benson corrects some errors of previous biographers and gives a valuable periodical bibliography of Clemens's writings in the newspapers and magazines of Nevada and California from 1861 to 1865. He also reprints several of the Western sketches, including the actual correspondence between Clemens and James L. Blair of the *Virginia Daily Union,* which resulted in the former leaving for California.

Blair, Walter. *Horse Sense in American Humor,* 195-217.

Booth, B. A., "Mark Twain's Comments on Holmes' Autocrat," *Amer. Lit.,* 21 (1950) :456-63.

———, "Mark Twain's Friendship with Emeline Beech," *Amer. Lit.,* 19 (1947) :219-30.

Branch, E. M. *Literary Apprenticeship of Mark Twain, with Selections from His Apprentice Writing.* 1950.

Sat. Rev. of Lit., 33:33, Sept. 23, 1950. This "discussion of Twain's very early literary career and unpublished writings" is followed "by seventeen selections from the writings themselves. . . ."

De Voto, Bernard. *Mark Twain at Work.* 1942.

Amer. Lit., 14:447. "This book attempts to tell how Mark Twain wrote *Tom Sawyer, Huckleberry Finn,* and *The Mysterious Stranger*—and to evaluate these works. An essay about each is supplemented with relevant documents . . . discovered among the Clemens papers. . . . Both the essays and the documents . . . challenge previous scholarship. . . ." Mr. De Voto points out various facts which collide violently with Van Wyck Brooks's biographical interpretations, finds errors in the notes of De Lancey Ferguson about the relationships between the manuscript of *Huckleberry Finn* and the book, and shows "how fallible" A. B. Paine was in his voluminous work on Clemens. Mr. De Voto makes important contributions in evaluating Twain's three works, but his study "can profitably be supplemented."

Gratton, C. H., in Macy, John, ed. *American Writers on American Literature,* 274-84.

Gibson, W. M., "Mark Twain and Howells; Anti-Imperialists," *N. E. Quar.,* 20 (1947) :435-70.

Hazard, L. L. *The Frontier in American Literature,* 198-202.

Hoben, J. B., "Mark Twain's A Connecticut Yankee: a Genetic Study," *Amer. Lit.*, 18 (1946) :197-218.

Hollenbeck, J. W., "Mark Twain, a Story Teller at Work," *Coll. Engl.*, 7 (1946) :303-12.

Lorch, F. W., "Mark Twain's Sandwich Islands Lecture at St. Louis," *Amer. Lit.*, 18 (1947) :299-307.

Mack, E. M. *Mark Twain in Nevada.* 1947.

AHR, 53:632. Dr. Mack's book is "a very readable account of Nevada during its early years," and "the most detailed account we have of Twain in the Territory. However, Clemens had a gift for exaggeration, hence a book based largely on his *Roughing It*, should be used with caution."

Orians, G. H., "Walter Scott, Mark Twain and the Civil War," *So. Atl. Quar.*, 40 (1941) :342-59.

Parsons, C. O., "The Devil and Samuel Clemens," *Va. Quar. Rev.*, 23 (1947) :582-606.

Snell, G. D. *Shapers of American Fiction,* 211-22.

Taylor, W. C. *Economic Novel in America,* 116-47.

Trent, W. P., and John Erskine. *Great American Writers,* 231-50.

Vogelback, A. L., "Mark Twain: Newspaper Contributor," *Amer. Lit.*, 20 (1948) :111-28.

Waggoner, H. H., "Science in the Thought of Mark Twain," *Amer. Lit.*, 8 (1937) :357-70.

Williams, S. T., "The Enigma of Mark Twain," *Yale Rev.*, 40 (1951) :340-43.

JESSE WOODSON JAMES— 1847-1882
—Robin Hood of the Border or Cut-throat Bandit?

BIOGRAPHY: Croy, Homer. *Jesse James Was My Neighbor.* 1949.

N. Y. Times, June 19, 1949, p. 12. "The most comprehensive biography that has ever been written of Jesse and Frank and their families. Some may object to Croy's wisecracks . . . , but 'Jesse James Was My Neighbor' is must reading for any student of the American scene."

Groves, P. R. *Jesse James.* 1946.

Love, Robertus. *The Rise and Fall of Jesse James.* 1926

Books, June 13, 1926, p. 16. "Mr. Love has pieced together the fragments, sorting evidence and restraining conjectures with a judicious hand; and the result is an interesting footnote to American history, for the James boys were distinctly a product of their time. Ishmaels born of the Civil War and bred on the frontier."

Huntington, George. *Robber and Hero.* 1895.

Tripplett, Frank. *The Life, Times, and Death of Jesse James.* 1882.

COLLECTIVE BIOGRAPHY: Ghent, W. J., in *DAB*, 9:585.

Dibble, R. F. *Strenuous Americans,* 15-48.

Holbrook, S. H. "Phonies of the Old West," *Am. Merc.,* 68 (1949) :230-32.

SPECIAL ASPECTS: "Battle Over a Jesse James Monument," *Lit. Dig.,* 95:44-50, Oct. 29, 1927.

Garwood, Darrell. *Crossroads of America,* (1948) :83-116.

Greene, Laurence. *America Goes to Press,* (1936) :245-52.

Wecter, Dixon. *Hero in America,* 341-63.

WILLIAM ALLEN WHITE—   1868-1944
—"The Sage of Emporia"

ORIGINAL SOURCES: Johnson, Walter, ed. *Selected Letters of William Allen White, 1899-1943.* 1947.

AHR, 52:800. These entertaining letters reveal their author as a lovable personality, but contributes little new.

Wilson, Gill, ed. *Letters of William Allen White and a Young Man.* 1948.

*White, W. A. *Autobiography of William Allen White.* 1946.

Weekly Bk. Rev., Mar. 3, 1946, p. 1. Eminently readable story of a country editor, magazine writer, and leading Republican who edited "The Gazette" for fifty years. Good sketches of contemporaries.

Excerpts in *Atlantic,* 177 (Mar., 1946) :39-47.

Also in Fuess, C. M., and E. S. Basford, eds. *Unseen Harvests,* (1947) :645-53.

Stone, Irving, and Richard Kennedy, eds. *We Speak for Ourselves,* 309-15.

BIOGRAPHY: Hinshaw, David. *A Man from Kansas: the Story of William Allen White.* 1945.

AHR, 51:553. Personal recollections of a friend supplemented by selected editorials from the *Emporia Gazette.*

Johnson, Walter. *William Allen White's America.* 1947.

AHR, 53:359. A vigorous and penetrating appraisal of the small-town editor who usually supported the Republican party on election day at least.

---

* Awarded the Pulitzer Prize.

Rich, Everett. *William Allen White: the Man from Emporia.* 1941.

New Repub., 105:560, Oct. 27, 1941. Fails to clarify White's transition from a "thorough-going bigot" to a man with a "progressive viewpoint." Does give a good description of him as a small-town citizen and editor.

Extract in Prochnow, H. V., ed. *Great Stories from Great Lives,* 204-12.

COLLECTIVE BIOGRAPHY: Cooper, A. C., and C. A. Palmer. *Twenty Modern Americans,* 309-26.

Huff, Warren and Edna. *Famous Americans,* 611-21.

Pick, F. W., "Great American Journalists," *Contem. Rev.,* 171 (1947) :27-31.

Sergeant, E. S. *Fire Under the Andes,* 165-89.

SPECIAL ASPECTS: Frederick, J. T., "William Allen White and Mark Twain," *Rotarian,* 68 (1946) :47-48.

Hicks, Granville. *Great Tradition,* 164-206.

Lewis, Lloyd. *It Takes All Kinds,* 226-29.

CHAPTER XXXIX. THE NORTHWEST

PIERRE JEAN De SMET—   1801-1873
        —Jesuit Missionary

ORIGINAL SOURCES: Chittenden, H. M., and A. T. Richardson. *Life, Letters and Travels of Father Pierre Jean De Smet, S. J.* 4 vols. 1905.

An important work including the journals and many letters hitherto unpublished.

BIOGRAPHY: Margaret, Helene. *Father De Smet: Priest of the Rockies.* 1940.

PHR, 10:230. "The general reader will enjoy this (popular) biography and will gain a vivid impressionistic picture of the great missionary," but the specialist will prefer Chittenden and Richardson.

COLLECTIVE BIOGRAPHY: Schafer, Joseph, in *DAB*, 5:255.

HISTORY: Bischoff, W. N. *The Jesuits in Old Oregon, 1840-1940,* (1945) :13-24, 32-53, 64-67.

Fuller, G. W. *History of the Pacific Northwest,* 137-42.

Monaghan, James. *Overland Trail,* 193-216.

BRIGHAM YOUNG— 1801-1877 —Mormon Leader

BIOGRAPHY: Cannon, F. J., and G. L. Knapp. *Brigham Young and His Mormon Empire.* 1913.

Boston Transcript, Dec. 18, 1913, p. 11. "A man whose career was stranger and more incredible than any invented by Dumas, Balzac, or Defoe is here portrayed by the writer best qualified to tell us of the rise of Mormonism. Ex-Senator Cannon has a personal acquaintance with the leaders of Mormonism which enables him to give a plain, unvarnished tale of the foundation by a New England Puritan of a Mohammedan empire in the far west." (Lit. D.) "Perhaps the most interesting feature of the book to the average reader is the discussion of polygamy to which the authors give several chapters."

Gates, Susa, and Leah Witdsoe. *The Life Story of Brigham Young.* 1930.

Sat. Rev. of Lit., 150:22, July 5, 1930. "Mrs. Gates, one of Brigham's fifty-six children, has written this biography with the object of vindicating her father's memory, and within the limits she has observed, has been unexpectedly successful. As to the tenets of Mormonism, by stating them with a minimum of argument, she has gone far to disarm criticism. . . . Allowance made for filial partiality, the biographer has done her work well."

Werner, M. R. *Brigham Young.* 1925.

Yale Rev., 15:410, Jan., 1926. "It reveals again the penchant for the picturesque, the eye for interesting detail, the gift for broad sweeping narrative that made this author's *Barnum* such a marked success."

COLLECTIVE BIOGRAPHY: Bechdolt, F. R. *Giants of the Old West,* (1930) :155-78.

De Voto, Bernard, in *DAB,* 20:620.

Dibble, R. F. *Strenuous Americans,* 144-82.

Seitz, D. C. *Uncommon Americans,* 24-42.

Thomas and Thomas. *Fifty Great Americans,* 136-44.

———. *Living Biographies of Religious Leaders,* (1942) :253-65.

HISTORY: Monaghan, James. *Overland Trail,* 318-40.

SPECIAL ASPECTS: Calverton, V. F. *Where Angels Dared to Tread,* (1941) :127-67.

Greeley, Horace, in Snyder, L. L., and R. B. Morris, eds. *Treasury of Great Reporting,* 107-09.

Linn, W. H. *The Story of the Mormons,* (1902) :see index.

Weyl, Nathaniel. *Treason,* 212-37.

CHARLES COULSON RICH— 1809-1883
—Mormon Pioneer and Colonizer

BIOGRAPHY: Evans, J. H. *Charles Coulson Rich, Pioneer Builder of the West.* 1936.

AHR, 43:163. An entertaining biography based on family journals. It gives "a kaleidoscopic picture of the Mormon movement from the rise of the church to the death of Rich in 1883."

SPECIAL ASPECTS: "Mormon Family Has a Reunion," *Life*, 23: 59-60, Oct. 27, 1947.

JANE GREY SWISSHELM—1815-1884—"A Vigorous and Entertaining Journalist"

ORIGINAL SOURCES: Larsen, A. J., ed. *Crusader and Feminist: Letters of Jane Grey Swisshelm, 1858-1865.* 1934.

AHR, 40:792. The introduction gives an excellent biographical sketch by the editor. The letters from Pennsylvania and Minnesota newspapers describe the reforms she promoted, her lecture tour through frontier Minnesota, and her impressions of wartime Washington.

Swisshelm, J. G. *Half a Century.* 1880.

COLLECTIVE BIOGRAPHY: Shippee, L. B. "Jane Grey Swisshelm: Agitator," *MVHR*, 7 (1921) : 206-27.

Stearns, B. M., in *DAB*, 18:253.

Thorp, M. F. *Female Persuasion*, 56-106.

HENRY BENJAMIN WHIPPLE— 1822-1901
—Pioneer Bishop of Minnesota

ORIGINAL SOURCES: Whipple, H. B. *Lights and Shadows of a Long Episcopate, Being Reminiscences and Recollections of the Right Reverend Henry Benjamin Whipple, Bishop of Minnesota.* 1899.

AHR, 6:177. The chief interest of this biography "centers about Bishop Whipple's great achievements in the cause of education and his grand work among the Indians."

COLLECTIVE BIOGRAPHY: Nute, G. L., in *DAB*, 20:68.

SITTING BULL— 1834-1890 —Medicine-man of the
Sioux

BIOGRAPHY: Vestal, Stanley. *Sitting Bull, Champion of the Sioux: a Biography.* 1932.

AHR, 39:383. A biography based on a comparative study of the recollections of those who knew the Sioux chief.

COLLECTIVE BIOGRAPHY: Britt, Albert. *Great Indian Chiefs*, (1938) : 188-224.

Eastman, C. A. *Indian Heroes and Chieftains*, (1918) : 107-31.

Edwards, R. M. *American Indians of Yesterday*, (1948) :42-43.

Ghent, E. J., in *DAB*, 5:7.

Johnston, C. H. L. *Famous Indian Chiefs*, 425-55.

Sweetser, K. D. *Book of Indian Braves*, 131-55.

JAMES BUTLER HICKOK—1837-1876—"Wild Bill"

ORIGINAL SOURCES: Buel, J. W. *True Story of Wild Bill Hickok*. (American Folklore and Humor, 1946.)

BIOGRAPHY: Willstach, F. J. *Wild Bill Hickok: the Prince of Pistoleers*. 1926.

Sat. Rev. of Lit., Nov. 27, 1926, p. 6. Pictures "Wild Bill" as a border cop whose shooting was always in line of duty. Contains some errors.

COLLECTIVE BIOGRAPHY: Connelley, W. E., in *DAB*, 9:4.

Cunningham, Eugene. *Triggernometry*, (1934) :249-73.

Johnston, C. H. L. *Famous Scouts*, (1910) :232-63.

SPECIAL ASPECTS: Wecter, Dixon. *Hero in America*, 341-63.

JAMES JEROME HILL— 1838-1916 —"Empire Builder" or "Robber Baron?"

BIOGRAPHY: Pyle, J. G. *The Life of James J. Hill*. 2 vols. 1917.

AHR, 23:196. A reliable and useful study but not a definitive biography.

COLLECTIVE BIOGRAPHY: Beard, A. E. S. *Our Foreign-Born Citizens*, 186-96.

Cunningham, W. J., in *DAB*, 9:36.

Dibble, R. F. *Strenuous Americans*, 257-86.

Also in Durling and Watt, eds. *Biography*, 336-54.

Grayson, T. J. *Leaders and Periods of American Finance*, 428-42.

Hubbard, Elbert. *Little Journeys to the Homes of Great Businessmen*, 399-435.

Husband, Joseph. *Americans by Adoption*, 104-20.

Josephson, Matthew. *The Robber Barons*, 231-38, 246-49, 320-21, 432-34, 437-38, 443-44, 449-50.

Quiett, G. C. *They Built the West*, 339-99, 439-541.

Wildman, Edwin. *Famous Leaders of Industry,* 2nd ser., (1921) : 147-57.

SPECIAL ASPECTS: Gras, N. S. B., and H. M. Larsons, eds. *Casebook in American Business History,* 403-20.

Holbrook, H. S. "Jim Hill Built an Empire," *Am. Merc.,* 45 (1947) :103-10.

GEORGE ARMSTRONG CUSTER— 1839-1876
—"The Murat of the American Army"

ORIGINAL SOURCES: Custer, Elizabeth. *"Boots and Saddles," or Life in Dakota with General Custer.* 1885.

Hunt, Frazier, and Robert Hunt, eds. *I Fought with Custer.* 1947.

AHR, 52:799. "The story of Sergeant Windolph, last survivor of the Battle of the Little Big Horn, as told to the Hunts, with explanatory material and contemporary sidelights on the Custer fight."

Merington, Marguerite, ed. *Custer Story; the Life and Intimate Letters of George A. Custer and His Wife, Elizabeth.* 1950.

Sat. Rev. of Lit., 33:45, Mar. 11, 1950. These letters provide "a rare and unusual contribution to the basic data of America's military and social history—a wife's eye view of war and soldiering and a soldier's on-the-spot confidences to his wife."

BIOGRAPHY: Van de Water, F. F. *Glory Hunter, a Life of General Custer.* 1934.

Nation, 140:23, Jan. 2, 1935. "This is a book which ought to be in all libraries since it is the only authentic life of Custer and the only true account available of the relations of the army to the Indians."

Extract in Prochnow, H. V., ed. *Great Stories from Great Lives,* 377-78.

Utley, R. M. *Custer's Last Stand; with a Narration of Events Preceding and Following.* 1949.

COLLECTIVE BIOGRAPHY: Creel, George. *Sons of the Eagle,* 288-98.

Dustin, Fred, in *Mich. Hist. Mag.,* 30 (1946) :226-54.

Ghent, W. J., in *DAB,* 5:7.

Holbrook, S. H. "Phonies of the Old West," *Am. Merc.,* 68 (1949) :234-35.

Johnston, C. H. L. *Famous Cavalry Leaders,* (1908) :359-93.

SPECIAL ASPECTS: Appell, G. C. "In Defense of Custer," *Infantry Jour.*, 61 (1947) :69-70.

Britt, Albert. "Custer's Last Fight," *PHR*, 13 (1944) :12-20.

"Custer's Clay Feet," *Infantry Jour.*, 61 (1947) :50.

Smitter, Wessel. "Red Warrior Who Licked Custer," *Cornet*, 26 (1949) :117-20.

CHIEF JOSEPH— 1840-1904 —Master Strategist

BIOGRAPHY: Fee, C. A. *Chief Joseph: the Biography of a Great Indian.* 1936.

PHR, 6:294. A biography carefully written from documentary material which "clearly pictures the life of the Nez Percé chief, so earnest in his efforts to maintain peace, yet, ironically enough, known to posterity as the leader of one of the most formidable war bands in history."

Howard, H. A. *War Chief Joseph.* 1941.

PHR, 10:484. A popular biography which gives "a highly fictionized account of Joseph's early life." The Indian war "is handled strictly from the point of view of the soldiers and civilians who fought against the Nez Percé, with the result that it becomes a highly partisan account."

COLLECTIVE BIOGRAPHY: Blankenship, Russell. *And There Were Men,* (1942) :54-78.

Brady, C. T. *Northwestern Fights and Fighters,* 3-223.

Britt, Albert. *Great Indian Chiefs,* 249-74.

Eastman, C. A. *Indian Heroes and Great Chieftains,* (1918) : 194-212.

Ghent, W. J., in *DAB*, 10:218.

Sweetser, K. D. *Book of Indian Braves,* 105-31.

HISTORY: Haines, Francis. *Red Eagles of the Northwest: the Story of Chief Joseph and His People.* 1939.

PHR, 8:233. "An enthusiastic and perhaps a slightly rose-tinted description of the Nez Percé nation, past and present, with special attention to the Idaho Indian wars." Chapters 25 and 30 deal with "what is probably the most famous phase of Nez Percé history, the flight of Chief Joseph and White Bird and their followers in 1877, their pursuit by Federal troops, and the final dramatic events in the Bear Paw hills."

SPECIAL ASPECTS: Cobb, I. S. *Incredible Truth,* (1931) :229-42.

CRAZY HORSE—1844-1877—"The Greatest Military Genius of the Sioux Confederacy"

ORIGINAL SOURCES: Brininstool, E. A., ed. *Crazy Horse, the Invincible Oglala Sioux Chief: the "Inside Stories, by Actual*

Observers, of the Most Treacherous Deed Against a Great Indian Leader." 1949.

AHR, 55:708. Source material intended to show that Crazy Horse was unsurpassed as an Indian warrior and that he suffered most unjustly at the hands of the United States.

BIOGRAPHY: Sandoz, Mari. *Crazy Horse: the Strange Man of the Oglalas*. 1942.

Sat. Rev. of Lit., 26:20, Jan. 2, 1943. "A full-bodied and historically accurate book, which seems likely to remain the standard work on its subject. Competent research and skilled writing combine to make a most readable volume."

COLLECTIVE BIOGRAPHY: Ghent, W. J., in *DAB*, 4:530.

Johnston, C. H. L. *Famous Indian Chiefs*, 425-55.

SPECIAL ASPECTS: Smitter, Wessel. "Red Warrior Who Licked Custer," *Cornet*, 26 (1949) :117-20.

VALENTINE TRENT McGILLYCUDDY—
1849-1939—Surgeon, Engineer, Indian Agent

BIOGRAPHY: McGillycuddy, Julia E. *McGillycuddy, Agent: a Biography of Dr. Valentine T. McGillycuddy*. 1941.

PHR, 10:365. The readable biography of an outstanding Indian agent who came in contact with Sitting Bull, Calamity Jane, and Wild Bill Hickok.

MARTHA JANE CANARY—1850?-1903—"Calamity Jane"

COLLECTIVE BIOGRAPHY: Aikman, Duncan. *Calamity Jane and the Lady Wildcats*, 3-127.

Holbrook, S. L. *Little Annie Oakley and Other Rugged People*, 31-38.

Also in *Am. Merc.*, 64 (1947) :218-22.

Rogers, Cameron. *Gallant Ladies*, (1928) :345-63.

BIOGRAPHIES OF CONTEMPORARIES: Buel, J. W. *True Story of Wild Bill Hickok*, (1946) :85-96.

*HAMLIN GARLAND— 1860-1940 —Author

ORIGINAL SOURCES: Stone, Irving, and Richard Kennedy, eds. *We Speak for Ourselves*, 303-08.

---

* For a more complete bibliography see Spiller, et al. *Literary History of the United States*, 3 (1948) :526-28; *Current Biography*, (1940) :324-26.

Wagenknecht, E. C., ed. *When I Was a Child,* 337-41.

COLLECTIVE BIOGRAPHY: Van Doren, Carl. *Contemporary American Novelist, 1900-1920,* 38-83.

Williams, B. C. *Our Short Story Writers,* 182-99.

SPECIAL ASPECTS: Hazard, L. L. *Frontier in American Literature,* 261-68.

Hicks, Granville. *Great Tradition,* 131-63.

Muldoon, S. J. *Psychic Experiences of Famous People,* (1947): 14-16.

Taylor, W. F. *Economic Novel in America,* 148-83.

Van Doren, Carl. *American Novel,* 225-44.

JOHN ALBERT JOHNSON— 1861-1909 —Three Times Governor of Minnesota

BIOGRAPHY: Helmes, W. G. *John A. Johnson, the People's Governor.* 1949.

AHR, 55:637. A good biography of a country editor who became "a really great American governor."

COLLECTIVE BIOGRAPHY: Buck, S. J., in *DAB,* 10:104.

CHAPTER XL. THE SOUTHWEST

CHRISTOPHER CARSON— 1809-1868 —The Most Picturesque and Most Important of the Mountain Men

ORIGINAL SOURCES: Brewerton, G. D. *Overland with Kit Carson; a Narrative of the Old Spanish Trail in 1848.* 1930.

Bookman, 72:xx, Feb., 1931. Lt. Brewerton was a keen young man who rode over the old Spanish Trail with Carson. "His characterization of Kit Carson is very acute though it is glassed with hero-worship."

Quaife, M. M., ed. *Kit Carson's Autobiography.* (Lakeside Classics, 1935).

BIOGRAPHY: Campbell, W. S. *Kit Carson, the Happy Warrior of the Old West: a Biography.* 1928.

Sat. Rev. of Lit., 4:817, Apr. 28, 1928. Having obtained "considerable material" on Kit Carson, Mr. Campbell has produced "a racy narrative; picturesque, strong in local color, and admirably written."

Grant, B. C., ed. *Kit Carson's Own Story of his Life.* 1926.

Peters, D. W. C. *Life and Adventures of Kit Carson, the Nestor of the Rocky Mountains.* 1858.

COLLECTIVE BIOGRAPHY: Creel, George. *Sons of the Eagle,* 200-11.

Cathermole, E. G. *Famous Frontiersmen,* (1886) :349-96.

Ghent, W. J., in *DAB,* 3:530.

Gray, A. A. *Men Who Built the West,* (1945) :149-66.

Holbrook, S. H. *Little Annie Oakley and Other Rugged People,* 177-81.

Hunt, R. D. *California's Stately Hall of Fame,* 139-45.

Johnston, C. H. L. *Famous Scouts,* (1910) :181-210.

Peattie, D. C. *Journey into America,* (1943) :207-20.

HISTORY: Sabin, E. L. *Kit Carson Days, 1809-1868: Adventures in the Path of Empire.* 1914. Revised ed., 2 vols. 1935.

Springfield Republican, Oct. 15, 1914, p. 5; *PHR,* 5:379. Kit Carson "was a simple, illiterate, frontier character, possessing all the strength and many of the superstitions of the class to which he belonged." After traveling widely, interviewing people who knew his man and studying the writings of contemporaries, Mr. Sabin, "a born story writer," has produced an interesting and painstaking book about Kit Carson, the Mountain Men and the fur trade.

SPECIAL ASPECTS: Lyman, G. D. *The Saga of the Comstock Lode: Boom Days in Virginia City.* 1934.

New Repub., 79:354, Aug. 8, 1934. "The wealth of material on the Comstock fairly matches the fabulous riches of Sun Mountain in boom days, and Dr. Lyman has drawn from it at first hand to make a narrative of breadth, richness, and vigor."

GEORGE CROOK— 1829-1890 —Indian Fighter

ORIGINAL SOURCES: Bourke, J. G. *On the Border with Crook.* 1891.

Schmitt, M. F., ed. *General George Crook: His Autobiography.* 1946.

AHR, 52:146. Crook fought in the Civil War, but "is best known as an Indian fighter during the two decades after Appomattox." His autobiography ends in 1876, but Mr. Schmitt brings the story down to the General's death in 1890. Crook found fault with civilians and soldiers. "He did occasionally put in a kind word for the Indians and often worked fearlessly in their behalf."

COLLECTIVE BIOGRAPHY: Fieberger, G. L., in *DAB*, 4:563.

SPECIAL ASPECTS: Bloom, L. B. "Bourke on the Southwest," *N. M. Hist. Rev.*, 10 (1935) :1-35.

Bourke, J. G. "General Crook in the Indian Country," *Century*, 41 (1891) :643-60.

GERONIMO—   1829-1909   —Apache Warrior

ORIGINAL SOURCES: Davis, Britton, ed. *The Truth About Geronimo*. 1929.

AHR, 35:680. The editor was a cavalry officer on duty in Arizona in the early 1880's. His memoirs throw light on many obscure incidents in Geronimo's life.

Quaife, M. M., ed. *Truth About Geronimo by Britton Davis*. 1929.

Yale Rev., 19:431. "The title of his book is badly chosen, for 'the truth about Geronimo' has been well known, even to the general reader, since the publication in 1891 of John G. Bourke's 'On the Border with Crook,' and Mr. Davis's contribution to the subject is mainly corroborative; it effects no change in the general outline of the story and but very little in its details. He has told more 'truth about Geronimo,' and that is all."

Stone, Irving, and Richard Kennedy, eds. *We Speak for Ourselves*, 202-08.

COLLECTIVE BIOGRAPHY: Edwards, R. M. *American Indians of Yesterday*, (1948) :88.

Ghent, W. J., in *DAB*, 7:220.

Johnston, C. H. L. *Famous Indian Chiefs*, 398-409.

WILLIAM H. BONNEY— 1859-1881 —Billy the Kid

BIOGRAPHY: Burns, W. N. *Saga of Billy the Kid*. 1926.

N. Y. Times, Mar. 7, 1926, p. 10. "Mr. Burns apparently has gone over all the evidence, and he has written an exciting biography. So far as the facts go, those familiar with the data on the Kid's life will say the story is accurate in the main. Where the evidence conflicts, Mr. Burns gives both sides and indicates his preference. With the principal events of the Kid's life, however, Mr. Burns deals in straight-forward fashion, and the narrative is a stirring one."

Otero, M. A. *The Real Billy the Kid*. 1936.

N. Y. Times, Mar. 22, 1936, p. 8. "His aim, Mr. Otero says, has been to write a story, without embellishment, based entirely on fact. And this he has done competently, painstakingly collecting an immense amount of material, some of which has never been printed before, and dealing at great length with the Lincoln County War, which led to the Kid's capture and death."

Garrett, P. F. *Authentic Story of Billy the Kid.* 1882, 1946.

Siringo, C. A. *History of Billy the Kid.* 1920.

COLLECTIVE BIOGRAPHY: Cunningham, Eugene. *Triggernometry,* (1934) :129-70.

Dobie, J. F., in *Southwest Rev.,* 14 (1929) :314-20.

Ghent, W. J., in *DAB,* 2:271.

Lewis, Lloyd. *It Takes All Kinds,* 101-19.

HISTORY: McCarty, J. L. *Maverick Town: the Story of Old Tascosa.* 1946.

AHR, 52:807. These "colorful recollections of the vital days of this 'ghost town'" illustrate a significant "phase of American frontier life. . . ."

SPECIAL ASPECTS: Thorp, N. H. *Pardner of the Wind: Story of the Southwestern Cowboy,* (1945) :168-93.

Wecter, Dixon. *Hero in America,* 341-63.

CHAPTER XLI. CALIFORNIA

HENRY MEIGGS— 1811-1877 —"Builder of South American Railroads"

BIOGRAPHY: Stewart, Watt. *Henry Meiggs: Yankee Pizarro.* 1946.

AHR, 52:347. The story of a remarkable man—a lumber dealer in California—in the days of the gold rush, and a fugitive from justice and railroad builder in Chile and Peru.

COLLECTIVE BIOGRAPHY: Green, M. M. "South America's Railroad Builder," *Am. Merc.,* 54 (1942) :230-37.

Holmes, O. W., in *DAB,* 12:501.

Reynolds, M. G. "Henry Meiggs—the Man Who Wrestled with the Andes," *Pan. Am. Union Bul.,* 82 (1948) :460-62.

Stewart, Watt, and H. F. Peterson. *Builders of Latin America,* (1942) :245-57.

COLLIS PORTER HUNTINGTON— 1821-1900 —"The Ablest of the Big Four"

COLLECTIVE BIOGRAPHY: Daggett, Stuart, in *DAB,* 9:408.

Lewis, Oscar. *The Big Four,* 211-82.

HISTORY: Cleland, R. G. *History of California: The American Period,* 383-401.

HUBERT HOWE BANCROFT— 1832-1918 —"The Henry Ford of Literary Mass Production"

ORIGINAL SOURCES: Bancroft, H. H. *Literary Industries.* 1890.

BIOGRAPHY: Caughey, J. W. *Hubert Howe Bancroft, Historian of the West.* 1946.

PHR, 16:91. "A definitive biography. Caughey's book is exhaustive, sympathetic, scholarly, and refreshingly readable. . . . Caughey is altogether right in demanding the recognition of Bancroft for his great achievements and notable contributions; but his defense of Bancroft's methods will probably not win an unqualified verdict of acquittal for his client, though it may well result in a hung jury."

COLLECTIVE BIOGRAPHY: Caughey, J. W. "Hubert Howe Bancroft, Historian of Western America," *AHR,* 50 (1945) :461-70.

Hunt, R. D. *California's Stately Hall of Fame,* 399-403.

Knapp, F. A. J. "Two Contemporary Historians: José Maria Iglesias and Hubert Howe Bancroft," *Pac. Hist.,* 20 (1951) : 25-30.

Morris, W. A., in *DAB,* 1:570.

HISTORY: Walker, Franklin. *San Francisco's Literary Frontier,* 302-15.

SPECIAL ASPECTS: Cannon, C. L. *American Book Collectors and Collecting,* 96-102.

Hunt, R. D. "Hubert Howe Bancroft: His Work and His Methods," *Hist. Soc. of So. Calif. Pubs.,* 8 (1911) :158-73.

Kraus, Michael. *History of American History,* 573-96.

Langlois, C. V., and Charles Seignobos. *Introduction to the Study of History,* (1912) :19, 20, 22, 31.

Morris, W. A. "The Origin and Authorship of the Bancroft Pacific States Publications: a History of a History," *Ore. Hist. Quar.,* 4 (1903) :287-364.

BEN HOLLADAY—1819-1887—"The Most Important of Western Stagecoach Owners"

BIOGRAPHY: Frederick, J. V. *Ben Holladay, the Stagecoach King.* 1940.

AHR, 46:683; *PHR,* 9:481. A scholarly study of the man who put efficiency into the stagecoach business, and sold out before the coming of the railroads. Professor Frederick emphasizes the history of the business organization but scattered remarks and the final chapter give an impression of Holladay's dynamic personality.

COLLECTIVE BIOGRAPHY: Hafen, L. R., in *DAB,* 9:141.

Quiett, G. C. *They Built the West,* 339-99.

SPECIAL ASPECTS: Boyd, W. H. "Holladay-Villard Transportation Empire in the Pacific Northwest, 1868-1893," *PHR,* 15 (1946) :379-89.

SAMUEL BRANNAN— 1819-1889 —California Pioneer

BIOGRAPHY: Scherer, J. A. B. *The First Forty-Niner and the Story of the Golden Tea Caddy.* 1925.

COLLECTIVE BIOGRAPHY: Bieber, R. P., in *DAB,* 2:601.

Dickson, Samuel. *San Francisco is Your Home,* 13-21.

DeFord, M. A. *They Were San Franciscans,* (1941) :77-96.

Hunt, R. D. *California's Stately Hall of Fame,* 237-42.

THEODORE DEHONE JUDAH— 1826-1863 —Engineer and Railroad Builder

COLLECTIVE BIOGRAPHY: James, G. W. *Heroes of California,* (1910) :221-30.

Lewis, Oscar. *The Big Four,* 3-48.

Wheat, C. I., in *Cal. Hist. Soc. Quar.,* 4 (1925) :219-71.

HISTORY: Caughey, J. W. *California,* (1940) :426-33.

Daggett, Stuart. *Chapters on the History of the Southern Pacific.* 1922.

Am. Econ. Rev., 12:638. Professor Daggett gives "a very thorough presentation of the history of the railroad in its important aspects," including federal land grants and physical construction.

FRANCIS BRETT HARTE— 1836-1902 —Literary Genius or Fraud?

ORIGINAL SOURCES: Booth, B. A., ed. "Bret Harte Goes East: Some Unpublished Letters," *Amer. Lit.,* 19 (1948) :318-35.

*Harrison, J. B., ed. *Brett Harte: Representative Selections.* (American Writers, 1941) .

Amer. Lit., 13:436. "This is . . . the first anthology to give some idea of the full scope of Harte's work. . . . An elaborate introduction includes a resumé of Harte's life, and what is the fullest scholarly and critical discussion of his writing yet to appear. In general, it may be said that Professor Harrison is a defender both of Harte's work and of his character."

Harte, G. B. H., ed. *Letters of Brett Harte.* 1926.

Sat. Rev. of Lit., 2:717, Apr. 17, 1926. These letters, written mostly during his residence abroad, reveal an honest personality, struggling bravely against ill health and financial worries.

Howells, W. D. "Reminiscences of Bret Harte," *Overland,* 40 (1902) :220-39.

Howe, M. A. D. "Bret Harte and Mark Twain in the 'Seventies: Passages from the Diaries of Mrs. James T. Fields," *Atlantic,* 130 (1922) :341-48.

BIOGRAPHY: Merwin, H. C. *The Life of Bret Harte.* 1911.

Nation, 94:164, Feb. 15, 1912. Fails to explain Harte's baffling personality but maintains that he was a "truthful chronicler of early California."

Stewart, G. R., Jr. *Bret Harte, Argonaut and Exile.* 1931.

Amer Lit., 4:223. "An adequate biography . . . a masterly piece of scholarly research. The last chapter . . . is perhaps the fairest estimate of Harte that has thus far been written."

COLLECTIVE BIOGRAPHY: Brooks, Noah. "Bret Harte: a Biographical and Critical Sketch," *Overland,* 40 (1902) :201-07.

Bowen, E. W., in *Sewanee Rev.,* 24 (1916) :287-302.

Brooks, V. W. *The Times of Melville and Whitman,* 258-82.

Dam, H. J. W., in *McClure's,* 4 (1894) :38-50.

Elliott, S. R. "Glimpses of Bret Harte," *Read. Mag.,* 10 (1907) : 122-27.

Howells, W. D. *Literary Friends and Acquaintances,* 289-304.

Hudson, W. H., in *Library of the World's Best Literature,* 12: 6985-7013.

Hunt, R. B. *California's Stately Hall of Fame,* 357-62.

James, G. W., in *Overland,* 78 (1921) :11-18.

McCracken, J. C. "Reminiscences of Bret Harte and Pioneer

---

* For more complete bibliographies see Harrison, pp. cxiii-cxxv; Stewart, G. R., Jr. *Bret Harte, Argonaut and Exile,* (1931) :337-65; Spiller, et al. *Literary History of the United States,* 3 (1948) :542-44.

Days in the West," *Overland,* 66 (1915) :365-68; 67 (1916) : 7-15.

Mervin, H. C., in *Atlantic,* 90 (1902) :260-68.

Pattee, F. L., in *Cambridge History of American Literature,* 2: 377-81.

Russell, F. A. *American Pilgrimage,* 183-98.

Stewart, G. R., Jr., in *DAB,* 8:362.

HISTORY: Caughey, J. W. *California,* 345, 384, 396-404.

SPECIAL ASPECTS: Blair, Walter. *Native American Humor,* 129-33.

Brooks, Noah. "Bret Harte in California," *Century,* 58 (1899) : 447-51.

Canby, H. S. "Bret Harte's Tragedy," *Sat. Rev. of Lit.,* 18 (1932) :485-88.

Cheney, Warren. "Francis Bret Harte," *Overland* (new ser.), 1 (1883) :69-81.

Collins, J. P. "Bret Harte's Genius," *Nineteenth Century,* 170 (1924) :531-43.

Erskine, John. *Leading American Novelists,* 325-69.

Hazard, L. L. "Eden to Eldorado," *Univ. of Cal. Chronicle,* 35 (1933) :107-21.

———. *Frontier in American Literature,* 181-208.

Hicks, Granville. *Great Tradition,* 34-48.

Nadal, E. S. "Writings of Bret Harte," *No. Am. Rev.,* 124 (1877) :81-90.

Pattee, F. L. *Development of the American Short Story,* (1923) : 220-44.

———. *History of American Literature since 1870,* (1922) :63-82.

Quinn, A. H. *American Fiction,* (1936) :232-42.

Rourke, Constance. *American Humor,* 224-27.

Taylor, W. F. "The Fiction of Regionalism," in *History of American Literature,* (1936) :255-58.

Walker, F. D. *San Francisco's Literary Frontier,* (1939) :64-69, 106-09, 117-22, 213-17.

BIOGRAPHIES OF CONTEMPORARIES: Clemens, S. L. *Mark Twain in Eruption.* (1940) :261-92.

De Voto, Bernard. *Mark Twain's America.* (1935) :162-63, 191-92.

Mark Twain is said to have known Harte well and despised him heartily. He declared that he was a fraud as a man, a Westerner, and a writer.

JOHN MUIR—1838-1914—Old Man of the Mountain

ORIGINAL SOURCES: Muir, John. *Boyhood of a Naturalist.* (Riverside Lit., 1913) .

——. "Out of the Wilderness," *Atlantic Harvest,* (1947) :164-79.

——. *The Story of My Boyhood and Youth.* 1913.

Dial, 54:293, Apr. 1, 1913. This book emphasizes the sternly Puritanical treatment to which the boy was subjected in the hard pioneer days of early Wisconsin.

Also in *Atlantic,* 110 (1912) :577-87, 813-25; 111 (1913) :266-77.

Wolfe, L. M., ed. *John of the Mountains: the Unpublished Journals of John Muir.* 1938.

Amer. Lit., 10:502; Herald-Tribune *Books,* May 15, 1938, p. 1. Muir left sixty journals, "ranging in date from 1867 to 1911. . . . In addition to these journals *John of the Mountains* draws from 'a mass of notes scribbled upon loose sheets and bits of paper . . . largely devoted to an expression of his inmost thoughts upon nature and her transcendental meanings' . . ." The present volume follows its author over California and up to Alaska and shows him in his old age "as a national spokesman for the conservation of our wild places."

BIOGRAPHY: Bade, W. F. *Life and Letters of John Muir.* 1924.

Outlook, 139:32, Jan. 7, 1925. Professor Bade has rendered important service to lovers of nature in collecting new material and "weaving it into a sympathetic account of Muir's life."

Wolfe, L. M. *Son of the Wilderness: the Life of John Muir.* 1945.

Amer. Lit., 18:47. A eulogistic biography which gives "a meticulous account of the facts of Muir's life, but does not fully bring to life their essential motivating forces," or resolve the seeming contradiction between his romanticism and his scientific practise.

COLLECTIVE BIOGRAPHY: Bade, W. F., in *DAB,* 13:314.

Beard, A. E. S. *Our Foreign-Born Citizens,* 256-65.

Faris, J. T. *Men Who Conquered,* 135-49.

Hunt, R. D. *California's Stately Hall of Fame,* 369-74.

Osborn, H. F. *Impressions of Great Naturalists,* (1924) :227-50.

Parkman, M. R. *Heroes in America,* 1-28.

Tracy, H. C. *American Naturists,* (1930) :100-15.

Wyatt, E. F. *Great Companions,* (1917) :341-65.

SPECIAL ASPECTS: Brooks, V. W. *Chilmark Miscellany,* 245-54.

Foerster, Norman. *Nature in American Literature,* 238-63.

Freeman, Catherine, and Dick Freeman. "Wilderness Belongs to the People," *Natur. Hist.,* 55 (1946) :72-79.

Peattie, D. C. "Everybody Needs Beauty," *Read. Dig.,* 55(1949): 86-90.

Spiller, et al. *Literary History of the United States,* 2:873-74.

Young, S. H. *Alaska Days with John Muir.* 1915

Outlook, 110:931, Aug. 18, 1915. "Dr. Young's narrative is not only of absorbing interest but is of value for the light it throws upon the personality of the great naturalist and writer, John Muir."

*HENRY GEORGE— 1839-1897 —"America's Best Nominee for an International Economic Hall of Fame"

ORIGINAL SOURCES: Brown, H. G. *Significant Paragraphs from Henry George's Progress and Poverty.* 1928.

Post, Louis. *The Prophet of San Francisco: Personal Memories & Interpretations of Henry George.* 1930.

N. Y. Times, Feb. 1, 1931, p. 20. "An absorbingly interesting book about a remarkable man. . . . It was perhaps inevitable that the memories of such a friend and disciple should take the form of a more or less detailed narrative of Henry George's activities after his coming to New York and also of some considerable account of the progress of the movement he started."

Wagner, D. C., ed. *Social Reformers,* (1934) :463-85.

BIOGRAPHY: De Mille, Mrs. A. A. *Henry George, Citizen of the World.* 1950.

N. Y. Times, Apr. 16, 1950, p. 35. A biography by his daughter which makes clear why many people followed Henry George and voted for him, although they did not understand his *Progress and Poverty.*

George, Henry, Jr. *The Life of Henry George.* 1900.

Bookman, 12:621. A charming, "simply written narrative of the struggling printer and journalist." The portrait was drawn by his son, but with surprising objectiveness.

Nock, A. J. *Henry George: an Essay.* 1939.

---

* See Spiller, et al. *Literary History of the United States,* 3 (1948) :530-32.

N. Y. Times, Aug. 27, 1939, p. 4. "A penetrating estimate of the famous social philosopher."

COLLECTIVE BIOGRAPHY: Coleman, McAllister. *Pioneers of Freedom,* 109-22.

Colum, Padraic. "Heroes of Democracy," *Cath. World,* 164 (1946) :122-30.

De Casseres, Benjamin, in *Am. Merc.,* 23 (1931) :103-12.

Geiger, G. R. "The Forgotten Man: Henry George," *Antioch Rev.,* 1 (1941) :291-307.

Hunt, R. D. *California's Stately Hall of Fame,* 339-44.

James, G. W. *Heroes of California,* (1910) :401-16.

Madison, C. A. *Critics and Crusaders,* 257-84.

———. "Henry George, Prophet of Human Rights," *So. Atl. Quar.,* 43 (1944) :349-60.

Mitchell, Broadus, in *DAB,* 7:211.

Parrington, V. L. *Main Currents in American Thought,* 3:125-36.

Seitz, D. C. *Uncommon Americans,* 256-75.

Tarbell, I. M. "New Dealers of the Seventies," *Forum,* 92 (1934) :133-36.

HISTORY: Caughey, J. W. *California,* 533-37.

SPECIAL ASPECTS: Barker, C. A. "Henry George and the California Background of *Progress and Poverty,*" *Cal. Hist. Soc. Quar.,* 24 (1945) :97-114.

Dombrowski, James. *Early Days of Christian Socialism in America,* (1936) :35-49.

Dorfman, Joseph, III. *The Economic Mind in American Civilization, 1865-1918,* 3 (1949) :141-49.

Gabriel, R. H. *Course of American Democratic Thought,* 198-204, index.

Geiger, G. H. *The Philosophy of Henry George.* 1933.

Nation, 137:166, Aug. 9, 1933. "The author . . . has done more than substantiate the claims of Henry George to be considered among the first order of minds in economic inquiry. He has everywhere emphasized the ethical hopes that drove George onward. He has made a convincing plea for the return of ethical motives to economic scrutiny, for the re-entry of idealism into economic methods." Chapter two gives an entertaining and informative biographical sketch.

Harrison, Frederick. *National and Social Problems,* (1908) :366-408.

Hofstadter, R. I. *Darwinism in American Thought, 1860-1915,* 86-102.

Mott, F. L. *Golden Multitudes,* 165-71.

Teilhac, Ernest. *Pioneers of American Economic Thought in the 19th Century,* (1936) :114-74.

Schneider, H. W. *History of American Philosophy,* 193-207.

Werkmeister, W. H. *History of Philosophical Ideas in America,* 241-61.

*AMBROSE GWINETT BIERCE— 1842-1914?
—A Super-journalist—Not a Literary Creator

BIOGRAPHY: Fatout, Paul. *Ambrose Bierce: The Devil's Lexicographer.* 1951.

Herald-Tribune Bk. Rev., Aug. 26, 1951, p. 8. Since he disappeared into revolutionary Mexico in 1913, "the facts of Ambrose Bierce's life have been the subject of a surprising amount of curiosity on the part of biographers and critics. . . . He was an uncommonly colorful and controversial character, a journalist, who for more than a third of a century" waged continuous and violent warfare in various San Francisco journals. "Mr. Fatout's book does full justice to his picturesque, irascible, and highly contentious subject." He "contends that the obvious contradictions in Bierce's nature mainly sprang from the fact that he was never able to free himself from the teachings of his Calvinistic childhood and that this accounts for much of the inner turmoil of his later years. . . ." Unfortunately the author throws "no additional light on the mystery of Bierce's final disappearance."

McWilliams, Carey. *Ambrose Bierce: a Biography.* 1929.

Current History, 8:8a. Mr. McWilliams, in a sound and scholarly book, sheds bright light on Bierce's eccentric personality and on his heroic literary career, tracing the record down to Bierce's still unexplained disappearance somewhere in war-torn Mexico."

Walker, Franklin. *Ambrose Bierce: the Wickedest Man in San Francisco.* 1941.

PHR, 10:387. A resumé of Bierce's life from his Ohio boyhood to his mysterious disappearance in Mexico with emphasis on his newspaper wars in San Francisco. Professor Walker maintains that "Bierce the satirist was a pure opportunist, with neither program nor principle: 'the role of devil's advocate suited him so well that he never again was able to dis-

---

* See Spiller, et al. *Literary History of the United States,* 3 (1948) :404-06.

card it.' . . . Mr. Walker has done an excellent little volume, at once accurate and entertaining."

COLLECTIVE BIOGRAPHY: Cooper, F. T. *Some American Story Tellers*, (1911) :331-53.

Hunt, R. D. *California's Stately Hall of Fame*, 423-28.

Josephson, Matthew. *Portrait of the Artist as American*, 139-98.

Monaghan, Frank, in *DAB*, 2:252.

Russell, F. A. *American Pilgrimage*, 99-118.

HISTORY: Walker, Franklin. *San Francisco's Literary Frontier*, 237-55, index.

SPECIAL ASPECTS: Boynton, P. H. *More Contemporary Americans*, 75-93.

Dickson, Samuel. *San Francisco is Your Home*, 179-85.

Fadiman, Clifton. "Portrait of a Misanthrope," *Sat. Rev. of Lit.*, 29:11-13, Oct. 12, 1946.

Hicks, Granville. *Great Tradition*, 131-63.

Littell, Robert. *Read America First*, (1926) :183-88.

Snell, G. D. *Shapers of American Fiction*, 78-104.

EDWARD HENRY HARRIMAN—   1848-1909
—Railroad Executive

BIOGRAPHY: Kennan, George. *E. H. Harriman*. 2 vols. 1922.

AHR, 28:166. Harriman is pictured as a great railroad builder hampered at every turn by demagogues.

Lovett, R. A. *Forty Years After; an Appreciation of the Genius of Edward Henry Harriman (1848-1909), Financier, Railroad Builder and Strategist, Industrial Statesman of One Epoch and Prophet of a New*. 1949.

COLLECTIVE BIOGRAPHY: Dixon, F. H., in *DAB*, 8:296.

Quiett, G. C. *They Built the West*, 339-99.

Wildman, Edwin. *Famous Leaders of Industry*, 2nd ser., (1921): 135-44.

SPECIAL ASPECTS: Grayson, T. J. *Leaders and Periods of American Finance*, 443-70.

LUTHER BURBANK— 1849-1926 —Experimenter
With Plant Life

BIOGRAPHY: Beaty, J. Y. *Luther Burbank, Plant Magician*. 1943.

Howard, W. L. *Luther Burbank, a Victim of Hero Worship*. 1946.

N. Y. Times, Sept. 15, 1946, p. 45. "Dr. Howard has performed a public service in defending Burbank's fame while chopping down the tall tales about him. Though he has less literary skill than many who have written about Burbank, his work as a whole towers above that of all of the others."

COLLECTIVE BIOGRAPHY: Bridges, T. C., and H. H. Tilton. *Master Minds of Modern Science*, (1931) :48-59.

Fox, D. R., and A. M. Schlesinger, eds. *Cavalcade of America*, 229-45.

Hagedorn, Hermann. *Americans*, 63-86.

Hylander, C. J. *American Scientists*, 106-22.

Kellogg, Vernon, in *DAB*, 3:265.

Law, F. H. *Modern Great Americans*, 22-36.

SPECIAL ASPECTS: Meyer, H. H., in Lotz, P. H., ed. *Vocations and Professions*, (1940) :1-12

Snyder, Mrs. E. E. *Biology in the Making*, (1940) :162-74.

JOHN HAYS HAMMOND— 1855-1936 —Mining Engineer

ORIGINAL SOURCES: *The Autobiography of John Hays Hammond*. 2 vols. 1936.

Sat. Rev. of Lit., 11:597, Apr. 6, 1935. A readable narrative of a business man who saw history at first hand; met hundreds of people from Mexican bandits to George V.

SEVENTH GENERATION, 1901-1933

CHAPTER XLII. NEW ENGLAND

OLIVER WENDELL HOLMES— 1841-1935 —The Great Dissenter

ORIGINAL SOURCES: Cohen, F. S., ed. "Holmes-Cohen Correspondence," *Jour. Hist. Ideas,* 9 (1948) :3-52.

Holmes, O. W. *Justice Holmes to Doctor Wu; an Intimate Correspondence, 1921-1932.* 1947.

——. "Twisting the Tail of the Cosmos; Musings from Private Letters," *Sat. Rev. of Lit.,* 31:8-9, May 8, 1948.

Howe, M. A. D., ed. *Touched with Fire: Civil War Letters and Diary of Oliver Wendell Holmes, Jr., 1861-1864.* 1946.

AHR, 53:629. The matters mentioned in these documents "are mostly trivial, and reveal, as the editor suggests, that the Civil War meant more to Holmes in retrospect than it did in action."

James, Henry. "Letters of Henry Adams to Mr. Justice Holmes," *Yale Rev.,* 38 (1949) :410-33.

Lerner, Max, ed. *The Mind and Faith of Justice Holmes: His Speeches, Essays, Letters, and Judicial Opinions.* 1943.

AHR, 49:457. A "thoughtful summary of Holmes's career and personality. . . ." These documents allow the reader to see the famous liberal from all sides. The author explains "why some able lawyers do not consider Holmes a great judge."

Perry, R. B., ed. "Common Enemy; Early Letters of Oliver Wendell Holmes, Jr., and William James," *Atlantic Harvest,* (1947) :647-60.

BIOGRAPHY: Biddle, Francis. *Mr. Justice Holmes.* 1942.

Sat. Rev. of Lit., 26:15, Jan. 9, 1943. "This sketch, in twelve chapters of the life and works of Mr. Justice Holmes is an exceptionally delightful, balanced, and interesting book. . . . The author, the distinguished Attorney-General of the United States, has maintained a fine balance between the anecdotal and other personal touches which enliven the book and the marshalling of the essential facts concerning Holmes's legal writing, judicial opinions and other activities."

Extract in Prochnow, H. V., ed. *Great Stories from Great Lives,* 35-37.

COLLECTIVE BIOGRAPHY: Allen, Devere. *Adventurous Americans,* 18-37.

Carnegie, Dale. *Dale Carnegie Biographical Roundup,* 103-09.

Cooper, A. C., and C. A. Palmer. *Twenty Modern Americans,* 365-81.

Cottler, Joseph. *Champions of Democracy,* 179-204.

Frankfurter, Felix, in *DAB,* 21 (sup. 1) :417.

Hagedorn, Hermann. *Americans,* 19-40.

Seagle, William. *Men of Law: from Hammurabi to Holmes,* (1947) :331-55.

Sergeant, E. S. *Fire Under the Andes,* 307-31.

——, in Beckwith and Coope, eds. *Contemporary American Biography,* 55-68.

Thomas and Thomas. *Fifty Great Americans,* 258-67.

——. *Living Biographies of Famous Americans,* 247-60.

SPECIAL ASPECTS: Brogan, D. W. *American Themes,* 166-74.

Cardozo, B. N., in Bryant, M. M., comp. *Essays Old and New,* (1940) :258-65.

Cohen, M. R. *Law and Social Order,* (1933) :198-218.

——. *Faith of a Liberal,* (1933) :20-31

Dewey, John. *Characters and Events,* (1929) :100-06.

Frankfurter, Felix. *Law and Politics,* 61-87.

——, in Thornton, J. E., comp. *Science and Social Change,* (1939) :441-61.

Garraty, J. A. "Holmes's Appointment to the U. S. Supreme Court," *N. E. Quar.,* 22 (1949) :291-303.

Laski, H. J. *Danger of Being a Gentleman,* (1940) :249-70.

——. *Studies in Law and Politics,* (1932) :146-62.

Lavery, Emmett, "Justice Holmes and Canon Sheehan," *Cath. World,* 172 (1950) :13-19.

Le Duc, A. S., "Man Who Rescued the Captain," *Atlantic,* 180 (1947) :80-86.

Levy, B. H. *Our Constitution: Tool or Testament,* (1941) :111-76.

Seagle, William, "The Significance of Justice Holmes," *So. Atl. Quar.,* 44 (1945) :154-64.

Smith, T. V. *Creative Skeptics,* (1934) : 177-228.

——, in Perry, C. M., ed. *Philosophy of American Democracy,* (1943) :119-52.

Wiener, P. P. *Evolution and the Founders of Pragmatism,* 172-89.

HENRY CABOT LODGE—   1850-1924
—Wilson's Nemesis

ORIGINAL SOURCES: Lodge, H. C. *Early Memories.* 1913.

Yale Rev., 3:814. Reminiscences of his life before he entered politics. The book is valuable for its estimate of Charles Sumner and the evaluation of Parkman as historian.

BIOGRAPHY: Lawrence, William. *Henry Cabot Lodge.* 1925.

N. Y. Times, May 24, 1925, p. 3. "Bishop Lawrence's book is in many respects a model short biography. He writes with vigor and forthrightness. . . . But, naturally the main interest in any life of Lodge is the story of his political antagonism to Woodrow Wilson and the League of Nations. On this point the Bishop is hardly likely to satisfy impartial opinion. This biography's chief merit is that it is the well-informed personal record of an intimate friend."

Schriftgiesser, Karl. *Gentleman from Massachusetts: Henry Cabot Lodge.* 1944.

Wk. Bk. Rev., Sept. 10, 1944, p. 1. Mr. Schriftgiesser is obviously no great admirer of Lodge, but he has written with a quiet restraint that makes his book all the more deadly. It is as searing a biography as has appeared in this country in years."

COLLECTIVE BIOGRAPHY: Munro, W. B., in *DAB,* 11:346.

ELIHU THOMSON—   1853-1937
—"Beloved Scientist"

BIOGRAPHY: Woodbury, D. O. *Beloved Scientist, a Guiding Spirit of the Electrical Age.* 1944.

AHR, 50:301. "*Beloved Scientist* is the story of a self-made scientist who evolved from a questioning experimenting boy into a high school teacher and later 'a guiding Spirit of the Electrical Age' during momentous decades. Problems in any field of science presented an alluring challenge to Elihu Thomson, for his broad interest embraced astronomy and geology and biology as well as chemistry and physics. He was, moreover, graciously endowed with a spirit and manner which won him the title 'Beloved.' "

COLLECTIVE BIOGRAPHY: Dunlap, O. E. *Radio's 100 Men of Science,* 106-09.

JOHN LAWRENCE SULLIVAN— 1858-1918
—"Boston's Strong Boy"

ORIGINAL SOURCES: Sullivan, J. L. *Life and Reminiscences of a 19th Century Gladiator.* 1892.

BIOGRAPHY: Dibble, R. F. *John L. Sullivan.* 1925.

Fleischer, N. S. *John L. Sullivan: Champion of Champions.* 1951.

Herald Tribune Bk. Rev., Aug. 26, 1951, p. 12. The best biography of "the greatest heavy-weight fighter in the world from 1882 to 1892."

COLLECTIVE BIOGRAPHY: Inglis, W. O., in *DAB,* 18:193.

———. *Champions Off Guard,* (1932) :18-108.

SPECIAL ASPECTS: Brisbane, Arthur, in Greene, Ward, ed. *Star Reporters,* (1948) :34-45.

Fleischer, N. S. *Heavyweight Championship,* (1949) :77-103.

Rice, Harold. *Within the Ropes, Champions in Action,* (1946) : 30-58.

Woolf, S. J. "New Yorkers: a Gallery of Memories," *N. Y. Times Mag.,* July 25, 1948, p. 11.

CARRIE CHAPMAN CATT— 1859-1947 —Feminist

BIOGRAPHY: Peck, M. G. *Carrie Chapman Catt: a Biography.* 1944.

Sat. Rev. of Lit., 27:22, Aug. 26, 1944. "It is difficult to write the biography of a living person, especially of a friend. Miss Peck is to be congratulated on the well-written, authoritative, and entertaining history she has evolved from a vast amount of documentary material and her own close association and knowledge."

COLLECTIVE BIOGRAPHY: Adams, Mildred, in *Nation,* 164:330-31, Mar. 22, 1947.

Allen, Devere, ed. *Adventurous Americans,* 165-78.

Burnett, C. B., in Stoddard, A. G., ed. *Topflight Famous American Women,* (1946) :179-97.

WILBUR LUCIUS CROSS— 1862-1948
—"Uncle Toby": "A Yankee in the Franklin Tradition"

ORIGINAL SOURCES: Cross, W. L. *Connecticut Yankee; an Autobiography.* 1943.

Wkly. Bk. Rev., Oct. 17, 1943, p. 1. Wilbur L. Cross has written an interesting book about his unusual life. He taught English at Yale, and was the editor of the *Yale Review* who revived that almost defunct magazine. After retiring at the age of 68, he was governor of Connecticut for eight years.

COLLECTIVE BIOGRAPHY: Devane, W. C., and others. "Wilbur L. Cross, 1862-1948," *Yale Rev.*, 38 (1949) :341.

Woolf, S. J. *Drawn from Life*, 106-15.

GAMALIEL BRADFORD—   1863-1932
—Compassionate Biographer

ORIGINAL SOURCES: Brooks, V. W., ed. *The Letters of Gamaliel Bradford, 1918-1931.* 1934.

Amer. Lit., 6:482. "A large portion of the letters are addressed to scholars like Perry Bliss and Garland Greever and to authors as different as Robert Frost and H. L. Mencken. *The Letters* form an admirable complement to the published *Journal.* In particular, they reveal Bradford as an excellent literary critic."

———. *The Journal of Gamaliel Bradford, 1883-1932.* 1933.

Amer. Lit., 6:233. "There are numerous passages which reflect Bradford's feeling about the subjects of his biographical sketches."

COLLECTIVE BIOGRAPHY: Britt, Albert. *Great Biographers*, 183-218.

Carver, George. *Alms for Oblivion*, 278-86.

Genzmer, G. H., in *DAB*, 2:556.

Longaker, J. M. *Contemporary Biography*, (1934) :67-87.

SPECIAL ASPECTS: Beach, J. W. *Outlook for American Prose*, (1926) :21-60.

Hough, L. H. *Vital Control*, (1934) :39-68.

WILLIAM LYON PHELPS—   1865-1943
—Educator and Literary Critic

ORIGINAL SOURCES: Barber, F. H. *Fellow of Infinite Jest; Recollections and Anecdotes of William Lyon Phelps.* 1950.

Phelps, W. L. *Autobiography with Letters.* 1939.

Booklist, 35:268, Apr. 15, 1939. "The life story of Yale's well-liked professor is sincere and provides pleasant . . . reading. He writes in an informal manner including some anecdotes and a great deal of appreciative comment on the drama. It is evident that as a teacher, writer, lecturer, traveller, and sports enthusiast, he has always enjoyed life and people. Parts of the book consist of letters from famous people. The book is too long, but it will be enjoyed by admirers throughout the country."

Stone, Irving, and Richard Kennedy, eds. *We Speak for Ourselves*, 227-73.

SPECIAL ASPECTS: Reilly, J. J. *Of Books and Men*, (1942) :51-59.

*EDWIN ARLINGTON ROBINSON— 1869-1935
—Poet

ORIGINAL SOURCES: Fussell, E. S. "Robinson to Moody: Ten Unpublished Letters," *Amer. Lit.*, 23 (1951) :173-87.

Robinson, E. A., in Farrar, J. C., ed. *Literary Spotlight*, 116-24.

Sutcliffe, Denham, ed. *Untriangulated Stars; Letters to Harry de Forest Smith, 1890-1905*. 1947.

N. E. Quar., 21:111. "The letters are not only a psychograph of Robinson, the poet. They are also another significant testimonial to the struggle of the artist in America, as they suggest antiphonally Robinson's firm refusal to compromise with the literary fashions of the period, and his resultant long probation. Thus, they are a symbolic unit, not only for Robinson scholars and enthusiasts, but for anyone concerned with the creative efforts in a materialistic culture."

BIOGRAPHY: Bates, E. W. *Edwin Arlington Robinson and His Manuscripts*. (Colby College Monographs, 1944.)

N. E. Quar., 17:323. An address by Robinson's chief copyist. It sheds light "upon Robinson's determined effort to establish himself as a dramatist. Her account of the poet's habits in preparation and revision of his manuscript is naturally important also."

Hagedorn, Hermann. *Edwin Arlington Robinson: a Biography*. 1938.

Books, Oct. 30, 1938, p. 7. "Granting Mr. Hagedorn's accuracy in dealing with the dates and the obvious facts of E. A. Robinson's career, his book has the character of a novel in which the central figure is made visible through the lives of those around him. In this respect Mr. Hagedorn's book is successful, and his oblique portrait of E. A. Robinson will, I think, remain invaluable to other and future biographers of more sharply defined critical insight, of greater social and psychological penetration or perhaps to a more direct and definitive study of the poet's life and work. The peculiar value of this book lies in the fact that it is a source book of the environment out of which Robinson wrote his poetry."

Neff, Emery. *Edwin Arlington Robinson*. (American Men of Letters, 1948).

---

* See also Spiller, et al. *Literary History of the United States*, 3 (1948) :705-08.

Sat. Rev. of Lit., 31:12, Nov. 13, 1948. The biography of one of America's greatest poets and of his almost superhuman struggle to keep alive while awaiting recognition. The book is a rare success in blending biography, literary criticism, and an account of the reception of Robinson's work.

Redman, B. R. *Edwin Arlington Robinson.* (Modern American Writers, 1927) .

Bookman, 64:628, Jan., 1927. "A pleasant estimate of the great poet. By pleasant, I do not mean that it is a good piece of work. It is the best estimate of Robinson that has been done, yet it lacks that deep sense of Robinson's New England character which will some day be present in a life."

Winters, Yvor. *Edwin Arlington Robinson.* 1947.

New Yorker, 22:98, Feb. 8, 1947. "In every way, the best analysis of Robinson yet written. Winters scrutinizes Robinson's technique and background sensitively but firmly, and the result is a clarification of Robinson's virtues and weaknesses that should be of great assistance to those who have found the poet dry and impenetrable."

COLLECTIVE BIOGRAPHY: Boynton, P. H. *Some Contemporary Americans,* 16-32.

Brooks, V. W. *New England: Indian Summer,* 491-519.

Ledoux, L. V., in *DAB,* 21 (sup. 1) :632.

Maynard, Theodore, *Our Best Poets,* (1922) :153-68.

Mims, Edwin. *Christ of the Poets,* (1948) :222-24.

Squire, J. C. *Contemporary American Authors,* 121-48.

Whipple, T. K. *Spokesmen,* 45-69.

Wood, Clement. *Poets of America,* (1925) :119-41.

SPECIAL ASPECTS: Beach, J. W. *Concept of Nature in Nineteenth Century English Poetry,* (1936) :522-46.

Cestre, Charles. *An Introduction to Edwin Arlington Robinson.* 1930.

Bookman, 72:192, Oct., 1930. "For those thousands of readers to whom Robinson 'needs no introduction,' the most valuable part of this book will be the chapter on the poet's treatment of the Arthurian legend. Here Professor Cestre stands stoutly against much expert opinion, and he has said things in praise of Merlin, Lancelot, and Tristram that will have to be carefully considered by every serious student of Robinson's work."

Cowley, Malcolm. "Edwin Arlington Robinson: Defeat and Triumph," *New Repub.,* 119:26-30, Dec. 16, 1948.

Crowder, Richard. "Emergence of E. A. Robinson," *So. Atl. Quar.*, 45 (1946) :89-98.

———. "E. A. Robinson's Craftsmanship: Opinions of Contemporary Poets," *Mod. Lang. Notes*, 61 (1946) :1-14.

Drinkwater, John. *Muse in Council*, (1925) :248-62.

Gorman, H. S. *Procession of Masks*, (1923) :15-39.

Gregory, Horace, and M. A. Zaturenska. *History of American Poetry, 1900-1940*, (1946) :107-32.

Hicks, Granville, *Great Tradition*, 207-56.

Isaacs, L. M. "E. A. Robinson Speaks of Music," *N. E. Quar.*, 22 (1949) :499-510.

Jones, Llewellyn. *First Impressions*, (1925) :13-36.

Kaplan, Estelle. *Philosophy in the Poetry of Edwin Arlington Robinson*. 1940.

New Repub., 103:126, July 22, 1940. "An earnest, electric piece, stressing Robinson's preoccupation with fate and faith, his transcendentalism and his love of truth. It shows the poet blowing a trumpet of hope in an orchestra of disillusionment."

Loggins, Vernon. *I Hear America*, 33-70.

Lowell, Amy. *Poetry and Poets*, (1930) :210-32.

———. *Tendencies in Modern Poetry*, (1927) :3-75.

Monroe, Harriet. *Poets and Their Art*, (1932) 1-11.

Morris, L. R. *The Poetry of Edwin Arlington Robinson: an Essay in Appreciation*. 1923.

Bookman, 57:464, June, 1923. This book is "a comprehensive appraisal of all Robinson's work since his first slim volume of verse."

Munson, G. B. *Destinations*, (1928) :57-66.

Untermeyer, Louis. *American Poetry Since 1900*, (1923) :42-66.

Wells, H. W. *American Way of Poetry*, (1943) :89-105.

Zabel, M. D. *Literary Opinions in America*, (1937) :397-406.

CALVIN COOLIDGE—   1872-1933
—"A Study in Inertia"

ORIGINAL SOURCES: Thompson, C. W. *Presidents I've Known*, 345-86.

BIOGRAPHY: White, W. A. *A Puritan in Babylon: the Story of Calvin Coolidge*. 1938.

AHR, 45:427. "Whatever its defects as either history or biography, this work has real values which appear when Mr. White draws on his personal store of Washington experiences to point up the Coolidge decade. His journalistic friends have lent him data to refresh his memory. His political friends have written and told him things, sometimes off the record." His assistant worked through the Taft papers in the Library of Congress.

Extract in Prochnow, H. V., ed. *Great Stories from Great Lives,* 108-20.

COLLECTIVE BIOGRAPHY: Booth, E. T. *Country Life in America,* 228-45.

Bradford, Gamaliel. *The Quick and the Dead,* 221-58.

Dulles, F. R. *Twentieth Century America,* 287-309.

Gardiner, A. G. *Portraits and Portents,* (1926) :12-21.

Hathaway, E. V. *Book of American Presidents,* 321-39.

Levin, P. R. *Seven by Chance,* 231-62.

Lowry, E. G. *Washington Close-ups,* 23-33.

Merz, Charles. "The Silent Mr. Coolidge," *New Repub.,* 47:51-54, June 2, 1926.

Nevins, Allan, in *DAB,* 21 (sup. 1) :191.

Tucker, R. T. *Mirrors of 1932* (1931) :55-74.

Wildman, Edwin. *Famous Leaders,* 327-40.

SPECIAL ASPECTS: Bliven, Bruce. "The Great Coolidge Mystery," *Harper's,* 152 (1925) :45-53.

Bradford, Gamaliel. "The Genius of the Average, Calvin Coolidge," *Atlantic,* 145 (1930) :1-13.

Brogan, D. W. *American Themes,* 106-09.

Bulow, W. J. "When Calvin Coolidge Came to Visit Us," *Sat. Eve. Post,* 219:22-23, Jan. 4, 1947.

Clapper, O. E. *Washington Tapestry,* 69-78.

Dennis, A. P. *Gods and Little Fishes,* 118-74.

Frank, W. D. *In the American Jungle,* (1937) :45-48.

Kent, F. R. "Assailing the President," *Forum,* 77 (1927) :14-21. Also in *Read. Dig.,* 5 (1927) :642-44.

Lippmann, Walter. *Men of Destiny,* 10-17.

Perling, J. J. *Presidents' Sons,* 292-300.

Pollard, J. E. *Presidents and the Press,* 713-33.

Slosson, P. W. "Calvin Coolidge: His Place in History," *Cur. Hist.,* 33 (1930) :1-6.

Starling, E. W. *Starling of the White House,* 204-81.

Stone, Irving, in Leighton, Isabel, ed. *Aspirin Age, 1919-1941,* 130-51.

White, W. A. *Masks in a Pageant,* 435-60

Whiting, E. E. "What the Coolidge Administration Has Accomplished," *Forum,* 77 (1927) :10-13.

Also in *Read. Dig.,* 5 (1927) :641-42.

Wish, Harvey. *Contemporary America,* 358-82.

Woolf, S. J. *Drawn from Life,* 42-50.

Young, K. H., and Lamar Middleton. *Heirs Apparent,* 257-69.

*AMY LOWELL— 1874-1925 —Stogies and Sonnets

ORIGINAL SOURCES: MacNair, H. F., ed. *Florence Ayscough and Amy Lowell; Correspondence of a Friendship.* 1946.

BIOGRAPHY: Damon, S. F. *Amy Lowell: a Chronicle, with Extracts from Her Correspondence.* 1935.

Amer. Lit., 8:105. "The most notable biography yet written of a recent American author. It is based upon adequate materials, and it is well proportioned and admirably written. It gives the reader not only a vivid impression of Miss Lowell's striking personality but many revealing glimpses of other poets both English and American."

COLLECTIVE BIOGRAPHY: Brooks, V. W. *New England: Indian Summer,* 520-43.

Lowes, J. L., in *DAB,* 11:453.

Maynard, Theodore. *Our Best Poets,* (1922) :194-215.

Sergeant, E. S. *Fire Under the Andes,* 11-32.

Untermeyer, Louis, in Balch, Marston, ed. *Modern Short Biographies,* 194-211.

Wood, Clement. *Poets of America,* 214-28.

SPECIAL ASPECTS: Boynton, P. H. *Some Contemporary Americans,* 72-88.

Cargill, Oscar. *Intellectual America,* 176-310.

Collins, Joseph. *Taking the Literary Pulse,* (1924) :48-72.

Farrar, J. C., ed. *Literary Spotlight,* 51-64.

Gregory, Horace, and M. A. Zaturenska. *History of American Poetry,* 182-91.

Hicks, Granville. *Great Tradition,* 207-56.

---

* See also Spiller, et al. *Literary History of the United States,* 3 (1948) :626-28.

Hughes, Glenn. *Imagism and the Imagists,* (1931) :197-223.

Loggins, Vernon. *I Hear America,* 71-112

Lowes, J. L. *Essays in Appreciation,* (1936) :157-74.

Monroe, Harriet. *Poets and Their Art,* (1932) :78-85.

Phelps, W. L. *Advance of English Poetry in the Twentieth Century,* (1918) :245-76.

Untermeyer, Louis. *American Poetry Since 1900,* (1923) : 135-56.

CHAPTER XLIII. NEW YORK AND NEW JERSEY

ELIHU ROOT—　　　　　　　　　　　　　　　1845-1937
　　—Roosevelt's Preference for His Successor!

BIOGRAPHY: Jessup, P. C. *Elihu Root.* 2 vols. 1938.

AHR, 45:673. "Jessup leaves no doubt of the influence of Elihu Root upon public policy or of the high quality of his statesmanship. Jessup's own legal training fitted him admirably to portray the logical and lucid quality of Root's mind. His thoroughness gives his work an unusually definitive character. He not only had access to Root's voluminous and valuable collection of papers but to Root himself through much of the period of preparation. . . . Jessup happily combines respect for and understanding of Root with a critical spirit. . . . Root's lack of social conscience and moral sensibility and the limitations of his class outlook prevented his great ability and force of character from making him a statesman of the first order. The failure of an otherwise excellent study to perceive this does not deprive Jessup's work of rank among the great American biographies."

COLLECTIVE BIOGRAPHY: Auerback, J. S. *The Bar of Other Days,* (1940) :221-24.

Gilbert, C. W. *Mirrors of Washington,* 163-80.

Law, F. H. *Modern Great Americans,* 220-33.

Woolf, S. J. *Drawn from Life,* 205-13.

HISTORY: Sullivan, Mark. *Our Times,* 3:9f, 120f, 278-81.

SPECIAL ASPECTS: Beck, J. M. *May It Please the Court,* (1930) : 136-47.

Butler, N. M. *Is America Worth Saving?* (1920) :183-94.

THOMAS ALVA EDISON— 1847-1931
—"The Wizard of Menlo Park"

ORIGINAL SOURCES: Runes, D. D., ed. *Diary and Sundry Observations*. 1948.

N. Y. Times, May 2, 1948, p. 5. The diary, that runs only from July 12 to July 21, 1885, is the most interesting document in the volume. It shows that "Edison was an avid but unsystematic reader." He says deafness "probably drove me to reading." He regarded this as a boon—it helped him to concentrate on problems. It even aided his courtship—he taught his sweetheart the Morse code, and his proposal was made and accepted in that code. Edison is most fascinating when talking of how he thought of his inventions. "The personality of an eager, creative man stands out on every page."

BIOGRAPHY: Simonds, W. A. *Edison, His Life, His Work, His Genius*. 1934.

N. Y. Times, Dec. 2, 1934, p. 11. "An intimate study of Edison's entire life, beginning with his inheritance and the background of his grandparents in Canada. The narrative of his long laboratory years is filled with anecdotes which throw new light upon the inventor's unique character and enquiring mind."

COLLECTIVE BIOGRAPHY: Bolton, S. K. *Famous Men of Science*, 195-208.

Bradford, Gamaliel. *The Quick and the Dead,* 79-111.

Burlingame, Roger, in *DAB,* 21 (sup. 1) :277.

———. *Inventors Behind the Invention,* (1947) :144-211.

Coakley, J. C. F. "Thomas Edison's 102 Years," *Pub. Utilities,* 43:156-59, Feb. 3, 1949.

Croffut, W. A. *American Procession,* 294-303.

Dunlap, O. E. *Radio's 100 Men of Science,* (1944) :79-84.

Hagedorn, Hermann. *Americans,* 41-61.

Henderson, Archibald. *Contemporary Immortals,* 1-23.

Hylander, C. J. *American Inventors,* 158-73.

Kennelly, A. E. "Thomas A. Edison, Inventor," *Elec. Engr.,* 66 (1947) :113-17.

Kettering, C. F., in *Sci. Mo.,* 64 (1947) :109-16.

Law, F. H. *Civilization Builders,* 171-75, 232-39.

———. *Modern Great Americans,* 92-105.

Matschoss, Conrad. *Great Engineers,* 314-32.

Morris, Charles. *Heroes of Progress in America,* 301-08.

Thomas and Thomas. *Fifty Great Americans,* 294-302.

———. *Life Stories of the Great Inventors,* (1948) :201-14.

———. *Living Biographies of Famous Americans,* 203-15.

Wildman, Edwin. *Famous Leaders of Industry,* 1st ser., (1920) : 115-27.

SPECIAL ASPECTS: Abrams, E. R. "Inquisitive Thomas Edison," *Pub. Utilities,* 39:134-42, Jan. 30, 1947.

Bush, Vennever. *Endless Horizons,* (1946) :146-50.

Chesterton, G. K. *Generally Speaking,* (1946) :14-20.

Farrar, L. D. "Philosophy of Thomas A. Edison," *Pub. Util.,* 39:200-09, Feb. 13, 1947.

Forbes, B. C. *Men Who are Making America,* 93-104.

Glenister, S. H. *Stories of Great Craftsmen,* (1939) :214-35.

Hathaway, E. V. *Partners in Progress,* 184-227.

Harrington, M. C., in Lotz, P. H., ed. *Vocations and Professions,* (1940) :97-108.

Jacks, M. M. "Edison Started Something," *Pop. Mech.,* 87 (1947) :153-57.

Maxey, G. W. "Thomas A. Edison, Individualist," *Vital Speeches,* 16:330-34, Mar. 15, 1950.

Muldoon, S. J. *Psychic Experiences of Famous People,* (1947) : 81-85.

Nerney, M. C. *Thomas A. Edison, a Modern Olympian.* 1934.

Booklist, 30:313, June, 1934. "Anecdotes which portray Edison principally as a zealous inventor but also as a social being with definite opinions on tariff, controlled currency, farm relief, and modern utopias, with an established belief in an intelligent God. The author spent two years arranging Edison's private papers."

Extract in Prochnow, H. V., ed. *Great Stories from Great Lives,* 190-97.

Sprague, H. C. *Frank P. Sprague and the Edison Myth.* 1947.

"Thomas A. Edison and the Founding of Science," *Science,* 105:142-48, Feb. 7, 1947.

Wallace, Archer. *Religious Faith of Great Men,* 139-73.

Wecter, Dixon. *Hero in America,* 415-44.

WALTER HINES PAGE—   1855-1918
—"Britain's Friend in Her Hour of Need"*
or Our Ablest Diplomat in History?

BIOGRAPHY: Hendrick, B. J. *The Life and Letters of Walter H. Page.* 2 vols. 1922.

AHR, 28:566. Civil War and Reconstruction did not prevent a young tarheel from being nurtured on British literature and becoming the keen and thoughtful editor of New York magazines. Page opposed the Democratic agitation against imperialism, and thus became the friend of President Roosevelt and Ambassador Bryce. When one of the "writers" he had discovered became president, it was natural for Wilson to send his charming literary friend to London as ambassador. Many exclaimed that Page was our ablest diplomat in Europe. Others thought writing brilliant letters was not enough. The ambassador must protect American property against British violations of international law. Some realized that Page was devoting himself to winning his friend, the President, over to the side of the Allies in the War. This fascinating biography includes the correspondence of Page, President Wilson and Colonel House.

———. *The Training of an American: the Earlier Life and Letters of Walter H. Page, 1855-1913.* 1913.

AHR, 34:139. The editor has supplemented Page's brilliant letters with running biographical comment which gives "the whole story something of the appearance of a biography." The opening pages on Page's boyhood have a special charm. The youth appears "in the character of a lover of nature" living a lonesome life surrounded by pine forests. His education spoils him for the sawmill. He tries journalism, finally becomes a successful editor. The war with Spain comes and Page stands out as a leader in the Southern educational awakening and a member of Roosevelt's Country Life Commission. Mr. Hendrick has told an effective tale.

COLLECTIVE BIOGRAPHY: Connor, R. D. W., "Walter Hines Page: a Southern Nationalist," *Jour. of Social Forces,* 2 (1924): 164-68.

Meneely, A. H., in *DAB,* 14:142.

HISTORY: Sullivan, Mark. *Our Times,* 3:319-21ff.

SPECIAL ASPECTS: Bryant, Arthur. *American Ideal,* (1936) :200-33.

Connor, R. D. W., in Odum, H. W., ed. *Southern Pioneers in Social Interpretation,* 51-67.

---

* Inscription on the tablet to Page in Westminster Abbey

Gratton, C. H. "The Walter Hines Page Legend," *Am. Merc.*, 6 (1925) :39-51.
An article hostile to Page.

Inge, W. R. *Lay Thoughts of a Dean,* (1926) :112-26.

Marcosson, I. F. *Adventure in Interviewing*, 36-56.

Mowat, R. B. *Americans in England*, 243-57.

Parks, E. W. *Segments of Southern Thought,* (1938) :273-89.

Thwing, C. F. *Friends of Men*, 91-107.

Willson, Beckles. *America's Ambassadors to England*, 441-62.

WOODROW WILSON—   1856-1924
—"The Greatest President Since Lincoln"

ORIGINAL SOURCES: Baker, R. S., and W. E. Dodd. *Woodrow Wilson. Public Papers, College and State; Educational, Literary and Political Papers, 1875-1913.* 2 vols. 1925.

Sat. Rev. of Lit., 1:785, May 30, 1925. "One cannot read these papers without feeling the charm and mastery of the man who wrote them. He had a gay wit that startles and fascinates. He dealt with hearer and reader in words of challenge and courtesy. He speaks to bankers and tells them what bankers might do and do not do. He has the same message for the lawyers, for the teachers, for the ministers. And when he speaks to the descendants of New England he gaily explains the virtues which New England did not possess. All in all, whether or not one agrees with him, one must admire and thrill at the gallantry of his spirit."

Harden, Maximilian. *I Meet My Contemporaries,* (1925) :14-63.

Link, A. S., ed. "A Letter from One of Wilson's Managers," *AHR*, 50 (1945) :768-75.

Thompson, C. W. *Presidents I've Known*, 253-321.

BIOGRAPHY: Baker, R. S. *Woodrow Wilson: Life and Letters.* Vol. I, *Youth, 1856-1890.* Vol. II, *Princeton, 1890-1910.* 1927. Vol. III, *Governor, 1910-1913.* Vol. IV, *President, 1913-1914.* 1931.

AHR, 33:898; 38:138. This authorized biography comes closest to being the definitive life of Wilson, but falls short of this. Mr. Baker showed "amazing industry" and great "talent for orderly arrangement" in using the enormous masses of material available to him. "He is always clear in his presentation and avoids anything like subtlety. . . ." He is very sympathetic toward Wilson, but not toward his opponents. At times he eulogizes Wilson, and "gives a false impression . . . in his continual emphasis upon the quality of grand strategy which he ascribes to Wilson." Mr.

Baker minimizes the role of Bryan, Col. House and Republicans who prepared the way for the Federal Reserve Act. At times the President framed his own policies, without consulting his advisors. "Wilson's title to real statesmanship is not spoiled by the futility of this particular aspect of policy any more than by the fact that he was prone to commit cardinal errors when he approached a problem without authoritative and well informed advisors." Mr. Baker emphasizes interpretation too much; he should let the documents speak for themselves.

———. Vol. V, *Neutrality, 1914-1915.* 1935.

N. Y. Times, Nov. 24, 1935. p. 3. "Mr. Baker's great biography grows in importance as it proceeds. It is natural that the present volume should be of greater general interest than its predecessors, for events were dramatic and problems were grave, but 'Mr. Baker is also more at home with his subject, his grasp is firmer, and there is more opportunity to speak out."

———. Vol. VI, *Facing War, 1915-1917.* 1937.

New Repub., 93:142, Dec. 8, 1937. "Mr. Baker is no hagiographer. He sees a number of Wilson's faults and is remarkably frank about them. As a historian he ranks well above some others dealing with the same materials. He may well be pardoned if he magnifies some of Wilson's achievements. Perhaps he would like to make of Wilson a heroic figure in the great drama of our age. The trouble is, of course, that the drama is a kind of Greek Tragedy."

———. Vol. VII, *War Leader, 1917-1918.* Vol. VIII, *Armistice, 1918.* 1939.

AHR, 46:441. "In these volumes Mr. Baker departs from the orthodox biographical presentation of those which had previously appeared, abandoning all attempts at interpretation in favor of a compilation of the raw materials of history. What we have now is only a 'day-by-day-chronicle' of the President's activities during this period, rather than his 'life.' " In spite of some drawbacks "it is a pleasure to note that by his new procedure Mr. Baker has in fact succeeded in making the role of our war President more real to us. . . . The complete absence of interpretation or analysis probably makes it easier to see Wilson as he really was. We have abundant evidence of the qualities which many of his severest critics never failed to acknowledge: courage, steadfastness, loyalty, a fine sense of propriety, and the ability to use tact in recalling others to it."

Extract in Prochnow, H. V., ed. *Great Stories from Great Lives,* 322-35.

Bell, H. C. F. *Woodrow Wilson and the People.* 1945.

New Repub., 113:164, Aug. 6, 1945. This book offers little on Wilson's pre-Princeton years or the New Freedom at home, but "deserves high praise as a personal study, particularly for its literary qualities."

Dodd, W. E. *Woodrow Wilson and His Work.* 4th edition. 1921.

N. Y. *Times,* Sept. 12, 1920, p. 21. Written by a friend, this biography is a discriminating and just appraisal. For a different view see *AHR,* 27:334.

Lawrence, David. *The True Story of Woodrow Wilson.* 1924.

N. Y. *World,* June 8, 1924, p. 7. "The book is rich in little minor revelations that are the very spice of history. . . . Mr. Lawrence has given us some graphic, illuminating pictures—one of an actual working day in Wilson's life at the White House, indicative of the superhuman exactions of the position."

Link, A. S. *Wilson: the Road to the White House.* 1947.

AHR, 53:130. Mr. Link "has made telling use of over a hundred contemporary newspapers and of the papers of Ray Stannard Baker." Making "little new contribution" during Wilson's years of education and of teaching, he describes the Baltimore Convention in colorful fashion, maintaining that Bryan was "really on the periphery during the Convention in so far as the Wilson managers were concerned. . . . Wilson, the Leader, will, it is to be hoped, come completely alive in the next volume."

McAdoo, Eleanor. *The Woodrow Wilsons.* 1937.

AHR, 42:171. Wilson's youngest daughter "gives information about personal attitudes and the Wilson family life such as we have about no other President, . . ." The author brings the book to a close with her mother's death in 1914.

Notter, Harley. *The Origins of the Foreign Policy of Woodrow Wilson.* 1937.

AHR, 44:166. Mr. Notter's thesis is that "all the essential elements of thought governing Wilson's foreign policy were determined, and in several instances specific policies were formulated, before he took the oath of office as President of the United States."

Reid, E. G. *Woodrow Wilson: the Caricature, the Myth, and the Man.* 1934.

AHR, 40:155. This little book by "a personal friend from Wilson's student days" gives us "revealing glimpses of the authentic Wilson." Is it "worthless gossip," or the best brief book on Wilson?

COLLECTIVE BIOGRAPHY: Agar, Herbert. *The People's Choice,* 267-311.

Allen, F. L., in *There Were Giants in the Land,* 144-52.

Bassett, J. S. *Makers of a Nation,* 268-92

Bernstein, Herman. *Celebrities of Our Time,* (1924) :335-47.

Bolitho, William. *Twelve Against the Gods,* (1929) :329-51.

Box, P. H. *Three Master Builders and Another,* (1925) :295-392.

Bradford, Gamaliel. *The Quick and the Dead,* 41-78.

———, in Beckwith and Coope, eds. *Contemporary American Biography,* 13-34.

Cottler, Joseph. *Champions of Democracy,* 285-310.

Dennis, A. P., in Peterson, Houston. *Great Teachers,* 131-52.

Dos Passos, J. R., in Beckwith and Coope, eds. *Contemporary American Biography,* 35-42.

Eddy, G. S., and Kirby Page. *Makers of Freedom,* 200-30.

Egbert, D. D., and D. M. Lee. *Princeton Portraits,* (1947) :73-79.

Hagedorn, Hermann. *Americans,* 137-59.

Hathaway, E. V. *Book of American Presidents,* 287-303.

Howe, M. A. D. *Causes and Their Champions,* 267-306.

Keynes, J. M. *Essays in Biography,* (1933) :3-30.

———, in Balch, Marston, ed. *Modern Short Biographies,* 389-410.

Law, F. H. *Modern Great Americans,* 261-74.

Lippmann, Walter. *Men of Destiny,* (1927) :129-39.

Merriam, C. E. *Four American Party Leaders,* 44-62.

Nevins, Allan. "Woodrow Wilson Relives in a Great Biography," *Cur. Hist.,* 35 (1932) :501-06.

Payne, J. M. *Virginia Born Presidents,* 213-32.

Osgood, C. G., in Thorp, Willard, ed. *Lives of Eighteen from Princeton,* (1946) :282-301.

Radek, Karl. *Portraits and Pamphlets,* (1935) :35-43.

Seymour, Charles, in *DAB,* 20:352.

Thomas and Thomas. *Fifty Great Americans,* 312-20.

———. *Living Biographies of American Statesmen,* 295-307.

Thwing, C. F. *Friends of Men,* 413-35.

White, W. A., in Balch, Marston, ed. *Modern Short Biographies,* 359-88.

Wildman, Edwin. *Famous Leaders of Character in America,* 195-205.

Williams, J. H. H. *Men of Stress: Woodrow Wilson, Andrew Carnegie, Lord Leverhulme.* 1948.

SPECIAL ASPECTS: Bailey, T. A. *Wilson and the Lost Peace.* 1944.
AHR, 50:365. "Professor Bailey undertakes to examine the relations of . . . Wilson to the establishment of world peace, beginning with Wilson's first pronouncements on the subject and concluding with his submission of the Treaty of Versailles to the Senate in 1919." He seeks to reveal actual

blunders made "so that the peace makers of the present may not repeat them."

——. *Wilson and the Peace Makers; Combining Woodrow Wilson and the Lost Peace and Woodrow Wilson and the Great Betrayal.* 2 vols. 1947.

Clapper, O. E. *Washington Tapestry,* 49-68.

Cousins, Norman. "Woodrow Wilson and His Clients," *Sat. Rev. of Lit.,* 33:24-25, Sept. 23, 1950.

Daniels, Josephus. *Wilson Era, Years of War and After, 1917-1923.* 1946.

N. Y. Times, June 8, 1946, p. 7. "To the story of the League of Nations fight Mr. Daniels contributes interesting sidelights and a highly quotable paraphrase of 'Who Killed Cock Robin?' In this matter and in all others of any importance he is whole heartedly and unreservedly for Wilson. Whether or not he adds any cubits to the towering stature of the War President, he adds here some pleasing touches to the portrait of the man. In this connection he reports numerous sallies of wit and some of the best of his stories."

Dennis, A. P. *Gods and Little Fishes,* 84-117.

Diamond, William. *Economic Thought of Woodrow Wilson.* 1944.

New Repub., 111:251, Aug. 28, 1944. "A modestly titled and brilliantly executed study of Wilson's thinking."

Dulles, F. R. *Twentieth Century America,* 128-45, 235-56.

Gilbert, C. W. *Mirrors of Washington,* 25-45.

Graham, M. W. *American Diplomacy in the International Community,* (1948) :122-73.

Hamlin, Fred. *Land of Liberty,* 290-311.

Hansen, Harold, in Leighton, Isabel. ed. *Aspirin Age,* 1-33.

Hapgood, Norman, in Brown, A. B., ed. *Great Democrats,* (1934) :665-76.

Hofstadter, Richard. *American Political Tradition,* 234-78.

Hugh-Jones, E. M. *Woodrow Wilson and American Liberalism.* (Teach Yourself History Library, 1948.)

AHR, 54:219. The author "has tried to write an interpretation of United States history from 1865 to 1921 by way of a biography of Woodrow Wilson. In spite of many generalizations and errors of fact and interpretation, the author gives "an admirable estimate of Wilson's place in the history of American liberalism."

Johnson, G. W. *American Heroes and Hero Worship,* 251-77.

——, in Odum, H. W., ed. *Southern Pioneers in Social Interpretation,* 29-49.

Kraus, Michael. *History of American History,* 453-91.

Lansing, Robert. *The Big Four and Others at the Peace Conference,* (1921) :37-76.

Lewis, Wyndham. *America and Cosmic Man,* (1949) :92-100.

Link, A. S. "Enigma of Woodrow Wilson," *Amer. Merc.,* 65 (1947) :303-13.

Ludwig, Emil. *Genius and Character,* (1927) :91-118.

Marcosson, I. F. *Adventures in Interviewing,* 145-53.

Martin, E. S. *What's Ahead and Meanwhile,* (1927) :145-53.

Martin, William. *Statesmen of War in Retrospect, 1918-1928,* (1928) :217-33.

Milton, G. F. *Use of Presidential Power, 1789-1943,* 197-250.

Morley, C. D. *Powder of Sympathy,* (1923) :213-17.

Mowat, R. B. *Americans in England,* 258-75.

Munson, G. B. *Twelve Decisive Battles of the Mind,* (1942) : 239-46.

Myers, W. S., ed. *Woodrow Wilson; Some Princeton Memories.* 1946.

Parkman, M. R. *Fighters for Peace,* (1919) :285-311.

Perry, Bliss. *Praise of Folly,* 151-70.

Pollard, J. E. *Presidents and the Press,* 630-91.

Saveth, E. N. *American Historians and European Immigrants, 1875-1925,* 137-49.

Sears, L. M., in Hutchinson, W. T., ed. *Essays in American Historiography,* 102-21.

Slocombe, G. E. *Mirror to Geneva,* (1938) :15-36.

Smut, J. C., in Smith, C. A., ed. *Essays on Current Themes,* (1923) :90-96.

Soward, F. H. *Moulders of National Destinies,* (1940) : 1-9.

Starling, E. W. *Starling of the White House,* 30-164.

Van Doren, Carl, and C. L. Carmer. *American Scriptures,* 43-50.

Villard, O. G. *Prophets True and False,* 158-68.

Wallace, Archer. *Religious Faith of Great Men,* 193-217.

Wecter, Dixon. *Hero in America,* 392-414.

Weyl, W. E. *Tired Radicals,* (1921) :81-101.

Wish, Harvey. *Contemporary America,* (1945) :167-92.

Zilliacus, Konni. *Mirrors of the Past,* (1946) :150-218.

Zweig, Stefan. *Tide of Fortune,* (1940) :263-85.

BIOGRAPHIES OF CONTEMPORARIES: Blum, J. M. *Joe Tumulty and the Wilson Era.* 1951.

N. Y. Times, July 29, 1951, p. 1. A detailed biography of the faithful secretary who served Wilson as "a sort of composite average American" on whom he tried out ideas and speeches. "The major interest in the latter part of the book is . . . in the roles that Tumulty played while Wilson was at the Versailles conference" and while he was ill.

Houston, D. F. *Eight Years with Wilson's Cabinet, 1913-1920; With a Personal Estimate of the President.* 2 vols. 1926.

N. Y. Times, Oct. 31, 1926, p. 3. "As a literary product, the work takes relatively high rank among the rapidly growing memorabilia of the Wilson Administration. Its deliberately phrased portions, as differentiated from the casually framed entries in note form, made more or less on the spur of the moment, which are reproduced, show considerable degree of polish, marked lucidity and general charm. The book is a worthy effort of one who had been the executive head of a college and two universities. It bears the stamp of a purpose well conceived and on the whole, well executed."

THEODORE ROOSEVELT— 1858-1919 —The People's President

ORIGINAL SOURCES: Abbott, Lyman. *Silhouettes of My Contemporaries,* 310-31.

Hagedorn, Hermann. *Americans,* 111-35.

Irwin, Will, ed. *Letters to Kermit from Theodore Roosevelt, 1902-1908.* 1946.

Morison, E. E., ed. *The Letters of Theodore Roosevelt. Vols. I and II: The Years of Preparation, 1898 to 1900.* 1951.

N. Y. Times, Apr. 22, 1951, p. 33. These volumes show that young Roosevelt was very free in saying what he thought, and that he simply could not spell. Many letters already published are reprinted, particularly the ones to Cabot Lodge.

Roosevelt, Theodore. *Theodore Roosevelt: an Autobiography.* 1913.

AHR, 19:670. This narrative touches only the high spots of Roosevelt's career. It presents his side of controversial questions, throws little light on the views of the opposition. "By far the most interesting and revealing chapters are the 'Vigor of Life,' 'In Cowboy Land,' and 'Outdoors and

Indoors.' They are sprinkled with interesting and amusing anecdotes, characterizations, and slight personal adventures that disclose the quality of the man and the undeniable personal charm and attractiveness that have won for him so many staunch and loyal friends, ranging from ambassadors through all types of citizenship to second-rate prize fighters. . . . The chapter on 'Outdoors and Indoors,' showing, as it does, Mr. Roosevelt as a lover of children and of nature, is quite the most charming and delightful chapter in the book. . . . It is these personal and intimate chapters that give the present volume its value, rather than Mr. Roosevelt's controversial treatment of past or present public questions."

————, in Strong, S. D., ed. *What I Owe to My Father*, 135-44.

Selections from the Correspondence of Theodore Roosevelt and Henry Cabot Lodge, 1884-1918. 2 vols. 1925.

AHR, 30:841. Some of these letters "show how shrewdly and carefully" Lodge groomed his friend "for political preferment."

Thompson, C. W. *Presidents I've Known*, 111-210.

Wise, J. S. *Recollections of Thirteen Presidents*, 311-65.

BIOGRAPHY: Bishop, J. B. *Theodore Roosevelt and His Times: Shown in His Own Letters.* 2 vols. 1920.

AHR, 26:552. "These two fine volumes will be indispensable . . ., but they exhibit the art of the official biographer at much less than its best. Mr. Bishop qualified for the task of writing the Roosevelt biography by many years of admiring friendship, during which he enjoyed both the frequent hospitality and the political patronage of his subject. He does not throw himself modestly into the background, content to be the transparent medium of revelation . . ., but he ventures to add his comment upon events, and occasionally his testimony as to character or facts."

Pringle, H. F. *Theodore Roosevelt, a Biography.* 1931.

AHR, 37:570. A revaluation which pays more attention to Roosevelt's "ideals and accomplishments" and less to his personal magnetism. The book is both scholarly and entertaining and is easily the best biography.

Thayer, W. R. *Theodore Roosevelt, an Intimate Biography.* 1919.

AHR, 25:306. "The character of Colonel Roosevelt is convincingly presented here; but Mr. Thayer adds little to our knowledge of his life." . . . The biography (by an intimate friend) is throughout an impressionistic picture rather than a work of scholarship."

COLLECTIVE BIOGRAPHY: Agar, Herbert. *The People's Choice*, 267-311.

Bassett, J. S. *Makers of a New Nation*, 215-44.

Booth, E. T. *Country Life in America*, 209-27.

Bradford, Gamaliel. *Portraits and Personalities,* 172-88.

———. *The Quick and the Dead,* 1-39.

Cortissoz, Royal. *American Artists,* 325-40.

Levin, P. R. *Seven by Chance,* 177-230.

Hathaway, E. V. *Book of American Presidents,* 259-73.

Law, F. H. *Modern Great Americans,* 204-19.

Merriam, C. E. *Four American Party Leaders,* 22-43.

Paxson, F. L., in *DAB,* 16:135.

Pringle, H. F., in Hamilton, E. B., ed. *How They Started,* 165-91.

Sherman, S. P. *Americans,* 256-87.

Street, J. L., in *There Were Giants in the Land,* 10-15.

Thomas and Thomas. *Living Biographies of American Statesmen,* 281-92.

Tracy, H. C. *American Naturists,* 147-54

White, W. A. *Masks in a Pageant,* 283-326.

HISTORY: Sullivan, Mark. *Our Times,* 3:see index.

SPECIAL ASPECTS: Beers, H. A. *Four Americans,* 7-31.

Bernstein, Herman. *Celebrities of Our Time,* (1924) : 326-34.

Blythe, S. G., in Greene, Ward, ed. *Star Reporter,* (1948) :70-77.

Boynton, P. H. *America in Contemporary Fiction,* 1-20.

Bryant, Arthur. *American Ideal,* (1936) :139-99.

Cohen, J. H. *They Builded Better Than They Knew,* (1946) : 73-90.

Dennett, Tyler. *Roosevelt and the Russo-Japanese War. A Critical Study of American Policy in Eastern Asia in 1902-1905.* 1925.

AHR, 31:156. "A brief but notable book which will have to be taken into account by all students of modern Far Eastern history. His chief new source has been the unpublished letters of President Roosevelt to which he has had access and from which he has gathered much important material."

Dewey, John. *Characters and Events,* 1:87-94.

Dulles, F. R. *Twentieth Century America,* 87-110.

Filler, Louis. *Crusaders of American Liberalism,* 43-54, 165-68, 320-28, 355-56.

Hagedorn, Hermann. *Roosevelt in the Bad Lands.* 1921.

AHR, 27:621. By using journals and family letters never printed before, and interviewing old timers, the author has written a stirring account of Roosevelt's ranching days in Dakota in the eighties.

Hay, John. *Addresses,* (1906) :217-25.

Higginson, A. H. *British and American Sporting Authors,* (1949) :260-63.

Hofstadter, Richard. *American Political Tradition,* 203-33.

Johnson, G. W. *American Heroes and Hero Worship,* 192-250.

Kraus, Michael. *History of American History,* 492-545.

Leary, J. L., Jr., comp. *Talks with Theodore Roosevelt from the Diaries of John J. Leary, Jr.* 1920.

AHR, 26:149. "It is Roosevelt the tribal chieftain that is revealed in this book, loving his friends and being served by them with devotion, hating his enemies and wishing that life were long enough for them all to be punished. . . . The compiler . . . is one of the group of newspapermen who surrounded Roosevelt in his later life."

Lewis, Wyndham. *America and Cosmic Man,* (1949) :85-91.

Livermore, S. W. "Theodore Roosevelt, the American Navy, and the Venezuelan Crisis of 1902-03," *AHR,* 51 (1945) :452-71.

Lodge, H. C. *Frontier Town,* (1906) : 162-68.

Marcosson, I. F. *Adventures in Interviewing,* 79-93.

Miller, R. C., in *Medieval and Historiographical Essays in Honor of James Westfall Thompson,* 423-38.

Milton, G. F. *Use of Presidential Power, 1789-1943,* 173-96.

Mowry, G. E. *Theodore Roosevelt and the Progressive Movement.* 1946.

PHR, 15:364. An "attractive study of Roosevelt and the Progressive party" which goes "beyond the comprehensive Pringle biographies of Roosevelt and Taft" to make "substantial additions to the political history of the years 1908-1912. The author's rather convincing picture of Taft tends to bring us back to the hostile contemporary estimate held by the Republican insurgents and away from Pringle's more friendly view of a bumbling but progressive statesman. Mowry finds Taft bumbling enough—lazy and careless to a fatal degree in preparing speeches—but mentally closer to the Old Guard than to the tentative but recognizable liberalism of Roosevelt."

———. "First President," *Am. Merc.,* 63 (1946) :578-84.

O'Gara, G. C. *Theodore Roosevelt and the Rise of the Modern Navy.* 1943.

AHR, 49:357. An accurate and readable study of Roosevelt's contribution to the building of the navy. The President's "notable failures" are noted too. Mr. O'Gara "failed to use" several rich manuscript collections.

Osborn, H. F. *Impressions of Great Naturalists*, 251-76.

Perling, J. J. *Presidents' Sons*, 247-73.

Pollard, J. E. *Presidents and the Press*, 569-600.

Root, Elihu. *Men and Policies*, 3-16.

———. *Miscellaneous Addresses*, 217-22.

Ross, E. D. "Roosevelt and Agriculture," *MVHR*, 14 (1927) : 287-310.

Saveth, E. N. *American Historians and European Immigrants, 1875-1925*, 112-21.

Thornton, H. J., in Hutchinson, W. T., ed. *Essays in American Historiography*, 227-51.

Wallace, Archer. *Religious Faith of Great Men*, 193-217.

Wecter, Dixon. *Hero in America*, 364-91.

Wish, Harvey. *Contemporary America*, 68-98.

VICTOR HERBERT— 1859-1924 —American Master of the Operetta

COLLECTIVE BIOGRAPHY: Hughes, Rupert, and Arthur Elson. *American Composers*, (1914) :see index.

Martens, F. H., in *DAB*, 8:573.

Thomas and Thomas. *Forty Famous Composers*, (1948) :355-64.

SPECIAL ASPECTS: Howard, J. T. *Our American Music*, 3rd ser., (1946) :653-54.

Taylor, Deems. *Well Tempered Listener*, (1940) :67-72.

NICHOLAS MURRAY BUTLER— 1862-1947 —America's Cultural Ambassador

ORIGINAL SOURCES: Butler, N. M. *Across the Busy Years: Recollections and Reflections*. 2 vols. 1939, 1940.

AHR, 45:676, Vol. I. A great autobiography which records the rise of a self-supporting college student of English descent to outstanding leadership in education and politics. The book throws much light on American political and educational history during the half century before its publication.

———. Vol. II. 1940.

Springfield Republican, Aug., 1940, p. 7. This volume ". . . is less a biographical chronicle than a conglomeration of letters, discussions, anecdotes and records, incidents and personal contacts."

*EDITH NEWBOLD WHARTON— 1862-1937
—Patrician Analyst of the American Scene

ORIGINAL SOURCES: Wharton, Edith. *A Backward Glance*. 1934.

Boston Transcript, Apr. 28, 1934. "Few literary autobiographies carry us through such diverse scenes as does Mrs. Wharton's; few reveal the sensitive and imaginative spirit of their writers so simply and yet so eloquently."

BIOGRAPHY: Lubbock, Percy. *Portrait of Edith Wharton*. 1947.

So. Atl. Quar., 47:585. An admiring but candid and gossipy portrayal of a wealthy woman and perfect hostess who was encouraged to write by William James himself.

Lovett, T. M. *Edith Wharton*. (Modern American Writers, 1925.)

Sat. Rev. of Lit., 1:841, June 20, 1925. "The estimate is just and his comparisons with her masters, Henry James and Thackeray, are excellently made. He allows too little, however, for the charm and interest of her aristocrats."

COLLECTIVE BIOGRAPHY: Burdett, Osbert, in Squire, J. C., et al. *Contemporary American Authors*, 151-76.

Cooper, F. T. *Some American Story Tellers*, 168-95.

Loggins, Vernon. *I Hear America*, 175-94.

Overton, G. M. *Women Who Make Our Novels*, 324-42.

Sherman, S. P. *Main Stream*, 204-12.

Van Doren, C. C. *Contemporary American Novelists, 1900-1920*, 84-131.

Williams, B. C. *Our Short Story Writers*, 337-57.

SPECIAL ASPECTS: Beach, J. W. *Twentieth Century Novel*, (1932) :287-303.

Boynton, P. H. *Some Contemporary Americans*, 89-107.

Bjorkman, Edwin. *Voices of Tomorrow*, (1913) :see index.

Collins, Joseph. *Taking the Literary Pulse*, 48-72.

Edgar, Pelham. *Art of the Novel*, 196-205.

Flanner, Janet. *Americans in Paris*, (1940) :185-96.

Hartwick, Harry. *Foreground of American Fiction*, 369-88.

Hatcher, H. H. *Creating the Modern American Novel*, 21-33, 87-98.

---

* See also Spiller, et al. *Literary History of the United States*, 3 (1948) :757-59.

Hicks, Granville. *Great Tradition,* 207-56.

Hind, C. L. *Authors and I,* 306-11.

James, Henry. *Notes on Novelists.* 1914.

Jessup, J. L. *The Faith of Our Feminists: a Study in the Novels of Edith Wharton, Ellen Glasgow, Willa Cather.* 1950.

Amer. Lit., 23:262. "The author apparently assumes that each writer was a feminist primarily concerned with preaching feminism." The reviewer dissents and says that "the attempt to fit the actualities of their books to this assumption involves distortion."

Lawrence, Margaret. *School of Femininity,* (1936) :248-80.

Michaud, Regis. *The American Novel Today,* 47-70.

Russell, F. T. "Melodramatic Mrs. Wharton," *Sewanee Rev.,* 40 (1932) :425-37.

Sedgwick, H. D. *New American Type,* (1908) :51-96.

Snell, G. D. *Shapers of American Fiction,* 140-56.

Van Doren, C. C. *The American Novel,* 260-80.

Wilson, Edmund. *Wound and the Bow,* (1941) :195-213.

———. "Edith Wharton: a Memoir by an English Friend," *New Yorker,* 23:101-04, Oct. 4, 1947.

Quinn, A. H. "The Gilded Era of Edith Wharton," *N. Y. Times Bk. Rev.,* Aug. 27, 1950, p. 1.

CHARLES EVANS HUGHES—   1862-1948   —"He
Missed the Presidency by an Eyelash"

Collective Biography: Filler, Louis. *Crusaders of American Liberalism,* 190-202.

Hyde, C. C. "Charles Evans Hughes: an Appreciation," *Am. Jour. Int. Law,* 43 (1949) :335-38.

Macartney, C. E. N. *Men Who Missed It,* 114-22.

McCune, Wesley. *Nine Young Men,* (1947) :240-42.

Umbreit, K. B. *Our Eleven Chief Justices,* (1938) :451-500.

Stone, Irving. *They "Also Ran,"* 97-117.

Villard, O. G. *Prophets, True and False,* 37-50.

Wildman, Edwin. *Famous Leaders of Character in America,* 269-81.

Woolf, S. J. *Drawn from Life,* 214-22.

History: Sullivan, Mark. *Our Times,* 3:51-68, 282-88.

SPECIAL ASPECTS: Davenport, F. M. "Did Hughes Snub Johnson? An Inside Story," *Am. Pol. Sci. Rev.*, 43 (1949) :321-32.

Gilbert, C. W. *Mirrors of Washington*, 67-86.

Hendel, Samuel. *Charles Evans Hughes and the Supreme Court.* 1951.

N. Y. Times, Feb. 11, 1951, p. 7. Mr. Hendel shows that Hughes contributed largely to constitutional issues that came before the Supreme Court while he was a member of that body. This book should be read by all students of law and government.

Lowry, E. G. *Washington Close-ups*, 168-79.

McElwain, Edwin. "Business of the Supreme Court as Conducted by Chief Justice Holmes," *Harvard Law Rev.*, 63 (1949) :5-26.

Pringle, H. F., in *Reader's Digest Reader*, 301-04.

WALTER JOHANNES DAMROSCH— 1862-1950
—Humanist of the Baton

ORIGINAL SOURCES: Damrosch, Walter. *My Musical Life.* 1924.

Springfield Republican, Feb. 26, 1924, p. 8. "Entertaining . . . including numerous amusing anecdotes about the great and the near-great in the musical life of two continents during the last half-century."

Stone, Irving, and Richard Kennedy, eds. *We Speak for Ourselves*, 84-92.

BIOGRAPHY: Finletter, Gretchen. *From the Top of the Stairs.* 1946.

N. Y. Times, Sept. 15, 1946, p. 6. "A vastly amusing book" written by one of Damrosch's daughters.

Excerpt in *Read. Dig.*, 49 (1946) :45-49.

COLLECTIVE BIOGRAPHY: Armsby, Mrs. L. B. *Musicians Talk*, (1935) :139-43.

Beard, A. E. S. *Our Foreign-Born Citizens*, 421-36.

Howard, J. T., and Arthur Mendel. *Our Contemporary Composers*, (1941) :10-22.

Saleski, Gdal. *Famous Musicians of Jewish Origins*, (1949) :221-26.

SPECIAL ASPECTS: Aldrich, Richard. *Concert Life in New York, 1902-1923*, (1941) :6-8, 705-07.

Ewen, David. *Dictators of the Baton*, (1943) :119-31.

———. *Man with a Baton,* (1937) :23-67.

Howard, J. T. *Our American Music,* (1946) :351-54.

Taylor, Deems. *Of Men and Music,* 144-53.

Woolf, S. J. *Drawn from Life,* 356-63.

JAMES HARVEY ROBINSON—   1863-1936
—Preceptor of the "New History"

BIOGRAPHY: Hendricks, L. V. *James Harvey Robinson, Teacher of History.* 1946.

AHR, 52:798. A thorough, well-balanced account of "the professional career of one of the world's most distinguished teachers." Robinson sought "to free history from its conventional role as the record of past politics," and to enrich "our knowledge of the past by the use of selected source material." He sought constantly to discover why we think the way we do.

SPECIAL ASPECTS: Barnes, H. E., in Odum, H. W., ed. *American Masters of Social Science,* 321-408.

Edman, Irvin, in Hintz, H. W., and B. D. Grebanier, eds. *Modern American Vistas,* (1940) :357-70.

Essays in Intellectual History, Dedicated to James Harvey Robinson by His Former Seminar Students. 1929.

Hendricks, L. V. "James Harvey Robinson and the New School for Social Research," *J. Higher Ed.,* 20 (1949) :1-11.

LILLIAN WALD— 1867-1940 —"The Understanding Friend of Slum Children, Fish Peddlers, Financiers, a President . . . and a . . . Prime Minister"

BIOGRAPHY: Duffus, R. L. *Lillian Wald: Neighbor and Crusader.* 1938.

MVHR, 25:584. "An effective portrait of a notable woman" who started the Henry Street Settlement, the public nursing service, and the Children's Bureau.

COLLECTIVE BIOGRAPHY: Beatty, Jerome, in *Reader's Digest Reader,* 333-36.

Hunting, H. B., in Lotz, P. H., ed. *Distinguished American Jews,* (1945) :10-20.

Yost, Edna. *American Women of Nursing,* (1947) :22-41.

SPECIAL ASPECTS: Duffus, R. L., in Logie, I. M. R., ed. *Careers in the Making,* 2nd ser., (1942) :203-13.

Hedin, A. I. S., in Handlin, Oscar, ed. *This Was America,* (1949) :464-71.

Knickerbocker, E. V., ed. *Present Day Essays,* (1923) :262-81.

Robinson, Victor. *White Caps,* 269-309.

HARVEY WILLIAM CUSHING— 1869-1939
—"Father of Modern Brain Surgery"

BIOGRAPHY: Fulton, J. F. *Harvey Cushing; a Biography.* 1946.

New Yorker, 22:142, Nov. 30, 1946. "A bulky, thorough, and readable biography. . . . The descriptions of some of Cushing's celebrated operations on the brain and spinal cord and of his discoveries in electro-surgery are so clear that even the layman can get an idea of the man's achievements."

Thompson, E. H. *Harvey Cushing: Surgeon, Author, Artist.* 1950.

Kirkus, 18:120, Feb. 15, 1950. "A careful, authoritative but still highly readable biography."

COLLECTIVE BIOGRAPHY: Gumpert, Martin. *Trail-blazers of Science,* (1936) :289-98.

Leonardo, R. A. *Lives of Master Surgeons,* (1948) :121-24.

Moulton, F. R., and J. J. Schifferes, eds. *400 Years of a Doctor's Life,* 277-78, 378-80.

SPECIAL ASPECTS: Match, R. "Father of Modern Brain Surgery," *Read. Dig.,* 52 (1948) :76-80.

Ward, Harold, ed. *New Worlds in Medicine,* (1946) :463-77.

DWIGHT WHITNEY MORROW— 1873-1931
—"The Diplomat Who Won the Mexicans"

BIOGRAPHY: Nicolson, H. G. *Dwight Morrow.* 1935.

Commonweal, 23:108, Nov. 22, 1935. "Of particular interest is the story of his mission to Mexico; and this Mr. Nicolson relates more fully than any other writer has done."

COLLECTIVE BIOGRAPHY: Beals, Carleton. "The Diplomat Who Won the Mexicans," *N. Y. Times,* Sept. 21, 1930.

Egan, Martin, in *DAB,* 13:234.

White, T. M. *Famous Leaders of Industry,* 3rd ser., (1931) :195-205.

SPECIAL ASPECTS: Allen, R. S., and Drew Pearson. *Washington Merry-Go-Round,* (1931) : 268-92.

Nicobon, H. G., in Hamilton, E. B., ed. *How They Started,* 226-64.

Salter, J. A. *Personality in Politics,* (1947) :160-74.

Wilson, Edmund. *American Jitters,* 1-5.

ALFRED EMANUEL SMITH— 1873-1944 —"The Happy Warrior"

BIOGRAPHY: Graham, Frank. *Al Smith, American: an Informal Biography.* 1945.

AHR, 51-553. Gossipy narrative of a colorful figure.

COLLECTIVE BIOGRAPHY: Duffus, R. L. "Al Smith: an East Side Portrait," *Harper's,* 152 (1926) :320-27.

Lippmann, Walter. *Men of Destiny,* 1-9, 35-44.

Stone, Irving. *They "Also Ran,"* 285-305.

White, W. A. *Masks in a Pageant,* 463-79.

ENRICO CARUSO— 1873-1921 —Tenor of the "Golden Voice"

BIOGRAPHY: Caruso, Dorothy. *Enrico Caruso, His Life and Death.* 1945.

Sat. Rev. of Lit., 28:10, June, 1945. "The story will give pleasure to those who enjoy true stories of married love, as well as those who like to read about famous singers. . . . Mrs. Caruso's lovingly drawn portrait of her husband is that of a great singer, who was also an extraordinarily picturesque and amiable character."

COLLECTIVE BIOGRAPHY: Thomas and Thomas. *Living Biographies of Famous Men,* 227-39.

SPECIAL ASPECTS: Aldrich, Richard. *Concert Life in New York,* (1941) :122-24, 161-64, 591-96.

Armstrong, William. *Romantic World of Music,* (1922) :140-54.

Gardiner, A. G. *Many Furrows,* (1924) :259-62.

Haggin, B. H. *Music in the Nation,* (1949) :274-75.

Henderson, W. J. *Art of Singing,* (1938) :303-09.

Huneker, J. G. *Bedouins,* (1920) :134-43.

———. *Variations,* (1921) :273-79.

Kent, George. "So Kind of Them to Remember," *Read. Dig.,* 48 (1946) :65-69.

Marek, G. R. *Front Seat at the Opera,* (1948) :264-67.

Parker, H. T. *Eighth Notes,* 59-63.

JAMES JOHN WALKER— 1881-1946 —Playboy
Mayor of New York, a "Great Little Guy"

BIOGRAPHY: Fowler, Gene. *Beau James: the Life and Times of Jimmy Walker.* 1949.

Herald-Tribune Bk. Rev., Apr. 10, 1949, p. 3. Gene Fowler was the logical man to paint "a vivid portrait of Jimmy Walker. He was around when James J. Walker rose to great power and when he had his great fall; moreover, Fowler was, and is, the sort of man to understand the contradictory aspects of Walker's character and not be shocked, or even greatly surprised, at the revelation of the most astonishing didos." Fowler's story adds up to lively reading," and he "does not sit too harshly in judgment on the glamorous figure of Walker."

COLLECTIVE BIOGRAPHY: Moley, Raymond. *Twenty-seven Masters of Politics,* (1949) :204-14.

FIORELLO HENRY LA GUARDIA— 1882-1947
—"Little Man Who Ran New York"

ORIGINAL SOURCES: La Guardia, F. H. *Making of an Insurgent: an Autobiography, 1882-1919.* 1948.

N. Y. Herald-Tribune Wkly. Bk. Rev., May 23, 1948, p. 4. "When Fiorello H. LaGuardia, who was one of the best and certainly the most exciting mayor New York ever had, began to write his autobiography he was already a very sick man. But none of the pain and anguish of those final days crept into the pages he had completed before death overtook him. This is a book filled with a zest for living and doing, written by a man who was looking back with detachment upon a useful and happy life."

BIOGRAPHY: Carter, J. F. *La Guardia: an Unauthorized Biography.* 1937.

New Repub., 92:376, Nov. 3, 1937. Interprets the mayor not as an "East Side alien" but as a product of the American West.

Limpus, L. M., and B. W. Leyson. *This Man La Guardia.* 1938.

Books, Oct. 30, 1938, p. 18. Sympathetic rather than critical.

COLLECTIVE BIOGRAPHY: Peragallo, Olga. *Italian American Authors and Their Contribution to American Literature,* (1949): 129-37.

Werner, M. R. "Fiorello H. La Guardia; an Intimate Portrait," *New Repub.,* 117:13-16, Sept. 29, 1947.

SPECIAL ASPECTS: Brown, J. M. *Seeing Things,* (1946) :54-62.

Ernst, M. L. *Best is Yet,* (1945) :174-78.

Gunther, John. *Inside U. S. A.,* 578-88.

Liebling, A. J. "Mayor into Columnist," *New Yorker,* 22:56-61, Feb. 23, 1946.

Nizer, Louis. *Between You and Me,* (1948) :68-72.

Pearson, Drew. "Only America Could Produce La Guardia," *Scholastic,* 51:19-20, Nov. 3, 1947.

Shuster, G. N. "Little Man Who Ran New York," *Commonweal,* 47:90-92, Nov. 7, 1947.

HENRY LOUIS GEHRIG— 1895-1933 —Lou Gehrig

BIOGRAPHY: Graham, Frank. *Lou Gehrig, a Quiet Hero.* 1942.

Books, Mar. 29, 1942, p. 7. A sports columnist's affectionate but restrained biography of a baseball star: "the life story of a quiet hero." Intelligible to those who know little about baseball.

Extract in Prochnow, H. V., ed. *Great Stories from Great Lives,* 64-69.

COLLECTIVE BIOGRAPHY: Atkinson, Leroy, and Austen Lake. *Famous American Athletes of Today,* 3rd ser., (1932) :83-103.

Busch, Niven. *Twenty-One Americans,* 321-32.

Graham, Frank, in Logie, I. M. R., ed. *Careers in the Making,* 2nd ser., (1942) :167-78.

Grayson, Harry. *They Played the Game,* (1944) :10-13.

GEORGE HERMAN RUTH—   1895-1948
—Babe Ruth

ORIGINAL SOURCES: Daniel, D. M., ed. *I Remember Ruth,* by H. G. Salsinger. 1948.

Hoyt, Waite. *Babe Ruth as I Knew Him.* 1948.

Ruth, G. H. *Babe Ruth Story as Told to Bob Considine.* 1948.

N. Y. Times, May 2, 1948, p. 33. "Bob Considine who wrote the book in the first person, has done much more than describe Ruth's vagaries and exploits. He has captured the team personality of the Yankees of the Twenties and Thirties, and he has lively stories to tell."

BIOGRAPHY: Meany, Thomas. *Babe Ruth; the Big Moments of the Big Fellow.* 1947.

N. Y. Times, Dec. 14, 1947, p. 22. "Mr. Meany takes the Babe from the streets of Baltimore to his last days . . . , recording his triumphs with a fine gift for anecdote and a distinct skill in recreating the high moments. . . ."

COLLECTIVE BIOGRAPHY: Johnston, C. H. L. *Famous American Athletes of Today,* 1st ser., (1928) :97-124.

Lieb, Frank, "Life Story of Babe Ruth," *Baseball Register,* (1948) :3-32.

Meany, T. W. *Baseball's Greatest Hitters,* (1950) :151-63.

Powers, J. J. A. *Baseball Personalities,* (1949) :106-30.

Sher, Jack. *Twelve Sport Immortals,* (1949) :280-304.

Shoemaker, R. H. *Best in Baseball,* (1949) :162-78.

SPECIAL ASPECTS: Broun, H. C., in Snyder, L. L., and R. B. Morris, eds. *Treasury of Great Reporting,* 414-16.

Carmichael, J. P. *My Greatest Day in Baseball,* (1945) :1-5.

Gallico, P. W. *Farewell to Sport,* 30-43.

Grayson, Harry. *They Played the Game,* (1944) :8-9.

Sher, Jack. "What Baseball Owes to Babe Ruth," *Read. Dig.,* 50 (1947) :1-5.

FRANCIS SCOTT KEY FITZGERALD— 1896-1940
—"A Man of Talent Who Did Not Fulfill His Early Promise"

BIOGRAPHY: Mizener, Arthur. *The Far Side of Paradise; a Biography of F. Scott Fitzgerald.* 1951.

Booklist, 47:204, Feb. 1, 1951. "The key to this sympathetic but clear-sighted biography is the author's observation that Fitzgerald was partly an enthusiastic, romantic young man, and partly, in the novelist's own phrase, a spoiled priest. This is the tragedy of a man whose beginnings bred in him an intolerable sense of inferiority and a need to excel which was diverted, except for his writing, into a compulsion to attract unfavorable attention; this in turn deepened his self-contempt. Even his successes were sensational, and his failures so frequent that they deepened his conflicts; eventually, there was guilt for his part in his wife's mental breakdown, and alcoholism. A tale of pursuit by furies, worthy of the Greeks."

COLLECTIVE BIOGRAPHY: Boyd, E. A. *Portraits,* (1924) :217-25.

Cargill, Oscar. *Intellectual America,* 311-98.

Millet, F. B. *Contemporary American Authors,* (1940) :354-56.

Mizener, Arthur, in Thorp, Willard, ed. *Eighteen from Princeton,* (1946) :333-53.

Rosenfeld, Paul. *Men Seen,* (1925) :215-24.

SPECIAL ASPECTS: Berryman, John, in *Kenyon Rev.,* 8 (1946) : 103-12.

Bishop, J. P. "Missing All," *Va. Quar. Rev.,* 13 (1937) :106-21.

———. *Collected Essays,* 66-77, 229-32.

Cowley, Malcolm. "Of Clocks and Calendars." *New Repub.*, 104 (1941) :376-77.

Fitzgerald, F. S., in Farrar, J. C., ed. *Literary Spotlight*, 125-34.

Geismar, M. D. *Last of the Provincials*, 287-352.

Gray, James. *On Second Thought*, (1946) :59-82.

Hatcher, H. H. *Creating the Modern American Novel*, 72-86.

O'Hara, John. "In Memory of Scott Fitzgerald," *New Repub.*, 104 (1941) :311-13.

Marshall, Margaret. "Notes by the Way," *Nation*, 152 (1941) : 159-60.

Mizener, Arthur. "F. Scott Fitzgerald's Tormented Paradise," *Life*, 30:82-88, Jan. 15, 1951.

———. "Fitzgerald in the Twenties," *Partisan Rev.*, 17 (1950) :7-38.

———. "Scott Fitzgerald and the Imaginative Possession of American Life," *Sewanee Rev.*, 54 (1946) :66-86.

Scully, Frank. *Rogues Gallery*, 267-76.

Trilling, Lionel. *Liberal Imagination*, (1950) :243-54.

Weir, Charles, Jr. " 'An Invite with Gilded Edges'; a Study of F. Scott Fitzgerald," *Va. Quar. Rev.*, 20 (1944) :100-13.

Wilson, Edmund. "Imaginary Conversations: Mr. Van Wyck Brooks and Mr. Scott Fitzgerald," *New Repub.*, 38:249-54, Apr. 30, 1924.

Wilkinson, B. "Scott Fitzgerald: Ten Years After," *N. Y. Times Bk. Rev.*, Dec. 24, 1950, p. 7.

GEORGE GERSHWIN—1898-1937—A Genius in Jazz

BIOGRAPHY: Armitage, Merle, ed. *George Gershwin*. 1938.

Books, 15:20, Oct. 16, 1938. In this memorial volume "the article that shines out, however, simple, dignified and poignant in its restraint, is Ira Gershwin's account of his brother's life."

Goldberg, Isaac. *George Gershwin, a Study in American Music*. 1931.

Booklist, 28:196, Jan., 1932. "An informal and interesting account of the life of George Gershwin, who at thirty-three has made a genuine contribution to American music and is credited with having raised jazz to a new plane."

Also in *Ladies' Home Jour.*, 48:12-13, Feb.; p. 20, Mar.; p. 25, Apr., 1931.

COLLECTIVE BIOGRAPHY: Ewen, David. *Book of Modern Composers*, (1942):481-92.

——. *Composers of Today*, (1949):98-102

Thomas and Thomas. *Forty Famous Composers*, (1948):408-18.

SPECIAL ASPECTS: Ewen, David. "Stature of George Gershwin," *Am. Merc.*, 70 (1950):716-24

Howard, J. T. *Our American Music*, (1946):446-52.

Marek, George. "Rhapsody in Blue—Twenty-five Years After," *Good House.*, 128 (1949):4.

Saleski, Gdal. *Famous Musicians of Jewish Origins*, (1949):62-66.

CHAPTER XLIV. THE SOUTH

WALTER CLARK— 1846-1924
—"The Jurist of the Populist Movement"

ORIGINAL SOURCES: Brooks, A. L., and H. T. Lefter, eds. *Papers of Walter Clark. Vol. I, 1857-1901.* 1948.

BIOGRAPHY: A. L. *Walter Clark, Fighting Judge.* 1944.

AHR, 50:355. An admirable biography of a "crusading Judge" who "gave his all to humanity."

COLLECTIVE BIOGRAPHY: Pearson, C. C., in *DAB*, 4:140.

Ashe, S. A., ed. *Biographical History of North Carolina*, (1908): 67-76.

WILLIAM CRAWFORD GORGAS— 1854-1920
—Sanitarian and Surgeon-General

BIOGRAPHY: Gibson, J. M. *Physician to the World: the Life of General William C. Gorgas.* 1950.

PHR, 20:174. Mr. Gibson's biography is "another revelation of 'little known facts about well known men.'" He gives "not only a comprehensive narrative of the sanitarian's famous work in wiping out yellow fever in the Canal Zone, but also his cleaning up Havana after 1898. Gorgas' investigation of pneumonia in South Africa, which led to health improvement among native miners, the great doctor's monumental work as Surgeon-

General during World War I, the first American conflict in which disease
did not kill more than the enemy, and his leadership against yellow fever
in Peru and Ecuador."

Gorgas, M. C., and B. J. Hendrick. *William Crawford Gorgas;
His Life and Work.* 1924.

N. Y. State Lib. "The story of the conquest of yellow fever is inextricably
interwoven with the career of General Gorgas. Not only does this record
of his life trace with simple dignity all the phases of his elimination of
this, but it gives an admirable picture of the man, his resolute determina-
tion in the face of all obstacles, his tireless devotion and his final achievements in Havana, in the Canal Zone and as Surgeon-General in the (first)
World War."

COLLECTIVE BIOGRAPHY: Jirka, F. J. *American Doctors of Destiny,* (1940) :182-200.

Lambert, S. W., and G. M. Goodwin. *Medical Leaders from
Hippocrates to Osler,* (1929) :289-310

Law, F. H. *Civilization Builders,* 338-43.

———. *Modern Great Americans,* 121-35.

Martin, T. W. "Doctor William Crawford Gorgas of Alabama
and the Panama Canal," *Newcomen Soc., Am. Branch,*
(1947).

Phalen, J. M., in *DAB,* 4:30.

Walker, Mrs. M. E. M. *Pioneers of Public Health,* (1930) :227-
38.

SPECIAL ASPECTS: Bierring, W. L. "William C. Gorgas, M. D.,"
in Fishbein, Morris. *History of the American Medical Assoc.,
1847 to 1947,* (1947) :707-11.

Snyder, Mrs. E. E. *Biology in the Making,* (1940) :207-37.

Wilson, C. M. *Ambassadors in White,* (1942) :125-55.

Yost, Edna. *Modern Americans in Science and Invention,*
(1941) :100-16.

LOUIS DEMBITZ BRANDEIS—   1856-1941
—Supreme Court Justice

BIOGRAPHY: Mason, A. T. *Brandeis, a Free Man's Life.* 1946.

Harvard Law Rev., 60:165. Especially recommended to law students and
lawyers, since it describes many of the factors "which determine the success or failure of a lawyer in the practise of his profession. The work is
particularly interesting and valuable in this aspect, since it portrays
vividly the career of a brilliant and successful advocate, shown by the

author to have been actuated in his private practise and in his public and community efforts by the highest of motives, who, nevertheless, came perilously near professional disaster as the result of a course of conduct which sharply divided the community into those who praised him beyond words as the 'People's Lawyer' and those who vigorously condemned the ethics of his conduct."

COLLECTIVE BIOGRAPHY: Cohen, J. H. *They Builded Better Than They Knew,* (1946) :190-200.

Goodhart, A. L. *Five Jewish Lawyers of the Common Law,* (1949) :24-38.

Hagedorn, Hermann. *Americans,* 205-24.

McCune, Wesley. *Nine Young Men,* (1947) :239-49.

SPECIAL ASPECTS: Bloom, S. F. "Liberalism of Louis D. Brandeis," *Commentary,* 6 (1948) :313-21.

Freund, P. A. *On Understanding the Supreme Court,* (1949) : 45-75.

Mason, A. T. "Louis Brandeis: People's Attorney," *Am. Merc.,* 64 (1947) :440-47.

Rand, I. C., in *Can. Bar Rev.,* 25 (1947) :240-50.

GEORGE WASHINGTON CARVER— 1864-1943
—One of America's Most Famous and Beloved Scientists

BIOGRAPHY: Holt, Rackham. *George Washington Carver: an American Biography.* 1943.

AHR, 49:326. "A skillful and sympathetic portrait of a great American." Born a slave, Carver overcame all obstacles, and became an outstanding agricultural chemist at Iowa State College. He was called to Tuskegee to help Booker T. Washington. He has probably revealed more of its neglected resources to the South than any other man. An interesting human document, this biography portrays the rise of a people held back by prejudices.

COLLECTIVE BIOGRAPHY: Borth, Christy. *Pioneers of Plenty,* (1939) :226-40.

Bullock, R. W. *In Spite of Handicaps,* (1927) :45-51.

Cooper, A. C., and C. A. Palmer. *Twenty Modern Americans,* 139-58.

Embree, E. R. *13 Against the Odds,* (1944) :97-116.

Hagedorn, Hermann. *Americans,* 225-43.

Lankard, F. G., in Lotz, P. H., ed. *Rising Above Color*, (1943): 1-10.

Ovington, M. W. *Portraits in Color*, (1927) :169-80.

Richardson, B. A. *Great American Negroes*, (1945) :151-63.

Thomas and Thomas. *Fifty Great Americans*, 348-57.

Yost, Edna. *Modern Americans in Science and Invention*, 147-62.

SPECIAL ASPECTS: Fenner, M. S., and J. C. Soule. "George Washington Carver—the Wizard of Tuskegee," *NEA Jour.*, 35 (1946) :580-81.

Hill, D. G., in Butler, G. P., ed. *Best Sermons*, (1947) :275-79.

Luce, C. B. "Saintly Scientist," *Vital Speeches*, 13:241-45, Feb. 1, 1947.

Wright, C. W. "George Washington Carver, an American Scientist," *Jour. Chem. Educ.*, 23 (1946) :268-70

IRVIN SHREWSBURY COBB— 1876-1944
—"Corn From Kentucky"

ORIGINAL SOURCES: Cobb, I. S. *Exit Laughing, an Autobiography.* 1941.

Atlantic, May, 1941. "*Exit Laughing* exceeds even my rosy expectations, what he has written is a smiling and anecdotal book, salty with common sense; shrewd and affectionate in its thumbnail sketches of men he liked. . . . Biting in his condemnation of a Democrat like Woodrow Wilson who disappointed his Southern fervor; amusing in his account of his writing habits, his quest for source material, and his encounter with English novelists; prejudiced, as in his hatred of motors and his fondness for Hollywood, and agreeably garrulous as a man who loves a good story and sometimes tells too many."

Stone, Irving, and Richard Kennedy, eds. *We Speak for Ourselves*, 33-36.

HUEY PIERCE LONG— 1893-1935 —"The Kingfish"

BIOGRAPHY: Beals, Carleton. *Story of Huey Long.* 1935.

N. Y. Herald Tribune, Nov. 18, 1935, p. 13. "Mr. Beals does not make the common mistake of under-estimating his enemy; and he does not believe that the evil of Huey Longism went into the grave with Huey. His comparisons of Huey with Latin-American dictators rather than with European Fascists have freshness and force."

Davis, Forrest. *Huey Long: a Candid Biography.* 1935.

N. Y. Times, Sept. 29, 1935, p. 5. "Mr. Davis follows Long through the tortuous channels of Louisiana politics, and half admiringly, records his rise to power. He watches him in the Senate, listens to his attacks upon the President. He considers Huey's social and economic philosophy."

Kane, H. T. *Louisiana Hayride; the American Rehearsal for Dictatorship, 1928-1940.* 1941.

Books, May 11, 1941, p. 5. "Although it is hardly the definitive work on Longism, 'Louisiana Hayride' is a clear, smooth-running and highly entertaining account of one of the most astonishing episodes in American political history."

Smith, Webster. *The Kingfish; a Biography of Huey Long.* 1933.

N. Y. Times, Apr. 16, 1933, p. 2. "Webster Smith is not one of Huey Long's admirers. But he cannot be accused of prejudice against him, or of unfairness, for he has told only the plain tale of the Kingfish's sensational career and amazing personality as Senator Long himself depicted it both in words and deeds. But he has written it down with a cynical sense of humor, an aloof derisiveness and a command of unconventional phraseology that make his book one of exceptional saltiness."

COLLECTIVE BIOGRAPHY: Basso, Hamilton, *Main Stream,* 179-98.

———. "Huey Long and His Background," *Harper's,* 170 (1935) : 663-73.

Hamlin, Fred. *Land of Liberty,* 251-72.

Moley, Raymond. *Twenty-seven Masters of Politics,* (1949) : 221-31.

Potter, D. M., in *DAB,* 21 (sup. 1) :506.

Rorty, James, in *Forum,* 94 (1935) :74-79, 126-27.

Sokolsky, G. E., in *Atlantic,* 156 (1935) :523-33.

SPECIAL ASPECTS: Carter, Hodding, in Leighton, Isabel, ed. *Aspirin Age,* 339-63.

———, in *Am. Merc.,* 68 (1949) :435-47.

Gunther, John. *Inside U. S. A.,* 809-12.

Johnson, G. W. *American Heroes and Hero Worship,* 147-91.

Michie, A. A., and Frank Ryhlick. *Dixie Demagogues,* (1939) : 108-41.

Parrington, V. L. *American Dreams,* 195-210.

Phillips, Cabell. "Lengthening Shadow of Huey Long," *N. Y. Times Mag.,* Nov. 7, 1948, p. 14.

Stolberg, John. "Dr. Huey and Mr. Long," *Nation,* 141:344-46, Sept. 25, 1935.

Swing, R. G. *Forerunners of American Fascism,* (1935) :62-107.

Thorning, J. F. *Builders of the Social Order,* (1941) :159-66.

Unofficial Observer. *New Dealers,* (1934) :336-75.

———. *American Messiahs,* (1935) :1-32.

Van Devander, C. W. *Big Bosses,* (1944) :192-211.

Wilson, F. J. "Undercover Man; the Kingfish Gets Hooked," *Collier's,* 119:86, May 17, 1947.

*THOMAS WOLFE—   1900-1938
—"Mountaineer or Bohemian?"

ORIGINAL SOURCES: Meade, R. D., ed. "You Can't Escape Autobiography; New Letters of Thomas Wolfe," *Atlantic,* 186 (1950) :8-83.

Middlebrook, L. R. "Further Memories of Tom Wolfe," *Am. Merc.,* 64 (1947) :413-20.

———. "Reminiscences of Tom Wolfe," *Am. Merc.,* 63 (1946) : 544-49.

Wolfe, Thomas. "Writing Is My Life," *Atlantic,* 178 (1946) :60-66; 179 (1947) :39-45, 55-61.

Terry, J. S., ed. *Thomas Wolfe's Letters to His Mother, Julia Elizabeth Wolfe.* 1943.

Commonweal, 38:127, May 21, 1943. "Everyone who admired Thomas Wolfe as a writer, or loved him as a man, had better read this book as soon as possible. . . . One of the more striking things in these letters, considering their author's just repute for a certain redundancy, is their extreme pithiness of utterance. He wrote for his mother's eyes alone as he never wrote for his public, and despite my admiration for him as a novelist, I can't but feel that here he writes better."

BIOGRAPHY: Muller, H. J. *Thomas Wolfe* (Makers of Modern Literature, 1947).

Nation, 165:652, Dec. 13, 1947. A critical study which asks the question: "and is Wolfe really the blundering, brilliant mountaineer hopelessly confused by the world of fashion? In so many ways he seems to have been just the arty young man he despised, and perhaps there is more Greenwich Village in him and less North Carolina in him than he realized. . . . The best parts of Muller's book are those that show simply and without apology his enjoyment of Wolfe's art."

COLLECTIVE BIOGRAPHY: Basso, Hamilton, in Cowley, Malcolm, ed. *After the Genteel Tradition,* 207-12.

---

* See also Spiller, et al. *Literary History of the United States,* 3 (1948) :784-86.

Loggins, Vernon. *I Hear America,* 113-41.
SPECIAL ASPECTS: Beach, J. W. *American Fiction, 1920-1940,*
(1941) :173-93.
Bishop, J. P. *Collected Essays,* (1948) :129-37.
Boynton, P. H. *America in Contemporary Fiction,* 204-24.
Burgum, E. B. "Thomas Wolfe's Discovery of America," *Va.
Quar. Rev.,* 22 (1946) :421-37.
Canby, H. S. *Seven Years Harvest,* 163-70.
Frohock, W. M. *Novel of Violence in America, 1920-1950,*
(1950) :47-66.
Geismar, M. D. *Writers in Crisis,* (1942) :185-235.
———. "Thomas Wolfe; the Hillman and the Furies," *Yale Rev.,*
35 (1946) : 649-65.
Johnson, P. H. *Hungry Gulliver; an English Critical Appraisal
of Thomas Wolfe.* 1948.
New Yorker, 23:85, Jan. 24, 1948. "An extremely acute appraisal of Thomas
Wolfe by an English critic."
Kazin, Alfred. *On Native Grounds,* 453-84.
McCole, C. J. *Lucifer at Large,* (1937) :231-53.
Muller, H. J. *Modern Fiction,* (1937) :404-18.
Norwood, Hayden. *The Marble Man's Wife: Thomas Wolfe's
Mother.* 1947.
Library Jour., 72:160, Jan. 15, 1947. "A revealing self-portrait of an extra-
ordinary individual. Of interest to Wolfe enthusiasts for the illuminating
glimpse into his heritage and for the sources of incidents and characters
appearing in his books."
Rothman, N. L., in Tate, Allen, ed. *Southern Vanguard,*
(1947) :52-77.
Snell, G. D. *Shapers of American Fiction,* 173-87.
Van Doren, Carl. *The American Novel,* 334-48.
Van Gelder, Robert. *Writers and Writing,* (1946) :114-19.

CHAPTER XLV. OHIO, INDIANA, MICHIGAN

EUGENE VICTOR DEBS—   1855-1926
—An American Socialist
ORIGINAL SOURCES: Abramowitz, Isidore, ed. *The Great Pris-
oners,* 707-08.

Schlesinger, A. M., Jr. *The Writings and Speeches of Eugene Debs.* 1948.

New Repub., 119:24, Nov. 1, 1948. "In summing up the man and his age, it is impossible for anyone who claims to be even slightly left of center to find a more impressive figure. . . . The figure of Debs and the burden of his thought have survived the perspective of years."

BIOGRAPHY: Ginger, Ray. *Bending Cross; a Biography of Eugene Victor Debs.* 1949.

AHR, 55:641. The best biography. It traces "the evolution of the man from organization Democrat and conservative craft unionist to revolutionary socialist. The author "implies that Debs was a curious mixture of Karl Marx, John Brown, and James Whitcomb Riley."

Morias, H. M., and William Cahn. *Gene Debs; the Story of a Fighting American.* 1948.

APSR, 42:1042. In this book the authors "render a service to those who may wish to draw a better perspective of the labor movement of our times, by presenting in easy style and exciting fashion the devotion and contributions of a truly great leader to labor's interests more than a generation ago. The work can hardly be called a biography. It is incomplete, sketchy, dramatizing particularly the events of the Great Northern Railway strike, the Pullman strike, the Debs campaigns for the presidency, and his imprisonment in the Atlanta penitentiary. In it there is nothing new, but its readable style makes a contribution for the popular reader."

Painter, F. R. *That Man Debs and His Lifework.* 1929.

AHR, 36:655. This book is not a well-balanced biography but it gives the important facts and may facilitate the work of a future biographer.

COLLECTIVE BIOGRAPHY: Eastman, M. F. *Heroes I Have Known,* (1942):45-68.

Ghent, W. J., in *DAB*, 5:183.

Harris, Frank. *Latest Contemporary Portraits,* (1927):103-11.

Madison, C. A. *Critics and Crusaders,* 486-506.

Thomas and Thomas. *Fifty Great Americans,* 303-11.

SPECIAL ASPECTS: Behrman, S. N. "Debs and the Day of Atonement," *New Yorker,* 23:42-45, Dec. 6, 1947.

Meyer, H. H., in Lotz, P. H., ed. *Vocations and Professions,* 42-52.

WILLIAM HOWARD TAFT—   1857-1930
—A Conservative President Who Lived to Be a Liberal

ORIGINAL SOURCES: Armstrong, W. P., ed. "Letters of Roommates: William H. Taft and George B. Edwards," *Am. Bar Jour.,* 34 (1948):383-85.

Barker, C. E. *With President Taft in the White House; Memories of William Howard Taft.* 1947.

Thompson, C. W. *Presidents I've Known,* 213-49.

BIOGRAPHY: Pringle, H. F. *The Life and Times of William Howard Taft: a Biography.* 2 vols. 1939.

AHR, 46:176. A definitive biography based largely on the Taft papers in the Library of Congress. The author holds steadily to "the pattern of biography," but necessarily reviews the "seventy-five years of American history" of which Taft was a part. He also gives valuable vignettes of many national figures.

COLLECTIVE BIOGRAPHY: Agar, Herbert. *The People's Choice,* 267-311.

Bassett, J. S. *Makers of a New Nation,* 245-67.

Hathaway, E. V. *Book of American Presidents,* 274-86.

Pier, A. S. *American Apostles to the Philippines,* (1950) :27-36.

Pringle, H. F., in *DAB,* 18:266.

Thwing, C. F. *Friends of Men,* 77-88.

Umbreit, K. B. *Our Eleven Chief Justices,* 393-450.

White, W. A. *Masks in a Pageant,* 327-44.

SPECIAL ASPECTS: Dulles, F. R. *Twentieth Century America,* 111-27.

Brown, W. G. "President Taft's Opportunity," *Century,* 78 (1909) :252-59.

Filler, Louis. *Crusaders for American Liberalism,* 320-40.

Frankfurter, Felix. *Law and Politics,* (1939) :37-47.

Lowry, E. G. *Washington Close-ups,* 264-75.

Perling, J. J. *Presidents' Sons,* 274-91.

Pollard, J. E. *Presidents and the Press,* 601-29.

Swisher, C. B. *American Constitutional Development,* 528-66.

Wish, Harvey. *Contemporary America,* (1945) :68-98.

BIOGRAPHIES OF CONTEMPORARIES: White, W. A. *A Puritan in Babylon: the Story of Calvin Coolidge.* 1938.

AHR, 45:427. Mr. White "made use of an assistant to work through the Taft papers in the Library of Congress, extracting thence samples of comment which reveal how pungent a biography of Taft may someday be written."

ALBERT JEREMIAH BEVERIDGE— 1862-1927
—A Gentleman from Indiana

BIOGRAPHY: Bowers, Claude. *Beveridge and the Progressive Era.* 1932.

AHR, 38:350. An excellent biography based largely on manuscript material. The book is both scholarly and readable. It contains many good sketches of contemporaries.

COLLECTIVE BIOGRAPHY: Thomas, B. P. *Portrait for Posterity,* 243-66.

SPECIAL ASPECTS: Kraus, Michael. *History of American History,* 546-72.

Strevey, T. E., in Hutchinson, W. T., ed. *Essays in American Historiography,* 374-93.

HENRY JONES FORD— 1863-1947
—"Father of the Automobile"

ORIGINAL SOURCES: Forbes, Mrs. R. T. *These Men I Knew,* (1940) :231-36.

BIOGRAPHY: Richards, W. C. *The Last Billionaire, Henry Ford.* 1948.

Sat. Rev. of Lit., 31:31, Apr. 3, 1948. "When historians come to write definitely of Henry Ford and his times, they will most certainly turn to 'The Last Billionaire' as a basic source. Persons who read it in the meantime will find it a vastly entertaining book about a fabulous tycoon, the like of which America had never seen before—and is apt never to see again."

Simonds, W. A. *Henry Ford, His Life, His Work, His Genius.* 1943.

Commonweal, 37:647, Apr. 16, 1943. William A. Simonds has been associated with Mr. Ford for over twenty years; one could scarcely expect this book to be critical. Yet this does not mean that it is useless. For it assembles within two covers a lot of facts and material with which Americans should be more widely acquainted. It is written in an easy if somewhat florid style, and it is probably not too far off in its major judgments —excepting for those judgments where friendship for Ford obviously would not lead to objectivity. Mr. Simonds, for instance, has nothing to say about the speedup or the turnover of labor in Ford's plants, about the inequities wrought by mass production in these factories, although he has a great deal to say about the high wages consistently paid by the company, about its fine policy of employing Negroes, and the remarkable things it has done with the employment of blind and crippled men. Ford's anti-Semitism is blankly denied."

Sward, K. T. *Legend of Henry Ford.* 1948.

New Yorker, 24:98, June 12, 1948. "Probably the most thoughtful work on Ford and his company yet published."

COLLECTIVE BIOGRAPHY: Bradford, Gamaliel. *The Quick and the Dead,* 113-48.

Busch, Niven. *Twenty-one Americans,* (1930) : 3-45.

Corwin, E. S., in *DAB,* 6:515.

Drucker, P. F. "Henry Ford: Success: Failure," *Harper's,* 195 (1947) :1-8.

Forbes, B. C. *Automotive Giants of America,* (1926) :94-109.

———. *Men Who are Making America,* 115-24

Hagedorn, Hermann. *Americans,* 245-66.

Henderson, Archibald. *Contemporary Immortals,* (1930) : 177-93.

Law, F. H. *Civilization Builders,* 51-88.

Thomas and Thomas. *Fifty Great Americans,* 339-47.

———. *Living Biographies of Famous Americans,* 295-307.

Villard, O. G. *Prophets, True and False,* 284-99.

Wildman, Edwin. *Famous Leaders of Industry,* 1st ser., (1920) : 131-43.

SPECIAL ASPECTS: Burlingame, Roger. *Inventors Behind the Inventor,* (1947) :115-43.

Ford, H. J. *Famous Fortunes,* 51-69.

Gardiner, A. G. *Portraits and Portents,* (1926) :147-54.

Gunther, John. *Inside U. S. A.,* 398-413.

Littell, Robert. *Read America First,* (1919) :246-67.

Myers, Gustavus. *History of Bigotry in the United States,* (1943) :333-48.

Stidger, W. L. *The Human Side of Greatness,* (1940) :1-11.

Stidger, W. L., ed. "Looking Under the Human Hood," *Rotarian,* 70 (1947) :9-11.

———. *Pew Preachers,* (1930) :39-48.

Thompson, C. L. "Problems of Industrial Expansion; Henry Ford: Mass Producer," *Cur. Hist.,* 17 (1949) :137-43.

Wecter, Dixon. *Hero in America,* 415-44.

WARREN GAMALIEL HARDING—   1865-1923
—Inept President Betrayed by His Friends

ORIGINAL SOURCES: Thompson, C. W. *Presidents I've Known,* 325-42.

BIOGRAPHY: Adams, S. H. *Incredible Era: the Life and Times of Warren Gamaliel Harding.* 1939.

AHR, 46:179. Harding appears as "a kindly, well-meaning 'joiner' " made a scapegoat in 1924. Largely dependent on the newspapers, "the book adds little to what Mark Sullivan has written." However, the *New Republic* (101:296, Dec. 27, 1939) says the book is "a vivid narrative" and "a sound original source for future historians . . ."

COLLECTIVE BIOGRAPHY: Agar, Herbert. *The People's Choice,* 267-311.

Clapper, E. O. *Washington Tapestry,* (1946) :55-68.

Harris, Frank. *Contemporary Portraits,* 4th ser., (1923) :262-80.

Hathaway, E. V. *Book of American Presidents,* 304-20.

Lippmann, Walter. *Men of Destiny,* (1927) :107-11.

Holbrook, S. H. *Lost Men of American History,* 320-47.

Levin, P. R. *Seven by Chance,* 244-54.

Nevins, Allan, in *DAB,* 8:252.

White, W. A. *Masks in a Pageant,* 389-434.

Wildman, Edwin. *Famous Leaders of Character in America,* 285-95.

SPECIAL ASPECTS: Adams, S. H., in Leighton, Isabel, ed. *Aspirin Age,* 81-104.

Dulles, F. R. *Twentieth Century America,* 287-309.

Gilbert, C. W. *Mirrors of Washington,* 3-21

Lowry, E. G. *Washington Close-ups,* 11-22.

Mencken, H. L., in Wilson, Edmund, ed. *Shock of Recognition,* 1233-37.

Pollard, J. E. *Presidents and the Press,* 697-712.

Slosson, J. W. "Warren G. Harding: a Revised Estimate," *Cur. Hist.,* 33 (1930) :174-79.

Starling, E. W. *Starling of the White House,* 165-203.

Wish, Harvey. *Contemporary America,* 245-71.

BIOGRAPHIES OF CONTEMPORARIES: Pringle, H. F. *Life and Times of William Howard Taft,* 1:953-56.

ORVILLE WRIGHT—   1871-1948

WILBUR WRIGHT—   1867-1912
                  —Aviation Pioneers

ORIGINAL SOURCES: Kelly, F. C., ed. *Miracle at Kitty Hawk: the Letters of Wilbur and Orville Wright.* 1951.

Herald-Tribune Bk. Rev., July 1, 1951, p. 1. This skilfully edited collection of letters, notes, and extracts from Orville's diary "is a complete contradiction of the picture of brothers Wright that emerges from the newspaper interviews and stories."

Also in *Atlantic,* 185 (1950) :23-29, 67-70; 186 (1950) :68-74.

BIOGRAPHY: Kelly, F. C. *The Wright Brothers. A Biography Authorized by Orville Wright.* 1943.

AHR, 49:129. "The definitive biography which declares that the brothers were 'equal partners' in their venture. While neither went through college or received an advanced scientific education, Mr. Kelly makes it clear that they were 'true scientists.' The press and the U. S. Army paid little attention to them, and it was not until Nov., 1909, that the Wright Company was incorporated and the business of making airplanes began. The book is a fascinating story that avoids being too technical."

Freudenthal, E. E. *Flight into History; the Wright Brothers and the Air Age.* 1949.

Herald-Tribune Bk. Rev., July 3, 1949, p. 5. "This is an interesting but an irritating book. It does throw some new light on those puzzling men. . . . Not a rounded out biography, it studies mostly two phases of their lives —their conduct of their business affairs, and their relationship with Octave Chanute."

COLLECTIVE BIOGRAPHY: Burand, W. F., in *Mech. Engr.,* 70 (1948) :581-85.

Charnley, M. V., in Keyes, R. K., ed. *Lives of Today and Yesterday,* 270-83.

Carnegie, Dale, in *Dale Carnegie Biographical Roundup,* 228-33.

Fraser, C. C. *Famous American Flyers,* (1944) :1-45.

Hathaway, E. V. *Partners in Progress,* 131-84.

Henderson, Archibald. *Contemporary Immortals,* 134-67.

Law, F. H. *Civilization Builders,* 67-73.

———. *Modern Great Americans,* 275-86.

Thomas and Thomas. *Fifty Great Americans,* 368-75.

———. *Life Stories of Great Inventors,* 245-54.

————. *Living Biographies of Famous Americans,* 219-28.

Wildman, Edwin. *Famous Leaders of Industry,* 1st ser., (1920) : 327-38.

SPECIAL ASPECTS: Hodgins, Eric, and F. A. Magoun, in Compton, Ray, and C. H. Nettles, eds. *Conquest of Science,* (1939) :169-82.

Stein, Gertrude. *Four in America,* 83-117. For Wilbur.

Van Doren, Carl, and C. L. Carmer. *American Scriptures,* 90-98.

WALTER PERCY CHRYSLER—   1875-1940
—Automobile Manufacturer

ORIGINAL SOURCES: Chrysler, W. P. *Life of an American Workman; in Collaboration with Boyden Sparks.* 1950.

Booklist, 47:155, Dec. 15, 1950. "An autobiography which appeared serially in the *Saturday Evening Post* 13 years ago, now published in book form as a timely example of opportunities offered by the American way of life. This is the success story of a boy born in a railroad town in Kansas when marauding Indians were still a danger, whose skill and ambition took him to the top in his first job as a railroad mechanic, whereupon he turned to something more difficult, and continued the process until he became an automobile manufacturer, and head of the huge Chrysler corporation."

Also in *Read. Dig.,* 58 (1951) :141-56.

COLLECTIVE BIOGRAPHY: Cooper, A. C., and C. A. Palmer. *Twenty Modern Americans,* (1942) :275-90.

Forbes, B. C. *Automotive Giants of America,* (1926) :30-43.

Mirrors of Wall Street, Putnam. (1933) :197-212.

White, T. M. *Famous Leaders of Industry,* 3rd ser., (1931) :17-27.

Woolf, S. J. *Drawn from Life,* (1932) :339-46.

SHERWOOD ANDERSON—   1876-1941   —Author

ORIGINAL SOURCES: Anderson, K. J. "My Brother, Sherwood Anderson," *Sat. Rev. of Lit.,* 31:6-7, Sept. 4, 1948.

BIOGRAPHY: Howe, Irving. *Sherwood Anderson.* (American Men of Letters, 1951) .

Sat. Rev. of Lit., Apr. 28, 1951, p. 17. "Perhaps the most satisfactory study of Anderson that has yet been written."

Scheville, James. *Sherwood Anderson; His Life and Work.* 1951.

New Yorker, 27:141, Apr. 14, 1951. "A coherent and understanding life story. It is less arresting than the legend—the small town poor boy who became a successful manufacturer, and then, one night, walked out of that life into Chicago's bohemia and became a great writer—but it makes a lot more sense. The critical portions are sound but a little pedestrian."

COLLECTIVE BIOGRAPHY: Cargill, Oscar. *Intellectual America,* 311-98.

Hansen, Harry. *Midwest Portraits,* (1923) :109-79.

Hind, C. L. *Authors,* 19-23.

Lovett, R. M., in Cowley, Malcolm, ed. *After the Genteel Tradition,* 88-99.

SPECIAL ASPECTS: Boynton, P. H. *America in Contemporary Fiction,* 113-30.

———. *More Contemporary Americans,* 157-77.

Calverton, V. F. *Newer Spirit,* (1925) :52-118.

Collins, Joseph. *Taking the Literary Pulse,* 29-47.

Daugherty, G. H. "Anderson, Advertising Man," *Newberry Lib. Bul.,* ser. 2, no. 2:30-38, Dec., 1948.

Edgar, Pelham. *Art of the Novel,* 338-51.

Frank, W. D. *In the American Jungle,* (1937) :93-96.

Fredenthal, David. "Winesburg, Ohio; a *Life* Artist Visits Sherwood Anderson's Town," *Life,* 20:74-79, June 10, 1946.

Geismar, M. D. *Last of the Provincials,* 233-84.

Hartwick, Harry. *Foreground of American Fiction,* 111-50.

Hatcher, H. H. *Creating the Modern American Novel,* 155-71.

Hazard, L. L. *Frontier in American Literature,* 290-98.

Hicks, Granville. *Great Tradition,* 207-56.

Hoffman, F. J. *Freudianism and the Literary Mind,* (1945) :230-55.

Kazin, Alfred. *On Native Grounds,* 205-26.

Loggins, Vernon. *I Hear America,* 143-74.

McCole, C. J. *Lucifer at Large,* (1937) :125-50.

Michaud, Regis. *The American Novel Today,* 154-99.

Pearson, N. H. "Anderson and the New Puritanism," *Newberry Lib. Bul.* ser. 2, no. 2:52-63, Dec. 1948.

Phillips, W. L. "How Sherwood Anderson Wrote *Winesburg, Ohio,*" *Amer. Lit.,* 23 (1951) :7-30.

Van Doren, C. C. *The American Novel,* 294-302.

West, Rebecca. *Strange Necessity,* (1928) :309-20.

Whipple, T. K. *Spokesman,* 115-38.

Wickham, Harvey. *The Impuritans,* (1929) :235-90.

KNUTE KENNETH ROCKNE— 1888-1931
—Football Coach

BIOGRAPHY: Wallace, Francis. *Notre Dame Story.* 1949.

Kirkus, 17:416, Aug. 1, 1949. "A magnificent, hero-worshipping, sentimental and at times, bally-hooing picture of its immortal, Rockne, a great coach and a great guy."

COLLECTIVE BIOGRAPHY: Beard, A. E. S. *Our Foreign-Born Citizens,* 310-21.

Kieran, John, in *DAB,* 16:67.

Thomas and Thomas. *Fifty Great Americans,* 440-48.

WENDELL LEWIS WILKIE— 1892-1944 —Lawyer and Utility Executive

COLLECTIVE BIOGRAPHY: Hagedorn, Hermann. *Americans,* 361-86.

SPECIAL ASPECTS: Binkley, W. E., in Salter, J. T., ed. *Public Men In and Out of Office,* (1946) :53-70.

Clapper, E. O. *Washington Tapestry,* 221-31.

Drummond, J. R., in Leighton, Isabel, ed. *Aspirin Age,* 444-75.

Roberts, Cecil. *And So to America,* (1947) :290-302.

ERNEST TAYLOR PYLE— 1900-1945 —Journalist

BIOGRAPHY: Miller, L. G. *The Story of Ernie Pyle.* 1950.

N. Y. Times, Aug. 27, 1950, p. 5. "Lee Miller's touching biography will help perpetuate the Ernie Pyle legend. It is a moving story about 'the little fella', sympathetically told. . . . This is a magnificent biography, as tragic a love story as has been written in our time. The little Hoosier was not a greater war correspondent than, say, Richard Harding Davis, Winston Churchill, or Floyd Gibbons; he was a different kind. He wrote himself into the heart of a great army and into the heart of the whole nation with simpler prose. Miller's biography will bathe his shrine in sympathetic glow."

COLLECTIVE BIOGRAPHY: Fisher, Charles. *Columnists,* (1944): 296-317.

Painter, F. C., in Drewry, J. E., ed. *More Post Biographies,* (1947) :274-88.

SPECIAL ASPECTS: Brown, J. M. *Seeing Things,* (1946) :46-53.

McNamara, John. *Extra! U. S. War Correspondents in Action,* (1945) :178-92.

Snyder, L. L., and R. B. Morris, eds. *Treasury of Great Reporting,* (1949) :619-23.

CHAPTER XLVI. ILLINOIS

JOHN MERLE COULTER— 1851-1928 —Botanist

BIOGRAPHY: Rodgers, A. D., III. *John Merle Coulter.* 1944.

AHR, 50:182. "A biography of a great scientist and educator that covers an important sector in the history of science in America in the late nineteenth and early twentieth century. Botany has apparently found in Dr. Rodgers a devoted and competent historian."

COLLECTIVE BIOGRAPHY: Chamberlain, C. J., in *DAB,* 4:467.

Jordon, D. S., ed. *Leading American Men of Science,* 211-31.

SPECIAL ASPECTS: Caldwell, O. W., and E. E. Slosson, eds. *Science Remaking the World,* (1923) :167-89.

Mathew, Shailer, et al. *Contributions of Science to Religion,* (1924) :141-61.

CLARENCE SEWARD DARROW —1857-1938 —Lawyer

ORIGINAL SOURCES: Stone, Irving, and Richard Kennedy, eds. *We Speak for Ourselves,* 344-53.

BIOGRAPHY: Stone, Irving. *Clarence Darrow for the Defense: a Biography.* 1941.

AHR, 48:377. The biography of a colorful lawyer who throughout life was usually "a crusader for the 'underdog.' American public opinion frequently opposed the stand which Darrow took. The book contains a number of historical inaccuracies."

Extract in Prochnow, H. V., ed. *Great Stories from Great Lives,* 343-45.

COLLECTIVE BIOGRAPHY: Rusterholtz, W. P. *American Heretics and Saints,* (1938) :251-72.

Wilson, C. T., in Beckwith and Coope. *Contemporary American Biography,* 174-82.

SPECIAL ASPECTS: Fuess, C. M., and E. S. Basford. *Unseen Harvests,* (1947) :38-53.

Mencken, H. L., in Greene, Ward, ed. *Star Reporter,* (1948) : 226-53.

——, in Snyder, L. L., and R. B. Morris, eds. *Treasury of Great Reporting,* 428-33.

JANE ADDAMS— 1860-1935 —Social Worker and Pacifist

ORIGINAL SOURCES: Addams, Jane. *Twenty Years at Hull House.* 1910.

Bookman, 32:493. Miss Addam's book starts out as an autobiography but as it proceeds the thread of personal narrative loses itself in a topical discussion of Hull-house."

——. *Forty Years at Hull House.* 1936

Christian Century, 53:194. "It is not so much that Jane Addams deserves to have her work and her personality remembered, though she deserves it richly, as that the world needs to remember them for its good."

Stone, Irving, and Richard Kennedy, eds. *We Speak for Ourselves,* 443-48.

BIOGRAPHY: Linn, J. W. *Jane Addams.* 1935.

Books, Oct. 6, 1935, p. 4. Professor Linn writes objectively, although it is obvious throughout that his fascinating, important and readable book was derived from personal sources in addition to the letters, clippings, notes, programs and memos that had accumulated from the day that Jane Addams received her first valentine and saved it."

COLLECTIVE BIOGRAPHY: Adams, E. C., and W. D. Foster. *Heroines of Modern Progress,* 280-307.

Allen, Devere, ed. *Adventurous Americans,* 141-53.

Baxter, E. M., in Lotz, P. H., ed. *Women Leaders,* 1-10.

Cooper, A. C., and C. A. Palmer. *Twenty Modern Americans,* 349-64.

Cottler, Joseph. *Champions of Democracy,* 259-84.

Hathaway, E. V. *Partners in Progress,* 246-59.

Hagedorn, Hermann. *Americans,* 161-80.

Henderson, Archibald. *Contemporary Immortals,* 119-33.

Kennedy, A. J., in *DAB,* 21 (sup. 1) : 10.

Malone, Dumas. *Saints in Action,* 84-113.

Parkman, M. R. *Heroines of Service,* 297-322.

Thomas and Thomas. *Living Biographies of Famous Women,* 261-73.

———. *Fifty Great Americans,* 330-38.

SPECIAL ASPECTS: Davidson, H. M. P. *Good Christian Men,* (1940) :213-44.

Gill, D. M., and A. M. Pullen. *Adventures of Service,* (1938) : 30-39.

JAMES HENRY BREASTED— 1865-1935 —Archaeologist

BIOGRAPHY: Breasted, Charles. *Pioneer to the Past: the Story of James Henry Breasted, Archaeologist.* 1943

AHR, 49:137. "This biography of one of the world's great Egyptologists by a son who, though often his father's lieutenant, turned his back on Egyptology to become a newspaper man . . . is exceptional in its objectivity."

COLLECTIVE BIOGRAPHY: Ware, E. W., in *DAB,* 21 (sup. 1) :110.

SPECIAL ASPECTS: Albright, W. F. "James Henry Breasted, Humanist," *Am. Scholar,* 5 (1936) :287-99.

FINLEY PETER DUNNE— 1867-1936 —Mr. Dooley

BIOGRAPHY: Ellis, Elmer. *Mr. Dooley's America: a Life of Finley Peter Dunne.* 1941.

AHR, 48:147. "A study of a humorist whose influence was national" and whose creations were "as real to the American public as the characters of Dickens were to the English-speaking public of their time. . . . Dr. Ellis's book is a real contribution to American social history."

Extract in Prochnow, H. V., ed. *Great Stories from Great Lives,* 237-38.

COLLECTIVE BIOGRAPHY: Brogan, D. W. *American Themes,* (1949) :47-50.

Masson, T. L. *Our American Humorists,* (1931) : 110-19.

SPECIAL ASPECTS: Blair, Walter. *Horse Sense in American Humor,* 240-55.

Canby, H. S. *Seven Years Harvest,* 49-53, 55-59.

Filler, Louis. *Crusaders for American Liberalism,* 55-67.

Kelleher, J. V. "Mr. Dooley and the Same Old World," *Atlantic,* 117 (1946) :119-25.

Morris, Lloyd. "Mr. Dooley: A Man of Great Renown," *New Repub.,* 118:19-24, Mar. 22, 1948.

Seldes, G. V. *Seven Lively Arts,* (1924) :111-26.

*THEODORE DREISER—1871-1945—"A Rebellious Determinist"

ORIGINAL SOURCES: Dreiser, Theodore. *Book About Myself.* 1922.

N. Y. Times, Dec. 24, 1922, p. 14. "The volume is important, for in it is seen in the making a novelist who has brought Americans face to face with vital facts and vital forces. In this history of Dreiser's early career as a newspaperman one beholds the furnace in which the creator of Sister Carrie was forged. Dreiser's experiences are worth reliving vicariously by the reader. They are a stimulus to thought. One is not likely to regard many things with complete complacency after reading this book."

Dreiser, Theodore. *Dawn: a History of Myself.* 1931.

Yale Rev., 20:857. "Dreiser writes here in the manner of his best naturalistic novels—without reticence, but with sombre dignity, he has produced a book the like of which has not been seen since Rousseau's 'Confessions.' . . . His autobiography has the merit and lapses of his best novels."

BIOGRAPHY: Elias, Robert. *Theodore Dreiser, Apostle of Nature.* 1949.

Herald-Tribune Wk. Bk. Rev., Jan. 16, 1949, p. 1. "A biography of genuine merit and importance, as absorbingly interesting as it is enlightening. In a number of explicitly autobiographical books, Dreiser revealed himself with greater candor than any other American writer of his generation. And it is obvious that he drew heavily on his personal experience for the substance of his novels. Nevertheless, Mr. Elias greatly increases our knowledge of the man and thereby enlarges our understanding of his work."

Dreiser, Helen. *My Life with Dreiser.* 1951

Booklist, 47:292, Apr. 15, 1951. "Theodore Dreiser's second wife reveals much about the American writer's temperament and private life in this account of their 26 years together. Dreiser the writer is not neglected, however, and there are sidelights on how he wrote *An American Tragedy* and other books during these years. The study is not a literary masterpiece but is an absorbing human recital and a first hand source on Dreiser."

Matthiessen, F. O. *Theodore Dreiser.* (American Men of Letters, 1951.)

Booklist, 47:293, Apr. 15, 1951. This critical study . . . examines Dreiser's life, especially his early life, for the origins of his writings and philosophy; it does not make him as real a person as does" the book by Helen

---

*See also Spiller, et al. *Literary History of the United States,* 3 (1948) :474-77.

Dreiser "but is a more objective evaluation of Dreiser's place in American literature."

Rascoe, Burton. *Theodore Dreiser* (Modern American Writers, 1925).

Ind., 115-247, Aug. 29, 1925. "Mr. Rascoe has written a downright, hard-hitting book, striking out lustily for an author who is just beginning to come into his own."

COLLECTIVE BIOGRAPHY: Cargill, Oscar. *Intellectual America*, 48-175.

Chamberlain, J. R., in Cowley, Malcolm, ed. *After the Genteel Tradition*, 27-36.

Ford, F. M. *Portraits from Life*, (1937) :164-82.

Van Doren, C. C. *Contemporary American Novelists, 1900-1920*, 38-83.

Waldman, M., in Squire, J. C., et al. *Contemporary American Authors*, 97-117.

SPECIAL ASPECTS: Boynton, P. H. *America in Contemporary Fiction*, 131-49.

———. *Some Contemporary Americans*, 126-44.

Cowley, Malcolm. "Sister Carrie's Brother," *New Repub.*, 116: 23-25, May 26, 1947.

———. "Slow Triumph of Sister Carrie," *ibid*, 116:24-27, June 23, 1947.

Duffus, R. L. *American Criticism*, (1926) :46-61.

Edgar, Pelham. *Art of the Novel*, 244-54.

Flanagan, J. T. "Theodore Dreiser in Retrospect," *Southwest Rev.*, 31 (1946) :408-11.

Hartwick, Harry. *Foreground of American Fiction*, 85-110.

Hatcher, H. H. *Creating the American Novel*, 34-57.

Hazard, L. L. *The Frontier in American Literature*, 235-40.

Hicks, Granville. *Great Tradition*, 207-56.

———, in *Am. Merc.*, 62 (1946) :751-56.

Huth, J. F., Jr. "Theodore Dreiser: the Prophet," *Amer. Lit.*, 9 (1937) :208-17.

Karsner, David. *Sixteen Authors to One*, 3-24.

Kazin, Alfred. *On Native Grounds*, 73-90.

Loggins, Vernon. *I Hear America*, 113-41.

Munson, G. B. *Destinations,* 41-56.

Ross, W. O. "Concerning Dreiser's Mind," *Amer. Lit.,* 18 (1946) :233-43.

Scully, Frank. *Rogues Gallery,* 108-24.

Shafer, Robert, in Foerster, Norman, ed. *Humanism and America,* (1930) :149-69.

Sherman, S. P. *On Contemporary Literature,* (1917) :85-101.

Snell, G. D. *Shapers of American Fiction,* 233-48.

Van Doren, C. C. *The American Novel,* 245-59.

Van Gelder, Robert. *Writers and Writing,* (1946) :164-68.

Whipple, T. K. *Spokesman,* 70-93.

CHAPTER XLVII. MISSOURI, KANSAS, NEBRASKA

WILLIAM JENNINGS BRYAN—   1860-1925
—"Financial Heretic, Effective Orator, Agrarian Spokesman"

ORIGINAL SOURCES: Thompson, C. W. *Presidents I've Known and Two Near Presidents,* 41-107.

BIOGRAPHY: Curti, Merle. *Bryan and World Peace* (Smith Studies, 1932) .

AHR, 38:388. An impartial study of Bryan's attitude toward peace in 1898 and 1913 to 1920.

COLLECTIVE BIOGRAPHY: Johnson, Allen, in *DAB,* 3:191.

Lowry, E. G. *Washington Close-ups,* 34-48.

Merriam, C. E. *Four American Party Leaders,* 63-84.

Seitz, D. C. *The "Also Rans,"* 320-28.

Villard, O. G. *Prophets, True and False,* 202-14.

White, W. A. *Masks in a Pageant,* 233-79.

Wildman, Edwin. *Famous Leaders of Character in America,* 239-50.

SPECIAL ASPECTS: Barnes, J. A. "Myths of the Bryan Campaign," *MVHR,* 34 (1947) :367-404.

Hofstadter, Richard. *American Political Tradition,* 183-202.

McGeehan, W. O., in Snyder, L. L., and R. B. Morris, eds. *Treasury of Great Reporting,* 433-38.

Osborn, H. F. *Evolution and Religion in Education*, (1926): 25-42, 93-112.

Poage, G. R. "The College Career of William Jennings Bryan," *MVHR*, 15 (1928): 165-82.

JOHN JOSEPH PERSHING— 1860-1948
—"Black Jack"

BIOGRAPHY: Palmer, Frederick. *John J. Pershing, General of the Armies: a Biography*. 1948.

AHR, 54:693. "The author was closely associated with General Pershing when both were observers in the Russo-Japanese War and again when he observed on the Commanding General's staff in France. Thus he is peculiarly fitted to prepare this study, provided he is not carried away by blind admiration for his chief. His admiration is conspicuous throughout, but there is no fulsome praise, and as a rule he merely states the facts as he saw them, leaving the reader to draw conclusions. . . . The chief value of the book is in the vivid account of Pershing's unending struggle to maintain an independent American army in France. The proof-reading was bad."

COLLECTIVE BIOGRAPHY: DeWeerd, H. A. *Great Soldiers of the Two World Wars*, (1941): 162-86.

Johnston, C. H. L. *Famous Generals of the Great War*, (1919): 141-63.

Law, F. H. *Modern Great Americans*, 176-90.

Parkman, M. R. *Fighters for Peace*, (1919): 229-54.

Pier, A. S. *American Apostles in the Philippines*, (1950): 115-28.

Simonds, F. H. *They Won the War*, (1931): 1-23.

Westrate, E. V. *Those Fatal Generals*, (1936): 274-83.

Woolf, S. J. *Drawn from Life*, 283-92.

SPECIAL ASPECTS: Liddell-Hart, B. H. *Reputations Ten Years After*, (1928): 287-316.

Lowry, E. G. *Washington Close-ups*, 254-63.

Marcosson, I. F. *Adventures in Interviewing*, 183-99.

Morley, C. D. *Pipefuls*, (1920): 137-42.

Wecter, Dixon. *Hero in America*, 392-414.

WILLA SIBERT CATHER— 1876-1947 —"Master
Painter of the American Scene"

ORIGINAL SOURCES: Greenslet, Ferris. *Under the Bridge*, 78, 116-21, 185.

BIOGRAPHY: Bennett, M. R. *The World of Willa Cather.* 1951.

Booklist, 47:252, Mar. 15, 1951. "These fragments of inheritance, place, childhood friends, scholarship, methods of writing and literary experience put together, give perspective on the novelist's life and work. Many relevant quotations from Miss Cather are interspersed. The author, a resident of Red Cloud, Nebraska, where Willa Cather spent the impressionable years from 11 to 17 has recreated the prairie town and its people in the latter 80's. Simply written, with no attempt at literary criticism, this source material cannot fail to interest admirers of a master painter of the American scene. The front end paper locates places mentioned in her books."

COLLECTIVE BIOGRAPHY: Canby, H. S., in *Sat. Rev. of Lit.,* 30: 22-24, May 10, 1947.

Kohler, David., in *Engl. Jour.,* 36 (1947) :337-47.

Overton, G. M. *Women Who Make Our Novels,* 76-97.

Porterfield, Austin, in Squire, J. C., et al. *Contemporary American Authors,* 45-67.

Sergeant, E. S. *Fire Under the Andes,* 261-82.

Trilling, Lionel, in Cowley, Malcolm, ed. *After the Genteel Tradition,* 52-63.

Van Doren, C. C. *Contemporary American Novelists, 1900-1920,* 84-131.

Zabel, M. D., in the *Nation,* 164:713-16, June 14, 1947.

SPECIAL ASPECTS: Bloom, E. A., and L. D. Bloom. "Willa Cather's Novels of the Frontier: a Study of Thematic Symbolism," *Amer. Lit.,* 21 (1949) :71-93.

Boynton, P. H. *America in Contemporary Fiction,* 150-63.

———. *Some Contemporary Americans,* 162-77.

Brown, E. K. "Homage to Willa Cather," *Yale Rev.,* 36 (1946) : 77-92.

Collins, Joseph. *Taking the Literary Pulse,* 118-29.

Daiches, David. *Willa Cather: a Critical Introduction.* 1951.

N. Y. Times, Mar. 4, 1951, p. 4. An admirably conscientious lecture series on Miss Cather and her works."

Edgar, Pelham. *Art of the Novel,* 255-67.

Footman, R. H. "The Genius of Willa Cather," *Amer. Lit.,* 10 (1938) :123-41.

Gardner, H. C. "Willa Cather's Spirit," *America,* 77:158, May 10, 1947.

Geismar, M. D. *Last of the Provincials,* 153-220.

Gray, James. *On Second Thought,* (1946) :144-48.

Hartwick, Harry. *Foreground of American Fiction,* 389-404.

Hatcher, H. H. *Creating the Modern American Novel,* 58-71.

Hicks, Granville. *Great Tradition,* 207-56.

Kazin, Alfred. *On Native Grounds,* 247-57.

Laurence, Margaret. *School of Femininity,* (1936) :339-82.

Loggins, Vernon. *I Hear America,* 195-224.

Monroe, N. E. *Novel and Society,* (1941) :225-45.

Snell, G. D. *Shapers of American Fiction,* 140-56.

Van Doren, C. C. *The American Novel, 1789-1939,* 281-93.

Whipple, T. K. *Spokesman,* 139-60.

CHAPTER XLVIII. MINNESOTA AND WISCONSIN

ROBERT MARION LA FOLLETTE—   1855-1925
—Fighting Bob: Uncompromising Progressive

ORIGINAL SOURCES: Middleton, George. *These Things are Mine; the Autobiography of a Journeyman Playwright,* (1947) :291-97.

BIOGRAPHY: Doan, E. N. *La Follettes and the Wisconsin Idea.* 1947.

New Yorker, 23:94, Dec. 20, 1947. "As an exposition of the Wisconsin Idea —the struggle for a progressive liberalism—the book is informative. The concluding section, however, which deals with the political career of Robert M. La Follette, Jr., sounds merely like a campaign biography."

COLLECTIVE BIOGRAPHY: Harris, Frank. *Contemporary Portraits,* 4th ser., (1932) :155-61.

Macartney, C. E. N. *Men Who Missed It,* 96-103.

Paxson, F. L., in *DAB,* 10:541.

Villard, O. G. *Prophets, True and False,* 187-201.

SPECIAL ASPECTS: Filler, Louis. *Crusaders of American Liberalism,* 205-11.

Frankfurter, Felix. *Law and Politics,* 314-19.

Hesseltine, W. B. "Robert Marion La Follette and the Principles of Americanism," *Wis. Mag. Hist.,* 31 (1948) :261-67.

Lowry, E. G. *Washington Close-ups,* 233-42.

Muggah, M. G., and P. H. Raihle. *Meet Your Neighbor,* 160-63.

FREDERICK JACKSON TURNER—   1861-1932
—Historian of the American Frontier

ORIGINAL SOURCES: Fisher, Estelle, ed. "Letters of Frederick Jackson Turner," *Wis. Mag. Hist.,* 31 (1948) :339-45.

COLLECTIVE BIOGRAPHY: Commager, H. S. *American Mind,* 293-309.

Becker, C. L., in Odum, H. W., ed. *American Masters of Social Science,* 273-318.

———, in Peterson, Houston, ed. *Great Teachers,* 231-50.

Craven, Avery. "Frederick Jackson Turner, Historian," *Wis. Mag. Hist.,* 25 (1942) :408-24.

SPECIAL ASPECTS: Becker, C. L. *Everyman His Own Historian,* (1935) :191-232.

Benson, Lee. "The Historical Background of Turner's Frontier Essay," *Agri. Hist.,* 25 (1951) :59-82.

Craven, Avery, in Hutchinson, W. T., ed. *Essays in American Historiography,* 252-70.

Hofstadter, Richard. "Turner and the Frontier Myth," *Am. Scholar,* 18 (1949) :433-43.

Mood, Fulmer. *The Development of Frederick Jackson Turner as a Historical Thinker.* (Reprinted from *Transactions of the Colonial Soc. of Mass.,* vol. 34, pp. 283-352) . 1943.

AHR, 49:263. Mr. Mood gives "a careful examination of Turner's career up to the age of forty, with special references to the influences that shaped his ideas about history in general and the history of the United States in particular. . . . Turner's famous 'interpretation' Mr. Mood neither criticizes nor defends, but he defends Turner against the charge of being 'provincial'—the charge that he began with courses on the general history of the United States and then narrowed his interest to the course on the history of the West."

Mood, Fulmer, ed. "Frederick Jackson Turner's Address on Education in a United States Without Free Lands," *Agri. Hist.,* 23 (1949) :254-59.

Paxson, F. L. *Great Demobilization,* (1941) :23-41.

Saveth, E. N. *American Historians and European Immigrants,* 122-37.

Essays in American History Dedicated to Frederick Jackson Turner. Holt, 1910.

CHARLES HORACE MAYO—1865-1939—Son of the Founder of the Mayo Clinic

BIOGRAPHY: Clapesattle, Helen. *The Doctors Mayo.* 1941.

AHR, 47:901. Fascinating but scholarly account of an old country doctor and his two sons who built a great American clinic.

Extract in Prochnow, H. V., ed. *Great Stories from Great Lives,* 96-101.

COLLECTIVE BIOGRAPHY: Cooper, A. C., and C. A. Palmer. *Twenty Modern Americans,* 235-54.

Jirka, F. J. *American Doctors of Destiny,* (1940) :296-313.

*SINCLAIR LEWIS—1885-1951—He Put Main Street on the Map

Van Doren, Carl. *Sinclair Lewis: a Biographical Sketch.* 1933.

Books, Jan. 29, 1933, p. 2. "This little book, I think, contains the most brilliant writing Mr. Van Doren has done to date. From the first sentence, 'Sinclair Lewis stood up like a restless, determined tall flame,' to the close of the book it is a masterly and refreshing example of adroit and purposeful writing. . . . In Mr. Van Doren's pages 'Red' Lewis comes energetically alive, full of astonishing nervous energy and a passionate enthusiasm for living."

COLLECTIVE BIOGRAPHY: Boyd, E. A. *Portraits,* (1924) :183-88.

Cantwell, Robert, in Cowley, Malcolm, ed. *After the Genteel Tradition,* 112-26.

Commager, H. S. *American Mind,* 247-76.

Waldman, N., in Squire, J. C., et al. *Contemporary American Authors,* 71-94.

Woolf, S. J. *Drawn from Life,* 312-20.

SPECIAL ASPECTS: Boynton, P. H. *America in Contemporary Fiction,* 164-84.

———. *Contemporary Americans,* 179-98.

Canby, H. S. *Seven Years Harvest,* 133-39.

Edgar, Pelham. *Art of the Novel,* 268-300.

Geismar, M. D. *Last of the Provincials,* 69-150.

Hartwick, Harry. *Foreground of American Fiction,* 250-81.

---

* See also Spiller, et al. *Literary History of the United States,* 3 (1948) :609-11.

Hatcher, H. H. *Creating the Modern American Novel,* 109-26.

Hicks, Granville. *Great Tradition,* 207-56.

Hind, C. L. *More Authors and I,* 186-92.

Karsner, David. *Sixteen Authors to One,* 67-80.

Kazin, Alfred. *On Native Grounds,* 205-26.

Lippman, Walter. *Men of Destiny,* 71-92.

Loggins, Vernon. *I Hear America,* 225-47.

Marble, Mrs. A. R. *Nobel Prize Winners in Literature, 1901-31,* 364-82.

Michaud, Regis. *The American Novel Today,* 128-53.

Van Doren, C. C. *The American Novel,* 303-14.

Van Gelder, Robert. *Writers and Writing,* (1946) :77-81.

Williams, Michael. *Catholicism and the Modern Mind,* (1928) : 239-50.

Zabel, M. D., ed. *Literary Opinions in America,* (1937) :541-51.

CHAPTER XLIX. THE WEST

EDWARD MANDELL HOUSE—   1858-1938
—Wilson's Unofficial Representative

ORIGINAL SOURCES: Rahv, Philip, ed. *Discovery of Europe,* 436-59.

Seymour, Charles, ed. *The Intimate Papers of Colonel House.* 2 vols. 1926.

AHR, 31:812. Colonel House, an intimate friend, did much of the President's thinking for him. He also served as Wilson's unofficial representative in Europe. These documents throw much light on his activities.

COLLECTIVE BIOGRAPHY: Unofficial Observer (pseud.). *New Dealers,* (1934) :336-75.

Villard, O. G. *Prophets True and False,* 169-86.

SPECIAL ASPECTS: Benjamin, R. S., ed. *Inside Story,* (1940) : 139-56.

Gilbert, C. W. *Mirrors of Washington,* 89-104.

Martin, Wm. *Statesmen of the War—Retrospect, 1918-1928,* (1928) :234-48.

Parrington, V. L. *American Dreams,* 187-91.

MIGUEL ANTONIO OTERO— 1859-1944
—Governor of New Mexico

ORIGINAL SOURCES: Dargan, Marion, ed. Otero, M. A. *My Nine Years as Governor of the Territory of New Mexico, 1897-1906*. 1940.

"Confronted with the problem of deciding between nineteen candidates for the governorship of New Mexico, President McKinley passed all up, and appointed a young man whom he knew personally. Thus Miguel Otero suddenly arrived at a position he had not sought. A son of one of the leading Spanish families of the territory, he showed he had ability as an administrator. His enemies gave him a hard fight, but he was reappointed as governor by Roosevelt. The territory prospered during his administration, and Otero worked to further the admission of New Mexico as a state."—Foreword.

Hammond, George, ed. Otero, M. A. *My Life on the Frontier, 1864-1882*. Vol. I. 1935.

N. Y. Times, Sept. 8, 1935, p. 9. "Of all the books that have come out of the Southwestern frontier this is one of the richest, most varied and most vivid, a valuable contribution to the story of the Southwest. . . . The book contains a vast amount of material told with such graphic detail, all of it well arranged and narrated in orderly style."

———. Vol. II. 1939.

Pacific Hist. Rev., 9:483. This volume "covers roughly the last two decades of the 19th century, although most of the events fall in the eighties. . . . It was a rough period of New Mexico history, and the author pays little attention to constructive factors which contributed to the making of New Mexico today."

SPECIAL ASPECTS: Dargan, Marion. "New Mexico's Fight for Statehood," *N. M. Hist. Rev.*, 14 (1939) :17-19, 22-28. See index in Vols. 14-16 for passing reference to Otero in these seven articles.

Thompson, A. W. "I Helped Raise the Rough Riders," *ibid.*, 287-99.

ANNIE OAKLEY— 1860-1926 —Markswoman

BIOGRAPHY: Swartwout, A. F. *Missie; an Historical Biography of Annie Oakley*. 1947.

COLLECTIVE BIOGRAPHY: Genzmer, G. H., in *DAB*, 13:603.

Holbrook, S. H. *Little Annie Oakley and Other Rugged People*, (1948) :1-7.

Also in *Life,* 22:67-69, Apr. 28, 1947.

MARY AUSTIN—1868-1934—"One of America's Best Minds"

ORIGINAL SOURCES: Austin, Mary. *Earth Horizon, Autobiography.* 1932.

Sat. Rev. of Lit., 9:278, Nov. 26, 1932. "Mary Austin's *Earth Horizon* compelled me to read it as nearly at one sitting as the necessity of snatching a little food and sleep would permit, and left me with such a sense of actual participation in the life of America for the years through which it took me that it seemed curious to find myself moved ahead so little on the calendar."

BIOGRAPHY: Doyle, H. M. *Mary Austin: Woman of Genius.* 1939.

Amer. Lit., 14:456. The author, Helen Macknight Doyle, was a woman physician, who became Mary Austin's friend at a trying period. She compiled her book "largely from her observations and diagnoses, based upon many frank conversations. Her attitude is that of a sympathetic psychiatrist trying to root out the sources of her patient's trouble. For example, she places severe blame upon the mother and husband for their coldness to Mary. To her clinical notes Dr. Doyle adds gleanings from local papers and records, and gossip from old folks who recall the eccentric Mrs. Wallace Austin."

Pearce, T. M. *The Beloved House.* 1940.

Amer. Lit., 14:456. This book is "a sympathetic yet penetrating interpretation of Mary Austin's leading ideas, together with some new biographical items." The author was "a member of the literary group in New Mexico over which Mrs. Austin presided, (and) qualifies both as a scholar and as a friend of his subject. His book reflects his double role. He contributes fresh biographical material for two periods of her life, her childhood in Carlinville, Illinois, and her later years in Santa Fe. The Carlinville items are, for the most part, interesting gossip gleaned by the writer during a brief visit there. The Santa Fe episodes, however, are more revealing and authentic. Casa Querida, the home of Mary Austin built in Santa Fe, became for him a symbol typifying America and the American continent —the Beloved House."

COLLECTIVE BIOGRAPHY: Hunt, R. D. *California's Stately Hall of Fame,* 565-69.

Martin, Anne, in *Nation,* 139:409, Oct. 10, 1934.

Overton, G. M. *Women Who Make Our Novels,* 8-22.

Rourke, Constance, in *New Repub.,* 73:166-67, Dec. 21, 1932.

Sargeant, E. S. "Mary Austin, a Portrait," *Sat. Rev. of Lit.*, 11:96, Sept. 8, 1934.

Steffens, Lincoln, in *Am. Mag.*, 72 (1911) :178-81, June.

Tracy, H. C. *American Naturists*, 244-63.

Wynn, Dudley, in *DAB*, 21 (sup. 1) :34.

SPECIAL ASPECTS: Farrar, J. C., ed. *Literary Spotlight*, 165-74.

Smith, Henry. "The Feel of Purposeful Earth. Mary Austin's Prophecy," *N. M. Quar.*, 1 (1931) :17-33.

Van Doren, Carl. "Mary Austin: Discoverer and Prophet," *Century*, 107 (1923) :151-56.

———. *Many Minds*, 3-17.

———, ed. *Modern American Prose*, 373-83.

Wynn, Dudley. "Mary Austin, Woman Alone," *Va. Quar. Rev.* 13 (1937) :243-56.

EUGENE MANLOVE RHODES—   1869-1935
—"Cowboy Novelist"

ORIGINAL SOURCES: Dearing, F. V., ed. *Best Novels and Stories of Eugene Manlove Rhodes*. Introduction by J. Frank Dobie, pp. vii-xxii. 1949.

BIOGRAPHY: Rhodes, May. *The Hired Man on Horseback: My Story of Eugene Manlove Rhodes*. 1938.

MVHR, 25:583. "An intimate biography of Eugene Manlove Rhodes by his widow. . . ." The casual reader will find this book charming and highly amusing. Readers who love the region of which Rhodes wrote "will find it difficult to lay the book aside until the last page is finished."

COLLECTIVE BIOGRAPHY: Dobie, J. F. "Gene Rhodes: Cowboy Novelist," *Atlantic*, 183 (1949) :75-77.

*JACK LONDON—   1876-1916
—"Sailor on Horseback"

ORIGINAL SOURCES: London, Jack. *John Barleycorn, an Autobiography*. 1913.

N. Y. Times, 18:445, Aug. 24, 1913. "There are faults in this book—the crudely melodramatic illustrations, for instance. And Mr. London's vocabulary seems strangely limited. But 'John Barleycorn' is a distinguished achievement, a book surely destined to a high place in the world's esteem.

---

* See also Spiller, et al. *Literary History of the United States*, 3 (1948) :619-20.

Whatever may be its value as temperance propaganda, it must at any rate be acknowledged to be excellent narrative and startlingly real autobiography."

BIOGRAPHY: London, Charmian. *The Book of Jack London.* 2 vols. 1921.

Bookman, 54:391. A frank and vivid narrative by his adoring widow.

London, Joan. *Jack London and His Times: an Unconventional Biography.* 1939.

Amer. Lit., 12:126. The best biography. "Miss Joan London has sufficient sympathy with the Marxian outlook to interpret her father's activities in the early socialist movement at the turn of the century, and sufficient scholarship to chronicle the rise of socialism as a political force, in relation to her father and his leftist books." She "proves that her father was a careful student of Benjamin Kidd, but failed to record the fact that Ina Coolbrith, last of the old California writers, knew and encouraged" him in his youth.

Stone, Irving. *Sailor on Horseback. The Biography of Jack London.* 1938.

Time, 32:71, Sept. 19, 1938. "In *Sailor on Horseback,* Irving Stone gives a good picture of London's incredible literary labors, a good account of his strenuous domestic life, a dim picture of the period in which his books flourished. . . ."

COLLECTIVE BIOGRAPHY: Hunt, R. D. *California's Stately Hall of Fame,* 435-40.

Spiller, et al. *Literary History of the United States,* 2:1033-37.

Russell, F. A. *American Pilgrimage,* 234-52.

Whipple, T. K., in *DAB,* 11:370.

Williams, B. C. *Our Short Story Writers,* 256-77.

SPECIAL ASPECTS: Foner, P. S., ed. *Jack London.* 1947.

New Yorker, 23:145, Dec. 13, 1947. "A collection of London's fictional, autobiographical and polemic writings on social themes, with a long introduction in which the editor reviews London's career, emphasizing his noisy and athletic politics. Dr. Foner attempts to explain the motives behind London's celebrated desertion of the Socialist party and deals sympathetically with his eventual spiritual and presumed suicide."

Hartwick, Harry. *Foreground of American Fiction,* 67-84.

Hatcher, H. H. *Creating the Modern American Novel,* 21-33.

Hicks, Granville. *Great Tradition,* 164-206.

Johnson, M. E. *Through the South Seas with Jack London.* 1913.

N. Y. Times, 19:89, Feb. 22, 1914. "It is of Jack London's adventurous voyage in the forty-five footer, known as the Snark, that Mr. Johnson writes, and though Mr. London himself has written concerning this voyage, it is a good thing to have a story of the affair from a member of his crew. Mr. Johnson says that after years of longing for a real adventure he found what he wanted aboard the Snark while it was sailing from San Francisco to Honolulu, and thence on to Sidney by the way of the Marquesas, Society, Samoan and the Fiji islands."

Kazin, Alfred. *On Native Grounds,* 91-126.

Loggins, Vernon. *I Hear America,* 249-81.

London, Charmian. *The Log of the Snark.* 1915.

Nation, 101:784, Dec. 30, 1915. "Mrs. London tells from a woman's point of view . . . the story of the interrupted round-the-world cruise which has already been described by her husband." However, her narrative is not likely "to make 'snarking' among the South Sea Islands a popular pastime."

Mott, F. L. *Golden Multitudes,* 233-40.

Pattee, F. L. *Sidelights on American Literature,* 98-160.

Snyder, L. L., and R. B. Morris, eds. *Treasury of Great Reporting,* 269-74.

Van Doren, C. C. *The American Novel,* 225-44.

WILL ROGERS—1879-1935—He Made His Country Laugh

ORIGINAL SOURCES: Day, Donald, ed. *The Autobiography of Will Rogers.* 1949.

So. Atl. Quar., 50:300. "This is an unusual interpretation of the word 'autobiography.' The contents consist principally of magazine articles, newspaper columns, or published interviews. Only small portions, it would appear, were designed by Will Rogers as his *Autobiography.* However, the selections, pieced together with some comment by Donald Day, provide a chronological survey of the humorist's career."

BIOGRAPHY: Lait, Jack. *Our Will Rogers.* 1935.

N. Y. Times, Oct. 13, 1935, p. 5. "Mr. Lait's book has the distinctive value of being written out of intimate personal knowledge of Will Rogers, for the two had been friends and companions and sometimes fellow workers, for many years. . . . Most of the volume is concerned with Rogers' personality and with his wit, portraying the one and discussing the other from the viewpoint of personal knowledge and illustrating his points by means of extensive quotations from all manner of Rogers' utterances."

Rogers, Betty. *Will Rogers, His Wife's Story.* 1941.

New Repub., 105:869, Dec. 22, 1941. "Mrs. Rogers writes simply and, for a wife, quite sensibly about her husband's homely ways and the casual development of a uniquely American career. Well peppered with typical Rogers commentary."

Extract in Prochnow, H. V., ed. *Great Stories from Great Lives,* 282-83.

COLLECTIVE BIOGRAPHY: Butterfield, Roger. "Legend of Will Rogers," *Life,* 27:78-82, July 18, 1949.

Same abridged in *Read. Dig.,* 55 (1949) :31-36.

Cooper, A. C., and C. A. Palmer. *Twenty Modern Americans,* 327-47.

Hagedorn, Hermann. *Americans,* 291-309.

Hughes, Elinor. *Famous Stars of Filmdom,* (1932) :307-27.

Hunt, R. D. *California's Stately Hall of Fame,* 471-76.

Karsner, David. *Sixteen Authors to One,* 281-90.

Thomas and Thomas. *Living Biographies of Famous Americans,* 263-73.

Wecter, Dixon, in *DAB,* 21 (sup. 1) : 635.

SPECIAL ASPECTS: Blair, Walter. *Horse Sense in American Humor,* 256-73.

Canby, H. S. *Seven Years' Harvest,* 49-53.

Feibleman, J. K. *In Praise of Comedy,* (1939) :217-73.

Lucas, E. V. *Only the Other Day,* (1937) :95-105.

CHECK-LIST OF BOOKS MOST FREQUENTLY USED
IN PART II

Abbott, Lyman. *Silhouettes of My Contemporaries*. Doubleday, 1921. 361pp. o. p. 1933.

Outlook, 130:71, Jan. 11, 1922. A collection of the "Snap-shots" which appeared in the *Outlook*, to which are added sketches of Fiske, Booth, Lincoln, and Theodore Roosevelt.

Adams, Elmer Cleveland, and Warren Dunham Foster. *Heroines of Modern Progress*. Sturgis, 1913. 324pp. $3.50.

Booklist, 9:359, May, 1913. Entertaining sketches of women reformers from Mary Lyon to Jane Addams.

Agar, Herbert. *The Price of Union*. Houghton, 1950. 750pp. $5.00.

AHR, 55:909. "The work of a brilliant writer and seasoned historian" who shows how, again and again in American history, "emergencies were matched by opportunists and political strategists like Jefferson, Jackson, Lincoln, Wilson, and the two Roosevelts," and also "how weak and inept presidents, like Pierce, Fillmore and Buchanan, were powerless to maintain party discipline and give direction to unruly Congresses." The book is "notable for penetrating thumbnail analyses of character and ability."

Aikman, Duncan. *Calamity Jane and the Lady Wildcats*. Holt, 1927. 347pp. o. p. 1950.

Outlook, 148:34, Jan. 4, 1928. Vivid pictures of "uncontrollable ladies who flourished in the old bawdy West."

Alden, Carroll Storrs, and Ralph Earle. *Makers of Naval Tradition*. Ginn, 1926. 332pp. o. p. 1950.

AHR, 31:361. A readable book which emphasizes twelve leaders "as the chief makers of naval tradition."

Allen, Devere, ed. *Adventurous Americans*. Farrar, 1932. 346pp. o. p. 1950.

New Repub., 70:157, Mar. 23, 1932. Anonymous sketches of twenty-four contemporary liberals.

Angle, Paul McClelland. *The Lincoln Reader*. Rutgers U. Press, 1947. 564pp. $3.75.

AHR, 53:124. "The best single volume about Lincoln" for the general reader.

Bacon, Robert, and James Brown Scott, eds. Root, Elihu. *Miscellaneous Addresses*. Harvard, 1917. 308pp. $5.00.

AHR, 24:132. "Mr. Root's style is that of the high class specialist, and a bit unbending for popular uses, but he masses facts impressively and can be refreshingly frank."

Balch, Marston, ed. *Modern Short Biographies and Autobiographies.* Enl. ed. Harcourt, 1940. 589pp. $2.25.

New Repub., 102:513, Apr. 15, 1940. These selections are representative of recent American writing in this field. Nineteen out of the twenty-six men and women included are Americans.

Bassett, John Spencer. *Makers of a New Nation* (Pageant of America, 1928). Yale, 344pp. $2.00.

MVHR, 16:282. This volume "covers the political history of the United States from 1861 to 1923. . . ." It is accurate and interesting.

———. *The Middle Group of American Historians.* Macmillan, 1917. 324pp. o. p. 1950.

AHR, 22:879. After considering a number of men from various colonies, Bassett treats "the Middle Group" in much greater detail: Sparks, Bancroft, Prescott, and Peter Force. The treatment is biographical and critical.

Beard, Annie E. S. *Our Foreign-Born Citizens; What They Have Done for America.* 3rd ed. Crowell, 1939. 448pp. $2.50.

Booklist, 35:275, Apr. 15, 1939. "Short sketches of 47 American celebrities of foreign birth."

Bechdolt, Frederick Ritchie. *Giants of the Old West.* Century, 1931. 245pp. o. p. 1950.

MVHR, 17:620. A lively study of the personalities and careers of nine men who took leading parts in the making of the old West.

Becker, Carl Lotus. *Every Man His Own Historian; Essays on History and Politics.* Crofts, 1935. 325pp. $3.50.

Yale Rev., 25:213. "A volume of essays on historical and political subjects, all of which, with one exception, have been previously published in magazines."

Beckwith, John A., and Geoffrey Gainsborough Coope, eds. *Contemporary American Biography.* Harper, 1941. 347pp. o. p. 1950.

This useful little volume contains samples of a great variety of biographical material relating to over twenty individuals. There are comparative readings in biography for Wilson, Justice Holmes, and Stephen Foster.

Bessey, Mabel A., ed. Gamaliel Bradford. *Portraits and Personalities.* Houghton, 1933. 283pp. o. p. 1950.

N. Y. Times, Nov. 6, 1933, p. 6. The editor has contributed introductory essays on the author and "The Place of Biography in the School Curriculum," plus suggestive questions and topics. Then there are seven new sketches by Bradford, and five drawn from his other volumes.

Bishop, Joseph Bucklin. *Notes and Anecdotes of Many Years.* Scribner, 1925. 236pp. o. p. 1933.

N. Y. World, Oct. 18, 1925. An experienced newspaper man portrays many famous characters he knew.

Blair, Walter. *Native American Humor, (1800-1900).* Am. Bk., 1937. 573pp. o. p. 1950.

MVHR, 24:586. A scholarly history of the development of American humor during the nineteenth century.

Blankenship, Russell. *And There Were Men.* Knopf, 1942. 305pp. o. p. 1950.

Books, Aug. 16, 1942, p. 5. Interesting sketches of different types of men who lived in the Pacific Northwest.

Bleyer, William Grosvenor. *Main Currents in the History of American Journalism.* Houghton, 1927. 464pp. $4.00.

AHR, 32:891. Concentrates largely on nine outstanding editors from the elder Bennett to W. R. Hearst.

Blumenfield, Ralph David, *R. F. D.'s Procession.* Macmillan, 1935. 285pp. o. p. 1950.

Books, Aug. 25, 1935, p. 16. "This is a sketchy, gossipy and uncritical book . . ."

Bowers, Claude G. *Party Battles of the Jackson Period.* Houghton, 1922. 506pp. $5.00.

AHR, 28:558. An entertaining history which emphasizes colorful leaders; neglects underlying economic issues and manuscript sources.

———. *The Tragic Era: the Revolution After Lincoln.* Houghton, 1929. 567pp. $5.00.

AHR, 35:382. Dramatic but scholarly history containing a number of excellent pen portraits. The indictment of the Radical Republicans would be more effective if the author had shown more restraint in his expressions.

Boynton, Percy Holmes. *More Contemporary Americans.* U. of Chicago Press, 1928. 231pp. o. p. 1950.

Booklist, 24:58, Nov., 1927. "This second volume of essays on literary appreciation and the American public discusses Herman Melville, Ambrose Bierce, Sherwood Anderson and Sinclair Lewis."

———. *Some Contemporary Americans: the Personal Equation in Literature.* U. of Chicago Press, 1924. 289pp. o. p. 1950.

Outlook, 138:64, Sept. 10, 1924. Brief but penetrating essays on twentieth century writers.

Bradford, Gamaliel. *American Portraits, 1875-1900.* Houghton, 1922. 248pp. $3.50.

AHR, 28:167. Sympathetic yet critical sketches whose value depends "upon the insight and judgment" the biographer shows in studying the published material and upon his skill in precipitating the results of his study into a brief sketch."

———. *As God Made Them; Portraits of Some Nineteenth Century Americans.* Houghton, 1929. 294pp. $4.00.

Books, Mar. 31, 1929, p. 5. "The understanding is high, the writing excellent. One may not always agree with the interpretation, but it is a relief in these days to find something of research presented in such readable fashion."

———. *Biography and the Human Heart.* Houghton, 1932. 283pp. $3.50.

Books, Dec. 4, 1932, p. 2. This posthumous volume is of interest chiefly for the sketches of Longfellow and Whitman and two essays on the technique of biography.

———. *Confederate Portraits.* Houghton, 1914. 291pp. $4.00.

AHR, 20:177. Readable character sketches which "reject all debatable matter." Quite likely, many readers found the sketches surprisingly sympathetic when they first appeared in the *Atlantic*.

———. *Portraits of American Women.* Houghton, 1919. 276pp. o. p. 1950.

Outlook, 124:79, Jan. 14, 1920. Sketches written with rare insight and literary skill.

———. *The Quick and the Dead.* Houghton, 1931. 283pp. o. p. 1950.

Outlook, 157:374, Mar. 11, 1931. When applied to leaders of the Seventh Generation, Bradford's formula sometimes produces sketches that are provocative.

———. *Union Portraits.* Houghton, 1916. o. p. 1950.

AHR, 22:187. Impressionistic sketches based "on a vast knowledge of detail." Some seem provocative and illuminate distinctly American characteristics.

Bridge, James Howard. *Millionaires and Grub Street; Comrades and Contacts in the Last Half Century.* Brentano, 1931. 304pp. o. p. 1950.

N. Y. Times, Sept. 20, 1931, p. 25. "For five years before his coming to this country, Bridge was the secretary of Herbert Spencer. Naturally enough, he devoted the first chapter of his book to his experiences with and description of this giant of the nineteenth century." His first job in America was with Andrew Carnegie, with whom he developed a close and lasting friendship. He also enjoyed pleasant relations with other well-known men.

Britt, Albert. *Great Biographers.* Whittlesey, 1936. 223pp. o. p. 1950.

N. Y. Times, Apr. 5, 1936, p. 2. "An interesting and valuable outline of biography."

Brogan, Denis William. *American Themes.* Harper, 1949. 284pp. $3.50.

AHR, 55:228. Ten essays out of thirty-nine deal with biographical subjects.

Brooks, Van Wyck. *A Chilmark Miscellany.* Dutton, 1948. 315pp. $4.00.

Booklist, 45:85, Nov. 1, 1948. "Selections from the author's pleasant writing, with its historical and literary flavor. Includes descriptions of New England and the South, essays on literary figures, and miscellaneous sketches."

———. *New England: Indian Summer, 1865-1915.* (Everyman's Library series 641A.) Dutton, 1940. 557pp. $1.25.

AHR, 47:380. Contains stimulating sketches of literary people, but little on the history of American thought.

———. *The Flowering of New England, 1815-1865.* (Modern Library ed.) Dutton, 1936. 550pp. $1.95.

AHR, 42:563. A brilliant, impressionistic study of literary history by America's most distinguished literary critic. Inclined to ramble; the reader needs to use the index for a complete portrait of any one writer.

———. *The Times of Melville and Whitman.* Dutton, 1947. 489pp. $5.00.

Amer. Lit., 20:459. "A history of the literary life in America" by a modern critic who has never ceased to grow.

———. *The World of Washington Irving.* Dutton, 1944. 495pp. $4.00.

AHR, 50:557. An entertaining book which presents a variety of colorful figures. Sometimes inaccurate as to minor details.

Brown, Rollo Walter. *Lonely Americans.* Coward-McCann. 1929. 319pp. o. p. 1950.

Bookman, 69:iv, May, 1929. "In each case Mr. Brown has approached his subject with knowledge, spirit and intimate sympathy, even writing of Lincoln and Whistler freshly. This is an important book."

Busch, Niven, Jr. *Twenty-one Americans; Being Profiles of Some People Famous in Our Time.* Doubleday, 1930. 332pp. o. p. 1933.

New Repub., 65:200, Dec. 31, 1930. "Sprightly but unofficial biographies. The sketches first appeared as 'Profiles' in *The New Yorker* and are intended to inform readers divertingly of the manners, apologies and achievements of the leaders in the building, golfing, theatrical and allied American industries."

Campbell, Walter Stanley (Stanley Vestal, pseud.). *Mountain Men.* Houghton, 1937. 296pp. o. p. 1950.

MVHR, 24:255. Episodes in the lives of trappers and trail breakers of the Rocky Mountain region.

Canby, Henry Seidel. *Classic Americans: a Study of Eminent American Writers from Irving to Whitman.* Harcourt, 1931. 351pp. o. p. 1950.

Nation, 133:545, Nov. 18, 1931. Interprets eight major writers in the light of social and intellectual background.

——. *Seven Years' Harvest; Notes on Contemporary Literature.* Farrar, 1936. 310pp. o. p. 1950.

New Repub., 89:364, Jan. 20, 1937. "Mr. Canby is admirable on Thomas Wolfe, and on the autobiographical novel in general; and he has some excellent things to say about the future of realism."

Cannon, Carl Leslie. *American Book Collectors and Collecting, from Colonial Times to the Present.* Wilson, 1941. 391pp. $3.00.

AHR, 47:343. Emphasizes the collector himself in some cases; in others the books he collected.

Cargill, Oscar. *Intellectual America; Ideas on the March.* Macmillan, 1942. 777pp. $6.00.

AHR, 47:897. Stimulating study of the influence of European movements on recent literary life in America.

Carpenter, Jesse Thomas. *The South as a Conscious Minority, 1789-1861; a Study in Political Thought.* N. Y. U. Press, 1930. 315 pp. $3.00.

Am. Pol. Sci. Rev., 25:466. "The first systematic survey of the development of this peculiar minority political philosophy."

Carver, George. *Alms for Oblivion; Books, Men, and Biography.* Bruce, 1946. 325pp. $3.00.

N. Y. Times, Aug. 11, 1946, p. 29. "An interesting account of biographical writing in England" from the medieval chronicler to Lytton Strachey.

Caughey, John Walton. *California*. Prentice-Hall, 1940. 680pp. (Text ed.) $5.00.

PHR, 9:490. "A straightforward, interesting narrative of the history of California from its discovery to the present day."

Channing Edward, Albert Bushnell Hart, and Frederick Jackson Turner. *Guide to the Study and Reading of American History*. Rev. ed. Ginn, 1912. 650pp. o. p. 1950.

AHR, 18:589. A new edition of a book which first appeared in 1897.

Choate, Joseph Hodges. *American Addresses*. Century, 1911. 360pp. o. p. 1950.

Nation, 94:115, Feb. 1, 1912. These addresses "are marked by the urbanity and the humor that have contributed to the author's high reputation as a public speaker."

Clapper, Olive Ewing. *Washington Tapestry*. McGraw, 1946. 303pp. $2.75.

N. Y. Times, Feb. 10, 1946, p. 4. "Mrs. Clapper races through the important episodes of the Thirties and early Forties with breath-taking speed. She manages, however, to say something intimate and interesting about a lot of people who strode across the Washington stage in those years." The book is best "when gossipy and feminine." It is "strikingly lacking in cynicism."

Cleland, Robert Glass. *History of California: American Period*. Macmillan, 1922. 512pp. $4.00.

AHR, 28:334. This book is "dignified, scholarly, and readable."

———. *This Reckless Breed of Men: the Trappers and Fur Traders of the Southwest*. Knopf, 1950. 361pp. $4.00.

AHR, 55:919. An excellent book written in lively style, but it does not give much space to the individual.

Clifton, John L. *Ten Famous American Educators*. N. E. A., 1933. 272pp. o. p. 1950.

Ed. Res. B., 13:105, Apr. 18, 1934. "Although several different writers contributed to the volume, there runs throughout a simplicity of style and a presentation of human-interest incidents that make it a delightful book to read."

Collins, Joseph. *Taking the Literary Pulse; Psychological Studies of Life and Letters*. Doran, 1924. 317pp. o. p. 1933.

N. Y. Tribune, June 29, 1924, p. 27. Composed mostly of criticisms and reviews which give "a good deal of the story" of the book.

———. *The Doctor Looks at Biography*. Doran, 1925. 344pp. o. p. 1950.

Sat. Rev. of Lit., 2:483, Jan. 9, 1926. Occasionally the doctor seems superficial or prejudiced, "but usually he is discriminating and just."

Commager, Henry Steele. *American Mind; an Interpretation of American Thought and Character Since the 1880's.* Yale U. Press, 1950. 476pp. $5.00.

New Repub., 112:19, Apr. 24, 1950. "(Commager) has accepted no easy job, and under the Damocles' sword that hangs over all encyclopedists, he has, written one of the most serious histories of American thought since Parrington."

Cooper, Alice Cecilia, and Charles A. Palmer. *Twenty Modern Americans.* Harcourt, 1942. 416pp. $2.50. (Text ed.)

Wkly. Bk. Rev., Apr. 18, 1943, p. 8. Emphasizes traits of character which made these Americans famous.

Cortissoz, Royal. *American Artists.* Scribner, 1923. 363pp. $3.00.

N. Y. Tribune, Nov. 25, 1923, p. 21. A useful book which records "the predilections of a great lover of American art."

———. *Art and Common Sense.* Scribner, 1913. 445pp. $1.75.

Int. Studies, 51:sup. 142, Dec., 1913. "We know of no art book of recent times that makes better or more instructive reading."

Coulter, Ellis Merton. *The Confederate States of America, 1861-1865.* (History of the South, 1950.) La. State U. Press, 644pp. $7.00.

Ann. Am. Acad., 271:196. "Written by one of the South's most distinguished historians, this book is by all odds the best survey of Southern civilization, 1861-1865, that has yet appeared. Here is told the story of Southern wartime society and economy as well as of war, politics, and diplomacy. The author brings to his task an unusually rich and comprehensive knowledge of his subject and a marked gift for lucid historical prose."

———. *The South During Reconstruction, 1865-1877.* (History of the South, 1947.) La. State U. Press, 426pp. $5.00.

AHR, 53:565. "This study sets a high standard for the forthcoming volumes in the series which, happily, will deal with less controversial periods and subjects. Though sometimes drawn too exclusively from Southern sources, the documentation is accurate and it is unlikely that future historians will materially alter the author's basic conclusions."

Cournos, John. *Modern Plutarch; Being an Account of Some Great Lives in the Nineteenth Century, Together with Some Comparisons Between the Latin and the Anglo-Saxon Genius.* Bobbs, 1928. 428pp. o. p. 1950.

Sat. Rev. of Lit., 5:317, Nov. 3, 1928. "The trouble with Mr. Cournos is not that he borrows something from Plutarch, but that he does not borrow enough. He seems to feel that his title was forced upon him in order to forestall a charge of plagiarism, but the scruple seems strained. . . . One can only record a belief that his technique is wrong and Plutarch's right, and a regret that the Plutarchian technique was not borrowed along with the Plutarchian 'idea.' "

Cowie, Alexander. *Rise of the American Novel.* Am. Bk., 1948. 877pp. $5.00.

Sat. Rev. of Lit., 31:19, June 26, 1948. "An informed and discriminating account of American novels and novelists by a reader who enjoys a good story at the same time that he is critical of its shortcomings, and who is able to communicate both his enjoyment and his criticism."

Cowley, Malcolm, ed. *After the Genteel Tradition; American Writers Since 1910.* Norton, 1937. 270pp. o. p. 1933.

Nation, 144:707. A symposium by twelve critics who seek to explain the decline of several literary reputations. The book is uneven, but contains some sound criticism.

Cowley, Malcolm, and Bernard Smith, eds. *Books That Changed Our Minds.* Doubleday, 1939. 285pp. $2.50.

Books, Jan. 7, 1940, p. 14. This symposium serves as a helpful guide to books which have been most influential in shaping American ideas.

Cox, Kenyon. *Old Masters and New.* Fox, Duffield, and Co., 1905. 311pp. o. p. 1950.

Cur. Lit., 39:504. Mr. Cox gives "a painter's estimate of Whistler and Sargent."

Creel, George. *Sons of the Eagle; Soaring Figures from America's Past.* Bobbs, 1927. 322pp. o. p. 1933.

Outlook, 146:128, May 25, 1927. "For those who like three cheers and a tiger whenever a familiar name is mentioned the volume will meet with favor. It is uncritical and exuberant."

Croffut, William A. *An American Procession, 1855-1914; a Personal Chronicle of Famous Men.* Little, 1931. 321pp. o. p. 1950.

Sat. Rev. of Lit., 7:700, Mar. 28, 1931. Interesting recollections of a New York reporter who claims "he has met and conversed with every President of the United States from Millard Fillmore to Woodrow Wilson, and with few exceptions in that span, with every American famous as author, inventor, explorer, statesman, editor, or warrior."

Curti, Merle Eugene. *The Growth of American Thought.* (Text ed.) Harper, 1943. 848pp. $4.75.

Springfield Republican, Oct. 23, 1943, p. 6. "An exciting event is the publication of *The Growth of American Thought*. This is a tremendous feat of scholarship, comparable in insight to Parrington's *Main Currents in American Thought* but far more ambitious in design. Scholars will be vicariously exhausted by the sheer bulk of materials digested, from old letters and scientific treatises to recent editorials in the *Saturday Evening Post* and the jungle prose of Father Divine. But the proof of research is in the reading. Ordinary readers will find fascination as well as rich mines of information and interpretation in this 800 page 'social history.' "

———. *The Social Ideas of American Educators.* Scribner, 1935. 613pp. $4.00.

AHR, 41:158. Adding much to our knowledge of the activities of men like Horace Mann, Henry Barnard, William T. Harris, and others.

DeFord, Miriam Allen. *They Were San Franciscans.* Caxton, 1941. 321pp. $4.00.

Nation, 154:45, Jan. 10, 1942. "Gossipy and readable stories."

Dibble, Roy Floyd. *Strenuous Americans.* Boni & Liveright, 1923. 370pp. o. p. 1950.

New Repub., 37:211, Jan. 16, 1924. Essays written after the manner of Lytton Strachey.

Dickson, Samuel. *San Francisco is Your Home.* Stanford U. Press, 1947. 262pp. $3.50.

Booklist, 44:200, Feb. 1, 1948. Colorful chapters "about the history, legends and famous people of San Francisco." The author has written the script for a radio program for years.

Dowdey, Clifford. *Experiment in Rebellion.* Doubleday, 1946. 455pp. $3.75.

AHR, 52:752. A dramatic account of the administration of Jefferson Davis written by a Richmond novelist. Especially good in interpreting the personalities of Davis and Benjamin. Vivid characterizations of contemporaries.

Dullus, Foster Rhea. *Twentieth Century America.* Reynal, 1945. 582pp. $4.50.

AHR, 51:387. A breezy text, especially good in evaluating personalities.

Durling, Dwight, and William Watt, eds. *Biography: Varieties and Parallels.* Dryden, 1941. 501pp. $1.40.

The selections are by various authors. Includes ten Americans; also a chapter and a bibliography on "The New Biography."

Eddy, Sherwood, and Kirby Page. *Makers of Freedom; Biographical Sketches in Social Freedom.* Doran, 1926. 311pp. o. p. 1950.

Bookman, 64:105, Sept., 1926. "Kirby Page and Sherwood Eddy . . . have chosen for their subjects eight epoch making figures from the history of world progress." These range from Francis of Assisi and John Wesley to Booker T. Washington and Susan B. Anthony.

Edgar, Pelham. *Art of the Novel; from 1700 to the Present Time.* Macmillan, 1933. 481pp. o. p. 1950.

Canadian Forum, 14:269, Apr., 1934. An interesting book, which is rather elusive at times.

Erskine, John. *Leading American Novelists.* (Biographies of Leading Americans.) Holt, 1910. 378pp. o. p. 1933.

Nation, 90:630. "Brief biographies of certain American story-writers."

Farrar, John Chipman, ed. *Literary Spotlight.* Doran, 1924. 356pp. o. p. 1933.

Nation, 119:574, Nov. 26, 1924. "A few of the portraits are complete, and the whole is a document of value. . . ."

Fenner, Mildred Sandison, and E. C. Fishburn. *Pioneer American Educators.* N. E. A., 1944. 160pp. o. p. 1950.

Grade Teach., 62:8, June, 1945. "In this well-written booklet are given the most interesting facts in the lives of eighteen of the early educators of America."

Filler, Louis. *Crusaders for American Liberalism.* Antioch Press, 1939. 422pp. $4.00.

Amer. Lit., 12:263. A fairly complete picture of the muckrakers of the early part of the twentieth century and their contributions to reform.

Fish, Carl Russell. *The American Civil War: an Interpretation. 1876-1932.* Longmans, 1937. 531pp. o. p. 1950.

AHR, 43:909. An excellent interpretative history which includes first-rate thumbnail sketches of the leaders on both sides.

Flynn, John Thomas. *Men of Wealth: the Story of Twelve Significant Fortunes from the Renaissance to the Present Day.* Simon, 1941. 531pp. o. p. 1950.

Books, June 1, 1941, p. 5. Sketches of capitalists who made millions by juggling stocks. Includes six Americans.

Foerster, Norman. *American Criticism; a Study in Literary Theory from Poe to the Present.* Houghton, 1928. 273pp. o. p. 1950.

Books, June 17, 1928, p. 4. "Mr. Foerster's exposition is so evenhanded, so good-tempered, so studiously objective and proportioned that no sane man could accuse him of bias. He may not have said the last word on the subject, but he has said his say on the final grounds."

———. *Nature in American Literature; Studies in the Modern View of Nature.* Macmillan, 1923. 324pp. o. p. 1950.

Bookman, 57:466, June, 1923. "Professor Foerster has succeeded in putting into his very able book a refreshing and rather unusual out-of-door quality. It is almost as though we were out in the country having talks illustrated by the things of nature themselves."

Fox, Dixon Ryan, and Arthur Meier Schlesinger, eds. *Cavalcade of America.* Bradley, 1937. 300pp. o. p. 1950.

Springfield Republican, Dec. 19, 1937, p. 7. "The pageant of American progress as set forth in the dramatic radio sketches sponsored by the Du Pont Company is presented to the reading public in this collection. It includes 16 plays by various writers who have herein made history live."

Freeman, Douglas Southall. *Lee's Lieutenants: a Study in Command.* 3 vols. Scribner, 1942-44. 773pp. 760pp. 862pp. $7.00 each.

AHR, 48:592; 49:121; 50:562. Lee's greatest biographer follows his *R. E. Lee* with this excellent study of the personalities of the army of northern Virginia and of the efforts of the high command to find and develop proper commanders.

Fuller, George Washington. *A History of the Pacific Northwest.* Knopf, 1931. 383pp. $3.75.

PHR, 1:118. A good history of the region. Includes an entertaining account of Whitman and DeSmet.

Gabriel, Ralph Henry. *The Course of American Democratic Thought; an Intellectual History Since 1815.* Ronald Press, 1940. 452pp. o. p. 1950.

AHR, 46:164. "This volume deals with democratic thought from the early Middle Period to the present time. Although primarily concerned with ideas it treats them in relation to the characteristics" of six periods in American development.

Geismar, Maxwell David. *Last of the Provincials; the American Novel, 1915-1925; H. L. Mencken, Sinclair Lewis, Willa Cather, Sherwood Anderson, F. Scott Fitzgerald.* Houghton, 1947. 404pp. $3.75.

Kirkus, 15:456, Aug. 15, 1947. "Of literary interest and argument."

Goebel, Dorothy Burne, and Julius Goebel. *Generals in the White House.* Doubleday, 1945. 276pp. o. p. 1950.

AHR, 51:386. Readable sketches based on wide reading but without citations.

Goodsell, Willystine. *Pioneers of Women's Education in the United States.* McGraw-Hill, 1931. 311pp. o. p. 1950.

Sch. & Soc., 34:774, Dec. 5, 1931. "Author Goodsell makes the story of Mrs. Willard, of Catherine Beecher and of Mary Lyon lively and engaging. She amplifies each with short, typical selections from the educational writings of her heroines."

Gras, Norman Scott Brien, and Henrietta Melia Larson. *Casebook in American Business History.* Crofts, 1939. 765pp. $5.00.

Springfield Republican, Jan. 21, 1940, p. 7. A useful book which gives "a background of biography in a number of the chapters."

Grayson, Theodore Julius. *Leaders and Periods of American Finance.* Wiley, 1932. 566pp. o. p. 1950.

Sat. Rev. of Lit., 9:20, July 30, 1932. "Professor Grayson has here undertaken to popularize the history of American finance by mixing summary accounts of episodes or periods with sketches of the work of representative financial leaders."

Greene, Laurence, comp. *America Goes to Press: the News of Yesterday.* Bobbs, 1936, 375pp. o. p. 1950.

Sat. Rev. of Lit., 13:7, Mar. 28, 1936. A compilation which shows "how colorful events of the past . . . have been covered." The book is "full of rattling good stories, told vigorously and dramatically" but often rather crudely.

Greenslet, Ferris. *Under the Bridge.* Houghton, 1943. 237pp. $3.00.

Book Week, Nov. 21, 1943, p. 1. "This charmingly written and witty autobiography of one of the most distinguished of American publishers reads as easily as an autobiographical novel and the adventures of its hero—which are described by Mr. Greenslet with admirable detachment and modesty as well as refreshing sincerity and humor—hold the reader's attention from the first word to the last."

Gregory, Horace, and Marya Zaturenska. *A History of American Poetry, 1900-1940.* Harcourt, 1946. 524pp. $4.00.

Booklist, 43:98, Dec. 1, 1946. "A chronological discussion of 40 years of American poetry in terms of the individual poets—their background and personality as well as their writings."

Gunther, John. *Inside U. S. A.* Harper, 1947. 979pp. $5.00.

Atlantic, 179:120. An encyclopedia book by a brilliant reporter. Includes lively profiles of the leaders who run the communities he visited. These are written with warmth and sympathy.

Hagedorn, Hermann. *Americans: a Book of Lives.* Day, 1946. 392pp. $6.00.

Sat. Rev. of Lit., 29:66, Apr. 13, 1946. Biographical sketches of seventeen people of the present century. Primarily intended to give foreigners a better understanding of America. The sketches are kindly and old fashioned; there is no debunking.

Hamilton, Elizabeth, ed. *How They Started, Nine Famous Men Begin Their Careers.* Harcourt, 1937. 286pp. o. p. 1950.

N. Y. Times, Oct. 3, 1937, p. 10. These nine extracts from biographies describe the way in which each of these famous men chose his life work.

Hartwick, Harry. *Foreground of American Fiction.* Am. Bk., 1934. 447pp. o. p. 1950.

Springfield Republican, July 14, 1934, p. 8. This study "is among the weightier analyses of current American fiction while there is an excess of generalized deduction, there is also considerable pungent interpretations, and much that is said about individual writers—Norris, Dreiser, Sherwood Anderson, Cabell, Hergesheimer, etc.—is incisive and illuminating."

Hatcher, Harlan Henthorne. *Creating the Modern American Novel.* Farrar, 1935. 307pp. o. p. 1950.

Booklist, 32:38, Oct., 1935. "The author passes judgment on about 450 twentieth century novels, indicating their subject matter and the conditions under which they were written."

Hathaway, Esse Virginia. *Partners in Progress.* McGraw, 1935. 303pp. o. p. 1950.

N. Y. Times, Nov. 24, 1935, p. 12. "The book offers an interesting interpretation of the past that is full of provocations and inspirations to thought."

Hazard, Lucy Lockwood. *The Frontier in American Literature.* Crowell, 1927. 308pp. o. p. 1950.

Outlook, 141:91, May 18, 1927. "A thoughtful work, planned and executed from an original point of view, rich in suggestion and amply repaying a careful study."

Henderson, Archibald. *Contemporary Immortals.* Appleton, 1930. 209pp. o. p. 1950.

N. Y. Times, Dec. 7, 1930, p. 46. Entertaining and informative. Eulogistic. Includes five Americans.

Hendrick, Burton Jesse. *Lincoln's War Cabinet.* Little, 1946. 482pp. $5.00.

AHR, 52:527. Character sketches which emphasize the "trouble makers" among Lincoln's advisors and generals. The conclusions reached sometimes challenge other recent studies.

———. *Statesmen of the Lost Cause; Jefferson Davis and His Cabinet.* Little, 1939. 452pp. o. p. 1950.

AHR, 45:923. An historical narrative which gives excellent treatment of the chief civil leaders of the Confederacy. Concludes that their incompetence was a decisive factor in its downfall. Well written, but this thesis is disputed by Patrick in *Jefferson Davis and His Cabinet.*

Hergesheimer, Joseph. *Swords and Roses.* Knopf, 1929. 327pp. o. p. 1950.

Yale Rev., 19:177. Giving "an artist's impression" rather than strictly orthodox history, "Mr. Hergesheimer has painted a series of portraits of men and women of the old South in war times together with one landscape entitled 'The Deep South'—for background, as it were."

Hesseltine, William Best. *Confederate Leaders in the New South.* La. State U. Press, 1950. 146pp. $2.50.

Ga. Hist. Quar., 35:169. This book is made up of three lectures which Professor Hesseltine delivered at Louisiana State University as the Fleming Lectures for 1949. Professor Hesseltine "finds two diverging symbols in the post war careers of Lee and Davis; the one pointing toward the New South and reconciliation and the other clinging to the civilization of the Old South. Around these symbols the 285 leaders crystallized more or less clearly. The references are brief and there is no index.

——. *Lincoln and the War Governors.* Knopf, 1948. 405pp. $4.50.

Wkly. Bk. Rev., May 30, 1948, p. 2. This scholarly volume describes the methods by which Lincoln reduced the states and their governors to mere agents of the Federal Government and thus consolidated the nation.

Hicks, Granville. *The Great Tradition: an Interpretation of American Literature Since the Civil War.* Macmillan, 1933. 317pp. $3.00.

New Repub., 76:368. An analysis of American writers of the sixth and seventh generations in terms of their relation to social and economic forces.

Hind, Charles Lewis. *Authors and I.* Lane, 1921. 336pp. o. p. 1933.

Booklist, 17:293, May, 1921. "Short pungent opinions, discussions and appreciations of over fifty authors mostly of the present. Entertaining."

Hofstadter, Richard. *Social Darwinism in American Thought, 1860-1950.* U. of Pa. Press, 1944. 191pp. $2.50.

Am. Soc. Rev., 9:711. A brief study, "remarkably meaty, and very well written."

Holbrook, Stewart Hall. *Little Annie Oakley and Other Rugged People.* Macmillan, 1946. 238pp. $3.50.

Kirkus, 16:426, Aug. 15, 1948. "A series of delightful pieces, pure Americana. . . . Lively reading."

Howe, Mark Antony De Wolfe. *Causes and Their Champions.* Little, 1926. 331pp. o. p. 1950.

Survey, 57:462, Jan. 1, 1927. Entertaining, graphic sketches based on wide reading.

———. *Classic Shades: Five Leaders of Learning and Their Colleges.* Little, 1928. 199pp. $2.50.

N. Y. Times, Oct. 21, 1928, p. 2. "The whole volume is so charmingly written as to be of broad interest to the 'general reader,' whether he is personally interested in the subject of education or not. The book's only fault is that there is not more of it."

Howells, William Dean. *Literary Friends and Acquaintances.* 1900. o. p. 1939. (Library ed. 1911.)

The best account of the classic age of Boston and Cambridge.

Hudson, Arthur Palmer, ed. *Humor of the Old Deep South.* Macmillan, 1936. 548pp. o. p. 1950.

Books, July 19, 1936, p. 10. An interesting book too well written to gather dust. It wil introduce readers to new sources.

Hunt, Rockwell D. *California's Stately Hall of Fame.* College of the Pacific, 1950. 675pp. o. p. 1950.

PHR, 19:301. Short, vivid biographies of 104 distinguished men and women who have played important roles in California's history make up this fascinating and useful volume."

Husband, Joseph. *Americans by Adoption; Brief Biographies of Great Citizens Born in Foreign Lands.* Little, 1920. 153pp. o. p. 1939.

Booklist, 17:69, Nov., 1920. "Stephen Girard, John Ericsson, Louis Agassiz, Carl Schurz, Theodore Thomas, Andrew Carnegie, James J. Hill, Augustus Saint-Gaudens, Jacob A. Riis are nine Americans by adoption whose lives are described both for what they gave to and received from our country." The sketches are "clear, inspiring, (and are) addressed primarily to young people."

Hutchinson, William Tecumseh, ed. *The Marcus W. Jernegan Essays in American Historiography.* U. of Chicago Press, 1937. 417pp. $5.00.

MVHR, 24:589. Probably the best single volume on "the leading historians of the last hundred years."

Hylander, Clarence John. *American Inventors.* Macmillan, 1934. 216pp. $2.50.

N. Y. Times, July 1, 1934, p. 9. "A useful, readable, up-to-date book, adequately illustrated by photographs and by drawings that are clear and enlightening."

———. *American Scientists.* Macmillan, 1935. 186pp. $2.50.

Springfield Republican, Apr. 29, 1935, p. 6. "Like many other books designed ostensibly for youth, this one can be read with profit by older people."

Irwin, Grace. *Trail-Blazers of American Art.* Harper, 1930. 228pp. o. p. 1950.

Booklist, 27:166, Dec., 1930. "A biographical account of each artist is given, as well as a discussion of his work and its relation to the history of art."

Johnson, Gerald White. *American Heroes and Hero Worship.* Harper, 1943. 284pp. $3.00.

Wkly. Bk. Rev., Oct. 3, 1943, p. 1. A brilliant and entertaining book that lays bare the ironies and paradoxes of American history.

———. *America's Silver Age: the Statecraft of Clay-Webster-Calhoun.* Harper, 1939. 280pp. $3.50.

Books, Apr. 30, 1939, p. 5. Stimulating account of the middle period of American history. Pictures Clay as the hero, and Calhoun and Webster as the villains. Some errors of fact.

Josephson, Matthew. *Portrait of the Artist as American.* Harcourt, 1930. 308pp. $3.00.

Nation, 130:627, May 28, 1930. "An arresting history of the American artist, admirably written, full of penetrating criticism; a series of brilliant and absorbing biographical sketches."

———. *Robber Barons: the Great American Capitalists, 1861-1901.* Harcourt, 1934. 474pp. $3.50.

Nation, 138:279, Mar. 7, 1934. Not a series of biographies, but a dynamic history with the stories of Vanderbilt, Gould, Huntington, Hill, Carnegie, Rockefeller, Frick, and Morgan all skillfully interwoven.

———. *The President Makers: the Culture of Politics and Leadership in an Age of Enlightenment, 1896-1919.* Harcourt, 1940. 584pp. $3.75.

AHR, 46:949. Journalistic survey with emphasis on biography. Based on wide research and many interviews with participants. Deflates Theodore Roosevelt but is unfair to Taft and Wilson.

Karsner, David. *Sixteen Authors to One: Intimate Sketches of Leading American Story Tellers.* Copeland, 1929. 290pp. o. p. 1933.

Books, Feb. 17, 1929, p. 14. Portrays literary celebrities of the 1920's in relation to their work.

Kazin, Alfred. *On Native Grounds: an Interpretation of Modern American Prose Literature.* Reynal, 1942. 541pp. $3.75.

Sat. Rev. of Lit., 25:5, Oct. 31, 1942. An excellent study which enters sympathetically into the inner life of many diverse writers.

Keiser, Albert. *The Indian in American Literature.* Oxford, 1934. 312pp. $3.00.

Books, Jan. 28, 1934, p. 17. "Mr. Keiser by proceeding without transition from Captain John Smith to Mary Rowlandson, and thence by seventeen jumps to Hamlin Garland, has run the risk of our unwillingness to believe that we are getting from him the whole story of how the Indian has appeared and conducted himself in American literature."

Kraus, Michael. *A History of American History.* Farrar, 1937. 607pp. o. p. 1949.

MVHR, 24:589. A very readable book, although it "does not emphasize biography." Its appraisals, however, "are quite in line with the consensus of professional opinion."

Kunitz, Stanley Jasspon, and Howard Haycraft, eds. *American Authors, 1600-1900; a Biographical Dictionary of American Literature.* Wilson, 1938. 846pp. $5.00.

N. Y. Times, Oct. 23, 1938, p. 12. A very readable reference book which gives essential information with skill and charm. The book is too inclusive and has too jaunty a style.

Law, Frederick Houk. *Civilization Builders.* Appleton, 1939. 356pp. $1.40.

Times (London) *Lit. Sup.*, Nov. 4, 1939, p. 647. "A very readable and stimulating account."

———. *Modern Great Americans; Short Biographies of Twenty Americans of Modern Times, Who Won Wide Recognition for Achievement in Various Types of Activity.* Appleton, 1926. 314pp. o. p. 1949.

Books, Mar. 13, 1927, p. 17. Brief but interesting sketches.

Lawrence, David Herbert. *Studies in Classic American Literature.* Viking, 1923. 264pp. o. p. 1949.

Nation, 117:Sup. 398, Oct. 10, 1923. "His book is honest, independent, and eccentric, a thousand miles . . . away from most books of critical essays. The core of the book is its tinglingly vital challenge not only to America but to all manner of human quackery and puffery. . . ."

Leech, Margaret. *Reveille in Washington, 1860-1865.* Harper, 1941. 483pp. $3.75.

AHR, 48:365. A colorful picture of Washington society in the 1860's. Excellent "thumbnail biographies" and scattered references, especially to the leading women of the city.

Leighton, Isabel, ed. *Aspirin Age, 1919-1941.* Simon & Schuster, 1949. 491pp. $3.95.

Christian Science Monitor, Aug. 20, 1949, p. 16. Some of these selections are interesting, but the book has "no point of view, no underlying thread of unity."

Levin, Peter R. *Seven by Chance: the Accidental Presidents.* Farrar, 1948. 374pp. o. p. 1949.

N. Y. Times, June 20, 1948, p. 3. Mr. Levin is shrewd in appraising Tyler, Johnson, and others who came to the presidency through the deaths of their predecessors. The natural conclusion is that the vice-president should be selected with greater care.

Lewis, Oscar. *The Big Four: the Story of Huntington, Stanford, Hopkins, and Crocker, and the Building of the Central Pacific.* Knopf, 1938. 415pp. $4.50.

AHR, 44:939. These sketches of railroad promoters give a colorful description of the ways in which they spent their wealth.

Lippmann, Walter. *Men of Destiny.* Macmillan, 1927. 244pp. o. p. 1949.

Books, Sept. 4, 1927, p. 1. "All of Mr. Lippmann's papers are lively reading and well worthy of publication. Mr. Lippmann is a great publicist. If there is an abler editorial in the country I am not aware of it."

Loggins, Vernon. *I Hear America: Literature in the United States Since 1900.* Crowell, 1937. 378pp. o. p. 1949.

Booklist, 34:126. Entertaining sketches, partly biographical, partly critical.

Long, Orie William. *Literary Pioneers: Early American Explorers of European Culture.* Harvard, 1936. 267pp. $3.00.

AHR, 42:562. Essays on six of the earliest Americans who studied in German universities. All of the men included were connected with Harvard.

Lonn, Ella. *Foreigners in the Confederacy.* U. of N. C. Press, 1940. 566pp. o. p. 1949.

Books, July 7, 1940, p. 6. "One of the most scholarly and original contributions to Civil War history." It presents quite "a gallery of heroes, rogues and eccentrics. . . ."

Lotz, Philip Henry, ed. *Vocations and Professions.* (Creative Personalities.) Assn. Press, 1940. 145pp. $2.00.

Christian Century, 57:219, Feb. 14, 1940. Brief sketches ranging from Luther Burbank to Harry Emerson Fosdick. Easy style.

———. *Women Leaders.* (Creative Personalities.) Assn. Press, 1940. 149pp. $1.25.

Christian Century, 57:675, May 22, 1940. Brief sketches. Mostly American women of the sixth and seventh generations. Gives questions for discussion.

Lowry, Edward George. *Washington Close-ups.* Houghton, 1921. 275pp. o. p. 1949.

New Repub., 29:186, Jan. 11, 1922. Intimate friendly sketches by a Washington correspondent. Perhaps he was too kind.

Macartney, Clarence Edward Noble. *Lincoln and His Generals.* Dorance, 1925. 226pp. o. p. 1949.

Books, Dec. 20, 1925, p. 11. "Dr. Macartney shows considerable restraint in dealing with Lincoln, but his criticisms are both keen and weighty."

———. *Men Who Missed It: Great Americans Who Missed the White House.* Dorance, 1941. 122pp. o. p. 1949.

These sketches are briefer and less comprehensive than those of Irving Stone and Don Carlos Seitz.

McLeish, Archibald, and E. F. Prichard, eds. Frankfurter, Felix. *Law and Politics; Occasional Papers, 1913-1938.* Harcourt, 1939. 352pp. o. p. 1949.

Books, Nov. 5, 1939, p. 1. These papers are of general interest, none of them are technical. They are readable, and penetrating and set a high standard of prose writing.

Macy, John, ed. *American Writers on American Literature.* Liveright, 1931. 539pp. o. p. 1949.

N. E. Quar., 6:642. Essays by thirty-seven contemporary critics. Somewhat uneven, but interesting—partly on account of the conflicting opinions represented.

Madison, Charles Allan. *American Labor Leaders: Personalities and Forces in the Labor Movement.* Harper, 1950. 474pp. $4.00.

Kirkus, 18:229, Apr. 1, 1950. Interesting and provocative portraits of influential leaders. Somewhat biased against those who have tried to clean communism out of the unions.

———. *Critics and Crusaders.* Holt, 1947. 572pp. $3.50.

AHR, 53:119. Sympathetic sketches of eighteen men and women which constitute an informal history of American radicalism.

Malone, Dumas. *Saints in Action.* Abingdon, 1939. 183pp. o. p. 1949.

Churchman, 153:17, Nov. 1, 1939. "Here are introductions to lively careers, fascinating and inspiring. The book is especially valuable to all who have no ready access to the more ambitious biographies."

Marcosson, Isaac Frederick. *Adventures in Interviewing.* Lane, 1919. 314pp. o. p. 1949.

Outlook, 124:161, Jan. 28, 1920. This book "is packed with big personalities described in a most entertaining way by a man who has a genius for interviewing and has had rare opportunities for its exercise."

Matthiessen, Francis Otto. *American Renaissance; Art and Expression in the Age of Emerson and Whitman.* Oxford, 1941. 678pp. $7.00.

Yale Rev., 31:200. "A dynamic book of literature in mid-nineteenth century America, and on its related intellectual life, provocative and perceptive in its close analysis of Emerson, Thoreau, Hawthorne, Melville, and Whitman, and boldly experimental in method."

Maurice, Sir Frederick. *Statesmen and Soldiers of the Civil War: a Study of the Conduct of War.* Little, 1926. 173pp. o. p. 1949.

MVHR, 14:111. A British military expert discusses the relations between Davis and Johnston, Davis and Lee; Lincoln and McClellan, and Lincoln and Grant.

Mencken, Henry Louis. *Mencken Chrestomathy.* Ed. and annot. by the author. Knopf, 1949. 627pp. $5.00.

Kirkus, 17:224, Apr. 15, 1949. "Here is a chance to read him for yourself. He will endear himself to few, for he debunks pretensions and shows the clay feet of idols. Even his obituaries make no concessions. Urbane and witty, he is frequently a healthy irritant."

Merriam, Charles E. *Four American Party Leaders.* Macmillan, 1926. 104pp. o. p. 1949.

AHR, 32:174. Keen and stimulating analyses of Lincoln, Bryan, Roosevelt, and Wilson.

Michaud, Regis. *The American Novel To-day; a Social and Psychological Study.* Little, 1928. 293pp. o. p. 1949.

Books, Feb. 5, 1928, p. 7. "Such contentions have been the steady refrain of American criticism for the past fifteen years. Mr. Michaud goes over them again, often with knowledge and insight. He does not, however, furnish anything like the firm, precise analysis and exposition of the movement which might have summed it up and left it in its place in history. . . . Then there are frequent contradictions, or at least volte-faces."

Miller, Perry Gilbert Eddy, ed. *The Transcendentalists; an Anthology.* Harvard, 1950. 521pp. $6.50.

Nation, 171:43. "From Perry Miller's extremely skillful editing of the documents the transcendentalist controversy emerges as one of the major intellectual battles of our history. He briefs us on its progress in masterly fashion, discriminating the moves so that we watch it almost with the excitement of watching a play."

Milton, George Fort. *The Use of Presidential Power, 1789-1943.* Little, 1944. 349pp. o. p. 1949.

AHR, 50:358. The author is strongly interested in personalities. Cited for eight men given special attention.

Minnigerode, Meade. *Certain Rich Men.* Putman, 1927. 210pp. o. p. 1949.

New Repub., 53:77, Dec. 7, 1927. Seven short sketches which convey an idea of the period from Stephen. Girard to James Fiske, as well as the characters of the men themselves.

Mirrors of Wall Street. Putman, 1933. 268pp. o. p. 1949.

Sat. Rev. of Lit., 10:94, Sept. 9, 1933. Some interesting revelations; but, on the whole, the author lets the bankers off rather lightly for 1933. Perhaps that is why he preferred to remain anonymous.

Mirrors of Washington. Putman, 1921. 256pp. o. p. 1949.

Am. Pol. Sci. Rev., 15:622. Fourteen political leaders are analyzed in daring style. In some instances the treatment is "caustic" or "almost bitter." A clever book, but not as well balanced as *The Mirrors of Downing Street.*

Monaghan, James. *Overland Trail.* (American Trails.) Bobbs, 1947. 431pp. $4.00.

Wkly. Bk. Rev., Nov. 30, 1947, p. 5. While the author is a professional historian, "he has written this book for the general reader in a simple narrative style."

Mott, Frank Luther. *American Journalism: a History of Newspapers in the U. S. Through 250 Years, 1690 to 1940.* Macmillan, 1941. 772pp. o. p. 1949.

AHR, 48:344. The best volume on the subject. Gives due emphasis to great editors from Franklin to William Allen White.

——. *Golden Multitudes, the Story of Best Sellers in the United States.* Macmillan, 1947. 357pp. $5.00.

New Repub., 117:25, Dec. 22, 1947. "Frank Luther Mott has brought to his study a sense of humor and a graceful, easy writing style that makes pleasant and interesting reading of what might have become dusty detail."

Mowat, Robert Balmain. *Americans in England.* Houghton, 1935. 284pp. o. p. 1949.

New Repub., 83:22, May 15, 1935. "*Americans in England* has the pleasant temper of an after-dinner speech. It shows only sweet kings and queens, lovely diplomats, dear fine artists and all that. . . . Nevertheless, Mr. Mowat's book about historical characters is not without lovable enjoyment these days. The scheme of the book is an interesting one."

Mumford, Lewis. *The Golden Day: a Study in American Experience and Culture.* Liveright 1926. 283pp. $2.50.

AHR, 33:142. This "brilliant and fascinating study of the American mind deals especially with Emerson, Thoreau, Whitman, Hawthorne and Melville."

Myers, Gustavus. *History of Bigotry in the United States.* Random House, 1943. 504pp. $3.50.

Atlantic, 172:123. "The scholarship and good sense in this book will provide source material for many years to come."

———. *History of the Great American Fortunes.* (3 vols. in 1, Modern Library ed.) Random House, 1937. 732pp. $2.45.

Nation, 90:485; 91:474. Mr. Myer's work is "full of that kind of bitter denunciation which we are in the habit of associating with the muck-raking literature of the present day."

Odum, Howard Washington, ed. *American Masters of Social Science: an Approach to the Study of the Social Sciences Through a Neglected Field of Biography.* Holt, 1927. 411pp. o. p. 1949.

AHR, 33:198. Rather diverse essays on nine outstanding teachers of history, economics, and sociology. The one on Veblen is critical, all the others are eulogistic.

———. *Southern Pioneers in Social Interpretation.* U. of N. C. Press, 1925. 221pp. o. p. 1949.

Outlook, 141:128, Sept. 23, 1925. "On the whole, the book is decidedly worth while, throwing a good deal of light on an interesting phase."

O'Higgins, Harvey Jerrold, and Edward Hiram Reede. *The American Mind in Action.* Harper, 1924. 336pp. o. p. 1949.

Lit. Rev., May 17, 1924, p. 756. "The book also has a value independent of its Freudian basis. Many readers will discount or reject its psychoanalytic conclusions, but will nevertheless be entertained and instructed by these portraits. In its vigorous portraiture and in the suggestiveness, not the finality, of his theories regarding the subconscious mind as a determinant of some great careers, lies the value of Mr. O'Higgins's book."

Orcutt, William Dana. *Celebrities Off Parade.* Willett, 1935. 287pp. o. p. 1949.

N. Y. Times, Oct. 6, 1935, p. 12. A publisher's reminiscences of his literary friends. Readable, humorous, penetrating.

Osborn, Henry Fairfield. *Impressions of Great Naturalists.* Scribner, 1924. 216pp. o. p. 1949.

Booklist, 21:149, Jan., 1925. "Lectures and articles on twelve outstanding naturalists by the author of several scientific books. Contains interesting biographical data, personal impressions and brief summaries of their work."

Overmyer, Grace. *Famous American Composers.* Crowell, 1944. 210pp. $2.50.

Theatre Arts, 28:556, Sept., 1944. Well written sketches of a dozen musical personalities from Francis Hopkinson to Aaron Copland. Includes singers as well as composers.

Parkman, Mary Rosetta. *Heroines of Service.* Century, 1917. 322pp. o. p. 1949.

N. Y. Times, 22:441, Oct. 28, 1917. Biographical sketches of eleven women who served as teachers, nurses, or social helpers.

Parrington, Vernon Louis. *American Dreams; a Study of American Utopias.* Brown U. Press, 1947. 234pp. o. p. 1949.

Wkly. Bk. Rev., July 18, 1948, p. 12. "An intelligent, informative, and readable survey of Utopian fiction in America from colonial times to the present. . . . Future writers on the subject may challenge its definitiveness, but they will nevertheless be indebted to Mr. Parrington for having blazed the trail."

Patrick, Rembert W. *Jefferson Davis and His Cabinet.* La. State U. Press, 1944. 401pp. o. p. 1949.

AHR, 50:566. A good discussion of the characteristics of the Confederate president and his official advisors. Concludes that he was an able administrator and chose efficient men upon whom he could place full responsibility."

Pattee, Fred Lewis. *Sidelights on American Literature.* Century, 1922. 342pp. o. p. 1949.

Int. Bk. Rev., Feb., 1923, p. 50. "Mr. Pattee possesses a peculiarly ingratiating style of writing which is plentifully interspersed with quotations from the writers he is considering."

———. *The Feminine Fifties.* Appleton, 1940. 339pp. o. p. 1949.

Library Quar., 10:618, Oct., 1940. "*The Feminine Fifties* is . . . a readable book, amusing, entertaining, casual, even—in a very restricted sense— illuminating. It will not satisfy the scholar, as it is manifestly incomplete as a social study. It is descriptive rather than interpretative. It suffers badly from inadequate documentation."

Peabody, Francis Greenwood. *Reminiscences of Present-day Saints.* Hougton, 1927. 308pp. o. p. 1949.

Springfield Republican, Nov. 21, 1927, p. 6. "It is very much worth while to make or renew one's acquaintance with these widely different personalities Dr. Peabody has so charmingly sketched."

Phelps, William Lyon. *Howells, James, Bryant, and Other Essays.* Macmillan, 1924. 206pp. o. p. 1949.

Booklist, 21:62, Nov. 24. These essays, reprinted from various periodicals, contain "biographical data and critical opinion presented in simple popular style."

Quiett, Glen Chesney. *They Built the West: an Epic of Rails and Cities.* Appleton, 1934. 569pp. o. p. 1949.

Special Libraries, 26:27, Jan., 1935. "A vivid picture of a developing country. None of the color, enterprise or daring of the leading figures is lost in this engrossing narrative. Well illustrated and indexed with good bibliographical references."

Rahv, Philip, ed. *Discovery of Europe; the Story of American Experience in the Old World.* Houghton, 1947. 743pp. o. p. 1950.

AHR, 53:139. "This anthology is a popular convenience on the subject of cultural interplay which will more and more be a stimulating experience for both general reader and students of European and American history. Without eccentricity in selection, arrangement, or notes, Rahv's materials extend from 1772 to 1939." Familiar passages from such as Franklin, Melville, Hawthorne, Henry James, and William E. Dodd "gain new meaning in this juxtaposition."

Ratner, Joseph, ed. Dewey, John. *Characters and Events; Popular Essays in Social and Political Philosophy.* 2 vols. Holt, 1929. 861pp. o. p. 1949.

Boston Transcript, June 15, 1929, p. 4. These lectures "show penetrating analysis, a humane outlook, and a wisdom which we like to think of as marking the philosophical mind."

Robinson, Victor. *White Caps; the Story of Nursing.* Lippincott, 1946. 425pp. $3.75.

Wkly. Bk. Rev., Feb. 2, 1947, p. 24. "An invaluable reference book for the nurse who honors her tradition. The general reader will find it equally rewarding."

Rosen, George, and Beate Caspari Rosen, eds. *400 Years of a Doctor's Life.* Schuman, 1947. 429pp. $5.00.

Sch. & Soc., 67:171, Feb. 28, 1948. "The excerpts are brief, as are the introductory paragraphs. Nevertheless it is possible to get a good idea of medical education through the past four centuries, as well as insight into the other activities of physicians and an inkling of what goes on within their minds. The Rosens' opus has considerable value for the prospective medical student, and for the lay reader."

Rourke, Constance Mayfield. *Trumpets of Jubilee.* Harcourt, 1927. 445pp. o. p. 1939.

AHR, 33:417. Entertaining sketches of five leaders of the early and middle nineteenth century.

Russell, Frank Alden (Ted Malone, pseud.). *American Pilgrimage.* Dodd, 1942. 270pp. o. p. 1950.

Sat. Rev. of Lit., 25:12, May 23, 1942. "Excellent little biographical and character sketches, not particularly critical, but thoroughly enjoyable, even if one is already reasonably familiar with the books and personalities discussed."

Salter, John Thomas, ed. *Public Men: In and Out of Office.* U. of N. C. Press, 1946. 513pp. o. p. 1949.

N. Y. Times, May 19, 1946, p. 33. Twenty-seven sketches, by as many authors, of men who are on the public stage today, or who have been only recently retired. Very readable.

Saveth, Edward Norman. *American Historians and European Immigrants, 1875-1925.* Columbia U. Press, 1948. 244pp. $3.00.

Introduction. "In the years from 1875 to 1925 historians had hardly more than occasional insight into the role of immigration into our national development. When they treated the subject of European immigration at all, they treated it as a side issue to which little attention need be paid. Consequently a large part of the present study is concerned with the attitude of the various American historians toward immigrants and immigration, more than with their constructive approach or interpretations. At the outset, there is some account of background factors shaping historians' attitude toward immigrants and of the influence of the Teutonic germ theory of institutional development upon the late nineteenth century American historians."

Schlesinger, Arthur Meir, Jr. *The Age of Jackson.* Little, 1949. 577pp. $5.00.

AHR, 51:510. A readable interpretation which develops the thesis that the Jacksonian reform movement owed its chief strength to the Eastern workingman. Excellent sketches of leaders.

Schneider, Herbert Wallace. *History of American Philosophy.* Columbia U. Press, 1946. 646pp. $4.50.

N. Y. Times, Dec. 22, 1946, p. 8. "Professor Schneider has introduced a host of interesting, neglected thinkers. But perhaps more important, his fresh honest study reveals the need and possibility of a knowledge of the meaning of our different basic activities. If I read him rightly, he would feel amply repaid for his long labors if his history provoked the study of things American in all its forms, to make possible an adequate American philosophy, and a history of philosophy to replace his. Until then his work must stand as our most embracing philosophic account of the history of American thought."

Seager, Allan. *They Worked for a Better World.* (People's Library.) Macmillan, 1939. 123pp. $0.75.

Books, June 11, 1939, p. 8. Sketches of five individuals who championed American ideals. They range from Roger Williams to Edward Bellamy.

Seitz, Don Carlos. *Famous American Duels; with Some Account of the Causes that Led up to Them and the Men Engaged.* Crowell, 1929. 345pp. o. p. 1949.

Outlook, 152:351, June 26, 1929. "The book is perhaps over-documented, but is intended for popular reading and written in an easy newspaper style."

———. *The "Also Rans"; Great Men Who Missed Making the Presidential Goal.* Crowell, 1928. 356pp. o. p. 1939.

Books, Apr. 22, 1928, p. 15. Entertaining sketches which should be read "in connection with Viscount Bryce's famous chapter on why great men are not chosen presidents. . . ."

Sergeant, Elizabeth Shepley. *Fire Under the Andes: a Group of North American Portraits.* Knopf, 1927. 331pp. o. p. 1949.

Nation, 124:345, Mar. 30, 1927. Excellent sketches of fourteen men and women of genius. The author shows a preference for writers and New Englanders.

Sherman, Stuart Pratt. *Main Stream.* Scribner, 1927. 239pp. o. p. 1949.

Christian Century, 44:694, June 2, 1927. "Many of the papers were published as book reviews, and they afford a fine illustration of the possibility—alas, too seldom realized—of developing a book review into a critical essay which has value on its own account."

Smith, Charles Alphonso. *Southern Literary Studies; a Collection of Literary, Biographical, and Other Sketches.* U. of N. C. Press, 1927. 192pp. o. p. 1949.

Outlook, 146:352, July 13, 1927. "Professor Smith played a considerable part in the literary life of the South, teaching in several southern universities."

Snell, George Dixon. *Shapers of American Fiction, 1798-1947.* Dutton, 1947. 316pp. $3.75.

Sat. Rev. of Lit., 30:21, May 31, 1947. "As a rule, such books represent the best that has been thought and said by everybody else on the same subject. But the present survey has enough points of interest to escape from this unhappy category. . . . Yet Mr. Snell's four categories of native fiction are valuable. They illuminate some obscure phases of the work of our best novelists, and they bring out some new connections between a series of apparently disparate individuals. . . . On the whole though, while *The Shapers of American Fiction* is not a distinctive work of literary criticism, it is an intelligent and very readable introduction to some of the major figures in our letters."

Snyder, Louis Leo, and Richard Brandon Morris, eds. *Treasury of Great Reporting; "Literature Under Pressure from the Sixteenth Century to Our Own Time."* Simon & Schuster, 1949. 784pp. $5.00.

AHR, 55:652. "From the reporting of four centuries, two historians have now winnowed out 175 of the world's top news stories. . . . Most great events had great observers. . . . The editors sketch the evolution of reporting and greatly heighten the continuity and interest by weaving around each story its background and consequences. There is must reading for every educator and newsman and exciting enough reading for anyone."

Spiller, Robert Ernest. *Americans in England During the First Half Century of Independence.* Holt, 1926. 416pp. o. p. 1949.

N. Y. Times, Oct. 17, 1926, p. 5. "An anthology of American travelers' opinions about England previous to 1815, any part of which may be dipped into separately and enjoyably. But for those who care to delve more deeply there is, between the lines, much food for thought and a deal of information."

Squire, John Collins, and others. *Contemporary American Authors.* Holt, 1928. 236pp. o. p. 1933.

Booklist, 24:394, July, 1928. "Essays by the editor and associated critics of the *London Mercury.* Some of the work here is brilliant."

Starling, Edmund W. *Starling of the White House; the Story of the Man Whose Secret Service Detail Guarded Five Presidents from Woodrow Wilson to Franklin Delano Roosevelt as Told to Thomas Sugrue.* Simon & Shuster, 1946. 334pp. o. p. 1950.

Sat. Rev. of Lit., 29:15, Mar. 2, 1946. The recollections of a "privileged observer and gifted raconteur" who was intimately associated with the occupants of the White House from Wilson to Franklin Roosevelt.

Stedman, Edmund Clarence. *Poets of America.* Houghton, 1896. 516pp. o. p. 1950.

Preface. Biographical and critical essays on American poets from William Cullen Bryant to Walt Whitman.

Stein, Gertrude. *Four in America.* Yale, 1947. 221pp. $3.75.

Library Jour., 72:1468, Oct. 15, 1947. "Posthumous publication of four essays in which Miss Stein considered George Washington, Ulysses S. Grant, the Wright brothers, and Henry James, as Americans and as creators. Long introduction by Thornton Wilder furnishes a gloss on some of the more difficult passages, discusses her aims as a writer, and recalls some of her conversations."

Stone, Irving. *They Also Ran: the Story of the Men Who Were Defeated for the Presidency.* Doubleday, 1943. 389pp. $3.50.

Sat. Rev. of Lit., 26:10, July 3, 1943. Lively, journalistic sketches of nineteen political leaders from Crawford to Wilkie. Grouped by professions without regard to chronalogy. Frequent comparisons and contrasts.

Stone, Irving, and Richard Kennedy, eds. *We Speak for Ourselves: a Self-portrait of America.* Doubleday, 1950. 462pp. $5.00.

Library Jour., 75:1664, Oct. 1, 1950. "An anthology of selections from autobiographies of Americans from all walks of life, statesmen, politicians, explorers, educators, doctors, theatre people, writers, preachers, etc."

Stowe, Lyman Beecher. *Saints, Sinners and Beechers.* Bobbs, 1934. 450pp. o. p. 1949.

N. E. Quar., 7:594. Lively sketches of a famous New England family written by a grandson of Harriet Beecher Stowe.

Strong, Sidney Dix, ed. *What I Owe My Father,* by Jane Addams and others. Holt, 1931. 184pp. o. p. 1949.

Christian Century, 48:1147, Sept. 16, 1931. "Moving and intimate portraits of men" who lived up to the responsibilities of fatherhood.

Sullivan, Mark. *Our Times, the United States 1900-1925,* Vol. III, *Pre-war America.* Scribner, 1930. 586pp. $5.00.

Nation, 131:740, Dec. 31, 1930. "The events of the period are at most but shadowy to the younger generation of Americans whose citizenship has only recently allied them with political, business, and social responsibilities. To this class of readers the volume and its series will afford an entertaining and instructive approach to contemporary history by a writer of skill in well-balanced selection, able to comprehend and articulate in concise fashion a segment of the many-sided American scene which has come under his intellectual ken."

Sweetser, Kate Dickson. *Book of Indian Braves.* Harper, 1913. 183pp. o. p. 1949.

Ind., 76:458, Dec. 4, 1913. Biographical sketches of famous Indians from Powhattan to Chief Joseph.

Thomas, Benjamin Platt. *Portrait for Posterity, Lincoln and His Biographers.* Rutgers U. Press, 1947. 329pp. o. p. 1949.

San Francisco Chronicle, Sept. 21, 1947, p. 12. "This book is not only important for the indirect picture it gives of the sixteenth President, but also for the insight it gives into the whole system of biographical writing. You will never read another book about another great man again without looking hard between the lines."

Thompson, Charles W. *Presidents I've Known and Two Near Presidents.* Bobbs, 1929. 386pp. o. p. 1933.

N. Y. Times, Feb. 24, 1929, p. 1. Entertaining, colorful sketches written by a Washington correspondent.

Thorp, Mrs. Margaret (Farrand). *Female Persuasion; Six Strong-minded Women.* Yale, 1949. 253pp. $3.75.

AHR, 55:691. The women Mrs. Thorp sketches in this little book "are chosen from various sections of the country and represent different philosophies of life and different interests. They have in common a breaking of precedent, a strength and toughness of mind, and undertaking of work hitherto unusual for women."

Thwing, Charles Franklin. *Friends of Men; Being a Second Series of Guides, Philosophers and Friends.* Macmillan, 1933. 479pp. o. p. 1949.

Christian Century, 50:692, May 24, 1933. "Biographical essays of more than ordinary penetration. . . . Dr. Thwing is no man's Boswell, but he has been the equal friend of many of the great, and the great friend of many who never rose above the ranks."

———. *Guides, Philosophers and Friends; Studies of College Men.* Macmillan, 1927. 479pp. o. p. 1949.

Boston Transcript, July 2, 1927, p. 3. "Here indeed is a fine and stately company, and happy indeed the reader who can make them in the best sense his 'guides, philosophers and friends.'"

Ticknor, Caroline. *Glimpses of Authors.* Houghton, 1922. 335pp. o. p. 1949.

Freeman, 6:430, Jan. 10, 1923. "Not much of it is new, but almost all of it is entertaining, and the reader renews an acquaintance not only with the members of the Fields's circle, but with Lew Wallace, Bellamy of *Looking Backward* . . . Uncle Remus, Howells . . . and many others."

Tracy, Henry Chester. *American Naturalists.* Dutton, 1930. 282pp. o. p. 1949.

Outlook, 154:547, Apr. 2, 1930. "Sketches of twenty American nature lovers and writers are included in *American Naturalists*—among them Audubon, Thoreau, Burroughs, Muir, Akeley, Andrews, Beebe and Seton. A book that all nature lovers will enjoy."

Tyler, Alice Felt. *Freedom's Ferment: Phases of American Social History to 1860.* U. of Minn. Press, 1944. 608pp. $6.50.

AHR, 49:735. A sympathetic sketch of the early reform movement. Brief references to individuals.

Unofficial Observer (pseud.). *American Messiahs.* Simon & Schuster, 1935. 238pp. o. p. 1941.

Nation, 141:80, July 17, 1935. Entertaining, provocative sketches of the spokesmen of unrest.

Van Doren, Carl Clinton. *The American Novel, 1789-1939,* rev. and enl. ed. Macmillan, 1940. 406pp. o. p. 1949.

New Repub., 102:285, Feb. 26, 1940. "Mr. Van Doren writes with so much more instinctive literary feeling than most academic historians that the book does not seem likely very soon to be superseded; the chapter on such writers as Cooper and Mark Twain are admirably vigorous and meaty. The book, in fact, is about as good as literary history can be when it is written almost wholly without benefit of general ideas."

Van Dyke, John Charles. *American Painting and Its Tradition.* Scribner, 1919. 270pp. o. p. 1949.

Rev. of Revs., 61:109, Jan., 1920. "Studies of nine representative American painters who belong to a definite period in American art, including practically the last quarter of the nineteenth century and the first fifteen years of the twentieth."

Van Gelder, Robert. *Writers and Writing.* Scribner, 1946. 381pp. $3.50.

Wkly. Bk. Rev., July 14, 1946, p. 6. Mencken says the best of an author is in his book; he advises against any attempt at personal contact. Here, however, is what over a hundred authors told the editor of the *New York Times Book Review* about their habits of work. These articles originally appeared in the *Times Book Review* between 1940 and 1946.

Villard, Oswald Garrison. *Prophets, True and False.* Knopf, 1928. 355pp. o. p. 1949.

Sat. Rev. of Lit., 5:71, Aug. 25, 1928. A shrewd observer and gifted writer discusses a score of American leaders in the nineteen twenties. They range from Al Smith and Herbert Hoover to Hearst and Ford.

———. *Some Newspapers and Newspaper-men.* Knopf, 1923. 335pp. o. p. 1933.

Nation, 117:584, Nov. 21, 1923. "Mr. Villard is unusually well fitted for his task. He inherited the ownership of a great newspaper. No one ever questioned his journalistic ability or his high views of the responsibilities of the profession. . . . It might be feared that Mr. Villard would write of his one-time rivals with bitterness or scorn. His judgments, it is true, are severe, but who will say that they are not just? Yet the characters in Mr. Villard's drama are not all villains; and if he has no heroes, he sees

with admirable clearness the journalistic ideal and sets it forth with real
eloquence."

Vincent, Leon Henry. *American Literary Masters.* Houghton,
1906. 517pp. o. p. 1950.

Preface. Biographical and critical essays on nineteen writers who figured
between 1809 and 1860.

Wagenknecht, Edward Charles, ed. *When I Was a Child; an
Anthology.* Dutton, 1946. 477pp. $4.00.

Kirkus, 14:574, Nov. 1, 1946. "The editor's accompanying notes, choice and
arrangement of materials add to the excellence of the collection. Worthwhile even in a welter of anthologies."

Walker, Franklin. *San Francisco's Literary Frontier.* Knopf,
1939. 400pp. o. p. 1949.

Books, July 23, 1939, p. 1. A social history of California from 1849 to 1869
enlivened by appearances and reappearances of major and minor literary
figures of the day.

Wallace, Archer. *Religious Faith of Great Men.* Round Table,
1934. 217pp. o. p. 1941.

Springfield Republican, June 6, 1934, p. 14. "The author's selection of
names and quotations is obviously guided by the desire to prove that the
truly great personalities of history were, in some sense of the word, be-
lievers. But there is no perversion or false interpretation.—The book has
some biographical interest and can be read with profit by workers with
young people and by speakers."

Werkmeister, William Henry. *History of Philosophical Ideas in
America.* Ronald, 1949. 599pp. $5.00.

Sch. & Soc., 70:32, July 9, 1949. "An attempt has been made to view the
development of American philosophy against a general background
which includes such diverse ideas as Puritanism and Deism, which, in
turn, has found expression in Transcendentalism and the Gospel of
Wealth."

Westrate, Edwin Victor. *Those Fatal Generals.* Knight, 1936.
302pp. o. p. 1949.

Boston Transcript, Mar. 28, 1936, p. 3. "Mr. Westrate is no radical muckraker, he does not aim to debunk and pull down, but he has, through
much research and careful study, weighed our military men in the balance
and evaluates the worth of each in no uncertain terms."

Weyl, Nathaniel. *Treason: the Story of Disloyalty and Betrayal
in American History.* Public Affairs Press, 1950. 491pp. $4.50.

N. Y. Times, Apr. 2, 1950, p. 6. "Even if some readers disagree with his
verdicts, no one will deny that Weyl has written his book with vigor,

warmth and humor. *Treason* is unfailingly interesting, and it moves with the certainty and pace of a first-rate work of fiction, perhaps because Weyl is also a novelist. . . . To the reader, most of the conclusions in *Treason* are sound; what's more, the book is not only entertaining and informative; at this hectic moment in our history it is also important."

Whipple, Thomas King. *Spokesmen: Modern Writers and American Life.* Appleton, 1928. 277pp. o. p. 1949.

Ind., 120:555, June 9, 1928. "Mr. Whipple breaks no new ground, but he writes with discernment and appreciation of nine outstanding figures in contemporary American literature."

White, William Allen. *Masks in a Pageant.* Macmillan, 1928. 507pp. $3.00.

Yale Rev., 18:368. Portraits of political leaders based on the personal contacts of a newspaper man. Entertaining but sometimes inaccurate. Biased in favor of Theodore Roosevelt; unfair to Taft and Wilson.

Wiener, Philip Paul. *Evolution and the Founders of Pragmatism.* Harvard, 1949. 288pp. $5.00.

Library Jour., 74:1320, Sept. 15, 1949. "Its main chapters tell the part played by six scholarly Harvard men—three of them natural scientists and three historians, or legalists, William James and Oliver Wendell Holmes being the best known today, who, beginning in the 1870's, thrashed out philosophic problems in their so-called Metaphysical Club. As the background for the importance of their contribution, Professor Wiener summarizes the religious and scientific developments and controversies of the period, with special reference to Darwin's theories."

Williams, Ben Ames, ed. *A Diary from Dixie.* By Mary Boykin Chesnut. Houghton, 1949. 572pp. $5.00.

AHR, 55:629. A reprint of a book first printed in 1905. Mrs. Chesnut was the wife of a United States Senator from South Carolina who was also a leader in the Confederacy. Her "diary's significance lies in its faithful portrayal of a society at war." Mrs. Chesnut "understood and appreciated life among the lowly," but viewed society from the standpoint of an aristocrat.

Williams, Blanche Colton. *Our Short Story Writers.* (Modern American Writers.) New ed. Dodd, 1920. 357pp. o. p. 1949.

Booklist, 17:154, Jan. 21, 1922. This book gives the life stories of Hamlin Garland, O'Henry, Jack London, Edith Wharton, "and tells how they are reflected in their writing."

Willson, Beckles. *America's Ambassadors to England, 1785-1929: a Narrative of American Diplomatic Relations.* Stokes, 1929. 497pp. o. p. 1949.

AHR, 35:135. These sketches abound in "rather well-authenticated gossip."

Wilson, Edmund, ed. *Shock of Recognition*. Doubleday, 1943. 1290pp. o. p. 1950.

Commonweal, 38:400, Aug. 6, 1943. "This is an ably edited, truly distinguished, richly rewarding anthology."

Winters, Ivor. *In Defense of Reason: Seven Studies in the History of American Obscurantism*. Morrow, 1947. 611pp. $4.00.

Nation, 164:718, June, 1947. "There can be no dodging the fact that Mr. Winters's criticism is powerful, informed, consistent, and, for the most part, just—with only those errors caused by too great a rigidity in the structure of his intellect. . . . That is, it is clear that Mr. Winters's criticism is of great use in getting at American literature both for what it says or tries to say and for how it says or fails to say it: Why is it, then, that his criticism is not in general use? The answer lies in the habits of our age. Mr. Winters's criticism is judicial; we have a horror of judgment because we do not know what it might destroy in our potential selves."

Wise, John Sergeant. *Recollections of Thirteen Presidents*. Doubleday, 1906. 284pp. o. p. 1933.

Wise was a Virginia politician and a gifted writer whose recollections cover all the presidents from Tyler to Theodore Roosevelt.

Wish, Harvey. *Contemporary America; the National Scene Since 1900*. Harper, 1945. 675pp. $4.50.

Nation, 161:290. "The book is competently written, mildly liberal in viewpoint, and exploits to good advantage the available secondary sources. It is, moreover, extremely readable and surprisingly free from major errors."

Wood, Clement. *Poets of America*. Dutton, 1925. 392pp. o. p. 1941.

Ind., 114:591, May 23, 1925. "He has the excellent habit of illustrating his critical opinions with adequate quotations from the poet criticized, and in most instances contrives to uphold his verdicts by chapter and verse. Altogether, a stimulating and interesting book."

Woolf, Samuel Johnson. *Drawn from Life*. McGraw, 1932. 387pp. o. p. 1949.

Book Rev. Dig., 1932, p. 1047. "Impressions and anecdotes of important men whose portraits were drawn from life by the artist-author."

Wright, Richardson Little. *Forgotten Ladies: Nine Portraits from the American Family Album*. Lippincott, 1928. 307pp. o. p. 1949.

Nation, 127:Sup. 638, Dec. 5, 1928. "Fascinating material about American women from the days of the Indian frontier to the Civil War, women who, indeed, do not deserve to be forgotten."

Young, Klyde H., and Lamar Middleton. *Heirs Apparent; the Vice-Presidents of the United States.* Prentice-Hall, 1948. 314pp. o. p. 1949.

AHR, 54:219. "The authors, one a journalist and the other an economist and explorer, have leaned heavily upon odd bits of information such as a quiz program or a believe-it-or-not column might feature. . . . What goes for an index is almost worthless. All in all, the book is a good example of how history should not be written."

SUBJECT INDEX

AGRICULTURE: Carver, G W., 435; Chapman, J., 200; Burbank, L., 396; Hammond, J. H., 197; Hampton, W., 318; Polk, L. L., 323; Porter, A., 210; Ruffin, E., 306; Spalding, T., 207; Wailes, B. L. C., 212; Watson, T. E., 327.

ARMY: Buckner, S. B., 336; Crook, G., 385; Custer, G. A., 381; Forrest, N. B., 335; Gaines, E. P., 208; Gorgas, J., 335; Grant, U. S., 359; Hampton, W., 318; Harrison, W. H., 199; Houston, S., 215; Jackson, A., 204; Jackson, T. J., 311; Lee, R. E., 307; Longstreet, J., 319; McClellan, G. B., 301; Morgan, J. H., 336; Mosby, J. S., 313; Pershing, J. J., 455; Pratt, R. H., 314; Roosevelt, T., 418; Scott, W., 188; Sherman, W. T., 338; Stuart, J. E., 312; Taylor, Z., 209; Thomas, G. H., 310.

ART, ARCHITECTURE: Audubon, J. J., 210; Homer, W., 250; McKim, C. F., 287; Morse, S. F. B., 178; Saint-Gaudens, A., 288; Sargent, J. S., 264; Thornton, W., 187; Whistler, J. A., 247.

COLONIST: Bidwell, J., 225; Rich, C. C., 379.

CRIME: Bonney, W. H., 386; Brown, J., 367; James, J. W., 375; Meiggs, H., 387; Murrell, J. A., 212.

BUSINESS, TRADE: Armour, P. D., 362; Astor, J. J., 172; Barnum, P. T., 230; Carnegie, A., 384; Chrysler, W. P., 446; Colt, S., 168; Cooke, J., 280; Cooper, P., 178; Duke, J. B., 328; Flagler, H. M., 322; Ford, H. J., 442; Gould, J., 281; Gregg, J., 223; Gugenheim, D., 306; Hanna, M. A., 343; Huntington, C. P., 387; Larkin, T. O., 221; McCormick, C. H., 357; McLoughlin, J., 217; Morgan, J. P., 283; Pattie, J. O., 222; Pinkham, L. E., 236; Train, G. F., 240; Vanderbilt, C., 179; Westinghouse, G., 304.

EDUCATION: Agassiz, J. L., 229; Bache, A. D., 183; Beecher, C. E., 202; Burgess, J. W., 286; Butler, N. M., 422; Carver, G. W., 435; Cooper, T., 193; Coulter, J. M., 449; Curry, J. L. M., 321; Eaton, A., 173; Eliot, C. W., 248; Gilman, D. C., 312; Harper, W. R., 366; Hopkins, M., 228; James, W., 258; Lieber, F., 198; Longstreet, A. B., 197; Lyon, M., 149; Mann, H., 147; Palmer, A. F., 264; Peabody, E. P., 228; Phelps, W. L., 402; Pratt, R. H., 314; Silliman, B., 144; Stowe, H. B., 233; Sumner, W. G., 285; Washington, B. T., 337; Webster, N., 141; Willard, E. H., 175.

ENGINEERING: Goethals, G. W., 265; Hammond, J. H., 397; Judah, T. D., 389; McGillycuddy, V. T., 383; Roebling, J. A., 183; Roebling, W., 285.

FINANCE: Astor, J. J., 172; Cooke, J., 280; Duke, J. B., 328; Flagler, H. M., 322; Frick, H. C., 305; Gould, J., 281; Gugenheim, D., 306; Hill, J. J., 380; Holladay, B., 388; Morgan, J. P., 283; Ralston, W. C., 225.

GOVERNMENT: Adams, C. F., 230; Adams, J. Q., 142; Altgeld, J. P., 366; Arthur, C. A., 280; Austin, S. F., 214; Bancroft, G., 150; Benjamin, J. P., 334; Beveridge, A. J., 442; Blaine, J. G., 244; Blair, F. P., 190; Brandeis, L. D., 434; Brown, A. G., 335; Brown, J. E., 319; Bryan, W. J., 454; Calhoun, J. C., 194; Clay, H., 209; Cleveland, G., 281; Coolidge, C., 405; Crockett, D., 213; Cross, W. L., 401; Curry, J. L. M., 321; Davis, J., 330; Douglas, S. A., 358; Fish, H., 268; Frémont, J. C., 224; Garfield, J. A., 342; Gaston, W., 193; Grant, U. S., 359; Grundy, F., 208; Hammond, J. H., 197; Hampton, W., 318; Hanna, M. A., 343; Harding, W. G., 444; Harrison, W. H., 199; Hay, J., 363; Hayes, R. B., 340; Hewitt, A. S., 187; Hill, B. H., 321; House, E. M., 460; Hughes, C. E., 424; Jackson, A., 204; Johnson, A., 329; Johnson, J. A., 384; Kennedy, J. P., 191; La Follette, R. M., 457; La Guardia, F. H., 429; Lane, J., 219; Lincoln, A., 345; Lodge, H. C., 400; Long, H. P., 436; Morrow, D. W., 427; Otero, M. H.,

503

INDEX